Georgia, Armenia & Azerbaijan

Georgia
p30

Armenia
p126

Azerbaijan
p197

Nagorno-Karabakh
p265

Azerbaijan
p197

THIS EDITION WRITTEN AND RESEARCHED BY

Alex Jones, Tom Masters, Virginia Maxwell, John Noble

Contents

PLAN YOUR TRIP

KAPULYA/GETTY IMAGES ©

HIKERS, SVANETI P82,
GEORGIA

JANE SWEENEY/GETTY IMAGES ©

FLAME TOWERS P211, BAKU,
AZERBAIJAN

ON THE ROAD

Contents

UNDERSTAND

SURVIVAL GUIDE

SPECIAL FEATURES

Welcome to the Caucasus

Breathtaking natural beauty, deeply hospitable people, quaint rural backwaters and cosmopolitan capitals make the South Caucasus region a thrilling, offbeat discovery.

Cultural Cornucopia

The region is smaller than the UK yet takes in three distinct countries (two Christian, one Islamic), three breakaway territories and at least 16 local languages. This is a cultural crossroads where Europe meets Asia and tomorrow mingles with yesterday. Russian, Persian, Turkish and other influences have been absorbed into proudly distinctive local cultures where social attitudes remain traditional, with family networks supreme. Travel weaves you between rapidly modernising capitals and slow-paced countryside where most families still live off their land.

A Feast for the Senses

Astonishing natural beauty is in your face throughout the Great Caucasus, soaring mountains that stride from the Black Sea to the Caspian in a sequence of dramatic peaks fronted by green river valleys and quaint, remote villages. The Lesser Caucasus and Talysh ranges have glories of their own, while at lower altitudes terrain incorporates idyllic patchworks of farms and woodland plus arid semi-deserts and rocky gorges. Savour all this with deep-rooted hospitality, fresh fruity cuisine and wines from the world's original home of viniculture.

The Great Outdoors

The mountain regions are strung with spectacular walking and riding routes with ruined castles, towers and ancient churches often perched in achingly picturesque locations. Each country has great day-trip hikes but high in the Great Caucasus, Georgia's Svaneti, Kazbegi and Tusheti regions are particularly ideal for longer-distance village-to-village treks. Each of the nations has ski resorts. Rafting and paragliding are possible in Georgia where climbers can scale Mt Kazbek and other 5000m peaks. Delve underground in Armenia's many caves, or explore Azerbaijan's Caspian hinterland where natural curiosities include mud volcanoes and fire phenomena.

Food for the Mind

Antique forts, monasteries, mosques, churches and excavations pepper the region. History buffs can delight in disentangling their Bagratids from their Bolsheviks. The cities boast well-presented museums, splendid galleries and a rich theatrical heritage. Tourism infrastructure can seem modest by European standards but linguistic and logistic challenges help push visitors to interact with friendly locals – ideal for those who want to go well beyond the beaten path.

Why I Love Georgia, Armenia & Azerbaijan

By Alex Jones, Writer

In 1995 I stumbled off a train into a Tbilisi still bruised by the recent civil war and with barely functioning basic amenities. Northern Armenia hadn't fully recovered from the 1988 earthquake and Baku had yet to show a glimmer of the future oil boom. Yet, while poverty seemed to reign in each country, I was constantly enveloped by the most extraordinary hospitality. Despite unsolved conflicts, I've watched the Caucasian states transform themselves beyond belief in the last 20 years. But disarming hospitality remains a core defining feature of each of the three remarkable nations that comprise this ever-fascinating region.

For more about our writers, see page 320

Above: Khor Virap Monastery (p175), Armenia, with Mt Ararat (Ağrı Dağ, Turkey) in the background

Georgia, Armenia & Azerbaijan

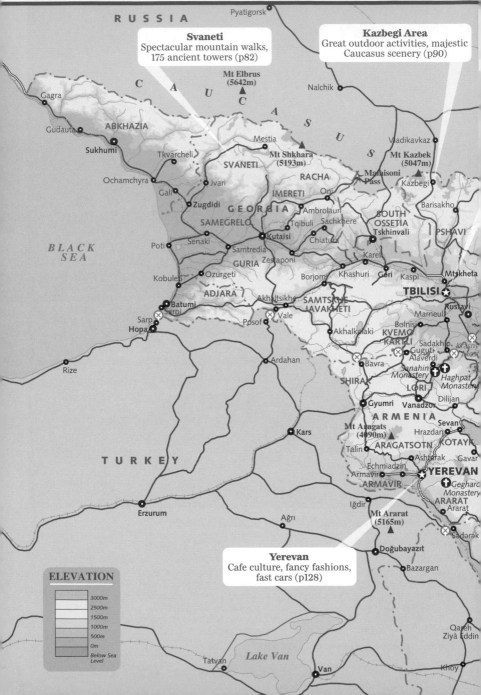

Svaneti
Spectacular mountain walks,
175 ancient towers (p82)

Kazbegi Area
Great outdoor activities, majestic
Caucasus scenery (p90)

Yerevan
Cafe culture, fancy fashions,
fast cars (p128)

ELEVATION

3000m
2500m
1500m
1000m
500m
0m
Below Sea
Level

RUSSIA

Pyatigorsk

Mt Elbrus
(5642m)

Nalchik

Gagra

Gudauta

C A U C

ABKHAZIA

Sukhumi

Tkvarcheli

Mestia

Vladikavkaz

A S U S

Mt Kazbek
(5047m)

Ochamchyra

Jvari

SVANETI

Mt Shkhara
(5193m)

RACHA

Mamisoni
Pass

Kazbegi

Gali

Zugdidi

IMERETI

Oni

Barisakho

SAMEGRELO

GEORGIA

Ambrolauri

SOUTH
OSSETIA

PSHAVI

Poti

Senaki

Tqibuli Sachkhere

Tskhinvali

BLACK
SEA

Samtredia

Kutaisi

Chiatura

Kobuleti

Ozurgeti

GURIA

Zestaponi

Karel

Khashuri Gori

Kaspi

Mtskheta

Batumi

Sarpi

ADJARA

Akhaltsikhe

Borjomi

SAMTSKHE-
JAVAKHETI

TBILISI

Sarp

Hopa

Vale

Posof

Akhalkalaki

Marneul

Rustavi

KVEMO
KARTLI

Bolnisi

Sadakhlo

Krasny
Most

Rize

Ardahan

Bavra

Guguti
Alaverdi

SHIRAK

Sanahin
Monastery

Haghpat
Monastery

LORI

Dilijan

Gyumri

Vanadzor

TURKEY

Mt Aragats
(4090m)

ARMENIA

Sevan

Hrazdan

KOTAYK

Kars

Talin

ARAGATSOTN

Ashtarak

Gavar

Echmiadzin

YEREVAN

Armavir

Geghard
Monastery

ARMAVIR

ARARAT

Erzurum

Ağrı

Iğdir

Ararat

Mt Ararat
(5165m)

Sadarak

Doğubayazıt

Bazargan

Qareh
Ziyà Eddin

Lake Van

Tatvan

Van

Khoy

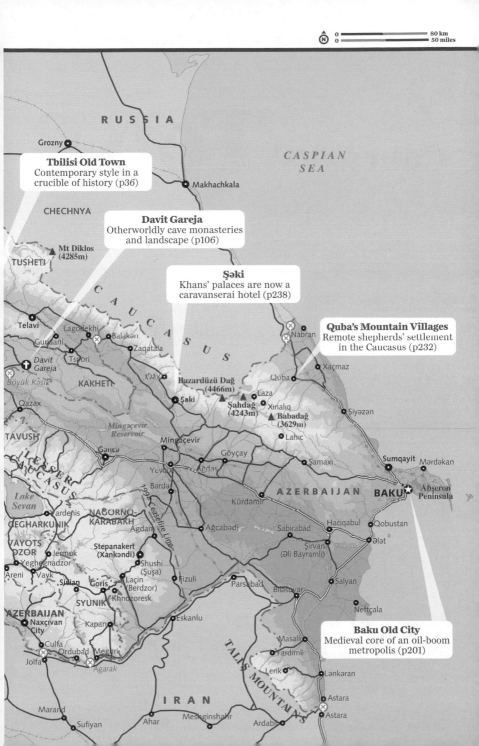

0   80 km
0   50 miles

Tbilisi Old Town
Contemporary style in a
crucible of history (p36)

Davit Gareja
Otherworldly cave monasteries
and landscape (p106)

Şəki
Khans' palaces are now a
caravanserai hotel (p238)

Quba's Mountain Villages
Remote shepherds' settlement
in the Caucasus (p232)

Baku Old City
Medieval core of an oil-boom
metropolis (p201)

RUSSIA

CASPIAN
SEA

Grozny

Makhachkala

CHECHNYA

Mt Diklos
(4285m)

TUSHETI

C
A
U
C
A
S
U
S

Telavi
Lagodekhi
Balakən
Nabran

Gurjaani
Zaqatala
Quba
Xaçmaz

Davit
Gareja
Tsnori
Qax
Bazardüzü Dağ
(4466m)
Laza

Böyük Kəsik
KAKHETI
Şəki
Şahdağ
(4243m)
Xınalıq
Babadağ
(3629m)
Siyəzən

Qazax
Mingəçevir
Reservoir
Lahıc

TAVUSH
Gəncə
Mingəçevir
Göyçay
Şamaxı
Sumqayıt
Mərdəkan

LESSER
CAUCASUS
Yevlax
Bərdə
Ağdaş
Kürdəmir
AZERBAIJAN
BAKU
Abşeron
Peninsula

Lake
Sevan
Vardenis
NAGORNO-
KARABAKH
Ağcabədi
Sabirabad
Haciqabul
Qobustan

GEGHARKUNIK
Agdam
Şirvan
(Əli Bayramli)
Ələt

VAYOTS
DZOR
Jermuk
Yeghegnadzor
Stepanakert
(Xankəndi)
Shushi
(Şuşa)
Fizuli
Parsabad
Salyan

Areni
Vayk
Sisian
Goris
Laçin
(Berdzor)
Biləsuvar

SYUNIK
Khndzoresk
Eskanlu
Neftçala

AZERBAIJAN
Naxçıvan
City
Kapan
Masallı

Culfa
Ordubad
Meghri
Yardımlı

Jolfa
Agarak
Lerik
Lənkəran

TALIS
MOUNTAINS
Astara

IRAN
Astara

Marand
Meshginshahr
Ardabil

Sufiyan
Ahar

Caucasus' Top 9

Tbilisi Old Town

1 Nowhere better blends the romance of Georgia's past with its striving for a new future than Tbilisi's Old Town (p36). Winding lanes lined by rakishly leaning houses lead past tranquil old stone churches to shady squares and glimpses of the ultra-contemporary Peace Bridge spanning the Mtkvari River. Casual cafes and bohemian bars rub shoulders with trendy lounge-clubs, folksy carpet shops, new travellers' hostels and small, quirky hotels. The aeons-old silhouette of Narikala Fortress supervises everything, while Georgia's 21st-century Presidential Palace, with its egg-shaped glass dome, looks on from over the river.

21st-Century Baku

2 Hot on the heels of Dubai, Baku has been rapidly transforming its skyline with some of the world's most audacious and spectacular new architecture. Counterpointed with the city's medieval Unesco-listed Old City core is a trio of 190m-tall skyscrapers shaped like gigantic glass flames that really appear to burn at night once the remarkable light show comes on. The majestic white curves of Zaha Hadid's Heydar Əliyev Cultural Centre (p211; pictured) form a similarly thrilling spectacle. And along the Caspian Sea waterfront a series of new projects is soon destined to add an other-worldly crescent-moon-shaped mega-hotel.

AARON GEDDES/GETTY IMAGES ©

JANE SWEENEY/GETTY IMAGES ©

Svaneti

3 The mysterious mountain valleys of Svaneti (p82; Ushgali village pictured) sit high in the Caucasus, surrounded by snowy peaks, alpine meadows and forests – a paradise for walkers in summer. Long isolated from the outside world, Svaneti has its own language and a strongly traditional culture, symbolised by the 175 *koshkebi* (ancient stone defensive towers) that stand picturesquely in its villages, and the 1000-year-old frescoes in its churches. Accessible only by a long road trip until recently, Svaneti also has daily small-plane flights from Tbilisi.

Davit Gareja

4 Set in remote, arid lands near Georgia's border with Azerbaijan, these much-revered cave monasteries (p106) were carved out of a lonely cliff-face long, long ago. They became a cradle of medieval monastic culture and fresco painting. Saints' tombs, vivid 1000-year-old murals, an other-worldly landscape and the very idea that people voluntarily chose – and still choose – to live in desert caves all combine to make visiting Davit Gareja a startling experience today. Though remote, the site makes an easy day trip from Tbilisi, Telavi or Sighnaghi.

MAYA KARKALICHEVA/GETTY IMAGES ©

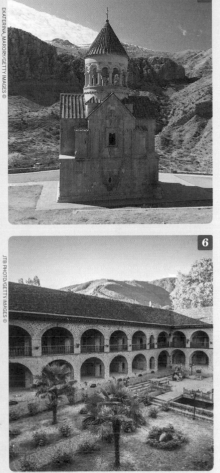

Armenian Monasteries

5 Armenia's rich collection of ancient churches and monasteries (p166) is a world treasure that has developed over thousands of years of architectural tinkering. At first glance their layout seems almost identical, each with a conical roof representing Mt Ararat. However, closer inspection reveals that each has its own unique character and design variation. Location also differentiates Armenia's monasteries, ranging from Tatev's mountaintop perch to Noravank's desert canyon and the iconic Khor Virap with the backdrop of Mt Ararat itself.

Şəki

6 Embodying the Caucasus' cultural contrasts and provincial charms, the small city of Şəki (Sheki; p238) features heavy fortress bastions, two mural-walled palaces of former khans and several historic brick mosques, while up the road in Kiş (Kish) is one of the region's oldest and best-preserved Christian churches. You can stay in a genuine caravanserai (pictured) that dates back to Silk Route days and visit an archaeological site displaying graves from the Bronze Age. The whole setting is majestic with lushly wooded hills backed by high snow-dusted peaks.

Kazbegi Area

7 Just a couple of hours' drive from Tbilisi, the small town of Kazbegi (p90) is the hub of one of the region's most spectacular, yet easily accessed, high-mountain zones. The sight of Tsminda Sameba Church (p92; pictured), silhouetted on its hilltop against the massive snow-covered cone of Mt Kazbek, is Georgia's most iconic image. Numerous walking, horse-riding and mountain-bike routes lead along steep-sided valleys and up to glaciers, waterfalls, mountain passes and isolated villages – just ideal for getting a taste of the high Caucasus.

Yerevan Street Life

8 Street life in Yerevan is slow-paced, often involving long hours spent lingering over coffee or beer in the city's numerous outdoor cafes. Cafe and wine-bar scenes get going late afternoon and build to a crescendo by evening, ending some time before dawn. The crowds mass especially around Opera Sq or Republic Sq (p133; pictured), occasionally passing by Northern Ave to preen and parade their latest fashions.

E_RASMUS/GETTY IMAGES ©

VAHANN/SHUTTERSTOCK ©

ALEX JONES ©

Quba's Mountain Villages

9 Behind the peaceable country town of Quba, woodland glades and sheep-nibbled hillsides lead up into the foothills of the Great Caucasus. Here, separated by dramatic canyons and wild river valleys, lie a scattering of remote shepherd villages, some speaking their own unique languages. Best known of these is Xınalıq (p233; pictured), where stacked, grey-stone houses constitute what, by some definitions, is 'Europe's highest village'. Slightly further afield, Laza has one of the most spectacular backdrops of any Caucasian mountain settlement and its rustic simplicity contrasts dramatically with the Caucasus' most glitzy ski resort, 4km away.

Need to Know

For more information, see Survival Guide (p289)

Currencies

Armenia: Dram (AMD)

Azerbaijan; Manat (AZN)

Georgia: Lari (GEL)

Languages
Armenian, Azerbaijani,
Georgian

Visas

Simple or unnecessary
for most visitors to
Georgia and many to
Armenia. Essential and
sometimes awkward for
visiting Azerbaijan.

Money

ATMs and money-
changing offices widely
available. Credit cards
rarely accepted outside
upper-market places in
the capitals.

Mobile Phones

Local SIM cards are
inexpensive.

Time

Four hours ahead of
GMT/UTC; in Armenia
and Azerbaijan clocks
are put forward one
hour during daylight
saving time (late March
to late October).

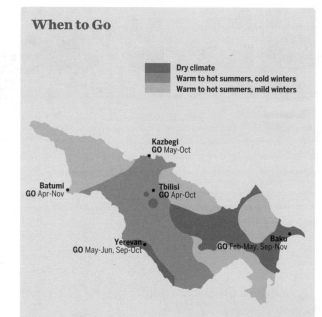

When to Go

Dry climate

Warm to hot summers, cold winters

Warm to hot summers, mild winters

Kazbegi
GO May-Oct

Batumi
GO Apr-Nov

Tbilisi
GO Apr-Oct

Yerevan
GO May-Jun, Sep-Oct

Baku
GO Feb-May, Sep-Nov

High Season
(Jul & Aug)

➡ Locals' holiday
time; tourist
accommodation is
crowded.

➡ Visit mountain
areas; the only
assured snow-free
months for hiking in
the high Caucasus.

➡ Capitals and
other lowlands
unpleasantly hot and
humid.

Shoulder
Seasons (May–
Jun & Sep–Oct)

➡ May and
October offer the
most pleasant
temperatures in the
lowlands.

➡ Upland areas can
be snowbound from
late September to
early June.

➡ May is rainy but
between showers the
flowers are magical.

Low Season
(Nov–Apr)

➡ Winter sports
January to March;
most non-ski
mountain lodgings
close.

➡ Inland often below
freezing December to
February.

➡ Tbilisi: wet and
slushy; Yerevan: icy;
Baku: cold till March.

➡ Wintry weather
often lasts into April.

Useful Websites

Abkhazia (http://abkhazia.travel/en) Abkhaz tourism.

Armenia Information (www.armeniainfo.am) ATDA tourist information.

Caravanistan (www.caravanistan.com) Visa tales collated.

Caucasian Knot (www.eng.kavkaz-uzel.ru) News from north and south Caucasus.

Eurasianet (www.eurasianet.org) Features on the region.

Georgia (www.georgia.travel) Official tourism site.

IWPR (iwpr.net/global/caucasus) News and bridge-building.

Karabakh (http://karabakh.travel/en) Nagorno-Karabakh tourism.

Thorn Tree (www.lonelyplanet.com/thorntree/forums/europe-eastern-europe-the-caucasus) Lonely Planet travellers' forum.

Visit Azerbaijan (azerbaijan.travel) Official tourism site.

Important Numbers

Country code Armenia	☏374	
Country code Azerbaijan	☏994	
Country code Georgia	☏995	
Emergency	☏103 (Georgia ☏112)	
International access code	☏00	

Daily Costs

Budget: Less than US$50

➡ Hostel bed: US$5–20

➡ Simple snack meals: from US$3

➡ Occasional museum: US$2–10

➡ Tea: US$0.40–2

➡ Cheap draft beer: US$0.50–1

➡ Bottled water when tap water unsafe: per L US$0.30

➡ City bus/metro fares: per day US$1.50

➡ Longer distance bus/train ride: US$5

Midrange: US$50–125

➡ Double midrange hotel room: per person US$25–40

➡ One midmarket restaurant meal: US$6–15

➡ Admission to a couple of museums: US$4–20

➡ Beverage and cake at a coffee shop: US$3–9

➡ Bottle of wine in local bar-cafe: US$4–20

➡ Mixture of city buses and taxis: per day US$8

➡ Longer distance shared-taxi ride: US$10

Top End: More than US$125

➡ Luxury hotel double room: per person from US$80

➡ Restaurant lunch: US$7–20

➡ Good-quality dinner: US$15–35

➡ Wine with dinner: US10–50

➡ Beer in an expat pub: US$3–6

➡ Rental car or private driver: per day from US$50

Arriving in the Region

David the Builder Kutaisi International Airport (p296) Prebook on www.georgianbus.com for direct minibus connections to various cities timed to fit with flight arrivals. Destinations include Kutaisi (US$2.10, 30 minutes), Tbilisi (US$8.50, four hours), Batumi (US$6.30, two hours), Mestia (US$17, four hours) and Kazbegi (US$23, 5½ hours).

Heydar Əliyev International Airport (Baku; p296) Bus H1 runs half-hourly by day, and a few times at night. Taxic cost around US$30 to central Baku (25 minutes).

Tbilisi International Airport (p296) Bus 37 runs around twice hourly (7am to 11pm), hourly on Sundays. Official taxi fares to central Tbilisi approximately US$10 (20 minutes).

Zvartnots Airport (Yerevan; p296) Minibus 18 (8am to 8pm) runs thrice hourly to central Yerevan. A taxi should cost under US$9 (20 minutes).

Getting Around

Marshrutky (minibuses) and buses Provide main transport within the region augmented on major routes by faster shared taxis.

Trains Usually slower than buses and with limited network, but handy overnight sleepers are inexpensive and more comfortable than going by road.

Car Drive on the right. Speed limits usually low, rarely over 90km/h. Parking is relatively easy outside the capitals.

Azerbaijan to Armenia There is no direct transport between Armenia and Azerbaijan.

For much more on **getting around**, see p299

What's New

Wines & Winebars

Caucasian wines, the world's oldest, are back with a vengeance. Yerevan is enjoying a recent proliferation of European-style wine bars, with casually stylish In Vino (p144) and Aperitivo (p145) leading the pack. Azerbaijan's Savalan-branded wines are a great unexpected discovery. And in Kaheti, heartland of Georgia's 7000-year-old winemaking tradition, ever more wineries are opening their gates to visitors – Kvareli's Winery Khareba (p104) is almost a wine theme park.

Baku Bonanza

The fast-changing Azerbaijani capital is a testing ground for a dazzling array of modernist construction projects. The all-white Heydar Əliyev Cultural Centre presents a particularly bamboozling statement of 21st-century architectural audacity. (p211)

Kutaisi Rising

Awakening from post-Soviet doldrums, historic Kutaisi hosts Georgia's new parliament, has a new international airport and has finally had its millenium-old Bagrati Cathedral rebuilt after a 320-year wait. (p64)

Swanky Sports

Azerbaijan is rapidly developing its sports-tourism potential, opening a plush national golf course (p231), two upmarket ski resorts and a Caspian kiteboarding centre (p229). Baku's Formula 1 Grand Prix premiers in 2016.

Russian Borders Open

After years of closure, several Russia–Caucasus border crossings are now open to foreigners, making both the Georgian Military Hwy (p88) and the weekly Baku–Moscow train (p297) viable access options.

Gəncə Rejuvinated

A major facelift is revamping Azerbaijan's second city, restoring its 17th-century bathhouse and historic caravansarai (p239) and rebuilding the İmamzadə (p249) as one of the Caucasus' biggest Islamic shrines.

Riding High

Tbilisi and Batumi have unveiled new urban cable cars, Baku and Tbilisi have revived their funicular railways, and Quba's upmarket Chalette steakhouse even offers its own cable-car access. (p232)

New Caspian Port

Azerbaijan–Kazakhstan ferries now leave from a lonely new seaport complex near Ələt, 75km south of Baku, but buy tickets before you go! (p226)

Ski Shahdag

Plush upmarket hotels and a rapidly expanding piste network are creating the Caucasus' glitziest winter sports destination: the Shahdag Mountain Resort near Laza. (p234)

For more recommendations and reviews, see lonelyplanet. com/georgia-armenia-azerbaijan

If You Like...

Walking & Horse Riding

Svaneti Many varied trails cross this spectacular region of green valleys, snowy peaks and picturesque villages. (p82)

Kazbegi Area Quick climbs, longer glacier hikes and lovely valley walks or treks over high passes to remote Khevsur villages. (p90)

Yeghegis Valley Wide sweeping valley dotted with old churches. (p178)

Quba hinterland Hike between some of Azerbaijan's loveliest mountain villages, but plan well ahead if venturing into the Shahdag National Park. (p232)

Tusheti Beautiful mountain area with fine village-to-village walking and the region's best longer trek: five somewhat challenging days to, or from, Khevsureti. (p95)

Janapar Trail Pretty series of village-to-village footpaths marked for hikers. (p272)

Borjomi-Kharagauli National Park Well-marked trails of up to three days across forested hills and alpine meadows. (p111)

Kasagh Gorge A 5km trail alongside the Kasagh River links the spectacularly sited monasteries of Hovhannavank and Saghmosavank. (p154)

Zaqatala One of the most accessible starting points for a day hike (or more) up onto spectacular upland pastures. (p244)

Religious Sites

Geghard Monastery Chapels and churches hewn from the rock, plus remarkable *khatchkars* (carved stone crosses). (p149)

Mtskheta The living heart of Georgian Christianity centred on magnificent Svetitskhoveli Cathedral. (p57)

İmamzadə, Gəncə Soon to be reborn as the Caucasus' most dramatic Muslim shrine. (p249)

Davit Gareja Monastic cave-cells carved into a desert cliff. (p106)

Tatev Great fortified monastery on a fairy-tale natural rock fortress. (p184)

Vardzia Fascinating remnants of a cave city that was the spiritual heart of medieval Georgian Christianity. (p114)

Debed Canyon The beautiful medieval monasteries of Sanahin (p164) and Haghpat (p165).

Mir Mövsöm Ziyarətgah Folk superstition meets Islam at Şüvəlan. (p225)

Garni Temple A 1st-century Hellenic temple. (p149)

Ateşgah Suraxanı's fire temple still burns, though it's now a museum. (p233)

Citadels & Fortresses

Svaneti Mountain villages bristling with defensive refuge towers. (p82)

Baku Old City Photogenic crenellated walls enclose a whole inner city complete with mysterious tower, 15th-century palace and medieval minarets. (p201)

Shatili Unique agglomeration of defensive towers forming a single fortress-like whole. (p94)

Akhaltsikhe Night-time floodlights make the giant Rabati citadel fortress glow and highlight the golden dome of the mosque within. (p113)

Tusheti Tower-house hamlets and forgotten fortress ruins linked by superb hiking trails. (p95)

Amberd Fortress Lonely ruin worth the two-hour hike. (p154)

Şəki A mural-decorated khan's palace lies inside sturdy fortress walls. (p238)

Modern Architecture

While there's plenty of new building, the region's most jaw-dropping contemporary architecture is concentrated in three cities: Baku, Batumi and to a lesser extent Tbilisi.

Heydar Əliyev Cultural Centre Smooth white curves of what could be an alien spacecraft morphing into a gigantic albino snail. (p211)

Le Meridien Hotel site, Batumi Think 21st-century Empire State Building then insert a mini Ferris Wheel in the side. (p77)

Flame Towers Three 190m flame-shaped skyscrapers dominate Baku's skyline. (p211)

Peace Bridge Glass filigree footbridge that, along with the Presidential Palace, creates a startling contrast with the rest of old Tbilisi. (p37)

Views & Landscapes

Kazbegi Tsminda Sameba Church silhouetted against the towering snow-covered cone of Mt Kazbek. (p90)

Laza Amphitheatre of peaks and waterfalls. (p234)

Voratan Pass Spectacular views over snowcapped mountains and wildflower-strewn pastures. (p174)

Ananuri Lake, fortress and church in perfect rural harmony. (p88)

Mt Ararat (Ağrı Dağ) Floating on the horizon above Khor Virap Monastery. (p175)

Şahdağ Panorama from Park Qusar. (p234)

Top: Ananuri fortress (p88), Georgia
Bottom: Mud volcanoes (p226), near Qobustan, Azerbaijan

Ushguli Snow-streaked Mt Shkara towering above a dozen tower houses. (p86)

Selim Pass Look down on the picturesque Yeghegis Valley from a 14th-century stone caravanserai. (p180)

Ramana Fortress Stare down across a majestically ugly landscape of old oil workings. (p226)

Offbeat Curiosities

Yanar Dağ A hillside that never stops burning. (p226)

Sataplia Nature Reserve Dinosaur footprints. (p68)

Mud Volcanoes Small but fascinating hills that burp forth cold bubbling mud. (p226)

World's Oldest Shoe In the History Museum of Armenia. (p133)

Yanar Bulağ A stand-pipe of spring water that 'catches fire'. (p255)

Winter Sports

The best snow is in January and February. Heli-skiing is available at Gudauri much later into the season.

Gudauri The South Caucasus' largest and best-established ski area set in spectacular high mountains. (p88)

Shahdag A rapidly expanding piste network, beautiful setting and glitzy hotels that appeal to nouveau riche weekenders. (p234)

Tsaghkadzor Armenia's best-known ski centre with 27km of pistes, mostly red and black runs. (p173)

Laza Ice climbing possible on the frozen waterfalls, but you'll

need to organise everything yourself. (p234)

Qəbələ Easily accessible resort whose network of 21st-century ropeways operates year round. (p237)

Bakuriani Budget-friendly skiing and tobogganing. (p112)

Village Getaways

Pretty mountain villages where homestays or other basic tourist infrastructure are just enough to let you experience rural lifestyles.

Shenaqo Summer-only delight in Tusheti. (p95)

Xınalıq Europe's highest permanent village. (p233)

Juta Summer-only accommodation beneath the rocky candelabra of Mt Chaukhi. (p93)

Odzun Plateau-perched overlooking Debed Canyon (p163)

Lahıc Quaint, if touristy, coppersmiths' village with hiking potential. (p235)

Mazeri Escape the Mestia crowds in Svaneti's remote Becho valley overlooked by magnificent Mt Ushba. (p87)

Art

All three countries have a solid artistic heritage. Baku's Old City has a specially concentrated wealth of small private galleries.

Yarat Azerbaijan's latest Contemporary Art Centre in a reclaimed ex-naval warehouse. (p209)

Sergei Parajanov Museum Eccentric house museum of artist-cum–film director. (p137)

Pirosmani Works of Georgia's beloved primitivist painter are copied on many a sign and restaurant hoarding. See originals at Tbilisi's National Gallery (p43) and the Sighnaghi Museum (p104).

National Gallery of Armenia Remarkable collection of Armenian art, including stunning paintings by Vardges Surenyants. (p136)

Mayak 13 Designed by one of Azerbaijan's foremost modern artists, this restaurant is more artwork than eatery. (p215)

Icons Georgia's churches and museums are full of beautiful old icons. Mestia's Svaneti History & Ethnography Museum has some especially original and touching ones. (p83)

Soviet Throwbacks

Lenin statues have long since disappeared from public plinths but a few notable reminders of the 70-year period of Soviet rule remain. And not just those WWII memorials and ranks of dreary suburban apartment blocks.

Stalin Museum Still going strong in Gori, the town where he was born. (p59)

Soviet Yerevan Envoy Hostel's themed tour. (p139)

Mother Armenia Gigantic statue towers more than 20m above Yerevan. (p129)

City Hall, Gəncə Multiarched archetype of Stalinist neo-Classicism. (p248)

Republic Sq, Yerevan Soviet triumphalist architecture reclaimed. (p133)

Duzdağ A Soviet-era salt mine now used as an asthma treatment centre. (p255)

Month by Month

January

The coldest month. Expect snow and below-freezing temperatures over much of the region. Winter sports get going. Georgians and Armenians celebrate Christmas, with the devout going on fasts of varying rigour for days or weeks beforehand.

⭐ New Year

Cities are prettily decorated, with fireworks launching the year. Georgians may gather for post-midnight feasts. In Armenia children receive gifts from Dzmer Papik (Santa Claus/Grandpa Winter) on New Year's Eve; families and friends visit and exchange gifts over several days until Christmas (6 January).

⭐ Armenian Christmas (Surb Tsnund)

6 January. Hymns and psalms ring out from churches, where part of the ritual is the blessing of water to mark Epiphany (Jesus' baptism), with which Christmas is combined. Families gather for Christmas Eve dinners, where the traditional main dish is fish and rice.

⭐ Georgian Christmas (Shoba)

7 January. Flag-carrying, carol-singing crowds make Alilo (Alleluia) walks through the streets, with children wearing white robes. For some, the festive season continues to 14 January, 'Old New Year', the year's start on the Julian Calendar used by the Georgian Orthodox Church.

◉ Martyrs' Day

20 January. A national day of mourning in Azerbaijan, commemorating the 1990 massacre of Baku civilians by Soviet troops. Bakuvians head up to Şahidlər Xiyabani (Martyr's Lane) in a major commemoration.

February

It is very cold, albeit somewhat less so on the Caspian coast. The winter sports season is in full swing.

🎿 Skiing

The season runs from about late December to the end of March, but February generally has the best snow conditions. The top resorts are Gudauri, Bakuriani and Mestia in Georgia, Shahdag and Qəbələ in Azerbaijan, and Jermuk and Tsaghkadzor in Armenia.

⭐ Surp Sargis Don

The Day of St Sargis, a handsome warrior saint, is popular among unmarried Armenians: tradition tells that the person who gives them water in their dreams on this night will be their spouse. It falls nine weeks before Easter (between 18 January and 23 February).

⭐ Trndez

This Armenian religious festival of the Purification falls on 14 February. Bonfires are lit and people leap over them for protection from the evil eye, illness and poisons. Trndez also signals the approach of spring.

March

It's starting to get a little less cold, but don't expect anything above 10°C, except perhaps on the coasts. Across Azerbaijan shops sell emerald-green fresh-grown wheatgrass (səməni) as signs of the coming spring.

★ Women's Day

8 March. Celebrated throughout the region with flowers and presents given to female colleagues and friends, and lots of flower stalls on the streets. It's a public holiday in Georgia and Armenia.

☆ International Muğam Festival

Mid-March. Baku celebrates Azerbaijan's Unesco-protected traditional musical heritage (www.mugam.az) and invites artists from similar genres to a series of concerts and discussions.

★ Noruz Bayramı

Azerbaijan's biggest celebration lasts many days but focuses on the equinox (night of 20 to 21 March) marking the Persian solar New Year and the coming of spring. Traditions include preparing special rice dishes and cleansing the spirit by jumping over bonfires on the four Tuesday nights before the equinox.

April

Temperatures may climb to 20°C in lowland areas. Spring rains and melting snows bring bigger, faster rivers and the start of the main white-water-rafting season in Georgia (until July).

◉ Armenian Easter (Zatik)

Happens on the same variable date as Roman Catholic and Protestant Easter. On Palm Sunday (Tsaghkazard), a week earlier, trees are brought into churches and hung with fruit. Easter tables in homes are laid with red-painted eggs on beds of lentil shoots grown during the Lenten fast.

◉ Georgian Easter (Aghdgoma)

The Eastern Orthodox Easter can happen up to five weeks after the Western one. Churches hold special services on Passion Thursday (with Last Supper ceremonies) and Good Friday, notably at Svetitskhoveli Cathedral, Mtskheta.

◉ Genocide Memorial Day

24 April. Thousands of Armenians make a procession to Yerevan's genocide memorial, Tsitsernakaberd. The date is the anniversary of the arrest of Armenian leaders in Istanbul in 1915, generally considered to mark the start of the massacres.

May

Spring rains are interspersed with clear air and emerald-green fields are dappled with wild flowers. Temperatures become pleasant and walking trails in mountain foothill areas start to open up. Generally an enjoyable time to visit the region.

★ Victory Day

The anniversary of the Nazi surrender to the USSR on 9 May 1945 is still commemorated throughout the region. It's particularly interesting in Nagorno-Karabakh, where 9 May is also the anniversary of the Armenian capture of Shushi in 1992, a turning-point in the Karabakh War.

June

One of the best months. Temperatures get up to 30°C in most areas; spring rains have eased off. Walking season in the mountains gets into its stride, although some high passes are only accessible in July and August.

⭐ Abano Pass Opens

The only road into the beautiful Georgian mountain region of Tusheti, via the nerve-jangling 2900m Abano Pass, normally opens from June to October, though exact dates depend on the weather.

◉ Ramazan

The Islamic fasting month of Ramazan (Ramadan) starts on different dates each year, eg starting 6 June 2016, 6 May 2019. In Azerbaijan Ramazan does not impact greatly on the traveller experience: some pious Muslims refrain from eating, drinking and smoking during daylight but most restaurants remain open. A few stop serving alcohol.

Caspian Oil & Gas Exhibition

Baku's biggest trade show is hardly a draw for tourists but beware that business-standard hotels can be heavily booked for these few days in early June and airline tickets might prove more expensive.

July

It can get oppressively hot in the cities and lowlands but this is a great time to head to the mountains or the seaside.

☆ Golden Apricot International Film Festival

Yerevan hosts the region's biggest international film fest (www.gaiff.am), under the theme Crossroads of Cultures and Civilisations. Lasts a week in early or mid-July.

☆ Art-Gene Festival

This very popular folk festival (www.artgeni.ge) tours Georgia and culminates with several days of music, cooking, arts and crafts in Tbilisi.

☆ Black Sea Jazz Festival

International jazz artists gather in Georgia's main coastal resort, Batumi, for a week of rhythm, improvisation and fun in late July (www.batumijazz.ge).

☆ Kvirikoba

Georgian countryside festivals usually combine Christian devotion with merrymaking and pagan roots. Kvirikoba, one of Svaneti's biggest gatherings, is no exception. Liturgy, blessings, bellringing, animal sacrifice and a boulder-tossing contest are followed by feasting and song. It's held on 28 July in the Kala community.

☆ Baku Grand Prix

From 2016 Baku hosts a mid-July F1 Grand Prix using the city's streetscape for a dramatic Monaco-style spectacle.

☆ Vardavar (Transfiguration)

The big summer holiday in Armenia, 14 weeks after Easter. In a throwback to the legendary love-spreading technique of pre-Christian goddess Astgik, kids and teenagers throw water on everyone, and no one takes offence (much). It's hilarious but don't carry anything that can't survive a soaking.

August

The weather is airlessly hot and it's the big local holiday month, with people flocking to coasts, lakes and mountains. Accommodation in these areas, and transport to them, are at their busiest.

☆ Batumi Season

Georgia's Las Vegas–wannabe coastal resort fills up with holiday-makers from Georgia, Armenia and beyond in July and, especially, August. Much of Tbilisi's nightlife migrates here for the season, adding to the party atmosphere.

☆ Gabala International Music Festival

This top-class international smorgasbord of mainly classical music (www.gabalamusicfestival.com) rings out at Qəbələ in Azerbaijan at the end of July.

☆ Tushetoba

A part-traditional, part-touristic, Georgian mountain festival at Omalo, Tusheti, on the first Saturday in August (or last in July). It features folk music and dancing, traditional sports like horse racing and archery, and the chance to shear your own sheep.

☆ Astvatsatsin

This Armenian festival devoted to the Virgin Mary is celebrated on the Sunday nearest to 15 August. It marks the beginning of the harvest season, with priests blessing grapes in churches.

☆ Mariamoba (Assumption)

One of the biggest holidays in Georgia, especially eastern Georgia, celebrating the Assumption of the Virgin Mary into heaven (28 August by the Julian calendar). People attend church services and light candles, then gather for family picnics. Sheep may be slaughtered at churches, and then eaten at the gatherings.

September

Temperatures subside a little from their August heights, making for

excellent weather. The main local holiday season is over. This is the last month of the walking season in many mountain areas.

✨ Alaverdoba

These late-September religious-cum-social festivities around Alaverdi Cathedral in Kakheti celebrate the harvest, especially of grapes. People come from remote mountain villages to worship.

◉ Gurban Bayramı

The Muslim Festival of Sacrifice commemorates Abraham's test of faith when God ordered him to sacrifice his son Isaac. Azerbaijanis visit family and friends, and the head of the household traditionally slaughters a sheep, which forms the basis of a grand feast.

October

Autumn is here, with temperatures ranging between 10°C and 20°C in most areas. This is the season of harvest festivals and still a nice time to be here. It's usually still warm and pleasant on the Caspian coast.

✨ Kakheti Grape Harvest

The picking and pressing of grapes in Georgia's main wine-producing region, Kakheti, lasts from about 20 September to 20 October. Feasts, musical events and other celebrations go hand-in-hand with the harvest, and it's easy for visitors to join in both the harvest and the partying.

Top: Villagers stop at a church on their way to Kvirikoba, a Georgian festival held in Svaneti (p82)

Bottom: Girls crushing grapes during Armenia's wine harvesting festival in the Vayots Dzor region (p174)

◉ High Fest

The region's top international theatre festival (www.highfest.am) brings a broad range of dramatic companies from around 30 countries to Yerevan, during the first week of October.

🎖 Armenian Harvest Festivals

Almost every village and small town in Armenia holds a harvest festival. You'll see singing, dancing and plenty of fresh fruits and vegetables, and the preparation of traditional dishes. In the wine-growing village of Areni (Vayots Dzor) the festivities focus on wine.

🎖 Svetitskhovloba (Mtskhetoba)

The Day of Svetitskhoveli Cathedral, 14 October, sees the town of Mtskheta and its people returning to the Middle Ages with medieval dress, decorations and re-enactments. The Catholicos, patriarch of the Georgian Church, prays for the 12 Orthodox Apostles to give their protection to Georgia.

☆ Baku Jazz Festival

Baku's late October jazz festival varies in stature year by year but has drawn some top-notch artists in past years including Al Di Meola, Herbie Hancock and Aziza Mustafadeh.

🎖 Tbilisoba

Tbilisi's biggest festivity sees the whole city coming out to party for a weekend in October. Amid music and dance events, food stands abound and the wine flows, celebrating the autumn harvest.

November

Winter is closing in. The days are rapidly shortening and inland city temperatures drop from the high teens to single digits. Some snow in the mountains.

🎖 Giorgoba (St George's Day)

Georgia celebrates two days of its patron saint, St George, 6 May and 23 November. Both see people attending church and family feasts; 23 November is the more widely celebrated, particularly in eastern Georgia. The president pardons some lucky convicts and concerts are held in Tbilisi.

December

Winter is well and truly here. Temperatures are down around 0°C in most places.

☆ Tbilisi International Film Festival

Mainly Georgian, regional and European movies are showcased over a week (www.tbilisifilmfestival.ge) in the first week of December.

Itineraries

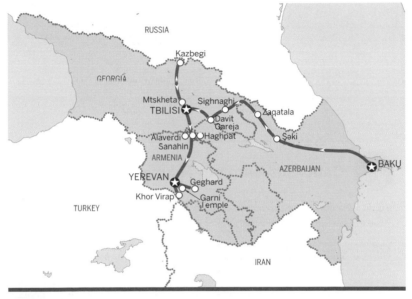

South Caucasian Highlights

You can get a basic taste of all three countries in two weeks, but do organise your Azerbaijan visa well in advance. Arrive in **Baku**, the ever-more glitzy Azerbaijani capital. Spend a couple of days exploring the art galleries and Old City core, plus make an excursion to **Qobustan** and the mud volcanoes. Take the night train to lovely **Şəki**, then hop west via **Zaqatala** into Georgia's wine region, Kakheti. Stop in **Sighnaghi** and drive on to the Georgian capital via the **Davit Gareja** cave monasteries. Spend three days in lovely **Tbilisi**, including an excursion to the old Georgian capital **Mtskheta**. Next head up to **Kazbegi** for two or three days' walking in the spectacular Great Caucasus.

Return to Tbilisi and head south into Armenia, hopping to the border via Marneuli and Sadakhlo then taking a taxi to the World Heritage monasteries of **Haghpat** and **Sanahin**. Continue from **Alaverdi** to the capital **Yerevan** with its wine bars and museums. Add excursions to **Garni Temple** and to **Geghard** and **Khor Virap** monasteries.

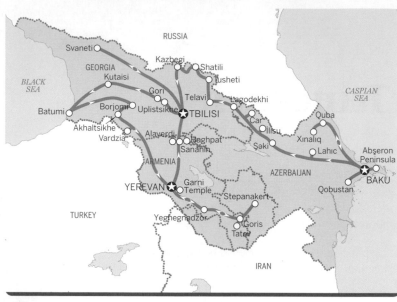

Caucasus Summer Hiking

Spend a few days in **Baku**, contrasting its world-beating 21st-century architecture with the medieval charm of its Unesco-listed Old City. Remember to register your Azerbaijani visa. As well as **Qobustan**, explore the offbeat **Abşeron Peninsula** with its fire phenomena, castle towers and oil-industry debris. Then head north to the mountain village of **Xınalıq** via the carpet-making town of **Quba**. Return to Baku and strike out northwest to quaint **Lahıc**, a good village base for summer walks and local encounters. Continue to lovely **Şəki** with its muralled khan's palace and caravanserai hotel, and consider adding days in other pretty Caucasus foothill villages such as **İlisu** above Qax, or **Car** near Zaqatala.

Enter Georgia at **Lagodekhi** and explore the classic wine region of **Kakheti** from a base at **Telavi**. Take the rough summer-only road to Omalo in remote **Tusheti** and, assuming you have a tent and decent fitness, hike (four days) from there to **Shatili**, ideally employing a horse to carry your backpack. Get driven to Roshka and make the strenuous day-hike to Juta en route to spectacular **Kazbegi**. Recharge with creature comforts in fabulous **Tbilisi** before another summer-only fix of mountains, spectacular valleys and fortified villages in **Svaneti**. Or hop across country for seaside fun at the quirky Black Sea resort of **Batumi**, visiting **Uplistsikhe**, Stalin's home town of **Gori**, and historic **Kutaisi** on the way. Two possible routes sweep back to fortress-dominated **Akhaltsikhe**, the longer but easier one via the old-world spa town of **Borjomi**, gateway to the Borjomi-Kharagauli National Park. From Akhaltsikhe, don't miss an excursion to the cave city of **Vardzia** before entering Armenia. Enjoy the cafe life of **Yerevan**, along with day trips to regional monasteries and **Garni Temple**, then head into southern Armenia. In around four days you could visit the **Yeghegnadzor** area (monasteries, lovely walks and wineries) and spectacular **Tatev** via slow-paced **Goris**. Goris is also the starting point for side trips to into the beautiful but highly disputed breakaway territory of Nagorno-Karabakh with its 'capital' at **Stepanakert**. Karabakh's Janapar Trail is a delightful village-to-village hiking route taking in castles and old churches. Return to Tbilisi via **Alaverdi** and the monasteries of **Haghpat** and **Sanahin**.

Countries at a Glance

Wherever you go in the South Caucasus, two of your strongest impressions will be the epic mountain scenery and wonderfully hospitable people. The spectacular Great Caucasus makes for wonderful hiking in Georgia, and Azerbaijan. Armenia and Nagorno-Karabakh are a crinkled jigsaw of mountains, valleys, plateaus and gorges, with good day walks.

Fans of ancient churches, monasteries, carvings and frescoes will adore Georgia, Armenia and Nagorno-Karabakh; Muslim Azerbaijan has its own sprinkling of palaces, mosques, forts and caravanserais.

Georgia is the most visited country, with a relatively good tourism infrastructure and rather more English spoken than in the other countries, though some Russian will still serve you in good stead. Travel is easy enough in Armenia, though fellow travellers are likely to be fewer. Azerbaijan is the least touristed by Westerners, mainly because of the visa hurdle. However, Azerbaijan's infrastructure has improved enormously in recent years: golf courses and ski resorts are appearing and the country is making growing attempts to attract world-class sporting events including 2016's Baku Grand Prix.

Visiting the breakaway republics Abkhazia and Nagorno-Karabakh remain politically sensitive adventures, reminding visitors of the region's precarious geopolitical position.

Georgia

Scenery
Hospitality
Outdoor Activities

Peaks & Vineyards
The Great Caucasus mountains will take your breath away with snowy peaks, green valleys and quaint stone villages. The lowlands are strewn with vineyards, rivers, forests and rocky canyons. And the Georgian habit of building churches and fortifications on picturesque perches only enhances the glories of the land's natural beauty.

Hearty Welcome
Georgians believe guests are gifts from on high, so providing hospitality is both customary and a pleasure. You'll often be delighted by the warmth of your welcome, at its best when you share locals' food and unfeasible quantities of their beloved wine.

Hikers' Paradise
Long-distance trails abound, some linking isolated mountain hamlets where medieval tower houses dominate the skyline. Villagers offer homestays and can supply horses should you tire of carrying a backpack. Rafting, paragliding and skiing are also possible in some areas.

p30

Armenia

Sacred Sites
Self-Driving Tours
Hiking

Churches & Monasteries

More than 1700 years of Christian heritage has left Armenia with a rich collection of ancient churches and monasteries, many still places of active worship. Most sacred is the heart of Armenian Christianity at Echmiadzin near Yerevan.

Rural Drives

Hiring a car will allow you to visit isolated medieval monasteries and picturesque mountain villages. Roads wend through wild-flower-strewn meadows, over magnificent passes and alongside swift-flowing rivers offering photo opportunities and picnic sites galore. Some rental deals allow you to drop off the car in Georgia.

Rustic Rambles

Armenia doesn't have alpine summits to challenge Georgia's but it offers plenty of scope for light hiking and backpacking. There are good walks around Dilijan, Ijevan and Tatev, and a more strenuous hike to the top of Mt Aragats.

p126

Azerbaijan

Scenery
Earth & Fire
Architecture

Deserts to Mountains

With dizzy Caucasian peaks, bald sheep-mown highlands, Caspian beaches, bucolic woodland meadows and craggy desert badlands, Azerbaijan packs in an astonishing variety of landscapes into a remarkably small space.

Spontaneous Combustion

If you're looking for offbeat curiosities, seek out Azerbaijan's gurgling mud volcanoes or investigate the unusual selection of fire phenomena, including 'inflammable' rivers, fire springs, burning hillsides and a classic fire temple that seems designed for a movie set.

Old & New

Baku's rash of dazzling 21st-century constructions contrast boldly with the city's stately century-old 'oil-boom' mansions, some grand Stalinist constructions and a Unesco-protected medieval Old City still enclosed within crenellated stone walls.

p197

Nagorno-Karabakh

Historic Sites
Architecture
Walking

Ancient Fortifications

Step back in time at Shushi, once one of the Caucasus' great cultural centres with fortifications and houses that date back to the mid-18th century. Much older is Tigranakert, an ancient city founded by Tigran the Great.

Forgotten Monasteries

Monasteries such as Gandzasar and Dadivank are fine examples of the centuries-old Armenian architectural craft. Amaras Monastery, founded by St Gregory the Illuminator in the early 4th century, is more modest in size but one of the world's oldest Christian sites.

Village Hikes

The well-marked Janapar Trail strikes out through the dramatic mountains, canyons and gorges of Karabakh, linking together a series of village-to-village day-hike footpaths that make it easy to get off the beaten track without carrying tents.

p265

On the Road

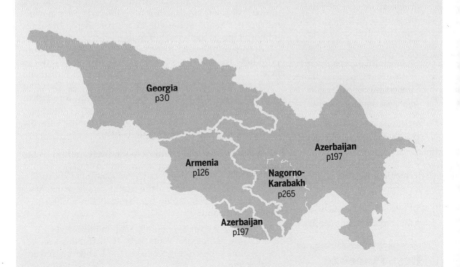

Georgia

📞 995 / POP 4 MILLION

Best Places to Eat

➡ Cafe Littera (p49)

➡ Shavi Lomi (p49)

➡ Old Boulevard (p80)

➡ Pheasant's Tears (p105)

➡ Mukhatsakatukha (p50)

Best Places to Stay

➡ Rooms Hotel (p91)

➡ Rooms Hotel (p47)

➡ Zeta Camp (p93)

➡ Skadaveli Guesthouse (p46)

➡ Roza Shukvani's Guesthouse (p84)

Why Go?

From its green valleys spread with vineyards to its old churches and watchtowers perched in fantastic mountain scenery, Georgia (Saqartvelo, საქართველო) is one of the most beautiful countries on earth and a marvellous canvas for walkers, horse riders, cyclists, skiers, rafters and travellers of every kind. Equally special are its proud, high-spirited, cultured people: Georgia claims to be the birthplace of wine, and this is a place where guests are considered blessings and hospitality is the very stuff of life.

A deeply complicated history has given Georgia a wonderful heritage of architecture and arts, from cave cities to ancient cathedrals to the inimitable canvases of Pirosmani. Tbilisi, the capital, is still redolent of an age-old Eurasian crossroads. But this is also a country moving forward in the 21st century, with spectacular contemporary buildings, a minimal crime rate and ever-improving facilities for the visitors who are a growing part of its future.

When to Go

➡ The ideal seasons in most of the country are from mid-May to early July, and early September to mid-October, when it's generally warm and sunny.

➡ July and August can be uncomfortably humid in the lowlands, with temperatures reaching 40°C. But this is an excellent time to be in the mountains, and it's high season on the Black Sea.

➡ Best months for hiking in the Great Caucasus are June to September.

➡ Early autumn brings the festive wine harvest in Kakheti, from about 20 September to 20 October.

➡ The eastern half of Georgia often suffers below-freezing temperatures between December and February.

FAST FACTS

Currency
Lari (GEL)

Language
Georgian

Emergencies
112

Visas
More than 90 nationalities need no visa for stays of up to one year. Those who need visas can apply online and receive them by email.

Resources
➡ **Agency of Protected Areas** (www.apa.gov.ge)

➡ **Civil.ge** (www.civil.ge)

➡ **Georgia** (http://georgia.travel)

➡ **Georgian Journal** (www.georgianjournal.ge)

➡ **Georgian National Museum** (http://museum.ge)

➡ **Georgian Wanderers** (www.facebook.com/groups/Georgianwanderers)

Exchange Rates

Australia	A$1	1.73 GEL
Canada	C$1	1.72 GEL
Euro zone	€1	2.60 GEL
Japan	¥100	2.02 GEL
NZ	NZ$1	1.61 GEL
UK	UK£1	3.54 GEL
USA	US$1	2.41 GEL

Daily Costs
➡ **Budget accommodation** per person 25 GEL

➡ **Two-course meal** 15–20 GEL

➡ **Museum** 3 GEL

➡ **Beer** per bottle 2–3GEL

➡ **100km marshrutka ride** 8 GEL

TBILISI

32 / POP 1.1 MILLION

Tbilisi (თბილისი) has come a long way since the Rose Revolution of 2003 ousted the post-Soviet Shevardnadze government.

To Tbilisi's eternal charms of a dramatic setting in the deep valley of the swift Mtkvari River, picturesque architecture, an ever-lively arts and cultural scene, and the welcoming Georgian lifestyle have been added a whole new 21st-century dimension of inviting cafes and restaurants serving ever-better food, up-to-date lodgings from backpacker hostels to international five-stars, funky bars and clubs, spruced-up museums, galleries, parks, plazas and whole streets, modernised transport and a sprinkling of eye-catching contemporary architecture. All of which make it a much easier, and more fun, city to visit and live in than it was less than a decade ago.

But the old Tbilisi is still very much here too. The Old Town, at the narrowest part of the valley, is still redolent of an ancient Eurasian crossroads, with its winding lanes, balconied houses, leafy squares and handsome churches, all overlooked by the 17-centuries-old Narikala Fortress. Neighbourhoods not far from the centre still retain a village-like feel with their narrow streets, small shops and community atmosphere. Small traders still clog up the pavements around metro stations selling fruit, vegetables, cheese and nuts fresh from the countryside.

The bus stations are still rooted in about the 1930s, too – but you can't have everything. Modern and ancient, Tbilisi remains the beating heart of the South Caucasus and should not be missed by any visitor.

History

Evidence of settlement in the area stretches back more than 6000 years, but Georgians like the legend that King Vakhtang Gorgasali of Kartli founded Tbilisi in the 5th century AD. The story runs that when the king was hunting, a wounded deer fell into a hot sulphur spring here and was miraculously healed. In fact, Gorgasali won the already-existing town back from the Persians, and moved his capital here from Mtskheta. But there's no doubt that it was Tbilisi's magnificent hot springs that gave it its name (Georgian *tbili* means warm).

The city's location, commanding a crossing of the Mtkvari River on age-old trade routes between Asia and Europe, has always been prized. In 645 Arabs captured Tbilisi and kept it as an emirate for four centuries, but in 1122 King David the Builder (Davit Aghmashenebeli) made it capital of his united Georgia, building a palace near the Metekhi Church. David invited Armenian

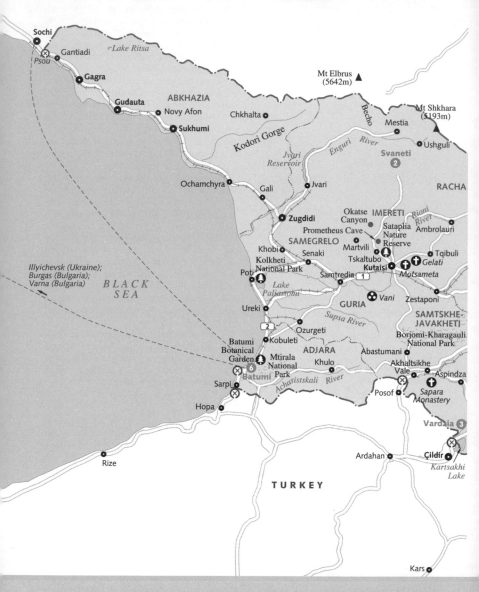

Karachaevsk

Sochi
Psou
Gantiadi
Gagra
Gudauta
Novy Afon
Sukhumi
ABKHAZIA
Chkhalta
Lake Ritsa
Kodori Gorge
Jvari Reservoir
Ochamchyra
Gali
Jvari
Zugdidi
SAMEGRELO
Khobi
Kolkheti National Park
Poti
Lake Paliastomi
Senaki
Ureki
Ozurgeti
2
Kobuleti
ADJARA
Batumi Botanical Garden
Mtirala National Park
Khulo
Batumi
6
Sarpi
Hopa
Rize

Mt Elbrus (5642m) ▲
Becho
Mestia
Enguri River
Svaneti 2
Mt Shkhara (5193m)
Ushguli
RACHA
Okatse Canyon
IMERETI
Rioni River
Sataplia Nature Reserve
Ambrolauri
Prometheus Cave
Martvili
Tskaltubo
Kutaisi **1**
Gelati
Tqibuli
Motsameta
Samtredia
Vani
Zestaponi
GURIA
Supsa River
SAMTSKHE-JAVAKHETI
Borjomi-Kharagauli National Park
Abastumani
Akhaltsikhe
Vale
Aspindza
Acharistskali River
Posof
Sapara Monastery
Vardzia 3
Ardahan
Çıldır
Kartsakhi Lake

BLACK SEA
Illyichevsk (Ukraine);
Burgas (Bulgaria);
Varna (Bulgaria)

TURKEY

Kars

Georgia Highlights

1 Enjoying the fascinating Old Town, fine restaurants, fun bars and good museums of **Tbilisi** (p31), the most charming Caucasian capital.

2 Discovering unique Svan culture, ancient defensive towers and wonderful walking amid Georgia's finest alpine scenery in **Svaneti** (p82).

3 Exploring **Vardzia** (p114), an entire medieval city carved out of a cliff face.

4 Catching the breathtaking sight of Tsminda Sameba Church silhouetted against legendary Mt Kazbek while

hiking around **Kazbegi** (p90).

⑤ Visiting the ancient cave monastery of **Davit Gareja** (p106) in its unique setting.

⑥ Soaking up the party atmosphere in **Batumi** (p76), Georgia's lovable Black Sea 'summer capital'.

⑦ Hiking the spectacular, pristine, high-mountain region of **Tusheti** (p95).

⑧ Spending days sipping the wines of **Kakheti** (p104) in the heartland of Georgian wine country.

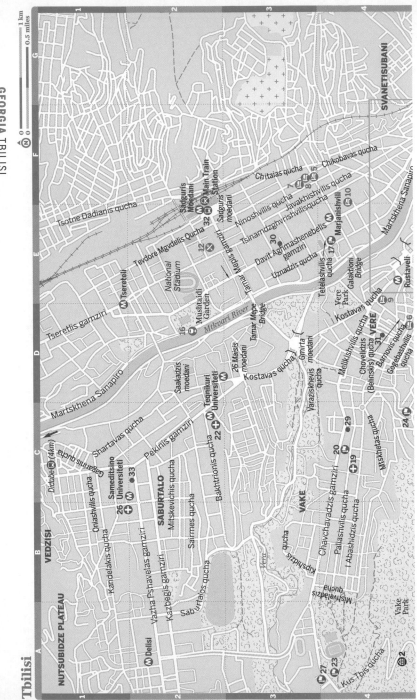

Tbilisi

Tbilisi

◎ Sights
1 Mtatsminda Park D5
2 Open-Air Museum of
   Ethnography A4
3 Tsminda Sameba Cathedral..............G5

🛏 Sleeping
4 Betsy's Hotel......................................D5
   Chubini Guest House ....(see 8)
5 Dodo's Guest House...........................F3
6 Hotel British House D4
7 Irina Guest House F3
8 Marina Guest House.........................F3
9 Rooms Hotel E4
10 Sky Hostel.......................................F4

✕ Eating
11 Chela..D5
12 Desertirebis Bazari............................E2
13 Maspindzelo......................................G6
14 Puri Guliani......................................D5
15 Rachasubani A5
   The Kitchen................................(see 9)

◎ Drinking & Nightlife
   Lounge Bar Funicular...............(see 14)
16 Mtkvarze D2
   Rooms Hotel Bar ....(see 9)

ℹ Information
17 Armenian Embassy............................E4
18 Azerbaijan Embassy..........................G6
19 CITO..C4
20 Dutch Embassy..................................C4
21 German Embassy G6
22 IMSS..C2
23 Iranian Consulate A4
24 Kazakhstan Embassy.........................C4
25 Medea Travel G6
26 MediClub Georgia..............................B1
27 Russian Interests Section of
   Swiss Embassy A4

ℹ Transport
28 Avlabari Minivan Stand G6
29 AZAL...C4
30 Georgian Airways E3
31 Jeep Rent..D4
32 Sadguris Moedani.............................E2
33 Vanilla Sky..C2

artisans and traders to settle here, and Armenians remained highly influential in Tbilisi until the 20th century. Under David and his great-granddaughter Queen Tamar, Tbilisi grew into a multi-ethnic city of 80,000 people, known for its production of weapons, jewellery, leather and silk clothing. The golden age was ended with a vengeance by the Mongols in 1235, who were followed by the Black Death, and then conqueror Timur (Tamerlane), who destroyed the city in 1386.

Tbilisi recovered somewhat under Persian rule during the 17th and 18th centuries, and in 1762 it became capital of a semi-independent eastern Georgia under King Erekle II. Erekle's protector Russia, however, withdrew its troops to fight the Turks, allowing Agha Mohamed Khan to inflict Persia's most devastating assault in 1795. His army killed tens of thousands and burnt Tbilisi to the ground. Russia annexed Georgia in 1800 and recreated Tbilisi in the imperial mould, laying out wide streets and squares. By 1899, it had 172,000 people, one-third of them Armenian and a quarter each Georgian and Russian.

The Soviet era saw huge growth as Georgians flooded in from the countryside. The city was a centre of opposition to the late Soviet regime and a battleground in the civil war that erupted after Georgian independence in 1991. The 1990s were dark years – literally, with frequent electricity blackouts – as living standards sank and corruption and crime became rife. But since the Rose Revolution of 2003 crime has almost disappeared and Tbilisi has enjoyed a flood of investment and refurbishment.

⊙ Sights

The Old Town, where Tbilisi began, is the most fascinating area for exploring. There's also plenty to see in the 19th-century city focused on Rustavelis gamziri, and in the Avlabari area on the left bank of the Mtkvari River. Most of the churches are open daylight hours every day.

⊙ Old Town ჯაღო

Tbilisi grew up below the walls of the Narikala Fortress, which stands on the Sololaki ridge above the west side of the Mtkvari. The buildings along the twisting lanes of the Old Town (Kala) have been renovated at a fairly fast lick over the past decade, but behind the pretty facades and off the main streets you'll still find picturesque dilapidation aplenty, with half-overgrown courtyards surrounded by carved wooden balconies – indeed some whole houses – leaning at rakish angles. Many buildings here date from soon after the Persian sacking of 1795, and still have the Eurasian character of earlier times.

The main thoroughfare of the Old Town is Kote Abkhazi, still widely known by its former name Leselidze, which winds down from Tavisuplebis moedani (Freedom Sq) to the busy square Meidan. Heading back north from Meidan, parallel to the river, is a string of narrow, traffic-free streets that formed the heaving commercial hub of the Old Town in medieval times – Sioni, Erekle II and Shavteli.

Jvaris Mama Church   CHURCH
(Map p38; cnr Kote Abkhazi & Ierusalimi) Little Jvaris Mama stands on a site where a church has stood since the 5th century. The current incarnation dates from the 16th century and its interior is covered in recently restored frescoes in striking reds, golds and blues. Entered from the same courtyard/garden is the large Armenian **Norasheni Church** (Map p38; Kote Abkhazi 41), dating from 1793. It was long disused but renovations began in 2015.

Meidan   SQUARE
(Map p38) In tsarist times Meidan was the site of Tbilisi's bustling main bazaar. Today it's busy with traffic but lined on two sides by restaurants and cafes, and it opens to the Metekhi Bridge over the Mtkvari – all overlooked by Narikala Fortress.

Armenian Cathedral
of St George   CATHEDRAL
(Map p38; Samghebro) This large cathedral just above Meidan was founded in 1251, though the current structure dates mainly from the 18th century. Its interior is surprisingly small but has colourful 18th-century frescoes. King Erekle II's famed Armenian court poet Sayat Nova was killed here during the Persian invasion of 1795 and his tomb is just outside the main door.

Tbilisi History Museum   MUSEUM
(Map p38; Sioni 8; admission 3 GEL; ⊙10am-6pm Tue-Sun) The eclectic exhibits here, housed in an old caravanserai, range from models and photos of old houses to high-society and ethnic costumes from the 19th century and realistic mock-ups of period craft workshops. There's a small restaurant.

On the lower floor is a set of contemporary craft workshops and showrooms, with some original jewellery, textiles and ceramics that are a class above regular touristic kitsch.

Sioni Cathedral   CATHEDRAL
(Map p38; Sioni 6) Sioni was originally built in the 6th and 7th centuries, but has been destroyed and rebuilt many times, and what you see today is mainly 13th century.

It is of special significance for Georgians because it's home to the sacred cross of St Nino which, according to legend, is made from vine branches bound with the saint's own hair. A replica of the cross sits behind a bronze grille to the left of the icon screen. The real thing is apparently kept safe inside.

★**Peace Bridge** BRIDGE
(Mshvidobis Khidi; Map p38) The street Erekle II, lined with cafes and galleries, gives access to the Peace Bridge, an elegant glass-and-steel footbridge over the Mtkvari, designed by Italian Michele De Lucchi and opened in 2010 – one of the most eye-catching of the many love-it-or-hate-it avant-garde structures that went up around Georgia in the Saakashvili years.

Residence of the Catholicos-Patriarch BUILDING
(Map p38) Opposite the small, leafy (but closed) park Erekle II moedani, high walls hide the residence of the Catholicos-Patriarch, head of the Georgian Orthodox Church.

★**Anchiskhati Basilica** CHURCH
(Map p38; Shavteli) Tbilisi's oldest surviving church is perhaps its loveliest. Built by King Gorgasali's son Dachi in the 6th century, it's a three-nave basilica whose weathered frescoes and walls of big stone blocks emphatically bespeak its age. The church's name comes from the icon of Anchi Cathedral in Klarjeti (now in Turkey), which was brought here in the 17th century (it's now in Tbilisi's Fine Arts Museum).

★**Clock Tower** TOWER
(Map p38; Shavteli 13; 🏠) One of old Tbilisi's most emblematic structures is one of its newest – the higgledy-piggledy clock tower, like something out of a fairy tale, outside the Gabriadze puppet theatre. Built by puppet master Rezo Gabriadze during a renovation of his theatre a few years ago, it evokes the spirit not only of the theatre beside it but also, somehow, of the whole Old Town. On the hour, an angel pops out of a door near the top and strikes the bell outside with a hammer.

Abanotubani ARCHITECTURE
(Map p38; Abano) A short walk south from Meidan, a collection of strange brick domes rises from the ground behind a small park. These are Tbilisi's famed sulphur baths, the Abanotubani. Alexanders Dumas and Push-

kin both bathed here, the latter describing it as the best bath he'd ever had. The domes are the roofs of subterranean **bathhouses** (p45). Outwardly more impressive, the above-ground Orbeliani Baths have a Central Asian feel to their blue-tile facade.

Botanical Gardens GARDENS
(Map p38; Botanikuri; admission 1 GEL; ⊙9am-6pm Mar, to 8pm Apr-Aug, to 7pm Sep, to 5pm Oct-Feb) It's easy to wander for a couple of hours in these tree-filled and waterfall-dotted gardens, which stretch more than a kilometre up the valley beneath the cliffs of Narikala Fortress. They were opened in 1845 on what had earlier been royal gardens.

On the way up to the gardens you pass a red-brick **mosque** (Map p38; Botanikuri) dating from 1895 – the only mosque in Tbilisi to survive Lavrenty Beria's purges of the 1930s. The interior is prettily frescoed and visitors are welcome to enter (after removing shoes).

◎ **Narikala Fortress & Around**

★**Narikala Fortress** FORTRESS
(Map p38; Orpiri; ⊙9am-9pm) FREE Dominating the Old Town skyline, Narikala dates right back to the 4th century, when it was a Persian citadel. The best way to reach it is by cable car (p39) from Rike Park. Or you can walk up from Meidan. The views over Tbilisi from the top of the fortress are superb.

Most of the walls were built in the 8th century by the Arab emirs, whose palace was inside the fortress. Subsequently Georgians, Turks and Persians captured and patched up Narikala, but in 1827 a huge explosion of Russian munitions stored here wrecked the whole thing. The Church of St Nicholas, inside the fortress, was rebuilt in the 1990s with funding from a police chief.

GEORGIAN STREET NAMES

The spelling of Georgian street names varies depending on whether words such as *qucha* (street), *gamziri* (avenue) or *moedani* (square) are present. In Georgian, Rustaveli Avenue is Rustavelis gamziri, but is often just referred to as Rustaveli. To simplify matters, we use noninflected names in addresses – for example, Rustaveli rather than Rustavelis gamziri – unless there is more than one street with the same name.

Tbilisi Old Town

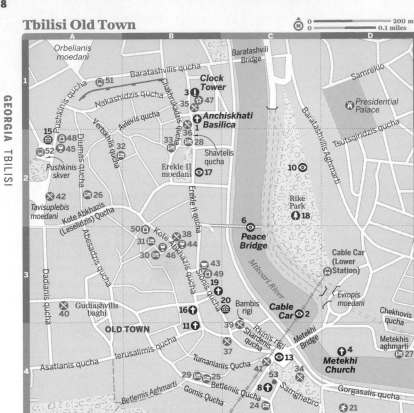

Kartlis Deda

MONUMENT

(Mother Georgia; Map p38) From Narikala (or the top cable car station), you can take a scenic walk west along the Sololaki ridge. The main landmark is the statue of Mother Georgia. This 20m-tall aluminium symbol of Tbilisi holds a sword in one hand and a cup of wine in the other – a classic metaphor for the Georgian character, warmly welcoming guests and passionately fighting off enemies.

Past Mother Georgia are the ruins of the **Shahtakhti fortress** (Shah's Throne; Map p40), which housed an Arab observatory, and then the enormous private **residence** of Bidzina Ivanishvili (Map p40), Georgia's richest man who was prime minister from 2012 to 2103. You can't see much of the palatial residence up close (the road discreetly passes underneath it) but from a distance it looks a bit like a space station.

◉ Avlabari

Avlabari is the dramatically located slice of Tbilisi above the cliffs on the east bank of the Mtkvari, across the Metekhi Bridge from the Old Town. At least twice, foreign invaders (the roaming Central Asian con-

Tbilisi Old Town

GEORGIA TBILISI

queror Jalaledin in 1226, and the Persians in 1522) used the bridge for forcible conversion of Georgians to Islam (those who resisted were tossed into the river).

★**Metekhi Church**   CHURCH
(Map p38; Metekhis aghmarti) The landmark Metekhi Church, and the 1960s equestrian statue of King Vakhtang Gorgasali beside it, occupy the strategic rocky outcrop above the Metekhi Bridge. This is where Vakhtang Gorgasali built his palace, and the site's first church, when he made Tbilisi his capital in the 5th century. The existing church was built by King Demetre Tavdadebuli (the Self-Sacrificing) between 1278 and 1289, and has been reconstructed many times since.

The building is thought to be a copy of King David the Builder's 12th-century church on this site, which was destroyed by the Mongols in 1235.

★**Cable Car**   CABLE CAR
(Map p38; one-way ride 1 GEL; ⊙ 11am-11pm) Tbilisi's most exhilarating ride – along with the Mtatsminda funicular (p43) – is the cable car, new in 2012, which swings from the south end of Rike Park high over the Mtkvari River and Old Town up to Narikala Fortress. To ride it, you need a Metromoney card (p53), available at the ticket offices if you don't have one.

Rike Park   PARK
(Map p38; ⊞) This attractive flowery expanse along the eastern riverbank, with its winding paths, pools and fountains, is joined to the west side of the Mtkvari by the Peace Bridge (p37). The two large metallic tubes at the park's north end are a **concert hall and exhibition centre** (Map p38; unfinished at the time of writing), designed by Italy's Massimiliano Fuksas.

Central Tbilisi

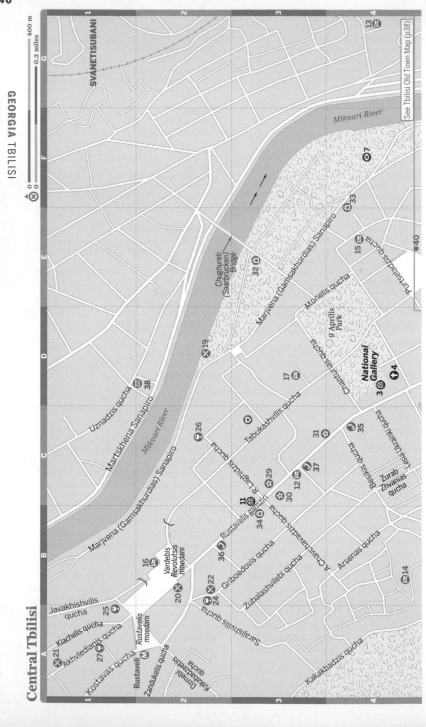

400 m
0.2 miles

SVANETISUBANI

See Tbilisi Old Town Map (p38)

Mtkvari River

Chughureti
(Saarbrucken)
Bridge

Marjvena (Gamsakhurdias) Sanapiro

Atonelis qucha

9 Aprilis
Park

National
Gallery

Chanturias qucha

Mtkvari River

Martskhena Sanapiro

Uznadzis qucha

Tabukashvilis qucha

Besikis qucha

Zurab
Zhvanias
qucha

Lesia Ukrainkas qucha

Marjvena (Gamsakhurdias) Sanapiro

R Lagidzis qucha

Rustavelis gamziri

A Chavchavadzis qucha

Griboedovis qucha

Zubalashvilebi qucha

Arsenas qucha

Sarajishvilis qucha

Kakabadzis qucha

Vardebis
Revolutsis
moedani

Javakhishvilis
qucha

Kiachelis qucha

Akhvledianis qucha

Kostavas qucha

Rustaveli

Rustavelis
moedani

Dzmebi
Kakabadzebis
qucha

Zandukelis qucha

Purtseladzis qucha

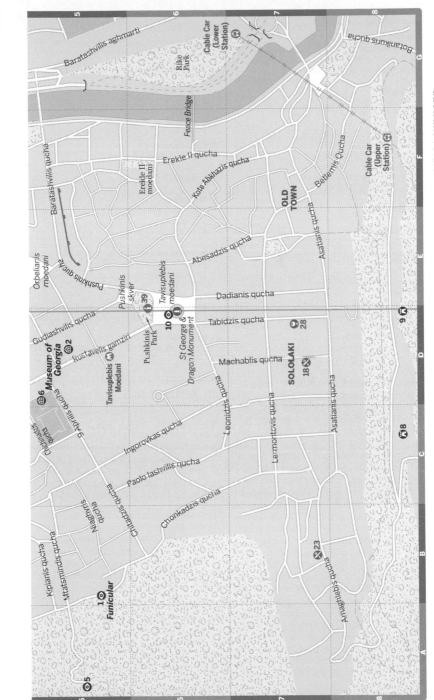

Central Tbilisi

Tsminda Sameba Cathedral CATHEDRAL
(Holy Trinity Cathedral; Map p34; Samreklo) The biggest symbol of the Georgian Orthodox church's post-Soviet revival towers on Elia Hill above Avlabari. Tsminda Sameba, unmissable by night and day, was consecrated in 2004 after a decade of building. A massive and lavish expression of traditional Georgian architectural forms in concrete, brick, granite and marble, it rises 84m to the top of the gold-covered cross above its gold-covered central dome. It's often very busy but retains a quiet, pious atmosphere, with many individuals praying, and candles burning before its numerous richly decorated icons.

The cathedral is five aisles wide but its emphasis is on verticality, with a result like one single, many-bulwarked tower. The huge dome creates a larger, much brighter central space than you'll find in most Georgian churches. Designed by Archil Mindiashvili, the building was paid for mostly by donations. Some controversy surrounded its construction on the site of an old Armenian cemetery.

◎ Rustaveli

Tbilisi's main artery, Rustavelis gamziri, is named after the national bard, Shota Rustaveli, and runs 1.5km north from Tavisuplebis moedani (Freedom Sq) to Rustavelis moedani. Laid out by the Russians in the 19th century, it's strung with elegant and important buildings. It's also a fast traffic route, dangerous to cross except by four pedestrian underpasses.

Tavisuplebis Moedani SQUARE
(Freedom Sq; Map p40) This busy traffic nexus was Lenin Sq in Soviet times. Georgia's last Lenin statue, toppled in 1990, stood where the golden St George (a gift to the city from its sculptor, Zurab Tsereteli) now spears his dragon.

Museum of Fine Arts MUSEUM
(Map p38; ☑2999909; Gudiashvili 1; admission 3 GEL, guide per group 10 GEL; ☉10am-6pm Tue-Sun) This museum's star turn is its Treasury section, enterable only with a guide (English/German/French speakers available). It contains a vast wealth of icons, crosses and jewellery in precious metals and stones from all

over Georgia and old Georgian churches on what is now Turkish territory. Many of Georgia's most sacred and revered objects are here. Don't miss the beautiful little pectoral cross of Queen Tamar, set with four emeralds, five rubies and six pearls – the only known personal relic of the great 12th-century monarch.

★ **Museum of Georgia** MUSEUM
(Map p40; www.museum.ge; Rustaveli 3; adult/student 5/1 GEL; ⊙10am-6pm Tue-Sun) The major highlight of the impressive main national museum is the Archaeological Treasury, displaying a wealth of pre-Christian gold, silver and precious-stone work from burials in Georgia going back to the 3rd millennium BC. Most stunning are the fabulously detailed gold adornments from Colchis (western Georgia). On the top floor, the Museum of Soviet Occupation has copious detail on Soviet repression and resistance to it.

The museum also stages temporary exhibitions from its large stored collections, such as Asian art and historical photography. In the lobby (free admission) are exhibits from Dmanisi, the archaeological site in southern Georgia whose 1.8 million-year-old hominid skulls are rewriting the study of early European humanity.

Parliament Building HISTORIC BUILDING
(Map p40; Rustaveli 8) The high-arched former Parliament building has seen momentous events, including the deaths of 19 Georgian hunger strikers at the hands of Soviet troops on 9 April 1989, and the Rose Revolution on 22 November 2003. It ceased to be the home of Parliament in 2012 when Georgia's new Parliament in Kutaisi opened, but many MPs want to return Parliament to Tbilisi, so the future is uncertain.

The building was constructed between 1938 and 1953 for Georgia's Soviet government. A small monument in front of it, and paving stones and glass panels set at irregular angles, commemorate the dead of 1989.

★ **National Gallery** GALLERY
(Map p40; Rustaveli 11; adult/student 5/1 GEL; ⊙10am-6pm Tue-Sun) For most visitors the highlight here is the hall of wonderful canvases by Georgia's best known painter Pirosmani (Niko Pirosmanashvili, 1862–1918), ranging from his celebrated animal and feast scenes to lesser-known portraits and rural-life canvases. There's also a good selection of work by other top 20th-century Georgian artists Lado Gudiashvili and David

Kakabadze. Enter from the park beside the Kashveti Church.

Zurab Tsereteli Museum of Modern Art MUSEUM
(Map p40; www.momatbilisi.ge; Rustaveli 27; admission 5 GEL; ⊙11am-6pm Tue-Sun) The art here is, apart from the odd temporary exhibition, all the work of one man – the museum's founder Zurab Tsereteli. This now Moscow-based Georgian is one of those lucky artists who becomes a financial success in his own lifetime, and the sculptures and paintings here are characteristic of his grandiose, larger-than-life work found in many countries.

Public Service Hall ARCHITECTURE
(Map p40; http://psh.gov.ge; Marjvena (Gamsakhurdias) Sanapiro; ⊙9am-6pm Mon-Fri) Nicknamed the Umbrellas, this building by Italian Massimiliano Fuksas is the biggest of a dozen Public Service Halls opened in new, contemporary buildings around Georgia by the Saakashvili government – one-stop shops for citizens to deal quickly with government bureaucracy in an open, corruption-deterring environment.

◉ Mt Mtatsminda

Mtatsminda is the hill topped by the 210m-high TV mast looming over central Tbilisi from the west. There's an amusement park up here, **Mtatsminda Park** (Map p34, http://park.ge; rides 1-5 GEL; ⊙9am-11pm; ⛷), but more exciting (for adults, anyway) is the spectacular ride up on the recently reconstructed **funicular** (Map p40; Chonkadze; one-way ride before/after midnight 2/3 GEL; ⊙9am-4am), as well as the views from the top. The restaurant building at the top of the funicular has a couple of great places to eat or drink (p51). To ride the funicular you need a 2 GEL plastic card, sold at the ticket office, on which you then add credit for your rides.

Walking trails lead across to Narikala Fortress (2.5km) and down past the national **pantheon** (Map p40) back to near the bottom of the funicular (1km).

◉ Vake ვაკე

Open-Air Museum of Ethnography MUSEUM
(Map p34; Kus Tbis qucha 1; adult/child 3/0.60 GEL; ⊙10am-6pm Tue-Sun Jun-Sep, 10am-5pm Tue-Sun Oct-May) This collection of traditional, mostly wooden houses, collected from all around Georgia, is spread over a wooded hillside with good views, and makes for an enjoyable

City Walk
Tbilisi New & Old

START RUSTAVELI METRO STATION
END NARIKALA FORTRESS
LENGTH 3.5KM; THREE HOURS

This walk takes you along Tbilisi's main avenue and into the narrow lanes of the Old Town, then up to Narikala Fortress with its great panoramas.

Start at the ❶ **monument to Shota Rustaveli** outside Rustaveli metro station. Pass the Stalinist ❷ **Academy of Sciences** at Rustaveli 52, with an informal souvenir market outside, then walk along Rustaveli to imbibe the busy atmosphere of Tbilisi's main artery. The street is strung with handsome and important buildings such as the Moorish-style ❸ **Opera & Ballet Theatre** (p52), built in 1896; the baroque-cum-rococo 1901 ❹ **Rustaveli Theatre** (p52); the ❺ **Parliament building** (p43); and the ❻ **Museum of Georgia** (p43). Rustaveli ends at wide ❼ **Tavisuplebis moedani** (p42) with its landmark St George and Dragon monument.

Head to the left down Pushkin, skirting the old ❽ **city walls**. At the bottom turn right into traffic-free Shavteli to Tbilisi's quirkiest building, the Gabriadze Theatre's rakishly crooked ❾ **Clock Tower** (p37). Continue to the city's oldest church and one of its prettiest, ❿ **Anchiskhati Basilica** (p37). ⓫ **Cafe Leila** (p49) across the street here is one of Tbilisi's most charming cafes and a perfect drinks stop. Continue south then turn left on to the most emblematic of Tbilisi's new structures, the elegant ⓬ **Peace Bridge** (p37) over the Mtkvari River, taking in the views of the also recently built Presidential Palace and Tsminda Sameba Cathedral up on the east side of the river.

Enjoy the flowers of ⓭ **Rike Park** (p39) before crossing back over the Peace Bridge and wandering down cafe-lined Erekle II to the revered ⓮ **Sioni Cathedral** (p36), home of the sacred cross of St Nino. Continue to busy ⓯ **Meidan** (p36) square where you turn right up to the recently renovated ⓰ **Armenian Cathedral of St George** (p36). It's five minutes more up to ⓱ **Narikala Fortress** (p37) – a steepish ending to your walk but well worth it for the views when you get there!

visit. The most interesting exhibits are in the lower section (near the entrance), where the buildings are kitted out with traditional furnishings, rugs and utensils, and the attendants can often explain things in English. A Georgian lunch at **Rachasubani** (Map p34; Kus Tbis qucha; mains 6-25 GEL; ⊘10am-11pm; 🕿) is a nice idea while you're here.

You can walk up to the museum through large, verdant Vake Park (reachable by bus 61 from Tavisuplebis moedani or northbound on Rustaveli), or stay on the bus until the petrol station 200m past the large Iranian embassy, then walk or take a taxi 1.4km up the road opposite.

🏃 Activities

Rafting and paragliding adventures can be had within an hour or two's drive of the city, and you can indulge in the Old Town's traditional steam baths any day.

Abanotubani

Any time of year is good for the unique experience of a traditional bath at Tbilisi's famed, steaming sulphur baths. There are several bathhouses to choose from. None could be described as modern or luxurious, but if you don't fancy the idea of stripping off among strangers at an inexpensive men's or women's public bath, most bathhouses also offer private rooms of various sizes with their own pools.

Abano No 5 (Map p38; per hr public baths 3 GEL, private rooms 40-80 GEL; ⊘24hr), said to be the oldest at around 300 years, has typical public baths but also a couple of decent private rooms. The fancier **Royal Bath** (Map p38; Grishashvili 1; rooms 45-80 GEL, scrub or massage 10 GEL; ⊘8am-11pm) has mosaic-domed private rooms only, and helpful Russian-speaking attendants (plus tea and beer). The popular and reasonably priced **Orbeliani Baths** (Map p38; Abano), with their impressive blue-tile facade and both public and private rooms, were closed for renovations at the time of writing but are always worth checking out.

Adventure Sports

Georgia's many rivers provide exciting runs for rafters of all levels. The season is from late April to mid-October (best until July on most rivers). A half-day trip with a one-to-1½-hour run on the Mtiuletis Aragvi or Pshavis Aragvi north of Tbilisi, suitable for beginners and up, typically costs 40 GEL per person for four or more people, plus 100 GEL to 150 GEL per group for transport. There are also challenges for experienced rafters on the Mtkvari River near Borjomi and Vardzia, and the Rioni River in western Georgia (June to November).

Georgian Adventures & Tours ADVENTURE SPORTS (📞599535589; www.facebook.com/georgian adventures) A reliable and recommended outfit for rafting and kayaking, with very experienced guides.

Adventure Club Jomardi ADVENTURE SPORTS (📞570100244, 599141160; www.adventure. ge; Robakidze 7; ⊘office 10am-6pm Mon-Fri; Ⓜ Didube) Jomardi is the longest-established rafting operator, with English-speaking guides available. It also rents sleeping bags (per day 5 GEL), sleeping mats (3 GEL), three-person tents (10 GEL) and mountain bikes (30 GEL to 50 GEL).

Irakli Kapanadze PARAGLIDING, SKIING (📞599690769, 595424298; i_kapanadze@yahoo. com) Irakli is a top mountain- and ski-touring guide and also a highly experienced paraglider who takes inexperienced flyers on tandem flights in areas near Tbilisi from March to October, for 50 GEL, and from Gudauri ski resort from late December to mid-April for 120 GEL to 220 GEL, transport included.

He can also provide logistical support for groups of experienced pilots who want to fly in good late-summer conditions (August to September) in areas including Gudauri and Svaneti.

🎉 Festivals & Events

Art-Gene Festival MUSIC, CRAFTS (www.artgeni.ge; ⊘Jul) This popular Georgian folk festival visits the regions then culminates with several days of music, dance, cooking, arts and crafts at Tbilisi's Open-Air Museum of Ethnography (p43).

Tbilisi International Festival of Theatre THEATRE (http://tbilisiinternational.com; ⊘Sep/Oct) Big program of shows by Georgian and international theatre groups and companies, over two weeks in September/October.

Tbilisoba FOOD, CULTURAL (tbilisoba.ge; ⊘Oct; 🏛) Tbilisi comes out to party for this festival of the autumn harvest and the city's founding, centred around the Old Town and Rike Park, over a weekend in

October. There are *mtsvadi* (shish kebabs), *khinkali* (spicy dumplings) and wine stalls everywhere, music and dance events, cheese, fruit and craft festivals and plenty more.

Tbilisi International Film Festival
FILM

(www.tbilisifilmfestival.ge; ⊙ Nov/Dec) Showcases recent Georgian and international movies, over a week usually in November or December.

🛏 Sleeping

There is a good range of places to stay in and around the areas of most interest to visitors, namely the Old Town and Rustavelis gamziri, including dozens of backpacker hostels (some of which vanish as fast as they appear – our recommendations have stood the test of time).

🛏 Old Town

Namaste Hostel
HOSTEL $

(Map p38; ☑2753446; www.facebook.com/pages/Namaste-Hostel-Tbilisi/585674301453197; Betlemi 26; dm 20-27 GEL, d 80-95 GEL; ❀🤖) This friendly, well-kept hostel has a great location with expansive views over the city. Its good facilities include panoramic terraces and a colourful, quirkily decorated lounge area with fireplace.

Old Town Hostel
HOSTEL $

(Map p38; ☑596122255, 571004002; tbilisioldtownhostel@gmail.com; Vakhtang Beridze 7; dm 20-25 GEL, d 60-70 GEL; ❀❀@🤖) A well-equipped hostel on a quiet lane, with a front yard for sitting out. It has four private rooms as well as the two dorms with good solid bunks and bright green bedding. The hostel offers out-of-town car trips.

Friends Hostel
HOSTEL $

(Map p38; ☑555507705, 577737771; www.friendshostel.ge; Betlemi 28-30; dm/d 15/40 GEL; 🤖) A small, friendly, cheap hostel in one of the quaintest parts of old Tbilisi, Friends has an open-plan arrangement with the three small private rooms entered through its 10-person dorm, so it's hard not to meet everyone else. There's a tiny bar, and lovely views.

★ Skadaveli Guesthouse
GUESTHOUSE $$

(Map p38; ☑595417333; www.ska.ge; Vertskhli 27; s 50 GEL, d 70-90 GEL; ❀❀🤖) This Old Town hideaway has just four very attractive, good-value rooms with contemporary furnishings and comfy beds – plus a lovely wood-columned verandah for sitting out, and a super-helpful host, all in amazing contrast to the quaintly dilapidated exterior of this 1860s building. An extra 10 GEL per room is charged for one-night stays; no children under 14 years.

★ Envoy Hostel
HOSTEL $$

(Map p38; ☑2920111; www.envoyhostel.com/tbilisi; Betlemi 45; incl breakfast dm 25-36 GEL, d/tr 95/130 GEL; ❀❀@🤖) Envoy has a great location just above Meidan square and is one of Tbilisi's best hostels. It's an old parquet-floored house, now with six dorms, four privates, a scenic roof terrace, a good modern kitchen-dining area, and an adequate number of showers and toilets.

Guests get a free two-hour Old Town walking tour, and on Saturdays it runs a minibus to its Yerevan hostel (p140) with stops at several of northern Armenia's main sights (135 GEL, 11 hours).

Hotel Urban Oasis
BOUTIQUE HOTEL $$

(Map p38; ☑591100004; www.facebook.com/pages/urban-oasis/806900292714768; Shavteli 8; d incl breakfast US$70-90, 3-room apt US$200; ℗❀❀🤖) Formerly a luxurious private home, Urban Oasis is full of interesting decorative details and antique furniture, with a carved stone fireplace and Steinway grand piano in the sitting room. The high-ceilinged rooms have a bright, airy, modern feel, with good beds and toiletries. Breakfasts are satisfying, and the big terrace has fine views across to Tsminda Sameba Cathedral.

Villa Mtiebi
BOUTIQUE HOTEL $$

(Map p38; ☑2920340; www.hotelmtiebi.ge; Chakhrukhadze 10; incl breakfast s €68, d €79-99; ❀❀🤖) A small hotel that maintains its building's original art-nouveau elegance. Rooms are soundproofed and service is welcoming and attentive.

Hotel Dzveli Ubani
HOTEL $$

(Map p38; ☑2922404; www.megzuri.com.ge; Diuma 5; s/d incl breakfast US$50/60; ❀🤖) This small hotel in a rambling Old Town house has modest but cosy and well-equipped rooms. The top-floor mansard rooms are the most appealing.

No12 Boutique Hotel
BOUTIQUE HOTEL $$$

(Map p38; ☑2552212; www.no12hotel.com; Vakhtang Beridze 12; incl breakfast s US$116-205, d US$152-226; ❀❀@🤖) On a quiet lane right in the heart of the Old Town, No12 offers attractive if smallish rooms with exposed brick panels, pretty tile-surrounded mirrors and coloured-glass lampshades. Staff are amiable and there's a nice upstairs terrace.

Rustaveli Area

★Why Not? Hostel
HOSTEL $

(Map p40; ✆599007030; www.whynohostels.com; Tabukashvili 15/4; incl breakfast dm 18-32 GEL, d 65 GEL; ✉🖥) The building looks pretty ramshackle from outside, but on the inside this is a fun, sociable hostel in a funky, spacious, two-level house. It has nice big common areas, and the five dorms (one for women only) all have solid wood bunks except the cheapest option, a large room with 16 mattresses on the floor.

Tea, coffee and washing machine are free, and it offers good-value out-of-town day trips.

Boombully Rooms & Hostel
HOSTEL $

(Map p40; ✆551100172, 2931638; http://boombully.com; Rustaveli 24; dm/s/d/tr €11.50/24.50/29/37.50; ✉✳🖥) Boombully has a good location, sociable atmosphere and friendly young management. There are three private rooms, comfy bunks in the one dorm (which might be converting to privates) and a pine-panelled kitchen, all around a spacious sitting area with a balcony overlooking Rustaveli.

Nest Hostel
HOSTEL $

(Map p40; ✆598161771; www.nesthosteltbilisi.com; Orbeliani 27/34; dm 20-25 GEL, d 70 GEL, tr 70-90 GEL, q 90 GEL; ✉✳🖥) From the well-travelled team that's behind Canudos Ethnic Bar (p52), this is a friendly, smallish hostel in a quaint house with an unusual spiral staircase and pleasant little yard. It's tucked down a tiny alley off Purtseladze near the corner of Orbeliani – hopefully they'll put a sign out by the time you get there.

Guest House Formula 1
GUESTHOUSE $$

(Map p40; ✆574456789; www.formula1georgia.com; Kote Meskhi 13a; incl breakfast s US$35, d US$39-49, tr/f US$59/89; ✳🖥) It's a bit of a hike uphill from the town centre, but handily located for the Mtatsminda funicular and run by a hospitable family. There are four cosy, carpeted rooms, the best being the top-floor family suite with its private terrace.

Betsy's Hotel
HOTEL $$$

(Map p34; ✆2931404; www.betsyshotel.com; Makashvili 32-34; s/d incl breakfast US$130/150; ✉✳@🖥🎿🎿) An American-owned stalwart of comfort and good service, Betsy's has a panoramic location on the slopes of Mt Mtatsminda. The rooms are bright and spick-and-span, with attractive Georgian carpets, appealing original art and well-equipped bathrooms, and most have great views over the city.

The bar (especially its Friday happy hour from 6pm to last customer) and restaurant are both highly recommended, and there's also a small outdoor pool.

Radisson Blu Iveria Hotel
LUXURY HOTEL $$$

(Map p40; ✆2402200; radissonblu.com/hotel-tbilisi; Vardebis Revolutsis moedani 1; r from US$398; P✉✳@🖥🎿) The Radisson has panoramic, luxurious rooms with super-comfy beds, most looking along the Mtkvari River and far beyond. Its several good restaurants, cafes and bars include a 24-hour summer terrace with great vistas, and there's an excellent spa, pool and fitness centre on the 18th and 19th floors (included in room rates), plus a big outdoor pool.

Vere

This mostly residential area northwest of Rustaveli has a couple of interesting options.

★Rooms Hotel
BOUTIQUE HOTEL $$$

(Map p34; ✆2020099; http://roomshotels.com/tbilisi; Kostava 14; r incl breakfast US$165-307; P✉✳🖥) Rooms is by far Tbilisi's most stylish hotel. Common areas lead into another in an appealing semi-open-plan, nonformal arrangement, while the wood-furnished rooms are well kitted out in contemporary styles but with quaint throwback details like transistor radios and even the occasional iron-footed bathtub.

An entrance lobby lined with shelves of books gives some idea what to expect and opens into a spacious, cosy lounge, followed by a bar, followed by the top-class restaurant, The Kitchen (p51) – and the long courtyard-garden has a wonderful summer bar. It's a 135-room hotel but the friendliness of the staff is of a kind you'd only expect in somewhere much smaller.

Hotel British House
BOUTIQUE HOTEL $$$

(Map p34; ✆2988783; www.british-house.ge; Chovelidze 32; s/d incl breakfast €85/100; ✉✳🖥) This elegant little hotel in a quiet, leafy part of Vere has a welcoming, home-like atmosphere, with antiques and original art abounding. Staff are obliging and the rooms are attractive and well-equipped, with carpets and quality furnishings including king-size beds.

East of the River

The Marjanishvili area has an appealing neighbourhood atmosphere, full of small shops.

Irina Guest House
HOSTEL $

(Irene Japaridze's Boarding House; Map p34; ☑ 599111669; guesthouse-irina.ge; 3rd fl, Ninoshvili 19b; dm/s/d/tr/q 20/35/50/75/100 GEL; ☺❄@☎) This long-standing backpacker favourite has beds and bunks squeezed into almost every available space, which guarantees a social experience. Altogether its two floors contain nine air-conditioned rooms, two kitchens, four showers and six toilets. There's free tea and coffee. It's just off Marjanishvili and well signed.

Dodo's Guest House
GUESTHOUSE $

(Map p34; ☑ 579954213, 2954213; dodogeorgia@gmail.com; Marjanishvili 38; dm 20-25 GEL, apt from €30; ☺☎🖥) With four large rooms full of beds and bunks, Dodo's has a kind of antiquated charm, and the family has been hosting and helping travellers for two decades. The bathroom and kitchen could use an upgrade, though. They also have a nice apartment with a kind of *fin-de-siècle* feel (minimum two-night stay).

Sky Hostel
HOSTEL, GUESTHOUSE $$

(Sky Guest House; Map p34; ☑ 551080205; www.facebook.com/skyguesthousetbilisi; Davit Aghmashenebeli 77; s/d/tr €18/22/30; ☺☎) This welcoming place has just four plain but bright and well-kept rooms sharing two bathrooms. There are no dorms but it has a kind of hostel feel thanks to its friendly hostess and shared kitchen/sitting room. It's the pink building at the far end of the Aghmashenebeli 77 courtyard.

Marina Guest House
GUESTHOUSE $$

(Map p34; ☑ 2959259; www.marinatbilisi.com; Chubinashvili 20; per person incl breakfast US$25; Ⓟ☺☎) Marina's good-sized rooms, for up to five people, have a slight oriental touch and are set along the beautiful 1st-floor balcony of this 19th-century house. Breakfasts are good and your hostess is welcoming and helpful.

Chubini Guest House
GUESTHOUSE $$

(Map p34; ☑ 599551655; georgekhmelevski@gmail.com; Chubinashvili 20; s/d/tr/q incl breakfast 60/80/120/140 GEL; Ⓟ☺☎; Ⓜ Marjanishvili) Chubini is a good option with two rooms and an apartment, all with private bathroom, on the ground floor of a handsome balconied 19th-century house, around a garden-courtyard set back off the street.

Green House Hostel
HOSTEL $$

(Map p40; ☑ 599265432; www.facebook.com/pages/Tbilisi-Green-House/119849388174351; Akhvlediani khevi 13; dm 30 GEL, d 70-80 GEL; ☺❄@☎) A lovely, spacious house in a quiet lane, Green House appeals to travellers in search of a peaceful hideaway not too far from the centre of things. It has a spacious kitchen, a leafy front yard and a piano in the comfy sitting room, and is run by a friendly couple full of helpful knowledge about Tbilisi and Georgia.

Hotel Old Metekhi
HOTEL $$$

(Map p38; ☑ 2747404; www.ometekhi.com; Metekhis aghmarti 3; r US$90-130; ☺❄☎) Perched on a rocky cliff above the Mtkvari, this recently renovated hotel offers good, carpeted rooms with well-equipped bathrooms. About half the 21 rooms have spectacular views over the river.

🍴 Eating

Tbilisi has a marvellous range of eateries from traditional Georgian to some fabulous fusion affairs. There's also a great cafe culture.

🍴 Old Town Area

Machakhela
GEORGIAN $

(Map p38; Kote Abkhazi 24; khachapuri 4-18 GEL; ⊙10am-11pm; ☎) A fine and inexpensive place to experience that quintessential Georgian dish, the *khachapuri* (cheese pie). It serves almost nothing else except salads (the Greek is fine). Every pie is freshly made and it offers most of the varieties that exist, in sizes from small to 'titanic', with a helpful picture menu for beginners.

Cafe Alani
GEORGIAN $

(Map p38; Gorgasali 1; mains 5-14 GEL; ⊙11am-11pm) This simple little restaurant with clean, modern design serves Ossetian food, which is similar to Georgian, and it's some of the best-value fare in town. Try the very tasty *chakapuli* (lamb with tarragon and plums) or *shkmeruli* (sizzling chicken in garlic sauce), and, if you have room, wind up with a *khabidzgina*, a filling Ossetian *khachapuri*. The house beer, Alani, slips down very nicely.

Racha
GEORGIAN $

(Map p38; Lermontov 6; mains 4-7 GEL; ⊙9am-10.30pm) One of Tbilisi's last *duqani* (cheap, traditional, basement eatery, literally 'shop'), Racha serves up tasty home-style staples such as *khinkali* (spicy dumplings), *mtsvadi* (shish kebabs), *khachapuri* and *badrijani nigvzit* (aubergine slices with walnut-and-garlic paste) at great prices. Perhaps not a place for beginners: the menu is a board written in Georgian and no one speaks any English. You can bring your own wine.

★**Shavi Lomi**   GEORGIAN, FUSION $$
(Black Lion; Map p40; ☑2931007; Amaghleba 23; mains 10-25 GEL; ☺noon-midnight) Shavi Lomi is a terrific Georgian fusion restaurant in a brick-arched basement, serving up Georgian ingredients in inventive European-style preparations. The menu is long and enticing, but we can definitely recommend the beef-and-wild-plum bouillon, rolled cheese bread with spinach, and rabbit in white-wine sauce! There's also a very good list of mainly Georgian wines. There are only about 10 tables so it's worth reserving. Find it by the outsize copy of Pirosmani's famous black lion painting on the exterior.

Entrée   CAFE $$
(Map p38; www.entree.ge; Kote Abkhazi 47; breakfast combos 5-15 GEL; ☺8am-10pm or later; ☎☑) Bright cafe with very good Euro style breakfasts, baked goods and coffee. Not bad for salads and pasta, either. There are several other branches around the city.

Cafe Leila   GEORGIAN, INTERNATIONAL $$
(Map p38; Shavteli 20; mains 10-20 GEL; ☺11am-midnight; ☎☑) Leila is a lovely place to relax with a mint lemonade, coffee and a light dish like hummus, soup or a salad. In a century-old building, it has delightful decor of interlaced stucco work inset with cute little Persian-style paintings.

Maspindzelo   GEORGIAN $$
(Map p34; Gorgasali 7; mains 8-22 GEL; ☺24hr; Ⓟ☎) Large and efficient but with friendly service, popular Maspindzelo, along the embankment from the sulphur baths, is a good bet for well-prepared Georgian classics – *khinkali, mtsvadi, ojakhuri* (a meat-and-potatoes dish) – at reasonable prices.

Samikitno   GEORGIAN $$
(Map p38; www.vdcapital.ge; Meidan; mains 7-18 GEL; ☺24hr; ☎) With large windows overlooking Meidan, this cheerful, informal place serves up decent Georgian standards from *khachapuri* to *mtsvadi, chakapuli,* and aubergine-and-walnut salad. The picture menu is a handy Georgian-food primer. There's another, larger branch on **Tavisuplebis moednai** (Map p38; Pushkin 5/7; mains 7-18 GEL; ☺24hr; ☎; Ⓜ Tavisuplebis Moedani).

★**Cafe Littera**   GEORGIAN, FUSION $$$
(Map p40; ☑599988308; Machabeli 13; mains 27-32 GEL; ☺noon-midnight) A real treat, Littera serves delectable 'nouveau Georgian' dishes in the lovely rear garden of the Georgian Writers' Union building. The frequently changing menu might include filet mignon with wild mushrooms, or sea bass with a spinach and soy-ginger redaction. Everything's delicious. It's a creation of Tekuna Gachechiladze, the pioneer of 'new Georgian' cuisine, and it's advisable to book. In winter it moves indoors.

KNOW YOUR KHACHAPURI

An excess of *khachapuri* is not the thing for slimmers, but Georgia's ubiquitous cheese pies are the perfect keep-me-going meal, as well as playing a part in many a feast. They're sold at street stalls and bakeries as well as in cafes and restaurants. Different regions have their own varieties, but you'll find many of them all around the country:

Khachapuri Acharuli The Adjaran variety is a large, boat-shaped calorie injection, overflowing with melted cheese and topped with butter and a runny egg.

Khachapuri Imeruli Relatively sedate and the most common Georgia-wide, these round, flat pies originating from Imereti have melted cheese inside only.

Khachapuri Megruli Round pies from Samegrelo, with cheese in the middle and more cheese melted on top.

Khachapuri penovani Square and neatly folded into four quarters, with the cheese inside the lightish crust – particularly tasty!

Khachapuri achma A large Adjaran concoction, with the dough and cheese in layers, lasagne-style.

Café Gabriadze
GEORGIAN $$$

(Map p38; Shavteli 13; mains 12-30 GEL; ☺10.30am-midnight) Quirkily attractive little Café Gabriadze, under the same management as the neighbouring Gabriadze puppet theatre, offers friendly service and good Georgian food with original twists. Decor is on theatrical themes, full of intriguing details.

Organique Josper Bar
INTERNATIONAL $$$

(Map p38; http://restorganique.com; Bambis rigi 12; mains 15-35 GEL; ☺11am-11pm; ☏) The narrow Old Town streets Sharden and Bambis rigi are lined with so-so, fairly touristic restaurants, but Organique Josper stands out for its excellent charcoal-grilled steaks and burgers, natural wines and good salads, all from organic raw materials. Decor is quite 'organique' too.

✗ Rustaveli Area

Caliban's Coffeehouse
CAFE $

(Map p40; Rustaveli 34; baguettes & baked goods 3-7 GEL; ☺10.30am-9pm; ☏) Caliban's is the cafe adjoining Prospero's Books, with a leafy courtyard and a comfy indoor area ideal for sitting with a laptop and a pot of coffee.

Puri Guliani
CAFE $

(Map p34; Funicular Complex, Mtatsminda; cakes & pastries 1.20-6 GEL; ☺1pm-midnight; ☏) Excellent cafe with awesome views at the top of the funicular, and strawberry tarts and chocolate cake worthy of the location.

Pasanauri
GEORGIAN $

(Map p40; Griboedov 37; khinkali 0.55-0.70 GEL, mains 7-20 GEL; ☺11am-midnight; ☑) A fairly modest place with around 10 wood-boothed tables, Pasanauri is frequently packed thanks to its *khinkali*, which are among the best in town. Top choice is the meaty 'Pasanauri special', but there are vegetable *khinkali* too, and other vegie options including rare vegetable *mtsvadi* and delicious *badrijani nigvzit*. Good draft Natakhtari beer too.

Khinklis Sakhli
GEORGIAN $

(Map p40; Rustaveli 37; khinkali 0.58-0.77 GEL; ☺24hr) With its green fish tanks and upholstered booths, the 'Khinkali House' is a down-to-earth Tbilisi institution where anyone and everyone goes by day or night to fill up on that national staple, *khinkali*, and draft beer.

★Mukhatsakatukha
GEORGIAN, EUROPEAN $$

(Map p40; Akhvlediani 15; mains 10-20 GEL; ☺11am-1am; ☏☑) Known to all as 'Mukha', this charming little restaurant fashions great European-style dishes from fresh local ingredients – the likes of pork escalope with mustard-and-cream sauce, or mussels *provençale*. It does great soups and good pasta too. It's also a fine place just for a drink.

TBILISI'S FOOD MARKETS

The upwardly mobile like to shop in the supermarkets that are sprouting all over Georgia, and they tend to think of the traditional market *(bazari)* as a not-too-hygienic place. But these are where most of Georgia buys the raw materials of their meals, and a visit to one of them tells you a lot about what makes Georgia tick. The quantities of varied, colourful produce, most of it freshly arrived from the countryside, are a feast for the eyes – piles of round cheeses, sacks of different-coloured beans, entire counters of walnuts, little mounds of spices, bowls of pickles, rows of plucked chickens, homemade sauces, big bunches of herbs and greens, piles of shiny fish, tubs of honey, every kind of fruit and vegetable that's in season, and of course plenty of wine.

Desertirebis Bazari (Deserters' Market; Map p34; cnr Tsinamdzghvrishvili & Abastumani; ☺7am-7pm) This sprawling conglomeration near the train station is Tbilisi's major central market. A wander round will reveal probably every food that Georgians eat. There's a relatively handsome modern building at the centre of things, but most traders prefer to remain on the streets and lots outside, apparently because they don't want to pay the fees for going inside. It is named after deserting soldiers who sold their weapons here in the early 1920s.

Other Markets

There's a big daily market outside Akhmetelis Teatri metro station in the far north of the city, and what are called markets, but are really collections of small shops and pavement-clogging street stalls, outside other metro stations such as Didube (where they're jumbled up with the city's main *marshrutka* terminal), Samgori and Ghrmaghele. Open daily, but are quieter on Sundays.

Dzveli Sakhli   GEORGIAN **$$**
(Old House; Map p40; ☑2365365; Marjvena San-
apiro 3; mains 6-50 GEL; ⊘11am-midnight) The
rambling 'Old House' serves authentic dishes
from all over Georgia and has a partly open-
air section right above the river, with Geor-
gian music and dance at 8pm nightly. Try
a smoked-veal *mtsvadi* in red wine, or the
trout in currant sauce. You can order wine by
the jug.

The Kitchen   AMERICAN, EUROPEAN **$$$**
(Map p34; ☑2020002; Rooms Hotel, Kostava 14;
mains 20-30 GEL; ⊘7am-4pm & 6-11.30pm; 🛜)
The spacious, Manhattan-style, open-kitchen
restaurant at the stylish Rooms Hotel cooks
up a short but very sweet menu of New
American fusion fare that changes every
week. It's a great place for steaks, among
other things. Reservations advised.

Chela   GEORGIAN **$$$**
(Map p34; Funicular Complex, Mtatsminda; mains
12-33 GEL; ⊘1pm-midnight; 🛜) Bustling
brasserie-like Chela specialises in very good
mtsvadi and other meaty grills, worthy
of the fantastic views from the top of the
funicular. It has a selection of good Geor-
gian wines too (21 to 86 GEL a bottle).

While you're here pop upstairs for a drink,
or at least a look, in Lounge Bar Funicular
(p52), home to Koka Ignatov's colourful 1960s
fresco *Tribute to Pirosmani*.

🍷 Drinking & Nightlife

Georgia is known for its hospitality, and
Tbilisi's nightlife does not disappoint.
Whether you're after a high-end cocktail,
a game of beer pong or dancing till broad
daylight, you're sure to find it here. The
evening entertainment scene has been rev-
olutionised in the last few years, with small
bars run by groups of friends mushrooming
all over the city.

Most bars and clubs are clustered in two
areas: the Old Town around Kote Abkhazi
(Leselidze), Erekle II and Sharden streets,
along with Tavisuplebis moedani (Free-
dom Sq); and the Rustaveli area including,
just off the avenue's northern end, the area
around Akhvlediani, a street which everyone
still knows by its Soviet name Perovskaya.
In general, the Old Town is slightly pricier
and partly about sitting outside to see and
be seen.

Tbilisi is lacking when it comes to night-
clubs, though Café Gallery has earned a rep-
utation as the best club in the Caucasus. Still,

if you don't like minimal techno you're likely
to be disappointed by the choice of tunes.

🍷 Old Town

Moulin Electrique   BAR, CAFE
(Map p38; Kote Abkhazi 28; ⊘10.30am-1am; 🛜)
Funky, friendly Moulin Electrique attracts a
mixed crowd of locals (who call it 'Bakha's',
after its owner) and foreigners. The outdoor
area next to Tbilisi's Ashkenazi synagogue is
a great place to while away the hours on a
summer evening, while the affordable cafe
food attracts the lunch crowd as well.

Zoestan   BAR
(Map p38; Vakhtang Beridze 5; ⊘5pm-2am) This
cosy basement bar is run by the eponymous
Zoe, a Frenchwoman with an encyclopedic
knowledge of Georgian folk music and a
voice to match. Hosting concerts most Sun-
days, it's a place to get into Georgian tradi-
tional music in a relaxed environment. No
smoking until 11pm.

Warszawa   BAR
(Map p38; Pushkin 19; ⊘10am-4am; 🛜) A tiny,
brightly lit Polish cafe-bar almost on Tavi-
suplebis moedani, Warszawa has the most
affordable drinks in town, and, at GEL 5,
quite possibly the world's cheapest steak tar-
tare. A late-night favourite, it's an ideal place
to meet fellow travellers. There is a comfier
wine-bar style section in the basement.

Vino Underground   WINE BAR
(Map p40; www.vinounderground.ge; Tabidze 15;
glass of wine 7-13 GEL, bottles 29-57 GEL; ⊘11am-
11pm; 🛜) Vino Underground is Tbilisi's
brick-vaulted temple to natural wine, so
you can be sure to get the authentic tastes
of traditional Georgian wine here. It has a
mind-boggling array to choose from: ask the
staff for some suggestions.

Café Kala   CAFE
(Map p38; Erekle II 8/10; ⊘10am-2am; 🛜) The
place that started the Old Town renaissance,
Kala is still one of the best places to go in
the area. While the food is only OK, it has
live jazz from 9pm nightly and is the best
people-watching spot in town.

🍷 Rustaveli Area

★Dive Bar   BAR
(Map p40; yard at Revaz Laghidze 12; ⊘6pm-1am;
🛜) Founded by a group of Georgians and
American Peace Corps volunteers, Dive has

become a Tbilisi institution, and is the best place to go for cheap beer and good times. With two beer pong tables, live music on Wednesdays and a large outdoor area, it's popular with locals and expats alike. Expect the bar staff to speak any language from Persian to German, and to politely tell you they don't do music requests.

Canudos Ethnic Bar   BAR
(Map p40; Samaias baghi, Javakhishvili; ⊙2pm-3am; 🛜) A Tbilisi fixture and often a 'final drink' destination. The crowd at Canudos skews younger and rowdier than at some spots. Loud music and lines for the toilet are a regular feature, but the fantastic outdoor area around a fountain makes this a great summer spot.

Café Gallery   CLUB
(Map p40; Griboedov 34; ⊙24hr; 🛜) A pleasant cafe and art gallery by day, at night Café Gallery becomes probably the best nightclub in the Caucasus. Weekends see the place's two storeys packed out by revellers dancing to a steady diet of minimal techno and house, until way past everybody's bed time.

Dublin   PUB
(Map p40; Akhvlediani 8; ⊙5pm-1am) A heady mix of young Georgians, raucous expats and live cover bands, Dublin has been keeping its neighbours awake since 1990. It has also given birth to dozens of clone bars on this section of Akhvlediani, so check which has the most going on.

Lounge Bar Funicular   COCKTAIL BAR
(Map p34; Funicular Complex, Mtatsminda; ⊙6pm-2am; 🛜) The most panoramic drinks in town, plus an oval bar and Koka Ignatov's fascinating 1960s fresco *Tribute to Pirosmani*.

🍸 Other Areas

Rooms Hotel Bar   COCKTAIL BAR
(Map p34; Kostava 14; ⊙9am-2am) For a bit of luxury, and the best cocktails in the Caucasus, head to the smoke-free bar at Rooms Hotel. Impeccable service, great interiors and good music, plus, in the summer, a fabulous garden bar: Rooms is the place to get a bit of Manhattan in Tbilisi.

Mtkvarze   CLUB
(Map p34; www.facebook.com/page.mtkvarze; Agladze 2; ⊙11pm-11am Fri & Sat, closed Aug) This former Soviet-era restaurant with a wraparound balcony overhanging the east bank of the Mtkvari River is a great place

for a nightclub. Mtkvarze (meaning 'on the Mtkvari') often hosts well-known DJs from Europe playing the Georgian favourite: minimal techno. All night food, too. See its Facebook page for what's on.

☆ Entertainment

You'll find listings online at www.info-tbilisi. com. Theatres and concert halls close for August, and some of them in July too.

Gabriadze Theatre   THEATRE
(Tbilisi Marionette Theatre; Map p38; 📋2986590; http://gabriadze.com; Shavteli 13; admission 10-30 GEL; ⊙box office 11am-7pm, closed Jul & Aug) If you think puppets aren't your thing, think again. The shows at this quaint little theatre, directed by maestro Rezo Gabriadze, are inspiringly original and moving. English subtitles appear on a screen. Try to see *Stalingrad* or *Ramona*. Pass by the theatre or ask someone to call about the schedule. Book ahead.

Rustaveli Theatre   THEATRE
(Map p40; 📋2726868; www.rustavelitheatre.ge; Rustaveli 17; ⊙closed Aug) The Rustaveli is internationally famed for the Shakespeare productions of Robert Sturua, who has directed here almost uninterruptedly since 1980. It occasionally does shows with simultaneous English translation: check at the box office.

Riffer   LIVE MUSIC
(Map p40; in the yard, Rustaveli 28; ⊙6pm-3am) This smoky, sweaty basement is the place for live guitar music in Tbilisi, and also boasts some of the best (and most extreme) karaoke nights you are likely to find anywhere. Set up by three well-known Georgian rockers, this is where to come to get into the emerging music scene.

Opera & Ballet Theatre   OPERA, DANCE
(Map p40; Rustaveli 25) Tbilisi's beautiful opera house, in a 19th-century neo-Moorish building, has been closed for renovations for several years, but may well reopen by the time you're there. When open, opera, ballet and classical concerts play to full houses here.

🛍 Shopping

Interesting shops purveying distinctive Georgian products, from wine to carpets to souvenir drinking vessels, are dotted along Rustaveli and around the Old Town.

★ Dry Bridge Market   ANTIQUES, CRAFTS
(Map p40; 9 Martis Park; ⊙10am-5pm Mon-Fri, 9am-6pm Sat & Sun) You'll find all kinds of

knick-knacks and intriguing miscellanea at this open-air flea market – original art, shaggy shepherds' hats, accordions, jewellery, silver, glass, daggers and Soviet memorabilia. It's best at weekends.

Prospero's Books
BOOKS, MAPS

(Map p40; ☑2923592; www.prosperosbookshop. com; Rustaveli 34; ☉9.30am-8pm) This English-language bookshop has a great selection of Georgia and South Caucasus titles, plus maps, and the excellent Caliban's Coffeehouse adjoins it.

Geoland
MAPS

(Map p40; ☑2922553; www.geoland.ge; Telegrapis chikhi 3; ☉10am-7pm Mon-Fri year-round, 11am-6pm Sat Jun-Sep) Georgia's best mapmaker, Geoland sells its own excellent 1:50,000 trekking maps (nine maps covering the Svaneti, Racha, Kazbegi, Tusheti and Borjomi areas), travel maps (six regional maps covering the country at 1:200,000), country map and Tbilisi city map, for 10 GEL each. It also prints off 1:50,000 sheets of all parts of Georgia, based on Soviet military maps, for 22 GEL each.

It sells camping gas and Garmin handheld and automotive GPSs too. The entrance is opposite the Public Service Hall on Marjvena (Gamsakhurdias) Sanapiro.

Gocha's Winery
WINE

(Map p38; Kote Abkhazi 27/15; ☉noon-11pm) A fair few wine shops are strung along Kote Abkhazi in the Old Town. They will all let you taste a few wines to help you decide which to buy. Gocha's has a good selection and an appealingly cave-like interior with a little bar to do your tasting.

Caucasian Carpets
CARPETS

(Map p38; Erekle II 8/10; ☉10am-8pm) Has the best selection of any Old Town carpet shop, with colourful rugs from Georgia, Azerbaijan, Iran and Central Asia, starting around US$250.

Aristaeus
FOOD

(Map p38; Pushkin 19; ☉10am-9.30pm) A great selection of Georgian cheeses, plus jars of artisanal jams and sauces.

❶ Information

MEDICAL SERVICES
CITO, IMSS and MediClub Georgia are private Western-standard medical facilities with English-speaking doctors.
CITO (Map p34; ☑2290671; www.cito.com; Paliashvili 40, Vake; initial consultation 40-115

GEL; ☉9am-6pm Mon-Fri, 9am-3pm Sat) Has a GP, specialists and a good laboratory.
IMSS (Map p34; ☑2920928; www.imss.ge; 5th fl, Neoclinic Bldg, Bakhtrioni 10a, Saburtalo; 30min consultation US$69; ☉24hr) Consultations and 24-hour inpatient care available with EU- or US-trained doctors. Has 24-hour emergency service.
MediClub Georgia (Map p34; ☑2251991; http://mcg.ge; Tashkent 22a, Saburtalo) Has 24-hour emergency and ambulance service, and a good inpatient clinic.

Pharmacies
Medicines are widely available at pharmacies (*aptiaqi* in Georgian, but often signed 'Apotheka'), including **Aversi** (http://pharma.ge/en), which has over 100 branches in Tbilisi, many open 24 hours.

MONEY
Tbilisi is full of ATMs issuing lari on MasterCard, Visa, Cirrus and Maestro cards.

Plenty of exchange offices (including at every metro station and the main bus stations and train station) provide lari in exchange for cash euros, US dollars and often roubles, sterling, Turkish lira, Armenian drams or Azerbaijani manat.

POST
Main Post Office (Map p40; www.gpost.ge; Davit Aghmashenebeli 44; ☉9am-5pm Mon-Fri, 10am-2pm Sat)

TELEPHONE
The three main mobile networks all have downtown shops.
Beeline (Bilaini; Map p40; www.beeline.ge; Rustaveli 16; ☉10am-7pm Mon-Fri, 10am-5pm Sat & Sun)

---

❶ METROMONEY CARDS

Metromoney cards, sold for 2 GEL at metro-station ticket offices, are essential for riding the metro, and also good for Tbilisi city buses and *marshrutky* (minibuses). You tap the card on a reader when you enter the metro or when you board buses and *marshrutky*. Fares are 0.50 GEL per metro or bus ride and 0.80 GEL for *marshrutky*. You can also pay with cash on buses (exact fare only) and *marshrutky*. Further metro or bus rides within 1½ hours of tapping in are not charged. You can put credit on the card with cash at metro-station ticket offices or in ubiquitous orange Express Pay machines, which have easy-to-follow instructions in English.

Geocell (Map p40; www.geocell.ge; Rustaveli 40; ☉10am-8pm Mon-Sat)

Magti (Map p40; www.magticom.ge; Rustaveli 22; ☉9am-9pm Mon-Fri, 9am-6pm Sat & Sun)

TOURIST INFORMATION

Tourism Information Centre (Map p40; ☑2158697; tictbilisi@gmail.com; Tavisuplebis moedani; ☉10am-6pm or later) Helpful staff can find the answers to most questions you throw at them. The airport desk is open 24 hours.

❶ Getting There & Away

Marshrutky (minibuses) are the main transport around Georgia. Along with some buses and minivans (smaller and more comfortable than *marshrutky*), they depart from several terminals around the city.

Trains are mostly slower and less frequent than road transport.

Flying or the train are overall the best options for getting direct to Baku; for northwest Azerbaijan you'll need *marshrutky*.

For Armenia, minivans from Avlabari metro station are a comfortable, convenient option.

AIR

Tbilisi International Airport (☑ arrivals 2310341, departures 2310421; www.tbilisi airport.com) is 15km east of the city centre. Direct flights head to/from more than 40 international destinations spread from Paris to Ürümqi (China). Many flights arrive and depart at unholy early-morning hours.

Within the South Caucasus, **Georgian Airways** (Map p34; ☑2485560; www. georgian-airways.com; Davit Aghmashenebeli 127; ☉10am-7pm Mon-Fri, 10am-3pm Sat-Sun) flies to Yerevan, and domestically to Kutaisi and Batumi. **AZAL** (Azerbaijan Airlines; Map p34; ☑2558888; www.azal.az; Chavchavadzis gamziri 28; ☉10am-7pm Mon-Fri, 10am-3pm Sat & Sun) and **Qatar Airways** (Map p40; ☑2439608; www.qatarairways.com; Vekua 3; ☉10am-6pm Mon-Fri) fly to Baku. Direct flights to Aktau (Kazakhstan) are operated by SCAT.

The terminal has ATMs, three 24-hour bank branches offering currency exchange, and car rental offices.

From Natakhtari Airfield, 25km north of Tbilisi, small-plane flights depart for Mestia (p86).

INTERNATIONAL MARSHRUTKY, BUSES & MINIVANS FROM TBILISI

DESTINATION	DEPARTURE	COST	DURATION (HR)	FREQUENCY
Athens	Ortachala	US$100	42	1 bus daily
Baku (via Tsiteli Khidi & Gəncə)	Ortachala	35 GEL	10	bus 3pm *
Istanbul (via Trabzon)	Ortachala	US$40 **	26	5 or more buses daily
Moscow	Ortachala	200 GEL	32	2 or more buses daily
Qax	Ortachala	10 GEL	4-5	*marshrutky* 8.40am, 11am, 1pm
Vanadzor (via Alaverdi)	Ortachala	20 GEL	3½	*marshrutka* 9.20am
Vladikavkaz	Ortachala	30-40 GEL	4	2 or more buses daily ***
Vladikavkaz	Didube	70 GEL	4	minivans leave when full
Yerevan (via Ijevan, Dilijan, Sevan)	Avlabari	35 GEL ****	6	minivans every 2hr 9am-5pm (☑ reservations 593229554)
Yerevan (via Alaverdi, Vanadzor)	Ortachala	30 GEL *****	6	*marshrutky* 8.20am, 9.10am, 10am, noon, 3pm, 5pm
Yerevan (via Alaverdi, Vanadzor)	Sadguris Moedani	35 GEL *****	6	*marshrutky* every 2hr 9am-5pm
Zaqatala	Ortachala	10 GEL	3-4	*marshrutky* 8.30am, 5.30pm

* Alternatively, take a *marshrutka* to the border at Tsiteli Khidi (Krasny Most; Red Bridge; 4 GEL, one hour, hourly 5am to 5pm from Sadguris Moedani), and pick up onward transport on the other side; start early in the day.

** Trabzon US$25 to US$30 (10 hours).

*** Also several buses weekly from Ortachala to several other southern Russian cities.

**** Ijevan 30 GEL; Dilijan or beyond 35 GEL.

***** Same fare to any point along route.

DOMESTIC MARSHRUTKY FROM TBILISI

DESTINATION	DEPARTURE	COST (GEL)	DURATION (HR)	FREQUENCY
Akhaltsikhe	Didube	8	4	hourly 8am-7pm
Bakuriani	Didube	10	4	9am, 11am
Batumi	Ortachala	25	6	6 Metro Georgia buses daily
Batumi	Didube	20	6	2-3 hourly 7.30am-8pm
Borjomi	Didube	6	3	hourly 8am-7pm
Dedoplistskaro	Ortachala	7	3	about hourly 8.30am-5pm
Gori	Didube	3	1¼	half-hourly 7am-7.30pm
Kazbegi	Didube	10	3	hourly 8am-7pm
Kutaisi	Didube	10	4	2-3 hourly 7am-7pm
Lagodekhi	Isani	7	2½	1-2 hourly 7.40am-6.15pm
Mestia	Sadguris Moedani	30	9	7am
Mestia	Navtlughi	30	9	7am
Mtskheta	Didube	1	30min	every 15min 7.30am-8.30pm
Sighnaghi	Navtlughi	6	2	every 2hr 9am-5pm, 6pm
Telavi	Ortachala	7	1¾	1-2 hourly 8am-6pm
Vardzia	Didube	15	6	10am
Zugdidi	Sadguris Moedani	15	5½	every 1½hr 9.30am-8pm
Zugdidi	Didube	15	5½	every 1½hr 8am-8pm

BUS, MARSHRUTKA & MINIVAN

Marshrutky may leave after or before scheduled times, depending how quickly they fill up, and all schedules are subject to change!

Didube (Tsereteli; Ⓜ Didube) The sprawling main hub for national services. Areas close to the metro exit have *marshrutky* to Akhaltsikhe, Bakuriani, Batumi, Borjomi, Kazbegi, Kutaisi, Mtskheta and Vardzia. Along a road to the right you'll find the Okriba bus station on your left, with more Batumi and Kutaisi *marshrutky* plus Zugdidi services, and a yard opposite with Gori *marshrutky*.

Ortachala (🖉 2753433; www.avtovagzal.ge; Gulia 1) Ortachala, 2.5km southeast of the Old Town, has services for Kakheti, Armenia, Azerbaijan, Turkey, Greece and Russia. *Marshrutky* to destinations in Kakheti, and Zaqatala and Qax in Azerbaijan, leave from out the front; other services, including comfortable **Metro Georgia** (🖉 2750595; www.geometro.ge) buses to Batumi, go from inside.

You can reach Ortachala on bus 50, 55 or 71 from Baratashvili in central Tbilisi. Heading into town from Ortachala, catch these going to the left on the street outside. *Marshrutky* 108 and 150 run between Ortachala and Didube.

Navtlughis Avtosadguri (Samgori; Ketevan Dedopalis gamziri; Ⓜ Samgori) About 300m west of Samgori metro station.

Sadguris Moedani (Map p34) In front of the main train station.

Avlabari Minivan Stand (Map p34; Avlabaris moedani) Outside Avlabari metro station.

Isani (Atskuri; Ⓜ Isani) In the street behind the State Audit Office building behind Isani metro station.

CAR

Self-drive car rental is viable if you're willing to cope with some local drivers' erratic behaviour.

Rental rates with local firms can be half what the international companies charge, though vehicles and backup may be correspondingly less dependable.

Four-wheel drive vehicles are recommended anywhere off main highways.

Jeep Rent (Map p34; 🖉 551106310; www. car-rent.ge; Office 50, Erekle Tatishvili 19; ☺ office 10am-6pm Mon-Fri, 10am-2pm Sat) A well-established, well-reputed local company, renting sedans (US$40 to US$60 per day) and higher-end 4WDs (US$80), with a dependable repair and replacement service. Pick-ups and drop-offs at Georgia's airports and road borders, and rentals into Armenia, are available at extra cost.

Minimum driver age is 23 and you'll need to leave a warranty deposit of US$200 to US$300.

Sixt (Map p38; 🖉 2439911; www.sixt.com.ge; Samghebro 5; ☺ office 10am-7pm Mon-Fri, 11am-3pm Sat) Also has a branch at the airport.

GEORGIA TBILISI

TRAIN

Tbilisi's **main train station** (Map p34; Sadguris moedani) is the railway hub of Georgia. Ticket counters, open 7am to 11pm, are on level 3 (the top floor) – there's usually someone who speaks English. You can buy tickets here for train trips starting anywhere in Georgia. Always bring your passport when buying tickets. Platforms are on level 2.

Schedules change often: some information is given in English on the **Georgian Railway website** (www.railway.ge) under 'Passenger Operations' – click 'Traffic Schedule' and/or 'Online Tickets': the main Tbilisi train station is listed here as Tbilisi-pass.

Train information is available in English on ☑ 1331.

For trains to Baku, Yerevan, Batumi and Zugdidi, it's advisable to book tickets a day or two ahead, and as far ahead as possible for July and August.

International Trains

The only international trains are the sleepers to Baku and Yerevan, though this should change when a new line to Kars in Turkey opens (conceivably in 2016).

The Baku train (3rd/2nd/1st class 41/62/120 GEL, 15 hours) leaves around 4pm or 5pm daily.

The Yerevan train (4th/3rd/2nd/1st class 32/44/70/100 GEL, 11 hours), via Vanadzor and Gyumri, normally departs around 8pm every two days. From mid-June to the end of September

it's usually replaced by a quicker 10-hour daily service, also leaving in the evening.

Fares can fluctuate with exchange rates and how far ahead you book.

Domestic Trains

➜ Overnight services depart around 9pm to Zugdidi (seat/2nd/1st class 7/21/30 GEL, nine hours), and around midnight to Batumi (4th/3rd/2nd/1st class 24/35/50/80 GEL, six hours, daily mid-June to end-September, every two days otherwise).

➜ Morning departures (between about 8am and 10am) head to Batumi (2nd/1st class 23/40 GEL, 5½ hours), Kutaisi (seat 7.50 GEL, 5½ hours) and Zugdidi (2nd class 15 GEL, 6½ hours). Extra trains to Batumi run during the summer holiday season.

➜ *Elektrichky* (slow trains with seating only) run to Borjomi (2 GEL, 4½ hours) in the morning and afternoon, and to Kutaisi (4 GEL, six hours) in the afternoon. For these, pay on the train.

❶ Getting Around

TO/FROM THE AIRPORT

Bus 37 (0.50 GEL, 7am to 11pm) runs from the airport to the main train station via Avlabari metro station and Tavisuplebis moedani and Rustaveli in the city centre; the same in reverse.

The official taxi fare from the airport to city centre or vice-versa is 25 GEL, but drivers will do their damnedest to get more out of you. Many hotels and some hostels offer airport pick-ups for 30 or 40 GEL.

PUBLIC TRANSPORT
Bus & Marshrutka

Yellow city buses and *marshrutky* provide an above-ground complement to the metro. Electronic boards at most bus stops list the destinations of approaching buses in English as well as Georgian. Buses only stop at predetermined stops, but you can get on and off *marshrutky* anywhere along their route. To get the driver to stop, shout '*Gaacheret!*' ('Stop!').

Bus routes and schedules are listed and mapped, partly in English, at http://ttc.com.ge.

Metro

The efficient Tbilisi metro operates from 6am to midnight, and the two lines reach most important parts of the city, meeting at Sadguris Moedani station. Signage and announcements are in English as well as Georgian.

TAXI

Taxis are almost always unmetered. Agree on the fare before getting in. The standard cost for a shortish ride (up to about 3km) is 4 GEL or 5 GEL. Longer rides cost up to 10 GEL.

Tbilisi Metro

AROUND TBILISI

A cradle of Georgian culture, the region west and south of the capital is known as Kartli, after the mythical father of the Georgian people, Kartlos, whose progeny made their home at Mtskheta. Nobody can understand Georgian spirituality without visiting Mtskheta, where St Nino converted the Iverian kingdom to Christianity in the 4th century. By contrast Gori is best known as the town where Joseph Stalin was born in 1879.

Mtskheta   მცხეთა

♪ 32 / POP 9800

Mtskheta has been Georgia's spiritual heart since Christianity was established here in about 327, and holds a near-mystical significance in Georgian culture. It had already been capital of most of eastern Georgia from about the 3rd century BC, and remained so to the 5th century AD, when King Vakhtang Gorgasali switched his base to Tbilisi. Mtskheta has always kept its status as a spiritual capital, and its Svetitskhoveli Cathedral is still the setting for important ceremonies of the Georgian Orthodox Church. With an alluring setting where the Mtkvari and Aragvi Rivers meet, Mtskheta makes an easy and enjoyable day trip from Tbilisi.

◉ Sights

★**Svetitskhoveli Cathedral**   CATHEDRAL
(Arsukidze; ⊘8am-8pm) This grand (and for its time, enormous) building dates from the 11th century, early in the golden age of Georgian church architecture. It has an elongated cross plan and is adorned with beautiful stone carving outside and in. Christ's robe is believed to lie beneath the central nave, under a square pillar decorated with colourful if faded frescoes of the conversion of Kartli.

Around Tbilisi

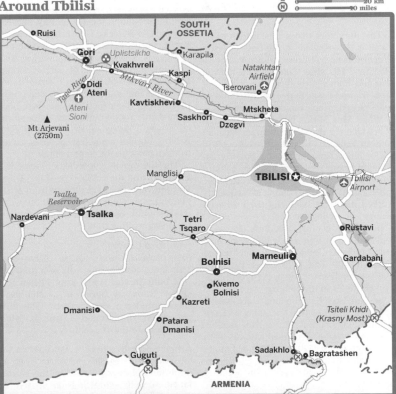

0   20 km
0   10 miles

- Ruisi
- SOUTH OSSETIA
- Gori
- Uplistsikho
- Karapila
- Kvakhvreli
- Kaspi
- Natakhtari Airfield
- Tserovani
- Didi Ateni
- *Tana River*
- *Mtkvari River*
- Kavtiskhevi
- Mtskheta
- ▲ Mt Arjevani (2750m)
- *Ateni Sioni*
- Saskhori
- Dzegvi
- Manglisi
- TBILISI
- Tbilisi Airport
- *Tsalka Reservoir*
- Nardevani
- Tsalka
- Tetri Tsqaro
- Rustavi
- Bolnisi
- Marneuli
- Gardabani
- Kvemo Bolnisi
- Dmanisi
- Kazreti
- *Tsiteli Khidi (Krasny Most)*
- Patara Dmanisi
- Guguti
- Sadakhlo
- Bagratashen
- ARMENIA

Mtskheta

The story goes that a Mtskheta Jew, Elioz, was in Jerusalem at the time of Jesus' Crucifixion and returned with the robe to Mtskheta. His sister Sidonia took it from him and immediately died in a passion of faith. The robe was buried with her and as years passed, people forgot the exact site.

When King Mirian built the first church at Mtskheta in the 4th century, the wooden column designed to stand in its centre could not be raised from the ground. But after an all-night prayer vigil by St Nino, the column miraculously moved of its own accord to the robe's burial site. The column subsequently worked many miracles and Svetitskhoveli means 'Life-Giving Column'.

In the 5th century Vakhtang Gorgasali replaced Mirian's church with a stone one, and the present building was constructed between 1010 and 1029 under Patriarch Melqisedek. It's still one of the most beautiful churches in the country.

Several Georgian monarchs are buried here. The tomb of Erekle II, king of Kartli and Kakheti from 1762 to 1798, lies before the icon screen (marked with his birth and death dates, 1720 and 1798). Vakhtang Gorgasali's tomb is behind this, with his sword-holding image carved on a raised flagstone.

★ **Jvari Church** CHURCH

(Holy Cross; ⊗8am-7pm) Visible for miles around on its hilltop overlooking Mtskheta from the east, Jvari is, to many Georgians, the holiest of holies. It stands where King Mirian erected a wooden cross soon after his conversion by St Nino in the 4th century. Between 585 and 604 Stepanoz I, the *eristavi* (duke) of Kartli, constructed the church over the cross.

Jvari is a beautifully symmetrical little building and a classic of early Georgian tetraconch design. It has a cross-shaped plan with four equal arms, rounded on the inside (with the angles between them filled in by corner rooms), and a low dome sitting on a squat, octagonal drum. The interior is bare, ancient stone, except for a carved wooden cross on the central plinth.

The site provides spectacular views over Mtskheta and the confluence of the Aragvi and Mtkvari rivers. The road up here from Mtskheta takes a highly circuitous 11km route; a taxi should cost 20 GEL for a return trip, including waiting time.

Samtavro Church CHURCH

(Davit Aghmashenebelis qucha; ⊗8am-8pm) This large church, now part of a nunnery, was built in the 1130s. King Mirian and Queen Nana are buried in its southwest corner, under a stone canopy. The little church in the grounds, Tsminda Nino, dates back to the 4th century.

Armaztsikhe-Bagineti ARCHAEOLOGICAL SITE

(admission free; ⊗24hr) Mtskheta was an important place as capital of the Iverian kingdom well before St Nino arrived. At Armaztsikhe-Bagineti, on the south side of the Mtkvari, you can inspect the excavated residence of Iverian rulers, including bathhouses, a royal sarcophagus, a wine cellar, a six-apse temple and what may have been a palace.

It's 3km from Svetitskhoveli – back across the Mtkvari bridge, then 900m along the Tbilisi road to an 'Armaztsikhe-Bagineti' signpost, from which it's about 800m along a path to the site.

🛏 Sleeping

Mtskheta is an easy day trip from Tbilisi, but if you fancy getting away from the city it has a few decent accommodation options.

Hotel Tamarindi HOTEL $
(⌨ 2512764, 579037772; www.hoteltamarindi.com; Arsukidze 23; s 40 GEL, d 50-80 GEL, f 100 GEL; ▣@🛜) This small hotel has three very comfy, large rooms and a good terrace looking across the street to Svetitskhoveli. Host Jemal speaks a little English and has a comfortable 4WD for outings.

Hotel Old Capital HOTEL, HOSTEL $$
(⌨ 593631786; giorgi.zurabishvili.73@mail.ru; Erekle II 7; dm 20 GEL, d 60-80 GEL, apt for 3-8 130-200 GEL, breakfast 5 GEL; ▣🛜) Just across the street from Svetitskhoveli, this friendly place has three neat, clean rooms and two new two bedroom apartments upstairs, all with private bathroom. There's a small hostel section at the side.

🍴 Eating

Mtskheta is famous for its *lobio* (beans with herbs and spices), which can be found in any local restaurant, served in a traditional clay pot.

Salobie GEORGIAN $
(mains 2-7 GEL; ⊙9am-11pm) Mtskheta's best-value and most popular eatery is 5km back along the road towards Tbilisi (the *marshrutky* pass the door). It's a rambling place with several rooms and terraces and staff bustling about serving all of Georgia's favourite basic dishes – *khachapuri, mtsvadi, khinkali* and, of course, *lobio* and *lobiani* (bean pie).

Old Taverna GEORGIAN $$
(Arsukidze; mains 5-12 GEL; ⊙10am-11pm) This little place serves decent Georgian fare such as *ostri* (spicy meat in a tomato-based sauce), *khachapuri* and mushroom dishes. In good weather it's lovely to sit outside facing Svetitskhoveli.

ⓘ Information

Tourism Information Centre (⌨ 2512128; ticmtskheta@gmail.com; Arsukidze 3; ⊙10am-7pm; 🛜) Has helpful English-speaking staff and free wi-fi.

ⓘ Getting There & Away

Marshrutky to Tbilisi leave about every 20 minutes, 8am to 8pm, from the bus stop on Davit Aghmashenebelis qucha. Trains to Gori (1 GEL to 6 GEL, one hour) stop at Mtskheta station, on the south side of the Mtkvari, 2km west of the town centre, at about 7am, 9.15am, 5pm and 9.30pm.

Gori გორი

☏ 370 / POP 49,000

Gori 80km west of Tbilisi, has long been synonymous with just one man: this is the town where Stalin was born and went to school. The large Stalin Museum is Gori's best-known attraction, but there are also some fascinating older sights, notably Uplistsikhe cave city, nearby.

In the 2008 war over South Ossetia (whose border reaches within 13km north of Gori), Gori was bombed by Russia, with at least 20 civilians killed, and most of the population fled before the town fell under Russian control for 10 days. Rows of single-storey refugee houses visible at Tserovani on the Tbilisi–Gori highway, and on Gori's northern edge, are reminders of that war.

The centre of town is the wide Stalinis moedani (Stalin Sq). The main street, Stalinis gamziri (Stalin Av), runs 600m north from here to the large Stalin Museum. The bus station is 500m west of Stalinis moedani, along Chavchavadze.

⊙ Sights

★**Stalin Museum** MUSEUM
(⌨ 225398; http://stalinmuseum.ge/new; Stalinis gamziri 32; admission incl guide in English 10 GEL, incl train carriage 15 GEL; ⊙10am-6pm Apr-Oct, 10am-5pm Nov-Mar) The museum makes no serious attempt to present a balanced account of Stalin's career or deeds. It remains, much as when it opened in 1957, a reverent homage to the Gori boy who became a key figure of 20th-century world history – although guides do now at least refer to the purges, the Gulag and his 1939 pact with Hitler. As well as the halls of memorabilia, the visit includes the tiny wood-and-mud-

brick house where Stalin lived for the first four years of his life.

The house, where Stalin's parents rented a single room, stands in front of the main museum building, under its own temple-like superstructure.

The museum charts Stalin's journey from the Gori church school to leadership of the USSR, the Yalta Conference at the end of WWII and his death in 1953. The first hall upstairs covers his childhood and adolescence, including his rather cringeworthy pastoral poetry, and then his early revolutionary activities in Georgia, his seven jail terms under the tsarist authorities (six of them in Siberia), the revolution of 1917 and Lenin's death in 1924. The text of Lenin's 1922 political testament that described Stalin as too coarse and power-hungry, advising Communist Party members to remove him from post of General Secretary, is on display.

One room is devoted to a bronze copy of Stalin's eerie death mask, lying in state. The next has a large collection of gifts from world leaders and other Bolsheviks. Off the staircase is a reconstruction of his first office in the Kremlin, plus personal memorabilia such as his pipes, glasses, cigars and slide rule. One small two-room section beside the foot of the stairs deals with political repression under Stalin.

To one side of the museum is Stalin's train carriage, in which he travelled to Yalta in 1945 (he didn't like flying). Apparently bulletproof, its elegant interior includes a bathtub and a primitive air-conditioning system.

Gori Fortress   FORTRESS
(☉24hr) **FREE** This oval citadel stands on the hill at the heart of Gori, a short walk west from Stalinis gamziri. It dates mostly from the Middle Ages, with 17th-century additions. With fine views, it's a good place to be around sunset. At its northeast foot, a circle of mutilated metal warriors forms an eerie memorial to those lost in 2008.

War Museum   MUSEUM
(Stalinis gamziri 19; admission 3 GEL; ☉10am-6pm Tue-Sun Mar-Nov, 10am-5pm Tue-Sat Dec-Feb) The War Museum, 400m south of the Stalin Museum, is mostly devoted to the Gori people's involvement in WWII, but also contains a small display on the 2008 war. In the lobby are a few pieces of Russian ordnance from that war, including a cluster bomb that was dropped on Gori's main square.

🛏 Sleeping

Guesthouses are the way to go here, with the smattering of hotels being pretty drab.

Guesthouse Svetlana   GUESTHOUSE $
(☏599583001; kasatik56@mail.ru; Abashidze 8; s/d 30/50 GEL, breakfast 5 GEL; ☻❀⬢) Good-size rooms with comfy beds in a large, well-kept house with parquet floors and excellent modern furnishings, plus a welcoming, English-speaking hostess, add up to one of the best bets in town. Dinner is available on request. It's in a small street off Samepo, 300m south from Chavchavadze.

Guesthouse Nitsa   GUESTHOUSE $
(☏599142488; liazauta@gmail.com; Kutaisi 58; per person with/without breakfast 30/25 GEL, dinner 10 GEL; ☻❀⬢) This friendly family, speaking English and a little French, provides four cosy rooms in their spacious house with its sweeping staircase and large lounge-dining room. A great assortment of homemade jams too! It's 200m east of the Stalin Museum.

Guesthouse Levani   GUESTHOUSE $
(☏598268045; www.facebook.com/guesthouse levani; Aghmeshenebelis gamziri 29; r per person 25-30 GEL, breakfast 5 GEL; ⬢) The few rooms here are relatively modest, but the warmth of your host, who speaks some French and a little English, makes up for that. The bathrooms are good. It's 400m southeast from the south end of Stalinis moedani, on the corner at the end of Zurab Antonov.

Hostel Kalifornia   HOSTEL $
(☏551300802; okalifornia@mail.ru; Rustaveli 79; dm 12 GEL, d 50-60 GEL; ⬢) You can sleep very cheap in the bunk dorm at this almost-new hostel a few steps north off Chavchavadze. It has two colourful mansard private rooms too – plus a kitchen, free tea and coffee, and a washing machine (5 GEL).

🍴 Eating

Cake House   CAFE $
(Stalinis gamziri 22; cakes & pastries 1-2.50 GEL; ☉10am-midnight; ⬢) A rattan-chaired cafe between the Stalin Museum and Stalinis moedani, serving super-sweet, gooey cakes, Turkish coffee and draft beer.

Sport Kafe   GEORGIAN $$
(Stalinis gamziri 11; mains 5-18 GEL; ☉11am-midnight; ⬢🅿) A large, bright and popular place just south of Stalinis moedani, Sport

STALIN & GEORGIA

Few would question the achievements of Iosif Jughashvili, the Gori cobbler's son who rose to rule the largest country on earth for a quarter of a century: were it not for the Soviet role in WWII, Nazi Germany may well have won, and in the space of a decade Stalin turned the USSR from a peasant economy into an industrial powerhouse – 'taking it with the plough and leaving it with nuclear weapons', as Churchill observed.

Yet Stalin's Gulag camps were responsible for the deaths of many millions, he is blamed for the 1932 Ukraine famine in which an estimated seven million died, and his ruthless secret police terrorised the Soviet population from the late 1920s until his death in 1953.

Stalin is still respected by some Georgians. When the government finally decided to remove the large Stalin statue from Gori's central square in 2010, they did it at night, with police sealing off the square. Yet any admiration for the man seems to be more a matter of pride in a local lad who rose to rule Russia – and a nostalgia for the days when the Soviet Union was a great power – than any thumbs-up for his murderous policies. Meanwhile Gori has reason to thank Stalin for the daily stream of tourists he brings to the town. Gori's souvenir shops now sell Stalin mugs, Stalin hipflasks and Stalin paperweights, and tourists pose for selfies before a small Stalin statue outside the museum. It's as if, with the passing of the decades, people are losing the memory of the horrors he perpetrated, and the leader of world communism has become just another capitalist commodity to be marketed to a pliable public.

GEORGIA AROUND GORI

prepares a big range of Georgian fare pretty well – including *chakhrakina,* a rare *khachapuri* species containing beetroot leaves and sour cream as well as cheese. It's a popular spot for evening drinks too.

The picture menu is helpful – just don't be deterred by some of the English translations (bowels on clay dish etc).

🛈 Information

Tourism Information Centre (☎ 270776; ticgori@gmail.com; Kutaisi 23a; ⊙10am-7pm Jun-Sep, 10am-6pm Oct-May) Behind the Stalin Museum.

🛈 Getting There & Away

Marshrutky to Tbilisi (3 GEL, one hour) leave about every 15 minutes, 7am to 6pm. There are four daily *marshrutky* to Borjomi (5 GEL, 1½ hours), two to Akhaltsikhe (7 GEL, 2½ hours) and one to Batumi (17 GEL, five hours, 9.30am). For Kutaisi, guesthouses or the tourist office can organise a taxi driver to take you out to the highway for 5 GEL and flag down a Kutaisi-bound *marshrutka* (7 GEL, three hours).

About 10 daily trains head east to Tbilisi (4 GEL to 32 GEL, one to 1¼ hours) from **Gori train station** (Gorijvari), across the Mtkvari from the south end of Stalinis gamziri. Westbound, there are two each to Borjomi, Kutaisi, Zugdidi and Batumi.

Around Gori

Uplistsikhe   უფლისციხე

This fascinating and once enormous **cave city** (admission 3 GEL, guide in English 15 GEL; ⊙10am-6pm; 🅿) sits 10km east of Gori above the north side of the Mtkvari River, with expansive views along the Mtkvari valley. Between the 6th century BC and 1st century AD, Uplistsikhe developed into one of the chief political and religious centres of pre-Christian Kartli, with temples dedicated principally to the sun goddess. After the Arabs occupied Tbilisi in AD 645, Uplistsikhe became the residence of the Christian kings of Kartli and an important trade centre on a main caravan road from Asia to Europe. At its peak it housed 20,000 people. Its importance declined after King David the Builder retook Tbilisi in 1122 and it was irrevocably destroyed by the Mongols in 1240. What you visit today is the 40,000-sq-metre Shida Qalaqi (Inner City), less than half of the original whole. Almost everything here has been uncovered by archaeologists since 1957.

⊙ Sights

Main Gate   GATE
To enter Uplistsikhe by its old main access track, go about 5m up the rocks opposite the cafe at the entrance, and follow the rock-cut

ST NINO & THE CONVERSION OF GEORGIA

While some of the legends that have grown up around St Nino are ridiculously far-fetched, there is no doubt that Nino is the historical figure to whom the 4th-century Christian conversion of Iveria (eastern Georgia) can be attributed. She is believed to have hailed from Cappadocia in Turkey and a widespread version has it that she was the daughter of a Roman general, raised in Jerusalem under the eye of an uncle who was the Christian Patriarch of Jerusalem, and that at the age of 14 she experienced a vision of the Virgin telling her that her destiny was to convert the Iverians to Christianity. Coming to Iveria in the 320s, Nino gained a royal convert at Mtskheta when her prayers were deemed to have saved Queen Nana of Iveria from serious illness. Then King Mirian was struck blind while hunting, only for his sight to be miraculously restored after he prayed to the Christian God – leading to mass baptism in the Aragvi River for the folk of Mtskheta. Mirian made Christianity Iveria's official religion in about 327. The vine-branch cross that the Virgin is believed to have given Nino (and which Nino later bound with her own hair) is kept at Sioni Cathedral in Tbilisi. She remains Georgia's most venerated saint, and is buried at Bodbe Convent in Kakheti.

path to the left. Metal-railed steps lead up through what was the main gate, with the excavated main tower of the Shida Qalaqi's defensive walls to the right.

Theatre
TEMPLE

Ahead from the cave city's main gate you'll find a cave overlooking the river with a pointed arch carved in the rock above it. Known as the Theatre, this is probably a temple from the 1st or 2nd century AD, where religious mystery plays may have been performed.

Main Street
STREET, TEMPLE

Uplistsikhe's old main street winds up to the right after you've passed through the main gate, with several important cave structures either side of it.

Down to the right is the large pre-Christian Temple of Makvliani, with an inner recess behind an arched portico. A little further up on the left is the big hall known as Tamaris Darbazi (Hall of Queen Tamar), where an ancient stone seat sits behind two columns cut from the rock, and the stone ceiling is carved to look like wooden beams. This was almost certainly a pre-Christian temple. To its left is an area with stone niches, thought to have been a pharmacy or dovecote.

A large cave building to the right of the Tamaris Darbazi was probably a sun temple used for animal sacrifices, later converted into a Christian basilica.

Uplistsulis Eklesia
CHURCH

(Uplistsulis Church) This triple-church basilica near the top of the hill was built in the 10th

century over what was probably Uplistsikhe's most important pagan temple.

Tunnel
TUNNEL

On your way back down out of the cave city, don't miss the long tunnel running down to the Mtkvari, an emergency escape route that could also be used for carrying water up to the city. Its entrance is behind a reconstructed wall beside the old main gate.

ⓘ Getting There & Away

A return taxi from Gori, including one hour's waiting time, costs 20GEL to 30 GEL. Marshrutky leave Gori bus station a few times a day for Kvakhvreli (1 GEL, 20 minutes), a 2km walk from Uplistsikhe.

Ateni Sioni ᲐᲢᲔᲜᲘᲡ ᲡᲘᲝᲜᲘ

This impressively ancient church (Map p57; Sioni Church at Ateni; ⊘10am-5pm; Ⓟ) has a beautiful setting above a bend of the pretty, grapevine-strewn Tana valley, 12km south of Gori. Ateni Sioni was built in the 7th century and modelled on Mtskheta's Jvari Church. Beautiful reliefs of stags, a hunting scene and a knight were carved into the exterior walls later. Inside, the 11th-century frescoes, depicting biblical scenes and Georgian rulers, are among the finest medieval art in the country. At the time of writing the frescoes were under restoration but you could still see them through a forest of scaffolding.

A return taxi from Gori to the church should cost about 20 GEL, or 30 GEL to 40 GEL if combined with Uplistsikhe. Alternatively, buses and marshrutky run from Gori bus station to Ateni Sioni (1 GEL, 30 minutes) once or twice hourly until 6pm.

WESTERN GEORGIA

Famous as the destination of Jason and the Argonauts in their search for the golden fleece, western Georgia is home to Georgia's second-largest city, Kutaisi, and is full of historical, architectural and natural riches. The region has always acted as a conduit for influences from the west, from the ancient Greeks to St Nino to the Ottoman Turks. It was for long periods ruled separately from eastern Georgia, but was also where the great united Georgian kingdom of the 11th and 12th centuries made its start.

Kutaisi ქუთაისი

☑ 431 / POP 149,000

Capital of several historical kingdoms within Georgia, Kutaisi is today being revitalised after years of post-Soviet decline. Georgia's parliament was transferred from Tbilisi to brand-new quarters here in 2012, and Kutaisi's airport has become a destination for international budget airlines. There are several interesting natural, historical and architectural attractions within day-trip reach of the city.

Kutaisi is built around the Rioni River, with the city centre, first developed in the 17th century, on its left bank. To its north, the right bank rises up to an older area where the landmark Bagrati Cathedral overlooks the city.

History

At the end of the 8th century AD, Leon II, king of Abkhazia, transferred his capital here from Anakopia. One of his successors, Bagrat II inherited the eastern Georgian kingdom of Kartli in the early 11th century, uniting western and eastern Georgia and becoming Bagrat III of Georgia. His descendant David the Builder was crowned

Western Georgia

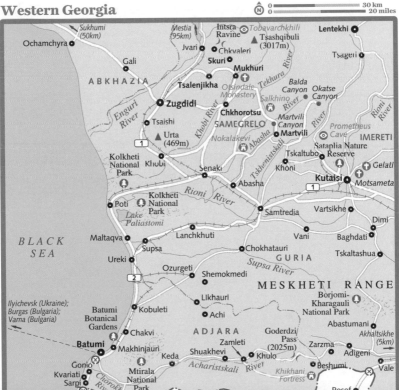

Georgian king in Kutaisi in 1089. Kutaisi remained the political and cultural centre of Georgia until 1122, when it was replaced by Tbilisi.

Kutaisi resumed as capital of western Georgia in the 15th century when the country was divided after the Mongol and Timurid invasions. It was occupied by the Ottomans in 1669, then captured by Georgian and Russian forces in 1770. In Soviet times it became Georgia's second-most important industrial centre. Post-Soviet industrial collapse sent many local people migrating to Russia, Greece and elsewhere.

◉ Sights

The Bagrati Cathedral is one of Georgia's most beautiful churches, and the attractively renovated central area around Kutaisis bulvari park and Pushkinis qucha is well worth exploring, with its colourful market, good museum, cafes and the grand **Colchis Fountain** (Tsentraluri moedani), adorned with large-scale copies of the famous gold jewellery from Vani.

★**Bagrati Cathedral**   CATHEDRAL
(Bagrati; ⊙variable hours, approx 9am-8pm) From the Jachvis Khidi (Chain Bridge) you can walk up cobbled streets to the stately Bagrati Cathedral on Ukimerioni Hill. The cathedral was built in 1003 by Bagrat III, with a tall drum and pointed dome resting on four free-standing pillars. In 1692 a Turkish explosion brought down drum, dome and ceiling to leave the cathedral in a ruined state. It was fully renovated between 2009 and 2012, with a mix of old and new stone and a few steel sections.

The cathedral gained Unesco World Heritage listing in 1994 following intermittent restoration efforts through the 20th century. Ironically the recent renovation has put it on Unesco's World Heritage in Danger list, due to threats to the 'integrity and authenticity of the site'.

Kutaisi

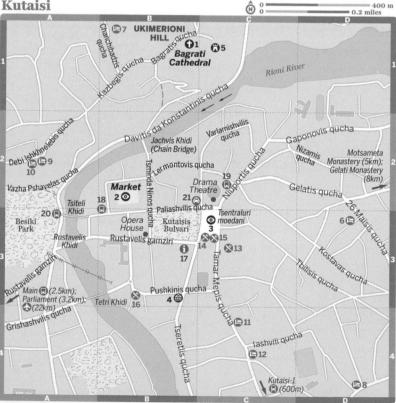

The **palace-citadel** immediately east of the cathedral dates back to the 6th century. It was wrecked in 1769 during Georgian-Russo-Turkish wars, but you can discern remains of wine cellars and a church.

★**Market**   MARKET
(btwn Paliashvili & Lermontov; ⊙7am-5pm or later) Kutaisi's indoor produce market is one of the largest, liveliest and most colourful in Georgia, full of cheese, walnuts, spices, herbs, fruit, vegetables, meat, *churchkhela* (strings of walnuts coated in grape-juice caramel), beans, wine, pickles and plenty more.

Kutaisi Historical Museum   MUSEUM
(⌇245691; Pushkin 18; admission 3 GEL, tour in English, German, Russian or Georgian 10 GEL; ⊙10am-5pm) The history museum has superb collections from all around western Georgia, but a guided tour is a good idea as labelling is poor. The highlight is the Golden Fund section, with a marvellous exhibition of icons and crosses in precious metals and jewels, including a large, reputedly miracle-working icon that used to reside in the Bagrati Cathedral.

Parliament Building   ARCHITECTURE
(⌇tours 32-2281693; tours www.parliament.ge/en/media; Irakli Abashidze 26) The six-storey-tall glass bubble of Georgia's parliament building, opened in 2012, rises 4km west of the city centre, reachable by bus 4, 38 or 100 from the city centre (west end of Paliashvili). Controversial from the moment a WWII memorial was blown up in 2009 to make way for it, the parliament is unpopular with many MPs, who would like to move parliament back to Tbilisi.

A brainchild of the Saakashvili government, intended to decentralise power from Tbilisi and boost economically depressed Kutaisi, the building has been criticised for its distance from the executive arms of government (still in Tbilisi), and for the expense of building and operating it.

Free one-hour tours inside the building are given at noon, 3pm and 5pm on Wednesdays, Thursdays and Fridays in weeks of plenary sittings. If you'd like to visit, telephone or email at least a couple of days ahead to check schedules and admission procedures, request (if you want) an English-speaking guide, and register your passport details.

🛌 Sleeping

Kutaisi's accommodation options have expanded hugely and you can expect new hostels, guesthouses and hotels to continue popping up, with the competition keeping prices good.

★**Giorgi's Homestay**   HOMESTAY $
(⌇243720, 595591511; giorgihomestay14@yahoo.com; Chanchibadze 14; per person with/without breakfast 30/20 GEL; ❄🔊📶) Giorgi Giorgadze and his family provide clean, pleasant and sizeable rooms in their ample house on Ukimerioni Hill. They have been hosting travellers a lot longer than most comparable establishments and understand what their guests need, offering plenty of travel tips and help, substantial breakfasts, sparkling bathrooms, and free tea and coffee.

Star Hostel   HOSTEL $
(⌇599988804; starhostel.ge@gmail.com; Tamar Mepe 37; dm/d incl breakfast 20/50 GEL; ❄📶)

Kutaisi

A good, clean, Georgian-run hostel 500m south of Tsentraluri moedani. Bunk dorms hold four to eight people and there are three doubles with bathroom. It offers reasonably priced taxi outings and rents bicycles (20 GEL per day).

Hotel Elegant
HOTEL $$

(☑598594910; dula50@mail.ru; Debi Ishknelebi 24; r per person with/without breakfast 40/30 GEL; P ⊖ ✳ ☎) One of several small or medium-sized hotels on a hilltop street overlooking the city centre from the northwest, the welcoming, family-run Elegant offers 10 pleasant, comfy, parquet-floored rooms in assorted colours. There's a lovely terrace for sitting out over a coffee or just enjoying the view.

Kiev-Kutaisi Hotel
HOTEL $$

(☑571026329; kiev.kutaisi@gmail.com; Tamar Mepe 25; d 50-60 GEL, breakfast 10 GEL; P ⊖ ✳ ☎ ☎) A small hotel with something of the feel of a family home, Kiev-Kutaisi is handily located just 400m south of Tsentraluri moedani. The welcome is friendly and English-speaking, and the rooms spotless and uncluttered. A family room and an apartment for six are available, as well as four doubles.

Gelati Guest House
GUESTHOUSE $$

(Hotel Gelati; ☑597986222, 597965326; www.gelati1.narod.ru; 26 Maisi 2nd Lane No 4; s/d 30/60 GEL, breakfast/dinner 7/15 GEL; ✳ ☎) Original art, moulded ceilings and other pretty touches give this friendly, English-speaking guesthouse a little something extra. The six rooms all have bathrooms.

Hotel Gora
HOTEL $$

(☑551929092; 195706@mail.ru; Debi Ishknelebi 22; d incl breakfast 80-100 GEL; P ✳ ☎) This professionally run 47-room hotel has a fine site looking down over the city centre, and makes the most of it with a nice big dining terrace. Rooms vary in size and the amount of care given to the decor, so it's worth checking a couple.

Hotel Edemi
BOUTIQUE HOTEL $$

(☑599563825; Solomon I-s 31; r 60-100 GEL, breakfast 10 GEL; ⊖ ✳ @ ☎) A lovely recent conversion of a large century-old townhouse, the Edemi provides good-sized, parquet-floored rooms with contemporary comforts including smart TVs, in decorative but uncluttered styles. It's a little out of the

city centre, 1km southeast of Tsentraluri moedani.

✗ Eating

The city centre has a decent selection of appealing cafes and small restaurants.

El Paso
GEORGIAN $

(Tsentraluri moedani; mains 4-8 GEL; ⊙9am-midnight) A plain but neat and clean central spot for good Georgian favourites including *lobiani* (bean pie), *khinkali* and *mtsvadi*.

Baraqa
GEORGIAN $

(Tamar Mepe 3; mains 6-10 GEL; ⊙10am-10pm; ☎) This pleasant, brick-arched place does good *khachapuri* and other dishes, including *kubdari* (a *khachapuri*-like pie with minced-meat filling) and wild mushrooms with cheese. Popular with locals at lunchtime and for ice cream any time.

Café Rennes
EUROPEAN, GEORGIAN $$

(Tsentraluri moedani; mains 10-20 GEL; ⊙11am-midnight; ☎) With chilled music and a vaguely Parisian theme, Rennes serves up well-prepared salads and soups as well as heartier fare like trout in pomegranate sauce or fillet steak in red wine, and good coffee, on its terrace out front or indoor cafe-bar area.

Palaty
EUROPEAN, GEORGIAN $$

(Pushkin; mains 7-20 GEL; ⊙11am-midnight; ☎) Frequent live music (typically jazz or folk) and a semi-bohemian ambience make Palaty a favourite spot with locals and visitors for evening drinks and food. Try a pasta or mushroom dish, *khachapuri* or even a steak.

❶ Information

Tourism Information Centre (☑241107; tickutaisi@gmail.com; Rustaveli 3; ⊙9am-7pm Mar-Nov, 10am-6pm Dec-Feb) Helpful office in the heart of town. There's also a desk at the airport.

❶ Getting There & Away

AIR

David the Builder Kutaisi International Airport (☑237000; kutaisiairport.ge/) at Kopitnari, 22km west of central Kutaisi, is a popular budget-airline entry point to Georgia. **Wizz Air** (http://wizzair.com) flies from Budapest, Katowice, Kiev, Vilnius and Warsaw, and **Pegasus Airlines** (www.flypgs.com) from Istanbul. There are also Moscow flights.

MARSHRUTKA

Marshrutky from Kutaisi's **main bus station** (Chavchavadzis gamziri 67), 3km southwest of the city centre behind a McDonald's, include the following services:

Akhaltsikhe (8 GEL, 3½ hours, three daily)
Batumi (10 GEL, two hours, hourly 9am to 5pm)
Borjomi (8 GEL, three hours, three daily)
Gori (8 GEL, 2½ hours, noon)
Mestia (25 GEL, 4½ hours, 10am)
Tbilisi (10 GEL, four hours, hourly 7am to 6pm)
Zugdidi (7 GEL, 1½ hours, 13 daily)

TRAIN

Kutaisi-1 station (Tamar Mepe), 1km south of the city centre, has slow trains to Tbilisi at 4.50am (4 GEL, six hours) and 12.25pm (8 GEL, 5½ hours); Batumi (2 GEL, four hours) at 5.30pm, and Zugdidi (2 GEL, 3½ hours) at 12.50pm.

❶ Getting Around

TO/FROM THE AIRPORT

Georgian Bus (☑ 555397387; www.georgian bus.com) runs minibuses between Kutaisi airport and several destinations around Georgia, including Kutaisi city (5 GEL, 30 minutes), Tbilisi (20 GEL, four hours), Batumi (15 GEL, two hours), Mestia (40 GEL, four hours) and Kazbegi (55 GEL, 5½ hours), timed to fit in with flight arrivals and departures. You can book and pay online, or at its airport desk – or, for trips to the airport, when you board the minibus. Minimum passenger numbers may be required for some destinations. The arrival and departure point in Tbilisi is Pushkinis skver, just off the north side of Tavisuplebis moedani.

Taxis between the airport and city centre cost 25 GEL.

BUS, MARSHRUTKA & TAXI

Bus 1 (0.30 GEL) and *marshrutka* 200 (0.40 GEL) run from the main bus station to Rustaveli in the city centre. Catch them across the road (Chavchavadze) from the bus station, going to the left. From the city centre to the bus station, catch bus 1 at the west end of Paliashvili. Taxis charge around 6 GEL from bus station to the city centre.

Around Kutaisi

Gelati & Motsameta
გელათი და მოწამეთა

Two beautiful and historic monasteries stand a few kilometres northeast of Kutaisi and you can easily visit them both in one outing.

◎ Sights

★**Gelati Monastery**　　　　MONASTERY
(◎ approx 8am-10pm; ℗) Georgians have always had a talent for choosing beautiful locations for their churches and this famous monastery complex, on a wooded hillside 8km northeast of Kutaisi, is an outstanding example. Gelati was a cultural hub of Georgia's medieval 'golden age', and many Georgian rulers were buried here, including the great 12th-century king, David the Builder. The interior of the main Cathedral of the Virgin is among the brightest and most colourful in Georgia, with fascinating frescoes.

King David founded Gelati in 1106 as a centre for Christian culture and Neoplatonist

---

JASON & THE GOLDEN FLEECE

In the Ancient Greek myth of the golden fleece, Jason, a prince of Thessaly, responds to his uncle Pelias' challenge to go to the land of Colchis to find the golden fleece. (Colchis was a historical kingdom occupying most of western Georgia in antiquity.) Jason had a special ship, the *Argo*, built to carry him and 49 other adventurous young Greek rowers (the Argonauts). After various tribulations, they reached Colchis and sailed up the Phasis River (present-day Rioni), where they were received by King Aeëtes in his capital (possibly Vani or Kutaisi). Aeëtes agreed to give up the fleece if Jason could yoke two fire-breathing bulls to a plough, and then sow the teeth of a dragon from which a crop of armed men would spring. Jason was helped by Aeëtes' daughter Medea, who had conceived a violent passion for him: he promised to marry her in return for help from her skills in magic. Medea gave Jason a charm which enabled him to survive Aeëtes' tests and to take the fleece from the dragon that guarded it.

The golden fleece itself is related to real Georgian mountain traditions: in Svaneti and Racha, people sifted for gold in mountain rivers by placing a sheepskin across the rocks to collect tiny nuggets. The legend is still widely commemorated in Georgia, not least by Argo beer, brewed in Tbilisi and drunk Georgia-wide.

learning. Medieval chroniclers described its academy as 'a second Jerusalem' and 'new Athens'. In 1510 the Ottoman Turks set fire to the complex, but Bagrat III of Imereti subsequently restored it. The monks were cast out by the communists in 1922, but the churches were reconsecrated in 1988.

The frescoes in the **Cathedral of the Virgin** were painted between the 12th and 18th centuries: the line of seven noble figures on the north wall includes David the Builder (holding the church) and Bagrat III of Georgia (with a cross over his left shoulder). A famous 1120s mosaic of the Virgin and Child, with Archangels Michael and Gabriel to the left and right respectively, looks down from the apse ceiling. If you visit during the Sunday-morning service from around 10am, you'll be treated to beautiful Georgian chants.

To the east of the cathedral, the **Church of St George** contains further colourful frescoes. Outside the cathedral's west door is the smaller Church of St Nicholas, built on an unusual arcaded base, and beyond that, the recently rebuilt **Academy**, where philosophy, theology, sciences and painting were studied, and important chronicles and translations written. **David the Builder's grave** lies inside the south gate: David wanted all who entered the monastery to step on his tomb, a notably humble gesture for such a powerful man. Ironically, reverent visitors today take great care *not* to step on it.

Motsameta Monastery   MONASTERY
Little Motsameta sits on a spectacular clifftop promontory above a bend of the Tskhaltsitela River, 5km from Kutaisi, 1.8km off the Gelati road. The river's name, 'Red Water', derives from an 8th-century Arab massacre. Among the victims were the brothers Davit and Konstantin Mkheidze, dukes of Argveti. Their bodies were thrown in the river but, the story goes, they were then miraculously brought up to the monastery site (by lions, in one common version).

The brothers' bones are kept in a side altar in the church. If you make a wish and crawl three times under it, your wish will supposedly be granted!

ℹ Getting There & Away
Marshrutky to Gelati (1 GEL, 30 minutes) leave from Brosse behind the Drama Theatre in Kutaisi at 8am, 11am, 2pm, 4pm and 6pm, passing the Motsameta turn-off en route. The last one back

from Gelati is at 4.30pm. If you're visiting both places, it's a mostly downhill road-walk of about one hour from Gelati to Motsameta, should the return *marshrutka* schedules not suit: you can cut 800m off the distance by heading to the left along the railway after 3.5km.

A taxi round-trip from Kutaisi to Gelati typically costs 25 GEL, or 30 GEL with Motsameta too.

Sataplia Nature Reserve
საათაფლიას სახელმწიფო ნაკრძალი

The star features of the 3.3-sq-km **reserve** (☑577101417; adult/student 6/3 GEL; ☉10am-6pm Wed-Mon; Ⓟ🖫), 9km northwest of Kutaisi, are a couple of dozen 120-million-year-old, fossilised dinosaur footprints (well displayed in a protective building), and an attractively lit 300m-long cave with a small underground river. The reserve is covered in thick, subtropical Colchic forest and has a couple of panoramic lookout points. It takes about an hour to walk round the main visitor route.

A taxi round-trip from Kutaisi combining Sataplia with Prometheus Cave costs 35 GEL to 40 GEL. Public transport is awkward: marshrutka 35 (0.40 GEL) goes from the west end of Paliashvili to the end of Javakhishvili on Kutaisi's western edge, where *marshrutka* 45 leaves for the remaining 5km to Sataplia when the driver considers he has enough passengers (four is usually sufficient).

Prometheus Cave
პრომეთეს მღვიმე

This 1.4km-long **cave** (☑577101417; www. prometheus.ge; adult/student 7/3.50 GEL, boat ride 7 GEL; ☉11am-6pm Tue-Sun; Ⓟ) at Kumistavi, 20km northwest of Kutaisi, is a succession of six large chambers followed by a 400m-long underground lake. Sections are truly impressive, and the guided visits along a well-made concrete path are enhanced by discreet coloured lighting and a little background classical music. Children under six years are not allowed in the cave.

Marshrutka 30 runs from the west end of Kutaisi's Tsiteli Khidi (Red Bridge) to the spa town of Tskaltubo (1 GEL, 30 minutes), where *marshrutka* 42 continues 8km to Prometheus Cave (1.50 GEL, 20 minutes) every hour or two.

Okatse Canyon ოკაცეს კანიონი

An exciting 700m-long walkway, new in 2014, projects from the edge of this 100m-deep canyon (Map p32; adult/student 6/3 GEL; ⊙10am-6pm; **P**) and culminates in a viewing platform that hangs right out over the middle. It's a 2km hike from the visitors centre near Zeda Gordi village, 42km northwest of Kutaisi. A jeep back to the visitors centre afterwards costs 15 GEL for five or six people.

Many people add on a visit to the nearby Kinchkha waterfall – a 7km jeep drive from the visitors centre (30 GEL per jeep round-trip) then a 2km (each way) walk. A round-trip taxi from Kutaisi costs around 60 GEL, and only a little more if combined with nearby Martvili.

Vani ვანი

The ancient city **site** (☑577500596; museum admission 1.50 GEL, museum & excavations tour per group 25 GEL; ⊙10am-6pm Tue-Sun; **P**), 40km southwest of Kutaisi, was one of the main centres of ancient Colchis, flourishing from the 8th to 1st centuries BC. Some speculate that it could have been the city of King Aeëtes, where Jason came in search of the Golden Fleece. The museum here, due to reopen by 2016 after reconstruction, has beautiful exhibits.

Excavations first started in the 1890s, after locals reported gold ornaments being washed down the hill after rains. Archaeologists have since found remains of monumental architecture and opulent burials. The museum's treasures include a mix of originals and copies of fabulous gold adornments with incredibly fine animal designs.

The site itself is not developed for visitors but you can make out some temple areas, defensive walls, a deep ritual well, a small city gate and a section of paved street. Taking a tour, available in English, Georgian or Russian, brings it all to life.

Marshrutky to Vani (3 GEL, 1½ hours) leave Kutaisi's main bus station hourly from 7am to 1pm (except 10am). From Vani's bus station, it's about a 15-minute walk to the museum. A taxi from Kutaisi costs about 50 GEL return.

Zugdidi ზუგდიდი

☑415 / POP 43,000

The bustling main city of Samegrelo (Megrelia) province, Zugdidi is 108km northwest of Kutaisi. The nearest city to the Abkhazian border, it has absorbed a high number of refugees since the 1990s. It's a stepping stone for getting to Svaneti or Abkhazia, and a base for exploring the less known attractions of Samegrelo.

The central boulevard, running southwest to northeast, is Zviad Gamsakhurdias gamziri, named after Megrelian Zviad Gamsakhurdia, post-Soviet Georgia's ultranationalist first president. The combined train and bus station is 1km west of here along Rustaveli.

◉ Sights

Dadiani Museum MUSEUM
(adult/student 2/1 GEL, treasure section adult/student 5/1 GEL, tour in English, German, Georgian or Russian 6 GEL; ⊙10am-6pm Tue-Sun, treasure section 11am-4pm Tue-Sun) The castle-like palace of the Dadiani family (old lords of Samegrelo), at the north end of Zviad Gamsakhurdia, is now a museum. As well as interesting 19th-century paintings of the Caucasus region and a fine collection of icons and crosses from the 10th to 20th centuries (in the Treasure section), it contains one of Napoleon Bonaparte's three bronze death masks, acquired via a marriage between a Dadiani and a Bonaparte relative.

The wooded botanical gardens beside the park are worth a stroll too.

🛏 Sleeping & Eating

Zugdidi Hostel HOSTEL $
(☑558102688; www.zugdidihostel.com; Rustaveli 8; dm/d/tr 20/45/60 GEL, breakfast 7-8 GEL; ☯☎) This hostel is run by super-friendly and helpful locals who offer some excellent day trips, plus visits to their farm with a Georgian feast, dancing and cooking classes.

The hostel has a bar and nice upstairs terrace in addition to fairly standard sleeping and cooking facilities. It's 1.5km east from Zviad Gamsakhurdia.

My Moon Hostel HOSTEL $
(☑557344868, 579792002; www.zugdidihostel.ge; Lermontovi 2nd lane No 5; dm/s/d incl light breakfast 20/30/50 GEL; ☯☎) Run by a lively, multilingual team of local musicians and friends, My Moon offers a sociable atmosphere in a beautiful, comfortable, pine-panelled house. Downstairs is a lively bar

with rock/blues/folk/pop music (sometimes live), games and quirky music-theme decor.

An excellent range of minivan trips and tours around Samegrelo is on offer. The hostel is 2km southeast of the town centre: free pick-ups from the bus/ train station are offered. The owners also run a second hostel in the **town centre** (🖉557344868, 579792002; www.zugdidi hostel.ge; Nikoladze 42; incl light breakfast, dm 20 GEL, d 40-50 GEL; ❀🛈), convenient for the bus and train stations; it's the sixth house past the Svaneti-style tower, in the street north off Rustaveli just west of the river.

Hotel Iberia Palace HOTEL $$
(🖉592750990, 592615252; www.iberiapalace.ge; Kikalishvili 6; s/d incl breakfast from 130/150 GEL; P❀❊🛈) Zugdidi's classiest lodgings are at this very comfy, well-run, 12-room central hotel opened above an electronics store in 2015. Rooms are spacious, bright and wood-floored, in whites and lime greens, with good toiletries.

The Host GEORGIAN $$
(Kostava 34; mains 7-15 GEL; ⊙9am-11pm; 🛈) This popular, three-floor, brick-walled establishment stands behind a McDonald's just off the fountain circle at the south end of Zviad Gamsakhurdia. Service is friendly and the range of good Georgian dishes includes Megrelian specialities such as *elarji* (cornmeal porridge with melted cheese) and *gebjalia* (boiled *sulguni* cheese with yoghurt and mint).

ℹ️ Information

Tourism Information Centre (ticzugdidi @gmail.com; Rustaveli 87, cnr Zviad Gamsakhurdia; ⊙10am-7pm Jul-Oct, 10am-6pm Nov-Jun)

ℹ️ Getting There & Away

The main *marshrutka* and bus terminal is at the train station. Departures (mostly *marshrutky*, a few buses) include the following:

Batumi (12 GEL, three hours, seven daily)
Kutaisi (7 GEL, 1½ hours, 10 daily)
Mestia (20 GEL, three hours, 8.30am)
Tbilisi (15 GEL, 5½ hours, about hourly, 7am to midnight)

Extra *marshrutky* to Mestia usually meet the trains arriving from Tbilisi (6.30am and 1.30pm at the time of writing), though they may not leave until they are full: Zugdidi's hostels can usually arrange for Mestia *marshrutky* to come and pick you up.

A night train to Tbilisi (seat/2nd/1st class 7/21/30 GEL, nine hours) departs Zugdidi at about 9pm (schedules can change). There's also a day train to Tbilisi (2nd class 15 GEL, 5½ hours, departing 5.50pm at the time of writing).

ABKHAZIA

The greatest tragedy to befall Georgia since its independence has been the bloodshed and misery that the breakaway of Abkhazia (Apsny or Apswa in Abkhazian, Apkhazeti in Georgian) has brought about. Once the jewel of the 'Soviet Riviera' along the Black Sea coast, today this de facto independent republic is still getting over the devastation of the 1992–93 war, with less than half its prewar population of 535,000. Russian tourism, investment and aid have boomed since the 2008 South Ossetia War and provided a lifeline for the Abkhazian economy. Parts of Abkhazia's towns still have a strangely underpopulated feel, but the coast and countryside are beautiful, and just being inside this curious territory with a throwback Soviet atmosphere is a fascinating experience.

Dangers & Annoyances

The area around the southern town of Gali, including the Abkhazian side of the Enguri River boundary, has a reputation for lawlessness. It's best to travel through this area by early afternoon, and avoid taking any transport in the area with no other passengers. The UK Foreign Office and US State Department, among others, advise against travel to Abkhazia.

ℹ️ Information

MONEY
Abkhazia's currency is the Russian rouble (worth around 1.5 US cents at mid-2015 rates). You can obtain roubles from ATMs in Sukhumi and Gagra and pay with international credit cards at some hotels and restaurants, and exchange cash US dollars, and often euros, at banks and moneychangers. Bring some roubles to keep you going on arrival.

TELEPHONE
Abkhazia uses the Russian country code 🖉7. Numbers starting 🖉940 are mobile numbers. At research time it was not possible to call from Georgia to Abkhazia except for the southern Gali district, which is within reach of Georgian mobile networks. It's easy to obtain a local SIM

SECRETS OF SAMEGRELO

The Samegrelo countryside, with the Caucasus foothills rising above 3000m in the north, is full of beautiful spots little known to outsiders. The best way to get out to them is on a trip with the enthusiasts from My Moon Hostel (p69) or Zugdidi Hostel (p69). Day trips for two to four people can cost between 100 GEL and 250 GEL.

The East
NOKALAKEVI
Some 60km from Zugdidi via Senaki, **Nokalakevi** (admission 3 GEL; ⊘10am-2pm & 3-6pm Tue-Sun) is a picturesque and historic ancient Colchian royal town and fortress. A tunnel leads down to the Tekhura River from the grassy grounds, and admission includes an interesting archaeological museum. Excavations are ongoing (see www.nokalakevi.org). About 1km upstream on the Tekhura you can take a dip in soothing thermal pools.

MARTVILI
Boat rides in the canyon near the small town of Martvili (მარტვილი) are hugely popular with locals. For less of a crowd experience head to the monastery, or – north of town – take a hike up Balda Canyon to Oniore waterfall (7km or 11km round-trip depending which route you take), or visit **Salkhino** (admission free; ⊘daily; Ⓟ), the former summer palace of the Dadianis, where the monks at the adjacent monastery may open their wine cellar for you to taste their excellent Ojaleshi wine.

Take a trip up the Abasha River through the **Martvili Canyon** (Inchkhuri Canyon, Gachedili Canyon; ⊘about Apr-Oct; Ⓟ Ⓗ), a 40m to 70m-deep canyon starting at Inchkhuri, 5km north of Martvili. It's a pretty, though not overwhelmingly exciting, ride: the price per small inflatable boat (five or six passengers) is 30 GEL to go 350m up the canyon and back, or 60 GEL for 700m.

Martvili's monastery, a medieval Georgian cultural centre, sits on a serene hilltop overlooking the town and the surrounding valleys and hills. Its church dates from the 7th century, with its original design based on the Jvari Church near Mtskheta. The interesting frescoes inside include portraits of the Dadiani royal house of Megrelia (Samegrelo), and a famous 17th-century Virgin on the apse ceiling.

The North
INTSRA RAVINE
Near Chkvaleri village there's a good 14km valley and forest hike in the Intsra ravine, and on nearby Kvira mountain you'll find Kuakantsalia, a large boulder that will rock at the push of a finger but won't topple even with the heave of a shoulder.

OTSINDALE MONASTERY
At Taia village, a few kilometres southeast of Mukhuri and 15km north of Chkhorotsu, this monastery stands on a superbly panoramic hilltop. Its church dates back to the 11th century: a solar disc on its ceiling and the nearby 'phallus stone' are survivors from pre-Christian rites here.

TOBAVARCHKHILI
The picturesque, remote mountain lakes of Tobavarchkhili, at around 2650m altitude, are best visited on a camping trip, as they're reached by a 33km 4WD drive north from Mukhuri, followed by a 12km walk to the lakes. A natural staircase climbs to the top of Mt Tsashqibuli (3017m), 4km southeast of the first lake. Legend has it that if you disturb the water of this lake, or make a noise near it, a thunderstorm will ensue.

It's possible to walk on from Tobavarchkhili over to Khaishi in Svaneti.

---

card: look for *'sim-karty'* signs at kiosks and shops.

TIME
Abkhazia is on Moscow time (GMT plus three hours), so put your clock back one hour if you enter by the Enguri boundary. There's no daylight saving time.

VISAS
The first step to visiting Abkhazia is to obtain a clearance letter to enter it. Instructions are on

THE ABKHAZIA CONFLICT

The Abkhaz are linguistically distinct from the Georgians, their language being one of the northwestern Caucasus family (although Russian is now the most common language in Abkhazia). During the Middle Ages, Abkhazia was an important component of Christian Georgia. It came under Ottoman rule in the 15th century. Russian conquest in the 19th century resulted in many thousands of Muslim Abkhaz fleeing to the Ottoman empire, and there is a big Abkhaz diaspora in Turkey today.

Under Soviet rule in 1921, Abkhazia signed a treaty of union with Georgia, but in 1931 it was downgraded to an autonomous region within Georgia. The number of ethnic Georgians in Abkhazia increased to the point where by 1989 46% of Abkhazia's population was Georgian and only 18% Abkhaz. The Abkhaz began to agitate for more rights in the late 1970s, and in 1990 Abkhazia's Abkhaz-dominated Supreme Soviet unilaterally declared Abkhazia a separate Soviet republic.

Real conflict broke out in August 1992 when the Georgian National Guard occupied Sukhumi, driving out most of its Abkhaz inhabitants. Abkhazia was plunged into a year of fighting, in which about 8000 people died. The Abkhaz were aided by fighters from the Russian Caucasus, and on some occasions by Russian armed forces. Both sides committed appalling atrocities. In September 1993 the Abkhaz attacked Sukhumi in violation of a truce and drove the Georgian forces and almost all of Abkhazia's Georgian population (about 230,000 people) out of Abkhazia. Only in the southern Gali district have significant numbers of Georgians (around 40,000) since returned.

After the 1992–93 war, Russia imposed trade sanctions on Abkhazia, but Vladimir Putin changed Russia's stance when he entered the Kremlin in 2000. Abkhazians were offered Russian passports from 2001, and in 2008 Russia removed trade sanctions. During the 2008 South Ossetia War, Russian forces came from Abkhazia to attack Georgian military installations in western Georgia. Soon afterwards, Russia recognised Abkhazia as an independent nation. (Only Venezuela, Nicaragua and a couple of small Pacific islands have followed Russia's lead.) Russia stepped up aid and investment and stationed anti-aircraft missiles and several thousand troops in the territory. In 2014 Abkhazia and Russia signed an Agreement on Alliance & Strategic Partnership, under which Abkhazia's defence, law enforcement, border control and economic management are to be merged with Russia's within three years.

Ethnic Abkhaz now constitute about half of Abkhazia's much reduced population. Most do not appear to want Russian rule (their ideal is genuine independence). They have, however, little choice but to obey Russia's will.

the website of the **Abkhazia Foreign Ministry** (☑840-2267069; http://mfaapsny.org; ulitsa Lakoba 21, Sukhumi): you fill in a form and email it to the foreign ministry's **consular service** (☑840-2263948, 840-2267069; http://mfaapsny.org; ulitsa Sakharova 33, Sukhumi; ☺9am-1pm & 2-6pm Mon-Fri) along with a copy of your passport's personal data page. Within seven working days you should receive your clearance letter (in Russian) by email: check it carefully as mistakes are sometimes made.

Having entered Abkhazia with your clearance letter, you must then go within three working days to the consular service office, in central Sukhumi, to obtain your visa. Abkhazia visas are single pieces of paper, not stuck into your passport. A 10-day single-entry visa costs the rouble equivalent of US$11.

Georgia permits foreigners to enter Abkhazia by the Enguri Bridge boundary near Zugdidi, but treats entry to Abkhazia from Russia by the Psou River border as illegal entry into Georgia, punishable by a heavy fine or imprisonment under Georgian law. If you enter Abkhazia from Russia, don't try to continue across Abkhazia's southern boundary into undisputed Georgia. You'll need at least a double-entry Russian visa in advance, so that you can return to Russia.

Sukhumi

☑840 / POP 63,000

Abkhazia's capital (Sukhumi or Sukhum in Russian, Sokhumi in Georgian, Akwa in Abkhaz) has a gorgeous setting on a bay backed by hills thick with luxuriant semi-tropical vegetation. In 1989 it had a multi-ethnic population of 120,000, but it was badly damaged during the war in 1992–93, when its large Georgian population was driven out. Reconstruction and new construction have accelerated in recent years, though numerous buildings still stand empty or ruined, including landmarks such as the old **Government House** (ploshchad Svobody), gutted when the Abkhaz took the city in September 1993.

◉ Sights

Naberezhnaya Makhadzhirov WATERFRONT
(Makhadzhirov Embankment; 🏛) Strung with pretty parks, part-derelict jetties, cafes and kitschy souvenir stalls, and fronted by stretches of stony beach, Sukhumi's 3km-long seafront promenade swarms with happy crowds during the summer holiday months.

Botanical Gardens GARDENS
(ulitsa Gulia 22, cnr prospekt Leona; adult/child R200/50; ☺9am-8pm; 🏛) With 50,000 sq metres of plants from around the world, the well-maintained botanical gardens, founded in 1840, are well worth a wander.

Abkhazian State Museum MUSEUM
(prospekt Leona 22; admission R100; ☺10am-6pm Tue-Sun) The recently refurbished museum has good archaeological sections as well as typical Soviet-style collections of stuffed animals and war memorabilia.

Alleya Slavy PARK
(Glory Alley) This park on the north side of ulitsa Lakoba is the burial site of many Abkhaz who died in the 1992–93 fighting.

🛏 Sleeping

Sukhumi has some good midrange hotels, though the best can get booked out in the high season (July and August). Numerous families rent rooms, starting at around R600 for a double with shared bathroom in high season: look for *'sdayutsya komnaty'* signs in Russian. There are several such options on a quiet, leafy stretch of ulitsa Akirtava, about 1km east of the city centre: coming from the south, you can get out of your *marshrutka* under the railway bridge as you approach central Sukhumi, and walk east along Akirtava.

Guesthouse GUESTHOUSE $
(📱9407724442; ulitsa Akirtava 55; r with/without bathroom R1200/600; ❄) The Kvitsinia family has a variety of decent, clean rooms in several buildings on their property, and a small guest kitchen. Some family members speak passable English.

★Hotel Sukhum BOUTIQUE HOTEL $$
(📱9409274182; www.otel-sukhum.ru; naberezhnaya Makhadzhirov 9; d incl breakfast R3500-6500; ❄❄🛜) This excellent small hotel sits beside the little Basla River, just upstream from the east end of the central seafront. It has a pretty riverside garden and bright, cheerful rooms in two buildings, one of which is also known as Eko Hotel Sukhum. The helpful owner speaks English and German.

There's a minimum two-night stay from May to September; outside that period, discounts are often available.

Hotel Leon HOTEL $$
(📱9407201100; www.leonhotel.net; naberezhnaya Makhadzhirov 6; r R3300-4000; ❄❄🛜) A very good, medium-sized, modern hotel just back from the eastern end of the central seafront. Rooms are furnished in pale wood and equipped with excellent showers, good aircon, and tea and coffee makers. The R300 breakfast is great value.

Hotel Inter-Sukhum HOTEL $$
(📱2260062; http://intersukhum.com; ulitsa Lakoba 109; s/d incl breakfast R1700/2200; ❄❄🛜) The rooms at this largeish hotel just west of the city centre are terminally bland, but they're clean and secure with small balconies and comfy beds, and the seafront is 100m away. The restaurant serves a buffet lunch or dinner for R300.

🍴 Eating

There are lots of cafes and restaurants on naberezhnaya Makhadzhirov, and others scattered elsewhere. Among the predominant Russian and Georgian dishes, many also serve some traditional Abkhazian dishes such as *abysta* or *mamalyga* (a thick maize porridge), *achapa* (a salad of greens or beans with chopped walnuts and spices), or *myaso po-abkhazsky* (Abkhaz-style meat; meat cooked in a spicy tomato sauce).

Nartaa RUSSIAN, GEORGIAN $
(naberezhnaya Makhadzhirov, btwn ulitsy Aidgylara & Konfederatov; mains R70-220; ☺10am-11pm) Wood-built Nartaa, with tables on various verandahs and small pavilions, does good food at small prices, including *shashlyk*, salads and a good *kartofel* (potato) side dish.

Dolce Vita RUSSIAN, EUROPEAN $$
(naberezhnaya Makhadzhirov, btwn ulitsy Aidgylara & Konfederatov; mains R290-890; ☺11am-2pm)

One of the more upmarket places, serving up good beef medallions in cream sauce, trout, gnocchi, burgers and more.

❶ Information

Maps of Sukhumi and Abkhazia are sold at souvenir shops (on naberezhnaya Makhadzhirov and elsewhere) and newsstands.

❶ Getting There & Away

ZUGDIDI

The 20-minute taxi ride from Zugdidi to Abkhazia's southern boundary at the Enguri Bridge (Enguris Khidi) costs 10 GEL. There are also *marshrutky* (1 GEL, about hourly 8am to 6pm) from the small street off the south side of Rustaveli, just west of the river. You show your documents at a Georgian police post at the southern end of the 1km-long bridge, then walk across the bridge and show them again at the **Abkhazian border post** (☉7am-7pm), where guards may need to call the Foreign Ministry in Sukhumi before letting you proceed.

From the border you might find a bus going all the way to Sukhumi (R250, two hours); a taxi should be R2000. Otherwise take a *marshrutka* or shared taxi (both R50, 30 minutes) or taxi (R200) to the sadly dilapidated town of Gali (Gal in Abkhazian), 15km northwest. Buses and *marshrutky* to Sukhumi (R200, two hours) leave Gali's bus station approximately hourly from about 8am to 5pm.

Returning south, buses and *marshrutky* to Gali leave Sukhumi's **bus and train station** (🚍 bus information 9409687535; ulitsa Dzidzaria), in the northwest of town, about hourly from 6am to 5pm. The last *marshrutky* from Gali to the boundary can leave any time from about 4pm.

OTHER DESTINATIONS

From Sukhumi's bus and train station, buses and *marshrutky* run northwest to Novy Afon (R50, 30 minutes), Gagra (R150, 1½ hours), and the Psou border (R200, two hours), about every half-hour from 6.30am to 3.30pm or later. There are also a few services into southern Russia, and a train to Moscow departs at least twice weekly (daily in the summer holiday season). The nearest passenger airport is Sochi International Airport, at Adler (Russia), 13km from the Psou border.

❶ Getting Around

Trolleybuses 1, 3 and 4 (R5) run from the bus and train station to ulitsa Lakoba in the centre, and 3 continues east to ulitsa Akirtava. A taxi between the station and centre costs R100 to R120.

Northwest of Sukhumi

The coast northwest of Sukhumi is beautiful, with thickly forested slopes reaching right down to the shore in places.

Novy Afon

This village 25km from Sukhumi makes a great outing from the city, though packed with tourists in July and August. **Novy Afon Monastery** (http://anyha.org; ☉9am-6pm or later), founded by Russian monks in the 1870s, stands out on the hillside with its multiple golden domes. It's about a 15-minute walk up from the main road – the path is lined with stalls selling wine, *chacha,* cheese, spices and tacky souvenirs. The monastery's cathedral, often thronged with worshippers, has sparklingly colourful murals. From there it's a five-minute walk down to the 10th-century stone **Church of Simon the Zealot** (Khram Simona Kananita; ☉usually closed), on the spot where the eponymous apostle was reputedly killed by Roman soldiers. A path leads up beside the waterfall here to Psyrtskha train station, from where you can walk 20 minutes up a pretty river valley to **Simon the Zealot's Cave** (Grot Simona Kananita), where the zealot lived.

West from the waterfall and church, it's 650m to the **Novy Afon Caves** (Novoafonskaya Peshchera; adult/child R500/free; ☉9am-7pm Jun-Oct, 10am-6pm Wed, Sat & Sun Nov-May; ♿), where guides lead visitors on a 1.4km, 1¼-hour underground journey through a series of impressive chambers. From here it's 2.5km uphill to **Anakopia** (admission R150; ☉10am-6pm), capital of Abkhazia in the 8th century AD. Taxis can take you halfway up for R100. Inside the hilltop citadel are a ruined 8th-century cathedral and a recently rebuilt 11th-century watchtower with awesome views.

Lake Ritsa

At Bzyb (or Bzypta), 70km from Sukhumi, a road heads off north up to Lake Ritsa, 2.5km long and surrounded by steep, forested Caucasus hills at an elevation of 880m. The 41km drive up to the lake, via gorges and waterfalls, is spectacular. Despite summer tourist crowds, Ritsa is a beautiful place. Stalin and Khrushchev both had *dachi* (country cottages), which are sometimes open to visitors, on its far side, and there are good walks to other lakes in these mountains.

There's no public transport to Lake Ritsa. The cheapest and easiest way there is to join a bus or minibus day-tour from Sukhumi, Gagra or other coastal towns. Tickets for these are sold at every hotel and numerous street stalls: the standard Ritsa trip is R900. It's around R1100 if you add Stalin's *dacha* or a walk to Little Ritsa Lake (Ozero Malaya Ritsa; about two hours there and back). With a walk to Mzy Lake (Ozero Mzy) or round the Valley of Seven Lakes (Dolina Semi Ozyor) – both round-trips of about five hours starting about 25km beyond Lake Ritsa – you pay about R1700.

Going independently, it costs around R5000 for a taxi day trip to Ritsa from Sukhumi and you must also pay a R350-per-person national park admission fee. If you're interested in guided multiday hiking in these mountains, a good outfit to contact is **Caucasus Explorer** (http://caucasus-explorer.com).

Gagra

📞 840 / POP 12,000

Abkhazia's main resort curves gently for about 8km round its bay below thickly forested mountains, about 85km from Sukhumi. Though the beach is stony, its setting is truly gorgeous, and Gagra is hugely popular with Russian tourists. The main **marshrutka stand** (ulitsa Demerdzhipa 30) is on the single main road towards the south end of town, next to Kontinent supermarket. The effective town centre is about 1km north of here along the main road and in the streets leading down to the beach. Plenty of *marshrutky* run the length of town.

The north end of town, called Staraya Gagra (Old Gagra), is much less built-up and crowded than the south: this was where in the early 20th century Russian Prince Oldenburgsky decided to establish a 'Russian Nice'. Large *belle époque* buildings dot the hillside, and the beach is backed by the tree-filled Primorsky Park. At the north end of the park the walls of the 4th-to-5th-century AD **Abaata fortress** (prospekt Ardzinba 115; admission R50; ⊙10am-10pm) enclose some of Oldenburgsky's resort buildings (now again a hotel), the lovely little 6th-century Church of St Ipatius and an interesting small historical museum.

🛌 Sleeping

Gagra has lots of hotels and guesthouses, and hundreds of houses rent out rooms in the July-to-September high season, with rates ranging from around R2000 a double in central areas near the beach down to about R700 in less central areas.

Hotel Abaata   HISTORIC HOTEL **$$**
(📞9409632799; www.abaata.ru; prospekt Ardzinba 115; d R3540-5560; 🅿️❋🀫) This is a recent restoration of Prince Oldenburgsky's century-old hotel installations inside the Abaata fortress. Rooms are comfortable, bright and functional, and the hotel has a good indoor-outdoor restaurant and its own bit of beach. Prices plummet from October to June.

Marco Club   HOTEL **$$**
(📞9407120899; www.abhaziahotel.ru; ulitsa Gumistinskaya 21a; r R2000-2500; ☮❋🀫) Marco Club has 42 plain, clean, medium-sized rooms two blocks from the beach in a green building with a 'Stolovaya' sign (referring to its cafeteria). Big discounts from October to June.

ADJARA

The idiosyncratic southwestern corner of Georgia, Adjara (აჭარა) has taken on the mantle of Georgia's holiday coast since the loss of Abkhazia. Batumi, Adjara's newly transformed capital, is the destination of choice for most Georgians – and many others – in search of summer fun, with a real party atmosphere in August. Many travellers enter Georgia at the busy Sarpi border post with Turkey, just south of Batumi.

Though Adjara's beaches are mostly stony, the semitropical climate is beautiful and the scenery gorgeous, with lush hills rising behind the coast, and peaks topping 3000m inland.

Under Ottoman control from the 16th century to 1878, most of Adjara's inhabitants were converted to Islam, but today Muslims comprise only about 30% of the population. Adjara has retained its Soviet-era status as an autonomous republic within Georgia: until 2004 its pro-Russian president, Aslan Abashidze, ran an authoritarian, corrupt regime backed by his own militia, but a standoff between Abashidze and President Saakashvili ended with Abashidze departing for exile in Moscow.

INLAND ADJARA

Mountainous inland Adjara is a different world from the coast. The heartland of Adjaran tradition, it's a region of beautiful old arched stone bridges, waterfalls, remnants of ruined castles, and wooden village houses clinging to steep slopes with the minarets of small mosques rising above them. The majority of Adjara's Muslims live here, principally in the Khulo district. A road runs 80km from Batumi up to the small town of Khulo, then continues unpaved for 50km (rough in parts) over the 2025m-high Goderdzi Pass (snowbound from about November to March) to Zarzma in Samtskhe-Javakheti, from where it's 30km (paved) on to Akhaltsikhe.

Sights & Activities

You'll get the most out of the region with your own 4WD vehicle, enabling you to get off the main road and up to the picturesque, remote villages. Along the main road there are typically lovely stone bridges at Makhuntseti and Dandalo. At Khulo a tiny podlike **cable car** (one-way 0.20 GEL; ☺9am-9pm) swings across the yawning valley to Tago village. One spectacular and remote destination worth journeying to is the ruined 13th-century Khikhani Fortress on a 2200m hilltop 33km southeast from Zamleti, which is on the main road 8km west of Khulo. The last kilometre to the fortress is a steep uphill walk.

A good time to visit is the first weekend of August, for the Shuamtoba festival at Beshumi, a few kilometres south of the Goderdzi Pass. This classic Georgian mountain festival features horse racing, folk music, fire-jumping and wrestling, and also happens to be a favourite occasion for couples to get married!

Sleeping & Eating

Khulo has four small hotels of which the most appealing is **Hotel Toma** (☑599091440; s/d 25/50 GEL, without bathroom 20/40 GEL; ℗), on the western edge of town. It has simple, clean rooms in blue, green or mauve, two guest kitchens and a ground-floor cafe.

You'll get more of a feel for local life in a village guesthouse, of which there are a couple in Kedlebi, about 5km northwest of Khulo, and several in Nigazeuli, 10km west along the main road then about 6km up to the north. They charge 40 GEL to 50 GEL per person with three meals.

Information

Batumi's Tourism Information Centres have information on inland Adjara, including its guesthouses, and good maps of walking or driving routes. Also see http://gobatumi.com/en/where-to-go/mountainous-ajara. Khulo's **Tourism Information Centre** (☑577150426; ☺9am-7pm May-Aug or Sep), on the central square, also has maps.

Getting There & Away

Marshrutky run every 20 or 30 minutes from Batumi's Old Bus Station to Khulo (5 GEL, two hours) and back, the last one leaving Khulo about 6pm (5pm in winter). From about April to October, a *marshrutka* departs Khulo for Akhaltsikhe (15 GEL, 3½ hours) at 10am.

Batumi ბათუმი

☑422 / POP 154,000

With a backdrop of mist-wrapped hills, Georgia's summer holiday capital has sprouted new hotels and attractions like mushrooms in recent years, but it still owes some of its charm to the *belle époque* elegance of its original boom time a century ago.

For travellers arriving from Turkey, Batumi makes a good introduction to Georgia, with its relaxed atmosphere, plentiful accommodation, good restaurants and nightlife.

Batumi developed in the late 19th century as the western terminus of a railway from Baku that then carried one-fifth of the world's oil production. A pipeline and refinery built by Ludwig Nobel, brother of Swedish dynamite inventor Alfred, soon followed. Batumi gained free-port status and became a fashionable resort at the southern tip of the Russian empire. In Soviet times the border with Turkey was closed, making Batumi a bit of a backwater, but it has since bounced back as a hub of commerce as well as tourism.

One of the first decisions of the post-Abashidze administration in 2004 was to make Batumi an attractive place to visit, a project that has notably succeeded. The seaside Boulevard park and the Old Town inland from it have been tastefully renovated, new architecture including a small forest of eye-catching tower buildings has sprung up, and Batumi has developed into one of the Black Sea's top resort magnets, with a great party scene in summer.

Sights & Activities

★ Batumi Boulevard PARK, BEACH
(www.boulevard.ge;) Everyone soon finds themselves strolling along Batumis bulvari, the park strip fronting the main beach, originally laid out in 1884 and now stretching 6km along the coast. With its trees, paths, fountains, cafes, beach bars and a few quirky attractions, this is the life and soul of Batumi. The beach itself is fine though stony – extremely busy in July and August, but kept clean.

Near the northeast tip of the *bulvari* you'll find a large **Ferris wheel** (per person 3 GEL; ⊙6pm-midnight), the 145m-high **Alphabet Tower** (a monument to Georgian script and culture), and a 7m-high, ethereally moving metal sculpture by Tamar Kvesitadze that is universally known as **Ali & Nino**, after the lover-protagonists of Kurban Said's marvellous novel of that name (see it after dark).

A bit further south rises Georgia's tallest building, the 200m-high **Batumi Tower**, looking a bit like a mini Empire State Building – with a mini Ferris wheel implanted in its side! Constructed under the Saakashvili government to be a technological university, it was sold off by his successors to be a Le Meridien hotel.

Southward, on what's known as the New Boulevard, an ornamental lake hosts the **Dancing Fountains** (⊙9pm-midnight Jun-Sep;) **FREE**, an entertaining laser, music and water show.

★ Evropas Moedani SQUARE
Broad Europe Sq is surrounded by beautiful *belle époque* buildings – renovated survivors from Batumi's original heyday plus new buildings in similar style. The square's musical fountains are a magnet for kids on hot summer evenings. Towering over it all is the **Medea monument** by sculptor David Khmaladze – to 'the person who brought Georgia closer to Europe', according to Batumi's mayor when it was unveiled in 2007.

Cable Car CABLE CAR
(Gogebashvili; return trip adult before/after 6pm 5/8 GEL, child 2 GEL; ⊙11am-midnight;) The 2.6km-long cable car carries you up to a shopping/cafe/restaurant complex on Anuria Hill for panoramic views over the city – especially pretty after dark.

Adjara Arts Museum MUSEUM
(Gorgiladze 8; admission 2 GEL; ⊙11am-6pm Tue-Sun) Well displayed and lit, the collection covers Georgian art including works by Pirosmani and Akhvlediani, as well as 19th- and 20th-century European and Russian painting.

Ortajame Mosque MOSQUE
(Chkalov 6) Batumi's only surviving mosque, built in the 1860s, is finely painted in pinks, greens and blues, with Koranic calligraphy on the walls – but is no longer big enough to accommodate the faithful who overflow on to the streets during Friday prayers. Batumi's Muslims have been seeking permission to build a second mosque.

Sheraton Pool SWIMMING
(Rustaveli 28; nonguests per 1/2 people 40/70 GEL; ⊙7am-10pm;) The Sheraton hotel has a lovely large open-air pool in a garden setting in the Bulvari park, with a poolside restaurant too.

Festivals & Events

Black Sea Jazz Festival JAZZ
(http://blackseajazz.ge; ⊙late Jul) Brings international stars and lots of music lovers to Batumi for several days in late July.

Sleeping

There's a large and growing range of accommodation, from hostels to five-star luxury hotels.

★ Gulnasi's Guesthouse GUESTHOUSE $
(557965859; homestay@mail.ru; Lermontov 24a; per person in 3 to 7-bed room 20 GEL, d with/without bathroom 60/50 GEL;) Gulnasi Miqeladze and her welcoming family run what's effectively a great-value budget hotel. The 18 rooms, on three floors, are

Batumi

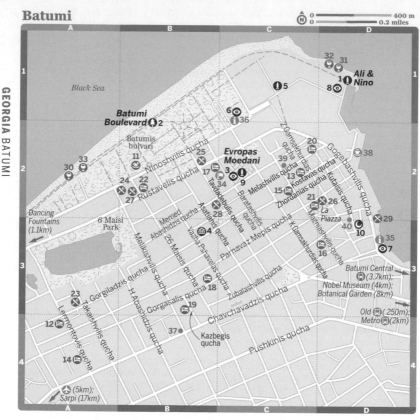

spotless and good-sized. There's free tea, coffee and wine tasting, a good big guest kitchen and generous breakfasts for 7 GEL. And they offer free pick-ups anywhere in Batumi on arrival.

The house is off the street, but there's a sign outside. The family is helpful with travel information and also offers day trips into rural Adjara (80 GEL to 100 GEL for up to five people, including picnic).

Hostel Batumi Globus   HOSTEL $
(☑276721; www.hostelbatumi-globus.com; Mazniashvili 54; dm 18-25 GEL, d 60-65 GEL; ☻✳🛜) A largeish hostel with a warm welcome, good kitchen, average dorms and rooms, and free laundry service. The big plus is the spacious, sociable courtyard with its barbeque stove.

Batumi Hostel   HOSTEL $
(☑294286; www.friendshostel.ge; Lermontov 10; dm 15 GEL, d 35-40 GEL; ☻🛜) A small,

crowded, friendly and cheap hostel with one 10-person dorm and four small doubles sharing bathrooms. Free use of the washing machine.

★Hotel Elegant   BOUTIQUE HOTEL $$
(☑274841; elegant-elegant@rambler.ru; Gorgasali 68; r incl breakfast 140-180 GEL; ☻✳🛜) This appealing little hotel has just six rooms, allowing for an attentive touch from the friendly management. The comfortable rooms are in a variety of tasteful styles, and the stained-glass panels and windows are an attractive feature.

Dzveli Batumi   GUESTHOUSE $$
(Old Batumi Hotel; ☑593333414, 277157; www.welcome.ge/dzvelibatumi; Kostava 24; incl breakfast s €25-30, d/ste €40/70; ☻✳🛜) Friendly and informative hosts Gocha and Irina offer a dozen well-equipped, carpeted rooms in an Old Town house, with assorted col-

Batumi

our schemes, homely touches and tasteful contemporary style.

Light House Hotel HOTEL **$$**
(☑278218; www.lighthouse.ge; Kazbegi 4; incl breakfast s 80-130 GEL, d 120-180 GEL; ⊖❋🛜) A stylish hotel on a quiet street, the Light House has just 15 rooms in eye-catching, modish styles and colours – a comfortable and friendly place to stay.

My Warm House GUESTHOUSE **$$**
(☑558176418; mywarmhouse@mail.ru; Melashvili 2; d 125-155 GEL; ⊖❋🛜) A welcoming, English-speaking, spotlessly clean guesthouse in the Old Town, with eight good-sized rooms sporting original touches such as coloured-glass wash basins. Some have balconies or their own kitchen and washing machine. Prices plummet in winter.

Hotel Brighton HOTEL **$$**
(☑274135; http://brighton.ge; Dumbadze 10; r incl breakfast 150-175 GEL; Ⓟ⊖❋🛜) This spick-and-span 15-room hotel has a great location just off Evropas moedani, helpful staff and a nice terrace overlooking the square. Rooms are nothing very fancy, just solidly comfortable.

Holland Hoek Hotel HOTEL **$$**
(☑270222; www.hhh.ge; Mazniashvili 18; d/tr/q incl breakfast 140/160/200 GEL, dm 25 GEL; ⊖❋🛜) New in 2015, Holland Hoek is proving popular with its good Old Town location, friendly welcome, bright, appealing rooms and strong line in colourful original art.

Piazza Boutique Hotel BOUTIQUE HOTEL **$$$**
(☑591005615; www.piazza.ge; Parnavaz Mepe 25; s/d incl breakfast from 205/220 GEL; ❋🛜) For a treat book into this hotel with 16 luxurious themed rooms (from shabby chic to Art Deco to English) in a 13-storey clock tower over a lively square with cafes, restaurants and nightly live music in summer (the hotel has soundproofing!).

Sheraton Batumi Hotel LUXURY HOTEL **$$$**
(☑229000; www.sheratonbatumi.com; Rustaveli 28; r incl breakfast from US$212; Ⓟ⊖❋🛜🏊) The faintly Chinese-looking Sheraton towers beside the Bulvari park and offers stylish, spacious, well-equipped rooms with super-comfortable beds. Many feature large ballerina photos in counterpoint to the large rock-star shots in the lobby. Facilities include outdoor and indoor pools (the latter

in the top-class spa) and a panoramic 20th-floor restaurant.

Room rates vary according to season and demand: check the website.

✗ Eating

Batumi is full of lively cafes and restaurants, and from July to September extra places open up on the main beach, some making creditable efforts at a tropical ambience.

★ **Old Boulevard**   GEORGIAN, EUROPEAN $$
(🖉 577242006; Ninoshvili 23a; mains 8-25 GEL; ☺ 9am-midnight or later; 🛜) The Old Boulevard has a refined atmosphere with deep sofas, floor-to-ceiling shelves of sculpture, and live classical guitar and piano in the evening. It cooks up great grills, seafood, Georgian classics and the odd surprise like hummus – and has an excellent wine list.

★ **Grill Town**   GEORGIAN $$
(Rustaveli 26-28; mains 10-25 GEL; ☺ 10am-1am; 🛜) This big, buzzing, contemporary place, with large windows and a terrace facing the park over the street, is hugely popular with just about everybody. It serves up very nicely done *mtsvadi, khachapuri, khinkali,* sausages, chicken dishes and other Georgian classics.

La Brioche   INTERNATIONAL $$
(Parnavaz Mepe 25; mains 10-25 GEL; ☺ 9am-2am; 🛜) One of several cafes and restaurants around the faintly Italian-style square La Piazza, Brioche is a particularly choice spot for breakfast, pancakes, desserts and good coffee. It also has a library-style cafe in the adjoining tower.

Cafe Retro   GEORGIAN $$
(🖉 599511722; Takaishvili 10; khachapuri 6.50-15 GEL; ☺ 9am-11pm) There's no better place than Batumi to decide whether you like *khachapuri Acharuli,* Adjara's large boat-shaped variety of Georgia's national fast food with a lightly fried egg on top. And there's no better place to try it than this neat place widely considered to make the best in town.

Privet iz Batuma   CAFE $$
(🖉 277766; Memed Abashidze 39; mains 6-18 GEL; ☺ 10am-12.30am or later; 🍽) A fashionable cafe with a pre-1917 theme, 'Hello from Batumi' is good for ice cream, cakes, salads, sandwiches, teas, coffees and alcoholic

drinks. The inside is air-conditioned and there are some pavement tables too.

Sanapiro   GEORGIAN $$
(Beregi; Gogebashvili 9; mains 9-20 GEL; ☺ 9am-1am) Right on the waterfront facing the harbour, this open-air pavilion is a local favourite for its fine location, respectable food (mainly Georgian standards) and efficient service.

★ **Fanfan**   GEORGIAN, EUROPEAN $$$
(Ninoshvili 27; mains 14-28 GEL; ☺ 10am-midnight; 🛜🍽) Shabby-chic in decor and favoured by cool, arty folk (though not exclusive to them), Fanfan also prepares delicious food – especially the seafood and the lemon tart.

In case you're travelling with your dog or cat, you'll be glad to know there's a menu section for them too.

🍷 Drinking & Nightlife

In summer Batumis bulvari is the party capital of Georgia, with long lists of international DJs providing high-energy and chill-out beats on the edge of the sea. An annually changing assortment of fresh-air beachside clubs and bars has thousands of people partying till dawn nightly from mid-July to mid-September. The clubs start to fill from 11pm, with admission typically starting at 10 GEL for women and 20 GEL for men. The two standout venues that have been around longer than most are **Sector 26** (www.facebook.com/batumisector26; Batumis bulvari) and **Iveria Beach** (www.facebook.com/iveriabeach; Batumis bulvari), joined more recently by **Boom Boom Beach** (www.facebook.com/boomboombeachbatumi; Batumis bulvari) and **Mandarin Beach** (www.facebook.com/mandarinbeachbatumi; Batumis bulvari). By day (from breakfast time onward) these places become beachside lounges with restaurant service and free entry, some with their own pools.

ℹ Information

Batumi Ajara (http://gobatumi.com) Useful official tourism site for Batumi and Adjara.

Tourism Information Centre (ticbatumi@gmail.com) The well-informed and helpful branches on Batumis bulvari (🖉 577909091; Ninoshvili 2; ☺ 9am-9pm Jul-Sep, 9am-7pm Oct-Jun) and beside the cable-car station (🖉 577909093; Gogebashvili; ☺ 24hr) do their best to answer your every question.

ℹ Getting There & Around

AIR

Batumi International Airport (☑235100; www.batumiairport.com), 5km south of town, has flights to/from Istanbul, Kiev, Moscow, Odessa, Tbilisi and Tel Aviv. Bus 10 (0.80 GEL) runs to/from Rustaveli in central Batumi. Taxis into town are normally 20 GEL.

LAND
Bus, Marshrutka & Taxi

Taxis to or from the Turkish border at Sarpi, 17km south, should cost 20 GEL. Bus 16 (0.80 GEL) and *marshrutka* 142 (1 GEL) run from the border to Batumi's Old Bus Station, and vice-versa, via Chavchavadze. The border is open 24 hours.

Going from Batumi into Turkey, there are bus services crossing the border, but you will often save time without adding expense by taking local transport to the border, crossing it on foot, then catching a waiting Turkish minibus to Hopa, about 20km south, where there are frequent departures to many points around Turkey.

Metro Bus Station (Batumi International & Intercity Bus Station; ☑242612; Gogoli 1) Departure point for comfortable Metro Georgia (☑577159400, 242244; www.geometro.ge) buses to Tbilisi and Turkey, and seven-passenger minivans as far as Trabzon (Turkey) and Yerevan (Armenia). Reached by bus 8 (0.80 GEL) and *marshrutka* 20 (0.60 GEL), northeast on Chavchavadze. Try to buy Metro Georgia tickets a day or two in advance; you can do this at Adjara Tour.

Old Bus Station (☑278547; Maiakovski 1) Departure point for *marshrutky* to Georgian destinations and some buses to Turkey. Reached by *marshrutky* 44 and 45 northeast on Chavchavadze.

Train

Batumi Central station is about 4km northeast of the city centre on the coast road. *Marshrutky* 20 and 28 run there, heading northeast on Chavchavadze. It's best to book ahead for trains (and essential in summer): you can buy tickets in town at the **Georgian Railway office** (Mazniashvili 5; ☉9am-1pm & 2-6pm) and **Adjara Tour** (☑228778; www.adjaratour.com; Chavchavadze 48; ☉9.30am-7pm Mon-Fri, 9.30am-6pm Sat & Sun). To Tbilisi (2nd/1st class 25/40 GEL, 5½ to 6½ hours) there are two day trains, and a night train departing at 1.40am every two days, plus an extra day train from about mid-June to September. Also from mid-June to the end of Septembe there is a daily train departing in the afternoon from Makhinjauri station, 5km north of Batumi, for Yerevan (Armenia; 3rd/2nd/1st class 45/65/80 GEL, 16 hours) via Tbilisi. Fares to Yerevan can fluctuate wildly according to exchange rates and how far ahead you book.

SEA

Ferry schedules and fares can fluctuate, and websites can be inaccurate: contact ferry companies direct for current details.

Ukraine & Bulgaria Both **UkrFerry** (www.ukrferry.com) and **Navibulgar** (www.navbul.com) operate several monthly ferries from Ilyichevsk (near Odessa, Ukraine) to Batumi and back (50 hours each way), and on the Varna (Bulgaria)–Batumi–Ilyichevsk–Varna route (about 2½ days Varna–Batumi, 4½ days Batumi–Varna). UkrFerry, the more comfortable option,

BUSES, MARSHRUTKY & MINIVANS FROM BATUMI

DESTINATION	BUS STATION	COST (GEL)	DURATION (HR)	DAILY FREQUENCY
Akhaltsikhe	Old	20	6	2 *marshrutky* via Khashuri & Borjomi
Istanbul	Metro	60-75	22	2 or more Metro Georgia buses
Kutaisi	Old	10	2	hourly *marshrutky*, 8am to 10pm
Mestia	Old	30	6	often a 2pm *marshrutka*, approx Jun-Sep; ask your accommodation to check
Rize	Old	15	3	Golden bus company half-hourly, 8.30am to 9pm
Tbilisi	Metro	25	6	6 Metro Georgia buses
	Old	20	6	hourly *marshrutky*, 8am to 10pm
Trabzon	Metro	20	4	minivans 8.30am & hourly from 10am to 6pm
	Old	20	4	Golden bus company 7 buses, 11am to 1am
Yerevan	Metro	25	12	hourly minivans by **Ika Tour** (☑557414164)
Zugdidi	Old	12	3	5 *marshrutky*

charges US$300/222 for a car/motorbike from Batumi to Ilyichevsk, plus US$115 to US$140 per person in two-berth cabins including meals. **UBG-Agency** (☑274119; Kutaisi 34; ☉10am-5pm) sells tickets for both companies, usually starting about two days before departure.

Bulgaria's **PBM** (www.pbm.bg) runs a weekly ferry on the Burgas–Batumi–Novorossiysk–Burgas route, taking 2¼ days Burgas–Batumi, 4¼ days back. The fare in either direction for a car/motorbike and driver (with a cabin berth and meals) is €250/100. Passenger fares are €100/150 in 4-bed/2-bed cabins , but private cars and foot passengers can't embark or disembark at Novorossiysk. Contact PBM's Poti-based Georgia agent, **Eurasia RoRo Line** (☑493-270370/1; info@erl.ge; Gegidze 20/11, Poti).

Russia Weather permitting, a hydrofoil operated by **Express Batumi** (☑593333966, 577556688; Baku 3) departs for Sochi (Russia; 235 GEL, five hours) at noon Thursday, returning Friday. In peak seasons a second weekly sailing is sometimes added.

Around Batumi

North of Batumi

Batumi's **botanic gardens** (☑270033; www.bbg.ge; admission 8 GEL; ☉9am-8pm), 8km northeast of town at Mtsvane Kontskhi (Green Cape), is well worth a trip. With many semitropical and foreign species, the 1.13-sq-km gardens cover a hillside rising straight out of the sea. It takes about 1½ hours to walk the main path at a leisurely pace.

You can get there by *marshrutka* 15, from Rustaveli and Gogebashvili, or 31 from Gogebashvili east of Chavchavadze.

South of Batumi

Gonio, 11km south of Batumi, and **Kvariati**, 4km beyond, on the road to the Turkish border at Sarpi, have pebbly beaches with generally thinner crowds and cleaner water than Batumi. Densely vegetated mountains slope right down to the coast at Kvariati.

Gonio Apsaros Fortress (adult/student 3/1 GEL, audio guide 5 GEL; ☉10am-6pm Jun-Sep, 11am-5pm Oct-May; ℗), an impressive piece of Roman-Byzantine military architecture, covers 47,000 sq metres within a rectangle of high stone walls with 18 towers. Built by the Romans in the 1st century AD, it was occupied by the Byzantines in the 6th century and by the Ottomans in the 16th century. An interesting little museum sits in its midst, with a cross outside marking what's believed to be the grave of the Apostle Matthias.

GREAT CAUCASUS

A trip into the Great Caucasus along Georgia's northern border is a must for anyone who wants to experience the best of the country. Spectacular mountain scenery, wonderful walks and picturesque old villages with strange, tall defensive towers are all part of a trip to the Great Caucasus.

Georgia's very identity hinges on this mighty range that rises in Abkhazia, runs the length of Georgia's border with Russia and continues into Azerbaijan. The most accessible destination is Kazbegi, reached by the dramatic Georgian Military Hwy from Tbilisi, but other areas are more than worth the effort of getting there – including enigmatic Svaneti and beautiful, pristine Tusheti.

It's notably cooler in the mountain villages, which can be a blessed relief in August, and in the hills you should be equipped for bad weather any time. The best walking season in most areas is from June to September. Some areas such as Khevsureti and Tusheti are only accessible for a few summer months.

Svaneti   სვანეთი

Beautiful, wild and mysterious, Svaneti is an ancient land locked in the Caucasus, so remote that it was never tamed by any ruler. Uniquely picturesque villages and snow-covered, 4000m-plus peaks rising above flower-strewn alpine meadows provide a superb backdrop to the many walking trails. Svaneti's emblem is the *koshi* (defensive stone tower), designed to house villagers at times of invasion and local strife (until recently Svaneti was renowned for its murderous blood feuds). Around 175 *koshkebi*, most originally built between the 9th and 13th centuries, survive here today.

Not so long ago Svaneti was still pretty well off the beaten track, but tourism development since the mid-2000s has brought new ski stations, flights from Tbilisi, a major improvement of the road up from Zugdidi, a huge increase in accommodation options and many more visitors, to the point where Svaneti's only town, Mestia, can get pretty

Svaneti

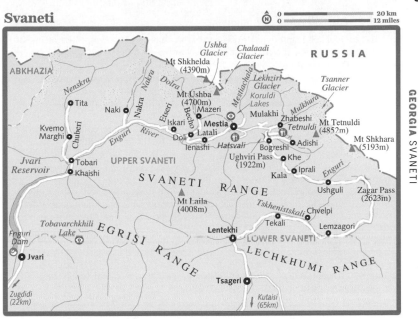

busy in summer. Svaneti's mystique and beauty, however, are in no danger of wearing thin.

During the many invasions of Georgia over the centuries, icons and other religious valuables were brought to this isolated region for safekeeping, and a significant number remain in private homes today. Svaneti also has a rich church-art heritage of its own, and many tiny village churches boast frescoes 1000 years old. This mountain retreat, with its own unwritten language, largely unintelligible to other Georgians, is regarded as a bastion of Georgian traditions, as can be witnessed at the numerous Svan festivals, of which probably the most famous is Kvirikoba (p22).

Svaneti is divided into Upper (Zemo) and Lower (Kvemo) Svaneti. Green and beautiful Upper Svaneti offers the best walking and climbing as well as the strongest traditions. The walking season lasts from about early June to mid-October, though some routes can be waterlogged early or late in that period.

Mestia   მესტია

📱 410 / POP 1900 / ELEV 1400M

The 'capital' of Upper Svaneti, Mestia is a conglomeration of at least 10 hamlets, dot-ted with picturesque Svan towers. The oldest of the hamlets, with most of the towers, are above the river on the northern side of town: Lekhtagi in the northwest, and Lanchvali and Lagami to the northeast. Recent government-sponsored tourism development has seen Mestia's central square Setis moedani rebuilt, and an airport and a rush of guesthouses and hotels (around 90 at last count) opening up.

⊙ Sights & Activities

★ Svaneti History & Ethnography Museum   MUSEUM

(📞 32-2157300; www.museum.ge; Ioselani 7; adult/student 5/1 GEL, English-, German- or Russian-speaking guide 25 GEL; ⊙ 10am-6pm Tue-Sun) Mestia's excellent main museum ranges over church treasures, manuscripts, weaponry, jewellery, musical instruments and historical photos – all well displayed, and labelled in English and Georgian – but the biggest highlight is the room of wonderful 10th- to 14th-century icons from Svaneti's churches, fashioned in silver or painted in tempera on wood. The best of these have a uniquely human and touching quality, and some, unusually, depict St George spearing emperor Diocletian instead of his normal dragon.

WALKS AROUND MESTIA

Many beautiful walks start from Mestia itself. Some routes are well signposted; others aren't. Your accommodation or Mestia's Tourism Information Centre (which gives out hiking maps) can help you find a guide if you want one.

Chalaadi Glacier This enjoyable route of six or seven hours return trip (11km each way) takes you out past Mestia's airport and up the Mestiachala valley. The last 1.5km or so, from a footbridge over the river, is uphill through woods to the foot of the glacier. Watch out for rocks falling off the glacier in summer.

You can also get to the footbridge by taxi (return 50 GEL including waiting time) or horse (40 GEL, plus 50 GEL for the guide and 40 GEL for the guide's horse).

Cross A moderately demanding half-day walk goes up to the cross that's visible 900m above Mestia on the north side of the valley. From the cross you can see the spectacular twin peaks of Mt Ushba (4700m).

From Setis moedani, walk 450m east along the main street then take the street up to the left (Beqnu Khergiani). Take the uphill option at all junctions, and after about 600m, on the edge of the village, the street becomes a footpath. Follow this up and after some 700m it bends to the right across the hillside, eventually meeting a 4WD track. You can follow the 4WD track, short-cutting some bends, all the way to the cross. The return trip from Mestia takes about five hours. With good weather and enough daylight, you can continue to the small, pristine Koruldi Lakes, about two hours beyond the cross and some 400m higher. A return trip by 4WD from Mestia to the cross, with waiting time while you go to the lakes and back, costs 80 GEL.

Mazeri via Guli Pass From about mid-June you can walk from Mestia to Mazeri in about 10 hours via the 2900m-high Guli Pass, with spectacular views of Mt Ushba. It's a demanding hike with 1500m of ascent then 1300m of descent: the route diverges from the Koruldi Lakes route at the Lamaaja ridge.

The museum, which reopened in 2013 after a thorough modernisation, is 600m south from Setis moedani, across two bridges.

🛏 Sleeping

Mestia has several good hotels as well as its dozens of guesthouses. Half-board rates include breakfast and dinner; most places are happy to provide 'only sleep', B&B or full-board arrangements if you like, adjusting prices accordingly. They can also arrange vehicles and/or guides for out-of-town trips and help with most things you might want to do.

★ Roza Shukvani's
Guesthouse   GUESTHOUSE $
(☑ 599641455; www.roza-mestia.com; Vittorio Sella 17; per person half board 40 GEL; ☎) Terrific Svan meals and a warm welcome from ever-helpful, English-speaking Roza and her family make this one of Mestia's best places to stay. The six spotless, spacious rooms (sharing three bathrooms) are on the house's upper floor, which is dedicated to guests. Vittorio Sella runs up off the main street about 60m west of Setis moedani.

Guest House Eka   GUESTHOUSE $
(☑ 599726719; www.svaneti-mestia.com; Vittorio Sella 8; per person half board 35-40 GEL; ☻☎) Hospitable, English-speaking Eka Chartolani, the archaeology curator at Mestia's museum, has five large rooms for up to four people (sharing bathrooms) and serves up delicious Svan/Georgian meals using a lot of home-grown produce. The house has nice views. Vittorio Sella runs up off the main street about 60m west of Setis moedani.

Nino Ratiani's Guesthouse   GUESTHOUSE $
(☑ 599183555; www.facebook.com/ninoratianis guesthouse; J Khaftani 1; per person half board 30-50 GEL; ℗☎) Particularly good Svan food (including many vegetarian dishes), a hospitable welcome, and a variety of rooms (some with bathroom) in two buildings, make Nino's one of the best and busiest budget stays in town. It's 400m along the street towards Zugdidi from Setis moedani.

Villa Gabliani   GUESTHOUSE $
(☑ 599569358; ciurigabliani1@rambler.ru; Gabliani 20; per person half board 45 GEL; ☎▣) These teacher sisters speak good English and German, and their house has six big, carpeted

rooms (sharing bathrooms) and a lovely verandah overlooking a garden of wild flowers and fruit trees, with the sound of a river below. It's 300m southwest of Setis moedani, near the hospital.

Manoni's Guesthouse
GUESTHOUSE $

(☑599568417, 577568417; manonisvaneti@ yahoo.com; Kakhiani 25; per person half board 30 GEL, camping per tent 5 GEL; Ⓟⴄ@🛜) A good-value guesthouse with eight quite comfy pine-panelled rooms of various sizes, and five shared bathrooms. Camping in the grassy garden includes hot shower and kitchen use. It's 1km east from Setis moedani, up a lane beside Kakhiani 31.

Guesthouse Davit Zhorzholiani
GUESTHOUSE $$

(☑599344948; www.svanetistay.com; Setis III chikhi No 1; half board s/d 80/120 GEL, r without bath 70-80 GEL; 🛜) This friendly family establishment, in a lane just off the east side of Setis moedani, has its own Svan tower and 13 excellent new rooms with private bath as well as eight older, smaller ones. There's a panoramic roof terrace and meals are plentiful and tasty. Amiable host Davit is an experienced mountain hiking guide.

Hotel Svan House
HOTEL $$

(☑592717230; svanhouse@gmail.com; Vakhtang Goshteliani 15; d incl breakfast 100 GEL; 🛜) A welcoming recent conversion of an old stone house, with eight good, clean, good-sized rooms along two wooden verandahs. It's 600m east of Setis moedani, up the hill a bit off the main road.

Villa Mestia
HOTEL $$

(☑568548445; www.villamestia.ge; Erekle Pharjiani 7; per person half board 50-60 GEL; ⴄ🛜🏊) This attractive three-storey house with a lovely tree-shaded garden (where you can take meals or drinks) has a degree of traditional charm thanks to its wooden doors, windows and furnishings, and stone-walled dining room. Rooms are comfy, all with bathroom and balcony. It's 500m from Setis moedani along the road towards Zugdidi.

Laleta
HOTEL $$

(☑599134011; www.svanetitours.com; Ienashi; per person half board 55-65 GEL; Ⓟ ⴄ🛜🏊) In large, green grounds just off the road in Ienashi, 7km west of Mestia, Laleta offers a relaxed rural alternative, with plain, comfy rooms (most sharing bathrooms) for up to five people. Some good walks and horse rides start right here, and different meals are cooked up fresh daily, with vegetarian dishes always available.

The helpful, English-speaking owners also run a budget hostel, **Kakuchela** (☑599134011; www.svanetitours.com; Ienashi, Latali; dm 15 GEL; ⴄ🛜), on the roadside nearby.

Guesthouse Ushba
HOTEL $$

(☑599555217; http://svanetistay.com; Tamar Mepe 7; per person half board 60 GEL; Ⓟ🛜) Has 11 good, recently built rooms of varied sizes and outlook but all with bathroom, plus a big terrace and bright sitting room with great views over the rushing river below. It's just 200m east of Setis moedani along the main street, and the on-site Cafe Ushba is convenient.

🍴 Eating & Drinking

Though most people eat most of their meals in their guesthouses, there are options for eating (and drinking) out.

Cafe Laila
GEORGIAN $

(Setis moedani; mains 4-12 GEL; ⏰8am-midnight; 🛜) A hugely popular gathering place on the central square – it can be hard to get a table on summer evenings when the

---

SKIING IN SVANETI

Skiers and Svaneti's tourism businesses have high hopes for the new **Tetnuldi ski resort** (http://tetnuldi.com), on the slopes of Mt Tetnuldi about 20km east of Mestia. Expected to open for the 2015–16 season, Tetnuldi was starting out with 25km of runs between 2260m and 3040m altitude and three French chairlifts, with a season expected to last from mid-December to mid-May.

The much smaller and lower Hatsvali ski station, 8km south of Mestia, works from late December to about early April, with a 300m beginners' slope, a 2600m blue run, a 1900m red run and one chairlift (lift passes and equipment rental both 20 GEL per day).

Svaneti is also good for ski touring – usually best towards the end of the season, and you should take a guide or ask local advice about conditions, as there are always potential hazards. Laleta is one hotel experienced in organising this activity.

SVAN COOKING

Svans eat many of the same dishes as other Georgians, but have their own specialities too. Typical dishes include *kubdari* meat pies, *chvishdari* (cheese cooked inside maize bread) and *tashmujabi* (mashed potatoes with cheese). The renowned 'Svaneti salt' is a blend of herbs, pepper and garlic frequently used to flavour meat dishes.

Georgian folk group is playing. The food is a respectable mix of Svan specialities and Georgia-wide favourites.

Café Lanchvali   CAFE, GEORGIAN $
(Lanchvali 8a; mains 5-8 GEL; ⊙10am-10pm; 🛜)
A lovely place to sit on the spic-and-span, timber-built, upstairs deck and enjoy a coffee, cool drink or inexpensive meal looking straight out at the museum tower in front.

ⓘ Information

There are three ATMs in town.
Tourism Information Centre (☑551080894; Setis moedani 7; ⊙10am-6pm)

ⓘ Getting There & Around

AIR
Vanilla Sky (Map p34; ☑599659099; www.vanillasky.ge; Vazha Pshavela 5, Saburtalo, Tbilisi; ⊙10am-6pm Mon-Fri, 11am-2pm Sat) flies a 15-seat plane from Natakhtari airfield, 25km north of Tbilisi, to Mestia and back five times weekly, weather permitting. The spectacular one-hour flight costs 65 GEL one-way, including transfers between Rustaveli metro station and Natakhtari. Call the Tbilisi office one hour ahead if you want to visit it. In Mestia tickets are sold at the **Vanilla Sky office** (☑598510895; Airport; ⊙10am-5pm Mon-Fri) at the airport, 2.5km east of the town centre (10 GEL by taxi). Guesthouses can call to make reservations.

MARSHRUTKA & TAXI
Marshrutky run to Mestia from Tbilisi, Kutaisi, Zugdidi and, from about June to September, often from Batumi. From Tbilisi you can also take a day or night train to Zugdidi and then a *marshrutka* from there. The road up from Zugdidi is normally kept open all year and traverses increasingly spectacular scenery as it heads up the Enguri and Mulkhura valleys.

Heading down from Mestia, *marshrutky* leave Setis moedani between 7am and 8am for Zug-

didi (20 GEL, three hours), Kutaisi (25 GEL, 4½ hours), Tbilisi (30 GEL, nine hours) and, in summer, Batumi (30 GEL, six hours). Further Zugdidi *marshrutky* may leave later if there are enough passengers.

Getting around Svaneti from Mestia usually means taxis. Your accommodation can arrange these.

Ushguli   უშგული

POP 290 / ELEV 2050M

Set in the topmost reaches of the Enguri valley beneath the snow-covered massif of Mt Shkhara (5193m), Georgia's highest peak, Ushguli is an unbelievably picturesque spot. With more than 20 ancient Svan towers, it has been on the Unesco World Heritage List since 1996. This community of four villages, a 47km, 2½-hour drive southeast from Mestia, reaches up to 2100m above sea level and has a claim to be Europe's highest permanently inhabited settlement. From lowest to highest, the four villages are Murqmeli, Chazhashi, Chvibiani and Zhibiani.

There's some wonderful walking around Ushguli: it takes about six hours to walk 8km up the valley to the foot of the Shkhara glacier and back. One tower in Chazhashi houses Ushguli's main **Ethnographic Museum** (admission 5 GEL; ⊙10am-6pm Tue-Sun), with a superb collection of gold, silver and wooden icons and crosses dating back to the 12th century from Ushguli's seven churches. At the top of Ushguli, beautifully situated on a hill looking up the valley to Shkhara, is the 12th-century **Lamaria Church**, with a defensive tower next to it.

🛏 Sleeping & Eating

Ushguli has experienced an accommodation explosion and now has about 40 guesthouses and small, basic hotels. Most are in the two upper villages, Chvibiani and Zhibiani, and there's also a rash of new places along the road up from the bridge at Chvibiani. As far as we know, nowhere in Ushguli offers rooms with private bathrooms.

Temraz Nijaradze   GUESTHOUSE $
(Gamarjoba Guesthouse; ☑595229814, 599209719; Zhibiani; per person incl 0/2/3 meals 20/40/50 GEL) The last house on the right of the street before Lamaria church, Temraz has four good, clean, wood-floored rooms, and serves up awesomely delicious local food. There are usually some English-speaking teenagers around in summer.

Tariel Nijaradze GUESTHOUSE $
(Guest House Caucasus Ushguli; ☑599317086; Chvibiani; per person incl 0/2/3 meals 20/40/50 GEL) Amiable Tariel's house is the first on the right as you walk up through Chvibiani. Of the six plain, clean rooms, two face north with great Shkhara views. Son Bakar speaks English.

Vila Lileo GUESTHOUSE $$
(☑599912256; Zhibiani; per person incl 2/3 meals 50/60 GEL; ☜) One of the largest and most professional establishments, with 30 beds in smallish rooms, and excellent Svan cooking. You can't miss its big red sign.

Kafe Koshki GEORGIAN $
(Chvibiani; mains 6-12 GEL; ☺10am-9pm, approx Jun-Sep) This neat wooden cafe with jolly yellow and red sunshades on its stone-flag terrace serves good basic fare such as *mtsvadi*, *khachapuri* and salads, and has Natakhtari beer on tap. Check out its spectacular traditional Svan man's chair, hand-carved with the Nijaradze family's history and all sorts of related motifs.

ℹ Getting There & Away

A taxi or 4WD day trip for up to four people from Mestia costs 150 GEL to 200 GEL, one-way trips are only a little less. The road is unpaved, and in poor condition, for the last 30km. It's normally open all year except after heavy snow and landslides, but non-4WD vehicles can only manage it from about June to October (and they need high clearance). The rough track on from Ushguli to Lentekhi in Lower Svaneti (75km, via the 2623m Zagar Pass) is passable from about May to September. 4WDs charge 300 GEL for the three-to-four-hour trip.

Becho ბეჩო

Becho, the community strung up the Dolra valley west of Mestia, is a very beautiful and relatively little-visited area with some wonderful walks. The spectacular, twin-peaked **Ushba** (4700m), Georgia's toughest and most dangerous mountaineering challenge, towers at the head of the valley. The highest village in the valley, **Mazeri**, is the best base. One lovely walk from Mazeri (demanding in its later stages) leads north up the Dolra River then steeply eastward up past waterfalls to the glacier on the west side of Ushba (nine or 10 hours there and back). Other trails lead over the hills to Etseri (the next community west) and Latali (east). In summer you can walk to Mazeri

from Mestia in a long, hard day via the Guli Pass (p84). A taxi day trip to Mazeri from Mestia costs 120 GEL to 150 GEL.

🛏 Sleeping & Eating

★**Grand Hotel Ushba** HOTEL $$
(☑790119192; www.grandhotelushba.com; Tvebishi; s/d incl breakfast €94/104, without bathroom €59/69; ℗☜☎) A comfortable mountain lodge in a gorgeous setting just past Mazeri, with a **restaurant** (mains 10 GEL; ☺6am-late) serving good Georgian dishes, salads and desserts. Rooms are attractive in combinations of pine, stone and white paint, though not as luxurious as you might expect for the prices. Still, it's one of the best places to stay in Svaneti and a great base for walking and other activities.

Staff will pick you up free from the main road 8km down the valley.

Guesthouse Shikhra GUESTHOUSE $$
(☑551098919; b.schampriani@gmail.com; Mazeri; per person incl breakfast/full board 35/50 GEL; ℗☜@☎) Friendly Shikhra is set in a lovely fruit orchard beside the main track through Mazeri. The seven rooms, sharing bathrooms, have comfy beds, and excellent home-style meals are available.

West of Becho

The valleys west of Becho, and the Svaneti Range above the south side of the Enguri valley, are full of off-the-beaten-track hiking possibilities. Even in these relatively remote communities you'll find a number of guesthouses, good to use as bases for local walks or as stops on longer treks. Recommended are the hospitable **Hanmer Guest House** (☑599629789; www.facebook.com/hanmer. house.svaneti; Iskari village, Etseri; per person with 0/1/2/3 meals 35/45/67/80 GEL), belonging

---

> ## ℹ SVANETI TRAILS
>
> The local municipality is improving access to some of Svaneti's less-visited areas by upgrading trail-marking along several routes: Mestia–Ushguli, Kala–Chvelpi–Lentekhi, Mestia–Becho–Etseri–Nakra–Chuberi, Khaishi–Tobavarchkhili–Lentekhi and Lentekhi–Latali. The improvements, due to be completed by 2016, should make exploring these beautiful regions significantly more practicable.

THE MESTIA–USHGULI TREK

The most popular longer trek from Mestia is the scenic four-day, 50km hike east to Ushguli, with village guesthouses for accommodation. Each of the first three days takes you up over a ridge, with an ascent of between 400m and 800m, followed by a descent to your destination, as you head across the lower folds of the main Caucasus ridge. The stages:

Mestia–Zhabeshi (14km, about seven hours) Takes you east up the Mulkhura valley to Zhabeshi, which has half a dozen places to stay including the friendly **Givi Kakhiani's Guesthouse** (☑599448047; iakakhiani@gmail.com; Zhabeshi; per person incl 3 meals 35-40 GEL; P).

Zhabeshi–Adishi (10km, about seven hours) An 800m ascent followed by 400m descent. Adishi has good guesthouse accommodation with English-speaking **Elizabeth Kaldani** (☑557283584; kaldanielizabeth@yahoo.com; Adishi; per person 20 GEL, full board 40-45 GEL), **Zhora Kaldani** (☑599187359; Adishi; per person with 0/1/2 meals 20/25/40 GEL) or **Mukhran Avaliani** (☑599186793; Adishi; per person with 0/1/2 meals 20/25/40 GEL).

Adishi–Iprali (15km, about seven hours) Iprali's popular **Family Hotel Ucha** (☑598790225, 595557470; Iprali; per person incl breakfast, dinner & lunch box 65 GEL; P) has a panoramic site and 17 good, clean, comfy rooms (which sometimes fill completely in July and August). Good meals too.

Iprali–Ushguli (10km, four to five hours) The easiest stage, though you're walking the 4WD road for much of it.

You can cut a day off the trek by taking a taxi to Zhabeshi, or a taxi to Bogreshi then walking 8km up the pretty Adishchala valley to Adishi for your first day.

to a British-Georgian couple, in Etseri, and **Guesthouse Nenskra** (☑551761919; http://svanetistay.com; Kvemo Marghi village, Chuberi; per person incl 2 meals 35-50 GEL) in Chuberi, the last main north–south valley before the boundary of Abkhazia.

Georgian Military Highway საქართველოს სამხედრო გზა

This ancient passage across the Caucasus towards Vladikavkaz in Russia provides the quickest access from Tbilisi to the high Caucasus, leading to the spectacular Kazbegi area – a highlight of any trip to Georgia. A track through the challenging mountain terrain was first properly engineered as a road in the 19th century with the Russian occupation of the Caucasus. As you head north from Tbilisi, the road clings to the side of the turquoise Zhinvali Reservoir and passes beautiful Ananuri and the Gudauri ski resort before crossing the 2379m Jvari Pass then descending the Tergi valley to the small town of Kazbegi, a superb base for walking, climbing and bird-watching.

Ananuri ანანური

This **fortress** 66km north of Tbilisi is a classic example of beautiful old Georgian architecture in a beautiful location, enhanced by the Zhinvali Reservoir spreading out below. Within the fortress are two 17th-century churches, the larger of which, the Assumption Church, is covered with wonderful stone carving, including a large cross on every wall. The fortress belonged to the *eristavis* (dukes) of Aragvi, who ruled as far as the Tergi valley from the 13th to 18th centuries.

Inside the Assumption Church are vivid 17th- and 18th-century frescoes including a *Last Judgement* on the south wall. You can climb the tallest of the fortress towers for fine views: it was here that the last defenders were killed in 1739 when a rival *eristavi* set fire to Ananuri and murdered the Aragvi *eristavi's* family.

Gudauri გუდაური

ELEV 2000M

About 110km from Tbilisi, the highway climbs 500m by a series of hairpins up to the **Gudauri ski resort** (www.facebook.com/gudauriofficial), Georgia's best and most popular ski station, which has recently improved and expanded facilities and is highly rated by many foreign skiers. The 57km of pistes (black, red, blue and green) are served by five chairlifts, rising from 1990m to 3285m, and one cable car. Normally the ski season lasts from shortly before Christmas to April, with the best snow in January and February. A one-day lift pass costs 30 GEL; equipment rental starts around 25 GEL.

Gudauri also offers good freeriding, and heliskiing with the Georgian-French company **Heliksir** (http://heliski.travel). Ski touring is best in March and usually possible

into May: one of Georgia's top mountain guides, Irakli Kapanadze (p45), organises trips for 100 GEL to 250 GEL per person per day from Tbilisi.

Public *marshrutky* from Tbilisi to Kazbegi will drop you in Gudauri (10 GEL, two hours) but you may have trouble finding one with free seats going down to Tbilisi. The central point of Gudauri is marked by the roadside **Smart supermarket** (⊘24hr), which has an ATM.

🛏 Sleeping & Eating

Gudauri has around 40 hotels, aparthotels and hostels, plus rental apartments. Most

Georgian Military Highway

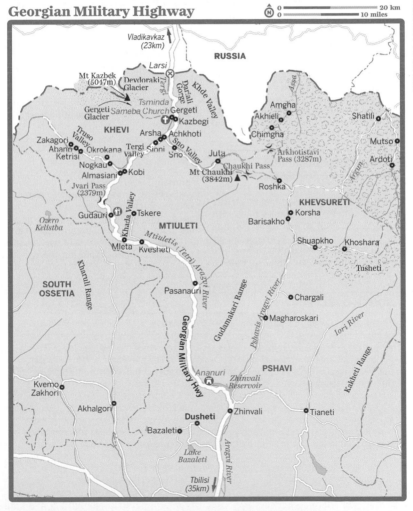

can help with ski rental and instruction, and transfers from Tbilisi.

Happy Yeti Hostel
HOSTEL $$
(☑571268800; http://happyyetihostel.com; dm incl breakfast & dinner US$35; ⓟ❸❄) Ukrainian- and Polish-run and dedicated to everybody having a good time, the Yeti revolves happily around its sociable bar-restaurant. It's 600m down the road from the resort centre.

Hotel Gudauri Hut
HOTEL $$
(☑595939911; www.gudaurihut.com; s/d half board US$80/120; ⓟ❸❄) A friendly, medium-sized hotel a short distance up the road from the centre of the resort, Gudauri Hut offers pleasant, clean, yellow-painted rooms with good views, plus three bars, a restaurant and sauna.

Hotel Shamo
HOTEL $$
(☑599500142; allgudauri.ge; d incl breakfast & dinner US$100-120; ⓟ❸❄) A relaxed, smallish hotel with a homey, log-cabin-type feel and excellent traditional Georgian meals. It's about 1km down the road from the resort centre, then 400m along a side road (indicated by a small sign).

Kazbegi (Stepantsminda)
ყაზბეგი (სტეფანწმინდა)
☑345 / POP 2500 / ELEV 1750M

This is most people's destination on the Georgian Military Hwy: a valley town with the famous hilltop silhouette of Tsminda Sameba Church and the towering snowy cone of Mt Kazbek looking down from the west. Now officially named Stepantsminda,

but still commonly known as Kazbegi, it's a base for some wonderful walking and mountain-biking.

The highway brings you straight into the main square, Kazbegis moedani. From here Kazbegis qucha forks to the right, while the main road leads down to a bridge over the Tergi River then continues 15km north to the Russian border in the Dariali Gorge. Immediately after the Tergi bridge a side road turns up to Gergeti village on the west side of the valley, almost a suburb of Kazbegi.

◉ Sights & Activities

Stepantsminda
Historical Museum
MUSEUM
(Kazbegis qucha 2; admission 3 GEL; ☉9am-6pm) The museum is set in the childhood home of writer Alexander Kazbegi (1848–93), 300m north of Kazbegis moedani. Kazbegi made the unusual decision to become a shepherd after studying in Tbilisi, St Petersburg and Moscow. Later he wrote the novels and plays that made him famous. The museum's ground floor contains photos, paintings and traditional artefacts documenting local life; the upstairs is devoted to the man.

Kazbegi's grave lies under a large stone sculpture near the fence outside: he asked to be buried in sight of Mt Kazbek.

Mountain Travel Agency
ADVENTURE SPORTS
(☑555649291; www.mtainfo.ge; Kazbegis moedani; ☉May-Nov) A one-stop shop for your mountaineering and camping needs and more. It rents mountain bikes (just 15 GEL per day at the time of writing and an excellent way of exploring the region) and equipment, including crampons, ice

---

SOUTH OSSETIA

The breakaway region of South Ossetia stretches up to the main Caucasus ridge north of the Georgian town of Gori. At research time, South Ossetia was not letting any foreigners in from Georgia and this looked unlikely to change soon. It may be possible to enter South Ossetia from Vladikavkaz in North Ossetia (Russia), although Georgia considers this illegal, and the British **Foreign Office** (www.fco.gov.uk) and US **State Department** (http://travel.state.gov) advise against travel to both South and North Ossetia.

The first step is to obtain clearance from the de facto **Ministry of Foreign Affairs** (☑7-997-4452243; www.mfa-rso.su; ulitsa Khetagurova 1, Zdanie Pravitelstva, 3 etazh, Tskhinvali) in Tskhinvali, South Ossetia's capital. At the time of writing clearances for independent travellers are near-impossible to get: you stand a better chance if you go with an agency such as **Caucasus Explorer** (http://caucasus-explorer.com) and are able to fork out around US$250 for the clearance.

You can look at South Ossetia any time you travel between Tbilisi and Gori, as the boundary comes to within 400m of the highway just west of Karapila village.

axes and harnesses (each 10 GEL per day), climbing rope (15 GEL), three-person tents (20 GEL), sleeping bags (8 GEL) and mats (5 GEL), and it sells cooking gas and trekking maps.

It also arranges mountain guides, including English speakers – €400/500 for four/five people for a Mt Kazbek ascent – plus packhorses, transport and accommodation bookings.

Fly Caucasus   PARAGLIDING
(⌨568114453; www.flycaucasus.com; 10min flight 160-200 GEL, 30min flight 350-400 GEL) Caucasus scenery is a paraglider's dream and you can do tandem flights year-round with this experienced English-speaking, Ukrainian-run outfit.

🛏 Sleeping & Eating

Kazbegi is very well supplied with guesthouses, all providing meals. Apart from the excellent Rooms Hotel, eating-out choices boil down to a handful of cafes around Kazbegis moedani.

Ketino's Guesthouse   GUESTHOUSE $
(⌨558131828, 571032439; www.facebook.com/ketino.kazbegi; Kvemo Gergeti; per person 20-25 GEL, full board 50 GEL; @ 🛜) A large, sociable, rambling house with a helpful, multilingual hostess and good food (vegan, vegetarian and kosher available). There are several dorm-type rooms, plus a couple of doubles, and four showers. Take the first street on the left going up the Gergeti road, and it's 250m along on the left.

HQ of Nove Sujashvili   HOSTEL $
(⌨593392278; Khevisberi, Kvemo Gergeti; dm 17-22 GEL, breakfast/dinner 5/10 GEL; P ➡ 🛜) A friendly, English-speaking brother-and-sister team run this popular little hostel, 250m along the second street on the left as you walk up the Gergeti road. The two dorms have their own bathrooms.

Nazi Chkareuli   GUESTHOUSE $
(Guest House Nazy; ⌨252480, 598382700; ssujashvili@yahoo.co.uk; Khevisberi 7, Kvemo Gergeti; per person with/without bathroom 30/20 GEL, incl 3 meals 15 GEL; P 🛜) Nazi's large house has two rooms with private bathroom and several dorm-style rooms with four or five beds. It's well-kept, the washing machine is free, and the meals are a bargain. Take the second street on the left going up the Gergeti road: it's almost immediately on the right.

★Anano Guesthouse   GUESTHOUSE $$
(⌨595099449; ananoqushashvili@yahoo.com; Vazha Pshavela 7; d/q 50/80 GEL, s/d with bathroom 50/60 GEL, breakfast per person 10 GEL; ➡🛜) Six bright, spick-and-span rooms with polished pine floors, good breakfasts and helpful English-speaking owners add up to one of Kazbegi's best guesthouses. From Kazbegis moedani take the uphill street passing Nunu's Guesthouse, turn left at the top and take the entry to the right after 30m.

Diana Pitskhelauri   GUESTHOUSE $$
(⌨599570313, 598522525; Vazha Pshavela 90; per person with/without breakfast 35/25 GEL, half board 50 GEL; P 🛜) Terrific meals, a welcoming hostess and bright, clean rooms (some with private bathroom) in modern buildings make this one of the best picks. From Kazbegis moedani take the uphill street passing Nunu's Guesthouse, then go 750m to the right. It's on the left at the end of the street.

Nunu's Guesthouse   GUESTHOUSE $$
(⌨558358535, 599570915; gvanci9191@gmail.com; dm/s/d 20/25/50 GEL, breakfast/dinner 10/15 GEL; @ 🛜) A good option just 50m up the uphill street from the marshrutka stand, with a friendly hostess, good meals and lovely mountain views from the balcony. It has vehicles for outings.

★Rooms Hotel   DESIGN HOTEL $$$
(⌨32-2710099; www.roomshotels.com; Gorgasali 1; incl breakfast s US$165-260, d US$183-277; P ➡ 🛜 ⊠) One of the best hotels in Georgia, Rooms is an inspired conversion of a former Soviet turbaza (group holiday residence). The once-spartan building is now clad almost entirely in appealing dark wood and makes brilliant use of its elevated position looking across the valley.

The rooms are contemporary, comfy and well equipped, but what's really special is the wonderful long front terrace gazing over at Mt Kazbek, plus the long, library-style lounge and 24-hour bar just inside, and the superb **restaurant** (mains 12-40 GEL; ☺8am-midnight; 🛜) 🍴 with gourmet Georgian, European and fusion dishes – the likes of local trout with walnut pesto, freerange chicken with Dijon sauce and spinach, and many other enticing concoctions.

There's also a very good indoor pool (and a casino should you need one of those). The

THE CHURCH ABOVE KAZBEGI

The 14th-century **Tsminda Sameba Church** (Holy Trinity Church; Gergeti) above Kazbegi has become almost a symbol of Georgia for its incomparably photogenic hilltop setting (at 2200m) with mighty Mt Kazbek rising behind it, and the fierce determination involved in building it on such a lofty, isolated perch. A rough, circuitous 6km motor track leads up to the church (return trip by taxi 40 GEL to 60 GEL), but you can walk up to the church in one to 1½ hours from Kazbegi.

Vakhushti Batonishvili wrote in the 18th century that in times of danger the treasures from Mtskheta, as well as St Nino's cross, were kept at Tsminda Sameba for safety. In 1988 the Soviet authorities constructed a cable-car line to the church, with one station right next to Tsminda Sameba. The people of Kazbegi felt it defiled their sacred place and soon destroyed it.

The beautifully weathered stone church is decorated with intriguing carvings, one on the bell tower appearing to show two dinosaurs.

There are several ways of walking up from Kazbegi. For the best distance-gradient compromise, walk up through Gergeti village to a T-junction 1.25km from the main road (80m after signs indicating the car track to the right). Go left at the T-junction, out past the last village buildings, and up beside a stream. About 120m past the last building, fork up to the right, passing to the right of a ruined stone tower; 200m after the tower take an initially lesser path diverging up to the right. This curves up round the hillside to reach the church in 1km.

cheaper back-view rooms are nice enough but don't have that Kazbek magic. Friday and Saturday nights are more expensive than Sunday to Thursday; and there are discounts for advance booking.

❶ Information

Liberty Bank (Kazbegis qucha 11; ⊘ 9.30am-5.30pm Mon-Fri, 9.30am-2.30pm Sat) The ATM here gives up to 400 GEL per withdrawal with Visa or MasterCard. The bank also exchanges euros and US dollars.

❶ Getting There & Away

Marshrutky to Tbilisi (10 GEL, three hours) are timetabled hourly from 7am to noon and at 1.30pm, 3.30pm, 5pm and 6pm. A taxi to or from Tbilisi can cost anywhere between 80 GEL and 120 GEL. Taxis waiting at the north end of the Tergi bridge often ask lower fares than those on Kazbegis moedani.

Vladikavkaz (Russia) is 45km north through the Dariali Gorge. To go through the **Larsi border point** (Verkhny Lars; ⊘ 7am-7pm), 15km from Kazbegi, you must be in a vehicle, or at least on a bicycle – no pedestrians. Taxis from Kazbegi to Vladikavkaz cost around 100 GEL. Driving time is under an hour, but the border itself can take anywhere from 20 minutes to a few hours depending on traffic and how slow/fast the Russians are processing people.

Around Kazbegi

There are many wonderful walks and riding routes in the valleys and mountains around Kazbegi.

◉ Sights

The walking and climbing season is from May or June to October or November, depending on the weather.

TRUSO VALLEY

The beautiful Truso Valley, source of the Tergi River, heads west off the Georgian Military Hwy 17km south of Kazbegi. It's dotted with ancient towers, abandoned Ossetian villages and strange mineral phenomena, notably the Abano mineral lake which bubbles with carbon dioxide. Take your passport: the South Ossetia boundary is close so there are Georgian soldiers in the valley. They may stop you going beyond Ketrisi, 14km up the valley, or you may be able to go as far as Zakagori, a further 3km.

A return taxi from Kazbegi (including waiting time while you explore) costs about 100 GEL to Kvemo Okrokana, 4km up the valley, or 150 GEL to Ketrisi. Mountain biking is also a popular means of exploring Truso.

SNO VALLEY & AROUND

The Sno Valley runs southeast off the Georgian Military Hwy from Achkhoti, 4km south of Kazbegi. The small village of Juta at 2150m, an outpost of Khevsur people from over the mountains to the east, is about 15km up the mostly unpaved valley road, and is a starting point for some great hikes. A taxi from Kazbegi to Juta costs about 80 GEL for a one-way or return trip.

🏃 Activities

★ Mt Chaukhi & Chaukhi Pass　　HIKING
One beautiful short walk from Juta goes southeast to the foot of Mt Chaukhi (3842m), a multi-pinnacled peak popular with climbers, 1½ hours from Juta. In a long, spectacular day of nine or 10 hours you can continue up to and over the 3338m Chaukhi Pass (passable from about July to mid-October) and down to Roshka in Khevsureti via the stunning **Abudelauri lakes**.

The trail over the pass itself and down to the lakes is not particularly obvious: a guide with a packhorse costs 100 GEL from Juta to the pass or 250 GEL to Roshka.

Gergeti Glacier Hike　　HIKING
If you're up for another 1000m of ascent after climbing to the famous Tsminda Sameba Church above Kazbegi, this walk rewards with spectacular views, especially of Mt Kazbek. The path heads straight up the ridge behind the church. Allow up to eight hours from the church to the glacier and down again.

An alternative route, less panoramic but more protected on windy days, forks off to the left from the main ridge path after about 500m. The two paths meet again at the Saburtse Pass at about 3000m altitude. From here you descend slightly to cross a small river before ascending to the side of the Gergeti (Ortsveri) Glacier. Stream water is normally OK to drink beyond the pass as there are no animals up here.

🛌 Sleeping & Eating

Juta has several places to stay, most only open from July to September.

★ Zeta Camp　　CAMPGROUND, LODGE $
(📞 577501057; www.zeta.ge; Juta; per person dm/tent/own tent 30/17/10, tr 135 GEL; ⊙ Jun-Sep; ⊜) A 10-minute walk above Juta with fabulous views up the green valley to Mt

Chaukhi, Zeta provides good tents with sleeping bags and mats, three good rooms in a wooden building, hot showers, and good food in its popular cafe (dishes 7 GEL to 14 GEL). A fun place to stay!

B&B Jago Arabuli　　GUESTHOUSE $$
(📞 593422951; Juta; per person 25 GEL, breakfast/dinner 10/15 GEL; ⊙ approx Jun-Sep; ⊜) Signposted from the bridge at Juta, this house has two fine four-bed rooms and a bathroom with a hot shower and seat toilet. The lady of the house, Maia, speaks English and it's worth calling ahead as they're sometimes fully booked.

Soso Arabuli　　GUESTHOUSE $$
(📞 555690045; Juta; per person half board 50 GEL; P ⊜) This is the red-roofed house just above the river about 300m upstream from the bridge at Juta. It's run by an amiable couple, here year-round, who provide cosy rooms, solid meals, a hot shower and an indoor squat toilet.

Khevsureti　　ხევსურეთი

Sparsely populated Khevsureti, bordering Chechnya (Russia), is home to some fantastic defensive architecture, a part-animist religion, and spectacular scenery of steep, forested valleys and blooming mountain pastures. Men in this remote area were still wearing chain mail well into the 20th century.

Today few villages have permanent inhabitants. There's no road access to most people's main destination, Shatili, 150km from Tbilisi, from about December to April when the Datvisjvari Pass (2676m) is closed. Shepherds bring their flocks up from Kakheti from about June to September, when tourism also provides an income for some families.

The road to Khevsureti turns northeast off the Georgian Military Hwy shortly before the Zhinvali Reservoir and runs up the Pshavis Aragvi valley towards Khevsureti's largest village, **Barisakho** (population 200), about 100km from Tbilisi. The asphalt gives out about 15km before Barisakho.

Roshka

Nine kilometres past Barisakho, a side-road climbs 7km west up to the tiny village of Roshka. A wonderful walk from Roshka takes you up to the three small, but very

MT KAZBEK

This 5047m extinct volcano (also called Mkinvartsveri or Mt Kazbegi), towering west of Kazbegi, has much folk history. The Greek Prometheus was supposedly chained up here for stealing fire from the gods, as was the Georgian Amirani, for challenging God's omnipotence. The Betlemi (Bethlehem) cave, 4000m above sea level, was believed to be the abode of many very sacred objects – Christ's manger, Abraham's tent and a dove-rocked golden cradle whose sight would blind a human being. There were taboos against hunting on the mountain and climbing it. Not surprisingly, the first to conquer Kazbek's peak were foreigners: Freshfield, Tucker and Moore of the London Alpine Club in 1868.

Today many thousands of people attempt to reach Kazbek's summit each year (it's especially popular with Poles), but this is a serious mountaineering challenge that requires fitness and acclimatisation to altitude: perhaps half of those who try do not reach the top. Unless you're suitably experienced, it's highly advisable to take a guide, which you can organise through agencies in Tbilisi or locally, including **Mountain Travel Agency** (p90). Climbers should register at the Emergency Management Department building at the bottom of the Gergeti road, on their way up to the mountain.

The ascent is technically straightforward, though there is some danger in crevasses. It takes three or four days from Kazbegi, with the first day hiking up from Kazbegi and over the Gergeti Glacier to the **Betlemi Hut** (Meteo Station; 32-2922533; www.facebook.com/bethlemihut; dm US$15, camping per tent US$5; May-Nov), a former weather station at 3650m altitude where you can sleep. The hut accommodates around 50 people indoors, which is often far from enough: in the busiest climbing season (late June to mid-September) there can be hundreds of people there. You can reserve places through **Mountain Travel Agency** (p90) in Kazbegi or **Geoland** (p53) in Tbilisi. Bring food, a warm sleeping bag and cooking gear. The wind can be fierce.

The second day is usually spent acclimatising, often with a climb to the Maili Plateau (4500m). On day three you start for the summit from Betlemi Hut around 2am. The ascent takes up to six hours, with the final 150m involving about three rope lengths of 35° to 40° ice. The descent to Betlemi Hut for the third night takes up to another six hours. Packhorses can reach the Betlemi Hut from about July to mid-September.

beautiful, coloured Abudelauri lakes with their backdrop of the jagged Chaukhi massif. It's about 2½ hours (5km) up to the first (green) lake, then 10 minutes on to the stunning turquoise lake, and a further hour (with no real path most of the way) up to the white lake, below a glacier coming down from the Chaukhi massif.

The excellent **Shota Tsiklauri's Guesthouse** (599399789; Roshka; per person incl breakfast & dinner 50 GEL; approx May-Oct;), at the very top of Roshka, provides four comfy guest rooms and fine food.

Shatili & Around

Shatili's **Old Town**, built between the 7th and 13th centuries, is a unique agglomeration of tall *koshkebi* (towers) clinging together on a rocky outcrop to form a single fortress-like whole. It was abandoned by the 1980s, and the new village, of about 20 houses, is just around the hill. But some towers have been restored as guesthouses. Shatili

is an increasingly popular weekend destination for Georgians. You might run into the **Shatiloba** (Aug or Sep, dates vary) festival, with folk music and dance, horse races and Georgian wrestling.

From Shatili the road continues 3km northeast then veers south just before the Chechnya border. At the bend, the **Anatori Crypts**, medieval communal tombs with human bones still visible, sit on a promontory above the gorge: in times of plague, infected villagers would voluntarily enter these tombs and wait for death. The road continues 9km up the Andaki valley to tiny **Mutso**, where the abandoned old village on a steep rock pinnacle contains several more bone-laden stone crypts. A foot trail continues over the very steep Atsunta Pass (3431m) into Tusheti.

Sleeping & Eating

Two of Shatili's old towers have been converted into guesthouses and sleeping there is a unique experience. Some of the houses along the village's one street and down near the river below also take guests. All can normally provide meals, though these may be fairly simple.

Dato Jalabauri's Guesthouse GUESTHOUSE **$$**
(☑598127614; www.facebook.com/Jalabauri; per person 25 GEL, half board 50 GEL; ☉ approx mid-May–Oct) An atmospheric *koshki*-guesthouse with 19 beds in small rooms reached by wooden staircases, plus a scenic balcony and a good hot shower. The family's own house is the nearest to the tiny church in the new part of Shatili.

Imeda's Koshki GUESTHOUSE **$$**
(☑598370317; per person 25 GEL, half board 50 GEL; ☉ approx mid-May–Oct) A tower-guesthouse near the foot of the Old Town, with nine rooms (some windowless) for up to five people, three hot showers and a terrace where good meals are served.

ⓘ Getting There & Away

A 20-seat *marshrutka* to Shatili (20 GEL, six to seven hours) leaves Tbilisi's Didube bus station (same area as the Kazbegi *marshrutky*) at 9am Wednesday and Saturday, starting back from Shatili at noon Thursday and Sunday from about June to October. Schedules may change; for information call driver **Temuri** (☑599272904), who speaks Georgian and Russian. There's also a bus from Didube to Barisakho (5 GEL, three hours) at 4pm Tuesday, Wednesday, Friday and Sunday. A minivan from Tbilisi to Shatili for up to seven people normally costs 350 GEL for a return trip, stopping one night. Shatili taxi driver **Niko Chincharauli** (☑599072155) charges 200 GEL one-way to Barisakho, 250 GEL to Roshka and 300 GEL to Tbilisi.

Tusheti თუშეთი

Tucked away in the Caucasus in Georgia's far northeast corner, Tusheti is an ever-more

GEORGIA TUSHETI

Khevsureti & Tusheti

THE TRANSCAUCASIAN TRAIL

It sounds an improbable dream: a way-marked walking trail running the whole 700km length of the Caucasus, from the Black Sea to the Caspian Sea. But it's a dream that is taking steps towards reality with a bold project, initiated by two former US Peace Corps volunteers in Georgia, to establish the **Trans-caucasian Trail** (www.transcaucasian trail.org).

This is a long-term project to map, mark and, where necessary build, the trail; provide maps and guides for hik-ers; bring sustainable tourism to remote regions; raise the profile of protected |areas; and promote connections be-tween communities along the way.

The first steps were taken in 2015 with the mapping of the route across Svaneti and from Kazbegi to Tusheti. Check the website for the latest progress.

popular summer hiking and horse-trekking area and weekend getaway for lowland Georgians, but remains one of the country's most picturesque, fascinating and pristine high-mountain regions. The single road to Tusheti, over the nerve-jangling 2900m Abano Pass from Kakheti, is 4WD-only and only passable from about late May to mid-October. Centuries-old *koshkebi* (stone defence and refuge towers) still stand in many villages, and evidence of Tusheti's old animist religion is plentiful in the form of stone shrines called *khatebi* (singular: *kha-ti*) decked with the horns of sacrificed goats or sheep. Women, including visitors, are not permitted to approach *khatebi*.

Today most Tusheti folk only go up to Tusheti in summer, to graze their flocks, participate in festivals, cater for tourists and generally reconnect with their roots. Many have winter homes around Akhmeta and Al-vani in Kakheti.

Tusheti has two main river valleys – the Pirikiti Alazani and the more southerly Gomtsari (Tushetis) Alazani – which meet below Omalo, the biggest village, then flow east into Dagestan (Russia). The scenery everywhere is a spectacular mix of snow-covered rocky peaks, deep gorges, tower-dotted villages and steep, grassy hillsides where distant flocks of sheep appear as slowly shifting patterns of white specks. The whole

area is under environmental protection as the Tusheti Protected Areas (1137 sq km).

◎ Sights & Activities

Most villages sit above near-sheer hillsides or nestle down by one of the rivers. There's a particularly splendid group of old towers, known as **Keselo**, on the crag at Zemo Om-alo, the upper part of Omalo. **Shenaqo**, a few kilometres east of Omalo, is one of the prettiest villages, with houses of stone, slate and rickety wooden balconies grouped be-low one of Tusheti's very few churches. Just outside Diklo, 4km northeast of Shenaqo, the **Dzveli Diklo** (Old Diklo) fortress – scene of a heroic last stand against Dagestani in-vaders in the 19th century – perches on a spectacular rock promontory. **Dartlo,** 12km northwest of Omalo in the Pirikiti Alazani valley, has another spectacular tower group-ing, overlooked by the single tall tower of **Kvavlo** 350m above.

Walking & Horse Riding

Routes are numerous though signage is er-ratic. The Tusheti Protected Areas Visitors Centre (p98) is helpful with information. It has lists of guesthouses along the routes, of which there are at least 40 in villages includ-ing Omalo, Shenaqo, Diklo, Chigho, Mirgve-la, Dartlo, Kvavlo, Chesho, Baso (Parsma), Girevi, Khakhabo, Shtrolta, Dochu and Ver-khovani. On some longer routes you need to camp. You can hire horses as mounts or packhorses in some villages for 35 GEL to 40 GEL a day, along with a horseman/guide for 50 GEL to 70 GEL per day – the visitors centre can arrange these for you.

Omalo to Shenaqo and Shenaqo to Dik-lo are two good short walks of a couple of hours each (one-way) on vehicle tracks. **Oreti Lake**, about 9km south of Omalo (four or five hours' walk), is a beautiful, pan-oramic destination and you can camp there overnight.

Omalo–Nakaicho Pass–Omalo   HIKING

A popular four-or-five-day route starts in Omalo, runs up the Pirikiti Alazani valley to Dartlo, Chesho and Parsma, then cross-es the steep 2900m Nakaicho Pass over to Verkhovani, and returns to Omalo down the Gomtsari Alazani valley.

The basic route does, however, involve quite a lot of road walking (not that traffic is heavy). Non-road alternatives are to ap-proach Dartlo from Diklo via Chigho, and to take the panoramic Gonta ridge route between the Nakaicho Pass and Gele (about 6km northwest of Omalo), instead of either of the two valley roads.

Omalo–Shatili
HIKING

The track up the Pirikiti Alazani valley beyond Chesho, via Parsma and Girevi, eventually leads to the 3431m Atsunta Pass, a very steep and demanding route over into Khevsureti. It's a trek of four or five days all the way from Omalo to Shatili in Khevsureti, with one night's camping required at the base of the Atsunta.

The pass is normally open for walkers and pack horses from about mid-June to mid-September. There is a potentially dangerous river crossing before the ascent to the pass, so a guide and horse are advisable, and it's less hazardous late in the season, though horses and guides can be in short supply after the end of August.

Omalo–Shuapkho
HIKING

This long westward route leads all the way up the Gomtsari Alazani valley to the Borbalo Pass (2990m), from where trails head west down to Shuapkho village in Pshavi, north down to Ardoti and Mutso in Khevsureti, and northwest to the Datvisjvari Pass.

Omalo Shuapkho should take four days on foot: you could spend the first night in a guesthouse (such as at Verkhovani), the second in the 12-person shelter on the way up to the pass, and the third camping.

🛏 Sleeping & Eating

Tusheti has plenty of guesthouses. They operate only when the road is open and some don't get going till July. Nearly all have shared bathrooms with (usually) hot showers. Only some have electricity in the rooms, though there's usually a plug in the kitchen or elsewhere for charging phones.

🛏 Omalo

Most people stay in the older Zemo (Upper) Omalo, where those picturesque towers are situated, but there are also options in Kvemo (Lower) Omalo, 1.5km down the hill.

Omalo 2005
GUESTHOUSE $

(☑599293756; www.facebook.com/hotelomalo 2005sastumroomalo2005; Zemo Omalo; per person incl 0/3 meals 25/50 GEL; ➔) At the top of Upper Omalo, beneath the towers, this was one of Omalo's first guesthouses, a whole decade old, and is built with traditional natural materials. Rooms are cosy, with electric light, and two have private bathrooms. The young owner Giorgi speaks fluent English.

Keselo
GUESTHOUSE $

(☑598941270, 577472111; arshaulidze@gmail. com; Kvemo Omalo; per person incl 0/1/2/3 meals 20/25/40/50 GEL; P➔) Green-fenced Keselo, scenically placed at the top of Kvemo (Lower) Omalo, has comfy beds in half a dozen rooms, and reasonable food.

Guesthouse Shina
GUESTHOUSE $$

(☑595262046; www.shina.ge; Zemo Omalo; per person incl breakfast & dinner 60-70 GEL; P➔) The fanciest place in Tusheti, this stone-and-wood house has rooms with private bathroom and electric light, plus a nice front garden and a dedicated restaurant area serving good meals.

Hotel Tusheti Tower
GUESTHOUSE $$

(☑599110879; tushetitower@gmail.com; Zemo Omalo; per person 25 GEL, incl breakfast & dinner 60 GEL; ➔) A small 17th-century tower

---

TUSHETI FESTIVALS

Tushetoba, held at Omalo on a variable Saturday in August (sometimes late July), is a semi-touristic festival featuring folk music and dancing, traditional Tusheti foods including *guda* sheep's cheese and *khinkali* dumplings, and mountain sports such as wrestling, archery and horse races (with riders no more than 15 years old because they're lighter so can go faster).

Atnigenoba, the end-of-summer festival that starts about 100 days after Georgian Easter (p21), is a non-touristic event bound up with Tusheti's ancient animist religion. It involves, among other things, ram sacrifices at the ancient shrines known as *khatebi*, separate-sex feasting, the drinking of sacred rye beer (specially brewed by men in large cauldrons) and more sports. The first day of Atnigenoba sees a huge gathering known as Lasharoba (dedicated to the deity Lashara), of people from all of Tusheti at Chigho. The second day sees Khitana at Jvarboseli, mainly for people from the Gomtsari Alazani valley. Further events go on in different villages for two more weeks.

ⓘ TUSHETI DOGS

The dogs guarding Tusheti's sheep and cattle are often fierce and sometimes dangerous. If you give the livestock as wide a berth as possible, the dogs are less likely to threaten you.

has been extended vertically to house four small stone-walled rooms with private bathrooms and electric light. Meals here are good and plentiful.

🛏 Shenaqo

Everywhere in Shenaqo has electricity thanks to its one-village hydro scheme.

Nino & Zauri Imedadze　　HOMESTAY $
(☑ 599001915; Shenaqo; per person incl 0/1/3 meals 20/30/50 GEL) Clean, basic rooms in a quaint, traditional wooden house, with a squat toilet and hot shower. Meals are large and delicious.

Old Tusheti　　GUESTHOUSE $
(☑ 558272006; per person incl 0/3 meals 20/50 GEL) Host Eldar Buqvaidze provides good, plentiful meals, plays the balalaika, and maintains a curious museum of traditional Tusheti artefacts. Ask about the magic rope for scaring off sheep. Cosy rooms hold up to four people each.

Darejan's Guesthouse　　GUESTHOUSE $
(☑ 599102944; Shenaqo; per person incl 0/3 meals 20/50 GEL; ☻) Just beside the church at the top of Shenaqo, Darejan offers seven bright, new, wood-floored and -walled rooms.

🛏 Dartlo

Hotel Dartlo　　HOTEL $
(☑ 598174966; www.dartlo.ge; per person incl 0/1/2/3 meals 20/30/40/50 GEL) At the top of the village, with fine views, it has six cosy wood-walled rooms with electric light, and offers 4WD tours – though 'hotel' is a bit of an exaggeration.

Hotel Samtsikhe　　HOTEL $$
(☑ 599118993; beselanidze@yahoo.com; per person incl 0/2 meals 25/60 GEL; ☻) Comprises six stone-and-wood houses, with 14 rooms in all, just above the ruined church at the foot of the village. Beds are comfy and the rooms have electric light.

🛏 Other Villages

Guesthouse Mirgvela　　GUESTHOUSE $
(☑ 577613386; mirgvela@yahoo.com; Mirgvela; per person incl 0/1/2/3 meals 20/30/40/50 GEL; Ⓟ ☻) Five kilometres northwest of Omalo at the junction of the Pirikiti and Gomtsari Alazani valley roads, Mirgvela makes a good place to start or end a long walk or ride. It has a big grassy lawn enjoying great views, and good pine-panelled rooms, some with private bathroom, plus generator electricity and good meals.

Lamata　　GUESTHOUSE $
(☑ 599700378; tushetiguesthouselamata@mail.ru; Verkhovani; per person incl 0/1/2 meals 10/25/40 GEL; ☼ 20 Jun-20 Sep) Your chance to sleep in a *koshki*. Three of the seven rooms are in the tower in front of the main house (but those in the main house are actually a bit comfier, and that's where the shower is). The family is friendly and the teenagers speak some English.

Family Hotel Panther　　GUESTHOUSE $
(Guesthouse Jiqi; ☑ 599585839; jangulashvili@yahoo.com; Chesho; per person incl 0/2/3 meals 20/40/50 GEL; ☻) This large house in Chesho has two scenic balconies and 10 double rooms sharing five bathrooms.

ⓘ Information

Tusheti Protected Areas Visitors Centre
(☑ 577101892; www.apa.gov.ge; ☼ 9am-6pm approx late May–mid-Oct) This helpful centre about 1km south of Omalo has plentiful displays on Tusheti, provides walking/riding route and accommodation information, and can help arrange guides, horses and vehicles.

ⓘ Getting There & Away

When the Abano Pass is open, 4WDs will carry three or four passengers from Telavi or Alvani (22km northwest of Telavi) to Omalo for 200 GEL – a spectacular four-hour drive (3½ hours from Alvani). Guesthouses and the Tourism Information Centre (p102) in Telavi can organise 4WDs to pick you up, and can often connect travellers with each other to share costs. Some accommodation places in Tbilisi can also arrange for 4WDs to meet you in Telavi or Alvani.

4WDs also wait for passengers at the central crossroads in Alvani; you may be able to share with others. It's best to be at Alvani by 9am; taxis from Telavi cost 15 GEL.

The road to Tusheti has been improved, but the asphalt still ends a few kilometres past Alvani, and the road still has all the same vertiginous precipices and steep switchbacks – not recommended for self-drivers.

KAKHETI

The eastern region of Kakheti (კახეთი) is Georgia's premier wine-producing area. Almost everywhere you go, you'll be invited to drink a glass of wine and it's easy to find yourself wandering around in a semipermanent mellow haze. Kakheti is also rich in history: here you'll find the incredible monastery complex of Davit Gareja, the picturesque hilltop town of Sighnaghi, and many beautiful churches, castles and mansions around the main town, Telavi.

Telavi   თელავი

🗐 350 / POP 20,000

The largest town in Kakheti, Telavi is set in the vineyard-strewn Alazani valley, between the Gombori Mountains and the Caucasus (visible to the northeast). It's the perfect base for exploring the region's viticultural, historical and architectural riches.

History

Telavi was one of Georgia's main medieval trade centres, but it was caught in the on-

slaught of the 13th-century Mongol invasion and then twice devastated by Persia's Shah Abbas I in the early 17th century (Abbas killed around 60,000 Kakhetians and carted another 100,000 off to Persia). In 1744 Persia's Nader Shah installed the local prince Erekle II here as ruler of Kakheti. Erekle united Kakheti with Kartli, to the west, as a more or less independent state, ruling with a progressive Westernising policy. He still occupies an honoured place in Kakheti annals.

👁 Sights

Batonistsikhe Castle   CASTLE, PALACE
Batonistsikhe was the residence of the Kakhetian kings in the 17th and 18th centuries. The complex includes a Persian-style palace where Erekle II was born and died, and

Kakheti

Telavi

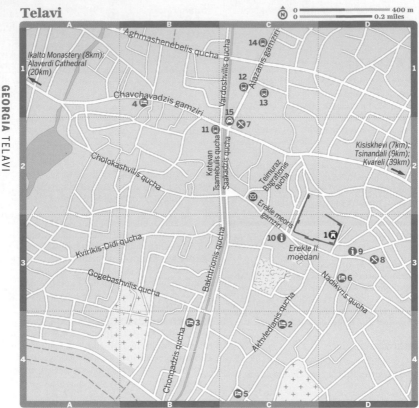

Telavi

⊚ Sights
1 Batonistsikhe Castle D3

🛏 Sleeping
2 Eto's Guesthouse C4
3 Hotel Neli Telavi..................................... B4
4 Marinella Guest House B1
5 Milorava's Guest House C4
6 Tushishvili Guesthouse D3

⊗ Eating
7 Bazari... C2
Bravo .... (see 6)

8 Chadiri Restaurant................................. D3

ℹ Information
9 Kakheti Wine Guild D3
10 Tourism Information Centre C3

ℹ Transport
11 Marshrutky to Ikalto.............................. B2
12 New Bus Station..................................... C1
13 Old Bus Station C1
14 Roki Bus Station C1
15 Shared Taxis to Tbilisi...........................C2

art and history museums, but at research time was completely closed for renovations, probably till at least 2017.

🛏 Sleeping

Most places can organise taxi trips around the area's sights and/or wineries at reasonable prices.

★**Tushishvili Guesthouse**   GUESTHOUSE **$**
(☑271909, 577756625; www.globalsalsa.com/
telavi; Nadikvari 15; per person with/without breakfast 30/25 GEL, dinner 15 GEL; P☻@☎) This
welcoming house is a long-time travellers'
favourite and justly so. Hostess Svetlana
serves fabulous dinners and is more than
helpful in organising local taxi trips and
providing transport information. Rooms are
comfy and well maintained.

Hotel Neli Telavi   GUESTHOUSE **$**
(Guesthouse Nelly; ☑599581820; www.facebook.
com/hotelneli; Chonqadze 11; per person incl breakfast 30 GEL, half board 50 GEL; P@☎) Five of
the eight big, bright rooms here have private
bathrooms. Best of all is the slightly more
expensive top-floor 'lux' room with great
panoramas. Nelly cooks excellent Georgian
meals with fresh, local ingredients, and the
natural wine flows.

Eto's Guesthouse   GUESTHOUSE **$**
(☑277070, 599782050; eto.neka@yahoo.com;
Akhvlediani 27; r per person 20-25 GEL, breakfast/
dinner 5/15 GEL; @☎) This friendly place has
four bright, clean rooms sharing a good
bathroom, and a lovely garden where you
can sit out under a big apricot tree. Meals
are made from fresh local produce and
guests can use the kitchen.

Milorava's Guest House   GUESTHOUSE **$**
(☑271257, 551505550; www.miloravagh.ge; Akhvlediani 67; r per person incl breakfast 30 GEL, half
board 40-45 GEL; ☎) Can accommodate six or
seven people in rooms with comfy beds in a
cottage beside the garden. Good meals and
an amiable, helpful host.

★**Villa Alazani**   GUESTHOUSE **$$**
(☑577414842; www.villaalazani.com; Kisiskhevi;
r/whole house incl breakfast €50/180; P☻☎)
This ample village house in Kisiskhevi,
7km southeast of Telavi, is a wonderful
rural hideaway. It has been beautifully re-
stored by its owners (a group of interna-
tional journalists and film-makers) with
wooden pillars, lovely spacious common
areas, a marvellous collection of antique
carpets, four good-sized bedrooms and a
spacious kitchen.
   A taxi from Telavi costs 5 GEL, and the
amiable Russian-speaking caretaker Te-
muri is normally available to taxi guests
around for excursions. Dinner, Georgian
music performances and cooking lessons
are available on request.

Schuchmann Wines Chateau   HOTEL **$$**
(☑577508005;   www.schuchmann-wines.com;
Kisiskhevi; r incl breakfast, wine tour & tasting 160-
220 GEL; P☻☎≋) A good hotel at one of
Georgia's top wineries, with spacious, balconied rooms in an attractive stone, wood and
brick building, plus ample dining areas and
excellent Georgian food. It's 7km southwest
of town in Kisiskhevi. A range of Kakheti
tours is on offer.

Marinella Guest House   GUESTHOUSE **$$**
(☑577516001; www.marinella.ge; Chavchavadze
131; s/d incl breakfast 50/70 GEL; P☻☎) Has
six cheerful, spotless, good-sized rooms in
a modern style, plus a nice breezy terrace.
English and German spoken.

✖ **Eating**
Restaurants are improving, and in a guest-
house you'll usually eat excellently.

GEORGIA TELAVI

MARSHRUTKY FROM TELAVI

DESTINATION	BUS STATION	COST (GEL)	DURATION (HR)	FREQUENCY
Alaverdi	Old	2	40min	every 15-20min, 8.45am-5.15pm
Alvani	Old	2	45min	every 15-20 min, 9am-5.30pm
Dedoplistskaro	Old	7	2	2.30pm
Dedoplistskaro	New	7	2	3.30pm
Kvareli	Old	3	1½	every 40 min, 9.30am to 5.30pm
Lagodekhi	New	6	1¾	7.30am, 8.30am, 8.40am, 1.30pm
Lagodekhi	Old	6	1¾	3pm
Sighnaghi	Old	5	1½	3pm
Tbilisi	New	7	1¾	every 40min, 7.40am-1pm
Tbilisi	Roki	7	1¾	every 30-45min, 6am-6pm
Tsinandali	Old	0.80	20min	every 30min, 9am-5pm

Bazari MARKET $

(cnr Chavchavadze & Alazanis gamziri; ⊙7am-6pm) Telavi's busy market bursts with fresh produce from the area's villages.

Bravo GEORGIAN $$

(Nadikvari 11; mains 6-14 GEL; ⊙10am-midnight; ⌨) Bravo does an excellent job on a wide range of Georgian favourites, all nicely presented, and there's a good terrace to enjoy them on. Plus delicious salads, home-made wine and pizza too, all served up by helpful staff.

Chadiri Restaurant GEORGIAN $$

(Chadari 1; mains 8-20 GEL; ⊙10am-11pm; 🔊) Chadiri does good Georgian dishes including specialities such as veal *khashlama* (meat braised with herbs and onions) and foil-baked trout. It has great valley and mountain views, and a revered 900-year-old plane tree outside.

ℹ️ Information

Tourism Information Centre (⌨275317; Erekle II 9; ⊙9am-6pm Mon-Thu & Sat, 10am-4pm Fri, 10am-5pm Sun) Helpful office upstairs in a building with verandah on the main square. It can help arrange shared 4WDs to Tusheti, among other things.

ℹ️ Getting There & Away

Telavi has several *marshrutka* and taxi departure points:

New Bus Station (⌨272083; Alazanis gamziri)

Old Bus Station (⌨271619; Alazanis gamziri)

Roki Bus Station (Alazanis gamziri)

Shared taxis to Tbilisi (10 GEL, 1¾ hours) wait at the top of Alazanis gamziri. *Marshrutky* to Ikalto (0.50 GEL) go about hourly, 8am to 6pm, from Chavchavadze.

Around Telavi

The villages and lovely countryside around Telavi are full of fascinating wineries and old castles, palaces, monasteries and churches. Public transport reaches most of them, but you can pack a lot more into your day by taking a taxi tour. Most Telavi accommodation places either have their own vehicles or can organise one to take you to several destinations in a trip for 70 GEL to 80 GEL. Knowledgeable, English-speaking **David Luashvili** (⌨593761216, 551300620; purgatorium@rambler.ru) is a recommended driver-guide.

Ikalto იყალთო

Ikalto Monastery MONASTERY

(⊙9am-6pm; 🅿) This monastery, beautifully situated in a cypress grove, was one of two famous medieval Georgian Neoplatonist academies, the other being Gelati near Kutaisi. Shota Rustaveli, the national poet, is thought to have studied here. The main Transfiguration Church was built in the 8th and 9th centuries. The roofless building along the south side of the compound was the Academy; an 8th-century stone wine press survives to its left (Georgian monasteries have always been enthusiastic winemakers).

The monastery is 2km uphill from the Telavi–Akhmeta road: turn off just after the 54/19 Km post. *Marshrutky* from Telavi terminate in Ikalto village, leaving you with a pleasant-enough 1.5km road walk up to the monastery.

Alaverdi ალავერდი

Alaverdi Cathedral CATHEDRAL

(⊙8am-6pm; 🅿) At the beginning of the 11th century, when Georgia was entering its cultural and political golden age, King Kvirike of Kakheti had a majestic cathedral built – at 50m tall, Alaverdi Cathedral remained the tallest church in Georgia for nearly a millennium. Situated 20km northwest of Telavi, its exterior is classically proportioned with majestic rounded arches but minimal decoration. Inside, the church has a beautiful spacious harmony, with light entering from 25 high slit windows.

Note the 16th-century St-George-and-dragon fresco over the west door. The *Virgin and Child* high in the apse is from the 11th century.

Also in the cathedral compound are the summer palace of Shah Abbas' governor (now the bishop's residence) and the Alaverdi Marani winery. The millennium-old winery, recently renovated, makes some of Georgia's best wines: it's not generally open to visitors but the cafe across the road sells bottles of traditionally made Alaverdi wine proudly bearing the slogan 'Since 1011', for a (by Georgian standards) whopping 75 GEL to 100 GEL.

The late-September religious-cum-grape-harvest festivities of **Alaverdoba** last several days, with people coming from remote mountain areas to worship, celebrate and enjoy the local wine.

Gremi   გრემი

Gremi Fortress   FORTRESS
(admission to tower 3 GEL; ⊘ 9am-6pm Tue-Sun; P) This picturesque brick citadel stands beside the Telavi–Kvareli road, 19km from Telavi. Kvareli-bound *marshrutky* will stop here. From 1466 to 1672 Gremi was the capital of Kakheti, but the town down to the west of the citadel was totally devastated by Shah Abbas in 1616. Within the citadel, the Church of the Archangels was built in 1565 by King Levan (who is buried inside) and contains frescoes from 1577. You can climb up inside the adjacent 15th-century tower-palace.

By the road below stands a large portrait of the Kakhetian Queen Ketevan, who was tortured to death by Abbas for refusing to renounce Christianity. A small roadside **museum** (admission 3 GEL; ⊘ 10am-6pm Tue-Sun; P) contains explanatory panels on old Gremi, plus artefacts from the site.

Nekresi   ნეკრესი

Nekresi Monastery   MONASTERY
Nekresi's early Georgian architecture and the views across the Alazani valley from its hillside-woodland site are marvellous. The monastery is 4km off the Kvareli road from a turning 10km past Gremi (Kvareli-bound *marshrutky* will drop you at the turn-off). Vehicles must park 1.5km before the monastery; from there *marshrutky* (1 GEL return trip) shuttle up and down the hill from about 9am to 5pm, approximately mid-April to mid-December.

Considerable repair and reconstruction has been done in recent years. The first church you come to is a three-church basilica from the 8th and 9th centuries, with a plan unique to early Georgian churches, the three naves being divided by solid walls into what are effectively three churches. Nekresi's tiny first church (one of the earliest in Georgia, dating from the 4th century) stands in the centre of the complex. Beside it stands a 9th-century bishop's palace, complete with wine cellar and a 16th-century tower. Immediately east is the main Church of the Assumption, another three-church basilica, from the 6th to 7th centuries, with 17th-century

murals adorning its smoke-blackened interior.

Tsinandali   წინანდალი

This village, home of a famous white wine and site of the storied Chavchavadze estate, lies 7km southeast of Telavi. The Shumi (p104) winery is next door to the estate, and the Schuchmann (p104) winery is just 4km west in Kisiskhevi village.

★ **Chavchavadze Estate**   PALACE, GARDENS
(www.tsinandali.com/index_en.html; gardens 2 GEL, museum & park incl guide in Georgian, English or Russian 5 GEL, with tasting 1/several wines 7/20 GEL; ⊘ 10am-7pm; P) Prince Alexander Chavchavadze (1786–1846) was one of the most colourful and influential characters in Georgian history, and the palace and gardens he created at Tsinandali are a don't-miss stop on any Kakheti tour. The palace tour takes you around half a dozen rooms restored in 19th century style and relates interesting episodes from the family story. The park is beautifully laid out in an English style, with venerable trees and exotic plants such as ginkgo, sequoia and yucca.

The multi-talented Chavchavadze was born into elite circles in St Petersburg as the son of Kakheti-Kartli's ambassador to Russia. He learned seven languages and was an influential Romantic poet and translator, helping to introduce European Enlightenment ideals to Georgia – as well as the grand piano, horse-drawn carriage and billiards. He rose to lieutenant-general in the Russian army but also joined Georgian rebellions against Russian rule (for which he spent time in exile). His homes at Tsinandali and in Tbilisi hosted illustrious visitors including writers Dumas, Pushkin, Lermontov and Griboedov – and he was a pioneer of European winemaking techniques in Georgia, helping to give Kakheti its current premier position in the Georgian wine world. (His famous cellars, containing 16,000 bottles, are being renovated for eventual opening for visits.)

In 1854 Lezgin tribesmen from Dagestan ransacked the Chavchavadze palace, kidnapping 23 women and children (what we see now is the house that was rebuilt after the Lezgin attack). Alexander's son David had to mortgage the house to ransom the hostages. He was unable to repay the loan and the house passed to Tsar Alexander III.

KAKHETI WINERIES

Visiting a few of Kakheti's wineries is a must while you're here. With about 60% of Georgia's vineyards (225 sq km), making wine by both the traditional *qvevri* method (p121) and modern European-style techniques, this is a region where wine plays a big part in daily life even by Georgian standards.

Kakheti's five main appellations of origin are Tsinandali (dry whites from Rkatsiteli grapes mixed with 15% to 20% Mtsvane); Mukuzani (quality dry reds from the Saperavi grape); Kindzmarauli (dry and semisweet Saperavi reds); Akhasheni (dry Saperavi reds); and Napareuli (whites and Saperavi reds).

Many wineries welcome visitors for tours and tastings. Some have restaurants and even hotels. The **Kakheti Wine Guild** (☑350-279090; www.kwg.ge; Rustaveli 1, Telavi; ☺10am-7pm) can help organise visits; it also sells over 100 types of wine direct. Here are four recommended and varied wineries within reach of Telavi, none requiring reservations for tastings and tours.

Shumi (☑598985130, 598503501; www.shumi.ge; Tsinandali; tour & 4-wine tasting free; ☺10am-6pm; ⓟ) This interesting smallish winery produces wines of numerous appellations under the Shumi and Iberiuli labels, and has a vineyard of about 400 vine varieties, along with a museum housing some astonishingly old wine-related objects. Tastings take place in a pretty garden.

Schuchmann (☑577508005; www.schuchmann-wines.com; Kisiskhevi; tour & tasting per person with 3/5/7 wines 15/25/35 GEL; ☺10am-evening; ⓟ) A very professional modern operation 7km southeast of central Telavi, producing 1.5 million bottles a year – 30% is *qvevri* wine (under the Vinoterra label) and the rest 'European' wine, fermented and aged in stainless-steel tanks, under the Schuchmann label.

There's also an excellent **hotel** (p101) here, and you can have lunch for 30 GEL to 50 GEL.

Twins Old Cellar (☑595226404; www.cellar.ge; Napareuli; tour & tasting 22 GEL; ☺9am-10pm; ⓟ) A family-run operation making *qvevri* and European wine, 23km north of Telavi. Visits include its comprehensive *qvevri* wine museum and tasting of three wines and one *chacha*. It also has a small **hotel** (☑595226404, 551747474; www.cellar.ge; Napareuli; r incl breakfast 80-120 GEL; ⓟ☺✳☺) overlooking vineyards, and a restaurant.

Winery Khareba (☑32-2497770; www.winery-khareba.com; Kvareli; tour with 2-wine tasting European/qvevri wines 10/12 GEL, without tasting 3 GEL; ☺10am-8pm May–mid-Nov, 10am-6pm mid-Nov–Apr; ⓟ) What's special here is the 7.7km of wine tunnels, dug out of a hillside in the early 1960s for storing and ageing wine at constant temperatures. Today the tunnels store more than 25,000 bottles of the Khareba company's European and *qvevri* wines. Tours go into part of the tunnels (where tastings also take place) then up to the viewing tower and restaurant.

It's a 4.5km drive east from Kvareli town centre.

Sighnaghi   სიღნაღი

☑ 355 / POP 2150

Sighnaghi is the prettiest town in Kakheti, sitting on a hilltop 60km southeast of Telavi and full of 18th- and 19th-century architecture with an Italianate feel. A big tourism-oriented renovation program has seen a rash of new accommodation spring up, but the town's original style has been maintained. Sighnaghi has wonderful views over the Alazani valley to the Caucasus beyond, and is a pleasant place to spend a night or two. Hopefully they will have stopped the rented quad-bikes roaring up and down the main street by the time you get there.

Sighnaghi was originally developed in the 18th century by King Erekle II, partly as a refuge for the area's populace against Lezgin and Persian attacks.

⊙ Sights & Activities

Sighnaghi Museum   MUSEUM
(Rustavelis chikhi 8; admission 3 GEL; ☺10am-6pm Tue-Sun) This well-displayed, modern

museum has good exhibits on Kakheti archaeology and history, and a room of 16 paintings by the great Kakheti-born artist Pirosmani – the biggest collection of his work after the National Gallery in Tbilisi.

Walls — ARCHITECTURE

Most of Erekle II's 4km defensive wall still stands, with 23 towers and each of its six gates named after a local village. Part of the wall runs along Chavchavadze on the hilltop on the northwest side of town, where you can enter the tiny Stepan Tsminda Church inside a tower. Another stretch runs down beside Gorgasali on the northeast side of town. Here you can climb up inside one tower and walk atop the walls down to two more.

Living Roots — HORSE RIDING

(www.travellivingroots.com; per 1/2/3hr 35/60/85 GEL) Living Roots does recommended horse rides, for all levels of experience, from its ranch in the hills just outside Sighnaghi. You can make arrangements through Pheasant's Tears.

🛏 Sleeping

Sighnaghi has a few good hotels and plenty of guesthouses (mostly with shared bathrooms), several of which are on or just off Gorgasali, the street leading north down to the Tsnori road.

David Zandarashvili's — GUESTHOUSE $$

(Hotel Family; ☑231029, 599750510; david zandarashvili@yahoo.com; Tsminda Giorgi 11; s/d/tr/q without bath 30/40/45/60 GEL, with bath s 50 GEL, D 60-80GEL, breakfast 7 GEL, dinner 20-25 GEL; ☺@🛜) The hospitable family here provides good rooms and views and great food and home-made wine, and their house is deservedly a travellers' favourite. Top-floor rooms, with private bathroom, are attractive and bright, especially those with balconies overlooking the valley. They offer reasonably priced day tours including to Davit Gareja.

Kusika Guest House — GUESTHOUSE $$

(☑599099812; kusikashvili.ilia@rambler.ru; Gorgasali 15; r 50 GEL, breakfast 10 GEL; 🅿✳🛜) This friendly little place has a vine-shaded courtyard with superb views over the Alazani valley to the distant Caucasus, and four cosy, clean rooms, two of them enjoying the same panoramas. The breakfasts are great and it's altogether a very nice find.

Nana's Guesthouse — GUESTHOUSE $$

(☑599795093; www.facebook.com/pages/nanas-guest-house/268413209818; Sarajishvili 2; dm 25 GEL, s 30-50 GEL, d 60-70 GEL, f 120 GEL, breakfast 7 GEL; ☺@🛜) English-speaking Nana Kokiashvili has four good, big rooms and wide balconies in her fine 18th-century house overlooking the central Bebris Park, and provides home-cooked, organic breakfasts and plenty of help organising transport and excursions.

Guesthouse MATE — GUESTHOUSE $$

(☑598899799; m.axmeteli@mail.ru; Gorgasali 20; per person 25 GEL, breakfast/dinner 10/15 GEL; 🅿☺✳@🛜) MATE is a very good-value guesthouse with a lovely garden and big meals with home-made wine served by the welcoming owner Manana. Rooms, for up to five people, are carpeted, comfy and slightly frilly (the best are the newer ones on the upper floor).

Central Guest House — GUESTHOUSE $$

(☑592404031; www.facebook.com/Sighnaghi CentralGuesthouse; 9 Apri No 30; dm/d/tr/ste 15/60/70/80 GEL, breakfast 10 GEL; 🅿☺✳@🛜) Just off one of the central squares, Erekle II moedani, and overlooking a deep, green valley, the Central offers six neat, clean, wood-floored rooms with private bathroom, in a recently converted 200-year-old house. The brick-walled dining room is decked with historical photos and artefacts, which your friendly English-speaking hostess Ana likes to explain to guests.

🍴 Eating & Drinking

★ Pheasant's Tears — GEORGIAN $$

(www.pheasantstears.com; Baratashvili 18; tasting of 4 wines & 1 chacha 15 GEL, meals 25 GEL, tasting & meal for 2 70 GEL; ☺11am-11pm; ☑) 🍷 Pheasant's Tears, a Georgian-American joint venture, makes top-class natural wines by the traditional *qvevri* method at its vineyards out of town. Here in Sighnaghi it offers wine tastings and delicious Georgian meals prepared from fresh, mainly organic and local produce, which you can enjoy in a pretty garden-courtyard.

Restaurant Nikala — GEORGIAN $$

(Lolashvili 9; mains 5-17 GEL; ☺11am-11pm; ☑) A decent little place on the main street for Georgian fare, including plenty of bean, mushroom and salad options.

ℹ Information

Tourism Information Centre (☑ 232414; Kostava 10; ☺ 10am-7pm Jun-Sep, 10am-6pm Oct-May) Just off Erekle II moedani.

ℹ Getting There & Away

Marshrutky depart from the yard behind the police station on Erekle II moedani to Tbilisi (7 GEL, 1¾ hours, six daily) and Telavi (4.50 GEL, 1½ hours, 9.15am to Saturday). For *marshrutky* to Lagodekhi and Dedoplistskaro, and further services to Telavi, head 7km east down the hill to Tsnori (by *marshrutka* 1 GEL, every half-hour 9.45am to 5.15pm Monday to Friday; by taxi 4 GEL from in front of Hotel Kabadoni).

Around Sighnaghi

Bodbe Convent (☺ 9am-6pm; Ⓟ), the revered final resting place of St Nino, is set among tall cypresses 2km south of Sighnaghi, a pleasant walk on country roads. The little church was originally built, over the saint's grave, by King Mirian in the 4th century. It has been rebuilt and renovated several times since. Nino's tomb, partly silver-covered, with a bejewelled turquoise cloisonné halo, is in a small chapel in its southeast corner.

A steep path leads 800m down to a small chapel built over St Nino's Spring, which reputedly burst forth after she prayed on this spot. Pilgrims queue up to drink and splash themselves with the holy water.

Davit Gareja
დავით გარეჯა

On the border with Azerbaijan, the ancient monastery complex of Davit Gareja (or Gareji) is one of the most remarkable of Georgia's historic sites. Its uniqueness is heightened by a lunar, semidesert landscape that turns green and blooms with flowers in early summer. Davit Gareja comprises about 15 monasteries spread over a remote area (most long abandoned), but visitors usually just see two – Lavra (which has been restored since Soviet times and is now again inhabited by monks) and, on the hill above it, Udabno, which has beautiful frescoes.

Lavra, the original monastery here, was founded by Davit Gareja, one of the 13 ascetic Syrian fathers who returned from the Middle East to spread Christianity in Georgia in the 6th century. The complex grew until monasteries were spread over a wide area. Manuscripts were translated and copied, and a celebrated school of fresco painting flourished here. The monasteries were destroyed by the Mongols in 1265, revived in the 14th century by Giorgi V the Brilliant, sacked by Timur, and then destroyed on Easter night 1615 when Shah Abbas' soldiers killed 6000 monks and trashed many of the artistic treasures. The monasteries never regained their former importance, though they remained active until the end of the 19th century. During the Soviet era, the military used the area for exercises and vandalised the monasteries.

It takes two to three hours to explore Lavra and Udabno. In July and August it can get fearfully hot here by the middle of the day, so an early start, getting here by 10am, is ideal.

◉ Sights

Lavra MONASTERY

The Lavra monastery is on three levels, with buildings from many periods. You enter by a gateway decorated with reliefs illustrating stories of the monks' harmony with the natural world. Inside you descend to a courtyard with the caves of Davit and his Kakhetian disciple Lukiane along one side, and the 6th-century cave church **Peristvaleba** (Transfiguration Church) on the other side. Davit's tomb sits to the right of the church's icon screen.

★ **Udabno Monastery** MONASTERY

Udabno comprises a series of caves along a steep escarpment looking down to grassy plains in Azerbaijan. Some contain fascinating frescoes painted in the 10th to 13th centuries. The exact line of the Georgia–Azerbaijan border up here has not yet been finally demarcated, and you may find Azerbaijan border guards patrolling here; they are not normally any hindrance to visiting the caves unless there is a flare-up of border tensions.

To reach Udabno, take the path uphill beside the church shop outside Lavra monastery. Watch out for poisonous vipers, including in the caves and especially from April to June. At a watchtower overlooking Lavra, take the path straight up the hill. In about 10 minutes you reach a metal railing. Follow this to the top of the ridge, then to the left along the far side of the ridge (where the railing deteriorates to a series of posts). The caves above the path here are the Udabno monastery.

VASHLOVANI PROTECTED AREAS

Down in remote far southeast Kakheti, Georgia's ever-changing landscapes take yet another twist. Beyond the town of Dedoplistskaro, expanses of wheat fields give way to a strange semi-desert zone where eroded badlands alternate with steppe grasslands, canyons, savannah, ancient wild pistachio forests and woodlands along the Alazani River (the border with Azerbaijan). It's a fascinating area for any nature lover. The 370-sq-km **Vashlovani Protected Areas** (ვაშლოვანის დაცული ტერიტორიები; www.apa.gov.ge) harbour a very high concentration of species including 46 mammals, 135 birds, 30 reptiles and 600 plants. The mammals include brown bear, wolf, otter, hyenas and goitered gazelles recently reintroduced from Azerbaijan. Vashlovani's most famous inhabitant, a solitary male leopard dubbed Noah who probably wandered in from Iran, has sadly not been seen since 2010.

The best times to visit, with moderate temperatures, plants in bloom and wildlife more active, are from April to mid-June and September to mid-November. July and August are excruciatingly hot.

Also well worth visiting near Dedoplistskaro are **Eagles Canyon** (Artsivis Kheoba), home to enormous vultures and black storks, and the ancient, crag-top Khornabuji Fortress.

The excellent **Visitors Centre** (☑577101849; nseturidze13@gmail.com; Baratashvili 5, Dedoplistskaro; ☉9am-6pm) in Dedoplistskaro has an interesting museum, good rooms (single/double 25/30 GEL) and a guest kitchen. All visitors must register here, and when you go to the reserve Georgian border guards will want to check your passport.

Sleeping

The Visitors Centre rooms are a good option before or after visiting the reserve.

If you have time, stay overnight in one of the six well-kept tourist bungalows on the banks of the Alazani River at **Mijnis Kure Bungalows** (r 40 GEL; ℗). Each bungalow has two single beds, electricity, and a bathroom with hot shower. You're a long, long way from civilisation here! There's a drinking-water well but bring mosquito repellent as well as food. Make reservations at the Visitors Centre.

Getting There & Around

The Visitors Centre can help arrange trips in the reserve (around 200 GEL for a day trip, 200 GEL to 300 GEL for two days). If you're driving yourself, you'll need a 4WD vehicle and a good GPS to navigate the labyrinthine, often very rough, tracks.

Marshrutky run from Dedoplistskaro to Telavi (7 GEL, two hours) at 7.30 and 8.30am, and to Tbilisi (7 GEL, three hours) about hourly from 7.30am to 4.30pm.

The most outstanding frescoes are about halfway along the hillside. Walk along till you reach some caves numbered with green paint. Seventy metres past cave 50, a side path heads up and back to cave 36, the monastery's **refectory**, where the monks had to kneel to eat at low stone tables. It's decorated with beautiful light-toned frescoes, the principal one being an 11th-century Last Supper. Further up above here are the **Annunciation Church** (cave 42), with very striking frescoes showing Christ and his disciples (you need some agility to get inside it); and **St George's Church** (cave 41).

Return to the main path and continue 25m to the left to Udabno's **main church**. Paintings here show Davit Gareja and his disciple Lukiane surrounded by deer, depicting the story that deer gave them milk when they were wandering hungry in this remote wilderness. Below them are Kakhetian princes.

The path eventually climbs to a stone chapel on the clifftop, then heads down back to the watchtower you passed earlier.

🛏 Sleeping & Eating

★**Oasis Club**　　　　HOSTEL, HOTEL $
(Khutebi Hotel; ☑574805563; www.facebook.com/theudabnohostel; Udabno village; incl breakfast dm 20 GEL; r per person 30-40 GEL; ℗◉☎☷) This unlikely Polish-run hostel-hotel-restaurant is indeed an oasis – of relaxation and fun, with occasional wild party nights, in what's almost the middle

of nowhere at semi-abandoned Udabno village (not to be confused with Udabno monastery), 14km before Lavra monastery on the road from Sagarejo.

For sleeping, you have a choice between the 20-bed hostel or cosy wooden hotel rooms with private bath. At the restaurant-bar (dishes 5 GEL to 12 GEL), cheerful staff serve up good salads, soups, *khachapuri* and other dishes, and plenty of beverages. It's great for a halt on the road even if you don't stay. The walking distance to Lavra cross-country is 8km.

Getting There & Away

From about mid-April to mid-October **Gareji Line** (☎551951447; www.facebook.com/gareji.line; return 25 GEL; ⊙mid-Apr–mid-Oct) runs a daily minibus between Tbilisi and Davit Gareja, departing at 11am from Pushkinis skver, just off Tavisuplebis moedani, and getting back there about 7pm. You get 2½ to three hours at Lavra and Udabno monasteries, plus a stop at Oasis Club on the way back. The ticket allows you to come back any day, so you can stay over at Oasis Club if you wish.

There are also day tours from Tbilisi with some hostels and agencies, or you can take a *marshrutka* from Navtlughi bus station to Sagarejo (3 GEL, one hour, every 20 minutes), and a taxi from there to Davit Gareja (return trip 60 GEL to 80 GEL).

From Sighnaghi, a taxi day trip to Davit Gareja costs around 100 GEL, or you could take a Tbilisi-bound *marshrutka* as far as Sagarejo and a taxi from there.

Marshrutky to Udabno village (6 GEL, 1½ hours) leave Navtlughi at 4pm on Monday, Wednesday, Friday and Sunday, making the return trip at 8.30am the same days.

Lagodekhi Protected Areas

ლაგოდეხის დაცული ტერიტორიები

This 244-sq-km **nature reserve** (www.apa.gov.ge) climbs to heights of more than 3000m in the Caucasus above the small town of Lagodekhi in eastern Kakheti near the Azerbaijan border. It features deep river valleys, alpine lakes and some of Georgia's best-preserved forests, and is home to several hundred East Caucasian tur, deer and chamois.

Activities

There are good half-day walks to two waterfalls, and from about late June to mid-October you can hike a very scenic 24km trail from Lagodekhi up to picturesque **Shavi Kldeebis Tba** (Black Rocks Lake) on the Russian border (three days there and back, with an ascent of 2200m), sleeping at a **mountain shelter** (bed/camping per person 15/5 GEL) about halfway to the lake. In 2016 a second trail between the lake and Lagodekhi is due to open, with another shelter, making the trip into a circular rather than there-and-back route.

Sleeping

Lagodekhi town has several decent accommodation options.

Kiwi House GUESTHOUSE $
(☎551245072; thekiwihouse.lagodekhi@gmail.com; Vashlovani 35; s/d 25/50 GEL, per person without bathroom 15-20 GEL, breakfast/lunch/dinner 5/10/15 GEL; P 🛜) A friendly English-speaking family home, with most guest rooms in a separate block at the back. Vegetarian meals available. It's 1.3km down the street from the reserve entrance.

Kavkasioni Guest House GUESTHOUSE $$
(Caucasus Hostel; ☎599856640; irina-orujashvili@mail.ru; Vashlovani 136, Lagodekhi; s/d 30/50 GEL, breakfast/dinner 10/15 GEL; ❄🛜) There's a warm welcome here, just 100m from the reserve entrance, and the seven rooms are bright and spotless, with shiny wood floors. Two have private bathrooms.

Information

Plentiful information is available at the English-speaking **visitors centre** (☎577101890; Vashlovani 197; ⊙9am-6pm) at the main reserve entrance, 2km up from the main road in Lagodekhi. It rents tents (per day 10 GEL), sleeping bags (5 GEL) and horses (50 GEL).

Getting There & Away

Marshrutky leave Lagodekhi's bus station for Tbilisi (7 GEL, 2½ hours, about hourly 6.30am to 5.30pm) and Telavi (6 GEL, 1¾ hours, five daily, 8am to 2.15pm).

A taxi to or from the Azerbaijan border at Matsimi, 4km southeast of Lagodekhi, costs 4 GEL. From the Azerbaijan side you can take a taxi to Balakən (AZN4) or Zaqatala (around AZN10).

You'll find moneychangers on both sides of the border and along the main road in Lagodekhi town, which also has several ATMs.

SAMTSKHE-JAVAKHETI

The tongue-twisting southern flank of Georgia is a highly scenic region whose biggest attractions are the spectacular cave city of Vardzia and beautiful Borjomi-Kharagauli National Park, which offers good mountain hiking. Landscapes are very varied, from the alpine forests and meadows around Borjomi and Bakuriani to the bare volcanic canyons of the Vardzia area.

Samtskhe-Javakheti (სამცხე-ჯავახეთი) was part of Tao-Klarjeti, a cradle of medieval Georgian culture that extended well into what's now northeast Turkey. Tao-Klarjeti fell under Ottoman rule from the 1550s to the 1870s, was briefly part of independent Georgia after the Russian Revolution, and was then divided between Turkey and Bolshevik Georgia in 1921. Javakheti is the more elevated southeastern half of Samtskhe-Javakheti. Bordering Armenia, it has a majority Armenian population.

Borjomi ბორჯომი

📍 367 / POP 14,000

Famous throughout the former Soviet Union for its salty-sour, love-it-or-hate-it fizzy mineral water, Borjomi is a small resort town in the green valley of the swift Mtkvari River. Russian soldiers discovered a health-giving mineral spring here in 1810, and Count Vorontsov, a Russian governor, later developed Borjomi as a resort, one that became particularly fashionable when Duke Mikhail Romanov (brother to Tsar Alexander II) built a palace at nearby Likani in the 1890s.

GEORGIA BORJOMI

Samtskhe-Javakheti

The town, which was considerably smartened up a few years ago, is popular with Georgian holidaymakers and people visiting Borjomi-Kharagauli National Park. It's also a good jumping-off point for Vardzia.

The main street, Rustaveli, runs along the northern bank of the Mtkvari. Just before you reach the heart of town (from the Tbilisi direction), a white suspension bridge crosses the river to the southern half of town, where Borjomi Park train station and the mineral water park are found. Rustaveli becomes Meskheti 300m west of the bridge, with the bus station another 300m along, and the national park visitors centre a further 1km.

◎ Sights & Activities

Mineral Water Park   PARK
(Tsentraluri Parki; 9 Aprili; admission May-Sep 0.50 GEL, Oct-Apr free; ☺10am-11pm; ♦) Borjomi's mineral water park, dating back to 1850, occupies a narrow, wooded valley. To find it, cross the little Borjomula River just east of Borjomi Park train station, turn right along 9 Aprili and go 600m. The original warm mineral spring, named Ekaterina Spring, sits beneath a pavilion straight ahead of the park entrance (you can fill bottles from it). The commercial Borjomi bottling plants today draw their water from other mineral springs – there are about 40 in the area.

If you walk about 3km upstream, beyond the 'attractions' of the park proper, you'll find a small, spring-fed swimming pool with a constant temperature of about 27°C.

Borjomi Museum of Local Lore   MUSEUM
(Tsminda Nino 5; adult/student 3/1 GEL, tour 15 GEL; ☺10am-6pm, closed Mon Sep-May) Housed in the former Romanov offices, off the western end of Rustaveli, this diverse collection includes the first-ever bottle of Borjomi mineral water (1890) and other displays on the waters, plus china and glass from the Romanov palace, and sizeable exhibits of stuffed wildlife and Soviet historical paintings.

Borjomi Plateau   WALKING
A **cable car** (one-way 3 GEL; ☺10am-11pm approx May-Sep; ♦) beside the Mineral Water Park entrance runs up to a hilltop Ferris wheel and the pine woods of the Borjomi Plateau (nice for a walk). About 2km south along the road from the Ferris wheel, a trail leads down to the 27°C pool above the Mineral Water Park and you can return to town that way.

🛏 Sleeping

Borjomi has a handful of hotels, and more than 100 guesthouses and homestays.

Hotel Victoria   GUESTHOUSE $
(☎222631, 593120283; raisa.gelashvili@mail.ru; Kostava 31; per person incl breakfast with/without bath 35/30 GEL; ☜) A friendly place with 10 good-value rooms for two to four people, including two duplexes (good for families), and all attractively pine-panelled. It's handily located 200m up the hill from the south side of the suspension bridge.

Marina Zulmatashvili's Guesthouse   GUESTHOUSE $
(☎222323, 598184550; marinasguesthouse@gmail.com; Shroma 2; per person with/without breakfast 30/25 GEL; ☻☜) One of the best-value guesthouses, in a welcoming, cosy home with four upstairs guestrooms. From the south side of the suspension bridge, go up Kostava until it bends left downhill. Here fork right, then turn right at the end, then take the first left. The house is 60m along on the left. If full, the owners can find you rooms in other houses nearby.

Guest House Besarioni   GUESTHOUSE $
(☎599779055; besikilursmanashvili@yahoo.com; Pirosmani 32; s 30-40 GEL, d 40-50 GEL, tr 60 GEL, breakfast 10 GEL; ℗☻☜) The friendly family here, speaking some English, have (for now) just two rooms sharing a bathroom, but everything is new and spotlessly clean. Guests can use the kitchen. It's up on the hill north of Rustaveli.

Borjomi Park Guest House   GUESTHOUSE $$
(☎555572557; Erekle 7; r 100 GEL, breakfast 10 GEL; ☻☜) More like a small hotel, this is a good midrange option where the clean, cosy rooms boast pine floors and a spot of art or photography to brighten things up. It's at the foot of the street leading up to the Mineral Water Park.

Green Rose Guest House   GUESTHOUSE $$
(☎599901117; Pirosmani 13; r 70-130 GEL, breakfast 10 GEL; ℗☻☜) One of many guesthouses in the streets up above the north side of Rustaveli, this is a solidly comfy option with clean, medium-size rooms (two have private bathroom) and a sizeable garden. The owner speaks a little English. No green roses, though!

✗ Eating

★ Cafe Old Borjomi   GEORGIAN **$$**
(Kostava 17; mains 6-15 GEL; ⊙11am-11pm; 🛜)
Very popular for its well prepared *mtsvadi,
khachapuri, shkmeruli* and trout in walnut
sauce, in a vaguely tavernish, wood-walled
space, Old Borjomi also manages friendly
service. There are only eight or 10 tables and
you may have to wait for one on summer
evenings.

Inka Cafe   CAFE **$$**
(9 Aprili 2; dishes 8-15 GEL; ⊙10am-10pm; 🛜) A
smart, wood-panelled cafe, with sepia-tint
photos of tsarist-era Borjomi, Inka does real
coffee (Americano; 4 GEL) and reasonable
khachapuri, omelettes, salads and cakes.

ℹ Information

Tourist Information Centre (📋221397; tic
borjomi@gmail.com; Rustaveli; ⊙10am-6pm
Mon-Sat, closed Sat Nov-Mar) In a glass pavilion
near the north side of the suspension bridge.

ℹ Getting There & Away

Marshrutka departures from Borjomi's **bus
station** (Meskheti 8) include the following:
Akhaltsikhe (4 GEL, one hour, about hourly)
Bakuriani (3 GEL, one hour, seven daily)
Batumi (17 GEL, five hours, 9am)
Gori (5 GEL, 1½ hours, 7.30am and 10.45am)
Khashuri (2 GEL, 30 minutes, half-hourly
9.30am to 5.30pm)
Tbilisi (6 GEL, three hours, hourly 7am to 6pm)

At Khashuri, 32km northeast of Borjomi, you can
change to *marshrutky* for Tbilisi, Kutaisi, Zugdidi
or Batumi.

Borjomi taxi drivers offer day trips to Vardzia,
with stops including Akhaltsikhe's Rabati and
two other forts, for 120 GEL for four people. The
Tourism Information Centre can book this for
you with English-speaking drivers.

Slow *elektrichka* trains leave Borjomi Park
train station, just east of the suspension bridge,
for Gori (2 GEL, four hours) and Tbilisi (2 GEL,
five hours) at 7am and 4.40pm.

Borjomi-Kharagauli National Park

ბორჯომ-ხარაგაულის
ეროვნული პარკი

The ranges of the Lesser Caucasus in southern Georgia are less well known and not as
high as the Great Caucasus, but they still
contain some very beautiful and wild country. **Borjomi-Kharagauli National Park**
(www.apa.gov.ge) provides the perfect chance
to get out into this landscape.

⚡ Activities

The park spreads over 851 sq km of forested hills and alpine meadows up to 2642m
high, north and west of Borjomi, and is
crisscrossed by 10 marked walking and
horse trails of various lengths. Diverse
wildlife includes brown bears, wolves and
chamois. The park is open all year but from
about December to March/April there is
snow in at least some areas (there are two
snowshoe trails). Overnight accommodation is available at six basic shelters, and
camping is possible too.

All visitors must obtain a permit beforehand from one of the two visitors centres –
which are also very helpful for information
and equipment rental. Several trails start
at the Likani ranger station, 5km from the
Borjomi visitors centre (about 6 GEL by taxi
from Borjomi town). A good day-hike of
13km, with an ascent and descent of 800m,
is Trail 6, which comes out on the Akhaltsikhe road at Qvabiskhevi. Trail 1 (Likani
ranger station to Marelisi ranger station) is
a 43km, three-day route crossing the park
from south to north via Mt Lomis Mta
(2198m). The longest and hardest route is
Trail 2 (Atskuri to Marelisi), a 54km north-
south route taking three or four days.

🛏 Sleeping & Eating

Four basic wooden **tourist shelters** (per
person 10 GEL) provide accommodation inside
the park. They have spring water but you
need to carry a sleeping bag, food and cooking gear. You can also sleep at two ranger
shelters (though they have no water), and
there are 10 **camping sites** (per person 5 GEL).

Some villages around the park's fringes have guesthouses, convenient for the
beginning or end of some trails. They include **Marelisi Guesthouse** (📋599951421;
Marelisi; per person incl breakfast 30 GEL) at
Marelisi on the north side of the park, recommended for its excellent food; and the
hospitable **Nick & George Guesthouse**
(📋597982007, 555259355; maiaaitsuradze@gmx.
com; Atskuri; per person 30 GEL, breakfast/lunch/
dinner 10/15/20 GEL; 🍴🛜) at Atskuri, with
good food and wine, and horses available
for rides and treks.

ℹ Information

The park's **Borjomi visitors centre** (☑577640444, 577640480; borjomikharagauli @gmail.com; Meskheti 23, Borjomi; ⊗9am-6pm Mon-Fri, 9am-4pm Sat & Sun) is 1km west of Borjomi bus station. It sells a good trail map (3 GEL), issues the free permits everyone must obtain for visiting the park (bring your passport or ID card), and can furnish all the information you need, including on horse rentals (60 GEL per day including guide) and drinking water sources. You can pay here for your nights in the park, and rent tents (10 GEL per night) and sleeping bags (5 GEL per night). Permits are also available at the **Kharagauli visitors centre** (☑577101894; borjomikharagauli@gmail.com; Solomon Mepe 19, Kharagauli; ⊗9am-6pm Mon-Fri, 9am-4pm Sat & Sun).

ℹ Getting There & Away

Marshrutky running between Borjomi and Akhaltsikhe will drop you off or pick you up at Likani, Qvabiskhevi or Atskuri, near where several trails begin or end.

Bakuriani   ბაკურიანი

☑367 / POP 2000 / ELEV 1700M

Thirty kilometres up a winding road through pine-clad hills southeast of Borjomi, Bakuriani is the cheaper and more family-oriented of Georgia's two main ski resorts. It has a mountain-village atmosphere and the area is also good for mountain walks in summer, with ski lifts operating in July and August.

🏃 Activities

The ski season lasts from mid-December to the end of March. Taxis to the lifts (10 GEL from the town centre) have ski racks.

Didveli   SKIING
(www.didveli.com; ski pass per day child/adult 20/30 GEL, Jul & Aug 1/3 lifts 5/10 GEL; ⊗lifts 11am-8pm mid-Dec–Mar, to 6pm Jul & Aug) The recently expanded and upgraded Didveli ski zone has 14km of blue, red and black runs, and a combination of cable car, chairlift, draglift and funicular rising from 1800m to 2700m. The lifts start 4km south of the town centre.

Kokhta Gora   SKIING
The Kokhta Gora zone, on the slopes of 2156m Mt Kokhta on the east side of town, was reopening after improvements for the 2016 season. The Otsdakhutiani beginners' slopes, with toboggan as well as ski runs, are between here and the town centre.

🛏 Sleeping & Eating

In the ski season almost every house in Bakuriani has rooms to let, some for as little as 15 GEL per person. Many guesthouses and small and large hotels are scattered around the town centre and along the roads towards the ski slopes. Some close outside the ski season, though plenty are open in July and August.

Hotel Apollon   HOTEL **$$**
(☑599334499; www.apollon.ge; Aghmashenebeli 21; per person full board ski season US$40-65, other seasons 60-65 GEL; 🅿🛜) Apollon provides good, pine-floored rooms with balconies and comfortable wooden beds, satisfying meals in a cosy dining room, friendly staff, and billiards and table tennis for your spare moments. It's 800m up the Didveli road from the town centre, and open all year.

Edelweiss Guest House   GUESTHOUSE **$$**
(☑599506349; www.welcome.ge/edelweiss; Mta 19; per person full board ski season 60-70 GEL, summer 50 GEL; 🅿☺🛜🏊) In the town centre, 200m up the hill from the bus station, Edelweiss has spacious rooms and a small summer pool. Open all year.

Crystal Hotel & Spa   HOTEL **$$$**
(☑595461461; www.hotelcrystal.ge; Didveli; r full board ski season from US$200, summer from US$120; 🅿☺🛜🏊) One of the most luxurious hotels in Bakuriani, this is also one of the closest to the Didveli ski lifts (1km away, with a free shuttle service). The clean-lined, contemporary rooms are all equipped with tea and coffee makers, rain shower heads, writing desks and balconies. And it boasts Bakuriani's only spa, with a pool.

Restaurant Retro   GEORGIAN **$$**
(Aghmashenebeli 7; mains 5-15 GEL; ⊗9am-midnight) On the main street, Retro has a nicely rustic-styled basement restaurant serving up good Georgian classics such as *khinkali, mtsvadi* and *khashlama*.

ℹ Information

Tourism Information Centre (☑240036; mari.m@bk.ru; Aghmashenebeli 1; ⊗10am-6pm Mon-Fri) On the main street; sells a good map (5 GEL) showing day walks.

ℹ Getting There & Away

From the bus station on Tamar Mepe in the town centre, *marshrutky* run to Borjomi (3 GEL, one hour) at least hourly from 8am to 5pm, and to

Tbilisi (10 GEL, four hours) at least five times daily. A taxi to or from Borjomi costs 25 GEL.

Slow but scenic trains run to Bakuriani (1 GEL to 2 GEL, 2½ hours) from Borjomi's Chyornaya Rechka station (2km east of Borjomi centre) at 7.15am and 10.55am, returning at 10am and 2.15pm.

Akhaltsikhe ახალციხე

 365 / POP 18,000

The capital and biggest town of Samtskhe-Javakheti, Akhaltsikhe means 'New Castle' in Georgian. The Rabati castle dominating the town from the north side of the Potskhovi River hasn't been new since the 12th century but it was lavishly restored a few years ago, helping to turn a town that was previously a sad case of post-Soviet decline into a reasonably attractive stop and jumping-off point for Vardzia.

Until the 19th century the Rabati area around the castle was all there was of Akhaltsikhe. It was celebrated for its ethnic and religious diversity and tolerance, in a frontier area where different empires, kingdoms and peoples met. Rabati today still has Georgian Orthodox, Armenian Apostolic and Catholic churches, a synagogue and a mosque, and Akhaltsikhe still has a large Armenian population.

The newer parts of town are mostly on the south side of the river: cross the bridge near the foot of Rabati and bear right at two forks and you'll be on the main street, Kostava.

◉ Sights

Rabati Castle   CASTLE
(Kharischirashvili 1; foreigner/Georgian/student 7/5/2 GEL, guide foreign language/Georgian 20/10 GEL; ☺9am-8pm; Ⓟ) The eastern end of this large, impressive castle (the first part inside the main entrance) includes a hotel, restaurant, **tourism information centre** (☑225028; Kharischirashvili 1; ☺10am-6pm) and a couple of shops. Tickets are only needed to go up into the monumental part at the west end, with its mosque, citadel and museum. A tour (available in English, French or German) is a good idea to bring things alive.

Ponds and colonnaded pavilions are set before the stone-and-brick **Ahmadiyya Mosque** and two-storey *medrese* (Islamic school), built in the 1750s. The mosque (no longer used for religious purposes) now sports a dazzling new gold dome. Up to

the left rise the citadel and the **Samtskhe-Javakheti History Museum** (☺10am-6pm Tue-Sun), which spans the aeons from the 4th-millennium-BC Kura-Araxes Culture to Ottoman weaponry and 19th-century regional costumes.

🛏 Sleeping & Eating

Hotel Old Rabati   HOTEL **$**
(☑551945549; Tsikhisdziri 6; r 40 GEL; Ⓟ❄🛜) A likeable little place on the street leading up to Rabati Castle. Though three of the four rooms have no natural light, they all have bathrooms and good beds, and the front terrace is a sociable conversation spot. The manager speaks just a little Russian and can find you decent rooms in nearby houses if hers are full.

Hotel Star   HOTEL **$**
(☑593224224; www.facebook.com/akhaltsikhe hotelstar; Parnavaz Mepe 16; d with/without breakfast 60/50 GEL; ➿❄🛜) A satisfactory option in the central part of town with 12 well-kept, green or pink rooms, and a nice little courtyard cafe for breakfast or a beer.

Lomsia Hotel   HOTEL **$$$**
(☑222001; www.lomsiahotel.ge; Kostava 10; incl breakfast s US$75-90, d/tr US$125/160; Ⓟ➿❄🛜) A very good new town-centre hotel with large, carpeted rooms equipped with bedside lights and tea and coffee makers. Everything is sparkling clean, staff are professional and English-speaking, and it also has Akhaltsikhe's most polished **restaurant** (☑8am-11pm; mains 7-15 GEL; 🛜), serving good Georgian and European dishes.

Restorani Iveria   GEORGIAN **$**
(Rustaveli; mains 5-8 GEL; ☺10am-midnight) Just a block off the central park, the Iveria does pretty good (and inexpensive) *mtsvadi, khinkali,* salads and soups, and has a nice little beer garden.

❶ Getting There & Away

Marshrutka departures from the busy **bus station** (Tamarashvili), on the north side of the river near the foot of Rabati, include the following:
Batumi (via Khashuri; 20 GEL, six hours, 8.30am and 11.30am)
Borjomi (3 GEL, one hour, 30 daily, 6am to 7pm)
Khulo (15 GEL, 3½ hours, 10am, about April to October)
Kutaisi (10 GEL, 3½ hours, three daily)
Tbilisi (8 GEL, four hours, 21 daily, 6am to 7pm)

GEORGIA AKHALTSIKHE

Vardzia (4 GEL, 1½ hours, 10.30am, 3pm and 5.30pm)

Yerevan (Armenia; 25 GEL, seven hours, 7am)

TURKEY
One daily bus (3pm) heads to Ardahan, Turkey (30 GEL, 2½ hours) via the **Vale–Posof border crossing** (☉10am-11pm Georgia time), 20km southwest of Akhaltsikhe. From Ardahan there are buses onward to Istanbul and other Turkish destinations the following morning.

Sapara Monastery
საფარის მონასტერი

This **monastery** has a dramatic position clinging to a cliff edge about 12km southeast of Akhaltsikhe, and rivals Vardzia as one of the most beautiful places in the region (and receives a fraction of Vardzia's visitors). In existence since at least the 9th century, it became the residence of the local ruling family, the Jakelis, in the 13th century. The largest of Sapara's 12 churches, St Saba's, with outstanding frescoes, dates from that time.

Taxis charge around 20 GEL return trip from Akhaltsikhe (60 GEL or 70 GEL if combined with Vardzia).

Vardzia   ვარძია

The 60km drive into the wilderness from Akhaltsikhe to the cave city of Vardzia is as dramatic as any in Georgia outside the Great Caucasus. The road follows the upper Mtkvari River, passing through narrow canyons and then veering south at Aspindza along a particularly beautiful valley cutting like a green ribbon between arid, rocky hillsides. There are several places of interest along the way: taxi drivers are often happy to stop at one or two of them for no extra charge. You can see Vardzia in a day trip from Akhaltsikhe or Borjomi, but the Vardzia area is a magical one, and an overnight (or longer) stay is well worthwhile.

◉ Sights

Khertvisi Fortress   FORTRESS
This impressive 10th- to 14th-century fortress perches on a rocky crag above the meeting of the Paravani and Mtkvari Rivers, 45km southeast of Akhaltsikhe where the Vardzia road diverges from the main road to Akhalkalaki and Armenia.

Tmogvi Castle   FORTRESS
Eleven kilometres past Khertvisi Fortress towards Vardzia, atop a high rocky hill across the river (which flows far below in a gorge), the remains of the once near-impregnable Tmogvi Castle date back at least a millennium. You can walk to it in an hour or so (4km) up the west side of the valley from Vardzia – and continue north to Khertvisi, on off-road trails most of the way, if you want.

Vanis Qvabebi   MONASTERY, CAVE
(Vani Caves) About 4km south of Tmogvi village and 2km before Vardzia, a track heads 600m up from the road to this cave monastery that predated Vardzia by four centuries. It's almost as intriguing as Vardzia itself and far less visited. A handful of monks have reoccupied the caves at the bottom left of the complex, after centuries of abandonment. You can climb up to the little white domed church, high up the cliff, by a series of wooden ladders inside the rock.

★Vardzia   MONASTERY, CAVE
(adult/student 3/1 GEL, guide 15 GEL, audio guide 5 GEL; ☉10am-6pm) The remarkable cave city of Vardzia is a cultural symbol with a special place in Georgian hearts. King Giorgi III built a fortification here in the 12th century, and his daughter, Queen Tamar, established a cave monastery that grew into a holy city housing perhaps 2000 monks, renowned as a spiritual bastion of Georgia and of Christendom's eastern frontier. Its inhabitants lived in rock-hewn dwellings ranging over 13 floors. Altogether there are over 400 rooms, 13 churches and 25 wine cellars, and more are still being discovered.

A major earthquake in 1283 shook away the outer walls of many caves. In 1551 the Georgians were defeated by the Persians in a battle in the caves themselves, and Vardzia was looted. Since the end of Soviet rule Vardzia has again become a working monastery, with some caves inhabited by monks (and cordoned off to protect their privacy).

Guides, available at the ticket office, don't speak English but they have keys to some passages and caves that you can't otherwise enter.

At the heart of the cave complex is the **Church of the Assumption**, with its two-arched, bell-hung portico. The church's facade has gone, but the inside is beautiful. Frescoes painted at the time of its construction (1184–86) portray many New Testament scenes and, on the north wall, Giorgi III and Tamar before she married (shown by the fact that she is not wearing a wimple). To be allowed in the church, women must wear long skirts and head covering, and men must wear long trousers. The door to the left of the church door leads into a long tunnel (perhaps 150m), which climbs steps up inside the rock and emerges well above the church.

🛏 Sleeping & Eating

Valodia's Cottage HOTEL **$$**
(☑595642346; www.accommodationvardzia.ge; Koriskhevi; s/d/tr/f US$23/35/45/45, breakfast US$5, lunch US$8-10, dinner US$12-15; ☺Apr-Nov; ℗🛜) In a beautiful riverside setting 2.5km south from Vardzia, Valodia's offers comfy rooms, some with balcony or terrace, in new pine or stone buildings. There's good Georgian food, much of it home-grown, and a lovely garden to eat in – a fine place for lunch even if you're not staying.

Hotel Taoskari HOTEL **$$**
(☑577749996; www.facebook.com/pages/vardzia-taoskari/237963042894724; r per person 30 GEL, breakfast 7 GEL; ℗🛜) Taoskari lacks atmosphere but is a reliable, not-too-expensive place to lay your head, just across the bridge from Vardzia.

ℹ Getting There & Away

The first *marshrutka* leaving Akhaltsikhe, at 10.30am, reaches Vardzia around noon, giving you just enough time to see the cave city and catch the last *marshrutka* back at 3pm (earlier ones are at 9am, 9.30am and 1pm, and there's one to Tbilisi at 9.45am). But a day trip is more comfortable by taxi, for 50 GEL return trip from Akhaltsikhe, or 120 GEL from Borjomi, with a few stops en route.

UNDERSTAND GEORGIA

Georgia Today

After 10 helter-skelter years of reform and modernisation, Mikheil 'Misha' Saakashvili and his United National Movement were ousted in the elections of 2012 and 2013 by the Georgian Dream coalition led by Bidzina Ivanishvili, Georgia's richest man. Ivanishvili stepped down after a year as prime minister and handed the reins to protégés, but by all accounts he remained very much a power behind the scenes. Under his watch, it has often been hard to discern what direction Georgia was moving in.

Sometimes it seemed Georgian Dream's main objective was simply to reverse the things it didn't like about the Saakashvili administration. It called a halt to the spending on grand showpiece infrastructure projects, and it gave the judiciary greater independence, addressing a widespread grievance against the previously Draconian court system. Yet it also launched a wave of court cases against former officials from the previous administration. Saakashvili himself went into self-imposed exile and in 2015 took up the post of governor of the Odessa region in Ukraine.

Georgia's relations with Russia warmed slightly but the big-bear neighbour continued to tighten its grip over the breakaway Georgian regions of Abkhazia and South Ossetia, signing alliances in 2014 and 2015 that tied the two territories ever closer to Russia, including in matters of defence and border control.

Georgian Dream has, however, continued Saakashvili's pursuit of closer ties with the

---

GEORGIA & ST GEORGE

St George (Tsminda Giorgi in Georgian) is Georgia's patron saint (as well as England's, Portugal's, Bulgaria's and Malta's) – but the legendary dragon-slayer was almost certainly not responsible for the country-name Georgia. Georgians know their country as Saqartvelo (land of the Kartvelebi), tracing their origins to Noah's great-great-grandson Kartlos. The English word 'Georgia' might stem from the Persian name for Georgians, *gurj*, which was picked up by medieval crusaders.

According to widely accepted accounts, St George was a senior officer in the Roman army who was executed in AD 303 in Nicomedia, Turkey, for standing up against emperor Diocletian's persecution of Christians. He soon became venerated as a Christian martyr and it was St Nino, the bringer of Christianity to Georgia in the 320s, who first popularised him among Georgians. Today Georgia celebrates two St George's Days each year – 6 May, the anniversary of his execution, and 23 November, commemorating his torture on a wheel of swords.

West, signing an association agreement with the EU in 2014. Part of the deal is that Georgia must enact a raft of reforms to bring it into line with European norms in areas including human rights and democracy. The prospect of too much Western liberal influence on Georgian culture, however, alarms the country's many social traditionalists, especially the Georgian Orthodox Church, which has enjoyed a massive revival since the end of the Soviet era and is the most powerful social force in the country. Some 40% to 45% of Georgians now attend religious services at least monthly, and the church is a highly conservative body. Clergy were involved in violently breaking up a Tbilisi rally marking the International Day against Homophobia and Transphobia in 2013. While many of the population at large have more liberal attitudes, conservative morality prevails. One survey in 2015 found almost 70% of Georgians believing it was never justified for women to have sexual relationships before marriage.

As the 2016 parliamentary election approached, the path forward was as uncertain as ever. While most Georgians would agree they were better off than 10 or even five years previously, many were now disillusioned with Georgian Dream, a common complaint being that the government was 'doing nothing'. There was no obvious rival movement to replace Georgian Dream. It was, however, a mark of how far Georgia had come in the past 10 to 15 years that the election, whatever its outcome, was unlikely to be anything other than democratic, free and fair.

History

Georgians live and breathe their history as a vital key to their identities today.

Early Kingdoms

In classical times the two principal kingdoms on the territory were Colchis in the west (site of Greek colonies), and Kartli (also known as Iveria or Iberia) in the east and south and some areas in modern Turkey and Armenia.

When St Nino converted King Mirian and Queen Nana of Kartli to Christianity in the early 4th century, Georgia became the world's second kingdom to adopt this faith, a quarter-century after Armenia. In the 5th century, western Georgia became tied to the Byzantine Empire, while Kartli fell under Persian control. King Vakhtang Gorgasali of Kartli (c 447–502) drove the Persians out and set up his capital at Tbilisi. But the Persians soon returned, to be replaced in 654 by the Arabs, who set up an emirate at Tbilisi.

The Golden Age

Resistance to the Arabs was spearheaded by the Bagrationi dynasty of Tao-Klarjeti, a collection of Christian principalities straddling what are now southwest Georgia and northeast Turkey. They later added Kartli to their possessions, and when these were inherited by King Bagrat of Abkhazia (northwest Georgia) in the early 11th century, most of Georgia became united under one rule. King Davit Aghmashenebeli (David the Builder; 1089–1125) made Georgia the major Caucasian power and a centre of Christian culture. It reached its zenith under Davit's great-granddaughter Queen Tamar (1184–1213), whose writ extended over much of present-day Azerbaijan and Armenia, plus parts of Turkey and southern Russia. Tamar is still so revered that Georgians today call her, without irony, King Tamar.

Death, Destruction & Division

The golden age ended violently with the arrival of the Mongols in the 1220s. King Giorgi the Brilliant (1314–46) shook off the Mongol yoke, but then came the Black Death, followed by the Central Asian destroyer Timur (Tamerlane), who attacked eight times between 1386 and 1403.

Devastated Georgia split into four main kingdoms: Kartli and Kakheti in the east, Imereti in the northwest and Samtskhe in the southwest. From the 16th to 18th centuries western Georgian statelets generally fell under Ottoman Turkish dominion, while eastern ones were subject to the Persian Safavids. In 1744 a new Persian conqueror, Nader Shah, installed local Bagratid princes as kings of Kartli and Kakheti. One of these, Erekle II, ruled both kingdoms as a semi-independent state from 1762.

Russian Rule

Russian troops crossed the Caucasus for the first time in 1770 to get involved in Imereti's liberation from the Turks. At the Treaty of Georgievsk (1783), Erekle II accepted Russian suzerainty over eastern Georgia in return for protection against his Muslim enemies. Russia went on to annex all the Georgian kingdoms and princedoms during the 19th century.

In the wake of the Russian Revolution (1917), Georgia was briefly independent, but was invaded by the Red Army and incorporated into the new USSR in 1922. During the 1930s, like everywhere else in the USSR, Georgia suffered from the Great Terror unleashed by Joseph Stalin, a cobbler's son from the Georgian town of Gori who had managed to take control of the largest country on earth.

Stalin died in 1953, and the 1960s and '70s are looked back on with nostalgia by older Georgians as a time of public order, peace and high living standards. Yet by the mid-1980s Mikhail Gorbachev began his policies of reform and the USSR disintegrated in just seven years.

Independence: From Dream to Nightmare

Georgia's bubbling independence movement became an unstoppable force after the deaths of 19 hunger strikers when Soviet troops broke up a protest in Tbilisi on 9 April 1989. Georgia's now anti-communist government, led by the nationalist Zviad Gamsakhurdia, declared independence on 9 April 1991. Almost immediately Georgia descended into chaos and civil war. Gamsakhurdia was replaced by a military council, which gained an international respectability when Eduard Shevardnadze, the Georgian who had been Gorbachev's foreign minister, agreed to lead it.

But internal conflicts got worse. A truce in June 1992 halted a separatist conflict in the region of South Ossetia, but an even more serious separatist conflict engulfed Abkhazia, where in September 1993 Georgia suffered a comprehensive defeat, leaving Abkhazia as well as South Ossetia de facto independent. Virtually all Abkhazia's ethnic Georgian population, about 230,000 people, was driven out of the territory.

The Rose Revolution

For a decade after the Abkhazia disaster, Georgia oscillated between periods of relative peace and security and terrible crime waves, gang warfare, infrastructure collapse and rampant corruption. Georgians eventu-

ally lost faith in Shevardnadze and flawed parliamentary elections in 2003 were the focus for a mass protest movement that turned into a bloodless coup, named the Rose Revolution after the flowers carried by demonstrators. Led by Mikheil 'Misha' Saakashvili, a US-educated lawyer heading the opposition United National Movement (UNM), protestors invaded the parliament building in Tbilisi on 22 November, and Shevardnadze resigned the next morning.

The 36-year-old Saakashvili won presidential elections in January 2004 by a landslide, appointed a team of young, outward-looking ministers and set about modernising the country, slashing taxes, regulations and bureaucracy, and launching 'zero-tolerance' campaigns against crime and corruption. Within months, the entire notoriously corrupt traffic police force was sacked and replaced with better paid, better trained, unbribeable officers. Within a few years crime almost disappeared and Georgia was one of the safest countries on the planet. Foreign aid and investment helped the economy, roads and railways were improved and electricity shortages ended.

But industry had died a death in the 1990s, and levels of poverty and unemployment stayed high. In response to growing protests, Saakashvili called a snap presidential election for January 2008, and won it with 53% of the vote.

War with Russia

The Saakashvili government had a strong pro-Western stance, with ambitions to join NATO and the EU. This spooked a Russia led by ex-KGB officer Vladimir Putin, who was quoted as saying he would 'hang Saakashvili by the balls'. Saakashvili began manoeuvring to bring the Russian-backed breakaway regions Abkhazia and South Ossetia back under Tbilisi's control. After a period of mounting tensions and sporadic violence in South Ossetia, Georgian forces started shelling the South Ossetian capital, Tskhinvali, on 7 August 2008, and entered the town the next day. But in two days they were driven out of South Ossetia by rapidly arriving Russian forces, which moved on to bomb or occupy Georgian military airfields and bases as well as the towns of Gori, Zugdidi, Poti and Senaki. The Russians halted just 45km short of Tbilisi. French President Nicolas Sarkozy negotiated a ceasefire, but the ethnic cleansing of most of South

Ossetia's 20,000 ethnic-Georgian population continued into November. The 'Five Day War' claimed about 850 lives (half of them civilians).

Before 2008 was over, Russia recognised both South Ossetia and Abkhazia as independent states. It went on to station missile systems and thousand of troops in both territories. By 2011 Russia was providing about half of Abkhazia's budget and virtually all of South Ossetia's, and both territories were very much Russian satellites.

Misha Loses his Way

The Saakashvili government carried on with its project to transform Georgia into a modern, westward-looking country, renovating shabby old town centres, building schools, opening a new parliament in the city of Kutaisi, and giving the country a seaside resort, Batumi, worthy of the name. International tourists began to arrive in increasing numbers.

But more and more Georgians began to feel alienated from the government and its path. Many felt too much power was wielded by a small, autocratic circle of politicians and their allies. Protesters frequently blocked Tbilisi's main avenue, Rustaveli. Perhaps most of all, it was the inequities of the justice system that turned people away from Saakashvili. Crime had been eradicated through a Draconian court system where acquittals were almost nonexistent and plea-bargaining was many accused's only hope of a relatively lenient sentence, whether or not they were really guilty of the crime of which they were accused. Critics say these same tactics came to be used not just against supposed criminals but also against others who opposed Saakashvili and his circle for one reason or another, be they political protesters, opponents in the media or citizens who objected to an infrastructure project.

In September 2012, shortly before a parliamentary election, videos showing violent abuse of prisoners in a Georgian jail appeared on national TV – a disaster for Saakashvili and the UNM. The election was won by the Georgian Dream coalition, an alliance of disparate groups held together chiefly by their dislike of Saakashvili, and led by Bidzina Ivanishvili, a Georgian multibillionaire who had made his fortune in business dealings in Russia in the 1990s. Ivanishvili became prime minister with Saakashvili remaining president for an acrimonious year until his term finished in 2013. The Saakashvili years were over.

Arts

Georgians are an incredibly expressive people. Music, dance, song, poetry and drama all play big parts in their lives.

Music & Dance

Georgian polyphonic singing is a tradition of multi-voice *a cappella* song that goes back thousands of years. It used to accompany every aspect of daily life, and the songs survive in various genres including *supruli* (songs for the table), *mushuri* (working songs) and *satrpialo* (love songs). It's still alive and well. Mostly male ensembles such as the Rustavi Choir perform in concert halls and at festivals such as Art-Gene, Tushetoba and Shatiloba, but polyphonic song is most electrifying when it happens at less formal gatherings such as around the table at a *supra* (feast), when the proximity, intimacy and volume can be literally spine-tingling. There are varying regional styles but it's typical for some singers to do a bass drone while others sing melodies on top.

Sagalobeli (ethereally beautiful church chants) have been part of Georgian life for at least 1500 years. Excellent choirs accompany services in the most important churches: the best time to catch them is Sunday morning between about 9am and noon.

Polyphonic singing may or may not be accompanied by some of Georgia's numerous folk instruments, which include the *panduri* and *chonguri* (types of lute), the *garmoni* (accordion) and various bagpipes, flutes and drums (check www.hangebi.ge for a rundown). For an easy introduction to Georgian folk music check out popular folk or folk-fusion artists such as groups Bani, Gortela and 33a, and singer Mariam Elieshvili.

Georgia's exciting folk dance ranges from lyrical love stories to dramatic, leaping demonstrations of male agility. Top professional groups such as Erisioni and Sukhishvilebi often tour overseas, but don't miss them if they are performing back home.

Jazz is also popular, with young pianist Beka Gochiashvili the rising star. Tbilisi and Batumi host annual jazz festivals. Minimal techno is still the optimal beat for many Tbilisi and Batumi clubbers: Gem Fest

(Georgian Electronic Music Festival; http://gem-fest.com), which launched with a stellar international DJ line-up in 2015, may become an annual event.

Georgia has produced many outstanding classical artists too. Nina Ananiashvili, artistic director of the state ballet, is one of the world's top ballerinas, while leading contemporary composer Gia Kancheli, born in 1935, has been described as 'turning the sounds of silence into music'.

Visual Arts

Many Georgian churches are adorned with wonderful old frescoes. The golden age of religious art was the 11th to 13th centuries, when Georgian painters employed the Byzantine iconographic system and also portrayed local royalty and saints. There were two main, monastic fresco schools: one at the Davit Gareja and the other in Tao-Klarjeti (modern southwest Georgia and northeast Turkey). During the same period artists and metalsmiths were creating beautiful icons and crosses with paint, jewels and precious metals that remain among Georgia's greatest treasures today. You can see them not only in churches but also in museums in Tbilisi, Kutaisi, Mestia and elsewhere.

Perhaps the last major artist in the fresco-painting tradition was one who painted scenes of everyday life in restaurants and bars in Tbilisi. The self-taught Niko Pirosmani (1862–1918) expressed the spirit of Georgian life in a direct and enchanting way. After his death in poverty and obscurity, his work was acclaimed by the leading, Paris-influenced Georgian modernists Davit Kakabadze, Lado Gudiashvili and Shalva Kikodze. Pirosmani, Kakabadze and Gudiashvili are well represented in Tbilisi's National Gallery. The Signaghi Museum has another good Pirosmani collection.

Georgia's contemporary art world is again blossoming after a depressed post-Soviet period. For copious information on artists, galleries and exhibitions, see www.art.gov.ge. The biggest names include Rusudan Petviashvili, painter and drawer of densely packed mythological/imaginary images by an unusual one-touch technique. She has her own galleries in Tbilisi and Batumi.

Literature

For a language with only a few million speakers, Georgian has an amazingly rich literature. In the 12th century Shota Rustaveli, a member of Queen Tamar's court, wrote *The Knight* (or *Man*) *in the Tiger's* (or *Panther's*) *Skin,* an epic of chivalry that every Georgian can quote from.

Nikoloz Baratashvili (1817–45) personified the romanticism that entered Georgian literature in the early 19th century. Some later-19th-century writers turned to the mountains for inspiration – notably Alexander Kazbegi, novelist and dramatist, and Vazha Pshavela, whom many consider the greatest Georgian poet after Rustaveli.

Mikheil Javakhishvili (1880–1937) brought the Georgian novel to the fore with vivid, ironic tales of city and country, peasant and aristocrat in tsarist and Soviet times, including *Arsena Marabdeli,* based on a real-life Georgian Robin Hood figure, and the picaresque *Kvachi Kvachantiradze.* Javakhishvili was executed by the Soviet regime. Nodar Dumbadze (1928–84) portrayed post-WWII life with humour and melancholy, and is one of the most popular Georgian novelists: *The Law of Eternity* and *Granny, Iliko, Ilarion and I* are among his novels available in English.

Leading post-Soviet writers include novelist Aka Morchiladze, whose *Journey to Karabakh* (1992) tells of two young Georgian men who suddenly, bewilderingly find themselves in the midst of the Nagorno-Karabakh conflict; and novelist, playwright and travel writer David Turashvili whose *Flight from the USSR* (2008) is based on a real-life attempt by a group of young Georgians to escape from the USSR by hijacking an Aeroflot plane.

Cinema

Georgian cinema enjoyed a golden age from the late 1960s to the 1980s, when Georgian directors created dozens of films distinct from the general socialist-realist run of Soviet movies. They won international awards with brilliant visual imagery, lively characters and use of allegory, fable and dreams to provide a platform for people's real concerns without upsetting the Soviet censors. Italian director Federico Fellini was a noted fan, praising Georgian cinema's ability to combine philosophy with childlike innocence.

Perhaps the greatest maestro was the Tbilisi-born Armenian Sergei Paradjanov (p190). Tengiz Abuladze's *Repentance* (1984) was a ground-breaking opening up of the Soviet past – a black portrait of a dictatorial politician clearly based on Stalin's Georgian henchman Lavrenty Beria. Other leading directors included Otar Iosseliani (*There Lived a Songthrush;* 1970), Eldar Shengelaia (*The Blue Mountains;* 1983) and Giorgi Shengelaia (*Pirosmani;* 1969).

Today home-grown Georgian cinema is making a comeback after the grim post-Soviet years, despite still-minuscule budgets. It gets a reasonable amount of screen time among the Hollywood stuff at Georgia's few cinemas. The tragic conflicts of the 1990s figure, directly or indirectly, in films such as Zaza Urushadze's *Tangerines* (a 2015 Oscar nominee), Levan Tutberidze's *A Trip to Karabakh* (2005) and Giorgi Ovashvili's enigmatic, Oscar-shortlisted *Corn Island* (2013).

Food & Drink

Georgian food is a unique expression of the land and its people – diverse, fresh, imaginative, filling, often spicy – and with hospitality and drinks often going hand-in-hand, eating is a central part of Georgian culture. The cuisine is based on the rich produce of Georgia's fertile soil, and Georgia's location on ancient spice routes has contributed a unique range of flavours and textures. Many staple dishes are vegetarian and some are vegan.

Georgians eat and drink at all times of the day. Restaurants keep long hours and have improved by leaps and bounds in recent years. But some of the best Georgian food you'll eat will still be in guesthouses, where you can enjoy home-cooked fare with that genuine touch of Georgian hospitality.

Staples & Specialities

A great staple for everybody is the *khachapuri,* essentially a cheese pie (p49).

Equally beloved are *khinkali* – big spicy dumplings which most Georgians adore and most visitors find they like too.

A great snack-on-the-go is *churchkhela,* a string of nuts (usually walnuts) coated in

HOW TO EAT A KHINKALI

Arguably Georgia's most beloved hunger-killer, the *khinkali* is a small bag of dough twisted into a hard nexus at the top, with a filling of spiced, ground-up meat, or potatoes or mushrooms or sometimes vegetables – and plenty of juice. You'll have a plate of at least five *khinkali* in front of you (it's impossible to order fewer). Many people like to sprinkle a good dose of pepper over the *khinkali* before starting.

Once they're cool enough to handle, pick one up by the hard nexus at the top, and bite a small hole just below it. Suck the juice out through the hole. Then eat the rest, except for the nexus, which you discard. Yum yum!

an often-pinkish caramel made from grape juice. You'll often see bunches of it hanging, sausage-like, at roadside stalls or markets.

Starters to a larger meal may include assorted salads, the delectable *badrijani nigvzit* (aubergine slices with walnut-and-garlic paste), *lobio* (bean paste or stew with herbs and spices) and *mkhali* (or *pkhali*), which are pastes combining vegetables with walnuts, garlic and herbs. The finest fresh bread to accompany a Georgian meal is *shotis* (or *tonis*) *puri* – long white loaves baked from wheat flour, water and salt (no fat or oil) in a round clay oven called a *tone.*

More substantial Georgian dishes include the *mtsvadi* (shish kebab) and a variety of chicken, pork, beef, lamb or turkey dishes in spicy, herby sauces or stews, with names like *chakapuli, chakhokhbili, kuchmachi, ojakhuri, ostri* or *shkmeruli.* Georgia's favourite spices and herbs include coriander, blue fenugreek, tarragon and ground-up marigold leaves.

Many dishes contain walnut, often ground up as an ingredient in sauces, dressings or pastes. A sprinkling of pomegranate seeds is a tasty and pretty-looking garnish. Wild mushrooms are also a favourite, and Georgia has a wonderful variety of local cheeses.

Religious-minded Georgians may abstain from meat, eggs and dairy products on Wednesdays, Fridays and during certain periods such as before Christmas and Easter. The 'fasting menus' offered for them by

EATING PRICE RANGES

The following indicators are for the price of a single main dish:

$ less than 9 GEL

$$ 9 GEL–16 GEL

$$$ more than 16 GEL

many restaurants make life easier for year-round vegetarians too.

The Supra & Toasts

While strictly speaking the word *supra* (feast, literally 'tablecloth') applies to any meeting where food and drink are consumed, the full works means staggering amounts to eat and drink. A selection of cold dishes and maybe soups will be followed by two or three hot courses as well as some kind of dessert, all accompanied by bottomless quantities of wine and rounds of toasts.

Bear in mind that Georgians toast only their enemies with beer. Wine or spirits are the only drinks to toast your friends with. However, at a *supra* you shouldn't drink them till someone proposes a toast. This can be a surprisingly serious, lengthy and poetic matter, even at small gatherings of a few friends. Larger gatherings will have a designated *tamada* (toastmaker), and some complex *supras* will involve an *alaverdi*, a second person whose role is to elaborate on the toast. If you are toasted, do not reply immediately but wait for others to add their wishes before simply thanking them – then wait a while before asking the *tamada* if you can make a toast in reply.

Drinks

Wine is a national passion and Georgians have been making and drinking it for at least 8000 years. Vodka is also common, and beer is a popular thirst-quencher: local brands include Natakhtari, Kazbegi and Argo.

Georgia's most famous nonalcoholic drink is Borjomi, a salty mineral water that was the beverage of choice for every Soviet leader from Lenin on. It polarises opinion. Nabeghlavi is a less salty alternative. Tap water seems safe to drink throughout the

GEORGIAN WINE

Wine (*ghvino*) is a national passion. After all, Georgians have been making and drinking it for at least 8000 years. Wine may well have been invented here, but perhaps more importantly, Georgians have continued to make wine by basically the same method ever since they started – fermenting it along with grape skins, pips and often stalks, in large clay amphorae known as *qvevri*, buried in the earth. This 'skin contact' is why traditionally made Georgian whites have a more amber/orangey tint than other white wines. 'European-style' winemaking – fermenting the grape juice without the pulp – has also been around in Georgia since the 19th century, but the basic local method practised by tens of thousands of families throughout Georgia has remained unchanged. It also yields the potent, grappa-like, firewater *chacha*, distilled from the pulp left after the wine is eventually drawn off.

Qvevri wine (also sometimes called 'unfiltered' wine) is beloved by followers of the fashion for 'natural wine' because it contains little or none of the additives (such as yeast, sugar or sulphur) commonly put into wine today. *Qvevri* wines certainly taste different from the wines most of the world is accustomed to. If there's one word that embraces their varied tastes, it could be, yes, 'natural'.

In Soviet times, larger-scale winemaking in Georgia was geared to the Russian taste for strong wine with lots of sugar, resulting in a decline in quality. Since the Soviet collapse Georgian commercial winemakers have been steadily upgrading their operations. The result is a wider and much better range of European-style wines, many of which are exported to the West and Asia. Today many winemakers produce both European-style and *qvevri* wines.

Wine is made all over Georgia, but more than half of it comes from the eastern Kakheti region (p104). Over 500 of the world's 2000 grape varieties are Georgian. Most commonly used for wine today are the white Rkatsiteli, Mtsvane and Kisi, and the red Saperavi.

Appellations of origin, such as Tsinandali and Mukuzani from Kakheti or Khvanchkara from Racha, denote the provenance of many of the country's better wines. Bottles of good commercially produced Georgian wine start at around 10 GEL in Georgian shops. Names on labels may denote the appellation of origin, or the type(s) of grape, or the producing company. You'll find further helpful information at **Georgian Wine Association** (www.gwa.ge) and **National Wine Agency** (http://georgianwine.gov.ge).

MENU DECODER

Georgian menus often look daunting, even if there's an English translation, but this list explains a lot of the items you'll find io most menus.

ajapsandali	stew of aubergines, potatoes, tomatoes, peppers and herbs
ajika	a paste of chilli or paprika with garlic and herbs
apkhazura	spicy meatballs/sausage
badrijani (nigvzit)	aubergine (in slices with walnut-and-garlic paste)
bazhe	walnut sauce
chakapuli	stew of veal or lamb with tarragon and plums
chakhokhbili	stew of chicken, turkey or sometimes pork with tomatoes, onions and herbs
chakhrakuli	lamb ribs stewed with tomato, herbs and spices
chanakhi	a lamb stew with layers of potatoes, aubergine and tomatoes
chashushuli	spicy stew of meat or mushrooms with veggies
chikhirtma	chicken broth
churchkhela	string of walnuts coated in a sort of caramel made from grape juice
kababi	doner kebab, shawarma
khachapuri	cheese pie
kharcho	soup with rice, beef and spices
khinkali	spicy dumpling with a meat, potato or mushroom filling
kuchmachi	stewed chicken/pig/calf innards with spices, herbs and usually walnuts
kupati	sausage
lobio	bean paste or stew with herbs and spices
matsoni	yoghurt
mchadi	maize bread
mkhali or pkhali	beetroot, spinach or aubergine paste with crushed walnuts, garlic and herbs
mtsvadi (ghoris/khbos)	shish kebab (from pork/beef), often just 'barbecue' on English-language menus
ojakhuri	meat goulash
ostri	spiced meat in a tomato-based sauce
satsivi	cold turkey or chicken in a spicy walnut sauce, traditionally a New Year dish
shkmeruli	chicken in garlic sauce
soko	mushrooms
sulguni	a salty cheese, sometimes smoked
suneli	a spicy paste
tqemali	plum sauce

country: we have never heard of anyone getting sick from drinking it. Various uncarbonated bottled waters are also available.

SURVIVAL GUIDE

ℹ Directory A–Z

ACCOMMODATION

Peak season in most of the country is July and August, when it's often worth calling ahead to secure a room. Seasonal variations in room rates are minor (except in ski resorts), though it's sometimes possible to secure a discount at quiet times.

Camping There are few organised camping grounds but equally few restrictions on wild camping. In the mountains, dogs or even bears or wolves might be a threat. If in doubt, ask locals.

Guesthouses Guesthouses are often enjoyable places to stay, not least for contact with local people and their home-cooked food. Bathrooms are typically shared. Average price: 25 GEL to 30 GEL per person; meals 5 GEL to 15 GEL each. Family and guest areas are often distinct.

ACCOMMODATION PRICE RANGES

The following price indicators indicate the cost of accommodation for two people, including taxes and breakfast:

$ less than 60 GEL

$$ 61 GEL– 200 GEL

$$$ more than 200 GEL

Homestays Slightly cheaper than guesthouses and you're more likely to share space with family members.

Hostels There are perhaps 50 travellers' hostels around Georgia (the majority in Tbilisi). They provide dormitory beds or bunks, sometimes a few private doubles, and shared bathrooms and kitchens. They're good places to meet other travellers, and many are run by young Georgians who enjoy hosting international guests. Typical price: 2 GEL to 25 GEL per person.

Hotels There are many small or medium-sized, midrange hotels with character in cities and towns around the country, and a handful of super-luxury top-end places in Tbilisi and Batumi. Double-room prices start around 60 GEL and are rarely above 200 GEL except in top-end places.

ACTIVITIES

➡ Peter Nasmyth's *Walking in the Caucasus: Georgia* is an excellent guide to over 50 day walks all around the country.

➡ Good resources for bird-watchers include *Bird-watching Guide to Georgia, Raptors & Owls of Georgia* and *Vultures of Georgia*, all by Lexo Gavashelishvili and others, and the Facebook group Birding Georgia.

➡ Walkers should give dogs a wide berth everywhere: Georgian mountain dogs are bred for fending off wolves.

BUSINESS HOURS

Typical opening hours:

Banks 9.30am to 5.30pm Monday to Friday

Bars noon to 2am

Cafes 10am to 10pm

Restaurants 9am to 11pm

Shops Food 9am to 9pm, other shops 10am to 7pm Monday to Saturday

EMBASSIES & CONSULATES

Georgian diplomatic missions in other countries are listed on the **Georgian Foreign Ministry website** (http://mfa.gov.ge). Foreign representation in Georgia includes the following.

Armenian Embassy (Map p34; ☑ 32-2950977; www.georgia.mfa.am; Tetelashvili 4, Tbilisi; ☺ consular section 10am-1pm Mon-Fri)

Azerbaijan Consulate (☑ 422-276700; www.azgenconsulate.ge; Dumbadze 14, Batumi; ☺ approx 11am-1pm Mon-Fri)

Azerbaijan Embassy (Map p34; ☑ consular section 32-2243004; www.azembassy.ge; Gorgasali 4, Tbilisi; ☺ consular section 10am-12.30pm Mon-Fri)

British Embassy (☑ 32-2274747; www.gov.uk/government/world/georgia; Krtsanisi 51, Tbilisi; ☺ 9am-5pm Mon-Fri)

Canadian Consulate (Map p40; ☑ 32-2982072; ccogeorgia@gmail.com; 3rd fl, Rustaveli 34, Tbilisi)

Dutch Embassy (Map p34; ☑ 32-2276200; georgia.nlembassy.org; Chavchavadzis gamziri 34, Vake, Tbilisi; ☺ consular department 9am-1pm & 2-5.30pm Mon-Thu, 9am-1.30pm Fri)

French Embassy (☑ 32-2721490; www.amba-france-ge.org; Krtsanisi 49, Tbilisi; ☺ 9am-1pm & 2-6pm Mon-Thu, to 4.30pm Fri)

German Embassy (Map p34; ☑ 32-2443700; www.tiflis.diplo.de; Sheraton Metechi Palace Hotel, Telavi 20, Tbilisi; ☺ 8.30am-5.30pm Mon-Thu, 8.30am-2.30pm Fri)

Iranian Consulate (Map p34; ☑ 32-2913656; info@iran.ge; Chavchavadzis gamziri 80, Vake, Tbilisi; ☺ 10am-1pm Mon-Wed & Fri)

Kazakhstan Embassy (Map p34; ☑ 32-2997684; www.kazembassy.ge; Shatberashvili 23, Vake, Tbilisi; ☺ consular section 10.30am-12.30pm Mon, Wed & Thu)

Russian Interests Section of Swiss Embassy (Map p34; ☑ consular service 32-2912782; www.georgia.mid.ru; Chavchavadzis gamziri 53, Vake, Tbilisi; ☺ 9am-1pm & 3-6pm Mon-Thu, 9am-2pm Fri)

US Embassy (☑ 32-2277000; georgia.us embassy.gov; George Balanchine 11, Didi Dighomi, Tbilisi; ☺ 8.30am-5.30pm Mon-Fri)

MAPS

➡ By far the best maps of Georgia, including hiking maps and regional maps, are published by Geoland (p53) and sold at its Tbilisi office and by Prospero's Books (p53), and erratically elsewhere.

➡ Tourist Information Offices hand out useful regional and country maps.

MONEY

➡ Georgia's currency is the lari (GEL). It has been fairly stable since it was introduced in 1995. One lari is divided into 100 tetri.

➡ Banknotes come in denominations of one, two, five, 10, 20, 50, 100 and 200 lari; coins run from one tetri to two lari.

→ ATMs, generally accepting MasterCard, Visa, Cirrus and Maestro cards, are plentiful in cities and towns.

→ There are also plenty of banks and small money-exchange offices in most towns and cities, where you can exchange US dollars, euros and sometimes sterling and the currencies of Georgia's neighbouring countries.

→ You can make purchases with credit cards at some hotels, restaurants and shops, though less frequently outside Tbilisi.

→ Common tipping practice in restaurants is just to round up the bill to the next round number.

See p31 for exchange rates and costs.

PUBLIC HOLIDAYS

New Year 1 and 2 January
Orthodox Christmas Day 7 January
Epiphany 19 January
Mother's Day 3 March
Women's Day 8 March
Orthodox Easter Sunday April or May (p294)
National Unity Day 9 April
Victory Day 9 May
St Andria's Day 12 May
Independence Day 26 May
Mariamoba (Assumption) 28 August
Svetitskhovloba (Day of Svetitskhoveli Cathedral, Mtskheta) 14 October
Giorgoba (St George's Day) 23 November

TELEPHONE SERVICES

Emergency ☑112
Georgia country code ☑995
International access code (calling from Georgia) ☑00
Landline numbers Seven digits in Tbilisi, six digits elsewhere; starting with 2.
Mobile phone numbers Nine digits, starting with 5.

Mobile Phones

→ Almost everyone in Georgia has a mobile phone and many businesses use them instead of landlines.

→ The three main networks – **Magti** (www.magticom.ge), **Geocell** (http://geocell.ge) and **Beeline** (www.beeline.ge) – have shops in all sizeable towns.

→ Magti is the overall best choice for coverage around the country.

→ You can easily obtain a Georgian SIM card for 1 GEL or 2 GEL, sometimes free, from the main networks. Take your passport when you go to get a SIM. The networks have 24-hour booths at Tbilisi airport where you can get one on arrival.

→ Call rates are low and there are bargain packages for international calls.

→ Internet packages are cheap: around 7 GEL to 10 GEL for 4GB, for example.

→ An easy way to top up your credit is with cash in orange 'Express Pay' machines or yellow-and-blue 'Pay Box' machines, widespread on the streets of all towns. Easy-to-follow instructions are available in English.

TOURIST INFORMATION

→ Georgia has a good network of Tourism Information Centres in main destinations.

→ The country's official tourism website is http://georgia.travel.

VISAS

→ Citizens of more than 90 countries and territories, listed at www.geoconsul.gov.ge, can enter Georgia without a visa for stays of up to one year.

→ Citizens of EU countries may enter Georgia with a national identity card instead of a passport; other nationalities must carry their passport.

→ Non-visa-free nationalities must obtain a visa in advance. For 'short-term' visits (up to 30 days), this is easiest done through the **e-Visa Portal** (www.evisa.gov.ge), where you upload documents and pay US$20.40 online by Visa or MasterCard. You receive the visa by email within five working days.

→ Short-term visas can also be – and longer-term visas must be – applied for at a Georgian consular office in your country of citizenship or residence. See www.geoconsul.gov.ge.

→ Entering Abkhazia or South Ossetia from Russia is considered a crime under Georgian law, punishable by a heavy fine or possible imprisonment. If you do this, don't try to continue into undisputed Georgia from either of the breakaway enclaves.

HOW TO DIAL GEORGIAN NUMBERS

CALLING	FROM LANDLINE	FROM MOBILE	FROM OTHER COUNTRIES
landline	☑0 + area code + number	☑0 + area code + number	☑IAC* + 995 + area code + number
mobile	☑0 + number	☑number	☑IAC* + 995 + number

* IAC: International access code

Visas for Onward Travel

Azerbaijan At the time of writing, the Tbilisi embassy is one of the most straightforward places to get an Azerbaijan visa, issuing 30-day visas within seven working days (often less). Take two photos, a passport photocopy and a hotel reservation (which can be an email from the hotel or a booking.com reservation). Fees are US$35 to US$60 for most EU nationalities, US$118 for UK citizens and US$160 for US citizens. Agencies near the embassy including **Medea Travel** (Map p34; ☏ 555100810; www.medeatravel.ge; Gorgasali 4th Lane No 3; ⊙10am-7pm Mon-Fri, noon-6pm Sat) will handle everything for you for about an additional US$50. The Batumi consulate is also well worth trying: its requirements and processing times fluctuate but travellers have obtained visas there without hotel reservations.

Iran The Iran visa situation was in flux at the time of writing. Thirty-day visas on arrival at all points of entry seemed likely to be made available to most nationalities. But UK, US and Canadian citizens still had not only to obtain a visa in advance but also to book a guided tour for their whole visit. This may all change. If you do need a visa, Tbilisi is a convenient place to collect it. You should apply several weeks ahead, through websites such as www.persianvoyages.com or http://caravanistan.com, for an Iranian foreign ministry authorisation code, costing around US$40. You nominate the Iranian embassy/consulate where you will collect the visa. Once you have the code, which in Tbilisi's case then sends you off to pay the visa fee at a bank (€30 to €200-plus for a 30-day tourist visa depending on your nationality) and return with proof of payment, your passport, two photos (women in headscarves), proof of insurance and your itinerary in Iran. Your visa should be ready the following working day.

Kazakhstan At the time of writing nationals of 36 countries need no visa for visits of varying periods (15 days for 10 EU states, the USA and Australia) – details at http://mfa.kz/index.php/en/kl-nlknlkna-lksn. Citizens of other EU countries, Canada, New Zealand and Israel can obtain 30-day tourist visas without a Letter of Invitation (LOI). The Tbilisi embassy normally issues these in three to five working days: get there at opening time as you'll have to spend about 45 minutes paying the fee at a bank.

Russia Travellers have obtained transit visas (normally for not more than three days for air travel or 10 days for land travel) at the Russian Interests Section of the Swiss embassy in Tbilisi, for US$60 with 10-day processing. You will need to talk to a consular official before applying, but required documents are likely to include proof of insurance and an onward visa. There is usually a knot of people crowd-

ing round the entrance to the building: push through and tell the guards you're a foreigner and need to ask for visa information. Thirty-day tourist visas may also be possible with an LOI, available via websites such as waytorussia.net.

Turkey Many nationalities don't need a visa for up to 30 or 90 days (see www.mfa.gov.tr/visa-information-for-foreigners.en.mfa). For others, e-visas are available rapidly online at www.evisa.gov.tr for between US$20 and US$80. Some nationalities can also obtain visas on arrival at Turkish airports or land borders; others can't. See www.evisa.gov.tr/en/info.

The Georgian Alphabet

GEORGIAN	ROMAN	PRONUNCIATION
ა	a	as in 'father'
ბ	b	as in 'bet'
გ	g	as in 'go'
დ	d	as in 'do'
ე	e	as in 'get'
ვ	v	as in 'van'
ზ	z	as in 'zoo'
თ	t	as in 'to'
ი	i	as in 'police'
კ	k	a 'k' pronounced very far back in the throat
ლ	l	as in 'let'
მ	m	as in 'met'
ნ	n	as in 'net'
ო	o	as in 'cot'
პ	p	as in 'tip' (with a stop on the outflow of air)
ჟ	zh	as the 's' in 'pleasure'
რ	r	as in 'rub', but rolled
ს	s	as in 'see'
ტ	t	as in 'sit' (with a stop on the outflow of air)
უ	u	as ln 'put'
ფ	p	as in 'put'
ქ	q	a 'k' pronounced very far back in the throat
ღ	gh	as a French 'r'
ყ	k	as the 'ck' in 'lick' (with a stop on the outflow of air)
შ	sh	as in 'she'
ჩ	ch	as in 'chip'
ც	ts	as in 'tsar'
ძ	dz	as the 'ds' in 'beds'
წ	ts	as in 'its' (with a stop on the outflow of air)
ჭ	ch	as in 'each' (with a stop on the outflow of air)
ხ	kh	as in Scottish 'loch'
ჯ	j	as in 'judge'
ჰ	h	as in 'here'

Armenia

♪ 374 / POP 3,019,000

Best Places to Eat

➡ Anteb (p143)

➡ Ankyun (p144)

➡ Cherkezi Dzor (p158)

➡ Zanazan Restaurant (p173)

Best Places to Stay

➡ Azoyan Guest House (p141)

➡ Avan Dzoraget Hotel (p163)

➡ Gohar's Guest House (p177)

➡ Maghay B&B (p161)

➡ Marriott Tsaghkadzor (p174)

➡ Tufenkian Historic Yerevan Hotel (p141)

Why Go?

Few nations have histories as ancient, complex and laced with tragedy as Armenia (Հայաստան). And even fewer have a culture that is as rich and resilient. This is a destination where you will be intrigued by history, awed by monuments, amazed by the landscape and charmed by down-to-earth locals. It's not an easy place to explore – roads are rough, transport is often hard to navigate and those who don't speak Armenian or Russian may find communication difficult – but travelling here is as rewarding as it is revelatory.

The simply extraordinary collection of medieval monasteries scattered across the country is the number-one attraction, closely followed by a dramatically beautiful landscape that is perfectly suited to hiking and other outdoor activities. And then there's the unexpected delight of Yerevan – one of Europe's most exuberant and endearing cities. Put together, they offer an enticing and hugely enjoyable travel experience.

When to Go

➡ Most of Armenia has a dry, high-altitude climate, though there are some verdant rainy pockets in the Lori, Tavush and Syunik regions. These receive the most rain in early spring.

➡ Spring temperatures are mild and the countryside is covered in wildflowers, making it a perfect time to go hiking.

➡ Autumn has long, warm days and stable weather conditions.

➡ Summer in Yerevan can be 40°C with little or no breeze for days at a time; weather in the north is cooler.

➡ Conditions in winter can be bleak, with temperatures falling to -10°C or even lower in many areas. Roads are often closed due to snow and ice.

Armenia Highlights

1 Enjoying time in the welcoming cafes, wine bars and restaurants of **Yerevan** (p128).

2 Marvelling at the ancient rock-hewn churches at **Geghard Monastery** (p149).

3 Hiking between spectacularly sited monasteries in the **Kasagh Gorge** (p154).

4 Visiting medieval fresco-covered churches of the dramatic **Debed Canyon** (p162).

5 Exploring somnolent villages, ruins and an old Jewish cemetery in **Yeghegis Valley** (p178).

6 Watching the sun slowly set over the dramatic cliffs surrounding **Noravank** (p176).

7 Enjoying a high-altitude picnic in front of a 14th-century caravanserai on scenic **Selim Pass** (p180).

8 Soaring up to fortified monastery at **Tatev** (p184) on the world's longest cable car.

FAST FACTS

Currency
Dram (AMD)

Languages
Armenian, Russian

English is widely spoken in Yerevan (especially by younger people), but not in regional towns and villages.

Emergencies
📖 112 or 911

Visas
Visitors from the US and from EU countries can visit Armenia for up to 180 days without a visa; citizens from most other countries can obtain an Armenian visa when entering the country.

Resources

➡ **Armenia Guide**
(www.armeniaguide.com)

➡ **Armenia Information**
(www.armeniainfo.am)

➡ **Armeniapedia**
(www.armeniapedia.org)

➡ **Ianyan Magazine**
(www.ianyanmag.com)

➡ **PanArmenian.net**
(www.panarmenian.net)

Exchange Rates

Australia	A$1	AMD346
Canada	C$1	AMD345
Euro zone	€1	AMD520
Japan	¥100	AMD406
NZ	NZ$1	AMD324
UK	UK£1	AMD710
USA	US$1	AMD484

Daily Costs

➡ **B&B or guesthouse room**
AMD15,000–30,000

➡ **Two-course evening meal**
AMD6000

➡ **Museum entrance** AMD500–1000

➡ **Beer (domestic) at a bar** AMD500

➡ **100km minibus ride** AMD1200

YEREVAN

📖 10 / POP 1.1 MILLION

Leave your preconceptions at home, because Yerevan (Երևան) will almost certainly confound them. This is a city full of contradictions – top-of-the-range Mercedes sedans share the roads with Ladas so old they should be in museum collections; old-fashioned teahouses sit next to chic European-style wine bars; and street fashions range from hipster to babushka with many weird and wonderful variations in between. Life here isn't necessarily easy (costs are high, transport is crowded and air pollution is a constant problem), but it's most certainly fun.

In summer, locals take to the streets every night, claiming tables at the city's many outdoor cafes, sauntering along its tree-filled boulevards and congregating around the much-loved musical fountain in Republic Sq. In winter, freezing temperatures encourage people off the streets and into the many *pandoks* (taverns) around town, where *khoravats* (barbecue meats), *oghee* (fruit vodka) and traditional music are enjoyed with gusto.

Few traces of the city's ancient past remain, with most of the building stock dating from the Soviet era. Fortunately, the stolid architecture is softened by a wealth of gardens and parks, as well as a number of handsome public squares. Areas outside the city centre are less attractive, blighted by huge derelict Soviet-era factories and run-down apartment blocks.

History

Yerevan's history dates back to 782 BC, when the Erebuni fortress was built by King Argishti I of Urartu at the place where the Hrazdan River widened onto the fertile Ararat Plains. It was a regional capital of Muslim khanates and Persian governors until the Russian annexation in 1828.

The Soviet rebuilding of the tsarist city removed most of its mosques and some of its churches, and hid others away in residential backwaters, but it kept some of the 19th-century buildings on Abovyan St and left the old neighbourhood of Kond more or less alone. Alexander Tamanyan developed the current grid plan in the 1920s with the idea that main boulevards (Mashtots, Abovyan and Nalbandyan) should point in the direction of Mt Ararat.

⦿ Sights

Most of Yerevan's sights are located in the city centre and can be easily reached on foot. We've organised our listings from the northern edge of the city centre towards the Hrazdan River at the southern edge.

⦿ City Centre

★ **Cafesjian Center for the Arts**   ARTS CENTRE
(Map p134; ☑ 56 72 62; www.cmf.am; Cascade, 10 Tamanyan St; adult/child 13-17yr/child 12yr & under AMD1000/750/free; ⊙10am-5pm Tue-Thu, to 8pm Fri-Sun) Housed in a vast flight of stone steps known as the Cascade, this arts centre is one of the city's major cultural attractions. Originally conceived in the 1920s by Soviet architect Alexander Tamanyan as part of his plan to modernise Yerevan, work on the monumental structure finally commenced in the 1980s but stalled after the 1988 earthquake. Eventually, Armenian-American philanthropist Gerard Cafesjian came to the rescue, funding its completion and transformation into a multi-level contemporary arts space.

The centre's two external garden galleries and five exhibition halls are accessed via an internal escalator that operates from 8am to 8pm daily. Next to the escalator are platforms where artworks from Cafesjian's personal collection of 20th-century and contemporary sculpture and furniture are displayed. There's a decidedly quirky theme at work here, with pieces such as Studio 65 for Gufram's *Marilyn 'Bocca' Lip Sofa*, Giogio Laveri's *Lipstick* and Richard Cresswell's *Butterfly Seat* three of many works catching the eye on the trip up and down. They and the garden galleries, which feature recessed fountains, modern *khachkars* (stone steles featuring carved crosses) and contemporary sculptures, can be visited free of charge. Visitors must have an admission ticket to enter the internal galleries.

On the ground floor, the large gift shop is one of the best places in the city to source quality souvenirs. There's also a welcoming and well-stocked art library with a small children's section.

In front of the Cascade, a sculpture garden features three huge bronze works by Colombian-Italian sculptor Fernando Botero: *Cat, Roman Warrior* and *Woman Smoking a Cigarette*. These sit alongside a whimsical wrought-iron teapot by Joana Vasconcelos, a bright blue kiwi by Peter Woytuk and many other works. The two streets edging the park are home to cafes, bars and restaurants with plenty of outdoor seating.

Mother Armenia Military Museum   MUSEUM
(Map p130; www.mayrhayastan.am; Haghtanak Park; ⊙10am-5pm Tue-Fri, 10am-3pm Sun) FREE
There's symbolism aplenty in this huge memorial above the Cascade. Twenty-two metres high, Mother Armenia's stern visage, military stance and massive sword project a clear message. Armenia has had its fill of invasions, massacres and repression, and will fight to preserve its nationhood and the lives of its citizens. Inside the pedestal is a military museum documenting Armenian involvement in WWII (300,000 Armenians died, half of those sent to fight) as well as the bloody 1988–94 Karabakh War with Azerbaijan.

The museum opened in 1950 and was originally topped with a 17m statue of Stalin. This was replaced with Ara Harutyunyan's Mother Armenia statue in 1967. One soldier was

ARMENIA YEREVAN

YEREVAN IN ONE DAY

Start off with a freshly ground *soorch* (coffee) at **Gemini** (p144) and then walk around the Opera House to the **Cafesjian Center for the Arts**. Wander through the sculpture garden in front of the center, take a trip up and down the art-edged escalator, and consider purchasing a souvenir from the gift shop. Next, marvel at the illuminated manuscripts at the **Matenadaran** (p131) or visit to the **Centre of Popular Creation** (p132) to see the best folk art collection in the country. After lunch, head to the **History Museum of Armenia** (p133), where the Bronze Age collection is impressive. After all of that culture, a relaxing drink is in order – wine aficionados should head to **In Vino** (p144) or **Aperitivo** (p145), beer drinkers to the **Beer Academy** (p145). For dinner, make your way to **Yerevan Tavern** (p143) for a feast of Armenian *khoravats* (barbecued food) accompanied by live Armenian music, or to **The Club** (p144) for French-Armenian fusion food. After dinner, stroll to Republic Sq to watch the sound-and-light show (summer only) or kick back at one of the mega-fashionable lounge cafes around Isahakyan St.

Yerevan

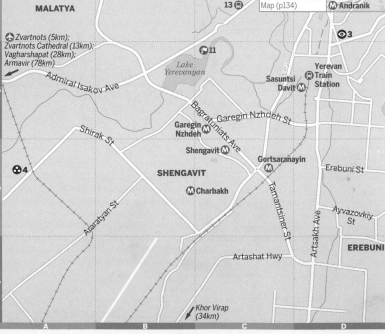

Ashtarak
(17km)

SILIKYAN

DAVTASHEN

Ashtarak Hwy

Fuchik St

Silikyan New Hwy

Silikyan
Old Hwy

Yeghvard Hwy

Vagharshan St

ARABKIR

Komitas Ave

Barbyus St

9 8

7

Halaban St

6
10 Barekamutyun

5

Kievyan St

Hrazdan River

Marshali
Baghramyan

Yeritasardakan

**Armenian Genocide
Memorial & Museum** 1

KOND

Tumanyan St

Charents St

Sebastia St

Hrazdan
Stadium

Republic Square
(Hanrapetutyan
Hraparak)

MALATYA

13

See Central Yerevan
Map (p134)

Zoravar
Andranik

Zvartnots (5km);
Zvartnots Cathedral (13km);
Vagharshapat (28km);
Armavir (78km)

3

Admiral Isakov Ave

Lake
Yerevanyan

11

Yerevan
Train
Station

Shirak St

Bagratuniats Ave

Garegin Nzhdeh St

Sasuntsi
Davit

4

Garegin
Nzhdeh

Shengavit

Gortsaranayin

Erebuni St

SHENGAVIT

Charbakh

Tamartsiner St

Ayvazovkiy
St

Azatutyan St

EREBUNI

Artashat Hwy

Khor Virap
(34km)

crushed to death and several were injured when Stalin's statue was wrenched off unannounced one night, leading to grim muttering about Stalin still killing from beyond the grave. Inside, one of the most interesting exhibits deals with Operation Nemesis, a covert action by the Armenian Revolutionary Federation (Dashnaktsutyun) carried out from 1920 to 1922 in which Ottoman political and military figures were assassinated for their roles in the horrific massacres of 1915-16.

Be warned that the staff here have a scam going whereby they try to charge every visitor AMD500 to enter. In reality, entrance is free and the charge only applies if you wish to take photographs.

Mother Armenia is located in the poorly maintained Haghtanak (Victory) Park, which is also home to a small fun fair popular with locals on weekends. To get here, take the elevator in the Cascade to the top courtyard and from there walk up the stairs to the huge concrete platform. From the top of the platform, walk to the main road, take the underpass and enter the park.

Matenadaran MUSEUM
(Map p134; ☑56 25 78; www.matenadaran.am/en; 53 Mesrop Mashtots Ave; adult/student AMD1000/200, guided tour AMD2500; ◎10am-4.30pm Tue-Sat) Standing at the top of Yerevan's

grandest avenue, this cathedral-like manuscript library is a source of enormous pride to all Armenians. The first *matenadaran* (book depository) for Armenian texts was built by St Mesrop Mashtots at Echmiadzin in the 5th century, and held thousands of manuscripts. Invasions over the centuries led to enormous losses through looting and burning, but 1800 exquisitely illustrated and bound manuscripts survived. These form the base of the stunning collection here.

At the base of the purpose-designed building, which dates from 1957, is a statue of Mashtots teaching his alphabet to a disciple. Six other statues of great scholars and writers stand by the door. The outdoor gallery has carved rock tombs and *khachkars* brought here from ancient sites around Armenia.

Inside, there are more than 23,000 manuscripts, fragments, documents and maps. The central hall focuses on the development of Armenian medieval sciences, literature and arts throughout the centuries. Other halls showcase Greek and Roman scientific and philosophical works, Iranian and Arabic manuscripts, and singular items such as the 13th-century Homilies of Mush, so heavy that it was ripped in half to be carried away to safety by two women after the 1915 massacres. The book was not put back together until years later, as one saviour had emigrated to America and taken it with her for safekeeping.

Centre of Popular Creation
MUSEUM
(Map p134; ☑56 93 80; www.cpc.am/en; 64 Abovyan St; admission AMD500, tours AMD2500; ☺11am-5pm Tue-Sat, 11am-4pm Sun) Its somewhat esoteric name means that many visitors to Yerevan overlook this museum. This is a great shame, as it is home to the best folk art collection in the country and is well worth a visit. Spread over two floors, the collection of woodcarving, silverwork, embroidery, carpets, lace and costumes is in mint condition and attractively displayed, with good lighting and English-language labels. The 19th- and 20th-century carpets and the intricate woodwork (some inlaid) are particularly impressive.

Yervand Kochar Museum
MUSEUM
(Map p134; ☑52 93 26; 39 Mesrop Mashtots Ave; admission AMD600, tour AMD2000; ☺11am-5pm Tue-Sat, 11am-4pm Sun) This fascinating museum does a great job of documenting the life and work of the prolific Armenian painter and sculptor. The museum showcases works created throughout Kochar's career, including *Lonely Woman,* painted in 1913 when he was only 13. Labels are in English and there is a short film about his most famous piece, the *Guernica*-like *Disaster of War* (1962).

Born in Tbilisi in 1899, Kochar studied art there and in Moscow before moving to Paris in 1923, where he exhibited work in shows alongside Georges Braque, Henri Matisse, Pablo Picasso, Joan Miró and many other avant-garde masters. In 1936 he relocated to Soviet-ruled Armenia, a move he no doubt regretted after he was imprisoned on politically motivated charges between 1941 and 1943. In later years, the Soviets recognised his work and bestowed a number of honours on him, including the People's Artist of the Soviet Union in 1976. He died in 1979.

Katoghike
CHURCH
(Map p134; cnr Sayat-Nova Ave & Abovyan St) The tiny 13th-century chapel incongruously known as the Katoghike (Cathedral) nestles beside the recently constructed Surp Anna Church. It has a fascinating history: the only Yerevan church to survive a devastating earthquake in 1679, it was incorporated into a new basilica in the 17th century and narrowly escaped being demolished when the

---

GETTING YOUR BEARINGS IN YEREVAN

Yerevan sits in a valley with the Hrazdan River cutting a serpentine gorge west of the city centre. Downtown streets are laid out on a grid intersected by pedestrianised Northern Ave (Hyusisayin Ave), where many upmarket shops are found. In the centre is Republic Sq (Hanrapetutyan Hraparak), where the History Museum of Armenia and National Gallery of Armenia are located. Opera Sq (Operayi Hraparak), home to the landmark 1930s Armenian National Academic Theater of Opera and Ballet building, is a short walk north.

The main bus station is the Kilikya Avtokayan west of town on the Vagharshapat/Echmiadzin Hwy, which also leads to Zvartnots Airport. *Marshrutky* (minibuses) to various parts of the country leave from Kilikiya and other destinations across the city, with a concentration around the Rossiya Mall on Tigran Mets Ave. The Yerevan train station is above Sasuntsi Davit metro station. Yerevan's metro has five stations in the city centre.

Soviets pulled that building down in 1936. A public outcry, highly unusual for that time, led to its preservation.

Hovhannes Tumanyan Museum   MUSEUM
(Map p134; ✆56 00 21; www.toumanian.am; 40 Moscovyan St; adult/child AMD500/300, guide AMD2500; ◷11am-4.30pm Tue-Sat, 11am-3.30pm Sun) This museum celebrates the life and work of the extraordinary writer, translator and humanist who is often described as Armenia's greatest poet. Tumanyan's most famous works are the libretto for Armen Tigranian's opera *Anoush* (1912), his poem 'The Conquest of Tmkaberd' and his novel *David of Sasoun*. The museum includes exhibits about these and other works, as well as photographs and letters documenting his life. On the upper floor there is a six-room reconstruction of his apartment in Tbilisi.

Born in 1869 in the village of Dsegh in the Lori region, Tumanyan was an extremely handsome and charismatic man who received his education in Tiflis (now Tbilisi) and was based in that city for most of his life. There, he hosted a circle of intellectuals in the garret of his house that included Avetik Isahakyan, Ghazaros Aghayan and Derenik Demirchian. Known as the 'Vernatoun', they were artistically prolific and socially progressive. In 1921 Tumanyan travelled to Constantinople to garner support and funds for Armenian refugees. Returning from that stressful trip, he fell ill in Tbilisi and was eventually transferred to Moscow for treatment. He died there in 1923.

Martiros Sarian Museum   MUSEUM
(Map p134; ✆58 17 62; http://sarian.am; 3 Sarian St) This museum preserves the studio and some of the works of 20th-century painter Martiros Sarian, known for his colour-saturated canvases. The museum was closed for renovation at the time of research.

Often described as the founder of the national style of painting, Sarian (also spelled Saryan) was born in Russia in 1880 and studied art at the Moscow School of Arts. Wanting to visit the homeland of his parents, he travelled to Armenia in 1901 and completed many paintings of the local landscape on that trip. After returning in 1915 to help refugees who had fled from the massacres in the Ottoman Empire, he relocated here permanently in 1928 after a two-year stint painting in Paris. Strongly influenced by the work of Henri Matisse and Paul Gauguin, Sarian soon became known for his vibrantly coloured landscapes and portraits.

Unlike many of his artistic peers he managed to stay in the good books of his Soviet masters, and was awarded the Order of Lenin three times. He died in Yerevan 1972.

Republic Square   SQUARE
(Hanrapetutyan Hraparak; Map p134) Originally named after Vladimir Lenin, Yerevan's main square was renamed in 1990. Designed by architect Alexander Tamanyan as the focal point of his 1924 urban plan for the city, the square's construction started in 1926 and continued until 1958, when the last of its Stalinist-style edifices was completed. The stone pattern in the centre of the square references an Armenian carpet, and the famous musical fountains are the city's most endearing attraction; these operate between sunset and 10pm in summer.

The pink tufa buildings on its northeastern, northwestern and southwestern edges were all purpose-built as government offices and remain so today. Other buildings include the Armenia Marriott Hotel on the southwestern corner and the National Gallery of Armenia/History Museum of Armenia at the northern (top) edge. Underneath the square is a large bunker constructed during the Cold War to protect high-ranking officials in the event of a nuclear attack. This is closed to the public.

★ History Museum of Armenia   MUSEUM
(Map p134; ✆52 96 01; www.historymuseum.am; Republic Sq; adult/student & child AMD1000/300, guide AMD5000; ◷11am-5.15pm Tue-Sat, 11am-4.15pm Sun) Its simply extraordinary collection of Bronze Age artefacts make this museum Armenia's preeminent cultural institution and an essential stop on every visitor's itinerary. Many of the items were excavated at the Necropolis of Lchashen near Lake Sevan in the 1950s, and it's hard to do them justice in words. The collection includes bronze sculptures, four-wheeled wooden chariots with metal decoration, carved stone fertility symbols, and a magnificent array of weapons and armour (arrows, quivers, helmets and shields).

Other exhibits of note include medieval *khachkars,* 18th- and 19th-century Armenian costumes, a 5500-year-old leather shoe discovered in a cave in Vayots Dzor region in 2008 (p176), carpets and embroidered amices (liturgical vestments). The only disappointing section is that concentrating on Soviet Armenia, which ostentatiously eschews English-language labelling (all other exhibits have Armenian, Russian and English labels).

Central Yerevan

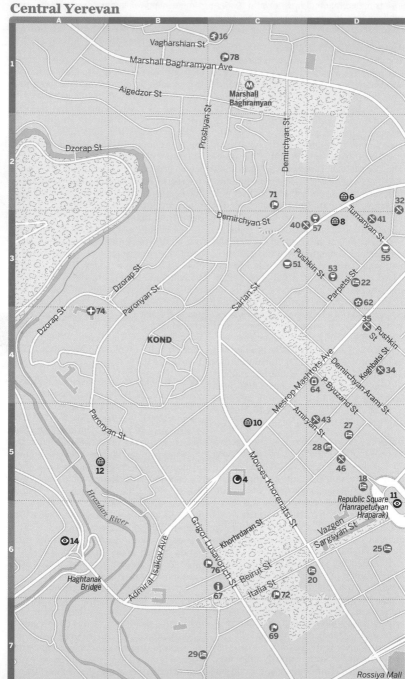

Vagharshian St
Marshall Baghramyan Ave
Aigedzor St
Marshall Baghramyan
Proshyan St
Demirchyan St
Dzorap St
Dzorap St
Dzorap St
Paronyan St
Paronyan St
Demirchyan St
Sarian St
Pushkin St
Parpetsi St
Pushkin St
Koghbatsi St
Mesrop Mashtots Ave
Demirchyan Arami St
P Byuzand St
Amiryan St
KOND
Movses Khorenatsi St
Grigor Lusavorich St
Admiral Isakov Ave
Hrazdan River
Haghtanak Bridge
Khorhrdaran St
Beirut St
Italia St
Vazgen Sargsyan St
Republic Square
(Hanrapetutyan Hraparak)
Tumanyan St
Rossiya Mall

16
78
6
32
71
41
40 57 8
55
51
53
22
62
35
34
74
64
10
43
27
28
12
46
18
4
11
14
25
76
20
67
72
69
29

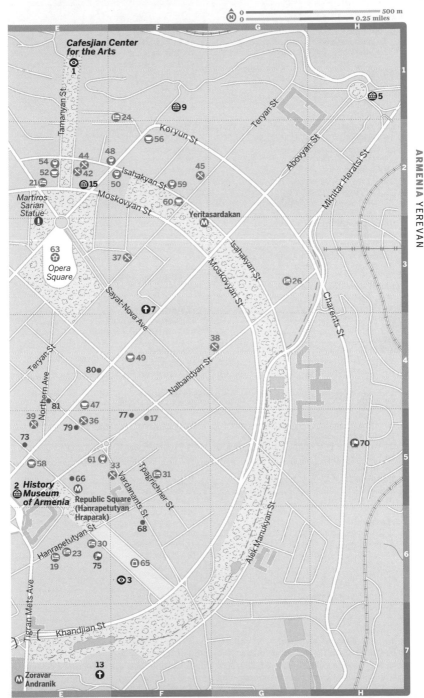

ARMENIA YEREVAN

Central Yerevan

National Gallery of Armenia   GALLERY
(Map p134; ☑ 56 74 72; www.gallery.am/en/; Republic Sq; adult/student & child AMD800/300, guide AMD5000; ⊙ 11am-5pm Tue-Sat, 11am-4pm Sun) Armenia's major art gallery holds a large but somewhat underwhelming collection of European and Russian art. Its major draw is, however, the collection of Armenian art displayed on the 4th and 5th floors. Highlights include works by Hakob Hov-

natanian (1806–81), Martiros Sarian (1880–1972) and Vardges Surenyants (1860–1921). Of these, the paintings by Surenyants are the most impressive. Depicting scenes from Armenian fairy tales and various historical events, they are colourful and delicately detailed, with an Orientalist feel. Don't miss them. The gallery occupies the top floors of the History Museum of Armenia. Entrance is free on the last Saturday of each month.

Modern Art Museum of Yerevan   GALLERY
(Map p134; ☑ 53 53 59; http://mamy.am; 7 Mesrop Mashtots Ave; admission AMD500, guide AMD2500; ☺ 11am-6pm Tue-Sun) When it opened in 1972, this was the first specialised museum of contemporary and modern art in the Soviet Union, and a source of enormous pride for the Armenian avant-garde. Many prominent local artists of the time donated works, and these form the core of the collection along with further artist donations from the 1980s. Recent acquisitions include some impressive works from the last decade – look out for paintings by Karen Petrosyan, Armen Gevorgyan and Laura Avetisyan.

The museum is accessed via a narrow lane running off Movses Khorenatsi St, parallel to Mashtots Ave.

Blue Mosque   MOSQUE
(Map p134; ☑ 10 42 84 98; 12 Mesrop Mashtots Ave; ☺ 10am-1pm & 3-6pm) There has been a mosque on this site since 1765, but like the other eight or so mosques that operated in Yerevan at the beginning of the 20th century it was closed during the Soviet era. Reconstructed in the late 1990s with Iranian funds, it is now the only functioning mosque in the city. Decorated with exterior tiles, it has a modest interior, graceful tiled dome, small minaret, and shady garden with fountains and flowerbeds. Visitors should dress appropriately – no bare legs or shoulders, and women should wear a headscarf when entering the prayer hall.

Sergei Parajanov Museum   MUSEUM
(Map p134; ☑ 53 84 73; www.parajanov.com/museum.html; 15/16 Dzoragyugh St; admission AMD700, tour AMD2500; ☺ 10.30am-5pm) For something totally unique, head to this museum near Hrazdan Gorge. Crammed with collages, drawings, photographs and assemblages created by the experimental filmmaker best known for his 1969 film *Sayat Nova* (aka *The Colour of Pomegranates*), it is as eccentric as it is engaging. Housed in an attractive 19th-century timber house, the collection

manages to successfully evoke Parajanov's prodigious talent, humour and humanity while at the same time illustrating the difficulties faced by artists, filmmakers and writers living under the Soviet regime.

Born in 1924 in Tiflis, Parajanov moved to Moscow in 1945 to study filmmaking. His early career was blighted when he was convicted of homosexuality (then illegal) in 1948, a charge that many of his friends and supporters considered bogus. After being released from jail and living in the Ukraine for a few years, he moved to Yerevan in the late 1960s. Two more criminal charges were levied against him in 1973 (for rape and producing pornography) and he was sentenced to five years of hard labour in a Siberian jail. He was eventually released after a high-profile international campaign for his freedom, supported by artists including Françoise Sagan, Jean-Luc Godard, François Truffaut, Luis Buñuel, Federico Fellini, Michelangelo Antonioni, Andrei Tarkovsky, Louis Aragon and John Updike. Parajanov died in Yerevan in 1990.

Armenian Centre for Contemporary Experimental Art   ARTS CENTRE
(Map p134; ☑ 56 82 25; www.accea.info; 1/3 Pavstos Buzand St; ☺ 11am-5pm Tue-Sat) FREE In a central location facing the popular Vernissage Market, this slightly down-at-heel arts centre is the hub of the city's avant-garde, hosting concerts, performances and talks. Experimental art in a variety of media is

ARMENIA YEREVAN

ARMENIA'S ARTISTIC HERITAGE

Armenia's artistic, literary and musical heritage is long, diverse and greatly revered by both locals and members of the diaspora. In Yerevan, a number of small museums memorialise the lives and work of famous artists and are well worth a visit. Prior familiarity with the work of these writers, painters, filmmakers and musicians isn't necessary because their personal stories closely reflect the tumultuous events of the past century and offer museum experiences that are as rich in history as they are in art. The most interesting are the **Hovhannes Tumanyan Museum** (p133), the **Yrvand Kochar Museum** (p132), the **Martiros Sarian Museum** (p133) and the **Sergei Parajanov Museum** (this page).

KHACHKARS

Listed by Unesco on its register of intangible cultural heritage, Armenian *khachkars* are outdoor steles carved from stone by craftspeople in Armenia and communities in the Armenian diaspora. Acting as memorial stones and focal points for worship, they are ornamented with carved crosses that are often depicted resting on the symbol of a sun or wheel of eternity. Other details can include geometric motifs, flowers, saints and animals. Carved using chisel, die, sharp pens and hammers, they can reach up to 1.5m in height and are believed by many Armenians to possess holy powers. There are thought to be more than 50,000 *khachkars* in Armenia.

In Yerevan, it's possible to watch *khachkars* being carved at a traditional stonemasons yard in Demirchyan Arami St between Teryan and Koghbatsi Sts. Medieval monasteries around the country all have an array of *khachkars*. Most stunning of all is the windswept cemetery filled with *khachkars* at Noratus (p173), near Lake Sevan.

exhibited in four exhibition spaces and often has political overtones. Yervand Kochar's 1959 figure *Melancholy* pines at the entrance.

Surp Grigor
Lusavorich Cathedral   CATHEDRAL
(Saint Gregory the Illuminator Cathedral; Map p134; http://lusavorich.am/; crn Khandjian & Tigran Mets Aves) Built to celebrate 1700 years of Christianity in Armenia and consecrated in 2001, this is the largest cathedral of the Armenian Apostolic Church in the world. The complex, which has a prominent location atop a hill on the eastern edge of the city centre, consists of three churches: the cathedral, the Chapel of St Tiridates the King, and the Chapel of St Ashkhen the Queen. These two royal figures supported St Gregory in converting Armenia to Christianity.

Some visitors find the interior disconcerting due to the presence of seats (1700 to be exact), the absence of candles (almost unheard of in Armenian Orthodox churches), the copious natural light and the minimalist decoration. The baldachin near the entrance was originally from Surp Gayane at Echmiadzin; it contains relics of St Gregory.

G.U.M Market   MARKET
(Gumi Shuka, Armenian Market; Map p130; 35 Movses Khorenatsi St; ☺7am-4pm) The displays of fresh and dried fruits at this covered market are pretty as a picture, so it's fortunate that the stallholders don't seem to mind tourists photographing their wares. In summer, the fresh fruit is magnificent, with peaches, cherries, apricots and berries of every description tempting shoppers. In winter, dried fruits and nuts, including the strings of syrup-coated walnuts known as *sujukh,* are popular purchases. Other produce includes fresh vege-

tables, aromatic herbs, pungent *basturma* (finely cured ham) and huge blocks of cheese.

◉ Outside the City Centre

Sights outside the city centre require a fair hike or a short cab or *marshrutka* ride.

★Armenian Genocide
Memorial & Museum   MEMORIAL
(Tsitsernakaberd; Map p130; ☑39 09 81; www.genocide-museum.am; Tsitsernakaberd Hill; ☺11am-4pm Tue-Sun) FREE Commemorating the massacre of Armenians in the Ottoman Empire from 1915 to 1922, this institution offers a powerful museum experience similar to that of Israel's Yad Vashem (Holocaust Museum). Designed by architects Arthur Tarkhanyan and Sashur Kalashyan working with artist Hovhannes Khachatryan, the two-storey exhibition space is built into the side of the hill so as not to detract from the monument above. The story of this horrific historical event is told through photographs, documents, newspaper reports and films.

From the museum, a broad pathway flanked by a 100m-long wall engraved with the names of massacred communities leads to the memorial, which was built in 1967. It consists of a 40m-high spire next to a circle of 12 basalt slabs leaning over to guard an eternal flame. The 12 tilted slabs represent the lost provinces of western Armenia, land lost to Turkey in a post-WWI peace deal between Ataturk and Lenin, while the spire has a fine split dividing it into larger and smaller needles, the smaller one representing western Armenia.

In the grounds there is a stand of trees planted by foreign leaders who use the term genocide to describe the events that occurred.

The complex is on Tsitsernakaberd Hill (Fortress of Swallows) across the Hrazdan Gorge from central Yerevan. The easiest way to get here is via taxi (AMD800 to AMD1200 from the city centre). Alternatively, take *marshrutka* 46 from Mesrop Mashtots Ave and alight at the steps of Hamalir (the Sports and Concert Complex). From here you can walk up the steps to the end of the park where the memorial and the museum are located. If driving, heading towards the Hrazdan stadium, turn right onto Athena St and look out for a blue sign with white lettering signalling the route.

★**Erebuni Historical & Archaeological Museum-Reserve**　　ARCHAEOLOGICAL SITE
(Map p130; ☑43 26 61; www.erebuni.am; 38 Erebuni St; adult/child & student AMD1000/300, guide AMD2500; ⏱10.30am-4.30pm Tue-Sun) This archaeological site dates from 782 BC, three decades before Rome was established. It gives an excellent insight into daily life in the palace of Argishti I, one of the greatest kings of Urartu. At the foot of the hill, a Soviet-era museum displays artefacts from the palace excavations including some extraordinary silver *rhythons* (drinking horns), as well as objects found when a Urartian tomb was uncovered in Yerevan in 1984 during construction of a factory.

The first stage of excavations here started in 1950, after a farmer unearthed an inscribed stone tablet. Archaeologists swooped in and soon found a large cuneiform slab with the inscriptions of Argishti I confirming the date when the fortress was constructed. They went on to uncover the remains of courtyards, halls, temples and rooms that were part of the royal palace. Dozens of Urartian and Achaemenid artefacts and mural fragments were also found, many of which are now displayed in the museum.

The view from the fortress takes in parts of the city and **Karmir Blur** (Red Hill; Map p130), where excavations have revealed similar ancient finds. Frescoes in the reconstructed palace wall are replicas. There are huge storerooms for wheat, along with *tonir* (oven pits) and gigantic pitchers for wine and oil. There's also a place for animal sacrifices, and workshops (still buried) for making tools.

To get here, take bus 16 or *marshrutka* 73 or 14 from Khandjian St, or from opposite the Zoravar Andranik metro station on Tigran Mets Ave. Alternatively, take *marshrutka* 11 from Republic Sq or *marshrutka* 37 or 58 from Mesrop Mashtots Ave. Get off at the large roundabout with an orange tufa statue of King Argishti in his chariot; it's a 15- to 20-minute trip from the city centre.

Yerevan Brandy Company　　DISTILLERY
(Map p134; ☑54 00 00; Admiral Isakov Ave; tour & tastings AMD4500-10,000; ⏱daily tours by appointment Sep-Jul, Mon-Fri only Aug) Occupying a commanding position on a hill overlooking the Hrazdan Gorge, this fortress-like distillery offers daily guided tours including generous tastings. The company cellars are full of barrels dating back to the 19th century, including one that won't be opened until a Karabakh peace deal appears. Tours take 75 minutes – the charge is AMD4500 if two recent vintages of brandy are tasted, AMD10,000 if you opt for three aged vintages.

To get here from the city centre, walk across the Haghtanak Bridge, hop aboard *marshrutka* 5 or 259 on Mesrop Mashtots Ave (AMD100) or take a taxi (AMD600). Book your tour at least one day in advance.

⛬ Tours

Envoy Hostel　　TOUR
(Map p134; ☑53 03 69; www.envoyhostel.com; 54 Pushkin St; per person AMD8500) For something a bit different, sign up for the informative and enjoyable minibus tour of Soviet-era Yerevan run by this hostel on Monday, Wednesday and Saturday between 11am and 3pm. It visits Republic Sq, the Yerevan train station, moribund factories, apartment blocks and other legacies of the USSR. Guides enjoy poking good-natured fun at their former Soviet masters.

The hostel also offers a walking tour of Yerevan (per person AMD2000), a range of guided tours to destinations around Armenia, airport transfers, and a popular hybrid tour/transfer between Yerevan and Tbilisi stopping at Sanahin, Haghpat and Akhtala monasteries en route (per person AMD29,500, 11 hours, Friday).

Hyur Service　　TOUR
(Map p134; ☑52 98 08; www.hyurservice.com; 96 Nalbandyan St; adult/child under 12yr AMD5000/2500) This reputable company offers a three-hour tour around the city centre on Mondays and Wednesdays at 7pm. Travel between sights such as the Opera House, Cascade, Republic Sq and Surp Grigor Lusavorich Cathedral is by both bus and foot, and is led by a professional guide. Hyur also offers private tours, airport transfers, tours around the country and apartment rental.

AURORA MARDIGANIAN

One of the most fascinating displays in the Armenian Genocide Museum (p138) is devoted to the tragic and eventful life of Aurora Mardiganian. Born in Chemeshgezak in Western Armenia (modern-day Çemişgezek in Turkey), Aurora was 14 years old when she and her family were forced from their homes and into a caravan of exiles by forces of the Turkish government in June 1915. On the march to Syria she saw every member of her family murdered and then was placed in a Turkish harem. Eventually escaping her captors, she was subsequently captured by Kurdish slave traders. Escaping yet again, she set out on a 600km walk to Erzerum, where she arrived in 1917. Erzerum had been taken by Russian troops by this time, so she was able to make her way on to Petrograd (now St Petersberg) with the help of the American Committee for Armenian and Syrian Relief (aka the Near East Foundation). The same organisation then assisted her migration to America.

In America, Aurora wrote an account of her horrific experience entitled *My two years of torture in ravished, martyred Armenia*. This was published in US newspapers and formed the basis of her memoir *Ravished Armenia: the Story of Aurora Mardiganian, the Christian Girl, Who Survived the Great Massacres* (1918), which was hugely successful in drawing the world's attention to the plight of the Armenians in Turkey. Even more influential was the 1918 silent movie *Ravished Armenia* (aka *The Auction of Souls*), which was based on Aurora's book and in which she actually starred. Aurora died in California in 1994.

★ Festivals & Events

Vardavar   CULTURAL
Celebrated on a Sunday in high summer 98 days (14 weeks) after Easter, this festival sees marauding gangs of bucket-equipped young people drenching bystanders with water. Sensible people stay indoors for the day.

Golden Apricot Yerevan
International Film Festival   FILM
(www.gaiff.am; ⊙ Jul) High-profile film festival held each year.

Yerevan Jazz Fest   JAZZ
(www.mezzoproductions.com; ⊙ Sep) Three-day jazz festival featuring local and international acts.

🛏 Sleeping

There has been a boom in hotel construction across Yerevan in recent times, and there has also been an increase in the number of hostels opening in the city centre. As a result, there are plenty of accommodation options to choose from. Low-season rates usually apply between November and March; rates are highest in September and October.

Note that we have used a nonsmoking icon to indicate where there are dedicated nonsmoking floors.

Envoy Hostel   HOSTEL $
(Map p134; ☑ 53 03 69; www.envoyhostel.com; 54 Pushkin St; dm AMD5300-8000, s with bathroom AMD17,000-23,000, without bathroom AMD12,000-20,000, d with bathroom AMD19,000-23,000, with-

out bathroom AMD17,000-20,000; ⊙❄@🛜) An excellent location and helpful staff make this long-time backpacker hub a popular choice. There are plenty of private rooms, plus nine mixed dorms with lockers (BYO padlock), hard beds and reading lights; we suggest avoiding those in the basement. Shared bathrooms are clean and well-maintained, though in short supply. The communal lounge and kitchen are major draws.

If you choose to stay here, be sure to take advantage of the free daily walking tour of the city and consider taking one of the hostel-run day tours around the country or into Georgia. Despite the address, the entrance is actually on leafy Parpetsi St, which is full of cafes, restaurants and bars.

Royal Hostel   HOSTEL $
(Map p134; ☑ 91 34 49 17, 11 36 10 00; 36 Khorhrdarani St; dm AMD4000-4500, s without bathroom AMD10,000-12,000, d without bathroom AMD12,000-14,000; ⊙❄@🛜) Opened in 2015, this friendly hostel is located in a residential pocket near the river. Originally a family home, it has three dorms sleeping between four and eight (two with air-con, which is necessary in summer) as well as a few private rooms. The communal kitchen and three shared bathrooms are very clean, and there's even a washing machine.

Cascade Hostel   HOSTEL $
(Map p134; ☑ 58 55 55; http://yerevan.pantika.de; 3rd fl, 2 Marshall Baghramyan Ave; dm AMD3500-5000, s without bathroom AMD8000-10,000, d/

tw without bathroom AMD12,000-13,300; ❄🛜)
High ceilings and parquet floors endow this
friendly and clean hostel with plenty of atmosphere, and its location near the Cascade
is close to cafes and bars. There are two adjoining dorms (one sleeping 12, the other six)
and two rooms sleeping up to four. Sadly,
bathroom facilities are inadequate, with only
one shower and two toilets for 24 beds. Other
facilities include lockers, a small communal
kitchen, a lounge and a washing machine
that guests can use at no charge. The hostel
entrance is at the rear of the building, near
the corner of Moskovyan and Tamanyan Sts.

Yerevan Hostel
HOSTEL **$**

(Map p134; 📞54 77 57; www.hostelinyerevan.com;
5 Tpagrichner St; dm AMD3500-7000, d AMD17,000-
25,000; ❄🛜) In the basement of a decrepit
apartment block, this hostel offers two eight-
bed dorms with uncomfortable bunks and
inadequate locker facilities, plus three overpriced doubles. From the dorms, guests need
to walk through common areas to reach the
clean but basic shared bathrooms. The staff
are very helpful and the location convenient,
which is why we are listing it here.

An annexe across the road has a six-bed
dorm with its own kitchen – it's better to
stay here than in the main building.

★ Azoyan Guest House
GUESTHOUSE **$$**

(Map p134; 📞98 56 66 40, 56 66 49; www.azoyan
guesthouse.am; 32 Hanrapetutyan St; s/d/tr
AMD27,000/32,000/34,000; 😊❄🛜) B&Bs
aren't often described as being elegant and
stylish, but both terms certainly apply here.
In a fantastic location between Republic Sq
and the Vernissage Market, it offers three
attractively decorated rooms with large
beds, satellite TV and work desk. There's no
lounge or outdoor area, but the makings of
a generous organic breakfast are supplied
in the communal kitchen.

★ Tufenkian Historic Yerevan Hotel
HOTEL **$$**

(Map p134; 📞60 50 10 10; www.tufenkianheritage.
com; 48 Hanrapetutyan St; s AMD35,000-91,000,
d AMD47,000-105,000; 😊❄📶🛜♨) Though it
calls itself an historic hotel, this impressive
five-star choice opposite the Vernissage Market was purpose-built and opened in 2012.
Rooms are spacious, with excellent bathrooms, comfortable beds and plenty of amenities. There's a small outdoor swimming pool,
the excellent Kharpert Restaurant (p144) and
a foyer cafe serving good coffee. Rates through

online booking sites are often slashed, offering sensational value.

★ My Hotel Yerevan
HOTEL **$$**

(Map p134; 📞60 07 08; www.myhotelyerevan.
am; 47 Nalbandyan St; s AMD25,000-22,000, d
AMD32,000-33,000; 🅿❄🛜) Tucked into a
corner of a residential courtyard on the city
edge, this recently opened hotel offers 12
attractively presented rooms with satellite
TV and tea and coffee facilities. Standard
rooms are on the small side, so it's worth
paying extra for the deluxe category. A buf-
fet breakfast is served in the basement and
there's a pleasant courtyard with resident
cat. To find it, look for the purple sign on
Nalbandyan St, enter the courtyard and
head to the left.

Hotel Meg
B&B **$$**

(Map p134; 📞58 10 08; www.hotelmeg.com; 1
Jrashat St; 1-room ste AMD33,200-62,400, 2-room
ste AMD45,500-72,000; 🅿😊🛜) An excellent
choice for families, the Meg offers new stylish and well-equipped suites with tiled floor,
kitchenette and satellite TV with DVD; the
two-room choice also has a couch and dining table. Breakfast is served in your suite.

The hotel is a little hard to find and is also
inadequately signed: walk up Mesrop Mashtots Ave towards the Matenadaran, turn
into the small compound on the opposite
side of the street to the Grand Candy Cafe,
head up the hill to the right and then into
the AD Sakharov Armenian Human Rights
Centre building on the left. The hotel is in
the basement.

Republica Hotel
HOTEL **$$**

(Map p134; 📞11-99 00 00; www.republicahotel.am;
7 Amiryan St; s AMD46,000 84,000, d AMD52,000-
91,000, ste AMD68,000-139,000; 😊❄🛜) A rel-
atively new midrange choice, the Republica
offers slightly cramped standard rooms and
an array of deluxe rooms and suites that
are worth the upgrade charge. Though the
hotel's claim to boutique status is a bit of a
stretch, its stylish ground-floor restaurant
(mains AMD2700 to AMD5900) and 100%
smoke-free policy deserve kudos. All rooms
have work desk and tea and coffee facilities.

Paris Hotel
HOTEL **$$**

(Map p134; 📞60-60 00 60; www.parishotel.
am; 4-6 Amiryan St; r AMD39,000-69,000, ste
AMD89,000-108,000; 🅿😊❄📶🛜) It may not
be the most stylish of the recently opened
hotels in the city centre, but the Paris
Hotel has a lot going for it. The great location

near Republic Sq, extremely helpful staff, secure parking, fitness centre and rooftop restaurant are all assets, as are the spacious rooms with tea and coffee facilities, satellite TV and work desk.

Europe Hotel　　　　　　HOTEL $$
(Map p134; ☑54 60 60; www.europehotel.am; 32-38 Hanrapetutyan St; s AMD35,000-62,000, d AMD40,000-73,000, ste AMD60,000-103,000; P❄@☎) Staff at this centrally located three-star choice are both friendly and efficient, and the hotel itself is run with an impressive degree of professionalism. Rooms have a slightly dated decor but are spacious and well-equipped, with comfortable beds. The breakfast buffet is generous, and there's a 24-hour lobby bar. Our only quibble is that communal areas reek of cigarette smoke.

Hyatt Place　　　　　　HOTEL $$$
(Map p134; ☑11-33 30 00; www.yerevan.place. hyatt.com; 26 V Sargsyan St; d AMD85,000-105,000, ste AMD135,000-250,000; P❄❄@☎) The exterior is hardly prepossessing, but enter this 2013 addition to Yerevan's five-star offerings and you're bound to be impressed. The location, professional service levels, large and well-equipped rooms (couch, work desk, iron and ironing board, tea and coffee facilities, iPhone dock, laptop safe) and stylish ambience are hard to beat. The breakfast buffet is fabulous, too.

Armenia Marriott Hotel　　HOTEL $$$
(Map p134; ☑59 90 00; www.marriott.com; 1 Amiryan St; r AMD83,000-250,000, ste AMD245,000-1125,000; P❄❄@☎❄) It's often described as Yerevan's best hotel, but we're unconvinced that this Soviet-era institution on Republic Sq deserves the accolade. Rooms in the original building are large but dowdy; those in the recently renovated attached building are much more attractive. The lack of a swimming pool and the extra charges for breakfast (AMD7200 to AMD12,000) and wi-fi (per hour AMD3000) are disappointing.

Best Western Congress　　HOTEL $$$
(Map p134; ☑59 11 99; www.congresshotel yerevan.com; 1 Italia St; s AMD46,000-60,000, d AMD60,000-97,000; ❄❄@☎❄) Overlooking a park close to Republic Sq, the Congress has one major advantage over its many recently opened four-star competitors: a huge swimming pool and health club. This, with the in-house pizzeria, makes it an excellent choice in summer, especially for families. Unfortunately, the tired rooms and average breakfast buffet move it out of strong contention at other times.

Nonguests can use the pool for AMD7500 on weekdays and AMD9000 on weekends. Use of the gym and sauna costs AMD5000 per day. The daily breakfast buffet costs AMD4200.

YEREVAN'S BUILDING BOOM

Recent visitors to Yerevan may be forgiven for thinking that they have arrived in a huge building site rather than one of the oldest cities in Europe. Cranes dominate the skyline, dust from excavations swirls in the streets and the drone of heavy machinery is constantly in the background. This building boom is unprecedented in Armenia's history, and while it might be good for the local economy, it's disastrous for the city's built heritage. Not long ago, the city centre was filled with handsome 19th-century office and apartment buildings, and surrounding neighbourhoods were characterised by their pretty timber houses. Now, most of those buildings and houses have been demolished.

Cultural critics such as Liana Aghajanian, a contributor to the online magazine Ianyan (www.ianyanmag.com), have warned that if this frenzy of development is allowed to proceed unchecked, Yerevan is likely to become 'a city without memory'. Many locals seem to share her concern – in 2014 there were major protests against the demolition of the Afrikyan Club House, a heritage-listed building in Teryan St. Other heated protests occurred in 2012 and 2013 when businessman Samvel Alexanyan, one of the wealthiest men in the country, pulled down most of the much-loved Pak Shuka, a produce market on Mesrop Mashtots Ave. Locals were outraged by his action (the market was on State List of Immovable Historical and Cultural Monuments of Yerevan as an officially recognized architectural monument) and by the fact that he was a member of parliament who ignored heritage laws.

One of the few 19th-century neighbourhoods to remain relatively intact is Kond in the southwestern corner of the city centre. Its ramshackle timber housing stock is – for now – almost exactly as it was a century ago. To explore its winding alleyways, enter up one of the steep cobbled slopes from Paronian or Sarian Sts.

✘ Eating

As is the case all over the country, *khoravats* is hugely popular here. However, it's also possible to dine at restaurants serving international cuisine and even at the occasional vegetarian establishment. Street snacks include *gharsi khorovats* (grilled meat wrapped in thin lavash bread), *msashot* (thin pizza topped with minced meat and spices, also known as *lahmajo* or *lahmajoon*) and *karkantak* (pastries stuffed with cheese, vegetables or meat). For international-style fast food try centrally located **Square One** (Map p134; ☑10 56 61 69; 1/3 Abovyan St; burgers AMD2500-2900, pastas AMD2000-2500; ☎) or one of the many branches of **Tashir Pizza** (www.tashirpizza.am) around town.

Most restaurants and cafes in the city levy a 10% service charge.

★ **Anteb**   ARMENIAN $
(Map p134; ☑53 09 88; 30 Koghbatsi St; mezes AMD400-2200, pides AMD700-2600, kebaps AMD2400-4400; ☺10.30am-11.30pm; ✱☑) Serving 'western Amenian' dishes that are very similar to those enjoyed in Turkey, this is one of the most popular eateries in the city centre. The decor and service are without frills, but this doesn't matter – everyone's attention focuses on the super-tasty mezes, salads, pides, *fatayer* (stuffed pastries), *lahmajoon* and kebaps on offer. The baklava is an essential finale.

Lagonid   MIDDLE EASTERN $
(Map p134; ☑58 49 93; 37 Nalbandyan St; mezes & salads AMD500-1500, mains AMD800-2800; ☺10am-11pm; ☎☑♨) Lagonid has been serving its robust rifts on Levantine dishes to loyal regulars for nearly 20 years, so it knows what makes diners happy. The food is fresh, the surrounds are pleasant, service is efficient and prices are extremely reasonable. It also delivers (AMD300 within the city centre, AMD400 to AMD1000 outside).

12 Tables   CAFE $
(Map p134; Alexander Spendiaryan St; sandwiches AMD900-2200, waffles & crepes AMD700-1600; ☺noon-midnight; ☎☑) Entered through an arty handicrafts shop, this cute-as-a-button basement tearoom has a whimsical, very feminine, decor and a well-priced menu of toasted sandwiches, baguettes, salads, pastas, waffles and crepes. There's a huge variety of leaf tea to choose from (all served in pots), as well as milkshakes, freshly squeezed juices and an exemplary house-made lemonade. The staff are very welcoming.

The Green Bean   VEGETARIAN $
(Map p134; ☑52 92 79; www.thegreenbean.am; 10 Tamanyan St; salads AMD1600-2300, bagels & sandwiches AMD1500-2900; ☺8.30am-11.30pm; ☎☑) Its heart is in the right place, so we wish that the coffee and food served at this modern cafe beneath the Cascade were better. Plenty of vegetarian and vegan salads and sandwiches are on offer (many produced using organically sourced produce), as well as organic teas and coffee (filtered and espresso). There's a second branch on **Amiryan St** (Map p134; 10 Amiryan St; ☺8.30am-10.30pm).

Wine Republic   INTERNATIONAL $$
(Map p134; ☑55 00 11 00; 2 Tamanyan St; pastas AMD2300-3600, burgers AMD1800-2900, cheese & meat platters AMD3500-5900; ☺noon-midnight; ✱☎) The interior walls of this recently opened bistro are clad in wooden panels stamped with insignia of vineyards around the world, signalling that it is serious about its wine. There are plenty of options by the glass and bottle, as well as a menu featuring cheese, salume, pastas, burgers and salads. Note that the entrance is actually on Isahakyan St.

Karma   INDIAN $$
(Map p134; ☑58 92 15; 65 Teryan St; mains AMD2200-3600; ☺11am-11pm; ✱☑) Meat dominates the menus at most of Yerevan's restaurants, so the generous array of vegetarian choices available at this Northern Indian restaurant comes as a very welcome change. The chef hails from the subcontinent, and the food is fresh and tasty. There's even Kingfisher beer on offer. Note: no credit cards.

Yerevan Tavern   ARMENIAN $$
(Pandok Yerevan; Map p134; ☑54 55 45; www.pandokyerevan.com; 5 Amiryan St; mains AMD700-6000; ☺10am-midnight; ✱) You'll need a big appetite and a willingness to be noisily entertained to make the most of this traditional dining experience. Popular with large groups of locals, it features a huge *khoravats* menu, brisk service and live music on most nights of the week. The menu is in Armenian only, but there are photographs of every dish, making ordering easy.

There are three other branches around town; most locals prefer this one or the larger branch in **Teryan St** (Pandok Yerevan; Map p134; ☑50 88 00; www.pandokyerevan.com; 91 Teryan St; ☺10am-midnight; ✱), near the Opera House.

CAFE CULTURE

Cafe-hopping is something of a sport in Yerevan, particularly in summer, and the cafe is a hybrid beast where coffee, alcohol and food are served, live music is often staged and impromptu dancing is not uncommon. To sample the local scene, head to Opera Sq (especially near the water feature known as Swan Lake), Isahakyan St, Tamanyan St in front of the Cascade, the park immediately southwest of Republic Sq and Luna Park next to Surp Grigor Lusavorich Cathedral.

Tapastan Yerevan   TAPAS $$

(Map p134; ✉52 19 32; 6 Sarian St; small plates AMD800-2500; ⊗noon-midnight; ☎✐) Graze on Venetian *cicchetti*, Basque *pintxos* and Armenian *patarner* at this popular place specialising in wine and tapas-style plates. The food is acceptable rather than inspired, but the international wine list, friendly staff and attractive surrounds make it well worth a visit.

Babig   LEBANESE $$

(Map p134; ✉11-99 43 43; www.babig-restaurant. com; 35 Pushkin St; mezes AMD700-3000, grills AMD2700-6000; ✱☎) Pastel-coloured walls, photographs of Lebanon and plenty of bric-a-brac impart a homely feel to this eatery. The menu is dominated by Lebanese staples such as mezes and grills, with a few additions out of left field (Lebanese burgers, anyone?). No credit cards.

★Ankyun   ITALIAN $$$

(Map p134; ✉54 46 06; www.ankyun.am; 4 Vardanants St; pizzas AMD4000-5200, pastas AMD3600-6200, mains AMD4200-13,000; ⊗noon-11pm; ✱✐★) Ask local foodies to nominate the best Italian food in town, and they inevitably choose this place. The chef uses seasonal ingredients to create pizzas, antipasti, pasta, grills and excellent versions of classic desserts such as tiramisu and pannacotta. The decor nods towards Tuscany, and you may even be offered a complimentary limoncello after your meal.

★The Club   INTERNATIONAL $$$

(Map p134; ✉53 13 61; www.theclub.am; 40 Tumanyan St; mains AMD3000-15,000; ⊗11am-midnight; ✱☎) Fusing western Armenian and French cuisine, the menu at this fashionable basement restaurant includes salads, traditional village dishes such as *dolma* (meat, rice and herbs wrapped in vine leaves) and *manti* (meat ravioli topped with yoghurt, garlic, tomato and butter), oven-baked fish and steaks sizzled on hot stones at the table. It's worth saving room for a dessert, as these are particularly good. There's live music most nights.

There are two additional spaces in its basement – a lounge with beanbag seating and a cafe serving pizzas (AMD1600 to AMD2400), burgers (AMD2100) and wraps (AMD690 to AMD990). These are accessed from a second entrance in the side street.

Kharpert Restaurant   ARMENIAN $$$

(Map p134; ✉60-50 10 30; www.tufenkianheritage. com/en/restaurants/kharpert-restaurant-in-yerevan/; 48 Hanrapetutyan St; mains AMD2000-9000; ✱☎✐) After a week or so in Armenia, many visitors find the local *khoravats*-dominated diet monotonous. Fortunately, this excellent restaurant in the Tufenkian Hotel can supply an antidote. Its seasonally driven menu includes modern rifts on traditional western Armenian dishes (soups, salads, pastries and stews), as well as universal favourites such as burgers and steaks. Surrounds are handsome; service can be perfunctory.

Dolmama's   ARMENIAN $$$

(Map p134; ✉56 13 54; www.dolmama.am; 10 Pushkin St; mains AMD6500-13,000; set menus AMD38,000-40,000; ⊗11am-11.30pm) Often described as Yerevan's best restaurant, Dolmama has various indoor spaces but the prime dining spot is the summer-only rear courtyard. The menu focuses on eastern Armenian dishes including *dolma*, *kashlama* (meat stewed in sweet wine) and *khorovats* with mulberry sauce. Consider opting for one of the set menus paired with wine.

🍷 Drinking & Nightlife

★Gemini   CAFE

(Map p134; ✉53 88 14; 31 Tumanyan St; ⊗9am-midnight) With the look and feel of a Parisian boulevard cafe, Gemini keeps its band of regulars happy with the city's best coffee (we love both the Armenian and iced varieties) as well as a variety of crepes (the Nutella is legendary). Beans are roasted and can be purchased at its nextdoor shop.

★In Vino   WINE BAR

(Map p134; ✉52 19 31; 6 Sarian St; ⊗11am-midnight; ☎) Our favourite of the wine bars that have recently opened in Yerevan, In Vino flaunts its Italianophile leanings but manages to do so without alienating supporters of Armenian produce. The range of Italian wines, cheese and *salume* (pork cold cuts such as salami and proscuitto) is impressive, and there are also local wines, cheeses, *basturma* and olives on offer.

Aperitivo   WINE BAR

(Map p134; ☑ 58 65 88; 41 Mesrop Mahtots Ave; ⊙ 11am-2am; ☎) Lined with bottles of wine from around the world, this stylish space has a shared bench, banquette seats and a few streetside tables where customers can enjoy a glass of wine or brandy accompanied by a cheese or meat platter, sandwich or salad. There's occasional live music on weekends.

Abovyan 12   CAFE

(Map p134; ☑ 58 06 58; 12 Abovyan St; ⊙ 10am-midnight) Bohemian is the first word that comes to mind when describing this hugely popular cafe near Republic Sq. Enter through the Dalan Handicrafts Shop or up the staircase to its right. Winter action is in the 1st-floor salons; in summer everyone moves to the large rear courtyard. There's occasional live music in both spaces. Better for drinking than eating.

Calumet   BAR

(Map p134; ☑ 099 88 11 73; 56a Pushkin St; ⊙ 5pm-midnight; ☎) This basement bar is owned by Hratch Davidian, a diaspora Armenian from Lebanon. The name is French for 'peace pipe', and its dated interior harks back to hippy days. There's well-priced draft Kilikiya and Stella, a Beatles-dominated soundtrack and welcoming bar staff. Enter through the wooden door on the street and head down the dimly lit stairs.

Beer Academy   BEER HALL

(Map p134; ☑ 060-50 45 04; 8 Moskovyan St; ⊙ 11am-midnight; ☎) Armenia's only microbrewery, this place has a large indoor drinking den and a pleasant outdoor terrace. The menu has been designed to complement its range of beers. Enter from Isahakyan St.

Stoyka   PUB

(Map p134; ☑ 43 84 18; 48 Nalbandyan St; ⊙ 7pm-late) A cheerful pub popular with young tourists, diaspora Armenians and locals, Stokya is known for late-night hedonism and a lethal array of drinks.

Jazzve   CAFE

(Map p134; 35 Tumanyan St; ⊙ 10am-midnight; ☎) A *jazzve* is a long-handled coffee pot in which rich Armenian coffee is brewed, and this popular chain of cafes specialises in coffee made this way. It also offers espresso coffees, a huge range of tea, snacks, ice-cream sundaes, smoothies and cocktails. There are other branches scattered around town.

Poplovok Jazz Café   CAFE

(Map p134; ☑ 52 23 03; 41 Isahakyan St; ⊙ 7am-7pm) In a pavilion overlooking Poplovok pond, this upmarket lounge-cafe is a male-dominated spot for a coffee during the day. At night the crowd is more diverse and live jazz is performed. It's on the Teryan St corner.

Mezzo   CLUB

(Map p134; ☑ 52 42 11; www.mezzo.am; 28 Isahakyan St; music surcharge applies; ⊙ noon-2am) Join Yerevan's bold, beautiful and Botoxed at this ritzy two-level club, where you can relax in one of the lounges, dine at the restaurant, choose a cigar from the walk-in humidor or dance to nightly live music in the parterre zone. Make sure you dress to the nines and bring a credit card with plenty of leverage.

Cafe Malócco   CAFE

(Map p134; ☑ 096 53 13 27; 1 Tamanyan St; ⊙ 9am-midnight; ☎) A popular local chain, Malócco serves Starbucks coffee and has a crowd-pleasing food menu of sandwiches, salads, pasta and steak. The food is unexceptional, so we prefer to claim a table overlooking the Cascade sculpture garden, order a lemonade and watch the street action. There are two other branches in the city centre.

Eden Café-Pub   PUB

(Map p134; ☑ 54 46 44; http://edencafepub.com/; 1a Tamanyan St; ⊙ 10am-3am; ☎) In the afternoon, Eden is so laid-back it's almost comatose. The pace picks up on warm summer nights, when regulars enjoy beers and *nargilehs* (waterpipes) at the streetside tables. There's live music in the smoky downstairs space on weekends.

Artbridge Bookstore Café   CAFE

(Map p134; ☑ 52 12 39; http://artbridge.am; 20 Abovyan St; ⊙ 8.30am-midnight; ☎) The dowager of Yerevan's arty cafes, Artbridge has been surpassed in both the quality and fashion stakes but retains a faithful core of regulars who appreciate its tranquil atmosphere, vegetarian-friendly menu and French-press coffee.

Grand Candy   CAFE

(Map p134; www.grandcandy.am/en/; 54 Mesrop Mashtots Ave; ⊙ 9am-9pm; ☻) Ask any Armenian child to name their favourite place, and they're likely to excitedly shout 'Grand Candy!' This sweets shop and cafe is painted in candy colours (of course), features a toy train running along tracks suspended from the ceiling, and has a ground floor crammed with sweets and chocolates. Needless to say, its mezzanine cafe is popular with families.

Bureaucrat   CAFE
(Map p134; 📋50 01 52; 19 Sarian St; ⊘11am-8pm Mon-Sat, noon-7pm Sun; 📶) This bookshop cafe's credentials are bohemian rather than bureaucratic, as it specialises in art books and is a popular spot for arty discussions. It's a good spot to read over an afternoon cup of tea.

☆ Entertainment

Yerevan Opera Theatre   CONCERT VENUE
(Map p134; 📋52 79 92; 54 Tumanyan St) The city's main entertainment venue was built in the 1930s and has two main halls: the Aram Khachaturian Concert Hall and the National Academic Theater of Opera and Ballet. Performance information is displayed on billboards outside, near Mesrop Mahtots Ave. There's also a ticket box here.

Malkhas Jazz Club   JAZZ
(Map p134; 📋53 53 50; 52 Pushkin St; admission AMD2000; ⊘11am-4am) Let's start by saying that in 2015 Kardashian sisters spent an evening here. This could be both a recommendation or a warning – we'll leave it for you to decide. Armenia's most famous jazz club, it's popular with oligarchs and its prices reflect this fact. Expect plenty of smoke, loud clients, good food and excellent live jazz. Live sets start at 9pm. Dress to impress.

🛍 Shopping

Cognac is a popular item to bring home, and there's a decent selection available in the duty-free store at Zvartnots Airport. For locally produced handicrafts and jewellery, try the gift store at the Cafesjian Center for the Arts or browse the wares at the Vernissage Market. Boxes of fruit-filled chocolates produced by local company Grand Candy also make good gifts.

Vernissage Market   MARKET
(Map p134; ⊘10am-4pm) An open-air market running between Hanrapetutyun and Khanjyan Sts, the Vernissage is where you should come to source locally produced handicrafts including traditional dolls, brass pots and *jazzves*, ceramics and woodwork, as well as second-hand goods. It has the most stalls on weekends; the pickings can be slim during the week. Quality varies, and bargaining is only occasionally successful.

Bookinist   BOOKS
(Map p134; 📋53 74 13; 20 Mesrop Mashtots Ave; ⊘10am-8pm Mon-Sat, 10am-7pm Sun) The city's best range of guidebooks, maps and novels in English and other languages.

ℹ Information

CULTURAL CENTRES
American Corner (Map p134; 📋56 13 83; www.americancorners.am; Yerevan City Central Library, 4 Nalbandyan St; ⊘9am-5pm Mon-Fri, 10am-4pm Sat) Has a library with books, American newspapers and free internet access. Also has occasional English-language film screenings and lectures. You'll find it next to the Republic Square (Hanrapetutyan Hraparak) metro station, behind Government Building No 3.

EMERGENCIES
Fire (📋101)
Medical Emergency (📋103)
Police (📋102)

INTERNET ACCESS
Free wi-fi is offered by the vast majority of Yerevan's hotels, cafes and fast-food joints. It's also available at the American Corner.

MEDICAL SERVICES
Pharmacies are marked by the Russian word *apteka;* there's one open late in every neighbourhood.
Nairi Clinic (Map p134; 📋53 75 00; www.nairimed.am; 21 Paronyan St) Has an emergency department and English-speaking staff.

MONEY
There are ATMs all over the city, including in the arrivals hall at Zvartnots Airport. Euros, US dollars and roubles can be changed nearly everywhere; the British pound and Georgian lari are less commonly traded.

TELEPHONE SERVICES
Beeline, VivaCell/MTS and Orange have offices all over the city.

TOURIST INFORMATION
It pains us to report that there is no official tourist information office in the city. The Tourism Unit at Yerevan Municipality's **Department of Culture and Tourism** (Map p134; 📋51 42 30; www.yerevan.am; Yerevan Municipality, 1 Argishti St; ⊘9am-6pm Mon-Fri) can supply maps, guidebooks and practical advice. The **My Yerevan** (www.myyerevan.am) and **Yerevan Municipality** (www.yerevan.am) websites carry some tourism-related content.

Not-for-profit outfit **One Armenia** (http://onearmenia.org/) produces a cute crowdsourced guide to Yerevan that is available online and in printed brochures available around town.

❶ Getting There & Away

AIR

Zvartnots Airport (☎49 30 00, flight information ☎187; www.zvartnots.aero), 11km from Yerevan, is Armenia's major airport. A multi-million-dollar overhaul of the airport was completed in 2011. There are regular flights to and from Russia (Moscow, Sochi, Krasnodar, Min Vody, Rostov), Ukraine (Odessa and Kiev), Iran (Tehran), France (Paris), Austria (Vienna), Turkey (İstanbul), the UAE (Dubai and Abu Dhabi) and Georgia (Tbilisi). At the time of research, there was discussion about the possibility of flights between Yerevan and Shiraz commencing. In summer there are also flights to/from Greece (Athens), Cyprus (Larnaca), Lebanon (Beirut) and Egypt (Hurghada).

The airport's arrivals hall has ATMs, a money exchange, a VivaCell/MTS booth, a post office and a Sixt car-hire desk.

BUS

The main bus station is the **Kilikya Avtokayan** (Map p130; ☎54 82 98, 56 53 70; 6 Admiral Isakov Ave), past the Yerevan Brandy Company on the road to Vagharshapat/Echmiadzin. To get here from the city centre, take *marshrutka* 5, 67 or 259 from Mesrop Mashtots Ave.

There are three types of transport operating from the bus station: large, often clapped-out, buses; the small minibuses known as *marshrutky;* and faster, more-comfortable and slightly more-expensive shared taxis (sometimes a car, often a minivan). From Kilikiya, there are services to many parts of the country as well as to international destinations.

Other services depart from the **Hyusisayin Avtokayan** (Map p130; ☎62 16 70; Tbilisian Mayrughi) on the Tbilisi Hwy, 4km from the city centre; from a stand near the Sasuntsi Davit metro station; from Sevan St behind the Yerevan train station; from a stand next to the Gortsaranayin metro station; and from the Raykom bus stand in Azatutyan Ave.

CAR & MOTORCYCLE

A number of agencies rent out cars in Yerevan, including big names such as Europcar, Sixt and Hertz. A three-day rental costs AMD65,000 to AMD190,000 depending on the make and model of the car. Many of the roads in Armenia are unsealed and in poor condition, so it is worth considering paying extra to hire a 4WD.

Policies on taking vehicles over the border to Georgia vary between companies, so be sure to clarify what is allowed. Some allow customers to pick up the car in Yerevan and drop off in Tbilisi (or vice versa).

Europcar (Map p134; ☎54 49 05; www.europcar.am; 8 Abovyan St; ◷10am-6pm Mon-Sat, 11am-5pm Sun) Enter via Pushkin St.

Hertz (Map p134; ☎58 48 18; www.hertz.am; 7 Abovyan St; ◷10am-6pm Mon-Fri)

INTERNATIONAL BUS & MARSHRUTKA SERVICES

The following services all originate and terminate at the Kilikya Avtokayan.

Batumi (Georgia) One daily *marshrutka* (AMD10,000, 10 hours) departing at 9pm between mid June and August only.

İstanbul (Turkey) One weekly bus (US$60 to US$70, 32 hours) departing 9am Saturday. Book tickets in advance through **Fairy Tour** (Map p134; ☎093 47 77 15, 54 66 25; http://fairytour.am/; 62 Hanrapetutyan St) or **Bogema Land** (Map p130; ☎26 54 26, 26 58 26; www.bogematravel.am; Apt 55, 16 Hrachya Qochar 16) in Yerevan.

Stepanakert (Nagorno-Karabakh) Hourly *marshrutky* (AMD5000, seven to eight hours), departing when full between 7am and 11am. The 7am service is the most reliable. There are also shared taxis departing between 7am and noon (AMD8000, five to six hours).

Tbilisi (Georgia) Daily *marshrutky* (AMD6500, six hours) departing once per hour between 8am and 11am. In addition, most of the hostels and hotels in town can organise seats in shared taxis (minivans) departing at 10.30am, 1pm, 3pm and 5pm daily (AMD8000, 5½ hours). These can pick up passengers at their hostel/hotel. The Envoy Hostel (p139) offers a hybrid tour/transfer between Yerevan and Tbilisi stopping at Sanahin, Haghpat and Akhtala monasteries en route (per person AMD29,500, 11 hours, Friday).

Tehran (via Tabriz; Iran) One daily bus (AMD25,000, 24 hours), departing at noon. A second service departs at the same time from Shahoumyan Sq near the Best Western Congress Hotel. It is essential to book seats in advance through Iranian travel specialist **Tatev Travel** (Map p134; ☎52 44 01; www.tatev.com; 19 Nalbandyan St; ◷9.30am-6pm Mon-Fri, 9.30am-3pm Sat). Note that the Tabriz stop is near the train station rather than in the centre of town.

TRAIN SERVICES FROM YEREVAN

Batumi (Georgia) Daily service between 15 June and 30 September at 3.30pm (1st/2nd class AMD22,000/14,000, 15½ hours). Stops in Tbilisi (1st/2nd class AMD15,000/9600, 10½ hours) en route.

Gyumri Daily services at 7.55am, 2.20pm and 6.15pm (AMD1000, 3½ hours).

Sevan Departs 8.30am daily except Wednesday between 15 June and 1 October (AMD600 to AMD1000, two hours). Travels to Shorzha on weekends, and to Tsovagyugh on weekdays. Stops on the highway near Sevanavank Peninsula en route.

Tbilisi (Georgia) See Batumi listing above for details of summer service. Between October and 14 June, trains leave on even days of the month at 9.30pm (1st/2nd class AMD14,000/8600, 10½ hours).

Sixt (☑ 91 37 33 66, 60 37 33 66; www.sixt.am; Arrivals hall, Zvartnots Airport; ☺24hr) There's also an office in the **North Avenue Hotel** (Map p134; ☑ 50 50 55; www.sixt.am; Foyer, North Avenue Hotel, 10 Northern Ave) in the city centre.

MARSHRUTKA

Yerevan is the hub of the national network, and *marshrutky* leave from spots around the city. Try to arrive about 30 minutes before departure if you are heading out of town to ensure you get a seat. If you have a bag or pack, you'll probably have to carry it on your lap.

TRAIN

Train services to Georgia and Gyumri depart from the atmospheric Soviet-era **Yerevan train station** (☑ information 184; Sasuntsi Davit Hraparak) off Tigran Mets Ave south of the city centre; the Sasuntsi Davit metro station is underneath the station building. Information boards are in Armenian and Russian, but some of the staff speak English. If you are travelling to Georgia you should book your ticket at least one day ahead, and take food and drinks with you for the trip. Services to Sevan depart from Almast train station northeast of the city centre.

ⓘ Getting Around

TO/FROM ZVARTNOTS AIRPORT

Marshrutky from Zvartnots Airport leave from a bus park near the main terminal. Exit the arrivals hall, turn right and walk up the stairs to find it. Yerevan minibus 18 (AMD200, every 20 minutes, 8am to 8pm) runs between the airport and Abovyan St in the city centre, stopping at both Sasuntsi Davit metro station and Rossiya Mall en route. You'll be charged an additional AMD100 for your luggage.

A taxi from the airport to the city centre should cost AMD3500 to AMD4000; agree on the price before getting into the taxi. From the city centre to the airport should only cost AMD3000. The trip takes about 15 to 20 minutes.

PUBLIC TRANSPORT

The main way around Yerevan is by *marshrutka*. There are hundreds of routes, shown by a number in the van's front window. They stop at bus stops but you can flag one down anywhere on the street. Trips cost AMD100; pay the driver as you leave. Ask to stop by saying '*kangnek*'.

There are also buses and electric trolleybuses following numbered routes. Tickets cost AMD100.

The **Yerevan metro** (one-way ticket AMD100; ☺6.30am–11pm) is clean, safe and efficient. It runs north–south through the city, stopping at these underground stations: Barekamutyun, Marshall Baghramyan, Yeritasardakan, Republic Square (Hanrapetutyan Hraparak), Zoravar Andranik near Surp Grigor Lusavorich Cathedral/Rossiya Mall and Sasuntsi Davit at the Yerevan train station. The line continues west and south on ground level to stations in the industrial suburbs. Trains run every five to 10 minutes and tickets cost AMD100.

TAXI

Taxis are cheap and plentiful, and range from well-loved Ladas to late-model Benzes. There are two types: street taxis and telephone or call taxis. Prices are AMD600 for the first 5km and then AMD100 per kilometre. Make sure the driver switches the meter on or you may be overcharged.

ⓘ YEREVAN MARSHRUTKA SHUFFLE

Every so often the authorities in Yerevan decide to shuffle around the departure points for *marshrutky* (minibuses) leaving the city. Departure times are also subject to change. It's a good idea to telephone the bus stations Kilikya Avtokayan or Hyusisayin Avtokayan, or consult with your hotel or guesthouse regarding possible changes to departure points and times.

AROUND YEREVAN

A number of high-profile sites can be visited on day trips from Yerevan. Garni and Geghard are east of the city and can easily be combined in one itinerary; the same applies to Zvartnots Cathedral, the Mother See of Holy Echmiadzin and Sardarapat to the west of the city. You can visit by public transport (*marshrutka,* bus or taxi) or sign up for a guided tour operated by Hyur Service (p139) or Envoy Hostel (p139).

⊙ Sights

Garni Temple   TEMPLE

(Գառնի; adult/student AMD1000/250, night visit AMD1200/450, guide AMD2500, parking AMD100; ⊙10am-8pm year-round, 8-11pm summer) Built by Armenia's King Trdat I in the 1st century AD, this Hellenic-style temple set on the edge of a gorge overlooking the Azat River was dedicated to the heathen sun god, Mitra. Largely destroyed by an earthquake in 1679, the Parthenon-like structure was rebuilt between 1969 and 1975. It features a monumental staircase and ionic columns topped by a frieze. Next to the temple are the ruins of a Roman-era bathhouse (closed to the public) and a 7th-century church.

Archaeologists have found Urartian cuneiform inscriptions dating back to the 8th century BC in the area around the temple, indicating that it has been inhabited since Neolithic times. The high promontory site is protected on three of four sides by a deep valley with rock cliffs, with a wall of massive blocks on the fourth side. Originally, the wall featured 14 towers and an entrance graced by an arch.

In the ruins of the church, look for the *vishap* (carved dragon stone). This is a marker to show the location of water. Some marks on the middle of the stone are in fact writing from King Argishti from the 8th century BC, which reads: 'Argishti, son of Menua, took people and cattle from Garni to Erebuni [the original site of Yerevan] to create a new community.'

Entrance to the site is free on the last Saturday of every month.

To reach Garni from Yerevan on public transport, you will need to make your way to GAI St, from where buses and *marshrutky* travel to Goght via Garni. To get there from the city centre, take bus 25, trolleybus 1 or *marshrutka* 44 from Mesrop Mashtots St, or *marshrutka* 5 from Opera Sq. Look out for a large park with an equestrian statue on the right-hand side of the road and then alight at the next stop, a Mercedes Benz showroom.

Marshrutka 266 and bus 204 (AMD250, 35 minutes) depart for Goght when full and operate between 9am and 6pm. They leave from a carpark to the right of the showroom, opposite the fresh produce market.

In Garni, alight at the crossroads with a bus shelter opposite a butcher shop and then walk south to the temple.

★ Geghard Monastery   MONASTERY

(Գեղարդ; ⊙9am-6pm) [FREE] Named after the holy lance that pierced Christ's side at the crucifixion, this World Heritage–listed monastery is carved out of the rock face of the Azat River Gorge. Legend has it as founded in the 4th century and its oldest surviving chapel dates back to the 12th century. The hugely atmospheric Surp Astvatsatsin (Holy Mother of God Church) dates from 1215 and features wonderful carvings; its adjoining *gavit* (vestibule) with its nine arches was built between 1215 and 1225.

Outside Surp Astvatsatsin, above the south door, is a coat of arms of the family of the Zakarian prince who built it. The theme is a common Near Eastern one, with the lion symbolising royal might.

On the left-hand side of the *gavit* are two entrances to chapels hewn from the rock in the 13th century. One contains a basin with spring water, *khachkars* and stalactite decoration. The second includes the four-column burial chamber of Prince Papaq Proshian and his wife, Hruzakan. The family's coat of arms, carved in the rock above, features two lions chained together and an eagle.

Outside, steps to the left of the entrance lead up the hill to a 10m passageway with carved *khachkars*. This gives access to a 13th-century burial vault that was carved out of the raw rock. Its proportions and acoustics are quite amazing. In the far corner is an opening looking down on the church below.

Behind the church are steps that lead to some interesting monastic cells and more *khachkars*. Outside the monastery, next to the stream, is a *matagh* (sacrifice) site that is used on Sundays after the morning service. A choir usually sings at that service, too.

As you approach the monastery, look to the left up the hill for caves housing monastic cells built by monks. Trees here are often dotted with strips of cloth, as are trees on the other side of the monastery near the river. It is said a person can say a prayer or make a wish and tie a strip of cloth to a tree

ARMENIA AROUND YEREVAN

Around Yerevan

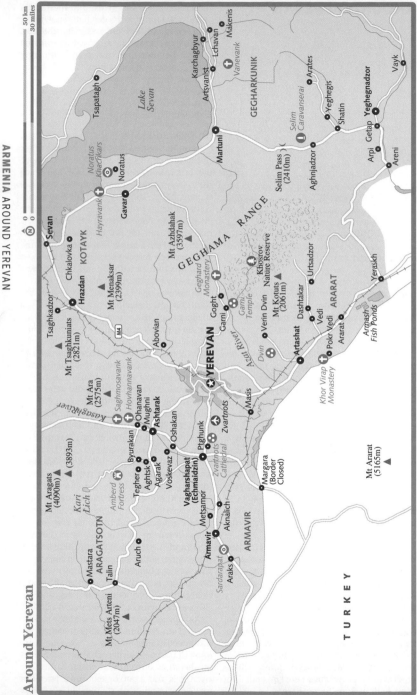

50 km
30 miles

Makenis
Lchavan
Karchagbyur
Vanevank
Artsvanist
Lake Sevan
Tsapatagh
Vayk
Arates
Yeghegnadzor
Getap
Yeghegis
Shatin
GEGHARKUNIK
Selim Caravanserai
Areni
Arpi
Aghnjadzor
Selim Pass (2410m)
Noratus Khachkars
Noratus
Martuni
Gavar
Hayravank
Sevan
Chkalovka
KOTAYK
Hrazdan
Mt Menaksar (2399m)
Mt Azhdahak (3597m)
GEGHAMA RANGE
Khostrov Nature Reserve
Urtsadzor
Yeraskh
Tsaghkadzor
Tsaghkuniats (2821m)
Geghard Monastery
Mt Kotuts (2061m)
ARARAT
Mt Tsaghkuniats (2821m)
Abovian
Goght
Garni
Temple
Verin Dvin
Dashtakar
Saghmosavank
Hovhannavank
Ohanavan
Mughni
Ashtarak
Oshakan
YEREVAN
Garni
Azat River
Dvin
Artashat
Vedi
Armash Fish Ponds
Mt Ara (2575m)
Kasagh River
Byurakan
Ptghunk
Zvartnots
Masis
Pokr Vedi
Ararat
Mt Aragats (4090m)
(3893m)
Tegher
Aghtsk
Agarak
Voskevaz
Zvartnots Cathedral
Khor Virap Monastery
Kari Lich
Amberd Fortress
Vagharshapat (Echmiadzin)
Metsamor
Margara (Border Closed)
Mt Ararat (5165m)
ARAGATSOTN
Mastara
Talin
Aruch
Aknalich
ARMAVIR
Armavir
Araks
Sardarapat
Mt Mets Arteni (2047m)
TURKEY

near the monastery to make it come true. On weekends, the ramp to the monastery is crammed with vendors selling souvenirs and food; you should be able to grab a snack of walnut *sujukh, gata* (sweet cake) or thin sheets of dried fruit puree.

Buses and *marshrutky* don't service Geghard. To get here from Yerevan, take a *marshrutka* or bus to the village of Goght, 6.4km northeast of Garni. These leave from the stop next to the Mercedes Benz showroom in GAI Ave. When you arrive in Goght, hire a taxi to take you the 4.2km from the bus stop to the monastery, drop you off and then collect you an hour later to return to the bus stop. This should cost AMD3000 to AMD3500.

If visiting both Geghard and Garni Temple, it makes sense to head to Geghard first and organise for the taxi driver to drop you back to Garni rather than Goght (AMD4000). After visiting the temple you can then return to Yerevan by bus or *marshrutka*.

Zvartnots Cathedral   RUIN
(Զվարթնոց; admission AMD700, parking AMD100; ⊙10am-5pm) Catholicos Nerses II (known as 'the Builder') sponsored construction of the 'Celestial Angels Cathedral' in the 7th century. Destroyed in the 10th century, its evocative ruins now stand in a semi-industrial landscape near Zvartnots Airport and were included on Unesco's World Heritage List in 2000. It was originally dedicated to – and housed relics of – Surp Grigor Lusavorich (St Gregory the Illuminator), the first Catholicos of the Armenian Church. A model in the on-site museum shows what it may have originally looked like.

The ruins lay buried until the 20th century, when they were excavated and the cathedral was partially reconstructed in a polygonal form with plenty of columns supporting carved arches. There are plenty of interesting sculptural remnants surrounding the main structure – look out for the carved eagle capital in particular.

The recently opened museum in the southwest corner of the site displays artefacts found during the excavation. It also has a series of informative panels about medieval Armenian architecture. Entry is included in the overall ticket price.

Around the cathedral are the ruins of the palace of the Catholicos and the wine press and stone tanks of a massive medieval winery.

Zvartnots is on the Vagharshapat–Yerevan Hwy, near the delightfully named village of Ptghunk, 17km from Yerevan and 4km from Echmiadzin. To get here, take bus 111 (AMD200, 30 minutes) from Yerevan's Kilikiya Avtokayan and look out for a pillar topped with an eagle on the left-hand side of the highway. This was created by noted Armenian sculptor Ervand Kochar and marks the entrance to the site.

Mother See of Holy Echmiadzin   MONASTERY
(Էջմիածին; ☑51 71 10; www.armenianchurch. org; Movses Khorenatsi St, Vagharshapat; Cathedral Museum AMD1500; ⊙Mayr Tachar 7am-8pm, Cathedral Museum 10.30am-1pm & 2-5pm Tue-Sat, 2-5pm Sun) Echmiadzin is the Vatican of the Armenian Apostolic Church, the place where Surp Grigor Lusavorich saw a beam of light fall to the earth in a divine vision, and where he built the first Mayr Tachar (Mother Church of Armenia). Though its rich history and symbolic importance make it a revered destination for Armenian Christians, we find the compound's churches and museums underwhelming and suggest that those who only have time for one day trip from Yerevan visit Geghard Monastery and Garni Temple instead.

The cathedral compound and its surrounding settlement functioned as the capital of Armenia from 180 to 340, when Christianity was first adopted by the Armenian nation. The seat of the Catholicos then wandered across western Armenia for centuries before returning here in 1441, with substantial rebuilding occurring in the 15th century.

The main cathedral, Mayr Tachar, stands in a quadrangle of hedges and lawn surrounded by 19th-century buildings. The original church was consecrated in AD 303 but later fell in ruin and was rebuilt in 480–483. More work and expansion occurred in the 600s, 1600s and 1700s, and a major restoration of the exterior was being undertaken at the time of writing. The three-tiered bell tower at the entrance of the church is richly carved and dates from 1654. Inside, the church is modest in scale, about 20m by 20m, but the roof gleams with frescoes. At the centre is an altar at the place where St Gregory saw the divine light strike the ground. Divine Liturgy is celebrated every Sunday starting at 11am (10.30am on feast days). Morning services are conducted at 7.30am from Monday to Saturday and 8am on Sunday. Evening services are conducted at 5.30pm daily.

At the rear of the church, through a door on the right of the altar, is the Cathedral Museum; buy your ticket from the office on the ground floor of the Palace of the

Catholicos in front of the cathedral (look for the 'Museums' sign). The Cathedral Museum houses precious objects and relics collected by the church, including the Holy Lance (Surp Geghard), the weapon used by a Roman soldier to pierce the side of Christ while he was still nailed to the cross. The spearhead is set into an ornate 17th-century gold-and-silver casing and was brought to Echmiadzin from Geghard Monastery. There are also clerical vestments and crowns, illuminated manuscripts, processional crosses, a hand-shaped reliquary of St John the Baptist, and a beautiful beaten-gold reliquary dating from 1300 that is said to contain a relic of the True Cross.

The Palace of the Catholicos (aka the Veharan) is the home of the present Catholicos, Karekin II, who was enthroned in November 1999. He is the supreme prelate of the 1700-year-old Armenian Apostolic faith. On its 2nd floor is the Pontifical Residence Museum, a series of galleries showcasing the art collections, treasured possessions and personal effects of the Catholicoses and kings of Armenia. This is visited on a guided tour (Armenian-language only).

Also in the grounds is the Rouben Sevak Museum, where paintings collected by Mr Sevak are displayed. It's not particularly noteworthy.

The gardens of Mayr Tachar have a 1915–23 Genocide Monument and many fine *khachkars* assembled from around the country. There are also a number of contemporary churches, seminaries and libraries in the compound, the most notable of which is the Holy Archangels Church next to the main gate. This was designed by Jim Torosyan and consecrated in 2011.

There are three other churches of note in Vagharshapat, the most notable of which is Surp Hripsime, built in 618 as a replacement for an earlier chapel on the site where St Hripsime was slain after she refused to marry the pagan King Trdat III, choosing instead to stay true to her faith (she was a Roman nun who had earlier fled here to escape marriage to the Roman emperor Diocletian). The small chamber at the back of this church has a niche that contains a few of the rocks purportedly used to stone Hripsime to death. The church is located on the main highway near the entrance to town (near the bypass).

Other churches include Surp Gayane, a short walk from Komitas Sq past the main gate of the Holy See. St Gayane was the prioress of the 32 virtuous maidens who accompanied St Hripsime to Armenia. The original 5th-century chapel over her grave was rebuilt as a church in 1630. It's a fine orange-toned building with a plain interior and some fine *khachkars* in its grounds.

Less interesting but still worth a visit is Surp Shogahat, a sturdy stone structure with simple, elegant lines. It was rebuilt on

PICNIC PROVISIONS

During the warmer months, Armenia's network of roads and highways serves a dual purpose. By the roadside, local farmers sell fruit, vegetables and other products to commuters keen on sourcing fresh produce – it's the local version of a farmers market, and a sensational source of picnic provisions. Each town and region tends to specialise in one crop or product, including the following:

Dilijan Freshly picked corn on the cob is cooked and sold on the road between town and the Sevan Pass, on the road to Lake Sevan.

Vanadzor Carrots are a popular purchase when driving between Vanadzor and Dilijan.

Voratan Pass Beekeepers tend their hives and sell jars of the golden bountry on the highway between the Voratan Pass and the turn-off to Tatev Monastery.

Areni Locally produced red wine and juicy apricots grown in orchards on the river plain are sold at stalls in this wine-growing town.

Debed Canyon Freshly picked berries (raspberries, mulberries and strawberries) tempt drivers around the town of Alaverdi.

There are wonderful picnic spots in rural settings throughout the country. Some of our favourites include the caravanserai on the Selim Pass between Lake Sevan and Yeghegnadzor; the stream along the road to Haghartsin Monastery outside Dilijan; the garden in the grounds of the Surp Gevorg Church in Mughni; and the forest surrounding Makaravank Monastery near Ijevan.

the foundations of a chapel to one of the companions of Hripsime and Gayane. You'll find it on Nalbandyan St, behind Surp Hripsime.

To get here, take bus 111 (AMD200, 30 minutes) from Yerevan's Kilikiya Avtokayan to Vagharshapat and alight at Komitas Sq, a big roundabout linking Mesrop Mashtots Ave and Movses Khorenatsi St (there's a statue in the middle of the roundabout, so it's hard to miss).

Sardarapat
MUSEUM

(Սարդարապատ; museum adult/child AMD1000/600, guide AMD5000, parking AMD100; ☉9.30am-5.45pm Tue-Sun) Set on a hill, the stunning orange tuff **memorial** at Sardarapat commemorates the battle in May 1918 when forces of the first Armenian republic turned back the Turkish army and saved the country from a likely annihilation. Designed by Russian-trained architect Raphael Israelyan and built in 1968, it is a popular pilgrimage destination for Armenians. The **State Ethnographic Museum** at the site is in two parts: battle paraphernalia in the first hall and an excellent ethnographic collection upstairs.

Sardarapat is about 10km southwest of Armavir, signposted near the village of Araks. *Marshrutky* leave from Yerevan's Kilikiya Avtokayan for Armavir (AMD400, 50 minutes, every 15 minutes from 7.30am to 8pm), from where you will need to negotiate with a taxi driver to take you to Sardarapat and return you to Armavir after two to three hours at the site. This should cost approximately AMD3000. There's a restaurant at the complex if you wish to have lunch or a coffee.

NORTHERN ARMENIA

North of Yerevan are the *marz* (provinces) of Kotayk, Aragatsotn, Shirak, Lori and Tavush. To their west lies the province of Gegharkunik, which links Lori and Tavush with the southern provinces along the edge of Lake Sevan.

Ashtarak
Աշտարակ

☑232 / POP 17,900

Ashtarak is a midsized regional town on the Kasagh Gorge, 22km northwest of Yerevan. It has an array of 19th-century buildings, streets filled with fruit trees, an 11th-century stone bridge (sadly dwarfed by a modern replacement) and four medieval churches in various stages of decrepitude. The best preserved of these is the small 7th-century **Karmravor Church**, which boasts intricate carvings and a cemetery with *khachkars*. While there is no compelling reason to visit the town itself, it does make a good kick-off point when visiting the Kasagh Gorge churches.

🛏 Sleeping & Eating

Ashtaraki Dzor
HOTEL $

(Dzor CJSC; ☑3 67 78; www.ashtarakidzor.am; Kasagh Gorge, Ashtarak; per person incl breakfast AMD10,000; P✳☎) This entertainment and accommodation complex is built on terraces down the walls of Kasagh Gorge and is popular with bus tours and large groups (wedding parties etc). The hotel rooms are reasonably comfortable and have river-facing balconies. It's about 4km north of the town centre.

❶ Getting There & Away

You need a car to explore this region properly. Getting from Yerevan to Ashtarak is no problem as regular *marshrutky* leave from the Kilikiya Avtokayan (AMD250, 40 minutes, one or two per hour from 8.40am to 6.40pm). However, once here you'll need to hitch, walk or hire a taxi to visit surrounding sites.

Around Ashtarak

Following the Kasagh Gorge Hwy north from Ashtarak to Spitak will take you past three important medieval monasteries: Surp Gevorg, Hovhannavank and Saghmosavank. Those wanting to walk part of the route can take the 90-minute trail at the bottom of the gorge linking Hovhannavank and Saghmosavank – it begins at the new cemetery on the northern part of Ohanavan village. Unfortunately, you won't be able to find a taxi or *marshrutka* at either Saghmosavank or Ohanavan for the return trip.

⦿ Sights

Surp Gevorg
MONASTERY

(Monastery of St George; Mughni) This handsome 17th-century church is located in the neighbourhood of Mughni, on the northern edge of Ashtarak. It features striped bands of stone around its central drum, a classic half-folded umbrella cupola, an arched exterior arcade, and elaborate carvings on and over its west and south doors. Inside, there are fresco fragments. The surrounding fortress walls have small towers, monks' cells and a refectory built into them.

Northern Armenia

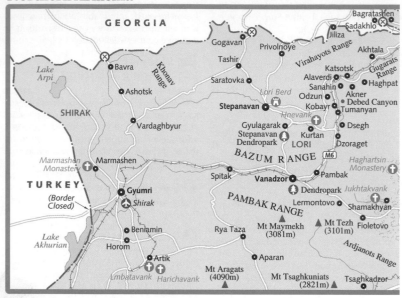

Mughni is an easy turn-off from the main highway that runs north to Spitak. Opposite the monastery is a bakery (open 9am to late) where you can purchase savoury and sweet pastries straight from the oven. These can be enjoyed in the charming garden behind the church, which has a pool, fountain and plentiful seating.

Hovhannavank   MONASTERY
(Monastery of John; Ohanavan) Perched on the edge of the Kasagh Gorge, this monastery in the village of Ohanavan was once an important educational and theological center where manuscripts were written and illuminated. It has two adjoining churches: a basilica dating from the 5th century and the 13th-century Church of St John. The church has an altar decorated with frescoes, as well as unusual cantilevered staircases on its north and south sides. The entrance to both buildings is via a splendid 13th-century *gavit*.

Saghmosavank   MONASTERY
(Saghmosavank) Located in the village of the same name, Saghmosavank (Monastery of Palms) was built on the edge of the Kasagh Gorge and comprises two main church buildings: the Church of Zion and the smaller Church of Karapet; both date from the 13th century. The monastery's *gavit* and

library date from the same period. Surrounded by a fortified wall and commanding wonderful views over the Kasagh Gorge and to Mt Aragats, it is the most attractive monastery in the gorge area.

Byurakan & Around
Բյուրական

The landscape around the village of Byurakan, about 14km northwest of Ashtarak on the southern slopes of Mt Aragats, includes an astronomical observatory and the impressive remains of the fortress of Amberd, 15km up the mountain. The **Surp Hovhannes Church** in Byurakan is an interesting early basilica model, and the 13th-century **Tegher Monastery** on the far side of the Amberd Gorge from Byurakan is about 5km uphill from Aghtsk in the old village of the same name. Other churches and villages in the vicinity have *khachkars* and *vishaps* scattered about.

◉ Sights

Amberd Fortress   FORTRESS
Constructed on a ridge above the confluence of the little gorges of the Amberd and Arkashen streams, this majestic stone fortress

through five observational instruments at this Soviet-era observatory complex, focusing on research into instability phenomena. Contact the observatory in advance to take a guided tour (AMD2000).

🛏 Sleeping

Byurakan Observatory
Guesthouse   HOTEL $
(☑ 094 91 09 92; www.bao.am; Byurakan; per person AMD6000; ☻ summer only) The observatory guesthouse is a lovely pink tuff building with basic but satisfactory rooms. For an extra AMD2000 you'll get a tour of the observatory at night.

🛈 Getting There & Away

There are four buses per day from Yerevan to Byurakan, departing at 10.30am, 12.45pm, 3.45pm and 5.30pm from the bus stand on Grigor Lusavorich St in Yerevan (AMD350). If you don't catch one of these there are also a few buses to Agarak, 6km south of Byurakan on the Ashtarak–Gyumri Hwy. From Agarak you could walk, hitch or hire a taxi. There are very few, if any, taxis in Byurakan itself so if you need a taxi to go to Aragats or Amberd, it's better to take one from Ashtarak or Yerevan. The four buses return to Yerevan at 7.30am, 9am, noon and 4pm.

dates back to the 7th century but its current buildings date from the 12th century. It's easy to see why the site was chosen – at 2300m above sea level it commands a position above the farms and trade routes of the Ararat Plain. The ruins of a chapel, 13th-century bathhouse and cistern stand downhill from the fortress.

The fortress is about a two-hour hike from the scout camp near the very end of Byurakan village, offering spectacular scenery along the footpath. Walk along the Mt Aragats road until you reach the ski house. Then take the left-hand fork of the road (the fortress can be seen from a distance, but you have to walk around a steep valley before reaching it). Although the fortress is geographically close to Byurakan, the paved road makes a 15km-long circuitous route.

The first part of the road heads uphill towards Kari Lich (Kari Lake) and then branches off to the left 5km before the fortress. As you walk or drive through this landscape look for the large green or white tents owned by Armenian shepherds who graze their flocks here in summer.

Byurakan Astrophysical
Observatory   OBSERVATORY
(Byurakan; ☑ 091 19 59 03; www.bao.am) A large research staff observes and studies the stars

Mt Aragats   Արագած Լեռ

Snow covers the top of the highest mountain in modern Armenia almost year-round, so climbing is best in July, August or September. Be careful – even in August, clouds can gather in the crater by about 10am, so it's good to start walking as early as possible (it's not unusual for hikers to start on mountain ascents at 5am). The southernmost of its four peaks (3893m) is easy enough for inexperienced climbers, but the northern peak (4090m) is more challenging and requires crossing a snowfield (experienced hikers only).

The well-respected **Spitak Rescue Center** (☑ 10-35 00 46) in Yerevan may be able to recommend experienced hiking and climbing guides.

🛈 Getting There & Away

There is no public transport to Kari Lich, the starting point for Mt Aragats walks. Hitchhikers usually take a bus to Byurakan and then try to thumb a lift, which is more likely on weekends.

Gyumri

Գյումրի

♫ 312 / POP 115,000

Armenia's second-largest city was almost levelled in the 1988 Spitak earthquake, and reconstruction works are still underway. It's not a particularly attractive place, but its bustling market and location on one of the main routes into Georgia means that it is visited by a reasonable number of tourists.

The townsfolk of Gyumri have a distinctive accent with hints of western Armenian, and a famously ridiculous sense of humour in tandem with conservative social mores. Other Armenians like to tease Gyumritsis about local delicacies such as *kalla* (cow's head) and the particularly rich stew of *khash* made here in the cold seasons (made from animal parts). The winters last longer here than in Yerevan, until April or May.

History

Gyumri was first settled around 400 BC, possibly by Greek colonists. The town was inhabited periodically until the early 19th century, when the Russians moved in and built a large military garrison. It even received a visit from Tsar Nicolas I who, in 1837, renamed it Alexandropol after his wife. As the third-largest city in the South Caucasus, after Tbilisi and Baku, Gyumri was an important trading post between the Ottoman Empire and the rest of Asia and Russia. As a transport hub, it was a stop on the rail journey from Tbilisi to Tabriz.

In 1920 the Turkish-Armenian war ended here with the signing of the Treaty of Alexandropol, an event that ceased the Turkish advance on Yerevan. In Soviet times the border was shut and Alexandropol became known as Leninakan.

The Spitak earthquake on 11 December 1988 put paid to much of Gyumri's historic splendour, and also destroyed the many factories established here by the Soviets. Besides levelling large parts of the city and surrounding villages, it killed 50,000 people and made many more homeless. The botched recovery effort would haunt the city for years as successive winters passed without heating or electricity. Things are better now, even though there is still plenty of reconstruction work to complete.

◉ Sights

The historic core of town, the **Kumayri** neighbourhood, is between Vardanants Sq and the City Park. Its grandest buildings are on Abovyan St, and plenty of restoration work was underway there at the time of writing. Another major restoration was underway at the

ARMENIA GYUMRI

Gyumri

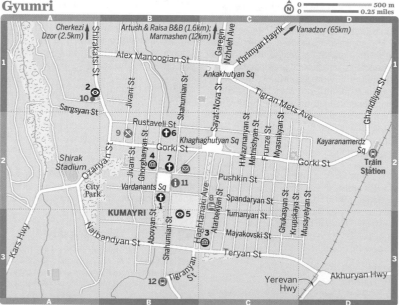

19th-century **Amenaprkich (All Saviours) Church** on the southern edge of Vardanants Sq. On the northern side of the square is another 19th-century church, Surp Astvatsatsin, locally called **Yot Verk** (Seven Wounds). The battered and worn roof cones from an earlier incarnation of the church stand outside. A couple of blocks north of Yot Verk, on Abovyan St, is modest **Surp Nishan**, built in 1870.

Museum of the Aslamazyan Sisters   MUSEUM

(✍4 82 05; http://aslamazyanmuseum.blogspot.com.au/; 242 Abovyan St; admission by donation; ☉10am-5pm Tue-Sun) Artists Mariam (1907–2006) and Yeranuhi (1910–98) Aslamazyan were born in Bash-Shirak village near Gyumri and two floors of this handsome 19th-century building showcase a large collection of their brightly coloured canvasses and ceramics. The sisters were huge travellers and painted scenes of their travels in many parts of the world, something that was extremely unusual for any Soviet artist of the time, let alone females. Note that the street numbers in Abovyan St are erratic – this is also number 31.

Museum of National Architecture and Urban Life of Gyumri   MUSEUM

(✍2 36 00; 47 Haghtanak St; adult/child AMD1000/300. sculpture museum AMD500, guide AMD2000; ☉11am-5pm Tue-Sat, 11am-4pm Sun) Though burdened with an unwieldy name and meagre budget, Gyumri's major cultural institution tries hard to provide a satisfying visitor experience. Set in a grand but crumbling 1872 mansion, its collection focuses on the traditional trades and crafts of Alexandropol, with displays on woodworking, blacksmithing, tinwork, lace, embroidery, shoemaking, hatmaking and silver-

smithing. An attached gallery of sculptures by Sergei Merkurov contains more Lenins and Stalins than you can shake a sickle at.

Shuka   MARKET

Gyumri's historic *pak shuka* (covered market) once occupied the land now occupied by Vardanants Sq. Levelled during the Soviet era, the stallholders moved their businesses a few blocks northeast, between Shahumian and Haghtanak Sts, where they remain today. The now uncovered *shuka* is one of the largest in Armenia, crammed with stalls selling fruit and vegetables, freshly ground coffee, pungent cheeses and *basturma,* bread, meats (beware the swinging carcasses), bottles of cognac and much more.

🕝 Tours

Shirak Tours   TOUR

(✍5 31 48, 5 03 86; www.shiraktours.am; 25 Haghtanaki St) Run by Alex Ter-Minasyan, this tour company based in the Berlin Art Hotel can organise sightseeing and adventure tours throughout the Shirak region.

🛏 Sleeping

Decent accommodation options are thin on the ground here. Though it's well located, we can't in good conscience recommend the massive, recently opened Alexandrapol Palace Hotel due to its ludicrously over-the-top decor. And the only other centrally located option worth mentioning, the Araks Hotel, is overpriced considering it is in sore need of refurbishment.

Artush & Raisa B&B   B&B $

(✍094 61 23 45, 093 35 03 14; www.gyumribnb.com; 1-2 Ayvazovski St; s/d AMD12,000/20,000; 🅿 🛜) English-speaking local guide Artush Davtyan runs this comfortable homestay with

ARMENIA GYUMRI

Gyumri

wife Raisa and adult son Martin. Six guest-rooms are available; four are in purpose-built blocks in the garden, two are in the main house and offer less privacy. Meals are enjoyed in the elegant piano room or gorgeous garden, which is filled with flowers and fruit trees. Dinner costs AMD4000.

★ Berlin Art Hotel   HOTEL $$
(☑2 31 48; www.berlinhotel-gyumri.am; 25 Haghtanak St; s/d AMD27,000/32,000; P✿❉☎) This gem of a hotel was built as an accommodation wing for the German hospital that shares the same premises. It's at the rear of the site and has a charming garden, cheerful dining room and simple but comfortable rooms with good beds and satellite TV. Paintings and sculptures by local artists adorn every wall.

The staff here are extremely helpful, and can answer any question about travel within and around the city. Shirak Tours, a respected local tour operator, is also based here.

✖ Eating

There are cheap street snacks available from shops and stalls at the *shuka*.

Polos Mukuch   ARMENIAN $
(☑3 45 11; 75 Jivani St; mains AMD2500; ✿9am-10pm) In a historic building opposite the beer factory, this popular place prepares a mix of Armenian and Georgian dishes – *kalla*, stodgy *khinkali* (spicy meat dumplings), *khashlama* (beef and potato stew) and kebabs are popular. Seating is in wooden cubicles, but many locals prefer to sit around the bar swilling beer (Gyumri, of course) chased with potent shots of *oghee*.

★ Cherkezi Dzor   ARMENIAN $$
(Fish Farm; ☑6 55 59; http://gyumrifish.am/; 1st Karmir Berd; fish per kg AMD3500-5600; ✿11am-11pm) Popular with Russian officers from the nearby army base, this restaurant is a great summer choice. Seating is in pavilions surrounding the fish pools where dinner will be caught to order. Those in the know choose trout (boiled is best) or sturgeon (barbecued). Bread is freshly baked in on-site ovens.

The restaurant is on the western side of town and a little hard to find. From the stadium, cross the opposite bank and walk north up the canyon for 1.3km. Alternatively, a taxi should cost AMD800 each way.

ℹ Information

There are plenty of ATMs in the city centre. You can read newspapers and use free internet at the

American Corner (☑5 21 53; http://gyumri.americancorners.am/en; 68 Shirakatsi St; ✿9am-5pm Mon-Fri) located next to the City Hall.
Tourist Information Office (☑055 59 15 53; http://travelgyumri.com/; 1 Vardanants Sq; ✿9am-7pm) English-speaking office that can answer tourist-related queries, supply maps of Gyumri and the Shirak region, and arrange cultural tours and events.

ℹ Getting There & Around

AIR

Shirak Airport, 5km southeast of town, is served by Vim Airlines (Moscow; three times weekly), Donavia (Sochi and Rostov-on-Don; weekly, August to October) and RusLine (Krasnodar; twice weekly). There are plenty of ticket agencies in town. A taxi to the airport should cost AMD1500.

BUS, SHARED TAXI & MARSHRUTKA

From Yerevan, regular *marshrutky* (AMD1500, two hours, every 20 minutes between 8am and 8pm) depart from Sevan St behind the Yerevan train station.

In Gyumri, buses, shared taxis and *marshrutky* leave from the bus station on Tigranyan St. Services include *marshrutky* to Yerevan (AMD1500, two hours, every 20 minutes between 7am and 7pm) and Vanadzor (AMD800, one hour, on the hour between 10am and 2pm), as well as one service per day to Stepanavan (AMD1500, 1½ hours, 9am). There's also a daily bus to Vanadzor (AMD500, 90 minutes, 4pm).

To Georgia, there is one daily *marshrutka* to Tbilisi (AMD5200, 3½ hours, 10.30am) and another for Akhaltsikhe (AMD4000, four hours, 10am). These will only depart if there is a minimum of five passengers. A seat in a shared taxi costs AMD2500 to Yerevan and AMD1500 to Vanadzor.

TRAIN

The train station is on Kayaranamerts Sq at the eastern edge of the city centre. A dedicated train service travels between Gyumri and Yerevan three times daily. From Gyumri the trains depart at 8.25am, 11.45am and 6.40pm (AMD1000, 3½ hours). The service from Yerevan to Georgia also stops here. Call or visit the **train station** (☑5 10 02) to confirm schedules and ticket prices.

Around Gyumri

Gyumri-based company Shirak Tours (p157) can organise sightseeing and adventure tours throughout the Shirak region and to Georgia.

Marmashen   Մարմաշեն

Marmashen's location deep in a river valley 10km northwest of Gyumri is unusual – medieval monasteries in Armenia were almost always constructed in elevated locations. There are three churches hewn from lovely apricot-coloured tuff clustered together here, the most impressive of which is the 10th-century **Surp Stepanos** (Church of St Stephen). A ruined 13th-century *gavit* is next to the church, and beautiful carved tombs and *khachkars* dot the surrounding landscape. The monastery is a popular picnic spot in summer.

To get here, take the main road north from Gyumri, follow the signs to Vahramaberd and pass through the village of Marmashen. When you arrive at Vahramaberd, turn left onto an unsealed road leading through farmland down into the valley. The monastery is near a lake and a small hydroelectric plant. A return taxi from Gyumri should cost around AMD5000 including 30 minutes at the monastery. Make sure the driver understands that you want to see the monastery and not the nearby village of the same name.

Harichavank Հարիճավանք

Once the summer residence of the Catholicos of Echmiadzin, the still-functioning **Harichavank Monastery** is located in the old town of Harich, about 4km from the town of Artik. Its chapel dates from the 7th or 8th century but was dramatically expanded with the addition of a *gavit* and domes in the 13th century. There is some beautiful geometric stonework over the main church door and around the dome of the *gavit*.

Inside, the church's caretaker can point out the anteroom/storeroom with a hole in the ceiling leading to a secret upstairs room. During times of invasion, the room was used to house women and children and sometimes even important local officials. A stone would be fitted exactly into the ceiling hole once everyone had climbed to safety.

Direct buses depart Gyumri's bus station for Harichavank (AMD400, 50 minutes) a few times daily. If you have your own vehicle, the monastery is about 15km off the main Yerevan–Gyumri road.

When you are in the area, consider checking out the well-preserved 7th-century **Lmbatavank** church southwest of Artik; it contains important early frescoes.

Stepanavan & Around
Ստեփանավան
♪ 256 / POP 12,600

Sitting on a plateau above the steep-sided gorge of the Dzoragets River, Stepanavan is known throughout the former Soviet Union as one of the birthplaces of Armenian communism. Students of Soviet history will find the town's museum interesting, but there is no cogent reason for other visitors to head this way, especially as there were major construction works at and around the Gogovan border crossing into Georgia at the time of writing, meaning that it was best avoided.

An early cell of the Bolsheviks led by local lad Stepan Shahumian operated from hideouts and caves in this region before the revolution. Shahumian died in a lonely corner of the Turkmenistan desert with the other 26 'Baku Commissars' in 1918, and all 26 were later sanctified in countless memorials across the region. (The Baku Commissars were Bolshevik leaders in the Caucasus in the early days of the revolution.)

⊙ Sights

Stepan Shahumian Museum MUSEUM
(♪ 2 21 91; Garegin Nzhdehi St; admission AMD400; ⊙ 9am-6pm Mon-Fri) This Soviet-era edifice was constructed in the 1970s on the site of the modest timber home of Stepan Shahumian and his wife Ekaterina Ter-Grigoryan, and the architects chose to preserve and display the house in the central atrium of the new building; it looks like a slightly sad dolls house. Inside, there are some of the Shahumians' original furnishings plus documents and photographs. There's also an upstairs gallery featuring works by local artists and a downstairs exhibit about the town.

Lori Berd FORTRESS
(Lori Fortress) Sitting on a promontory between the gorges of the Dzoragets and Miskhana Rivers, this ruined fortress has huge round towers and massive stone blocks along its exposed side. Originally the base of David Anhogin (949–1049), it eventually became a local power base for the Orbelians and Zakarians, powerful families of Armenian nobles. It's surrounded by farmland, an ancient cemetery and hillocks that are actually Bronze Age tumulus tombs. The bridge in the gorge below dates from the 14th century.

To reach the fortress, head out of town across the bridge and veer right at the roundabout, following the course of the river past the Lori Berd village and then veering right again at a sign. The remaining 2km is on a poor-quality road. A taxi from Stepanavan takes about 15 minutes and

WORTH A TRIP

A 7TH-CENTURY MONASTERY

Travelling between Stepanavan and the Debed Canyon (p162), one of two possible routes passes the monastery of **Hnevank**, located on a winding road 7km from Kurtan. Standing inside the gorge on the southern side of the canyon, near the confluence of the Gargar and Dzoragets Rivers, the complex has been ruined and rebuilt several times; most of what is visible today dates from the 12th century. It is particularly attractive in spring and summer when it is surrounded by wildflowers.

should cost around AMD1000. From the fort, you can walk back to Stepanavan along a 4.5km trail in the steep-sided gorge; this starts on the north side of the fort.

Stepanavan Dendropark　　　FOREST
(Sojut; ☉10am-7pm) **FREE** This cool and tranquil 35-hectare arboretum 11km south of Stepanavan was established in the 1930s and has a vast array of conifers and deciduous trees. It's especially popular in May when locals with respiratory problems come to inhale the pollen (not recommended for allergy sufferers!). You'll need a car to get here; the road is dreadfully potholed so a 4WD is preferable. The Cinderella-style carriage beside the road signals the **Hekyat Restaurant** (Fairytale Restaurant; ☑093 30 31 00; Gyulagarak; mains AMD4000; ☉9am-7pm), which is popular with locals.

To reach the Dendropark, head towards Vanadzor until you reach the village of Gyulagarak. Cross the bridge here, pass the ruined village church and then take the first street right onto the dirt road.

🛏 Sleeping & Eating

Locals hardly ever eat out, so there are few eateries in town. For quick snacks, try the pizza joint on the main street or the bakery on Surb Nshan St behind the museum. The best spot for a coffee or tea break is at the kiosk-cafe in Shahumian Sq (summer only).

Armine's Guesthouse　　　GUESTHOUSE $
(☑093 19 60 96, 2 21 58; armine5@yahoo.com; 11 Million St; s/d AMD8000/14,000; ☎) The only Stepanavan accommodation worth considering, this guesthouse has two clean and relatively comfortable bedrooms with basic bathrooms. There's also a washing machine

(AMD2000 per load), a communal kitchen and a lounge with satellite TV. It's operated by the extremely helpful Armine, who works at a nearby NGO and can answer all of your queries about travel in the region.

To find it, look for the pink building with the information logo on the western side of Shahumian Sq. The guesthouse is inside.

Slobodka Restaurant　　　ARMENIAN $
(mains AMD1800-2500; ☉noon-11pm) The chef at this recently opened restaurant behind the museum doesn't speak any English but she is happy to show guests what's in the refrigerator and on the stove. *Khoravats* and *dolma* are the staples, and extremely tasty.

❶ Information

There is a tourist information office in a municipal building on the eastern side of Shahumian Sq, but staff don't speak English and they keep very irregular hours. You can find limited tourist information at www.stepanavaninfo.com.

ATMs can be found in the bank buildings located between the Culture House and Lori Hotel on Garegin Nzhden St next to Shahumian Sq.

❶ Getting There & Around

From Yerevan, *marshrutky* (AMD1500, three hours, 9am, 11am, 1.30pm, 2.30pm, 3.30pm) depart from Kilikya Avtokayan.

In Stepanavan, all transport departs from a parking lot below the Stepan Shahumian statue. Services depart when full, and so there are no official departure times. *Marshrutky* leave for Yerevan (AMD1500, three hours) between 7.30am and 3pm. For Vanadzor (AMD400, one hour) there are usually four buses daily. Two daily buses go to Alaverdi (AMD700) and one daily bus goes to Gyumri (AMD1500, 1½ hours). Two *marshrutky* a day go to Tbilisi (AMD3000). A taxi anywhere in town from the main square costs AMD400.

Vanadzor　　　Վանաձոր

☑322 / POP 82,400

Lining the banks of the Pambak River, Vanadzor (formerly Kirovakan) is a post-industrial Soviet city that is the administrative centre for the Lori region. The town is a useful base for those visiting the medieval monasteries of Debed Canyon.

◎ Sights

Vanadzor's **shuka** is one of Armenia's busiest regional markets. The old village neighbourhoods of **Dimats** and **Bazum** are east of the town centre, over the Tandzut River. The centre of town was almost totally rebuilt during

Vanadzor

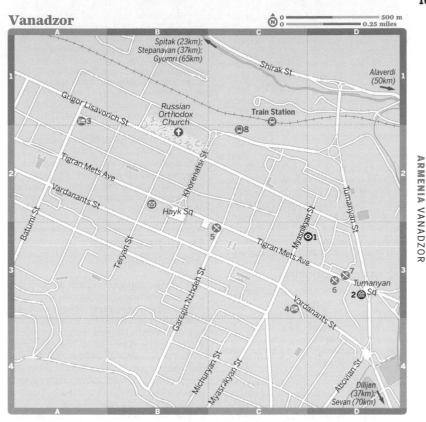

the Soviet era, but some elegant stone villas and country houses dating from the 19th century can be found south along Myasnikyan St.

The Debed Canyon monasteries can be visited on a day trip by taxi for around AMD15,000 to AMD20,000. This can be organised directly with drivers, or through Maghay B&B.

Vanadzor Museum of Fine Arts MUSEUM
(☑ 4 39 38; www.vanart.org; Tumanyan Sq; admission AMD500, guide AMD2000; ☺ 10am-6.30pm Tue-Sat, 10am-4pm Sun) There are nearly 2000 works of art on display at this branch of the National Gallery of Armenia, including paintings, sculptures, drawings, prints and decorative arts. Most are the work of artists from the Lori region.

🛏 Sleeping

★ **Maghay B&B** B&B $
(☑ 077 79 40 29; marined61@rambler.ru; 21 Azatamartikneri St; s/d AMD15,000/20,000, without bath-

room AMD13,000/16,000; P@☎) Ashot and Marine run one of the best B&Bs in Armenia, so you'll need to book ahead to score one of their seven rooms (five garden rooms with private bathroom; two in the main house sharing a bathroom). There's a communal kitchen where a delicious organic breakfast is served, and a newly built dining pavilion in the pleasant garden (dinner AMD4000 to AMD7000).

Two of the rooms with private bathroom have satellite TV, and all are clean and comfortable. To find the B&B, take the lane off Vardanants St where the large grey concrete bakery is located and head to its left and then behind it. A green sign on Vardanants St indicates the way.

Hotel Argishti HOTEL $$
(☑095 44 25 56; 1 Batumi St; r AMD25,000; P🛜) On a quiet street near the train station, the Argishti is overpriced for what it offers, but the English-speaking staff on reception will usually offer a discount of AMD5000 if asked. Rooms are clean and relatively comfortable, but have few frills. Wi-fi is patchy and breakfast is lacklustre.

✖ Eating & Drinking

The best meals in town are available at Maghay B&B. Nonguests are welcomed, but should call ahead to make a reservation.

There are plenty of cafes and fast-food joints on the main street, Tigran Mets Ave, including a branch of the popular **Tashir Pizza** (65 Tigran Mets Ave).

Oasis EUROPEAN, ARMENIAN $
(☑4 06 46; 48 Tigran Mets Ave; mains AMD1400-3200; ☺10.30am-11pm; 🛜) The food's nothing to get excited about (pizzas are stodgy, burgers are rubbery and the salads could be fresher), but this is the most popular dining spot in town. Its wide 1st-floor balcony is popular with students, who enjoy coffee and cake, luridly coloured cocktails and draft beer.

Jazz Cafe CAFE $
(☑098 11 72 82; 1st fl, 34 Tigran Mets Ave; mains AMD1500-3000; ☺9am-10.30pm; 🛜) This modern cafe is the most fashionable nightspot in town (it closes at 10.30pm, which shows just how vibrant the local nightlife is). A pianist plays every evening except Saturday, when a jazz band takes the stage. The food is adequate.

ⓘ Information

There are plenty of ATMs on Tigran Mets Ave.

ⓘ Getting There & Around

From Yerevan, *marshrutky* (AMD1200, two hours, half-hourly between 8.30am and 7pm) depart from Kilikiya Avtokayan.

In Vanadzor, the bus and train stations are at the bottom of Khorenatsi St, opposite the Russian Orthodox Church. *Marshrutky* to Yerevan (AMD1200, two hours, half-hourly from 7am to 5pm) take a 132km route via Spitak and Aparan. There are two morning *marshrutky* to Dilijan (AMD600, up to one hour), four daily *marshrutky* to Gyumri (AMD800, one hour) and two daily *marshrutky* to Noyemberyan via Alaverdi (AMD500, up to one hour). A *marshrutka* to Tbilisi (AMD4000) leaves at 8.30am.

Shared taxis charge AMD2000 per person to Yerevan and AMD5000 to Tbilisi.

The train service (p148) between Yerevan and Georgia makes a five-minute stop at Vanadzor. You should check the schedule and purchase your ticket from Vanadzor's train station at least one a day in advance.

Debed Canyon
Դեբեդի Ձոր
☑253

This canyon manages to pack in more history and culture than anywhere else in the country. Nearly every village along the Debed River has a church, a chapel, an old fort and a sprinkling of *khachkars* somewhere nearby. Two World Heritage–listed monasteries, Haghpat and Sanahin, are the main attractions, but there's much more to see. Derelict Soviet-era infrastructure is sadly noticeable along the riverbank, but the scenery is quite idyllic elsewhere.

The road through the canyon is busy, as this is the main artery linking Armenia with Georgia. Tourist facilities include the excellent hotel and restaurant in Dzoraget and a scattering of B&Bs in the villages. Ramshackle roadside *khoravats* stands are almost the only eating options outside the B&Bs, but in summer fresh fruits, including delectable berries, are sold by the side of the main road.

The canyon is best explored by car. Those using public transport should be able to travel between Alaverdi and most of the villages by *marshrutka,* but services vary in frequency and rarely operate on Sundays. Sanahin is easily reached by cable car from Alaverdi, and there are regular *marshrutky* to Haghpat and Odzun. There is one *marshrutka* per day to Akhtala, and one or two buses travel between Dsegh and Vanadzor most days. Hitchhikers should have no problem sourcing lifts on the main highway, but lifts on village roads are few and far between.

Dsegh   Դսեղ

Nestled on a wildflower-strewn plateau high above the gorge, this agricultural village is known throughout the southern Caucasus as the birthplace of Armenia's national poet, Hovhannes Tumanyan. Those who have already visited the Hovhannes Tumanyan Museum (p133) in Yerevan will find this timber **house** (admission AMD300; ☺10am-5pm Tue-Sun) where he grew up interesting, but those unfamiliar with his life and work will find the lack of English-language labelling frustrating. The house itself gives an interesting glimpse into local life during the tsarist era.

ⓘ Getting There & Away

The 7.6km road to Dsegh is clearly signed off the main highway 30km north of Vanadzor. The Hovhannes Tumanyan House Museum is located near Dsegh's central square, which sports a statue of Tumanyan, a cafe and a shop. A clapped-out bus travels between Vanadzor and the village once or twice daily (AMD400). There are a number of signed B&Bs if you are stranded here overnight.

Dzoraget

The only notable feature about this village and its surrounding area is the excellent Avan Dzoraget Hotel near the confluence of the Debed, Pambak and Dzoraget Rivers.

🛏 Sleeping & Eating

★**Avan Dzoraget Hotel**   HOTEL $$$
(☎060 50 10 10; www.tufenkianheritage.com; Dzoraget; s AMD27,000-100,000, d AMD35,000-110,000; P☺@☎🏊) Prepare to be impressed by this hotel right on the river's edge. There are 54 rooms spread over two buildings – opt for one with a river view if at all possible. Rooms are large and well equipped, and hotel facilities are excellent: indoor swimming pool, sauna, hot tub, gym and terrace restaurant. Kids love the ping-pong table (per hour AMD1400).

Avan Dzoraget Restaurant   ARMENIAN $$
(www.tufenkianheritage.com; Avan Dzoraget Hotel, Dzoraget; salads AMD1200-3300, mains AMD1800-10,000; ☺8am-10pm; P☎🍴) Few Armenian dining experiences are as pleasant as this one. Graze on your choice of an impressive array of salads and appetisers, many of which are vegetarian, or opt for a main dish such as locally caught rainbow trout. Seating is in an elegant indoor space or on the river-facing outdoor terrace. Service is friendly and efficient.

ⓘ Getting There & Away

Marshrutky (AMD500) travel between Vanadzor to Noyemberyan via Alaverdi twice daily and can drop you on the highway next to the bridge leading to the Avan Dzoraget Hotel.

Kobayr   Քոբայր

You'll need to watch the road carefully to spot the sign leading to the hamlet of Kobayr (also spelt Khober or Kober), around 6km north of the Avan Dzoraget Hotel and Restaurant. Leave your car in the small lot next to the railway line and clamour up the steep path, dodging chickens and other farm animals on the way. The climb takes 10 to 15 minutes.

Perched above the hamlet of Kobayr is the 12th-century **monastery** of the same name. The main church has some partially restored frescoes and a detached 3th-century bell tower; the church was being restored at the time of research. There are also three chapels, one with a scenic balcony.

ⓘ Getting There & Away

Kobayr is about 18km from Alaverdi and 33km from Vanadzor. *Marshrutky* travelling the route between Vanadzor, Alaverdi and Noyemberyan can be flagged down on the highway but only pass twice daily.

Odzun   Օձուն

Perched on a broad shelf that terminates at a sheer plunge down to the Debed River, Odzun is a substantial settlement of about 6000 residents that is best known for its magnificent church of St Astvatsatsin.

◎ Sights

St Astvatsatsin Church   CHURCH
(Surp Astvatsatsin) Built on the site where legend tells us St Thomas buried Christ's swaddling clothes in the 1st century, the core of St Astvatsatsin dates from the 5th century but had considerable additions in the 8th century. The current building features plenty of carved bas reliefs, a central cupola, a handsome external pillared arcade on its southern side and two 19th-century belfries. The unusual funerary monument next to it is thought to date from the 6th century.

The priest lives nearby, and is always happy to show visitors through the church. He can often to be found in the small garden cafe opposite, which serves tea, good Armenian coffee and home-made cakes.

One and a half kilometres to the southeast of the church, at the edge of the canyon, is the three-chambered **Horomayri Monastery**, the well-camouflaged remnants of which are visible below the cliff on the right.

🛏 Sleeping

Sergo Davtyan B&B   B&B $
(Chez Sergo; 📞 091 42 75 40; www.odzunbandb.
am; House 4, 22 St; per person AMD10,000; 🛜) French-speaking Azniv and Sergo Davtyan and their English-speaking adult son are justifiably proud of their eight-room B&B, which is the best in Odzun. Though it looks like a concrete bunker outside, the interior is very pleasant, with an elegant lounge-dining room on the ground floor. The clean and very light bedrooms on the 1st floor have modern bathrooms.

❶ Getting There & Away

Five *marshrutky* per day travel from Odzun to Alaverdi (AMD200) between 8am to 3.30pm. Odzun is on the road to Stepanavan, and the Alaverdi to Stepanavan bus passes through here at 10.30am and 3.30pm (AMD700).

Alaverdi   Ալավերդի

Blighted by a huge smokestack belching smoke into the valley, Alaverdi is the administrative and transport hub of this area but doesn't have much else going for it. Rows of shabby Soviet-era apartment blocks are cut into the strata by the highway and the railway line, and a half-decommissioned copper smelting plant (the source of the smoke) dominates the town's northern edge.

Tamara's bridge, about 1km north of the bus stand, was built by order of Queen Tamar of Georgia in the 12th century. This humpbacked stone bridge was used by road traffic until 30 years ago. There are four kitten-faced lions carved on the stone railing. In summer, two outdoor cafes operate next to the bridge.

🛏 Sleeping & Eating

Iris Guesthouse   GUESTHOUSE $
(📞 094 89 42 92, 091 08 88 12; irina israyelian@gmail.com; 65 Baghramyan St; dm AMD7000, d AMD18,000, d/tw without bathroom AMD15,000/16,000; 🅿🛜) Very popular among backpackers, this house has several guestrooms and great views of the river. Owner Irina Israeliyan is an enthusiastic

host and can prepare meals upon request (organic dinner AMD4000). The guesthouse is located right on the highway, about 2km south of Alaverdi (look for the small yellow and orange signs pointing to the left as you travel north).

Flora   ARMENIAN $$
(Yerevan Hwy; set menus AMD3200-4100; ⊙10am-10pm) Also called Armen's, this huge place is popular with tour groups and has a number of dining spaces inside and on the rear terraces. The menu holds no surprises (*khorovats*, cheese and salad) and the quality only just makes the grade. To get here, cross Tamara's bridge, climb the stairs on the far side and turn right.

❶ Getting There & Away

From Yerevan, *marshrutky* (AMD1700, three hours) depart from Kilikya Avtokayan at 9.30am, 1pm, 2pm, 3pm and 4pm. Shared taxis from Kilikya charge AMD2500 to AMD3000 per passenger and depart when full.

In Alaverdi, buses and *marshrutky* leave from a parking bay next to shops on the main road – taxis wait here too. A bus ticket and information window is located in the back of the lot. There's one *marshrutka* to Akhtala at noon (AMD300), *marshrutky* to Yerevan at 8am, 9.30am, 11.30pm and 2pm (AMD1700, three hours), two daily *marshrutky* to Vanadzor (AMD500, up to one hour), two daily buses to Stepanavan (AMD700) and five *marshrutky* per day to Haghpat (AMD200). The Haghpat service operates between 8.30am and 5pm Monday to Saturday.

A seat in a shared taxi costs AMD5000 to Tbilisi and AMD3000 to Yerevan. A private taxi will cost AMD5000 to the Georgian border, AMD15,000 to Tbilisi and AMD20,000 to Yerevan.

Sanahin   Սանահին

Home to one of Armenia's World Heritage-listed medieval monasteries, this village is cut into the canyon wall above Alaverdi and is an essential stop for all visitors to the Debed Canyon. Taking the cable car from Alaverdi is an enjoyable start to any visit here, and it also saves the fuss of finding a park near the monastery, which can be very busy on weekends in the high season.

◎ Sights

Sanahin Monastery   MONASTERY
Sanahin is packed with ancient graves, darkened chapels and medieval study halls. The inner sanctum of the cross-shaped Surp Astvatsatsin Church (Holy Mother of God

Church) is the oldest structure, dating back to 934. Its adjoining *gavit* is one of the later buildings, built in 1181. In its heyday, the monastery was renowned for its school of illuminators and calligraphers and also for its medical school. Its name means 'older than that one', referring to nearby Haghpat Monastery.

Sanahin's large library (scriptorium) was built in 1063. Square in plan and vaulted, it has 10 niches of varying sizes in which codices and books were stored. At the southeastern corner of the library is a small church dedicated to St Gregory the Illuminator. The 11th-century Academy of Gregory Magistros is located between the two main churches. The cemetery, located to the southeast of the main buildings, contains a 12th-century mausoleum housing the Zakarian princes.

Mikoyan Museum MUSEUM
(admission AMD300; ⊙10am-1pm & 2-6pm) This Soviet-era museum is a shrine to brothers Anastas and Artyom Mikoyan. Anastas survived 60 years in the Politburo, outlasting even Stalin – we reckon he deserves a museum. Artyom was the designer of the USSR's first jet fighter in WWII, the MiG. There's an early MiG jet outside the museum (no climbing allowed!) and plenty of photos, medals, uniforms and aircraft plans and drawings inside.

The museum is located downhill from Sanahin Monastery, off Mikoyan St.

ⓘ Getting There & Away

A cable car (AMD300) climbs the lip of the inner canyon from Alaverdi's copper mine up to Sarahart, from where it's a short walk to Sanahin. It runs according to work shifts at the mine – 7.15am to 10am, 11am to 2pm, 3pm to 7.30pm and 11.15pm to midnight.

From the cable-car station, walk up to the main square of Sarahart and take a left; after 900m you'll reach a T-junction in Sanahin village (separate from Sarahart). The monastery is uphill and the Mikoyan Museum downhill.

The Yerevan–Georgia train (p148) passes through Sanahin and stops at the station for one minute; you'll need to inform staff if you wish to alight. Buy your ticket in advance and tell platform staff if you wish to take the train north.

Haghpat Հաղպատ

The second of the Debed Canyon's World Heritage–listed monastery complexes is found in this picturesque village east of Alaverdi.

Occupying a commanding position overlooking the gorge, this **monastery** has atmosphere and architectural splendour in spades.

Founded around 966 by Queen Khosrvanuch, who funded construction of the domed Surp Nishan (Church of the Holy Cross) at the centre of the complex, it saw a building boom in the 12th and 13th centuries. Surp Nishan's frescoes and the porch, *gavit*, bell tower, library and chapter house were added at this time. The monastery's name means 'huge wall', acknowledging its hefty fortifications.

Other buildings in the complex include two 11th-century churches and a freestanding 13th-century *gavit* at the rear of the site. This has glorious acoustics and frames a magnificent view over the landscape. An inscription on Surp Nishan's *gavit* reads in part: 'You who enter through its door and prostrate yourself before the Cross, in your prayers remember us and our royal ancestors, who rest at the door of the holy cathedral, in Jesus Christ.'

🛏 Sleeping

Hotel Gayane HOTEL $
(☑093 41 37 05; s/d/4-bed cottage AMD8000/16,000/32,000; P✳︎☎︎☷︎) An excellent choice for families visiting this region, Gayane started as a B&B in a farmhouse but has since expanded to include four simple self-catering cottages and a new multistorey building with hotel-style rooms. Seven original B&B rooms are old-fashioned but have satellite TV; there are 18 rooms with views in the new building. Home-cooked dinners are available (AMD3000).

Facilities include a pool, billiard table and table-tennis table. The hotel complex is located at the end of a lane off an unsealed road off the main road a couple of kilometres down from Haghpat Monastery.

ⓘ Getting There & Away

Haghpat is 6km from the Yerevan Hwy, signed from the northern approach but not from the south.

Marshrutky from Alaverdi (AMD200) run five times daily between 8.30am and 5pm; there are no services on Sundays. It's a 7km walk to Sanahin Monastery via Akner village.

Akhtala Ախթալա

This small village 18km northeast of Alaverdi has one major claim to fame: the magnificent frescoes in its 13th-century **church**.

The fortifications here date to the 10th century, but the main church was built in the first half of the 13th century and is one of the few medieval churches in Armenia to retain

ARMENIA DEBED CANYON

ARMENIA'S MEDIEVAL MONASTERIES

Armenia's tourism industry has two major assets: the country's spectacular natural scenery and its extraordinary array of medieval monasteries. Fortunately, most of these monasteries are set in extremely scenic surrounds, meaning that any travel itinerary based on monastery visits will most definitely live up to a 'Best of Armenia' description.

The unique architecture of Armenia's medieval monasteries developed when elements of Byzantine ecclesiastical architecture were combined with the traditional vernacular architectural and building styles of the Caucasus. Spanning the period from the 10th to 13th centuries, many of these monasteries were built in elevated locations and were heavily fortified to protect them from marauding armies. Locally sourced stone – often tuff – was a logical and widely used building material.

The various architectural forms utilised in the churches within the monasteries – basilica, domed basilica and cruciform – are common throughout the Christian world, but Armenian monasteries have a number of distinctive elements, including conical 'umbrella-style' domes and cupolas mounted on a cylindrical drum. Another common feature is the *gavit*, a grand space built as the narthex (entrance room) to a major church; these sometimes doubled as a mausoleum. Most distinctive of all is the profusion of ornately carved stone decoration, including the carved memorial stones known as *khachkars* (p138). Of the 60-plus medieval monasteries in the country, the complexes at **Haghpat** (p165), **Sanahin** (p164), **Geghard** (p149) and **Echmiadzin** (p151) are all inscribed on Unesco's World Heritage list as representatives of the highest flowering of Armenian religious architecture. Other outstanding examples include **Saghmosavank** (p154), **Hovhannavank** (p154), **Haghartsin** (p169), **Goshavank** (p169), **Akhtala** (p165), **Noravank** (p176) and **Tatev** (p184).

When visiting an Armenian monastery it is respectful to dress modestly (no shorts, short skirts or bare shoulders); women should consider covering their heads but this isn't essential. Members of the Armenian Orthodox faith tend to exit church backwards so as not to turn their back on God; you may wish to do the same.

most of its original frescoes. These include a stunning Virgin Mary in the apse, and depictions of the Last Supper, Last Judgement, Crucifixion and Resurrection on other walls. Note the fresco of bearded Persians, said to have been painted so that invading armies would spare the church.

When you enter the monastery through the main gate, look left and you'll see two large caves that were used for smelting copper. Surrounding the church are a well-preserved chapel and a graveyard with old and new headstones – be careful where you walk, as weeds and grass hide dangerous drops into underground structures.

❶ Getting There & Away

A daily *marshrutka* to Akhtala (AMD200) departs Alaverdi at noon, but returns immediately, meaning that you will be stranded here after your visit. It's a 3km walk to the highway.

Dilijan Դիլիջան

📁 268 / POP 13,500

It's billed as the 'Switzerland of Armenia', and although that may be a bit of a stretch,

alpine Dilijan has undeniably attractive scenery and an extremely pleasant climate.

During Soviet times this was the peaceful retreat for cinematographers, composers, artists and writers to come and be creative; today it's a centre for tourism with a number of fine B&Bs and hotels.

There is certainly enough natural beauty to inspire creative thought: the lush oak and hornbeam forests surround the town with snowcapped peaks in the distance. In summer the villagers herd cattle down from the mountain pastures through the town, and people gather mushrooms and mountain herbs from the rich deciduous forests. The local architecture features a lot of steep tiled roofs and wooden beams, along with some cute gingerbread-style structures. Even the local Soviet monuments have a touch of flair.

The medieval churches of Haghartsin (p169) and Goshavank (p169) can be visited on an easy day trip from Dilijan.

◉ Sights

Art Gallery & Museum of Dilijan   MUSEUM
(📞2 44 50; 28 Myasnikyan St; admission AMD500, tour AMD2000; ◉10am-5.30pm Tue-Sat, 11am-5pm

Sun) Housing an eclectic collection of European and Armenian art from the 16th to 20th centuries, this gallery is housed in a grandiose building on the road to the upper town and is Dilijan's major cultural institution. Some of the older works from Italian and French artists had been housed in museums in Moscow and St Petersburg but were moved to Dilijan during WWII for safekeeping. The stand-out Armenian work is Arpenik Nalbandyan's Cézanne-like *Children from Khndzoresk*.

Diljan Historic Centre   AREA

(Sharambeyan St) This somewhat Disneyfied collection of stone and wooden traditional buildings includes workshops for local craftspeople, a hotel, souvenir shops and a restaurant. As you walk along the main road up to Dilijan's main shopping strip, look for a building housing the Armenian Apostolic Church and a wooden sign for the Tufenkian Old Dilijan Hotel on the left-hand side of the road. Walk down the stone stairs next to the sign to find the complex.

Monuments

A crownlike monument to the **50th Anniversary of Soviet Armenia** stands near the main roundabout in the lower town. The **WWII Memorial**, with the huge silver figures of a soldier holding a dying comrade, is on a hillock south of the river.

Walks

There are pleasant walks to the 11th-century **Surp Grigor Church** and **Jukhtakvank** monastery, both located near the Dilijan mineral-water plant, 3.2km along the Vanadzor road and about 3.5km up to the right. They are well signposted and a trail continues past Jukhtakvank, through pastures and woods, and back to Dilijan (a three-hour hike). If you are keen to cycle rather than walk, mountains bikes can be hired at the Tufenkian Old Dilijan Complex (AMD10,000 per day).

🛏 Sleeping

Daravand Guesthouse   B&B $

(☑78 57, 094 42 09 65; www.daravand.com; 46 Abovyan St; s/d AMD17,000/25,000, without bathroom AMD11,000/19,000; ℗) Owner Razmik is a diaspora Armenian with an Iranian upbringing and a German education, and he runs his guesthouse with great verve. Rooms are clean and well maintained, featuring good beds and small bathrooms. The downstairs lounge has attractive decor and the wide balcony has

a great view – both are lovely places to relax. Dinner costs AMD5000 per person.

The guesthouse is on the road towards Jukhtakvank, 360m off the main Dilijan–Vanadazor Hwy. Head towards the railway bridge and look out for a red garage on the right-hand side of the road; the guesthouse is reached by a switchback road next to this. If you're travelling by public transport, the local bus starts and ends its journey from the highway turn-off.

Nina B&B   B&B $

(☑091 76 77 34; nina-mail08@mail.eu; dm AMD7000, d AMD20,000, cottage per person AMD8000; ℗⬤) Most backpackers end up at this friendly B&B on the winding road behind the Art Gallery. It offers two dorms, four private rooms and two self-catering cottages (one in the garden and another down the road). Furnishings are dated, beds uncomfortable and bathrooms basic – it's clean, though. Dinners of soup, salads and either dolma or khoravats (AMD4000 to AMD7000) are a highlight.

Tufenkian Old Dilijan Complex   HOTEL $$

(☑094 03 08 83; www.tufenkianheritage.com; Sharambeyan St; s AMD27,000-38,000, d AMD34,000-44,000, ste AMD67,000; ⬤) The main business in the Dilijan Historic Centre offers comfortable but somewhat bland rooms in one building, and more atmospheric but less comfortable suites in a wooden annexe overlooking the valley. Breakfast is served in the disappointing Haykanoush Restaurant.

🍴 Eating

There are a couple of fast-food *shwarma* places next to the bus stand in the lower town.

Flying Ostrich By Dolmama   ARMENIAN $$

(☑060 65 50 80; 6 Sayat Nova St; mains AMD3500-6000; ⬤8.30am-midnight; 🖥) There was great excitement in town when this branch of Yerevan's upmarket Dolmama Restaurant opened next to the Aghstev River in 2014. Serving what it describes as 'traditional Armenian food with a twist', it offers indoor seating in a restored barn and outdoor seating in an attractive cobbled courtyard.

Getap Restaurant   ARMENIAN $$

(☑099 88 83 34; www.getap.am; Dilijan–Ijevan Hwy; grills AMD800-6000; ⬤9am-9pm; ℗⬤) Armenians adore dining at restaurants offering small wooden pavilions situated next to rivers and lakes – it's one step up from the equally adored picnic. Located on the highway to Ijevan, this place has plenty of pavilions and is popular with bus groups. Service is friendly and the extensive menu is dominated by *khoravats*.

Haykanoush ARMENIAN $$
(Sharambeyan St; mains AMD1500-5000; ⊗ 9am-10pm) Pickings are slim when it comes to Dilijan's dining scene, so we're including this restaurant in the Dilijan Historic Centre despite our reservations. Its decor is pleasant, but on our most-recent visit we found its service incompetent and food disappointing. This is unusual as it is part of the usually impressive Tufenkian hotel and restaurant chain – maybe things will improve.

❶ Information

There are plenty of ATMs, mobile phone offices and shops (including a *shuka*) in the upper town.

❶ Getting There & Around

From Yerevan, *marshrutky* (AMD1000, two hours) depart when full from Hyusisayin bus station between 9am and 6pm. The bus stand is in front of the cafe near the main roundabout in the lower town. *Marshrutky* between Ijevan and Yerevan stop here en route five times per day between 8am and 4pm (to Ijevan AMD500, to Yerevan AMD1000). One bus (AMD400, 70 minutes) and two *marshrutky* (AMD600, up to one hour) travel to Vanadzor each morning. A private taxi costs AMD5000 to Ijevan and AMD15,000 to the Georgian border.

Enquire about *marshrutky* to Tbilisi at the privately run **travel information office** (❷ 077 34 76 77) in the building next to the bus stand.

There are taxis at the main roundabout (the fare is AMD600 around town). During the day a local bus trundles between the western side of town around Kalinin St up to Shahumian St (AMD100). A taxi to Haghartsin and Goshavank and back will cost around AMD10,000 including waiting time.

HIKING FROM HAGHARTSIN TO SHAMAKHYAN

From Haghartsin, it's possible to walk on trails over the mountain to Shamakhyan, a village 3km northwest of Dilijan. Be prepared for sudden bursts of rain at all times of the year.

Walk past Haghartsin Monastery to find the trailhead, which is marked with a sign that reads: 'Dilijan NP Eco-Tourist Route'. After five minutes' walk the 4WD trail reaches a creek and continues up the opposite bank. From here it's a one-hour uphill hike to the ridge. The path is a bit overgrown in places but the route is fairly obvious.

At the ridge you'll find another set of 4WD tracks and you should follow these to the right. After a short distance, Dilijan will appear in the distance to your left. After about 30 minutes of level walking the 4WD tracks start to head downhill below the treeline. After about 15 minutes of downhill walking (still on the 4WD tracks) you'll see a fence made from branches. Stay on the road as it hooks left and continues downhill. Five minutes after seeing the fence an open meadow appears on the right. Just downhill from here is an artillery range used by the army.

At this point you should walk right, off the main 4WD track, and down towards the meadow. Cross the gully and walk along the hillside in a southwesterly direction (veering away from the artillery range). The trail disappears for a while but after 10 minutes you hit an obvious 4WD trail heading downhill (now the artillery range is more or less behind you). Continue downhill to a creek and a farmhouse on the opposite bank. There is a wood footbridge a little bit left of the 4WD track.

On the other side of the creek is a small picnic area. Continue along the 4WD trail for another 20 minutes and at the next clearing veer to the right. Shamakhyan village soon comes into view. The road leading to the village can be very muddy, so look for the small break that leads down to the creek and up the other bank to the village. The walk takes less than four hours. From the village you can walk down to the highway and catch a lift back to Dilijan.

Alternatively, you can extend the hike by walking from Shamakhyan to Jukhtakvank. Start by walking uphill from the taxi stand and follow this road as it wraps above the town to the cow farm *(kirova ferma)*. Just past the barns and sheds is a sign that says 'Nature Trail Jukhtak Vank – Shamakhyan'. Continue along this obvious 4WD trail for about 50 minutes and you'll eventually reach Jukhtakvank. Note that few locals know this trail, so if you ask for directions most people will tell you to walk down to the highway and turn right up the next valley for Jukhtakvank. However, the shortest route is definitely along the 'Nature Trail'. Along the trail are some information panels that describe the flora and fauna of the area.

From Jukhtakvank you can walk 3km downhill to the main highway.

Around Dilijan

Haghartsin   Հաղարծին

Hidden in a verdant valley 13km northeast of Dilijan, Haghartsin ('Dance of the Eagles') was built between the 10th and 13th centuries and has three churches: one named for Gregory the Illuminator; another for the Virgin Mary (Surp Astvatsatsin); and the third for St Stephen (Stepanos). There are stunning *khachkars* (don't miss the one on the southern wall of Surp Astvatsatsin), a sundial on the wall of St Gregory, a ruined *gavit* and a refectory with stunning arched ceiling.

The **monastery** was built by order of two brothers, princes of the Bagratuni kingdom, and their family seal can be seen on the back of St Stepanos.

A recent restoration of the site funded by the Sheikh of Sharjah in the UAE has seen the church buildings lose their historic patina, and many visitors find their bright and shiny appearance disconcerting. No doubt they will blend back into their surrounds in the future.

The monastery is 4km off the main Dilijan–Ijevan Hwy. There is no *marshrutka* service, but it's an extremely pleasant walk from the highway, with plenty of picnic spots and lookouts along the way.

Goshavank   Գոշավանք

Founded in 1188 by the saintly Armenian cleric Mkhitar Gosh, who was buried in a little chapel overlooking the main complex, this monastery features a main church (Surp Astvatsatsin), smaller churches to St Gregory of Narek and St Gregory the Illuminator, and a *matenadaran* (library) that is said to have held 15,000 books. A fourth church topped by a bell tower was built on top of the library in 1991; entrance was via the external cantilevered staircase.

Goshavank is considered one of the principal cultural centres of Armenia of its time; historians believe it was abandoned after the Mongol invasion in 1375. It then appears to have been reoccupied between the 17th to 19th centuries and restored from 1957 to 1963. Another major restoration was underway at the time of research. When here, take note of the splendid *khachkar* between the second St Gregory chapel and the *gavit*.

Goshavank is 6.5km off the main Dilijan–Ijevan Hwy, on the road to Chambarak. A taxi from Dilijan or Ijevan (both 23km away)

should cost around AMD4500 one-way. Attendants charge cars AMD100 to park in the church carpark.

Ijevan   Իջեւան

☑ 263 / POP 18,900

Surrounded by forested mountains and with the Aghstev River running through its centre, Ijevan is the attractive capital of Tavush *marz*. Ijevan means 'caravanserai' or 'inn' and the town has been on a major east–west trade route for millennia. The local climate is warmer than in Dilijan, and the town is the centre of a wine-growing district producing some acceptable white table wines. The town has some handsome early-20th-century buildings, a bustling open-air *shuka* and a wine factory.

Buses and *marshrutky* stop on the main highway. From the bus stand, walk over the bridge to reach the central square with its musical fountain. The *shuka* is in the streets north of the fountain, around a small church. There are plenty of banks with ATMs on Meliqbekyan St east of the central square.

◎ Sights

Locals enjoy whiling away the afternoon in the **Sculpture Park** in the centre of town.

Ijevan Wine Factory   WINERY
(☑ 3 64 57; 9 Yerevanyan St; tour AMD2500, tasting AMD3000; ⊙ 10am-5pm Mon-Sat) Put aside all expectations of a picturesque winery, because Ijevan's wine factory is just that – a large industrial complex where the local grape harvest is transformed into dry white and sparkling wines under the Haghartsin, Gayane and Makaravank labels. The tour explains how the factory's wine and cognac is produced, and the tasting includes three wines.

The factory is about 1.5km from the town centre, on the road to Dilijan.

🛏 Sleeping & Eating

There are a couple of decent budget accommodation choices to choose from, but decent eating options are hard to find. Most travellers eat at the restaurant below the Hotel Dok or grab a *lahmajo* at one of the cafes on Aboyyan St next to the river or Ankahutyan St opposite the Sculpture Park.

Anakhit Guesthouse   B&B $
(☑ 077 29 29 79, 077 01 22 74; 4 Tavrizyan St; s/d/f without bathroom AMD5000/12,000/18,000; 🅿 🛜) Travelers rave about this family-run B&B near the *marshrutka* stand, describing it as a

WORTH A TRIP

SHAMSHADIN & AROUND

North of Ijevan, one road turns northwest at Azatamut through the captured Azeri enclaves of Upper and Lower Askipara (now Verin Voskepar and Nerkin Voskepar) to Noyemberyan and the Georgian border. Another road turns right just before the border to Berd in Shamshadin region. There are still landmines along this frontier, so it's unwise to explore the shattered villages around here.

Travelling north on the Yerevan–Georgia Hwy, you'll come to a Y intersection. Take the left branch towards Noyemberyan and then take another turn-off left towards Achajur village. The uphill road is edged by vineyards and offers lovely views across the countryside. At the village, follow signs to the 11th-century **Makaravank** monastery. It's 6.5km from the village to the monastery along an unsealed and potholed road. Those in 4WDs should be able to drive all the way, but those in 2WDs will probably need to park on the side of the road at some stage and continue by foot. There is no public transport and the road is rarely used, meaning that hitchers are unlikely to have any luck sourcing a ride.

The beautiful church here is set deep in a forest, giving it a very peaceful atmosphere. There are some fine carvings on the exterior and interior of the structures, including ornate altar daises carved with eight-pointed stars, floral motifs, fish, birds and geometrical forms.

The Shamshadin region east of Ijevan is a fertile stretch of woodlands, vineyards and farms carved by three valleys: the Khndzorut, Tavush and Hakhum. With Azerbaijan on two sides and rugged mountains dividing it from the rest of Armenia, it's also quite isolated.

As the crow flies it's just 21km from Ijevan to Berd; the mountains in between them, however, have forced the construction of a roundabout road that loops for 67km north and then south. About 44km into the trip you'll spot **Nor Varagavank** up the hillside – the 3km detour is worth the trip to see the ruined monastery. The oldest sections were started in 1198 by David Bagrtuni, son of King Vasak I; a Surp Astvatsatsin church was added in 1237. The monastery once contained a fragment of the True Cross until it was lost in fighting in 1915.

Berd (population 8000) itself is nothing special but does have a restaurant and a couple of hotels. The main reason to come here is to hike along the old road from Ijevan. The 35km road twists and winds through the mountains and past some attractive old villages. The hike takes about 12 hours in total, best spread over two or three days. There are no hotels, but you can ask in the villages for a homestay. It's best to have a taxi driver take you the first 5km or so out of Ijevan to get you on the right track. Just make sure they are taking you on the old road that heads east of town rather than the new road going north.

A daily *marshrutka* (AMD500) leaves from Ijevan to Berd (on the new road) in the morning. It returns from Berd mid-afternoon. A shared taxi between Berd and Ijevan costs AMD1500 per person.

real home away from home. Owner Anakhit offers a warm welcome and is known for her cooking – breakfasts with their home-made jams and local honey are a highlight. Rooms are simple but comfortable, and there's a lovely terrace with view. Daughter-in-law Anna speaks English and French.

Hotel Dok HOTEL **$**
(☑4 01 71, 094 51 51 54; lusmel@yandex.ru; 1st fl, 40 Ankaxutyan St; r AMD10,000-20,000; ☜) The clean, bright rooms at this hotel offer excellent value for money, and there's a popular restaurant downstairs that serves Armenian and international cuisine. It's located on a roundabout on the eastern edge of the *shuka*. Look for the 'Fur' sign, enter the small foyer,

go through the left door and follow the stairs to the 1st-floor reception desk.

❶ Getting There & Away

From Yerevan, *marshrutky* (AMD1500, three hours) depart when full from Hyusisayin bus station between 9am and 6pm.

In Ijevan, *marshrutky* leave from the wooden bus shelter next to the Dan Garden Cafe on the highway. Departure information is displayed in a window of the ticket office set back from the street.

Marshrutky to Yerevan (AMD1500, three hours) leave five times daily from 7.30am to 3.30pm; these stop in Dilijan (AMD500, 40 minutes) en route. There are also a few daily *marshrutky* to Vanadzor (AMD1000, 90 minutes). Unfortunately, there are no bus services to Georgia; a private taxi to the border should cost AMD10,000.

Lake Sevan Սևանա Լիճ

📝 261 / POP 36,200

Set 1900m above sea level, the great blue expanse of Sevana Lich (Lake Sevan) covers 940 sq km, and is 80km long by 30km at its widest. The largest lake in the Caucasus, it's also one of the largest freshwater high-altitude lakes in the world. Its colours and shades change with the weather and by its own mysterious processes, from a dazzling azure to dark blue and a thousand shades in between. The lake supports a healthy fish population, including the endangered *ishkhan* (prince trout), named for a row of spots like a crown on its head. Other species include introduced crayfish and *sig* (white fish).

The level of the lake fell when Sevan's outlet, the Hrazdan River, was tapped for hydroelectric plants and irrigation in the 1950s and it is now about 20m lower than its original natural level. Other Soviet plans to drain the lake down to one-sixth of its size thankfully went nowhere. The retreating waters uncovered forts, houses and artefacts dating back some 2000 years, and made Sevan Island a peninsula.

The exposed land has been designated the Sevan National Park, although some of it is disappearing again as conservationists have convinced the government of the need to raise the level of the lake. Since 2002 it has risen more than 2m, an environmental achievement that has led to cleaner water and more fish.

Though the natural landscape is beautiful, most of the man-made structures around it are badly maintained eyesores. Armenians with money head to the Georgian beaches for their summer vacations, leaving Lake Sevan to campers, groups of Russian package tourists and noisy day-trippers. The quality of the resorts on the western side of the lake is universally low, and it's difficult to reach the only quality resort on the eastern edge due to its potholed highway. Fortunately, the quality of the highway on the eastern edge is good.

Sevan Սևան

This bustling town is 6km inland from the lake's western shore and is the administrative centre for the region. It was founded in 1842 as the Russian village of Elenovka but there

are few reminders of the past. Taxis to Yerevan, the peninsula and lakeshore hotels leave from the main street, which also has shops, ATMs and a *shuka*.

ℹ️ Information

The **Tourist Information Centre** (📝 2 22 86; 164 Nairyan St; ⊙ 9am-1pm & 2-6pm, reduced hours in winter) is located in the Qaghaqapetaran (city municipality building) on the main street. Staff speak Armenian, Russian and French, but no English. It has no English-language maps or brochures about the town or region.

ℹ️ Getting There & Away

Yerevan is only 67km away by freeway. *Marshrutky* (AMD800, one hour, 9am to 6pm) depart from Yerevan's Hyusisayin bus station when full.

Marshrutky travelling the route between Dilijan and Yerevan pick up passengers on the corner of Nairyan and Sayat-Nova Sts in Sevan (to Yerevan AMD600, to Dilijan AMD500).

The taxi stand is on the corner of Nairyan and Sargis Sevanetsi Sts. A private taxi costs about AMD7000 to Yerevan, AMD4000 to Dilijan and AMD3000 to Tsaghkadzor. A taxi to one of the hotels on or near the peninsula costs AMD1000. A four- or five-hour tour of Sevanavank, Hayravank and the *khachkars* of Noratus should cost around AMD7000.

Sevanavank Peninsula

The main beach strip is along the sandy south side of this peninsula, crowned by the much-photographed churches on the hill at the end. Don't expect clean water or a tranquil beach experience – bars pump out loud music and beachgoers play beach volleyball, waterski, ride jetskis and have fun on paddleboats. You'll need to pay a fee to use any of the beaches (AMD2000 to AMD3000 per person depending on the beach).

⊙ Sights

Sevanavank   MONASTERY
(parking AMD200) A pagan temple once occupied this elevated site overlooking the lake, but was replaced by a now-ruined church in the 4th century. Two further churches, **Surp Astvatsatsin** and **Surp Arakelots** (aka Surp Karapet), were built in the 9th century. A *gavit* was added to Surp Astvatsatsin at a later date; now ruined, it is filled with handsome *khachkars*. Accessed via a long flight of steps, the monastery is one of Armenia's most popular tourist sites and is horrendously overcrowded in summer.

Sevan

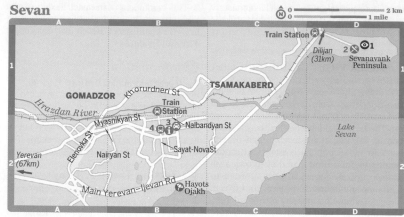

Sevan

◎ Sights
1 Sevanavank...................................... D1

✴ Eating
2 Ashot Yerkat Restaurant D1

❶ Information
3 Tourist Information Centre................B2

❶ Transport
4 Buses & Marshrutkas to
Yerevan..B2

Legend tells us that St Mesrop Mashtots had a vision of 12 figures walking across the lake, who showed him the place to found a church. Queen Mariam, wife of Vasak of Syunik, built the churches in 874, and they were heavily restored in the 17th century. In the 19th century the monastery was a place to reform errant monks – there was a strict regime and no women were allowed.

Views from the top of the hill are expansive and can be spectacular; in summer and autumn a thick carpet of cloud pushes over the Areguniats mountains to the north and evaporates at the lake's edge.

🛏 Sleeping & Eating

It's incumbent on travel writers to tell it like it is, so we feel compelled to say that there isn't one hotel or resort on the western side of the lake worthy of recommendation – stay elsewhere if at all possible.

Sevan's beach resorts start to fill up – and raise their prices – around late May. Prices may jump by 40% in the high season. The season slows down again in early Septem-

ber. In spring and autumn resorts remain open with reduced rates and in winter most are shut entirely.

Local restaurants and cafes crank up the volume of their stereos extra loud when tourists arrive, so you may have a hard time finding a quiet place to enjoy the birdsong and lapping waters of the lake.

Ashot Yerkat Restaurant　ARMENIAN **$$**
(☑ 2 50 00; mains AMD800-25,000; ☺ 10am-9pm) Located off the stairs leading to the monastery, this place has a huge dining terrace with partially obscured lake views. You'll need to share one of the long tables, as the restaurant is set up for the large tour groups that dominate its client base. The menu includes kebabs, grilled fish dishes (including extremely expensive *ishkhan* trout) and salads.

❶ Getting There & Away

A taxi between Sevan and Sevanavank costs AMD1000 each way. You'll be charged AMD2500 for a return trip with a 30-minute stop at the monastery.

A train leaves Yerevan's Almast train station at 8.30am daily except Wednesday between 15 June and 1 October travelling to Shorzha on weekends, and to Tsovagyugh on weekdays. It stops on the highway near the peninsula en route (AMD600, two hours).

Around Lake Sevan

About 30km south of Sevan is the typical *tufa* monastery of **Hayravank** – 1100 years old, sturdy as the day it was built, and with *khachkars* in the cemetery attesting to centuries of Armenian life. The monastery is clearly signed from the highway, and the promontory it stands on commands a fine view of Lake Sevan.

Further south is one of the most extraordinary cultural sights in the country. Head to the agricultural village of **Noratus** (sometimes spelt Noraduz) and follow the 'khachkars' sign to the villlage's cemetery, which is home to hundreds of carved memorial stones dating from the medieval period. Big and small, upright and recumbent, the *khachkars* are a truly extraordinary sight. According to one legend, an Arab army was once forced to take cover nearby as the commander mistook the field of *khachkars* for a battalion of enemy soldiers. They only moved on after a scout discovered the 'soldiers' were nothing more than harmless stone tablets. Also in the village is the 10th-century church of **Surp Grigor Lusavorich**, which has an unusually tall cylindrical form. Noratus is a good area to find a **beach** away from the bustle of Sevan.

The provincial capital of Gegharkunik *marz* is **Gavar** (population 19,000) on the cold slopes of the Geghama mountains west of Lake Sevan. It has shops, a few cafes and at least one hotel.

A paved road from **Martuni** (population 12,000) at the lake's southern edge, heads south over the Selim Pass (p180) to Yeghegnadzor in Vayots Dzor but this is impassable in winter (November to April).

About 20km east of Martuni is the handsome little **Vanevank** church (903), in a gorge south of the town of Artsvanist. Turn off at Karchagbyur and head up the valley through Lchavan to the centre of Makenis village to find the 10th- to 13th-century churches of **Makenyats Vank**, close to a gorge.

Further on, the road cuts inland to **Vardenis**. From here, a famously rough road used only by fearless truckers heads over the Sodk Pass (2400m) into the wilds of Kelbajar and northern Karabakh. Another road continues around the eastern side of the lake to the farming village of Tsapatagh, home to the upmarket **Avan Marak Tsapatagh Hotel** (☑ 060 50 10 10; www.tufenkianheritage.com; Tsapatagh; s AMD31,000-46,000, d AMD37,000-52,000, ste AMD52,000; ☺ May-Sep; P ☎ ☼) and the excellent **Zanazan Restaurant** (www.tufenkianheritage.com; Tsapatagh; mains AMD1800-10,000; ☺ 9am-10pm; P ☑ ♨). The hotel can organise hiking, mountain-biking, cycling and off-road tours.

The road along the eastern edge of the lake is in poor condition but can be traversed by 2WD. It continues north until it meets the Yerevan–Dilijan Hwy.

Tsaghkadzor Ծաղկաձոր

☑ 223 / POP 1300

Back when Armenia was part of the USSR, Soviet athletes came to Tsaghkadzor (Gorge of Flowers) to train for the Winter Olympics and other sporting competitions. The ski centre on the slope of Mt Tegenis is still here, and during the ski season (December to March) the village is hugely popular with wealthy Armenians keen to take to the slopes by day and relax in one of the luxury hotels at night. In summer, Tsaghkadzor is delightfully cool and makes an excellent base for those wanting to explore Lake Sevan, which is only 25km away.

From the Yerevan Hwy, the access road goes through the town of Hrazdan and continues up to the village's central square. From the square, take Khachatur Kechavetsi St uphill to the **Kecharis Monastery**, a complex comprising the Surp Grigor Church (1003), an attached 13th-century *gavit,* the small Surp Nishan chapel (1051) and a 13th-century *katoghike* (cathedral).

The road straight up from the monastery leads to the ski base where you can take the **ropeway** (chairlift; per section AMD2000; ☺ 10.30am-5.30pm) up the mountain. This operates year-round. You can hire ski equipment at the ski base or from Kecharis Hotel.

The forests around the base of the mountain provide some nice walks, especially in late spring and early summer when the wildflowers are blooming. Horse riding can be organised through Kecharis Hotel.

🛏 Sleeping

Kecharis Hotel & Resort HOTEL $$
(☑ 6 04 09; www.kecharis.am; 20 Orbeli St; s, d & tw AMD32,000-34,000, f AMD38,000; P @ ☎) This is the type of place where local families return year after year. It offers 34 rooms (12 of which are family duplexes), a gym and sauna, a restaurant serving buffet meals (AMD3500), two coffee shops, and a busy basement entertainment complex featuring a bowling alley and pool tables (both charged), a bar and two extra restaurants.

The location is convenient, being on the central square close to the town's shops.

ARMENIA TSAGHKADZOR

Guests can take advantage of free minibus transfers to the ropeway.

★ **Marriott Tsaghkadzor**　　HOTEL **$$$**
(☎10-29 41 11; www.tsaghkadzormarriott.com; 2 Tsandzaghbyuri St; r AMD63,000-88,000, ste AMD213,000; P☺✳☎☒) This recently opened and very impressive hotel on the northern edge of town offers spacious, beautifully appointed rooms in the main building and in seven freestanding villas. The facilities are wonderful: huge indoor pool, sauna, spa, gym, tennis courts, tearoom, terrace restaurant (mains AMD4900 to AMD7500), two lounge bars, business centre, and childrens' playroom with X-box and arcade games.

❶ Getting There & Away

Tsaghkadzor is only about 40 minutes' drive northeast of Yerevan. There is no *marshrutky* service; a taxi from Yerevan costs about AMD7000.

There are frequent buses and *marshrutky* between Yerevan's Raykom station and Hrazdan (AMD500), 6km down the valley – a taxi up to Tsaghkadzor from here will cost AMD1000.

SOUTHERN ARMENIA

Armenia's southern regions stretch from Karabakh to the east and the Azeri enclave of Naxçivan to the west. Vayots Dzor (Gorge of Woes) centres on the headwaters of the wine-growing Arpa valley. The name comes from a history of ruinous earthquakes across these mountainous valleys and cliffs. It's a great area to explore off-the-beaten-track trails by foot, horse or 4WD.

The province of Syunik, in the extreme south of the country, is accessed via the high-altitude Voratan Pass. The landscape here is surrounded by high pastures that are home to grazing animals, drifts of wildflowers and clusters of beehives. Its main

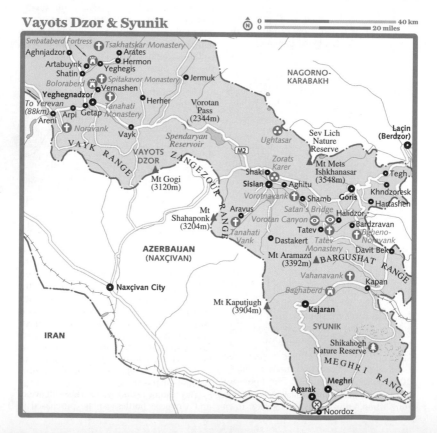

settlement, Goris, is a popular stop for travellers heading into Karabakh or Iran.

Pokr Vedi (Khor Virap)

Located 32km south of Yerevan at the foot of Mt Ararat, this village is best known as the home of one of Armenia's major pilgrimage destinations, the monastery of Khor Virap (Deep Dungeon). Sadly, pollution means that the mountain's snowy peak can rarely be seen from the village and monastery.

◉ Sights

Khor Virap Monastery   MONASTERY
(Խոր Վիրապ) The buildings here have been repeatedly rebuilt since the 6th century. Legend tells us that the pagan King Trdat III imprisoned St Gregory the Illuminator (Surp Grigor Lusavorich) here for around 12 years. These days, pilgrims queue to climb down a metal ladder into the well where the saint was incarcerated. To join them, wear sturdy shoes and head to the small church in the compound's southwestern corner (the well is to the right of the altar).

After his cruel treatment of the saint, the king was cursed by madness (or, in a more colourful version of the tale, cursed by sprouting the head of a boar) and was miraculously cured by St Gregory. Historians contend that Trdat may have switched allegiances to tap into the strength of Armenia's growing Christian community in the face of Roman aggression. In any case, the king converted to Christianity and St Gregory became the first Catholicos of the Armenian Apostolic Church. He set about building churches on top of pagan temples and teaching the faith. The main **Surp Astvatsatsin Church** dates from the 17th century. Look for the carving of the saint curing the possessed King Trdat on its eastern facade, facing visitors as they enter the compound.

Just outside the monastery walls are some excavations on the site of Artashat, Trdat's capital, founded in the 2nd century BC.

The monastery is on a hillock close to the Araks River, overlooking river pastures, stork nests and vineyards. It's reached via a 4.5km road off the main highway, which passes through Pokr Vedi (sometimes also called Khor Virap).

Armash Fish Ponds   FISH PONDS
The Armash Fish Ponds, 25km downstream from Khor Virap near the border town

of Yeraskh, are home to a great variety of migrating birds in spring and autumn, as well as local species.

❶ Getting There & Away

Three *marshrutky* per day travel from Sasuntsi Davit metro station in Yerevan to Pokr Vedi (AMD400, 50 minutes, 9am, 11am and 2pm), from where you will need to walk to the monastery. Going the other way, the *marshrutky* leave Pokr Vedi at 1.20pm, 3.20pm and 5pm.

Areni   Արենի

Few grape varieties can thrive in Armenia's climatic extremes, but the Areni grape is an exception to the rule. Most of the country's vineyards are on the Ararat Plain, but the valleys from the village of Areni up to Yeghegnadzor comprise a quality wine-growing region. When you drive into the village you'll see plenty of roadside stalls selling large bottles that look as if they're filled with cola. These are in fact filled with red wine, camouflaged so that Iranian truck drivers can smuggle the bottles over the border. Summer fruits (especially apricots) are also sold from the stalls.

◉ Sights

Surp Astvatsatsin Church   CHURCH
(Mother of God Church) Looking down on the village from its elevated location across the Arpa River, this small church was built in the 14th century and features wonderful carvings both inside and out; the Virgin Mary on the western exterior wall is particularly fine. Some of the headstones in the graveyard feature wine-making scenes, reflecting the industry's 6000-year-old history in this area.

Be careful when exploring the graveyard – we disturbed a snake on our most recent visit.

Hin Areni Wine Factory   WINERY
(☑ 091 40 70 33; www.hinareniwine.am; Yerevan Hwy; tour AMD500, tour & tasting AMD1500; ☺ 9am-9pm) Prominently located on the main highway, Hin Areni is a professional outfit that produces a quaffable red using Areni grapes and a dry white using *voskehat* (golden seed) grapes; both varieties are grown in nearby vineyards. The factory can be visited on a short tour that is best taken in late September and early October during the grape harvest.

The tasting includes four different wines and vintages; bottles can be purchased in the tasting room, also. The wines sold at the next-door Areni Winery Showroom aren't as impressive as those produced and sold here.

Noravank   Նորավանք

Founded by Bishop Hovhannes in 1105 and sensitively renovated in the 1990s, **Noravank** (New Monastery) is one of the most spectacular sites in Armenia and should be included on every visitor's itinerary. Around sunset, the reddish hues of the dramatic cliffs surrounding the monastery are accentuated by the setting sun, and the reddish-gold stone of its churches acquire a luminous sheen – it's a totally magnificent sight.

The complex includes the 13th-century **Surp Karapet Church**, built next to the ruins of an earlier church also dedicated to St John the Baptist. Attached to this is a small 13th-century chapel dedicated to **Surp Gregor**; it's home to a carved lion-human tombstone dated to 1300.

The main, much-photographed, structure is the 14th-century **Surp Astvatsatsin Church** (1339), built on top of the mausoleum of Burtel Orbelian, who is buried here with his family. Historians say the church is reminiscent of tower-like burial structures created in the early years of Christianity. There's a wonderful carving of Christ flanked by Peter and Paul above the door.

There are picnic spots and springs around Noravank, as well as an excellent on-site **restaurant** (mains AMD2500, open 9am to 9pm). Parking costs AMD100. The valley really warms up in the middle of a summer's day, so come early, or late in the afternoon.

Noravank features on many travel-agency tours from Yerevan, which is about 90 minutes away by road – many combine a visit with a stop at Khor Virap and a winery. Marshrutky from Yerevan or Yeghegnadzor can drop you at the turn-off on the highway near the Edem restaurant. From here, it's 6km to Noravank. Hitching is a fairly easy process, especially on weekends. About 4km from the turn-off to Noravank is an unusual cave-cafe dug out of the side of the cliff. There is no sign, but you'll see the metal grating between the boulders on the right side of the road.

Yeghegnadzor   Եղեգնաձոր

📞 281 / POP 7500

An overgrown country town built on twisting lanes that wind into the hills, Yeghegnadzor (yeh-*heg*-nadzor) is the peaceful administrative centre of Vayots Dzor. The town is a mainly Soviet-era confection of wide civic spaces and *tufa* apartment blocks,

THE WORLD'S OLDEST SHOE

In 2008 an archaeologist exploring a cave in Vayots Dzor found an ancient leather shoe buried under a pile of animal dung. She estimated that the shoe was around 700 years old and dated from the Mongol period. But once the shoe reached the laboratory a new story began to unfold. Testing dated the shoe to around 3500 BC, thus making it the world's oldest leather shoe (300 years older than a shoe found on a frozen mummy in the Alps in 1991).

The shoe is about a women's size 7 (US), designed for the right foot and is made from leather sewn together like a moccasin. It was found stuffed with grass as if its owner wanted to maintain the shape of the shoe. (The whereabouts of the left shoe are unknown.) The shoe is now on display at the History Museum of Armenia (p133).

The cave where the shoe was found is known as Areni-1 and is located not on some distant mountaintop, but rather just behind the Edem restaurant, where the main southern highway intersects with the road to Noravank. At the time of writing the cave was closed to casual tourists as researchers continue to excavate. However, it's possible that the cave will reopen for tourism by the time you read this; inquire at **Vayk Hotel** (p179).

Areni-1 is just one of thousands of caves around Areni and Arpi, some of which contain a kilometre or more of chambers. About 1km up the canyon from Areni-1 is Magili Karandzav, one of the deepest caves in the area and significant as the home of a large colony of fruit bats; Neolithic-era stone tools have also been found here.

Some caves are filled with a wonderful collection of stalactites and stalagmites, including the Arjeri, Mozrovi and Jerovank caverns. These caves are not for the inexperienced, so it's best to visit on a guided tour (the caves are also locked to casual visitors). The Vayk Hotel should be able to help you with this.

with few local industries or businesses; most locals rely on remittances or agriculture for their income. There isn't much to see in the town itself, but it does make a good base from which to explore the region – you could easily spend a couple of days here while visiting Noravank and the Yeghegis Valley.

There are shops and ATMs scattered along Narekatsky and Momik Sts.

Sights

There is a good walk from town down to the river and a 13th-century stone bridge, designed by the same architect who built Noravank. To get there, walk down the highway, turn right and walk for 400m, then turn left down a dirt track (just before the 256km post) and follow it for 1.3km to the bridge.

Yeghegnadzor Regional Museum of Vayots Dzor MUSEUM
(☎2 33 92; www.iatp.am/culture/tangaran; 4 Shahumian St; admission AMD300; ⏲9am-5pm Mon-Sat) The interesting building with its horseshoe-shaped entrance augers well, but the collection in this modest museum holds little of interest. Its only artefact of note is a 14th-century *khachkar* with intricate carving.

Sleeping

★Gohar's Guest House B&B $
(☎093 82 64 71, 094 33 29 93; sargisyan@hotmail.com; 44 Spandaryan St; s AMD10,000-12,000, d AMD16,000-18,000, f AMD25,000, incl breakfast; @ 📶 🏊) This friendly B&B in the upper part of town is owned by Gohar Gevorgyan, who keeps a clean and tidy house and uses organic home-grown produce to cook delicious meals (dinner AMD5000). Rooms are on a dedicated upper floor, with the family living below. There's a communal kitchen, washing machine, vine-covered terrace and small swimming pool.

Gohar speaks Armenian and Russian and her daughter and granddaughter speak English and French. To get here, walk up Spandaryan St towards the football field. When you reach the T-junction, turn left and then a quick right (so that you are walking next to the field). The guesthouse is on the right-hand side of the road.

Camping Crossway CAMPING GROUND $
(☎094 00 16 06, 094 78 93 91; Yerevan Hwy; sites AMD2000, sleeping platform AMD2000, dm AMD5000; P 📶 🏊) Newly opened, this camping ground near the entrance to town is set against a dramatic backdrop of pink mountains and is surrounded by farmland. There are two four-bed hostel dorms, sleeping platforms (mattresses and sleeping bags provided) and campsites (BYO tent). Facilities include a communal kitchen, dining pavilion, campfire area, ablution block, washing machine (per load AMD3000) and small swimming pool.

Hotel Arpa HOTEL $$
(☎2 06 01; www.hotelarpa.am; 8 Narekatsky St; s/d/deluxe d AMD17,000/26,000/29,000; P ❄ 📶) There's no sign on this modern hotel; it's the tall building on the lower (southern) side of an asphalted parking lot opposite the Ferris wheel park. Standard rooms are small but modern and clean with good beds; the deluxe version is larger. Management speaks German and Russian.

Eating & Drinking

If you have your own transport, there are several riverside restaurants along the main highway that set a good Armenian table for around AMD3000 per person, including kebabs, *khoravats,* salads and drinks. Most also serve a regional speciality of 'buried' cheese made from goats milk and herbs and aged in clay pots. These restaurants are open 8am until late outside of winter. There are many stands selling watermelon, fruit, honey, nuts, and homemade wines and conserves at Arpi between Areni and Yeghegnadzor.

Park Cafe BAR
(Aygi; ⏲10am-midnight May-Oct) Yeghegnadzor's nightlife is limited to this outdoor cafe in the gardens surrounding the Ferris wheel. Young locals eye off members of the opposite sex, parents bring young children for an after-dinner ice cream and the occasional foreign tourist is eyed with bemusement by both staff and customers. Those in need of sustenance can order pizza (AMD2000 to AMD2400) or sandwiches (AMD300 to AMD700).

Getting There & Away

To Yerevan, *marshrutky* (AMD1200, two hours) leave when full from the crossroad on the main highway. In Yerevan they depart from the stand next to the Gortsaranayin metro between 8am and 6pm. Hourly *marshrutky* to Vayk (AMD200) and one 2pm bus to Jermuk (AMD700) also depart from the crossroad.

Marshrutky and taxis from local village destinations arrive at the bus and taxi stop at the top end of Narekatsky St in the morning, carrying people from the region who work in town. They return to their destinations in the late afternoon. Taxis cost AMD3000 to Noravank, AMD7000 to Yeghegis, AMD12,000 to Jermuk, and AMD15,000 to Tatev or Goris.

Around Yeghegnadzor

There are a number of interesting sights within easy reach of Yeghegnadzor.

The village of Vernashen, 5km uphill from Yeghegnadzor, is home to the **Museum of Gladzor University** ($\boxtimes$ 2 37 05; admission AMD500; ⊙9am-5pm Tue-Sun) housed in the decommissioned 17th-century church of Surp Hagop. It has displays on monasteries across the country, plus old manuscripts and descriptions of Armenia's various schools and universities. If the museum is closed, get the key from the lady living next door. A taxi from Yeghegnadzor should cost AMD500.

Several kilometres away, and only accessible by foot or 4WD, the 14th-century **Spitakavor Monastery** was built on the site of a 5th-century basilica and has a church, *gavit* and bell tower. The exterior of the church features some unusual carving.

The 20th-century Armenian military commander Garegin Nzhdeh is buried in the graveyard. Nzhdeh fought in the Balkan Wars against the Ottoman Empire and commanded a force of Armenian volunteer fighters in WWI. In 1921 he was prime minister of the short-lived Republic of Mountainous Armenia.

To get here, head past the Museum of Gladzor University to a T-junction. The road to the left leads to the monastery; it's about 9km along a winding dirt track for vehicles or 6km along a more direct walking path. Walk past the museum and through the village, cross the stream and carry on straight up the western bank of the gorge keeping the stream and small dam on your right (ignore the vehicle road, which switches back). Continue up the track, veer left into grazing pasture and then head right. You'll then see the monastery above you.

Meanwhile the impressive main church at the **Tanahati Monastery** was dedicated to St Stepanos (Stephen) and was built in the 13th century on the site of a ruined 8th-century monastery. There are significant stone reliefs of animals on the exterior of the church, including the crest of the powerful Orbelian family (a bull and a lion) on the tambour and one of the Proshian family (an eagle holding a lamb in its talons) above the door. To get here

take the road to the right at the T-junction past the Museum of Gladzor University. It's 6km to Tanahati Vank (Monastery).

Yeghegis Valley   Եղեգիս

The beautiful Yeghegis Valley is surrounded by towering peaks and is home to many picturesque villages with medieval churches. It and the surrounding valleys are well worth exploring for a day or two.

To reach the area, turn north off the Yerevan–Goris Hwy at Getap and after 12km turn right (east) towards Shatin village. The sights are well signposted off the road.

About 2km up from Shatin village, a road branches up the valley to the west towards Artabuynk. About 1km past the village of Artabuynk a sign points to the left for the 10th-century Tsakhatskar Monastery, a crumbling agglomeration of churches and old *khachkars*. From the stream, continue up the main track to the right (the side of the valley with the power poles); the monastery eventually comes into view on the left. It can only be accessed by 4WD.

From the monastery, head back down the way you came and at the fork in the path head left up the slope to **Smbataberd** fortress. The stretch up to the fort takes about 30 minutes. On the other side of Smbataberd you can look down on the valley.

Yeghegis (yer-ghiz) village is reached by taking the right fork after Shatin. It has three churches in the village on the left-hand side of the main road: the 18th-century **St Astvatsatsin** with its grass-covered roof; the 13th-century **Surp Karapet Church**; and the very unusual 14th-century **Surp Zorats**, where worshippers gathered before an outdoor altar. It's believed this courtyard was created so that horses and soldiers could be blessed before going off to battle. Surp Karapet and Surp Zorats are difficult to find: start at St Astvatsatsin and walk uphill, then turn right, veer left and then turn right again when you see some *khachkars*. Surp Karapet is down another road to the right; Surp Zorats is straight ahead, around a corner (left) and then in a field on the right.

On the northeastern edge of the village, look for a blue sign saying 'Arates 9.7km'. Park here and walk down a switchback dirt road to find a metal footbridge crossing the river. Cross the bridge to find an 800-year-old **Jewish cemetery** – Hebrew inscriptions are clearly visible on some of the grave markers. The engravings are biblical verses and the names of the deceased. Prior to the discovery of the cemetery there had been no evidence of Jews inhabiting Armenia. The cemetery was in use for about 80 years – the oldest tombstone is dated 1266 and the newest is dated 1346. Researchers theorise that this community of Jews arrived from Persia, having travelled up the Silk Road. The reason for their disappearance remains a mystery.

The next village up the valley is **Hermon**, where a rough track north (on the left) leads to Arates and **Arates Vank**, a monastery with three ruined churches dating from the 7th to the 13th centuries. Arates is about 10km beyond Yeghegis.

Public transport to the area is limited. *Marshrutky* and taxis travel from the villages to Yeghegnadzor in the morning and return in the late afternoon. Taxis from Yeghegnadzor cost the standard AMD100 per kilometre; you'll need to negotiate waiting times with the driver.

The excellent **Lucytour Hotel Resort** (☑281-2 10 80; www.lucy-tour.com; Hermon; dm AMD7000, s/d/tw AMD13,000/23,000/20,000, f AMD44,000; ⓅⓈⓈ) at Hermon is a huge complex offering beds in dorms and private rooms, an indoor swimming pool, sauna, gym with trampoline, free use of bicycles and telescopes, volleyball and basketball courts, and fishing in a stocked fish pond. There's a guest-only coffee shop and restaurant (dinner AMD4000) and staff can organise guided hikes, horse-riding and quad-bike tours. Wi-fi is available in the reception area only.

Vayk வ்ய்ப்

☑282 / POP 9400

The rugged hills and valleys around this highway settlement are dotted with churches, monasteries and chapels built between the 8th to the 12th centuries.

🛏 Sleeping & Eating

Amrots Hotel HOTEL **$**

(☑2 22 22; www.amrotshotel.com; 2 Yerkrabanner St; s/d/tr AMD14,000/19,000/23,000; ⓅⓈ) A prominent location on a hill above the highway has endowed this recently opened hotel with its name (Amrots means Castle) as well as panoramic views of the surrounding countryside. Rooms are comfortable and very clean, with satellite TV and a pleasant decor. There's an air-conditioned dining room (mains AMD400 to AMD7000), a terrace cafe (cappuccino AMD600) and a lounge bar. Excellent value.

Vayk Hotel HOTEL **$**

(☑9 28 09; vaykhotel@gmail.com; 10a Jermuk Hwy; s/d/tr AMD12,000/18,000/21,000; ⓅⒺⓐⓈ) English-speaking owner Argishti is an enthusiastic and knowledgeable host, and can answer most questions about travelling in the region. Rooms are simply furnished, cramped and a bit dark, but the satellite TV and air-conditioning compensate. Meals are supplied for guests only (mains AMD1500 to AMD3000).

❶ Getting There & Away

Marshrutky to Yerevan (AMD1200, less than two hours, every two hours 8am to 7pm) leave from the highway.

Jermuk Ջերմուկ

☑287 / POP 4600

Known as the home of Jermuk mineral water, this upmarket spa town 2080m above sea level on the upper Arpa River is a popular vacation spot in summer due to its blissfully cool climate and in winter for its modest ski slopes. While here, many visitors take advantage of mineral-water treatments and hot springs – some of them very hot. The surrounding landscape is excellent for walks and hikes. The town is entered via a bridge spanning a deep gorge high above the Arpa River; turn left at the end of the bridge, and then right at the small lake to reach the Hyatt Place Jermuk hotel, Gallery of Waters, and Jermuk Armenia Hotel and Health Spa.

🏃 Activities

The spa business gets most of its customers in the July and August holidays. Some of its sanatoriums have immersion pools and treatment areas. The spa attendants take their job seriously – in the old days people would sign up for 18-day courses with medically supervised immersions in Jermuk's waters. The local action centres on the **Gallery of Waters**, a colonnaded structure with a row of stone urns fed with mineral water by pipes set in the wall. The various waters are said to have different properties, good for curing stomach and liver problems, heart disease and cancer.

Jermuk Ski Resort SNOW SPORTS

(ski lift return AMD1000; ⊙11am-7pm late Oct-early Apr) Next to the town, Jermuk's ski fields are small (there's 2.6km of sloped) but the facilities are modern and the equipment is in good condition.

THE SELIM PASS

Linking the provinces of Gegharkunik and Voyots Dzor, this road over the Vardenis mountain range is the most spectacular driving route in the country. Climbing to an elevation of 2410m, it is covered in heavy snow in winter and so is only open from May to October. Just below the highest point of the pass, on the Voyots Dzor side, is the **Selim Caravanserai**, built in 1332 by order of Prince Chesar Orbelian to offer shelter to caravans following the ancient Dvin-Partav trading route. A sturdy basalt building on a windswept plateau, it comprises a three-nave hall, vestibule, domed chapel and small rooms where travellers once slept. The facade features two bas-relief statues with Orbelian dynasty insignia. Destroyed sometime between the 15th and 16th centuries, it was reconstructed in the 1950s and is open to the elements. Picnic tables outside command wonderful views over the Yeghegis Valley.

Sadly, no public transport travels this road. A taxi between Yeghegnadzor and Martuni on the edge of Lake Sevan will cost around AMD20,000.

Jermuk Armenia Hotel and Health Spa
SPA

(☑ 2 12 90; www.jermukarmenia.com; 2 Miasnikyan St; ☺ 9am-5pm) This Soviet-era institution has hot baths, mud treatments, sauna, hydrotherapy rooms and various other treatment rooms. Treatments cost AMD600 to AMD2500.

🛏 Sleeping & Eating

There are lots of informal pensions and spas open in July and August, but options thin out in winter. In July and August prices can double based on demand.

Nairi Hotel
HOTEL $$

(☑ 2 20 08; www.jermuknairi.am; 7 Myasnikyan St; s AMD18,000-22,000, d AMD28,000-36,000) Functional rooms with satellite TV are on offer at this reliable midrange choice. Full board costs an extra AMD6000 to AMD7000.

Hyatt Place Jermuk
HOTEL $$$

(☑ 060 74 12 34; www.jermuk.place.hyatt.com; 7 Shahumyan St; r from AMD70,000; 🅿 ☺ ❄ 🛜 🐕) Opened in June 2015, this pink monolith on the lake opposite the Gallery of Waters is the most luxurious hotel in Southern Armenia. Rooms are large, well-appointed and extremely comfortable. Facilities include a large indoor pool, medical centre and spa, sauna, gym and restaurant.

Gndevank Restaurant
ARMENIAN $

(☑ 2 16 90; mains AMD2000-3000; ☺ 9am-midnight) This *khoravats* joint is the most popular eatery in town. Coming across the main bridge, turn right (away from the town centre); it's about 400m straight ahead in a wood-fronted building.

ℹ Getting There & Away

Jermuk is 177km from Yerevan, about two hours by the main highway and then 26km off the main highway on a spur road. In the high season *marshrutky* (AMD2000, 2½ hours) depart from Yerevan's Kilikya Avtokayan at 1pm and 4pm. Services leave Jermuk for Yerevan at 8am and 11am. The bus stand is next to the bank near the Hyatt Place Jermuk hotel.

There's also one bus per day to Yeghegnadzor (AMD700, one hour).

Sisian
Սիսիան

☑ 283 / POP 12,300

Sisian sits on a high plateau where it snows as late as March or April. The autumn ends early here too. It has a core of early-20th-century buildings and is divided into two districts by the wide Vorotan River. The town's buildings are poorly maintained, unemployment is high and the river is often full of rubbish – a sad fate for a place that was prosperous and proud in the Soviet era. The region was inhabited long before the town was built, evidenced by nearby Neolithic observatories and animal petroglyphs. These days, the only compelling reason to visit is to see the petroglyphs at Zorats Karer (aka Karahunj) and Ughtasar (Pilgrimage Mountain).

The centre of town is on the northern side of the Vorotan. *Marshrutky* leave from the junction on the northern end of the bridge. The main street, Sisakan St, runs parallel to the river, one block inland.

◉ Sights

The road up from town passes a Soviet war memorial with a Karabakh War monument – local men were some of the first to volunteer to join their kin over in the next mountain range when the war began, and paid a heavy price for it.

Sisavan Church   CHURCH

Originally built in the 6th century, Sisavan Church was restored as recently as the 20th century. It combines an elegant square-cross floor with some striking sculptures of royal and ecclesiastical patrons inside and out.

Sisian History Museum   MUSEUM

($\boxed{\nearrow}$2 33 31; www.sisianmuseum.am; 1 Adonts St; admission AMD500, tours AMD2000; ⊘11am-6pm) Townsfolk are very proud of their museum, which showcases a modest array of carpets, archaeological artefacts and ethnographic displays. It faces the sculpture park, making a visit to both an easy proposition.

Sculpture Park   PARK

The sculpture park in town one block from Sisakan St displays stone carvings from different millennia, including sarcophagi, phallus stones, ram stones and megaliths. You can spot the evolution of the pagan *khachkars* to roughstone crosses and finally medieval Armenian *khachkars*.

🛏 Sleeping & Eating

Hotel Dina   HOTEL $

($\boxed{\nearrow}$093 33 43 92; www.dinahotel.am; 35 Sisakan St; s/d AMD8000/14,000; $\boxed{P}$$\boxed{\widehat{?}}$) Its handsome exterior and pretty front garden raise hopes that are dashed when the dowdy rooms at this centrally located hotel are inspected. They're clean, but not particularly comfortable. That said, it's generally acknowledged to be the best sleeping option in town. The managers speak some English and can help with tours and onward transport.

Jrahars   ARMENIAN $

($\boxed{\nearrow}$30 53 86; Israeliyan St; mains AMD2500; ⊘10am-10pm) The food at this *khoravats* joint by the river just next to the bridge is basic and not particularly fresh, so we're disappointed to report that it is the town's best eatery.

❶ Getting There & Away

The taxi and *marshrutka* stand is on Israeliyan St, near the bridge. There is one daily *marshrutka* from Yerevan's Kilikya Avtokayan (AMD2000, four hours) at 9am; you'll need to check with the driver about its departure time from Sisian. Semi-regular *marshrutka* travel to and from Goris (AMD800, 45 minutes). *Marshrutky* travel to Stepanakert (AMD3000, 2½ hours) via Goris

and Shushi at 10.30am on Monday, Wednesday and Friday.

There are two access roads into the town from the Yerevan Hwy; the western one has the best driving surface.

Local tours can be negotiated directly with the taxi drivers or through Hotel Dina.

Around Sisian

Two hundred and twenty upright basalt stones up to 3m high set along sweeping lines and loops, some punctured with sight holes aligned with stars, make up the ancient site of **Zorats Karer** (also known as Karahundj or Carahunge, which means 'speaking stones'). The site, situated on a rise above the river plains ringed by mountains, is dotted with tombs dated to 3000 BC. The astronomical design of Zorats Karer is most evident at the solstices and equinoxes. Lines of stones define an egg-shaped area with a burial tumulus in the centre, with a north arm stretching 170m and a southern alley 160m long. About 70 stones are pierced with finger-sized holes. The builders had a deep knowledge of astronomy, including the zodiac and the lunar phases, combined perhaps with worship of stars such as Sirius. The site won't blow you away (there's no balancing stones like you'd see at Stonehenge) but the pleasant 45-minute walk here from town and excellent panoramas make it a worthwhile trip. Zorats Karer is 6km north of Sisian, signposted on the left about 700m before the main highway. The stones are in the fields about 100m from the turn-off.

The **Shaki Waterfall** lies about 4km from Sisian near the village of the same name. About 18m high, it sluices down a wide expanse of stones above the Shaki River. The water is used for Shaki's hydroelectric power station, so the waterfall isn't always 'on'.

About 6km down the Vorotan River from Sisian in **Aghitu** (Aghudi) village is a distinctive 7th-century **tower-tomb**. There are dragon stones nearby from the 2nd to 3rd century BC. The road continues as the canyon deepens past Vaghatin to **Vorotnavank**, 12km from Sisian on the south side of the Vorotan. Vorotnavank is a striking 9th- to 11th-century fortress and church complex built by Queen Shahandukht and her son Sevada.

The petroglyphs of **Ughtasar** (Pilgrimage Mountain) in the mountains north of Sisian are even older than Zorats Karer. They lie at an altitude of 3300m around a lake on

Mt Tsghuk, accessible between June and September – and even then only if it's not a cold summer. Carvings of leaping, dancing animals and hunters adorn rocks and boulders everywhere around the small lake. It's a haunting place surrounded by isolated peaks, and you can only wonder why ancient people would hike to such an inhospitable place to leave their mark on stone. The tracks are steep, rocky and hopeless without a 4WD and a guide. Hotel Dina (p181) in Sisian should be able to help you do this.

The ruins of **Tanahati Vank** are 17km southwest of Sisian past the Tolors Reservoir. A university was established here in 1280. Called Karmir (Red) Vank by locals, Tanahat Monastery is on a high promontory by a gorge. The monks here were so pious and ascetic they refused soup, cheese and oil, eating only vegetables, hence the name Tanahat, meaning 'deprived of soup'.

Goris   Գորիս

📙 284 / POP 18,000

The endlessly winding roads that leap through the gorges of the mountains of Syunik come to a major junction at Goris, making this an inevitable stop between Yerevan and Stepanakert or the Iranian border. The town's tree-lined avenues and grand 19th-century stone houses attest to its prosperous past, but these days Goris is poor, rundown and depressed. Come here if you are keen to visit Tatev Monastery or are en route to Karabakh or Iran. Otherwise, it's not worth the long drive or *marshrutka* trip.

Locals are skilled at making fruit *oghee*, including the deliciously potent mulberry and Cornelian cherry *(hone) oghee* – you should be able to source some at the *shuka* on Syuniki St. Shops and ATMs are located on Gushan Ashoti and Syuniki Sts.

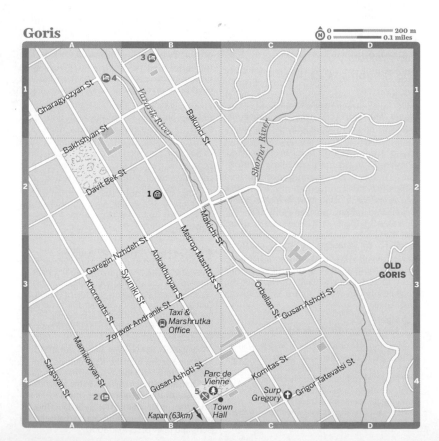

◉ Sights

Locals say the cave shelters and stables of **Old Goris** carved into the hillside on the east side of town were built and inhabited in the 5th century. Several trails lead up over a saddle where there are more volcanic pinnacle clusters to explore. Many of the rooms are linked together, and arched 'shelves' grace some walls. The caves are sometimes used to house cattle – watch your step.

Museum of Axel Bakounts   MUSEUM
(☑2 29 66; 41 Mesrop Mashtots St; admission AMD300; ⊙10am-5pm Tue-Sun) This pretty villa with its stone walls, timber verandah and courtyard garden was the home of writer Axel Bakounts (or Bakunts), who died in Stalin's 1937 purges. It features his personal effects and furnishings from the late 19th and early 20th centuries. The surrounding neighbourhood sports plenty of 19th-century houses.

🛌 Sleeping

Hotel Zanger   HOTEL $
(☑098 77 89 77; zangerhotel@yahoo.com; 13 Bakunci St; s/d AMD12,000/18,000, without bathroom AMD10,000/14,000; 🅿🛜) The luridly painted pink exterior is slightly off-putting (and extremely unsympathetic to its historic surrounds), but this recently opened hotel on a quiet street offers well-priced, clean and comfortable rooms with satellite TV so is worthy of recommendation. There's a rear courtyard where breakfast can be enjoyed during summer, and a breakfast room for the colder months.

Hostel Goris   HOSTEL $
(☑2 18 86, 093 28 79 02; jirmar28@yandex.eu; dm AMD5000, d without bathroom AMD14,000; 🛜) Operated by local artist Jirayr Martirosyan and his family, this cramped hostel has long been the number-one backpacker pick in Goris. Recent traveller feedback hasn't been laudatory, and we were unimpressed on our recent visit – it needs renovation. Three double rooms share a somewhat grubby bathroom on the 1st floor and there are two dark dorms downstairs. Dinner costs AMD4000.

To find it, look for the small sign off Khorenatsi St and head uphill towards the multistorey Goris Hotel. The hostel is next to this, facing the carpark.

Mirhav Hotel   HOTEL $$
(☑2 46 12; hotelmirav@yahoo.com; 100 Mesrop Mashtots St; s/d/tr AMD22,000/27,000/33,000; 🅿🛜) It claims boutique hotel status, but the regular presence of tour groups and large extended families means that the label isn't deserved. That said, this is the best sleeping option in Goris, offering attractively decorated common areas, a range of room types in two buildings, a rear garden and an excellent restaurant.

🍴 Eating & Drinking

Deluxe Lounge Cafe   INTERNATIONAL $
(☑091 22 44 77; Parc de Vienne; mains AMD1200-2500; ⊙11am-11pm) The Parc de Vienne is Goris' entertainment hub, and this sleek lounge cafe is where most of the action unfolds. The menu is dominated by international dishes – many Mexican – and the seating is in a dining pavilion or on a large outdoor terrace.

Mirhav Restaurant   ARMENIAN $$
(☑2 46 12; Mirhav Hotel, 100 Mesrop Mashtots St; mains AMD3200; 🖉) You'll need to book and order in advance to enjoy a meal in the Mirhav Hotel's restaurant, but it's worth the trouble. The menu here is more interesting than the average Armenian eatery, featuring stews, pilafs and tasty vegetarian dishes (the salads and fried vegetable dishes are particularly good). Tables are in a pleasant indoor dining space or rear garden.

ℹ Getting There & Away

There is only one *marshrutka* per day between Yerevan and Goris (AMD2500, six hours), which leaves Yerevan's Sasuntsi Davit metro station at 7am and returns from Goris when full. In Goris, the *marshrutka* and taxi office is in Syuniki St near the post office, and vehicles leave from a stand close by.

Regular shared taxis (per person AMD4500, 4½ hours) depart from the stand outside Yerevan's Sasuntsi Davit metro station between 9am and 1pm and return from Goris in the afternoon.

Marshrutky travel from Tatev to Goris (AMD700) on Monday and Friday at 9am. They return to Tatev at 3pm. A private taxi between Goris and Tatev costs AMD8000.

ARMENIA GORIS

GORIS TO MEGHRI HIGHWAY

Travellers continuing from Goris to Meghri on the Iranian border will need to steel their stomach against approximately 160km of nonstop hairpin turns as the road climbs and dips through the mountains of southern Syunik. Most people coming this way are overlanders heading to Iran or curious road-trippers wanting to cover every inch of Armenian soil.

The first stretch is a 68km drive from Goris to Kapan. The most interesting sight along this route is the **Bgheno-Noravank monastery**, which was lost to the world until 1920 when writer Axel Bakounts happened upon it in the forest. The main church dates to 1062 and contains intricately carved biblical reliefs. It's a great camping spot or a logical break for cycle tourists. The turn-off from the highway has a sign directing you towards Bardzravan, a nearby village. After 3.1km, turn off the road to the right and the church is visible after 150m.

Further down the highway, there is a military base (Karmerkar) and a turn-off for the 3km access road to the village of **Davit Bek**. The village is another pleasant stopover and sports a couple of old churches and a pristine river with cascades and swimming holes. From the village there is a pleasant 40-minute walk to a pagan temple.

On the final plunge towards Kapan a bizarre turquoise lake comes into view. This is an artificial lake created by the tailings of a nearby copper mine so while it might look like the Caribbean Sea, swimming is not recommended.

Kapan marks the halfway point to Meghri and is thus a logical place to spend the night. From Kapan there are two roads to Meghri: a 75km road via Kajaran; and a newer, more scenic 94km route through the **Shikahogh Nature Reserve**. The most attractive part of the reserve is the valley of the Tsav River, where at the hamlet of Nerkin Hand there's an ancient grove of massive plane trees. The oak and hornbeam forests either side of the Tsav comprise the nature reserve, though you'll need a Niva or Villis 4WD to explore the 100 sq km of gorges and forests.

One daily *marshrutka* departs from Sisian at 10.30am on Monday, Wednesday and Friday, stopping at Goris en route to Stepanakert (AMD2000). It departs around 11.10am from the intersection of the highway and Mesrop Mashtots St (AMD2000). If you miss this one, you can wait at the same spot for a *marshrutka* to pass through from Yerevan (four or five pass through every afternoon); they'll pick you up if there is space.

A *marshrutka* to Kapan (AMD1500, 1½ hours, 11am) departs from the *marshrutka* and taxi office in Syuniki St.

Around Goris

There are several historic villages around Goris, many with ancient artificial caves that are still used as stables.

Khndzoresk, 10km east of Goris, perches above the ruins of Old Khndzoresk, which was dug into a grassy gorge of soft volcanic sandstone. Whole walls of rock are dotted with caves; you could spend several hours exploring the area.

There are more caves around **Tegh** on the Stepanakert road, and around **Hartashen**, a tough but rewarding 3km on foot from Old Goris or about 8km by road. A smattering of **standing stones** similar to the ones

at Zorats Karer is visible from the main road towards Sisian.

The **Sev Lich Nature Reserve**, 14km northeast of town on the shoulder of Mt Mets Ishkhanasar, protects a lake (Sev Lich means 'Black Lake') at 2666m. The track up requires a 4WD and a guide. The reserve can also be reached from Sisian.

Tatev   Տաթեւ
✆ 284 / POP 900

The rural village Tatev sprouted around its famous **monastery** in medieval times.

The monastery's location is quite spectacular, perched on a basalt plateau overlooking the Vorotan River with jaw-dropping views over to the peaks of Karabakh. The bishops of Syunik built its main church, **Surp Poghos-Petros** (St Paul and St Peter), in the 9th century to house important relics. There are faint signs of **frescoes**, intricate carvings and portraits of the main donors on the northern side. The 11th-century **Surp Grigor Church** nestles next to it, and there's a miniaturised chapel above the gatehouse.

At the monastery's peak some 600 monks lived and worked in the complex, and national icon Surp Grigor Tatevatsi (St Gregory of Tatev; 1346–1409) is buried here.

In the courtyard, look for the 8m octagonal pillar topped by a *khachkar*. The 9th-century monument is said to have predicted seismic activity (or the roar of hooves by approaching armies) by shifting.

The fortifications, added in the 17th century, have been restored and are full of dining halls, towers and libraries. Outside the main gate there is an **oil press exhibit** with a display of seeds, tools and ancient machinery used in the process of oil extraction.

There is also plenty of scope for short hikes in the surrounding area. One trail from the village leads to **Svarants** (population 250), a hamlet 20 minutes' walk away on the other side of the valley. Another trail heads north to the top of **Petroskhatch mountain**, 4km from Tatev (the return-trip hike takes under three hours).

The most popular hike is downhill from Tatev to **Mets Anapad**, an overgrown 17th-century church. This takes 2½ hours.

Organised hikes in the gorge leave Tatev at 10am and 2pm (two-hour trail, AMD10,000) and at 11am (seven-hour trail, AMD20,000). Book at the Wings of Tatev Aerial Tramway (p185) ticket office in Halidzor.

If you're hiking or driving to Tatev rather than taking the aerial tramway, stop off to see **Satan's Bridge**, located on the road halfway between the cable car and Tatev village. Legend tells that centuries ago villagers fleeing a rebel army were blocked by the raging river. Before the invaders attacked, a bridge was magically created by a huge falling rock and the people were saved.

Just uphill from the monastery is the **Tatev Tourism Information Centre & Cafe** (☑9 73 32, 093 88 02 30; www.tatevinfo.com; ⊙10am-9pm) run by the extremely helpful English- and Italian-speaking Anna Arshakyan. This is the place to ask about hikes in the area (Anna can organise guides), travel around the region and B&Bs where you can spend the night.

❶ Getting There & Away

The most enjoyable way to reach the monastery is on the **Wings of Tatev Aerial Tramway** (☑060 46 33 33; www.tatever.com; one-way/return AMD2500/3500 Dec-Feb, AMD3000/4000 Mar & Oct-Nov, AMD3500/5000 Apr-Sep, child under 110cm AMD100; ⊙10.30am-5.30pm). This travels 5.7km from Halidzor village up to Tatev and is purported to be the world's longest cable car.

The aerial tramway operates from Tuesday to Sunday from 9.30am. It leaves once per hour (on the half-hour) but will also leave as soon as 15 passengers are assembled. The last car travels down to Halidzor at 7.45pm.

A taxi from Goris to the cable car should cost AMD10,000 return (plus AMD1000 per hour waiting time).

Shared taxis travelling from the stand near Yerevan's Sasuntsi Davit metro station to Goris will stop at Halidzor on request (AMD6000). These depart Yerevan when full between 9am and 1pm. Note that there is no taxi stand at Halidzor, so you will need to prearrange onward travel from Tatev.

Marshrutky travel from Tatev to Goris (AMD700) on Monday and Friday at 9am. They return to Tatev at 3pm.

Kapan   Կապան

☑285 / POP 41,900

The largest city in Syunik, Kapan is wedged between high mountains and splintered by numerous valleys. The name itself is derived from the Armenian word *kapel* (to lock), a reference to the interlocking mountain chains that converge here.

During the 18th century Kapan was a base for Davit Bek, an Armenian freedom fighter who took on Muslim invaders encroaching Armenia's southern border. The village grew rapidly during the Soviet era when Russian geologists, seeing the potential for mineral extraction, arrived with blueprints for a massive mining complex. There is so much unrefined metal underground that compasses won't work in some parts of town.

Mighty **Mt Khustup** (3210m) is visible high above the town. The approach to the peak is via the village of Verin Vachagan, about 3km southwest of Kapan. It's approximately 7km to the base of the peak, where a small church has been built. You can get fine views from here; another three hours of hiking is required to reach the peak.

The main site in the immediate area is the remains of 9th-century **Vahanavank**, about 7km from Kapan just off the Kajaran road. The monastery was once the religious centre for Syunik's kings. An attempt to restore the monastery in 1978 was later abandoned and what remains is a roofless structure of red limestone.

🛏 Sleeping & Eating

Hotel Lernagorts   HOTEL $

(☑2 80 39; lernagorts@mail.ru; 2 Demirchyan St; r per person AMD5000-10,000; 🛜) This place has been around since Soviet times and not much has changed since then. Rooms are dated, have uncomfortable beds and often smell of cigarette smoke. They're clean and cheap, though, so worth considering if you're on a tight budget.

Hotel Mi & Max
HOTEL **$$**

(☑2 03 00; mimaxhotel@rambler.ru; 8th & 9th fl, 2 Demirchyan St; s/d/deluxe AMD18,000/25,000/30,000; ✳🉂) This hotel within a hotel proves the old adage that it's not always wise to judge by initial appearances. Occupying the top floors of the worn Soviet-era Hotel Lernagordz, Mi & Max offers modern, light-filled rooms with good beds, satellite TV and a stylish decor. The deluxe versions have a sitting area and larger-than-usual bathroom.

Elegant Restaurant
ARMENIAN **$**

(☑2 15 05; 32 Shahumian St; mains AMD600-3200; ☺11am-midnight; ✳🉂) As classy as Kapan gets, this large restaurant functions as a cafe, bar and restaurant and is popular with locals wanting to enjoy a night out on the town. The menu is varied, with a good choice of salads. You'll find it at the eastern end of Shahumian St.

❶ Getting There & Away

From Yerevan, a daily *marshrutka* departs from the stand near Sasunti Davit metro station (AMD5000, eight hours) at 7am.

From Kapan, one daily *marshrutka* to Yerevan (AMD5000, six/eight hours in summer/winter) leaves from in front of Hotel Lernagordz at 7am. Shared taxis depart when full from the same location for AMD6000.

There's usually at least one daily *marshrutka* to Goris (AMD1500, 1½ hours) leaving from the bus stand on the main highway near the Davit Bek statue.

If you're heading to Iran, one daily *marshrutka* to Agarak (AMD2000) departs from the same spot between 2pm and 3pm, travelling via Meghri (AMD1500).

Meghri
Մեղրի

☑286 / POP 4600

Strategic Meghri, Armenia's toehold on Iran, is worth exploring for its fine stone houses and stark but beautiful scenery. The town sits deep in the rocky, lushly irrigated gorge of the Meghri River surrounded by sawtooth peaks. The 24-hour border crossing is at the Araks bridge near Agarak (population 4500), 8km from Meghri.

The brick domes of **Surp Hovannes** at the Meghri town monastery date from the 17th century. In the centre of the main part of town is the fine **Surp Astvatsatsin Church** with a distinctive octagonal dome, built in the 17th century with later frescoes. There's also the **Surp Sargis Church** across the river in Pokr Tagh, the smaller side of town, with two rows of columns and some delicately restored frescoes.

In Iran, just across the river from Agarak, is the ancient village of Noordoz (also spelt Noghdoz or Norduz) – the minarets of the local mosque are visible in the distance. This is a sensitive border area so be careful where you point your camera.

❶ Getting There & Away

One daily *marshrutka* leaves from the stand at Yerevan's Sasuntsi Davit metro station at 7am travelling to Agarak via Meghri (AMD7000, nine/11 hours in summer/winter).

From Meghri, a Yerevan service departs at 9am from Hotel Meghri, just off the central square, on Block 2. One bus to Kapan (AMD1500) also departs in the morning. A taxi to Kapan should cost AMD8000 to AMD10,000 (90 minutes) from Agarak or Meghri. A taxi between Meghri and Agarak costs about AMD2000.

On the other side of the border, buses are rare or nonexistent; a taxi to Jolfa (Julfa, Culfa; 40 minutes) should cost less than US$15. A shop just outside Iranian immigration exchanges currencies.

UNDERSTAND ARMENIA

Armenia Today

Despite its limited resources, Armenia has become a master at geopolitics. What other country in the world can say it maintains good relations with the USA, Russia *and* Iran? Each international giant has made moves to forge ties. The US has a huge embassy in Yerevan (on 8.9 hectares of land) and USAID and the State Department fund a range of economic and cultural assistance programs. Iran continues to bolster trade ties with Armenia and sign multi-billion-dollar energy deals; in June 2015 the two countries signed an agreement to build a third power transmission line that will almost triple electricity exchange between them. Russia, the main energy supplier until now, has upped the ante with a deal to jointly fund a new nuclear reactor at Metsamor to replace the current and outdated nuclear facility located there. The new reactor will be jointly funded by Russian and Armenia; construction is due to commence in 2018. Russia also maintains a military base of 3000 soldiers near Gyumri and posts troops along Armenia's borders with Turkey and Iran.

But while Armenia shoulders up to the big boys of international trade and energy, it remains mired in old feuds with its neighbours that make the Montagues and the Capulets seem like bosom buddies. Chief among these feuds is that with Azerbaijan. Official fighting between the two countries ended in 1994, but the matter still feels closer to war than peace. A sniper war still brews along the border, with both sides suffering regular casualties. The status quo – with Armenia officially occupying 16% of Azerbaijan and negotiations at a standstill – is likely to last for some time.

The long-simmering argument about the Ottoman Empire's treatment of Armenians between 1915 and 1922 underpins every dealing modern-day Armenia has with its other feuding neighbour, Turkey. The Armenians believe that the events consitute a genocide; the Turks won't accept that label. In 2015 official events in Armenia and across the diaspora marked the centenary of the start of that horrific sequence of events using a powerful slogan: 'I Remember and Demand'. This call for international recognition of what the Armenians consider a genocide was aimed primarily at Turkey, but also at the international community (to date, 24 states have responded positively to Armenia's demand). While the disagreement festers it is unlikely that diplomatic relations between Armenia and Turkey will normalise, meaning that the border will remain closed. An added complication is Karabakh – Turkey is on record as saying that it will only normalise relations with Armenia if the conflict is settled.

On the domestic front, the weakening economy and plummeting standard of living have led to many locals becoming disenchanted with President Serzh Sargsyan, elected for his second five-year term in 2013. In June 2015, the government's announcement of a planned 17% to 22% hike in electricity charges, the third increase in two years, triggered huge street demonstrations in Yerevan. Dubbed 'Electric Yerevan', the protests continued for two weeks before President Sargsyan announced that the electricity hikes – and similar hikes to water distribution charges – would not go ahead in the near future. Cynical locals, many of whom had carried banners at the demonstrations saying 'No to Graft' and 'Stop Corruption', fear that the price hikes will be cross-subsidised through tax increases and that the economic situation of most Armenians will continue to worsen.

The economy certainly is in a fragile state. Armenia posted 3.4% economic growth in 2014, down from 7.1% in 2012. The Russian ruble's sharp depreciation in December 2014 led to a significant decrease of export from Armenia to Russia, hitting the mineral and agriculture sectors hard and leading to rising unemployment (nearly 18% in 2014). It was estimated that 32% of the population were living below the poverty line in 2014. This is obvious when travelling in rural regions across the country – Yerevan may be relatively prosperous, but Armenians trying to make a living out of agriculture or mining work are doing it very hard indeed.

A SURNAME PRIMER

The vast majority of Armenian surnames end in '-ian' or '-yan'; spelling depends on whether the root ends in a vowel or consonant (Saro + yan = Saroyan or Gregor + ian = Gregorian). The suffix means 'from' or 'of', either from a town (Marashlian from Marash; Vanetsian from Van), from a parent (Davidian, son of David), from an occupation (Najarian, son of a carpenter; Boyajian, from the Turkish word 'boyaj' for someone who dyes fabrics), or from status or personal traits (Melikyan, son of a king; Sinanian, from a Turkish term for a well-endowed gent). Names with the prefix 'Ter' mean that a married priest (Ter Hayr) was an ancestor, eg ex-president Levon Ter-Petrossian. Western Armenian names may spell it 'Der', as in Der-Bedrossian. There are also families with the suffix '-runi', such as Siruni and Artsruni. These families were once aristocrats.

History

In the Beginning...

Like all ancient countries, Armenia has a murky origin. According to Bible lore Armenians are the descendants of Hayk, great-great-grandson of Noah, whose ark grounded on Mt Ararat after the flood. In recognition of their legendary ancestry, Armenians have since referred to their country as Hayastan, land of the Hayk tribe. Greek records first mention Armenians in the 6th century BC as a tribe living in the area of Lake Van.

The Armenian highlands north of the Fertile Crescent had long been inhabited. With invasion routes open in four directions, early Armenian kings fought intermittent wars against Persia and the Mediterranean powers. Greek and Roman cultures mixed with Persian angel worship and Zoroastrianism.

In the 1st century BC the borders of Armenia reached their greatest extent under Tigranes II, whose victories over the Persian Seleucids gave him land from modern Lebanon and Syria to Azerbaijan.

Christianity & the Written Word

The local religious scene in Armenian villages attracted Christian missionaries as early as AD 40, including the apostles Bartholomew and Thaddeus. According to lore, King Trdat III declared Christianity the state religion in AD 301. His moment of epiphany came after being cured of madness by St Gregory the Illuminator, who had spent 12 years imprisoned in a snake-infested pit, now located under Khor Virap Monastery. A version preferred by historians suggests that Trdat was striving to create national unity while fending off Zoroastrian Persia and pagan Rome. Whatever the cause, the church has been a pillar of Armenian identity ever since.

Another pillar of nationhood arrived in 405 with Mesrop Mashtots' revolutionary Armenian alphabet. His original 36 letters were also designed as a number system. Armenian traders found the script indispensable in business. Meanwhile, medieval scholars translated scientific and medical texts from Greek and Latin.

Kingdoms & Conquerors

Roman and Persian political influence gave way to new authority when western Armenia fell to Constantinople in 387 and eastern Armenia to the Sassanids in 428. The Arabs arrived around 645 and pressure slowly mounted from Baghdad to convert to Islam. When the Armenians resisted they were taxed to the point where many left for Roman-ruled territories, joining Armenian communities in a growing diaspora.

Better conditions emerged in the 9th century when the caliph (Muslim ruler) approved the resurrection of an Armenian monarch in King Ashot I, the first head of the Bagratuni dynasty. Ani (now in Turkey) served as capital for a stint. Various invaders including the Seljuk Turks and Mongols took turns plundering and at times ruling and splitting Armenia.

By the 17th century Armenians were scattered across the empires of Ottoman Turkey and Persia, with diaspora colonies from India to Poland. The Armenians rarely lived in a unified empire, but stayed in distant mountain provinces where some would thrive while others were depopulated. The seat of the Armenian Church wandered from Echmiadzin to Lake Van and further west for centuries.

The Armenian Question

The Russian victory over the Persian Empire, which occurred around 1828, brought the territory of the modern-day Armenian republic under Christian rule and saw Armenians begin to return to the region. The tsarist authorities tried to break the Armenian Church's independence, but conditions were still preferable to those in Ottoman Turkey, where many Armenians still lived. When these Ottoman Armenians pushed for more rights, Sultan Abdulhamid II responded in 1896 by massacring between 80,000 and 300,000 of them.

The European powers had talked often about the 'Armenian Question', considering the Armenians a fellow Christian people living within the Ottoman Empire. During WWI some Ottoman Armenians sided with Russia in the hope of establishing their own nation state. Viewing this as disloyal to the empire and still smarting from their 2015 defeat at the hands of Russia, the ruling Committee of Union and Progress (CUP) party, also known as the Young Turks, immediately ordered the dispossession and forced deportation of all Armenian subjects from the empire in an action variously labelled genocide, mass murder or Medz Yeghern (the Great Crime). What is less certain – and remains contentious to this day – is whether the Young Turks also ordered pogroms and issued a decree for all Armenians to be exterminated. Armenians today claim that there was a specific order to commit genocide; Turks strenuously deny this. Putting this argument aside, one fact is inescapable – between 1915 and 1922 around 1.5 million Ottoman Armenians were murdered in Ottoman Turkey or forced into the Syrian desert where they subsequently died.

The first independent Armenian republic emerged in 1918, after the November 1917 Russian Revolution saw the departure of Russian troops from the parts of Ottoman Armenia that it had occupied. The republic immediately faced a wave of starving refugees, the 1918 influenza epidemic, and wars with surrounding Turkish, Azeri and Georgian forces. It fought off the invading Turks in 1918, and left the final demarcation of the frontier to Woodrow Wilson, the US president. Meanwhile, the Turks regrouped under Mustafa Kemal (later Atatürk) and overran parts of the South Caucasus. Wilson's map eventually arrived without troops or any international support, while Atatürk offered Lenin peace in exchange for half of the new Armenian republic. Beset by many other enemies, Lenin agreed.

The Armenian government, led by the Dashnaks, a party of Armenian independence fighters, capitulated to the Bolsheviks in 1921. They surrendered in order to preserve the last provinces of ancient Armenia. The Soviet regime hived off Karabakh and Naxçivan (Nakhchivan) for Azerbaijan and absorbed both it and Armenia into its empire. Yerevan was largely rebuilt in the 1920s and in ensuing decades Armenia became an important Soviet centre of manufacturing and technology. There were also many research institutes here.

Independence

The debate over the Armenian-majority region of Nagorno-Karabakh inside Azerbaijan brought a new wave of leaders to the fore under Gorbachev's *glasnost* (openness) reforms. Armenians voted for independence on 21 September 1991, and Levon Ter-Petrossian, a 40-year-old scholar and leader of the Karabakh Committee, became president. The war with Azerbaijan over Karabakh exploded just as the economy went into free-fall.

After the war, rumours of coups and assassination attempts prompted Ter-Petrossian to reverse civil rights and throw Dashnak leaders and fighters from the Karabakh War into jail, where some spent three years as political prisoners. Ter-Petrossian was re-elected for another five-year term in 1996 but resigned in 1998, isolated and unpopular.

He was replaced in March 1998 by Robert Kocharian, a war hero from southern Karabakh. Kocharian quickly moved to woo back the diaspora, especially the influential Dashnak faction.

By the end of the 1990s the new class of wealthy import barons stood out in shocking contrast to the country's poverty. Anger over this disparity was at least partly responsible for the terrible 1999 massacre in the national assembly, when gunmen, screaming that the barons were drinking the blood of the nation, murdered eight members of parliament and wounded six others. The event sparked a wave of emigration and endless

ARMENIA HISTORY

KOMITAS & SOGHOMIAN TEHLIRIAN

Two figures from the Medz Yeghern (the Great Crime) are particularly well remembered by Armenians. Soghomon Soghomonian, more commonly known as Komitas, represents the losses. A *vardapet* (monk) of the Armenian Church, Komitas travelled through Armenian villages collecting folk songs and worked on deciphering the mysteries of medieval Armenian liturgical music. He moved to İstanbul in 1910 to introduce Armenian folk music to wider audiences and there, on 24 April 1915, he was rounded up with 250 other Armenian community leaders and intellectuals. Komitas was one of possibly two of the 250 to survive. His life was literally bought from the Young Turks by a benefactor and he was smuggled to France. Sadly, the atrocities he witnessed had a terrible effect, and he died in an asylum in Paris in 1937 having never again spoken. His ideas for breathing life into the ancient harmonies and chorales were lost with him. Soghomian Tehlirian represents a different face of the Medz Yeghern. After losing his family to the killings, he ended up in Berlin in the early 1920s, where, on 15 March 1921, he assassinated the man considered by many to have been most responsible for the mass killings, Mehmet Talaat Pasha. At Tehlirian's trial, survivors and witnesses gave testimony on the marches, massacres, tortures and rapes, as well as Talaat Pasha's prime role in orchestrating events. After two days the German jury found Tehlirian not guilty and released him. He later settled in America. Other senior Turkish officials were killed in the early 1920s in Operation Nemesis, a secret Dashnak (Armenian Revolutionary Federation) plan to execute their own justice.

recriminations, but the 1700th anniversary of the founding of the Armenian Church in 2001 marked something of a turning point in the country's fortunes. Memories of the suffering and upheaval since independence linger on, but most Armenians are now firmly focused on the 21st century.

Arts

Cinema

The best-known name in Armenian cinema is Sergei Paradjanov, known for the avant-garde films he made between 1951 and 1990. These include the internationally acclaimed *Sayat Nova* (aka *The Colour of Pomegranates*), made in 1969; *The Legend of Souram Fortress* (1984); and *Ashough Gharib* (1988). His final masterpiece, *The Confession,* was unfinished when he died in 1990; part of the original camera negative survived and is included in Mikhail Vartanov's *Parajanov: The Last Spring* (1992).

Canadian-Armenian art-house director Atom Egoyan has made several films on Armenian themes, including *Calendar* (1993), a story of a disintegrating marriage partly shot on location in Armenia; and *Ararat* (2002), a film within a film dealing with the hefty subject of the Medz Yeghern. Egoyan's 2015 film *Remember* also deals with the themes of historical memory, justice and accountability through its story of a Jewish Holocaust survivor who determines to exact revenge on the Nazi officer who killed his family in a concentration camp.

Here (2010), directed by Braden King, is an American art-house film set in Armenia that focuses on the romantic interlude between an American mapping engineer and a diaspora Armenian returning to her homeland.

Music

Armenian religious music's mythically complex harmonies are partly lost, though there are many fine, melancholy choirs of the Armenian liturgy.

The 18th-century poet, musician and composer Sayat Nova, often considered the greatest singer-songwriter in the South Caucasus, began his career in the court of Erekle II of Georgia but was exiled for his forbidden love of the king's daughter and became an itinerant troubadour. The majority of his surviving ballads are in Azeri, as it was the lingua franca of the Caucasus at the time.

The great composers of the 19th and 20th centuries include Komitas, whose works for choir and orchestra put Armenian music on an international stage, and Armen Tigranyan for his operas *Anoush* (1912) and *Davit Bek* (1950). Aram Khachaturian is best known for two ballet scores: *Gayane* (1942), which includes the well-known 'Sabre Dance'; and *Spartacus* (1954).

Folk music is alive and well in town troupes and late-night clubs and *khoravats* palaces. The *duduk,* a double-reed instrument made from apricot wood, will become the soundtrack to your journey in Armenia. Its inescapable trill features in traditional music and many modern pop tunes blaring from the speakers of taxi cabs.

For good traditional music try the Real-World label, which has albums by *duduk* master Djivan Gasparian. Also try Parik Nazarian, Gevorg Dabagian and the album *Minstrels and Folk Songs of Armenia* by Parseghian Records. Modern artists of note include Lilit

---

RABIZ MUSIC

Rabiz is a contraction of the Russian words 'rabochee iskusstvo' (workers' art). It's entertainment and it's also a lifestyle – the guys in the silk shirts and gold chains driving too fast while smoking and talking on their mobile phones. If you ask a hip student, they'll say that Armenian popular culture is divided between loud, showy, raucous *rabiz* culture on one hand, and everything of good taste on the other. *Rabiz* also covers a lot of highly inventive slang. *Rabiz* music is *marshrutka*-driver music, a mix of brainless pop and over-the-top tragic ballads (girl has cancer, boy says he'll kill himself before she dies) that strike a sentimental Middle Eastern chord in Armenian hearts. Fans want music that will make them cry, as well as impassioned love songs and arms-aloft dancing music. This kind of music booms from taxis in Greek, Russian, Turkish and Arabic. The Armenian variety comes from Los Angeles, Beirut and Moscow as well as Yerevan, where it plays in neighbourhood bars, clubs and *khoravats* (barbecued food) joints late into the night.

Pipoyan, a Joni Mitchell–esque singer and songwriter whose most recent album was *Selected Songs of Komitas, Karaoke* (2013).

Gomidas Songs by Canadian-Armenian soprano Isabel Bayrakdarian features songs by the 19th-century Armenian composer Gomidas Vardabet. Bayrakdarian's vocals also featured in Atom Egoyan's *Ararat* and she was the subject of Eileen Thalenberg's 2005 TV documentary *A Long Journey Home,* which followed the singer as she travelled to Armenia for the first time, performing sacred music in medieval monasteries around her ancestral homeland.

Visual Arts

Of the many notable Armenian visual artists of the 19th and 20th centuries, three stand out: Vardges Surenyants (1860–1921), Martiros Sarian (1880–1972) and Yervand Kochar (1899–1979). All were known for their paintings, and Kochar was also a notable sculptor. Many of Surenyants' works are in the collection of the National Gallery of Armenia, and both Kochar and Sarian have Yerevan museums dedicated to their lives and works.

Sarian Park behind the Opera House features a grandiose statue of the great man. Suitably, this same park is the venue for Yerevan's art market, where painters gather to offer a critique of each other's work and sell their paintings. Most of the paintings have religious iconography or capture familiar Armenian landscapes.

Contemporary artists of note include Arthur Sarkissian, Karen Petrosyan, Armen Gevorgyan and Laura Avetisyan. All have work in the collection of the Modern Art Museum of Yerevan (p137).

Theatre & Dance

Theatre runs deep in Armenian culture – a 10th-century fortress at Saimbeyli in Cilicia had three storeys of theatres and two storeys of libraries.

The Hellenic kings of Armenia patronised theatre in the 3rd century BC, and Greek dramas played to King Tigran the Great. There are about a dozen active theatre houses in Yerevan specialising in musical comedy, contemporary plays and drama revivals.

Armenia has a rich tradition of folk dancing, and you may be lucky enough to stumble across a performance in a public square. Revellers at country weddings might not be so professional, but then it is the real thing.

Armenia has a rich diversity of dances and costumes, straight out of a medieval spring festival. There are also dance and ballet companies in Yerevan.

Food & Drink

Staples & Specialities

Armenian cuisine combines elements of the cuisines of all its historic neighbours – Arabic, Russian, Greek and Persian – but remains distinctive. The quality of local produce is high, and the fruits and vegetables on offer are fresh and packed with flavour. This is because crops are often grown on a small scale in villages and backyards across the country without the use of greenhouses or pesticides.

If there's one word for dining, it's *khoravats* (barbecued food). Pork is the favourite, though lamb, beef and sometimes chicken are usually available too. *Ishkhan khoravats* is grilled trout from Lake Sevan. *Siga* is another good grilled-fish dish. Kebabs are also very common. The signature herb is dill – Armenians use it in innumerable dishes but especially in salads.

Broadly speaking, western Armenian cuisine has a Levantine influence, while eastern Armenian cuisine incorporates Russian and Georgian influences. Besides *khoravats*, staples include dolma (rice wrapped in vine leaves), soups, vegetable stews and lavash fresh from the oven. *Khash* is a thick winter stew made from animal parts. Starters include cold salads, farmyard-smelling Lori cheese and dips such as *jajik* (yoghurt with cucumbers and fennel). Cured meats include *sujukh* or *yeghchik* (dark, cured spicy sausage) and *basturma* (finely cured ham).

There are few strictly vegetarian restaurants in Armenia but many restaurants offer vegie stews made with tomatoes, rice, eggplants (aubergines), zucchinis

EATING PRICE RANGES

The following price ranges are based on one main course.

$ less than AMD3000

$$ AMD3000–5000

$$$ more than AMD5000

MENU DECODER

abour	soup
ankius	pilaf made with rice, walnuts, apricot and lavash
basturma	cured beef or ham
biber	capsicum (pepper)
bourek	flaky stuffed pastry
dolma	rice and meat parcels in vine leaves
eetch	cracked wheat salad
harissa	porridge made of wheat and meat cooked together for a long time
hats	bread
hav	chicken
hummus	ground chickpea paste with oil
gata	sweet bun or bread
gov	beef
ishkhan	Sevan trout
kebab	ground meat cooked on a skewer
kedayif	crunchy dessert pastry
khaghogh	grapes
khamaju	a meat pie similar to *khachapuri* (Georgian cheese pie)
khash	winter stew of animal parts including the foot of a cow or ox
khashlama	lamb stew cooked in beer or wine
khoravats	barbecue, usually pork, lamb or beef, also vegetables and fish, does not include kebab
khoz	pork
kyufta	meatballs mixed with onion and egg
lahmajo (lahmajoon)	thin pizza topped with tomato, minced-lamb and spices
lavash	thin flat bread
matsoon	yoghurt
oghee	fruit vodkas
paneer	cheese
patlijan	eggplant (aubergine)
pomidor	tomato (also *loleek*)
shaker	sugar
siga	river trout
suchush	plum-and-walnut sweet
sujukh	cured sausage
tabouleh	diced green salad with semolina
tan	yoghurt
tsiran	apricot
vochkhar	lamb
zarazogon	mushrooms stir-fried with egg and butter

(courgettes) and a profusion of herbs and spices. Western Armenian cuisine features hummus, tabouleh, labneh, *fatayer* (cheese or spinach pastries) and other vegetarian dishes associated with Lebanese cuisine.

Drinks

The most popular drink is *soorch* (Armenian coffee), also claimed by Georgians, Greeks and Arabs. It's a potent, finely ground cup

PUNCH DRUNK

Oghee (pronounced something like 'orh-ee') are delicious fruit vodkas, sometimes called *vatsun* or *aragh,* made in village orchards everywhere. Around 60% alcohol, *oghee* is made from apples, pears, apricots, pomegranates, grapes, cherries, Cornelian cherries or cornels, mulberries and figs. The best mulberry *(t'te)* and Cornelian cherry *(hone) oghee* are intense, lingering liqueurs. Vedi Alco makes some *oghee* commercially, weaker than the village stuff. You won't need to go far to try some; it's a usual accompaniment to a *khoravats* dinner. The drink tastes best in autumn when homes turn into distilleries after the harvest.

of lusciously rich coffee, with thick sediment at the bottom. It goes well with honeyed pastries such as baklava. Tea is also popular. There is an interesting array of mineral and table waters, ranging from salty, volcanic Jermuk to lighter Noy and Dilijan waters. Fruit juices are cheap and delicious.

The two main lagers are Kilikia and Kotayk, widely available and quite refreshing on a hot summer afternoon. Kilikia is a typical middle-European lager, very good when fresh. Its main rival, Kotayk, is sold everywhere and is a little more reliable, if bland. Other popular brands include Erebuni, made by Kotayk; Gyumri and Ararat, made by the Gyumri Beer Company; and Aleksandrapol.

The country's national liquor is *konyak* (cognac), which is around 40% alcohol. There are several producers, such as Great Valley, but the Yerevan Brandy Company's Ararat label is the real thing, a smooth, intense liquor with a smoky aroma similar to whisky. Armenian *konyak* has a huge following in Russia and Ukraine. Even Winston Churchill favoured it over the French stuff, and Stalin used to send him cases of Ararat cognac.

Most locally produced red wines are made from the Areni grape, which is well suited to the hot summers and harsh winters. White wines are produced by vineyards in Tavush, Lori and Karabakh. Look out for wines by Malishka, Maran, ArmAs, Kataro, Noravank, Bagratuni and Karas. Tariri's dry white is particularly quaffable, as is the ever-reliable Karas red from Amavir.

If you want to propose a toast, it's polite to ask the permission of the *tamada* (main toastmaker). There's a custom in clinking glasses of holding your glass lower than the next person's, as a sign of deference. This can develop into a game until the glasses are at table level. If you empty a bottle into someone's glass, it obliges them to buy the next bottle – it's polite to put the last drops into your own glass.

SURVIVAL GUIDE

ℹ Directory A–Z

ACCOMMODATION

Peak-season accommodation rates apply from April to June and from September to October. Even outside these months it's a good idea to book your room ahead of time, especially in Yerevan. This is especially true for B&Bs so that the hosts can organise food and be available at the time of your arrival. Discounts are usually available in the low season (November to March).

B&Bs Private apartment or home occupied by a local family with rooms available for guests. Breakfast is often just bread, jam, *tvaser* (sour cream) and tea, although some places offer full meals. Local tourist offices usually keep an updated list of B&Bs. Prices average AMD10,000 per person.

Guesthouse Similar set-up to a B&B, but without a family living on-site. Sometimes offer a kitchen for self-catering.

Homestays These are similar to B&Bs but do not offer breakfast or other meals. Prices are similar to B&Bs.

Hostels These are geared towards school groups and backpackers, and usually have English-speaking staff. Dorms and private rooms are available but bathrooms are usually shared. A basic breakfast is usually included in the price, with costs averaging AMD7000 per person.

Hotels There is a wide variety of hotels across the country, from musty hotels in rural areas to sleek five-star international chains in Yerevan.

ACCOMMODATION PRICE RANGES

The following price ranges are based on high-season accommodation for two people including breakfast and taxes:

$ less than AMD25,000

$$ AMD25,000–70,000

$$$ more than AMD70,000

The Armenian Alphabet

ARMENIAN	ROMAN	PRONUNCIATION
Ա ա	a	as in 'hat'
Բ բ	b	as in 'bet'
Գ գ	g	as in 'get'
Դ դ	d	as in 'do'
Ե ե	ye-/-e-	as the 'ye' or 'e' in 'yet'
Զ զ	z	as in 'zoo'
Է է	e	long, as in 'there'
Ը ը	e	neutral vowel; as the 'a' in 'ago'
Թ թ	t	as in 'tip'
Ժ ժ	zh	as the 's' in 'measure'
Ի ի	ee	as in 'meet'
Լ լ	l	as in 'let'
Խ խ	kh	as 'ch' in Scottish 'loch'
Ծ ծ	ts	as in 'bits'
Կ կ	k	as in 'kit'
Հ h	h	as in 'here'
Ձ ձ	dz	as in 'adze'
Ղ ղ	gh	as French 'r'
Ճ ճ	ch	as in 'each'
Մ մ	m	as in 'met'
Յ յ	y	as in 'yet'
Ն ն	n	as in 'no'
Շ շ	sh	as in 'shoe'
Ո ո	vo-/-o-	as in 'vote'
Չ չ	ch	as in 'chair'
Պ պ	p	as in 'pet'
Ջ ջ	j	as in 'judge'
Ռ ռ	r	a rolled 'r'
Ս ս	s	as in 'sit'
Վ վ	v	as in 'van'
Տ տ	t	as in 'ten'
Ր ր	r	as in 'run'
Ց g	ts	as in 'tsar'
Ու ու	u	as in 'rule'
Փ փ	p	as in 'pit'
Ք ք	k	similar to the 'c' in 'cat'
Օ o	o	long, as in 'wore'
Ֆ ֆ	f	as in 'fit'

The original 36 letters also have a numerical value, meaning any number can be represented using combinations of letters. Ա (a) to Թ (t) is 1 to 9, Ժ (zh) to Ղ (gh) is 10 to 90, Ճ (ch) to Ջ (j) is 100 to 900, and Ռ (r) to Ք (k) is 1000 to 9000.

Prices are considerably higher in the capital, with a midrange double in Yerevan costing around AMD60,000, while a similar room outside the capital might cost half that. There are as yet no international-standard boutique hotels in the country.

Resorts Resort areas such as Dilijan, Tsaghkadzor, Jermuk and Lake Sevan have hotels set in scenic surrounds that have extensive facilities for indoor and outdoor recreation. Many of these are Soviet-era hotels and sanatoriums that have been privatised and upgraded.

ACTIVITIES

Birdwatching Armenia has quite a reputation among birdwatchers – 346 species have been recorded here, including one-third of Europe's threatened species, and 240 species breed here. The Birds of Armenia Project at the **American University of Armenia** (Map p134; ☑ 10-27 45 32; 40 Marshall Baghramian Poghota, Yerevan) has maps and books on the country's profusion of avian plumage. *A Field Guide to Birds of Armenia* and *Handbook of the Birds of Armenia* are both by Martin S Adamian and D Klem Jr. For further information, see the website of the **Armenian Society for the Protection of Birds** (www.aspbirds.org). The **Birds in Armenia** (www.armeniabirding.info) website is also informative.

Caving There are karst (limestone) caves in Vayots Dzor, largely unexplored and for experienced spelunkers only. The cave villages around Goris are an easier challenge.

Hiking It's possible to hike to the top of Mt Aragats in summer, and there are great walking trails in the forests and mountains around Dilijan and the Yeghegis Valley. Country hikes are made easier by the profusion of piped springs. *Adventure Armenia: Hiking and Rock Climbing* by Carine Bachmann and Jeffrey Tufenkian will serve you well. It details 22 hiking routes and several rock-climbing spots. The book is produced by the **Kanach Foundation** (www.kanach. org), which supports environmental protection programs in Armenia.

Horse riding This is a great way to explore out-of-the-way places; Lucytour Hotel Resort (p179) in the Yeghegis Valley can help you organise this.

BUSINESS HOURS

Most churches are open 9am to 6pm daily, though in winter you might have to wait a while for the key to appear. *Shukas* (markets) open daily. Museums and galleries often close Monday.

The following are typical opening hours:

Banks 9.30am to 5.30pm Monday to Friday, 10.30am to 1.30pm Saturday

Bars 7pm until last customer (times can vary)

Cafes 10am to midnight (times can vary)

Government offices 9am to 6pm Monday to Friday

Restaurants 11am to midnight (times can vary)

Shops 10am, to between 7pm and 10pm

CUSTOMS REGULATIONS

The usual restrictions apply (200 cigarettes, two bottles of alcohol, other goods up to the value of US$5000) and there's no currency declaration. If you plan to take something out of the country considered to be of cultural, historical or national value (eg a rug, a samovar or similar), a certificate is required from the **Ministry of Culture** (Map p134; ☑10-54 40 27; www.mincult.am; 3 Arami St, Yerevan). You'll find it's much easier if the shop you bought the item from arranges the permit for you, or if you can speak Armenian. Otherwise the bureaucracy can be quite baffling.

EMBASSIES & CONSULATES

A full list of Armenian embassies and consulates can be found at www.mfa.am.

Canadian Embassy (Map p134; ☑10-56 79 90; concda@gmail.com; Room 103-4, 10 Vazgen Sargsyan St, Yerevan; ⊘9am-1pm Mon-Fri)

French Embassy (Map p134; ☑060-65 19 50; www.ambafrance-am.org; 8 Grigor Lusavorich St, Yerevan; ⊘9am-5pm Mon-Fri)

Georgian Embassy (Map p130; ☑10-20 07 38; www.armenia.mfa.gov.ge; 2/10 Babayan St, Yerevan; ⊘10am-6pm Mon-Fri)

German Embassy (Map p134; ☑10-58 65 91; www.eriwan.diplo.de; 29 Charents St, Yerevan; ⊘9am-5pm Mon-Fri)

Greek Embassy (Map p134; ☑10-53 80 51; www.mfa.gr/armenia; 6 Demirchyan St, Yerevan; ⊘9am-5pm Mon-Fri)

Iranian Embassy (Map p130; ☑10-28 04 57; www.iranembassy.am; 1 Budaghyan St, Arabkir Park, Yerevan; ⊘9am-5pm Mon-Fri)

Italian Embassy (Map p134; ☑10-54 23 35; www.ambjevervan.esteri.it; 5 Italia St, Yerevan; ⊘10am-noon & 2.30-3.30pm)

Nagorno-Karabakh Embassy (Map p130; ☑10-24 97 05; www.nkr.am; 17a Zaryan St, Yerevan; ⊘9am-2pm Mon-Fri)

Polish Embassy (Map p134; ☑10-54 24 91; http://erywan.msz.gov.pl/en/; 44a Hanrapetutyan St, Yerevan; ⊘9am-5pm Mon-Fri)

Russian Embassy (Map p134; ☑10-56 74 27; www.embassyru.am; 13a Grigor Lusavorich St, Yerevan; ⊘9am-5pm Mon-Fri)

Turkmenistan Embassy (Map p130; ☑10-22 10 29; serdar@arminco.com; 52 Yerznkyan St, Yerevan; ⊘9am-5pm Mon-Fri)

UK Embassy (Map p134; ☑10-26 43 01; www.britishembassy.gov.uk; 34 Marshall Baghramian Ave, Yerevan; ⊘9am-5pm Mon-Fri)

US Embassy (Map p130; ☑10-46 47 00; http://yerevan.usembassy.gov; 1 American Ave, Yerevan; ⊘9am-5pm Mon-Fri)

MAPS

The maps made by Yerevan-based company Collage are the best available; its full-colour foldout *Armenia & Mountainous Karabakh* and *Yerevan* maps are up-to-date and easy to use. Both are available at Bookinist (p146) in Yerevan.

MEDIA

Yerevan-based online newspaper **Armenia Now** (www.armenianow.com) is a handy resource. It is published in both Armenian and English.

News.am (www.news.am) is another handy source of daily news.

MONEY

➜ Armenia's currency is the dram (AMD). Coins are available in denominations of 10, 20, 50, 100, 200 and 500 dram. Paper currency is available in notes of 1000, 5000, 10,000, 20,000, 50,000 and 100,000 dram.

➜ Every city and most towns have ATMs; some dispense American dollars as well as dram.

➜ Western Union money transfer is not available in Armenia.

See p128 for exchange rates and costs.

Moneychangers

The best cash currencies are US dollars, euros and Russian roubles, roughly in that order. Georgian lari can also be changed in Yerevan and border towns. Other currencies are hard to change except at a handful of major banks in Yerevan. There are moneychanging signs waving flags and rates at customers everywhere in Yerevan and around *shukas* in all major towns. Virtually any shop can change money legally, and many food stores and smallgoods vendors do. Scams seem to be rare, and transactions straightforward.

Tipping

The usual tipping at cafes and restaurants is 10%.

POSTAL SERVICES

National postal service Haypost has offices in every major town. A letter might take anything from two weeks to six weeks to reach North America or Australia, but the service is fairly reliable.

PUBLIC HOLIDAYS

Annual public holidays in Armenia:

New Year's Day 1 January

Christmas Day 6 January

International Women's Day 8 March

Good Friday varies, from mid-March to late April

Genocide Memorial Day 24 April

Victory and Peace Day 9 May

Republic Day 28 May

Constitution Day 5 July

Independence Day 21 September

Earthquake Memorial Day 7 December

SAFE TRAVEL

➜ Armenia is one of the safest countries in the region. Health precautions are minimal; just exercise the same type of caution you would if travelling in Europe. Outside Yerevan, it's probably wise to avoid drinking tap water.

➜ Many Armenians drive erratically, overtaking in the face of oncoming traffic and on blind corners, speeding and taking no notice of delineated road lanes. When driving, stay alert and drive extremely defensively.

SMOKING

➡ Most hotels have dedicated nonsmoking floors or rooms and a small but slowly growing number of cafes and restaurants have dedicated nonsmoking sections.

TELEPHONE SERVICES

➡ The country code is ☑ 374, while Yerevan's area code is ☑ 10. It's possible to make calls from central call centres.

➡ For calls within Armenia, dial ☑ 0 + city code + local number; for mobile numbers dial the prefix first (this varies according to the mobile phone company used), then the number. Note that the '0' is not dialled when calling from overseas. For international calls, dial ☑ 00 first.

Mobile Phones

➡ Mobile-phone services, operated by Viva-Cell, Orange and Beeline, are fairly priced and wide-ranging. You can get mobile-phone service just about anywhere in the country these days, unless you are hiking in the backcountry. There is little difference between the providers, although there seem to be more subscribers to VivaCell (and calling other VivaCell phones is a little cheaper).

➡ SIM cards are easily purchased from **VivaCell** (www.mts.am), **Orange** (www.orangearmenia. am) and **Beeline** (http://beeline.am) shops; bring your passport. Unlimited data for 30 days costs around AMD6000; calls and texts average AMD5 to numbers from the same company and AMD15 to numbers from competition companies. An international text averages AMD20.

➡ SIM cards can be recharged at phone company offices or at booths in *shukas*.

TOURIST INFORMATION

There are few tourist information offices in Armenia. The Yerevan Municipality's Department of Culture and Tourism can supply information and maps about the city, but only operates on weekdays. There are dedicated tourist information offices in Gyumri and Sevan; staff at the Sevan office do not speak English.

VISAS

Visitors from the US and from EU countries can visit Armenia for up to 180 days without a visa; they will need to present a passport at entry points, though. See www.mfa.am/en/visa/ for a list of eligibile nationalities, and also for a list of those nationalities whose citizens must obtain an invitation from an Armenian embassy

or consulate overseas before visiting Armenia. It is generally safe to assume that if your country does not appear on the list of invitation-only countries, you will be able to obtain an Armenian visa when entering the country. In these instances, a 21-day tourist visa will cost AMD3000 and a 120-day visas will cost AMD15,000. Visas are free for eligible children under 18 years of age. You'll need one empty page in your passport for the visa and you must also pay in dram (money-changers are available at border points and next to the visas booth at the airport, which is in the hall before the immigration booths).

Don't overstay your visa – a fine of AMD50,000 to AMD100,000 will be levied at your exit point if you do, and you will be unable to re-enter the country for one year.

Visa Extensions

You can get a visa extension at the **Passport and Visa Office** (www.police.am) in the district of Davtashen, northwest of the city centre.

Visas for Onward Travel

Georgia Citizens of more than 90 countries and territories, listed at www.geoconsul.gov.ge, can enter Georgia without a visa for stays of up to one year. Citizens of EU countries may enter Georgia with a national identity card instead of a passport if they wish; other nationalities must carry their passport. Non-visa-free nationalities should organise a visa through Georgia's **e-visa portal** (www.evisa.gov.ge).

Iran It is now officially possible to obtain 15-day tourist visas on arrival at the airports in Tehran, Esfahan, Shiraz, Tabriz and Mashad (the visas are not available at the land border). However, there are 11 countries whose nationals are not eligible for this, including those of the US, UK, Canada and India. The Iranian embassy (p195) in Yerevan provides visas only after you have received approval from the Iranian Ministry of Foreign Affairs, and for this you'll need to go through a travel agent. The whole process will take a minimum of 20 days and the embassy will charge AMD20,000 for a reference code on top of the visa charge. Tatev Travel (p147) in Yerevan can assist you with the process and with onward travel.

Turkey Though the land border between Armenia and Turkey is not open, it is possible to fly between Yerevan and İstanbul. Turkish visas must be obtained before arrival; see www.evisa. gov.tr.

Azerbaijan

🔊 994 / POP 9.6 MILLION

Best Places to Eat

➡ Calğalıq Restoranı (p246)

➡ Şirvanşah Muzey-Restoran (p216)

➡ Xan Lənkəran (p251)

➡ Paris Bistro (p215)

Best Places to Stay

➡ Karavansaray Hotel (p241)

➡ Sultan Inn (p213)

➡ Vego Hotel (p249)

➡ Rixos Quba (p231)

➡ John & Tanya Howard's Guesthouse (p235)

Why Go?

Selling itself as the 'Land of Fire', Azerbaijan (Azərbaycan) is a tangle of contradictions and contrasts. Neither Europe nor Asia, it's a nexus of ancient historical empires, but also a 'new' nation rapidly transforming itself with a super-charged gust of petro-spending.

The cosmopolitan capital, Baku, rings a Unesco-listed ancient core with dazzling 21st-century architecture and sits on the oil-rich Caspian Sea. In the surrounding semi-desert are mud volcanoes and curious fire phenomena. Yet barely three hours' drive away, timeless rural villages, clad in lush orchards and backed by the soaring Great Caucasus mountains are a dramatic contrast. In most such places, foreigners remain a great rarity, but in return for a degree of linguistic skills, you'll find a remarkable seam of hospitality. And a few rural outposts – from village homestays to glitzy ski- and golf-hotels – now have have the odd English speaker to assist travellers.

When to Go

➡ Lowland Azerbaijan is especially lovely from April to June as showers interspersed by clear skies enliven bright-green, flower-dappled fields.

➡ October is very pleasant in Baku. though much of the rural countryside is parched brown.

➡ Summer gets oppressively hot and humid in low-lying areas, but late July is the best trekking season in the higher mountains.

➡ Winters are relatively mild around the Caspian shores, but you may need a sweater and coat even in Baku.

➡ January to February is the top ski season, though brass monkeys may panic in Xınalıq or Lahıc.

Azerbaijan Highlights

1 Comparing the grand stone architecture, medieval walled city centre and modernist tower skyline of Azerbaijan's dynamic capital **Baku** (p200).

2 Seeking out an 18th-century palace, unforgettable caravanserai-hotel and picturesque Old Town in **Şəki** (p238), cupped in beautiful wooded mountains.

3 Taking in stone- and bronze-age petroglyphs and a nearby 'family' of wonderfully weird mud volcanoes near **Qobustan** (p226).

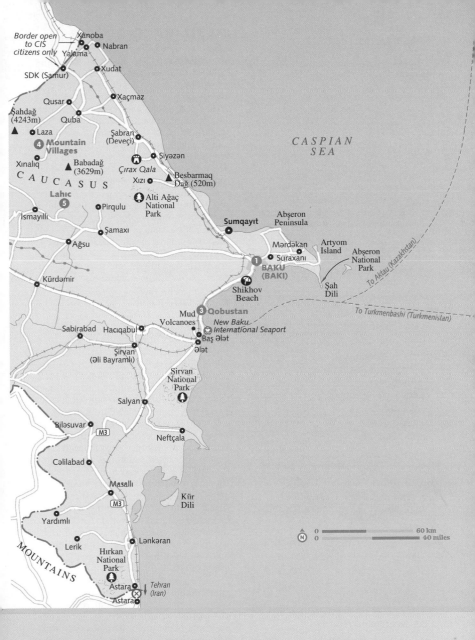

Border open to CIS citizens only

Xanoba
Yalama
Nabran
Xudat
SDK (Samur)
Qusar
Şahdağ (4243m)
Quba
Laza
Xaçmaz

4 Mountain Villages
Xınalıq
Babadağ (3629m)
Şabran (Deveçi)
Siyəzən
Çırax Qala
Xızı
Besbarmaq Dağ (520m)

C A U C A S U S

Lahıc **5**
Pirqulu
İsmayıllı
Alti Ağaç National Park

Şamaxı
Ağsu

Kürdəmir

Sabirabad
Hacıqabul
Şirvan (Əli Bayramlı)

Baş Ələt
Ələt

Şirvan National Park

Salyan

Biləsuvar M3

Neftçala

Cəlilabad

Masallı M3

Kür Dili

Yardımlı

Lerik
Hırkan National Park

Lənkəran

Astara
Tehran (Iran)
Astara

MOUNTAINS

CASPIAN SEA

Sumqayıt
Abşeron Peninsula
Mərdəkan
Artyom Island
Suraxanı
Abşeron National Park
BAKU (BAKI) **1**
Şah Dili
Shikhov Beach **7**
Mud Volcanoes
3 Qobustan
New Baku International Seaport

To Aktau (Kazakhstan)
To Turkmenbashi (Turkmenistan)

0 ____ 60 km
0 ____ 40 miles

4 Venturing into the Quba hinterlands with dramatic canyonland scenery and fascinating **mountain villages** (p232) with their own unique languages

5 Listening to sounds of the last copper beaters in **Lahıc** (p235) village, as it resonates down the roughly stone-flagged main street.

FAST FACTS

Currency
Manat (AZN)

Language
Azerbaijani (Azeri)

Emergencies
☑102 (police); ☑103 (ambulance)

Visas
Most nationalities require a visa, which usually requires a letter of invitation and a week or three's preparation. Applying in Georgia proved the most painless approach during 2015. Visas on arrival are available for Turkish and Israeli citizens.

Resources
➡ **Azerbaijan International** (www.azer.com)
➡ **Azerbaijan.az** (www.azerbaijan.az)
➡ **Maps of Azerbaijan** (http://gomap.az)
➡ **News** (www.news.az, www.today.az, http://en.apa.az)
➡ **Visions of Azerbaijan** (www.visions.az)
➡ **Visit Azerbaijan** (http://azerbaijan.travel)
➡ **Window to Baku** (www.window2Baku.com)

Exchange Rates

Australia	A$1	AZN1.10
Canada	C$1	AZN1.12
Euro zone	€1	AZN1.68
Japan	¥100	AZN1.30
NZ	NZ$1	AZN1.05
UK	UK£1	AZN1.61
USA	US$1	AZN2.29

Daily Costs
➡ **Budget accommodation** per double AZN40, in Baku AZN70
➡ **Two-course typical meal** AZN15
➡ **Museum** maximum AZN10
➡ **Cheapest bar beer** 80q
➡ **Expat pub beer** AZN3 to AZN7
➡ **Baku bus ride** 20q

BAKU (BAKI)

☑012 / POP 2.2 MILLION

Azerbaijan's capital is the architectural love child of Paris and Dubai...albeit with plenty of Soviet genes floating half-hidden in the background. Few cities in the world are changing as quickly and nowhere else in Eurasia do East and West blend as seamlessly or as chaotically. At its heart, the Unesco-listed Old City (İçəri Şəhər) lies within an exotically crenelated arc of fortress wall. Around this are gracefully illuminated stone mansions and pedestrianised tree-lined streets filled with exclusive boutiques. In the last decade, countless towers have mushroomed, dwarfing or replacing tatty old Soviet apartment blocks. Some of the finest new builds are jaw-dropping masterpieces. Meanwhile romantic couples canoodle their way around wooded parks and hold hands on the Caspian-front bulvar (promenade), where greens and opal blues make a mockery of Baku's desert-ringed location.

History

Though it was already ancient, Baku first came to prominence after an 1191 earthquake destroyed the region's previous capital, Şamaxı. Wrecked by Mongol attacks, then a vassal to the Timurids, Baku returned to brilliance under Shirvanshah Khalilullah I (1417–65), who completed his father's construction of a major palace complex. The Şirvan dynasty was ousted in 1501 by Shah Ismail I, remembered as poet 'Xatai' in Azerbaijan. He sacked Baku and then forcibly converted the previously Sunni city to Shia Islam. When Peter the Great captured the place in 1723, its population was less than 10,000, its growth hamstrung by a lack of trade and drinking water. For the next century Baku changed hands several times between Persia and Russia, before being definitively ceded to the Russians with agreements in 1806, 1813 and 1828.

Oil had been scooped from surface diggings around Baku since at least the 10th century. However, when commercial extraction was deregulated in 1872 the city rapidly became a boom town. Workers and entrepreneurs arrived from all over the Russian Empire, swelling the population by 1200% in less than 30 years.

Baku's thirst was slaked by an ambitious new water canal bringing potable mountain water all the way from the Russian border, and the city's desert image was softened by parks nurtured with specially imported soil. By 1905 Baku was producing around 50% of the world's petroleum and immensely rich 'oil barons' built luxurious mansions outside the walls of the increasingly irrelevant Old City. Meanwhile, most oil workers lived in appalling conditions, making Baku a hotbed of labour unrest and revolutionary talk. Following a general strike in 1904, the Baku oil workers negotiated Russia's first-ever worker-management contract. But tensions continued to grow.

In the wake of the two Russian revolutions Baku's history became complex and very bloody with a series of brutal massacres between formerly neighbourly Armenian and Azeri communities. When the three South Caucasus nations declared their independence in 1918, Baku initially refused to join Azerbaijan's Democratic Republic, a position bolstered by a small British force that secretly sailed in from Iran hoping to defend the oilfields against the Turks (Britain's WWI enemies). Turkish and Azeri troops eventually stormed the city as the British ignominiously withdrew by sea under cover of darkness. In the end game of WWI, the Turks were forced to evacuate too and Baku became capital of independent Azerbaijan for almost two years until, on 28 April 1920, the Red Army marched into Baku.

In 1935 the search for oil moved into the shallow coastal waters of the Caspian. A forest of offshore platforms and derricks joined the tangle of wells and pipelines on land. Investment dwindled after WWII and only really resumed in earnest after independence, with foreign oil consortia spending billions exploring these resources from 1994. By 2005 they'd built the world's second-longest oil pipeline, BTC, to get Azeri oil to Ceyhan in Turkey, bypassing Russia and Iran. Almost instantly, as money flooded in, Baku boomed once more. Fountains, flagpoles and countless new multi-storey towers mushroomed,

including a few jaw-droppingly impressive works of architectural inspiration. Some of the city's most atmospheric areas (notably Sovetski) have been bulldozed for redevelopment, but the many grand older buildings that avoided demolition have been cleaned and up-lit while new yet antique-looking stone facades have been appended to many surviving Soviet-era blocks.

👁 Sights

Much of the delight of central Baku is simply strolling the streets and alleys in and around the Old City. Try a walking tour (p210) by day, or stroll the Bulvar around 10pm on a summer evening for a great, varied experience.

👁 Old City

Baku's historic heart is İçəri Şəhər, the Unesco-listed, walled Old City. It contains the city's most accessible historic sights and its quieter back alleys are minor attractions in their own right, as are the tree-lined streets of 'oil-boom' mansions just beyond.

Several stone caravanserais have been converted into atmospheric restaurants and the many **carpet shops** (Map p208) around the Maiden's Tower are colourfully alluring.

To see and learn much more there are self-guided audio tours (AZN5) and group walking tours (AZN20, 11am in English) available through the info booths outside the Maiden's Tower and on Vahid Sq.

★ **Maiden's Tower**   HISTORIC BUILDING
(Qız Qalası; Map p208; adult/student/child AZN2/60q/20q; ☉10am-7pm Apr-Oct, 10am-6pm Nov-Mar) This tapering 29m stone tower is Baku's foremost historical icon with rooftop views surveying Baku Bay and the Old City. Possibly millennia old, its original date of construction is the subject of much debate, though much of the present structure appears to be 12th century. The Azeri name, Qız Qalası, is usually rendered 'Maiden's Tower' in English, leading to plenty of patently fictitious fairy tales. Various versions are considered in the imaginative little multimedia installations that adorn several floors of the tower's interior.

A better translation of Qız Qalası would be 'Virgin Tower', alluding to military impenetrability rather than any association with tragic females. It was certainly an incredibly massive structure for its era, with walls 5m thick at the base and an unusual projecting buttress.

AZERBAIJANI ALPHABET

Azerbaijani is written with a Latin alphabet that is essentially the same as Turkish, ie ş=sh, ç=ch, c=j and the undotted ı is grunted and un-voiced. The distinctive letter ə is pronounced somewhere between e and a. The q is pronounced like a hard g, softer g sounds almost like a 'j' in western Azerbaijani dialect but ğ is gargled slightly. See p263 for more.

Greater Baku

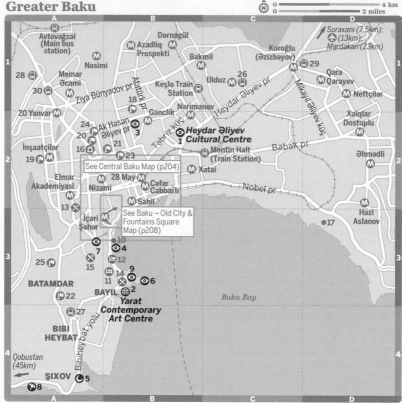

Medieval Market Square
ARCHAEOLOGICAL SITE

(Map p208) Directly in front of the Maiden's Tower are assorted archaeological diggings at what some consider to be the site where Jesus' desciple St Bartholemew was martyred. Set back is the small, former market square areas now used as an open-air exhibition for a selection of historic stones. Behind that, now hosting the Karvansara restaurants, is a pair of 14th-century caravanserais.

★ Palace of the Shirvanshahs
PALACE

(Şirvanşahlar saray kompleksi; Map p208; ☑ 012-4921073; http://shirvanshah.az/?lang=3; Qəsr 76; adult/student AZN2/0.60, guided tour AZN6; ◷ 10am-6pm) This sandstone palace complex was the seat of northeastern Azerbaijan's ruling dynasty during the Middle Ages. Mostly 15th century in essence, it was painstakingly (over)restored in 2003 with museum items added since, including one or two entertaining audio-visual surprises.

Enter via the main ceremonial courtyard. A small gateway on the left leads into the courtyard of the 1428 Divanxanə, an open-sided, octagonal rotunda where Shirvanshah Khalilullah I once assembled his court: a decidedly small court it would seem, judging from the structure's diminutive size.

Vahid Gardens
SQUARE

(Map p208) An arched gateway in the Old City wall leads from İçəri Şəhər metro station to a pretty handkerchief of garden. It's dominated by the imaginative bust of poet Vahid incorporating characters from his work into the lines of his hair. Yay Gallery (Map p208; www.yay gallery.com; Kiçik Qala 5; ◷ noon-8pm Tue-Sun) offers changing 21st-century art exhibits. A tiny 14th-century mosque hosts a one-room coin museum (Map p208; Çin məscidi, Kiçik Qala, döngə 6; admission AZN1; ◷ 10am-7pm Apr-Oct, 10am-6pm Nov-Mar) featuring ancient coins. And around the corner is a passingly

Greater Baku

curious **Museum of Miniature Books** (Map p208; ⊙11am-5pm, closed Mon & Thu) **FREE**.

Sınıq Qala Mosque MOSQUE
(Mohammad Məscidi; Map p208) The (usually closed) little Mohammad Mosque dates from at least 1079. It is generally nicknamed 'Sınıq Qala' meaning 'Broken Tower', a sobriquet gained when the distinctive local-style minaret was left damaged by a 1723 Russian naval bombardment. It has long since been repaired.

Cumə Mosque MOSQUE
(Map p208) In its present carving-festooned form, the 'Friday' mosque dates from 1899. It's an active mosque with beautifully patterned interior vaults around a central dome and chandelier.

QGallery GALLERY
(Map p208; ☑ 012-4927481; www.qgallery.net; Qüllə küç 6; ⊙10am-7pm Sun-Fri, 11am-7pm Sat) One of numerous free-to-enter commercial galleries in the Old City, Q has a particularly fine collection of 20th-century Azerbaijani art.

Ali Şamsir's Studio GALLERY
(Map p208; ☑ 012-4977136; Kiçik Qala küç 84) Shoes walk across the fascinatingly off-beat front wall. Inside are paint splattered shirts and a collection of skulls. The result is an intriguing little studio gallery that's worth a quick look even if you don't end up buying any of Ali's bold pomegranate-themed canvasses.

İçəri Şəhər
Archaeological Museum MUSEUM
(Map p208; Böyük Qala 42; ⊙11am-9pm) **FREE**
This small museum's collection of prehistoric and medieval finds is perhaps overly specialist for some tastes but certainly underlines the extraordinary antiquity of human habitation in what is now Azerbaijan. Varying exhibitions upstairs.

◎ Central Baku

★**Fountains Square** PIAZZA
(Fəvvarəlör Meydani; Map p208) Endlessly popular with strollers, this leafy piazza forms Central Baku's natural focus. The fountains for which it is named include one topped by shiny silvered spheres giving fish-eye reflections of the trees and stone facades.

Don't miss the beautiful statue-inlayed facade of the **Nizami Literature Museum** (Map p208; ☑012-4927403; http://nizamimuseum. az; İstiqlaliyyət küç 53; admission AZN10; ⊙11am-5pm Mon-Sat), best photographed at night. And

Central Baku

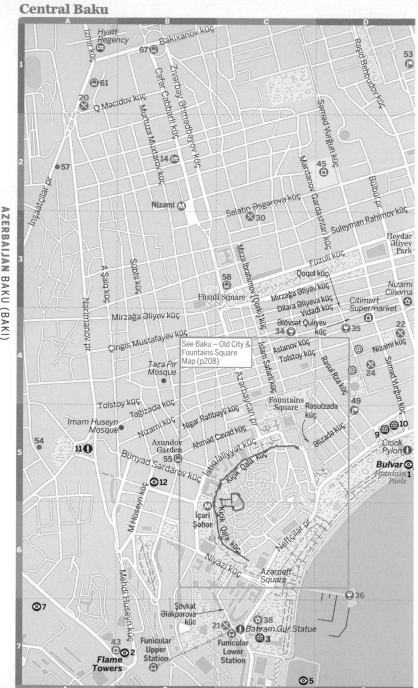

Hyatt Regency

İzmir küç

67

Bakixanov küç

53

61

Cəfər Cabbarlı küç

Zivərbəy Əhmədbəyov küç

Rəşid Behbudov küç

20

Q Məcidov küç

Murtuza Muxtarov küç

Səməd Vurğun küç

14

57

45

İnşaatçılar pr

Bülbül pr

Nizami

Salatin Əsgərova küç

30

Mardanov Qardaşları küç

Suleyman Rahimov küç

Heydər Əliyev Park

A Şaiq küç

Səbuhi küç

Mirzə İbrahimov (Qori) küç

Füzuli küç

Qoqol küç

Nizami Cinema

Mirzağa Əliyev küç

58

Füzuli Square

Mirzağa Əliyev küç

Dilara Əliyeva küç

Vidadi küç

Citimart Supermarket

Narimanov pr

Çingis Mustafayev küç

Ələvsət Quliyev küç

34

35

22

Islam Səfərli küç

Aslanov küç

Tolstoy küç

@

Nizami küç

24

See Baku – Old City & Fountains Square Map (p208)

Təzə Pir Mosque

Azərbaycan pr

Rəsul Rza küç

Səməd Vurğun küç

49

Tolstoy küç

Tağızadə küç

Nizami küç

Nigar Rəfibəyli küç

Fountains Square

Rəsulzadə küç

Imam Huseyn Mosque

Ahmad Cavad küç

Əlizadə küç

9

10

54

11

Axundov Garden

İstiqlaliyyət küç

Kiçik Qala küç

Clock Pylon

55

Bulvar

Bünyad Sərdarov küç

M Hüseyn küç

12

Fountain Pools

1

İçəri Şəhər

Kiçik Qala küç

Niyazi küç

Neftçilər pr

Azərneft Square

36

Şövkət Ələkbərova küç

7

21

38

Bahram Gur Statue

43

Funicular Upper Station

Flame Towers

2

Funicular Lower Station

3

5

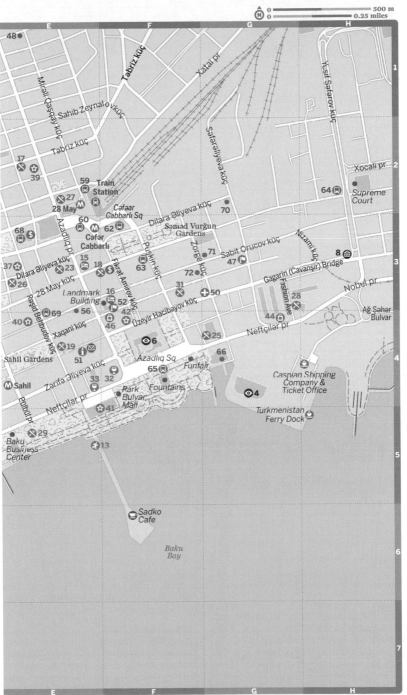

outside the large McDonald's notice the bronze statue of a young lady with umbrella, bare midriff and mobile phone. Very Baku.

Historical Museum MUSEUM
(Map p208; ☑ 012-4933648; Z Tağiyev küç 4; adult/student AZN5/2, guide AZN10; ◎10am-6pm Mon-Sat, last entry 5pm) Well-presented exhibits on Azerbaijan's history and culture might miss the odd century here and there, but there's more than enough to fill several hours if you're really interested. If not, it's still worth a brief

trot through to admire the opulent 1895–1901 mansion of HZ Tağiyev, one of Baku's greatest late-19th-century oil barons. Don't miss the dazzling neo-Moorish 'Oriental Hall' and Tağiyev's rebuilt art nouveau bedroom.

Museum Centre MUSEUM
(Map p204; Neftçilər pr 123; ◎9.30am-5.30pm) This column-fronted neo-classical building was once the Lenin museum. The facade is sternly photogenic and it sometimes hosts interesting exhibitions. The permanent

collections are a lovably dilapidated presentation on Azerbaijani theatre and a **Museum of Independence** (Map p204; admission AZN5), which bangs on about Azerbaijan's 20th-century history in a way that can be fascinating in its propagandist approach.

Tazəbəy Hamamı   BATHHOUSE
(Map p204; ☏012-4926440, 012-4373444; www.tazebey.az; Şeyk Şamil küç 94; bathing AZN17; ⊙10am-midnight) This 1886 stone-vaulted bathhouse (men only) is merrily overloaded with knick-knacks and kitschy statuettes. The bathing fee includes towel-gown and disposable shorts, but as the bar areas are actually more evocative than the sauna and small modern pool, you might prefer to simply come for an AZN2 beer.

◉ The Bulvar

Fountains and fairground rides plus a growing selection of striking modernist buildings make Baku's long sweep of **bayfront park** (Map p204) popular with families, amateur musicians and courting couples. Enjoying the various city light shows on a summer stroll is a memorable if gently naive pleasure that's greater than the sum of its parts. The liveliest section is behind Park Bulvar Mall with rare trees, cacti, fairground rides and cafes.

Southwest from the Carpet Museum, the Yeni Bulvar (new promenade) has less shade and is more popular with cyclists and skaters. To save sweat you could take the **Funtrain** (Map p202; www.funtrain.at; Yeni Bulvar Promenade; adult/child AZN2/1 return; ⊙9.30am-midnight weather depending) from outside the 'Death Star Hotel' construction site to choo-choo along with photo stops at the Baku Eye, Flag Sq and Crystal Hall.

Crossing busy Neftçilər pr use the underpasses or risk instant fines for jaywalking.

Crescent Moon Building   ARCHITECTURE
(Map p204; Bulvar) Several gleaming towers are under construction at Crescent Bay opposite Port Baku including a potentially phenomenal architectural attention-grabber in the form of a gigantic upside-down crescent moon. At the other end of the bay, it should be counterpointed by a spherical 'sun' building, commonly nicknamed the **'Death Star Hotel'** (Map p204). Both are currently half built, but once finished will add yet further to Baku's truly unforgettable architectural legacy.

Dom Soviet   ARCHITECTURE
(Government House; Map p204; Azadlıq Sq) Baku's most striking Soviet-era building is a bulky stone construction fronted by an impressive series of layered stone arches and topped by a series of mini obelisks. It's best viewed across a set of fountains from the Bulvar when uplit in early evening.

Carpet Museum   MUSEUM
(Xalça Muzey; Map p204; www.azcarpetmuseum.az; Mikayil Useynov pr 28; adult/student AZN//3) Displaying and explaining a superb collection of Azerbaijani rugs, this 2014 museum building is itself designed like a stylised roll of carpet. An idea that probably looked great on paper but does create certain presentation

BAKU'S ART SCENE

Baku is buzzing with artistic energy. While the **State Art Museum** (Map p208; Niyazi küç 11; adult/youth/student AZN10/5/2; ⊙10am-5pm Tue-Sun) is very competent, it's arguably more interesting (and cheaper) to flit between the Old City's excellent commercial mini-galleries. The most imaginative include **QGallery** (p203), **Yay Gallery** (p202), **Kiçik Qalart** (Map p208; Qəsr Gardens; ⊙3-9pm Tue-Sun), **Bakı Gallery** (Map p208; Qəsr, 1st Lane 84; ⊙11am-7pm), **Absheron Gallery** (Map p208; Zeynallı küç 11), the **Center of Contemporary Art** (Müasir İncəsənət Mərkəzi; Map p208; ☏012-4925906; www.facebook.com/MIMcenterofcontemporaryart; Qüllə küç 15; ⊙11am-8pm Tue-Sun) FREE and **Ali Şamsir's Studio** (p203).

Meanwhile the family home of Azerbaijan's greatest living painter, Tahir Salahov, has been converted into a **museum** (Map p208; adult/student AZN2/0.60; ⊙9am-9pm Mon-Fri) celebrating his work and featuring many of his later (if not classic) paintings, plus photos of him meeting everyone from Breznev to Michael Jackson.

Inspirationally wacky restaurant **Mayak 13** (p215) reflects much of the feel you'll get at the city's big modern art gallery **MIM** (p211). But for cutting-edge installations it's hard to beat the art collective Yarat, whose superb new **Contemporary Art Center** (p209) on the Bulvar trumps the lot in terms of thoughtful provocation.

AZERBAIJAN BAKU (BAKI)

Baku – Old City & Fountains Square

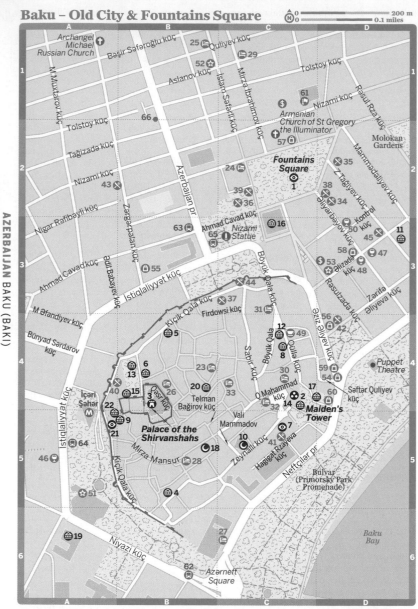

difficulties, with some exhibits awkwardly placed on sloping or curving surfaces.

World's Second-Tallest Flagmast GIANT FLAG (Map p202; Dövlət Bayrağı Meydanı) A gigantic flag flaps above the Bulvar's southern tip, hoisted on a 162m flagpole that was the world's tallest when erected in September 2010. Just eight months later it was superseded by a competitor in Dushanbe, Tajikistan. You can stroll around but not climb the huge base-mound.

Baku – Old City & Fountains Square

Crystal Hall ARCHITECTURE
(Map p202; Yeni Bulvar) It's squat and hardly beautiful but at night this diamond-faceted sports and concert venue twinkles mysteriously across the bay in subdued colours. In 2012 it hosted the most lavish Eurovision Song Contest ever held, and what was then the biggest international happening to have been held in Azerbaijan.

Baku Eye FERRIS WHEEL
(Şeytan çarxı; Map p202; Bulvar; adult/child AZN5/3; ☺1pm-1am) Officially opened in 2014, this 60m big wheel performs attractive light shows after dark. It spins very slowly, so a ride takes nearly 15 minutes including stops, with a video loop of the structure's construction playing should you tire of the fine bay and city views.

★**Yarat Contemporary Art Centre** GALLERY
(Map p202; www.yarat.az; Europa Park; ☺11am-8pm Tue-Fri & Sun, 11am-11pm Sat; ☐5) FREE Yarat means 'create', a spirit that's in ample evidence in this centre's many thought-provoking installations that don't shy away from socio-political commentary. Even the cafe is inspired, set around a repurposed metalpress rescued as part of the revamping of this former naval factory building.

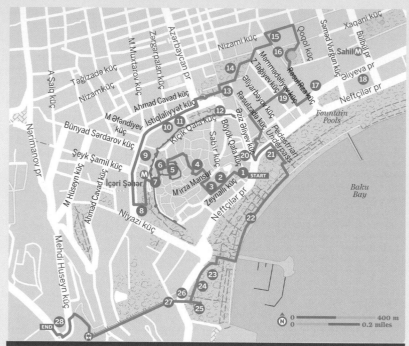

City Walk
Exploring Baku

START MAIDEN'S TOWER
END FLAME TOWERS
LENGTH 4KM; AT LEAST THREE HOURS

From ❶ **Maiden's Tower** (p201) wander colourfully touristy ❷ **Zeynallı küç** to the ❸ **Cumə Mosque** (p203), then pick your way through the Old City's most lived-in ❹ **backstreets** to the ❺ **Palace of the Shirvanshahs** (p202). Peep into a few art galleries, the free ❻ **Museum of Miniature Books** and the tiny ❼ **Coin Museum** (p202). Exit İçəri Şəhər onto grand İstiqlaliyyət küç near the handsomely renovated ❽ **Filarmoniya** (p219) concert hall. Curving northeast you'll pass the noble, late-19th-century ❾ **Baku City Hall**, the equally grand ❿ **Institute of Manuscripts** and ⓫ **İsmailiya Palace**. Beyond lies the Old City's sturdy, castle-style ⓬ **Double Gateway**, while on your left is the statue-inset facade of the ⓭ **Nizami Literature Museum** (p203).

Behind the museum, ⓮ **Fountains Sq** (p203) is a great place for people-watching and cafe life. Wander beneath outdoor chandeliers that hang over pedestrianised shopping street ⓯ **Nizami küç**, cross ⓰ **Molokan Gardens**, pass the boutiques of ⓱ **Rasul Rza küç** and spy the Soviet-acropolis-style ⓲ **Museum Centre**, a former Lenin museum. The tree-lined streets to the northwest are full of pubs, restaurants and century-old 'oil-boom' mansions, including one that houses the ⓳ **Historical Museum** (p206).

Peruse more glitzy ⓴ **boutiques** on Əziz Əliyev küç then use the pedestrian underpass beneath endlessly busy Neftçilər pr to emerge beside the dinky old ㉑ **Puppet Theatre**. Stroll along the ㉒ **Bulvar**, gazing across the Caspian's oil-rainbowed waters and passing ㉓ **Veneziya** where gondolas punt on a small loop of artificial canals. Admire the ㉔ **International Muğam Centre** (p218) and visit the big new ㉕ **Carpet Museum** (p207). Cross back to the ㉖ **Bahram Gur** dragon-slaying statue-fountain and take the free ㉗ **funicular** to reach the huge and impressive ㉘ **Flame Towers** (p211).

Well worth the journey, it's part of a new public space between Flag Sq and the sleek new Aquatics Centre.

Flame Towers Area

For views over the city centre it's worth climbing to the ridge that's so unmistakably marked by Baku's most iconic towers. Access is by bus 18, free funicular or a short sweaty stairway climb (around 15 minutes from the Bulvar).

★ Flame Towers   ARCHITECTURE

(Alov Qüllələri; Map p204; Mehdi Hüseyin küç; light show dusk-midnight; 🚃 6, 18) Completed in 2012, this trio of sinuous blue-glass skyscrapers forms contemporary Baku's architectural signature. The three towers range from 28 to 33 storeys – so huge that they're most impressive seen from a considerable distance, especially at night when they form a vast palate for a light show which interchanges between fire effect, pouring water and the national flag.

Şahidlər Xiyabani   CEMETERY, VIEWPOINT

(Martyr's Lane; Map p202; Gülüstü Park; ⊙ 24hr) The most notable feature of the park that stretches south from the Flame Towers is a sombre row of **grave-memorials** – Bakuvian victims of the Red Army's 1990 attack along with early martyrs of the Karabakh conflict. There's also a memorial to Turkish WWI soldiers, and (more controversially) to the British and Commonwealth troops killed fighting them. The viewpoint beside the **eternal flame** offers splendid panoramas across the bay, city and back towards the Flame Towers.

Fəxri Xiyaban   CEMETERY

(Alley of Honour; Map p204; Parlament pr 7; ⊙ 10am-7pm; 🚃 6) Since 1948 this attractively tree-shaded graveyard has been set aside as the last resting place for Azerbaijan's foremost public figures. Many of the memorials are impressive works of statuary. Former president Heydar Əliyev's tomb here is the first place that any visiting dignitary is likely to be taken to on an official visit to Baku.

Nəriman Nərimanov Statue   STATUE

(Map p204; Nərimanov pr) No, it's not Lenin. This truly gigantic Soviet-era statue actually honours Nəriman Nərimanov, Azerbaijan's first communist-era leader.

East of the City Centre

By public transport, bus 1 from the train station gets you to MIM and on to the Heydar Əliyev Cultural Centre. From there bus 11 continues eastbound to Koroğlu metro station for Abşeron destinations.

**★ Heydar Əliyev
Cultural Centre**   ARCHITECTURE

(Map p202; www.heydaraliyevcenter.az; Heydar Əliyev pr 1; adult/student AZN5/2 plus AZN5 per exhibition; ⊙ 11am-1pm & 2-6pm Mon-Fri, till 5pm Sat; 🚃 11, 24) Vast and jaw-droppingly original, this Zaha Hadid building is a majestic statement of fluid 21st-century architecture forming abstract waves and peaks that seem to melt together. The real delight is simply pondering and photographing the extraordinary exterior from ever-changing angles. The interior hosts concerts and several exhibition spaces including a permanent collection featuring the gifts received by Azerbaijan's presidents.

The entrance is from near the western corner. Bus 11 stops near both southwestern and east sides bus 24 passes a block west of the main entrance.

MIM   GALLERY

(Modern Art Museum; Map p204; www.mim.az; Yusif Səfərov küç 5; adult/student AZN5/2; ⊙ 11am-9pm, last entry 8pm; 🚃 30, 46, 49) This joyous tailor-made gallery creates a wide variety of intimate viewing spaces, in many of which you can recline on leather bean-bag sofas as you contemplate the extensive collection of predominantly post-1980 Azerbaijani art. Some earlier 20th-century canvases also appear, along with three original Picassos. Eastbound buses 30, 46 and 49 from the train station stop across a thundering major road from the gallery. To find the returning buses walk two blocks north.

Azər-İlmə   CARPET FACTORY

(Map p202; ☎ 012-4659037, 050-2509607; www.azerilme.az; Şəmsi Rəhimov küç 2; ⊙ 9am-1pm & 2-6pm; 🚃 63, 88) Hand-woven carpets using wool coloured with vegetable dyes are created before your eyes in this amazingly grand suburban gallery-workshop that includes a museum-like selection of traditional handicrafts. Tours are free with no sales pressure. Ideally call ahead, English spoken.

Take northbound bus 88 to where it turns left in front of Kontinental Supermarket, then walk two blocks right along Ak Həsən Əliyev küç to Kral Wedding Palace. Azər-İlmə is beside that to the south.

Southwest of the City Centre

Bibi-Heybət Mosque   MOSQUE

(Bibiheybət Məscidi; Map p202; Salyan Hwy) Worth a quick stop en route to Qobustan, this 1998 neo-Ottoman-style mosque replaced a 13th-century original demolished by the Soviets 'for road widening' in 1934. The interior is impressive and the rear terrace has curious views across an oil-rig port.

Shikhov Beach · BEACH
(Şıx çimərliyi; Map p202; 🚌124) The nearest beach to central Baku is most fascinating for photographers who want to snap bathers gambolling on the 'sand' with the romantic backdrop of giant offshore oil rigs.

🏃 Activities

Mirvari · BOAT TRIP
(Map p204; standard/deluxe AZN3/10; ☺ during fine weather May-Oct, typically 7-11pm) If the weather is encouraging, you can take a 30-minute pleasure-boat cruise around the bay on a sleek three-level new motor-yacht that includes a cafe and upmarket semi-private sections. The main attraction is watching the city lights, so most departures are at night.

The starting point is the access to the new Sadko pier cafe, which was nearing completion at the time of writing.

🎉 Festivals & Events

Caspian Oil & Gas Show · FAIR
(www.caspianoil-gas.com; ☺ early June) The biggest of many international trade fairs held at **Baku Expo Center** (Baku Ekspo Mərkəzi; www.bakuexpocenter.az; Binə Hwy), beyond the Buta Palace near Suraxanı. The rates for business hotels tend to rise for its duration.

Baku Jazz Festival · MUSIC
(☺ Oct) The world-class Baku Jazz Festival is usually held in October. Headline acts have included Herbie Hancock and Aziza Mustafazadeh.

🛏 Sleeping

Unlike Tbilisi, Baku has no real hostel culture – just a couple of backpacker bunk rooms tucked into private apartments, while a couple more budget hotels offer beds in a few shared rooms. In pricier hotels service is usually friendly and well meaning but often over-familiar.

AirBnB (www.airbnb.com) has limited offerings in Baku and many options are way out of the city centre, but there can be some bargains to be found. Rental agents that focus on the expat market sometimes offer short-stay options.

🛏 Old City

In addition to our recommendations, there are at least half a dozen other lower-midrange minihotels dotted about the Old City with rooms in the AZN50 to AZN80 range, many a little musty or ragged. Booking. com advertises a selection of sweetly unreconstructed room rentals from AZN25.

★ Buta Hotel · GUESTHOUSE $
(Map p208; 📞012-4923475; www.butahotel.com; Qasr küç 16; s/d/tw incl breakfast AZN60/70/80; ❄️ 🛜) This well-kept little gem is entered via a lounge decked with cushions and traditional copperwork. Climb the stairs past etchings and a few antiques to well-presented modern rooms with well-functioning showers, assorted art and clean, wood-effect floors. Breakfast is in the 4th-floor rooftop dining room: superb views but no lift.

Giz Galasi Hotel · HOTEL $
(Map p208; 📞012-4971785, Jabir 050-5246968; www.gizgalasi.com; Mirzə Mansur 34; s/d/tr/ste from AZN50/70/90/110; ❄️ 🖥 🛜 📺) Previously a private guesthouse for BP staff, the good-value Giz Galasi has 16 rooms with high ceilings, kettle, fridge and drinkable centrally filtered tap water. There are phenomenal views from Suite 8 and from the small rooftop area. Unusually there's a lift and a tiny (5m by 2m) pool. Sauna AZN20. English-speaking manager Jabir also acts as facilitator for a few inexpensive homestay rooms and apartments nearby.

The Horizon · HOTEL $
(Map p208; www.thehorizonhotel.az; Old City; s/d from AZN60/65; ❄️ 🛜) The Horizon has unusually spacious rooms with hardwood-effect furniture, framed artworks and very comfy beds. There are no views and some carpets could do with a clean, but at this price it's a great deal in the Old City.

Altstadt Hotel · GUESTHOUSE $
(Map p208; 📞012-4933492; www.altstadt-az. com; Ilyas Əfəndiyev küç 3/2a; s/d/tr incl breakfast AZN40/50/60; ❄️ 🛜) This simple eight-room guesthouse is peaceful and has the cheapest rooms with private bathroom you'll find in the Old City. It has a few rough edges including creaky floors, wobbly shower curtains and some carpet scuffing, but guests can use the hob and kettle in the appealing little bar-styled breakfast room.

★**Sultan Inn**   BOUTIQUE HOTEL **$$**
(Map p208; ☑012-4372305; www.sultaninn.com;
Böyük Qala küç 20; s/d AZN129/153.40; ✳☎)
This luxurious 11-room boutique hotel hits a
fine balance between opulent elegance, cosy
comfort and trendy modernism. The perfect-
ly central Old City location is a great plus and
the restaurant spies down upon the Maiden's
Tower.

Museum Inn   BOUTIQUE HOTEL **$$**
(Map p208; ☑012-4971522; www.museuminn.az;
Q Mahammad küç 3; s/d from AZN110/130; ✳☎)
Selling points of this eight-room hideaway
are the Maiden's Tower views, the vine-
draped rooftop, and the playful Disney-
Tuscan interior with lashings of ironwork
and stone cladding. Rooms come with stripy
wallpaper and rugs on cork floors, but beware
that two of them are windowless. No lift.

★**Shah Palace Hotel**   HERITAGE HOTEL **$$$**
(Map p208; ☑012-4921044; www.shahpalace.az;
Qoşa Qala 47; s/d AZN160/180) Entering this up-
market charmer gives a little of the frisson
of arriving in a fairy-tale Middle Eastern pal-
ace. The four-storey colonnaded courtyard is
filled with birdsong and retains historic well-
shafts from which archaeological finds have
been kept. Rooms are liable to overload the
senses with all the gilt and brocade, but if it's
glitz you want, this place is hard to pass up.
 There's a small sauna and splendid
hamam (bathhouse). Paying by credit card
costs 18% extra.

Four Seasons Baku   HOTEL **$$$**
(Map p208; www.fourseasons.com/baku; Neftchilar
pr 77; r from AZN370; ✳@☎⛲) This majestic flower-filled Beaux-Arts palace fits
perfectly with central Baku's nouveau-
Parisian self image, while the indulgent pool
and spa feel more Roman.

🛏 City Centre

★**Baku Palace Hotel & Hostel**   HOTEL **$**
(Map p208; ☑012-5961071; www.bakupalacehotel.
com; Islam Safarli 23; dm/s/d/tr US$18/48/52/56)
Far and away the best hostel in Baku, this
large converted luxury apartment has oodles
of communal sitting space with chandeliers,
sofas and even a piano. The shared kitchen
offers free tea and coffee and a small courtyard is handy for storing bicycles.
 Big four-bed dorms with private bath-
roooom have good showers but no lockers
and only one key per room. The hostel is

upstairs behind an unassuming old stone
facade.

Hotel Amber   HOTEL **$**
(Map p204; www.amberhotel.az; Cəfər Cabbarlı 29;
s/d from AZN60/70; ✳☎) Get boutique-style
rooms for budget prices at this 22-room discovery near Nizami metro station. Even the
standard rooms are plush and sizeable; the
more expensive 'luxe' rooms add double balconies but are more susceptible to road noise.

Hotel Hale Kai   HOTEL **$$**
(Map p208; ☑012-5965056; www.hotelhalekai.
com; Mirzə Ibrahimov küç 18; r incl breakfast
AZN70-120; ✳☎) Smart, central, American-
owned 23-room hotel with decor inspired
by Frank Lloyd Wright and featuring
Modigliani-style paintings by a Georgian
artist. Rooms are big and even the smaller
ones come with kitchenette. The small lob-
by bar has an art deco vibe.

Azcot Hotel   GUESTHOUSE **$$**
(Map p208; ☑012-4972507; www.azcothotel.
com; Nigar Rəfibəyli küç 38b; s/d from AZN80/85;
✳☎) In a fabulously central 1885 mansion, period settees, large Chinese vases
and tasteful landscape paintings make
the bright new corridors feel homely. The
spacious rooms have kettles and minibars.
But don't expect a big business hotel; the
experience is more like having a room in a
five-storey private mansion.
 Full English breakfast available as well as
buffet.

🛏 Train Station Area

Hotel Guesthouse Inn   GUESTHOUSE **$**
(Map p204; ☑012-4934167; www.guesthouse
baku.com/; Azadlıq pr 16/21; dm/s/d AZN22/47/52)
A couple of the nine comfortable if no-
nonsense rooms are sold 'per bed' as a
pleasant alternative to a hostel dorm. There
is a small but well-equipped shared kitche-
sitting room where guests can meet each
other. The tiny reception works 24 hours.
 The guesthouse entrance is hidden off
Azazliq pr in an inner courtyard.

Landmark Hotel   BUSINESS HOTEL **$$$**
(Map p204; ☑012-4652000; www.thelandmark
hotel.az; Nizami küç 90a; d/ste AZN215/239, break-
fast per person AZN23; ✳@☎⛲) Stunning
views complement suave decor softened with
patchwork bedboards and cobble-tiled bath-
rooms with giant rainhead showers. The art
collection is worthy of a gallery, and a whole

floor of the tower is given over to a gym and infinity pool with more great views. Check in on the 19th floor.

Bus Station

Komfort Inn
HOTEL $

(Hotel Comfort Inn; Map p202; www.comfortinn hotel.az; Main Bus Station; r incl breakfast from AZN40; ❇☂; ☐16, 37, 96) The bus station is miles from town so it's worth considering sleeping here if you have an early morning bus to catch. This once-stylish hotel, entered from the bus station's 5th floor, is very slightly worn but fully equipped and great value costing little more than a hostel if you share a twin room.

East of City Centre

There are many new hotels in the area known as Montin (eastern Gənclik) and around Nəriman Nərimanov metro station. Their proximity to the Heydar Əliyev Mərkəzi might sound like a plus, but beware that you'll be over 3km east of the Old City with limited strolling options and unforgiving traffic congestion to deal with.

Southern Bulvar Area

Several hotels in Bayil are reasonably handy for the southern boulevard once you've found an underpass beneath the unforgiving coastal highway.

Hotel Riviera
BOUTIQUE HOTEL $$

(Map p202; ☑012-4911010; www.riviera.az; Qurban Abassov 1; s/d/ste from AZN80/100/150; ☐5) Two-dozen floral rooms with interesting shapes and plenty of decorative arches crown a site whose wide-ranging restaurant forms several layered terraces overlooking Baku Bay. Sea-view rooms cost extra.

BLESSED BREAD

If you look behind any apartment block, you're likely to see bags of discarded stale bread hanging on trees or hooks, separate from the domestic trash. That's because bread is considered holy and can't be binned or even placed on the ground, leaving superstitious Azeris with a disposal problem. Eating bread with someone is considered to seal a bond of friendship. If you drop a piece of bread on the ground, it's good form to kiss it as an apology!

East Legend Hotel
HOTEL $$

(Map p202; ☑012-4916717; www.eastlegent.az; Xanlar küç 38, Bayil; s AZN60-75, d AZN70-85; ❇☂✖; ☐5) More guesthouse than hotel, this professionally managed little place crams in warmly comfy rooms, pseudo-antique elements, gym and sauna plus a tiny swimming pool in the central quadrangle. Baku Bay views are memorable from the rooftop restaurant.

It's on a quiet leafy street one short block west of Crown Hotel, accessible by southbound bus 5.

Eating

Baku is a culinary treat. Dinner prices can be high but good midrange restaurants typically offer weekday lunch-deal menus for AZN10 or less. Some budget restaurants have full meals for AZN5. Always check before ordering tea: in some lounge-style places a tea-and-jams set might cost AZN30.

Old City & Fountains Square

Firuzə
AZERBAIJANI, INTERNATIONAL $

(Map p208; ☑012-4934934; Əliyarbəyov küç 28a; mains AZN4-10.50, fish mains AZN9-22, beer from AZN2.80, fresh fruit juices AZN4.50; ☉11am-2am; ❇) Fountains Sq's secret subterranean budget favourite is an unusually attractive stone-walled basement draped in local carpets with table cloths embroidered in a similar style. Good air-con and a nonsmoking section add further appeal to a phenomenally wide-ranging menu of Azerbaijani and international favourites.

Kafe Araz
AZERBAIJANI $

(Map p208; İslam Səfərli küç 3; snacks 80q-AZN5, mains AZN5-20, beer from AZN2.30; ☉24hr) This popular fair-weather meeting point occupies a shaded, open-air terrace on the edge of Fountains Sq. It's great for outdoor beers or generous AZN7 portions of fruit-and-lamb *ənənəvi plov*.

Sehrli Tandir
AZERBAIJANI $

(Map p208; Kiçik Qala; mains AZN4-6, qutab/ləvəngi AZN1/10; ☉9am-11pm; ❇) Enter this cabin-restaurant past a flaming clay oven in which fresh bread, *ləvəngi* (stuffed shicken or fish casserole) and *qutab* (Azeri stuffed pancakes) are baked. The two cosy dining rooms are ideal for all-day Azeri breakfasts and also serve a range of *yeməkxana* classics such as *piti* (stew), dolma (rice wrapped in leaves), *buğlama* (steamed stew) etc. Tea by the glass AZN1.

★**Mayak 13**   FUSION **$$**
(Map p208; https://instagram.com/mayak_13; Kiçik
Qala 54; mains AZN8-22, sturgeon AZN32, beer/
wine/coffee from AZN5/10/5; ◷noon-10.30pm;
❄✿) If you liked Altay Sadikhzade's cartoon-
esque work at MIM, you'll adore his eccentric
Mayak 13 cafe designs. Marvelously absurd
rope-tied abstracts represent ripped sails and
intersperse a gamut of nautical bric-a-brac.
Merrily naive lighthouses, landscapes and
portraits splatter bare stone walls. The small
selection of beautifully prepared Azer-Euro
fusion dishes are classily served but be pre-
pared for nouveau-cuisine sized portions.

★**Paris Bistro**   FRENCH **$$**
(Map p208; ☑012-4048215; www.parisbistro.az;
Zərifə Əliyeva pr; mains AZN12-25, snacks AZN3-15,
coffee/water/wine from AZN3/2/6; ◷24hr; ❄✿)
It's hard to believe you're more than a few
metres from the Champs-Élysées in this perfectly pitched French masterpiece. It hits all
the right Parisian notes down to the plane
trees which curve out from an ever-busy park-
facing street terrace. Waiters in white aprons
busy themselves delivering garlic escargots,
scallops in pastis or flaming creme brulée.

Reduced menu after 11pm. Coffee and
snacks anytime.

Cafe City   INTERNATIONAL **$$**
(Map p208; www.cafecity.az; İslam Səfərli küç
1a; mains AZN9-17, beer/coffee/cocktails from
AZN2.80/2.90/6; ◷9am-midnight, to 2am Fri &
Sat; ❄✿) Fashion-conscious without undue
pretensions, Cafe City adds tasteful carved
screenwork to three elegant old-Baku build-
ings, including branches at **Sahil** (Map p204;
Rəşid Behbudov küç 8) and **Statistika** (Map
p204; İnşaatçılar pr 117). The picture menu of-
fers a mouthwatering array of international
cuisine and there's an AZN8 breakfast deal.
The original location has an in-demand sum-
mer terrace just off Fountains Sq.

Cizz-Bizz   AZERBAIJANI, INTERNATIONAL **$$**
(Map p208; ☑012-5055001; www.facebook.com/
cizzbizzoldcity; Kiçik Qala küç 114; mains AZN6.60-
11 plus AZN3.30 garnish, coffee/cocktails from
AZN3/6; ◷9am-2am daily, kitchen to 10pm; ❄)
Stone floors, hanging flower baskets, a shady
terrace and contrived but well-thought-out
attempts at old-world decor all combine to
make spaciously open Cizz-Bizz an under-
standable magnet for Old City tourists. The
food covers a range of Azerbaijani bases and
adds alternatives including tempura, trout,
and chicken in white-wine sauce.

Kutabs (Azeri-filled pancakes; AZN1)
come in five varieties.

Terrace Garden   AZERBAIJANI, INTERNATIONAL **$$**
(Floor 3; Map p208; Sultan Inn, Böyük Qala küç 20;
mains AZN11-25, beer from AZN3.50; ◷noon-10pm,
drinks till 11pm; ❄✿) An unusually wide and
high-quality selection of Azerbaijani classics
along with European options and offbeat cre-
ations served on a comfortable glass-walled
rooftop looking across to the Maiden's Tower.

There's a stylised fireplace pyramid beside
the bar.

Zakura   JAPANESE **$$**
(Map p208; ☑012-4981818; www.zakura.az; Əliza-
də küç 9; mains from AZN7; ◷11.30am-10.30pm;
❄✿) While Baku has more upmarket Japanese options, Zakura combines stylish
simplicity with great-value food. The AZN0
weekday lunch deal is one of Baku's foremost
dining bargains.

Ali & Nino Cafe   INTERNATIONAL, CAFE **$$**
(Map p208; ∠ Iağiyev küç 24b; meals AZN5.50-14, cof-
fee/cocktails from AZN1.90/5; ◷9am-11pm; ❄✿)
Just off Fountains Sq, this small, split-level
cafe uses sepia portrait photos to evoke Baku
of the WWI era of the eponymous novel by
Gurban (Kurban) Said. A picture menu spans
a gamut of styles from Georgian to Mexican.
Good, inexpensive coffee and cocktails too.

Adams Curries/Panchos   INDIAN **$$**
(Map p208; www.facebook.com/adams.curries;
Aliyarbeyov 12; mains AZN8-15, rice AZN3-8, beers
AZN2-4; ◷11am-1am; ❄) Despite scrappy
decor and a misleading sign ('Panchos
Mexican'), the attraction here is excellent
Indian food. It's a longstanding stalwart of
the Baku expat scene with regular Saturday
night curry buffets.

Muğam Club   AZERBAIJANI **$$$**
(Map p208; ☑012-4924085; Heqiqet Rzayeva küç
9; meals/beers from AZN20/5, kebabs AZN15-20;
◷11am-11pm) This historic two-storey car-
avanserai wraps its stone walls around a
colourful courtyard featuring two dwarf fig
trees and a trickling fruit fountain. It's very
photogenic and the Azerbaijani food is good
but prices are steep and this is a place that's
squarely aimed at feasting groups rather
than individuals or couples.

Some evenings from 8pm there's a dinner
show (adds 15% to your bill). This might be
wailing Muğam or an impressive cabaret
showcasing various Caucasian musical and
dance styles. Book ahead.

AZERBAIJAN BAKU (BAKI)

Paul's STEAK $$$
(Map p208; ☑ 055-5200092; www.pauls-baku.
com; Zərgəpalan küç; sausage/steak from
AZN14.50/22.50, beers AZN4.50-7; ☺ 6pm-late Mon-
Sat; ☎) It's inconspicuous, unpretentious and
the menu is short. But if you want perfectly
cooked, high-quality steak, sausages or pork
ribs at down-to-earth prices this German-
Austrian run yard-garden can't be bettered.
Excellent Weissbier on tap too. For winter
there's a wooden cottage area inside, in sum-
mer much seating is outdoors shaded by
plane trees. Reservations advised.

✖ Central Baku

As well as the following options, there are
numerous high-quality eateries in the JW
Marriott Absheron Hotel (Map p204; www.
marriott.com; Azadlıq Sq 674), modernist cafes
in the fashionable if rather soulless wind
tunnel of the new **Port Baku dining strip**
(Map p204; www.portbaku-dining.az/en; Fashion
Ave) as well as a big food court plus restau-
rants at **Park Bulvar Mall** (Map p204; www.
parkbulvar.az; Bulvar; ☺ 10am-midnight; ✱).

Bakı Ailəvi Restoran AZERBAIJANI $
(Map p204; 28 May küç 74a; mains AZN1.50-5;
☺ 10am-midnight; ✱☎) Of numerous inex-
pensive eateries dotted along the southern
edge of Səməd Vurğun Gardens, the Bakı
wins hands down on visual appeal with its
red, white and gilt vaulting. Weekday soup-
salad-main-drink lunches (AZN5) are gener-
ous and decent quality.

Baku Roasting Company CAFE $
(Map p202; www.bakuroasting.com; Ələskər Ələk-
bərov 12; coffee AZN3-5.40, cakes AZN5, lunch AZN9;
☺ 9am-9pm Tue-Sun, 9am-5pm Mon; ✱☎; Ⓜ Elm-
lər Akademiyası) This low-key American-style
cafe serves Baku's best coffee along with
bagels, breakfast burritos and a soup-
sandwich lunch combo. It's somewhat out-
side the city centre in the main student area.

50 Qapiq CENTRAL ASIAN $
(Map p204; Salatın Əsgərova küç 160; plov AZN3, tea
AZN0.25; ☺ 24hr) Feel like you're in a Bukhara
backstreet in this buzzing, all-male hang-out
for big platefuls of Uzbek-style *plov* (yellow
rice with carrot and lamb) served with cop-
per mini-flagons of *ayran* (lightly salted
yoghurt and water), 25q *armudi* (glasses)
of tea or AZN1.50 glasses of fresh-squeezed
pomegranate juice. *Piti, buğlama,* kebabs
and *pomidor-yumurta* (scrambled eggs
and tomatoes) also available. No dish costs
more than AZN4.

Nənəmin AZERBAIJANI, TAKEAWAY $
(Map p204; Süleyman Rəhimov küç; pirojki/qutab
from 20/30q; ☺ 8am-8pm) Queue at this take-
away window for excellent fresh-cooked *qutab.*

Entrée CAFE, BAKERY $
(Map p204; www.facebook.com/Entree.az; Dilarə
Əliyeva küç; snacks/meals from AZN2.50/7; ☺ 8am-
10pm; ✱☎) Entrée is the most appealing
of Baku's flourishing new trend towards
bakery-cafes. The big, suave Dilarə Əliyeva
branch is its flagship with a glass-walled
kitchen, comfy seating and excellent coffee.

★ Şirvanşah Muzey-Restoran AZERBAIJANI $$
(Map p204; ☑ 050-2420903; www.facebook.com/
shirvanshakh; Salatın Əsgərova küç 86; mains
AZN5-15; ☺ noon-11pm; ✱) On an unassuming backstreet, this superb discovery started
life as a 19th-century bathhouse but is now
a veritable ethnographic museum of handicrafts and knick-knacks that's sometimes
used as a film set. Over a dozen rooms are
themed to different historical eras from rustic craftsman's workshops to Soviet *apara-
chik's* office. The reliable Azerbaijani food
covers a similarly wide range.

Trin Trava RUSSIAN $$
(Map p204; ☑ 050-4712023, 012-4939904; www.
trin-trava.com; Xaqani küç 90; mains AZN7-14,
fish dishes AZN9-18; ☺ 12.30-10.30pm; ✱☎)
One room is styled like an *izba* (Siberi-
an cottage), another designed to resem-
ble a 1950s Soviet apartment, and the
food takes creative Slavic twists with
offerings including 'Hussar' (honey-
glazed salmon) and 'Trembling Bunny' (rab-
bit in sour cream). Next door its Blini pub
serves filled pancakes (AZN1 to AZN3) with
glasses of *kvas* (50q).

Dafne TURKISH, CAFE $$
(Map p204; www.facebook.com/dafnebydalida; 3rd
fl, Nizami küç 97d; mains AZN9-16, beer/cocktails/
coffee from AZN3.50/6/4.50; ☺ noon-2.30am)
Dafne is a suave but not exclusive lounge-
cafe for fine Turkish food and expertly mixed
cocktails, with most seating spread across a
large open-air rooftop. The entrance is easy
to miss.

La Strada Trattoria ITALIAN $$
(Map p204; www.lastrada.az; Dilarə Əliyeva küç;
pasta AZN8-15.50, bread AZN1.50, mains from
AZN12.50; ☺ noon-11.30pm; ✱) This relaxed
Italian restaurant produces scrumptious
pastas and thin-crust pizzas. Wine boxes,
herb jars and checkerboard floors bring life
to its high, whitewashed vaults, rattled now

and again by metro trains rumbling deep beneath. AZN10 weekday menu (noon to 3pm).

Imereti GEORGIAN $$
(Map p204; Xaqani küç; mains AZN7-11, xacapuri 8, wine per L AZN15; ⊙11am-11pm; 🏵) There are several fancier places but this unpretentious little basement remains our favourite inexpensive Georgian restaurant in central Baku. Note that there's a different more upmarket Imereti Restaurant on Raslu Rza küç.

Sahil AZERBAIJANI $$$
(Map p204; 📞012-4048212; www.sahil-dining.az; Bulvar; mains AZN10-40, kebabs AZN8-26; ⊙noon-10.30pm) Faultless Azerbaijani cuisine in a suave but relaxed setting right on the Bulvar. If you're on a budget, just sip slowly on an AZN8 margarita.

Chinar ASIAN FUSION $$$
(Map p204; 📞012-4048211; www.chinar-dining. az; Şövkət Ələkpərova küc 1; snacks AZN7-19, mains AZN14-44, beers/cocktails from AZN4.30/9.25; ⊙noon-2am, reduced kitchen after 11pm; 🏵) This fashion-conscious lounge-restaurant sports a 'theatre kitchen' producing top sophisticated dishes from yoghurt-mint tandoori chicken to fillet steak with foie gras. But the main focus is imaginative Asian-fusion food.

✖ Southern Bulvar

Mangal STEAK, AZERBAIJANI $$$
(Map p202; 📞012-5051011; www.facebook.com/ Mangal.Steak.House1; Mirzə Mustafayev 3; steak AZN35-100, Azerbaijani food AZN10-250; ⊙10am-2am) The main section is a vast hall steakhouse designed to feel like an outdoor village square. Hidden behind is a second stone-walled restaurant serving Azerbaijani cuisine and playing live Muğam music nightly. There's also a 'secret' terrace facing the giant flagmast. Top-notch but pricey.

✖ Batamdar

Teleqüllə INTERNATIONAL $$$
(Map p202; 📞012-5370808; www.telequlle.az; Ak Abbaszadə küç 2; mains AZN20-50, kebabs AZN10-25, small/large beers AZN6/8; ⊙11am-midnight; 🏵) Dining at this revolving restaurant is the only way to gain access to Baku's iconic Soviet-era TV Tower. Views are sensational and the upscale menu includes sturgeon in pomegranate and tenderloin in cognacgorgonzola sauce. Reservations are usually required. Beware: non-diners are charged AZN30 per person minimum fee for a drink, tea or coffee.

Take bus 63 from the Flame Towers to the Zoological Institute stop, then walk seven minutes steeply down to the entrance – good views from the approach and terrace.

🍷 Drinking & Nightlife

Expat bars are concentrated to the south and west of Fountains Sq between Tolstoy küç and Əlizadə küç. For much cheaper beer (from AZN1) try the bars on Qoqol küç around the Aslanov junction, but beware of basement 'Disko Klubs', which are predominantly seen as prostitute pick-up spots. Plush new lounge bars and super-expensive tea parlours are scattered far more widely out into the suburbs.

🍸 Old City & Fountains Square

★**Old School Cafe** BAR, CAFE
(Map p204; www.facebook.com/oldschool.cafe andshop; Topçubaşov küç; beer/vodka/tea from AZN2/3.20/1.60; ⊙noon-2am) A wonderfully off-beat hang-out for intellectual young Bakuvians, the sign is a typewriter, the interior decked with old clocks and cameras. Although there are occasional live concerts, this is more a place for earnest conversation over a *kəklikotu* (mountain herb) tea

Qadım Bakı TEA HOUSE
(Old Baku Tea House; Map p208; 📞012-4370818; Qüllə küç 22; tea AZN20; ⊙11am-midnight) This cosy stone cavern is smothered in carpets and lit by colourful Moroccan lamps plus daylight filtered through the stained glass of a few *shebeke* windows. Some snacks are served (*qutab, düşbərə* or dumplings, etc) but the main point is to linger over a classic spread of tea, jams and *paxlava* (baklava). An AZN20 set serves three people.
Shisha (waterpipes) cost AZN25 for up to two hours' smoking. No alcohol.

Otto PUB
(Map p208; www.facebook.com/ottoefes; Əlizadə küç 3; small/large beers AZN3/4; ⊙noon-3am) With bare stone vault-walls and big windows that slide open to allow a cooling breeze, Otto morphs from pub into low-key nightclub as the evening progresses. It's lively, fun and sometimes raucous, but late at night heavy-handed bouncers might refuse entry to unaccompanied males.

Brewery MICROBREWERY
(Map p208; İstiqlaliyyət küç 31d; small/large beers AZN2/3; ⊙11am-11pm or last customer) Baku's brewpub creates three varieties of very

acceptable ale, served in a stone-vaulted basement with heavy wooden furniture. Germanic and international meals (meals AZN12 to AZN 20, T-bone AZN30) are available.

Yacht Club Terrace — WINE BAR
(Yaxt Klub; Map p204; Bulvar; beer/wine from AZN5/6; 🛜) Push politely past security behind Azneft Sq, walk down the pier and around a squat glass cylinder of unmarked hotel to find this open terrace that stands on stilts above Baku Bay. Watch the Geneva-style water fountain and admire the city lights as you sip decent wines that are far cheaper by glass than by bottle. Excellent, 'molecular-organic' cuisine (mains AZN11 to AZN35) too.

Finnegans — PUB
(Map p208; Əlizadə küç; beer/Guinness from AZN5/7; 🕙11am-1am) Old faithful Anglo-Irish bar with big wrought-iron lamps in high vaults and some of the best live pub music in town.

Wednesday nights are especially good here. If things aren't hopping or you want a cheaper beer, there are numerous alternatives within stumbling distance.

Room — WINE BAR
(Map p208; www.facebook.com/RoomFineArtWine Dine; Əliyarbəyov küç 10; 🕙5pm-very late) This cosy, fashion-conscious place straddles wine bar, lounge-pub and cafe, appealing to upwardly mobile 20-somethings with DJ nights on Wednesdays and Fridays.

🍷 Central Baku

Secrets — PUB
(Map p204; Qoqol küç; beers from AZN1; 🕙noon-midnight) Secrets is the most appealing of several bars hereabouts that serve AZN1 beers, though others open later.

Bar 360 — BAR
(Map p204; 25th fl, Hilton Hotel, Azadlıq pr 1b; 🕙5pm-2am) Upmarket rotating bar with ever-changing views across the city. Check for changing happy-hour deals. Currently all cocktails cost AZN11 before 8pm.

Pasifico — LOUNGE
(Map p204; 📞012-4048212; www.facebook.com/ PASIFICOBAKU; 3rd fl, Bulvar; 🕙bar 6-11pm, club 11pm-3am Fri & Sat) Sea-view lounge turns club after 11pm on weekend nights with relatively mellow DJ beats.

E11even — LOUNGE
(Map p204; www.eleven.az; 11th fl, Park Inn Hotel; 🕙6pm-midnight Sun-Thu, 6pm-3am Fri & Sat) Dressy lounge-club.

☆ Entertainment
For extensive what's-on listings see www. bakucitylife.com.

Live Music
The Muğam Club (p215) often provides a cabaret of traditional music and Caucasian dancing to accompany your meal. Mangal (p217) has Muğam. Many other upmarket restaurants, typically those at beaches or in large suburban gardens, present Azeri pop stars singing at full blast. Many Westerners consider this more like punishment than entertainment.

International Muğam Centre — CONCERT VENUE
(Map p204; Neftçilər pr 9) This stylish new concert hall hosts a sparse schedule of concerts in an eclectic variety of styles.

THE INSIDE EDGE

Locals that you meet beyond the very centre of Baku are often fascinated by foreigners. Accepting invitations for long chats over tea can be a great way to gain insight to local youth culture, which is very much group based, if frequently sex-segregated. However, as in many a big, vibrant city, getting in touch with the 'real' cultural Baku can take some effort. The city's more interesting happenings tend to be under-publicised with much information spread by word of mouth. Though only in local languages, websites such as Citylife.az (www.citylife.az) and more off-beat MyEvents (http://myevents.az) are useful starting points. There are several innovative Facebook groups: BagBaku (p221) has various activities aimed at helping foreigners meet English-speaking locals for conversation and shared events including free/inexpensive city walks. Camping Azerbaijan (📞051-8868380; Facebook Camping Azerbaijan) also brings together locals and foreigners for weekend hiking getaways, mostly to the Quba mountain villages. BakuExpats (www. facebook.com/BakuExpatCommunity) is mostly aimed at longer term residents and is useful for answering questions about life in the city.

Le Chateau
JAZZ

(Map p208; www.facebook.com/lechateaubaku; Islam Safarli küç; ☺5pm-2am) Most evenings live jams (typically 9pm to 11pm) form a nonchalant backdrop to the lively wave of conversation in this smokily informal dive bar. No admission, cheap beer (from AZN1.50).

Baku Jazz Center
JAZZ

(Map p204; ☑012-4939941; http://jazzcenter.jazz.az; Rəşid Behbudov küç 19; admission AZN8-20; ☺7pm-midnight Tue-Sun, live music from 9pm most nights) The venue is a somewhat staid dining hall with mostly table seating, but the quality of the live performances is often very high. Although focussed on jazz, you might find a variety of other styles on offer, especially when a lack of backing band forces singers to use a pre-recorded backing track. Generally no tickets are sold – the music charge is added to your final bill.

Elektra/Enerji
DANCE, EVENTS

(Map p202; ☑012-4048208; www.saffron.az/en/restaurants/enerji; National Flag Sq) This new club and events venue opened in 2015 with a performance by rapper DMX. It's the latest development in the repurposed former naval dockyard that promises to form a social hub at the southern extension of the Bulvar.

Theatre & Classical Music

Baku has a vibrant arts scene. The theatre season runs from mid-September to late May. Tickets for various venues are sold at ticket booths **opposite Dom Soviet** (Teatri və Konsert Biletləri; Map p204; Üzeyir Hacıbəyov küç; ☺10am-2pm & 3-6pm) and on **Rəsulzadə küç** (Teatri və Konsert Biletləri; Map p208; Əlizadə küç 4; ☺10.30am-3pm & 4-6.30pm).

Opera & Ballet Theatre
OPERA, BALLET

(Azərbaycan Dövlət Akademik Opera və Balet Teatrı; Map p204; ☑012-4931651; www.tob.az; Nizami küç 95; ☺mid-Sep–May) This 1910 theatre has a classically grand interior albeit slightly in need of refreshing. It produces a mixed bag of shows, some grandiose, others more mundane repertory performances, but most are easy enough to follow without local-language ability.

Mime Theatre
MIME

(Dövlət Pantomima Teatrı; Map p204; ☑012-4414756; pantomima.az; Azadlıq pr 49; tickets AZN5) Superbly creative mime performances in a tiny theatre fashioned from a former chapel. Generally weekends only.

Filarmoniya
CONCERT VENUE

(Azərbaycan Dövlət Filarmoniyası; Map p208; ☑012-4972901; www.filarmoniya.az; Istiglaliyyat küç) With its twin Mediterranean-style towers, this 1910 Baku landmark was originally built as an oil-boom-era casino. The interior is as impressive as its architecture and there's an eclectic, if unpredictable, concert program.

Other Entertainment

Park Bulvar Mall
ENTERTAINMENT CENTRE

(Map p204; Bulvar; bowling alley per person per game AZN10 ; ☺bowling alley 10am-2am) On this mall's 4th floor there's a bowling alley and multiplex cinema showing some films in 3D.

🛍 Shopping

Pedestrianised Nizami küç, commonly still known by its Soviet-era moniker of Torgovaya (Trade St), remains a popular strolling/shopping area. Where else in the world will you find outdoor chandeliers? But more exclusive are the boutiques along the Bulvar, southern Rəsul Rza küç, western 28 May küç and Əziz Əliyev küç. Big 21st-century shopping centres include Park Bulvar Mall, 28 Mall and Port Baku Mall.

Carpets & Souvenirs

Carpets, along with Azeri hats and traditional copperware, might prove cheaper purchased in the provinces but they are conveniently sold though Ali Baba–esque shops around Baku's İçəri Şəhər, especially along Zeynallı küç. These are great places to browse with very little sales pressure. Beware that antique carpets cannot be taken out of Azerbaijan and any new carpet bigger than 600 sq cm will need an export permit. As long as the carpet doesn't look old, that's a relatively easy formality organised within 24 hours through the Carpet Museum (p207) but certification costs AZN46 (or half price if you're prepared to wait a week). No service on Wednesdays or Sundays. Dealers often organise permits for their clients.

Several stands in the Old City sell a selection of (often tacky) souvenirs, along with old Soviet-era badges, medals and buttons. More of the same are available in subterranean shops beneath the passage leading east from Fountains Sq.

Caviar

During WWI British soldiers found caviar to be 'cheaper than jam'. These days officially packed 113g pots of 'legal' caviar sold at **Xəzər Balıqı** (Map p204; Xaqani küç)

BAKU BLING

In the past decade as oil revenues have burgeoned, so too has the ostentation of Baku's nouveau riche. A premonition of Baku's drive towards unbridled luxury was the conversion of the once-quirky old Karvan Jazz Club into a **Dolce & Gabbana** (Map p208; Əziz Əliyev küç 4-6; ⊙ 11am-9pm) boutique. Across Əziz Əliyev küç you'll find **Tiffany** (Map p208; Əziz Əliyev küç 1c) and **Bvlgari** (Map p208; Əziz Əliyev küç 1a; ⊙ 11am-8pm), with Dior Accessories around the corner in a sturdy 1909 stone building. Next door, the **Tom Ford** (Map p208; www.tomford.com/men/; Neftçilər pr 105) male couture store occupies a classic mansion that once hosted Charles de Gaulle during a secret 1944 stopover en route to Moscow during WWII.

Ten years ago, potholed roads were largely the domain of battered old Ladas. But today a **Rolls Royce** (Map p208; www.rolls-roycemotorcars-baku.az; Əlizadə küç 5; ⊙ 9am-6pm Mon-Fri, 10am-4pm Sat) dealership now fills the century-old former Gorodskoi Bank building with its splendid 'dripping face' stonework. **Baku Lamborghini** (Map p204; www.facebook.com/BakuLamborghini; Parlament pr 78; ⊙ 10am-7pm) sits at the base of the Flame Towers, while Ferrari and Bentley have showrooms close to **Port Baku Mall** (Map p204; www.portbakumall.az; Neftçilər pr 151; ⊙ 10am-10pm). With Alexander McQueen and Stella McCartney boutiques, Port Baku has often been cited as the city's foremost luxury mall, though since 2015, department store **Harvey Nicholls** (Map p202; www.harveynichols baku.com; Izmir küç; ⊙ 10am-9pm Mon-Sat, 11am-9pm Sun) might chose to dispute that.

In reality most such boutiques and showrooms are ghostly quiet for most of the time, despite eagerly attentive staff.

cost AZN120/165 for sevruga/beluga. That's barely a third of the price you'd pay in Western Europe. At Baku's central market, **Təzə Bazar** (Map p204; Səməd Vurğun küç), you might find cheaper 'illicit' caviar in the fish section, but quality is harder to assure.

Bookshops

Chiraq Books   BOOKS
(Map p208; 🗷 012-4923289; www.chiraqbookstore.com; Zərgərpalan küç 4; ⊙ 10am-8pm Tue-Sat, 10am-5pm Mon) English-language bookshop with decent range of classics, bestsellers, travel guides and locally relevant titles, and a good souvenir section.

Kitab Evi   BOOKS
(Book House; Map p208; Nigar Rəfibəyli küç 41b (29); ⊙ 11am-7pm Mon-Sat) Stocks detailed Azerbaijan 1:500,000 topographic and road maps (AZN5), slightly dated postcards plus many booklets that would be free if you'd asked at the tourist office.

ⓘ Information

DANGERS & ANNOYANCES

The crime rate is very low. Avoid photography of official buildings and on the metro. Police are unforgiving with jaywalkers (AZN20 fines).

INTERNET ACCESS

Wi-fi is available in the majority of hotels and in numerous cafes with Bakuvians addicted to selfies and Foursquare check-ins. BakCell subscribers can use free wi-fi hotspots around Foun-tains Sq. Internet cafes are often hidden away in basements. For an all-night session pay just AZN2 from midnight to 8am at several places including the following:

PS3 Internet (Map p204; Qoqol küç 22d; per hr 60q; ⊙ 24hr) All-night Internet, hidden up steps between Double Coffee and club Raï.

VIP-Zone (Map p204; Xaqani küç; per hr 80q; ⊙ 24hr) Handy central Internet basement on the north side of Molokan Gardens.

MEDICAL SERVICES

A list of medical service providers appears on the US embassy's website at http://azerbaijan.usembassy.gov/medical_services.html.

MediClub (Map p204; 🗷 012-4970911; www.mediclub.az; Üzeyir Hacibəyov küç 45) Attractively appointed English-speaking clinic. Doctors' consultations from AZN34. Ambulance service available.

MONEY

ATMs Are ubiquitous. Exchange facilities are widespread and don't charge commission. Rate-splits are excellent for US dollars (under 1%), good for euros and competitive for Russian roubles. British pounds are less in demand but can sometimes be changed with around a 4% split.

Moneychangers For the best-value exchange deals try small bank-shops on the southern side of Səməd Vurğun Gardens, which also exchange British pounds and many 'nonstandard' currencies, albeit at poorer rates.

POSTAL SERVICES

Main Post Office (Mərkəzi Poçt; Map p204; Üzeyir Hacibəyov küç 72; ⊙ 8am-8pm Mon-

Fri, 8am-6pm Sat & Sun) Come here for Poste Restante.

TELEPHONE SERVICES

Pay phones are few and far between but mobile-phone shops are ubiquitous.

TOURIST INFORMATION

BagBaku (☑ 051-3703111; www.facebook.com/BagBaku) Informal group to help locals and foreigners meet and socialise.

Tourist Information Office (Map p204; ☑ 012-5985519; www.tourism.az; Üzeyir Hacıbəyov küç 70; ⊙ 9am-1pm & 2-6pm Mon-Fri) Gives away a range of glossy pamphlets and a full-colour *Baku Guide* magazine but don't count on detailed help for testing questions.

ⓘ Getting There & Away

AIR

Baku's **Heydar Əliyev International Airport** (www.airport.az; Bina; 🚌 H1, 116) is the busiest in the South Caucasus, with flights to/from plenty of European, Russian and Central Asian cities, plus Dubai, New York, Qatar, Tehran, Trabzon and Tbilisi. **AZAL** (Azerbaijan Airlines, SW Travel; Map p204; ☑ 012-5988880; www.azal.az; Nizami küç 66-68; ⊙ 8am-8pm) offers domestic flights to Gəncə (AZN31; daily), Naxçıvan (AZN70; four times daily) and Qəbələ (AZN35; Friday and Sunday).

BOAT

The **Caspian Shipping Company** (Map p204; ☑ Vika 055-2665354; www.acsc.az; ⊙ call ahead; 🚌 30, 46, 49) operates services to Turkmenbashi, Turkmenistan, and Aktau, Kazakhstan. While passengers are accepted and each boat has a few cabins, be very aware that these are cargo ships without luxury nor any set timetable. They could run several times weekly, or not at all. And journey times could extend to several days if there's a queue at the arrival dock. For Aktau, flying on SCAT or AZAL is often cheaper overall. Even with a bicycle.

Buying the ferry tickets is a dark art. Start by phoning every morning and again around 3pm until a sailing is confirmed. Get your name on the passenger list for a scheduled boat then, at an arranged time, seek out the far-from-obvious ticket office to pay. It's accessed through guarded gates at the western end of Ağ Şəhər Bulvar. State your business and staff should let you walk the 300m to the office. Vika speaks English and talking to her is your key for success. Using an agency is likely to be an expensive waste of money and time. Most Turkmenbashi-bound ferries currently leave from behind the office. However, most of those bound for Aktau, Kazakhstan, depart from New Baku International Seaport (p226) near Ələt, a massive 75km south of Baku.

BUS & MARSHRUTKA

Apart from minibuses to **Biləsuvar** (Map p204; Bakixanov Underpass, Tbilisi pr), which start from the Baku roundabout where Bus 65 goes under the Bakixanov overpass, most intercity services start from the **main bus station** (Avtovağzal; Map p202; www.bbak.az; Sumqayıt Hwy; Ⓜ Avtovağzal). Big and confusing, it is part shopping mall. Departures are from the 3rd floor but ticket booths (*kassa*) plus various private offices for Iranian and Turkish bus companies are hidden on the 1st floor.

For international routes, prepurchase around two days ahead notably for the following destinations:

İstanbul (US$60 to US$70, 32 to 40 hours, several daily at around noon)

Tehran (AZN40, around 16 hours, 9am)

Tabriz (AZN25, around 11 hours, 9am)

For Tabriz you could alternatively take one of five daily Naxçıvan-bound buses (AZN16, 14 hours, *kassa* 1) and change to a cheap shared taxi at Iranian Julfa.

Overnight routes to Georgia (Marneuli, Lagodekhi or Tbilisi) are available from *kassa* 11 at shorter notice.

Domestically, don't worry prebooking for shorter routes (under five hours). Longer-route tickets might be worth buying an hour ahead. Online bookings are theoretically possible up to 10 days ahead via www.bbak.az but only in Azerbaijani.

BAKU BUS STOPS

Some key stops as they appear on bus sign boards:

➜ **28 May** Loosely interpreted to mean anywhere near the train station.
➜ **Axundov Bağ** A triangular garden just north of İçəri Şəhər.
➜ **Azneft** The big traffic circle directly southwest of the Old City.
➜ **Beş Mərtəbə** Füzuli Sq.
➜ **M xxxx** Suggests a stop near xxxx metro station.
➜ **MUM** Handy for the western side of Fountains Sq.
➜ **Təzə Avtovağzal** Main bus station.
➜ **Vurğun Bağ** Vurğun Gardens, just south of the train station.

LOCAL KNOWLEDGE

FINDING A DRIVER

If funds aren't too limited, it can prove much more enjoyable to visit by chauffeured car. However in Baku, most competent, English-speaking drivers tend to get snapped up by oil companies rather than working in tourism so finding a driver-guide is far from easy.

➡ Ask at hostels rather than at travel agencies.

➡ Enquire through BagBaku (p221).

➡ Head for a shared-taxi stand and engage a driver who would be doing the trip anyway, then pay four times the per-person fare. But don't expect spoken English.

➡ Ask a car-rental company. AzRent (p223) adds AZN20 to the per-day car-rental fee to be chauffeur driven for up to 12 hours.

Approximately hourly services run to:

Gәncә (AZN9, seven hours)
İsmayıllı (AZN4, four hours)
Lәnkәran (AZN5, five hours)
Qırmızı Körpü (Georgian border; AZN10, 10 hours)
Quba (AZN4, 2½ hours) and **Qusar** (AZN4, three hours) for Shahdag
Şәki (AZN7, 6½ hours; mostly via Ağdaş)
Zaqatala (AZN8, eight hours)

Departure gates are flagged on electronic boards and via www.Navigator.az, but accuracy is approximate.

If the bus to your destination is full, still double-check with the driver or ask at kassa 7, which deals separately with timetabled minibuses. If all these are full too, there may still be an untimetabled marshrutka (minibus) from one of the uncovered bays opposite the main departure platforms. These services are essentially the only options for some closer or minor destinations and are especially useful for Şәki as untimetabled minibuses take the prettier route via Qәbәlә, unlike timetabled services.

The main bus station is nearly 10km north of central Baku. From 2016 the nearby glass-pyramid-shaped Avtovağzal metro station should become operational. Meanwhile by bus, the most painless approach is to take bus 37, which runs direct from Azneft via Hyatt/

Statistika. From the city-centre area it's easier to use the very frequent route 65 from bus stops Azneft (Map p208), İçәri Şәhәr (Map p208), MUM (Map p208) or Beş Mәrtәbә (Map p204) but you'll need to change at 20 Yanvar metro station or **Şamaxinka** (Map p202; Moskva pr, previously Tbilisi pr), switching to bus 16, 37 or 96. Those three city buses currently terminate at a parking area within the bus station compound, accessible through a hidden footbridge from the 2nd floor of the bus-station mall. However, a new city bus stand is under construction in what will eventually be the Avtovağzal metro station forecourt.

CAR & TAXI

Shared taxis to Quba, Şamaxı (per seat/car AZN6/24) and Qәbәlә (AZN12/50) leave from Şamaxinka, the junction-terminus of frequent bus route 65.

Driving within Baku is bamboozling but renting your own vehicle makes sense for exploring the hinterland.

Avis (Map p204; ☑ 050-2230248, 012-4975455; www.avis.az; İ Qutqaşınlı 50; cars per day/week/month from US$60/364/825, 4WD from US$125/721/1500; ⊙ 9am-6pm Mon-Fri, 9am-2pm Sat) Reliable car-rental agent. Prices include insurance and collision damage waiver (CDW) with a US$150 deductible. Or pay $10 per day more for zero deductible.

TRAINS DEPARTING BAKU

DESTINATION	VIA	DEPARTS	ARRIVES	FARE (AZN)
Astara	Lәnkәran	11pm	8.55am	8 kupe
Balakәn	Şәki	9.30pm	10.15am	10 kupe
Gәncә	'express'	9am alternate days	3pm	6 seat**
Kharkov (Ukraine)	Xaçmaz	1.33am Tue/Sat	4.30am Thu/Mon	124* kupe
Moscow Kurskaya	Xaçmaz	1.33am Thu	4.15am Sat	148* kupe
Qazax	Gәncә	10.40pm	11.50am	10 kupe
Tbilisi	Gәncә	8.30pm	12.15pm	20/30 platskart/kupe

*exact fares vary by date **day train, no sleeper berths

AzCar (Map p202; ☑ 012-5105173; www.azcar. az; Sultanova 23b) Rental cars from AZN55 per day, minimum two days. Yusif speaks English.

AzRent (Map p204; ☑ 012-5397110; www. azrent.az; İnşaatçılar pr 80) Car rental from AZN40. English spoken.

TRAIN

All overnight trains give you a sleeping berth: *kupe* in a 2nd-class compartment, *platskart* in an open bunk. Bed sheets are included in the modest fare. You'll need your passport both to buy a ticket and to board the train. At the time of research the main train station is undergoing a major redevelopment.

❶ Getting Around

TO/FROM HEYDAR ƏLIYEV INTERNATIONAL AIRPORT

Bus H1 takes around 45 minutes running between the airport's international terminal and the train station. Departures are half-hourly from 7am to 11pm plus a few times through the night. Cost is AZN1.30, which must be loaded onto a BakıKart (p224), available from a vending machine nearby.

Prebooked **Taxi189** (☑189; www.taxibaku. az; ⊘24hr) charges AZN15 to AZN18 to/from central Baku. Unbooked cabs more likely ask AZN30, though you might find a ride for half that by walking to the very back of the airport car park and finding unofficial cars.

PUBLIC TRANSPORT
Bus

City buses cost 20q per ride. For most services you pay cash as you get off. However, the sleek new red buses only accept prepaid BakıKart credit.

Many Baku bus routes are shown in detail on www.gomap.az – click 'Avtobuslar' in the left-hand panel and choose the route. Most are accurate but some are missing, while others have since been changed or discontinued (notably buses 1, 90 and 100)

The Google maps app routefinder works fairly well in Baku and www.niim.az claims to give real-time info about the next bus arriving at any stop, though it often seems unduly pessimistic. Beware that routes seem to change every year or two and the maps don't always stay updated.

City Sightseeing Bus (Map p204; www. city-sightseeing.com/tours/azerbaijan/baku. htm; starts Azadlıq Sq; AZN25; ⊘10am-7pm Apr-Oct) This hop-on, hop-off tourist service runs every 45 minutes on a 15-stop route. In most cases you'd probably do better mixing walking, funicular and the odd taxi if you can forgo the multilingual commentary.

Funicular

Funicular (Funikulyor; ⊘10am-1pm & 2-10pm Tue-Sun) The snazzy little funicular whisks you up from near Çinar Restoran to the Flame Towers area in just three minutes. Time between

Baku Metro

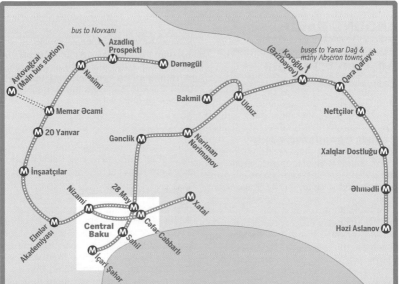

ℹ️ BAKIKART

Since September 2015, Baku has started phasing in a prepaid card system called the BakıKart, which can be purchased at metro stations and at certain bus stops. There are two versions of the card – a plastic one costing AZN2 plus credit that can be reused, and a disposable paper one allowing up to four credits (ie four rides will cost AZN1). For now the system is only used by the metro and the newest red buses, but it is likely that the system will be extended in the future.

---

departures can vary considerably according to custom.

Metro

The metro links the Old City (İçəri Şəhər metro station) via the train station (28 May metro station) with a series of suburban stations, most usefully Koroğlu, Qara Qarayev and Neftçilər metro stations, each with bus connections to certain Abşeron towns. Fares cost 20q per ride regardless of distance: prepay credit onto to a smart card (AZN2 deposit, refundable).

Taxi

BakıTaksi (☏9000; www.bakitaksi.az) The deep-purple London-style cabs are usually Baku's best value and the only ones to use a meter. Flagfall is AZN1, plus 70q per km, dropping to 40/20q per km after 10/20km.

AROUND BAKU

Abşeron Peninsula

☏012

The Abşeron confounds easy definition. Much of the once-agricultural land is blanched by salt lakes and sodden with oil run-off. Platoons of rusty oil derricks fill horizons with abstract metallic 'sculptures'. And wherever you look, new housing is filling up the remaining areas of former sheep pastures and almond groves. Yet despite mesmerising ugliness and a traditionally conservative population, the Abşeron still manages to be Baku's seaside playground. Meanwhile several historic castle towers peep between the *dachas,* fires that inspired Zoroastrian and Hindu pilgrims still burn, and beneath the cultural surface lie some of Azerbaijan's oddest folk beliefs. It's a perversely fascinating place.

For a day's exploration by public transport start from Baku's Koroğlu metro station (south exit) taking bus 184 to its Suraxanı terminus. Having visited the fire temple, continue with bus 104 for 15 minutes, getting off where it turns a right angle to the south. Walk one minute north to an obvious highway bus stop (Heydar Əliyev pr 402). From there bus 136 continues to Mərdəkən and Mir Mövsöm Ziyarətgah, or bus 101 gets you to within 300m of Qala's ethnographic complex. Bus 182 links Qala with Mərdəkən. Return by bus 136 to Koroğlu metro station for bus 217 for Yanar Dağ or bus 204 to Ramana. These leave from the metro station's south exits: use the highway underpass.

Suraxanı

The unique **Suraxanı Fire Temple** (Atəşgah Məbədi; ☏012-4524407; Atamoğlan Rzayev küç; adult/student AZN2/1; ⊙9am-6pm; 🚌184) is an 18th-century fire temple whose centrepiece is a flaming hearth above which arches a pillared stone dome with four side flues. These flues also spit dragon breath...but only on special occasions, notably the four Tuesdays leading up to Novruz. The fire altar sits in a roughly triangular courtyard surrounded by simple stone cells of former devotees with well over a dozen now hosting a well-explained museum. Allow around an hour to see it all.

Although the site was originally a place of worship for Zoroastrians, the fortified complex you see today was built by 18th-century Indian Shiva devotees.

From the bus 184 terminus, cross the rail tracks via the almost disused commuter train station, then turn left and walk three minutes passing a baronial-hall-style cafe-restaurant.

Qala

Qala's windswept village-scape is interesting in itself with several rustic old buildings in various stages of restoration.

⊙ Sights

Qala Ethnographic Museum Complex   MUSEUM
(☏012-4593714; Qala Village; admission/tour/ fortress AZN2/8/2; ⊙9am-6pm) Historic little Qala has a fascinating windswept village-scape. But it's now dominated by a faux fortress monument opposite which

Abşeron Peninsula

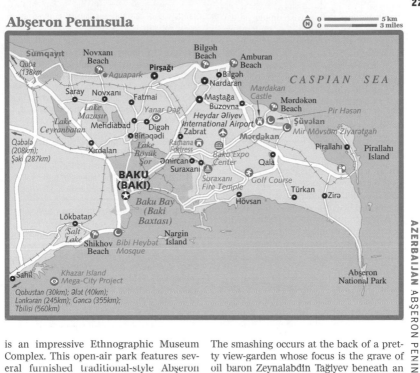

is an impressive Ethnographic Museum Complex. This open-air park features several furnished traditional-style Abşeron buildings (house, smithy, potters workshop) set amid a wide range of archaeological finds and petroglyphs, both original and reconstructions.

Information booths in Baku's old city sell AZN20 tickets for return excursions to Qala departing at 11am from outside the double gates. By public transport, Türkan-bound bus 101 from Baku's Ulduz metro passes within 300m of the museum complex. Walk west along Sulh street to find it. Bus 182 loops round to Mərdəkən.

Mərdəkən & Şüvəlan

Together forming one extensive semi-urban sprawl, neither Mərdəkən nor Şüvəlan are particularly attractive towns but they hide some of the Abşeron Peninsula's more intriguing places of legend and superstition.

◎ Sights

Pir Həsən   ISLAMIC
Pir Həsən is a shrine area where superstitious locals queue up to have bottles smashed over their heads. Honestly. It's considered a cure for nervousness of spirit.

The smashing occurs at the back of a pretty view-garden whose focus is the grave of oil baron Zeynalabdin Tağıyev beneath an egg-shaped stone pavilion, surrounded by archaeological fragments.

To find Pir Həsən turn north at the traffic light directly west of central Mərdəkən's arboretum ('Dendroloji Parki'). Swing west again on Ramin Qazimov küç and then turn north once more.

Mardakan Castle   FORTRESS
(Böyük Mərdəkan Qəsri; admission/'tour' AZN2/5; ◎8am-8pm) FREE This 22m square-plan tower is the more interesting of Mərdəkən's two crenellated fortress keeps. If you want to get in and up the five flights of unlit steps to the rooftop, seek out key-holder, Vidadi, who lives in one of the closest houses.

The tower is accessed off Kolxoz küç, about 15 minutes' walk from Pir Həsən following Ramin Qazimov küç west. Buses back to Baku pick up from Yesenin küç around three minutes' walk south.

Mir Mövsöm Ziyarətgah   ISLAMIC
(🖳136) One of Azerbaijan's most impressive new Muslim shrines, this complex is topped with a beautifully patterned Central Asian–style dome and has an interior spangled with polished mirror mosaic facets. Most Azeris

firmly believe that a wish made here will come true. And when it does they return in droves, offering suitable donations to show their gratitude.

At the back of the complex is a cemetery with a fascinating mix of Islamic, atheist and Christian graves. It's at the east end of Şüvəlan, around 4km east of central Mərdəkən. Bus 136 to/from Baku via Mərdəkən stops outside.

Ramana

On a rocky outcrop **Ramana Fortress** (📖 204 from Koroğlu metro station) is one of the Abşeron's most dramatic castles, but adding to the interest of the visit is the view of many grungy old oil workings, nodding donkeys and run-off pools that it surveys. Finding the key-holder is hit-and-miss.

Yanar Dağ

In the 13th century Marco Polo mentioned numerous natural-gas flames spurting spontaneously from the Abşeron Peninsula. The only one burning today is **Yanar Dağ** (Fire Mountain; admission AZN2; ⊙9am-8pm or longer), a 10m-long sliver of heat-blackened hillside where tongues of fire have been licking away since being accidentally ignited by a shepherd's cigarette back in the 1950s. It's best viewed at dusk.

A rubbish-disposal plant looms nearby and there are no 'facilities', but the site remains one of the Abşeron's stranger and more compulsive curiosities. Bus 217 (30q, 40 minutes) from Koroğlu metro station and bus 147 (30q, 30 minutes) from Azadliq metro station both terminate opposite the site.

Baku to Qobustan

The most popular day trip from Baku takes visitors to the petroglyph reserve above Qobustan, 60km south of the capital, and on to the isolated mud volcanoes above Ələt. En route you'll pass Bibi-Heybət Mosque (p211) and Shikhov Beach (p212).

❶ Getting There & Away

BagBaku (p221) and some budget hotels organise drivers to visit Qobustan and the mud volcanoes for AZN20/80 per person/car. Agencies might ask as much as AZN240.

Standard Baku taxis will happily take you to Qobustan but few will know how to find the mud-volcano site. No cars will attempt the latter in wet conditions.

By public transport take city bus 5 or 88 to their terminus at **Yiriminçi Sahə** (20-ci Sahə) roundabout, then swap to the Ələt-bound bus 195 (80q, one hour). Get off at the south end of Qobustan town, just before the overpass bridge. From here taxis want AZN10 return to the petroglyphs (plus AZN1 car-entry ticket), which should include a two-minute diversion to see a passingly interesting stone inscribed with some Roman graffiti. You'll need to pay around AZN25 total if also including the mud volcanoes.

Walking from relevant bus 195 stops is possible but unpleasant: you'll be looking at a several hours' on foot through sun-blasted, relatively barren terrain.

New Baku International Seaport (Ələt) Most cargo-ship ferries to Kazakhstan and a few headed for Turkmenistan depart from here but as yet there are neither ticket office nor any facilities, not even a shop or tea window, so bring all supplies. A taxi to/from Baku should cost around AZN30. Alternatively take bus 195 (80q): after passing through Baş Ələt, get off by the big roundabout, from where waiting taxis charge AZN5 for the last 3km.

Qobustan

The Unesco-listed **Qobustan Petroglyph Reserve** protects thousands of stick-figure stone engravings dating back up to 12,000 years. Themes include livestock, wild animals and shamen. They were carved into what were probably caves but over time have crumbled into a craggy chaos of boulders.

A visit starts 3km west of Qobustan at a state-of-the-art new museum, which gives context to what you will see on the mountain ridge 2km above. English-speaking staff offer guided tours to assist you spotting and deciphering the petroglyphs. But alone you'll still be able to spot the key scratchings. Don't miss the spindly reed boat sailing towards the sunset. Comparing this with similar ancient designs in Norway led controversial ethnologist Thor Heyerdahl to suggest that Scandinavians might have originated in what is now Azerbaijan.

Even if you have no particular interest in ancient doodles, Qobustan's eerie landscape and the hilltop views towards distant oil-workings in the turquoise-blue Caspian are still fascinating.

Ələt

On top of utterly unpromising little Daşgil Hill is a weird collection of baby **mud vol-**

canoes (Palcik Vulkanlar), a whole family of 'geologically flatulent' little conical mounds that gurgle, ooze, spit and sometimes erupt with thick, cold, grey mud. It's more entertaining than it sounds – even when activity is at a low ebb, you get the eerie feeling that the volcanoes are alive. And normally the peaceful site is completely deserted.

From the big Ələt junction roundabout some 15km south of Qobustan, follow 'Şpal Zavodu' signs but keep straight ahead (north) after crossing the railway. Keep to this unpaved track for 3km then climb the hill to your right (tough if wet).

NORTHERN AZERBAIJAN

Most of Azerbaijan's scenic highlights lie in the spectacular, snowcapped Great Caucasus or its luxuriantly forested foothills. Some of these zones are accessible from the Baku–Balakən road, others from the Quba–Qusar area, but unless you're prepared to hike via 3000m passes there's no direct way to cross between these two regions.

Baku to Quba

Northern Azerbaijan's real highlights start behind Quba. Nonetheless there are some interesting diversions en route suitable for those with a vehicle.

◉ Sights & Activities

Candycane Mountains LANDSCAPE
(Giləzi–Xızı road) An eye-catching area of vivid pink-and-white striped hills is commonly nicknamed the 'Candycane Mountains' by Baku expats. Look carefully and you find that the colourful landscape is littered with little fossils. The area is around 15km off the Baku–Quba Hwy east of Giləzi. Take the road that leads via Xızı to the gently attractive woodlands of the Altıağac National Park.

Beşbarmaq Dağ MOUNTAIN
(Five Finger Mountain; Siyəzən spur road, Km3.5; for-eigners/locals AZN4/2) Atop a super-steep grassy ridge, Beşbarmaq Dağ is a distinctive split crag whose mystical crown of phallic rocks attracts (mostly female) pilgrims. In around 20 minutes they climb a steep partially laddered trail from a ridgetop car park, kissing the stones and sometimes speaking in tongues en route hoping to score spiritual merit, good fortune and/or divine assistance in getting pregnant. Holy men lurk in rocky nooks ready to help out – but only with prayers.

The peak's looming 520m silhouette flips the bird at passing traffic high, high above Km88 of the Baku–Quba Hwy. At that point, Baku–Xaçmaz and Baku–Quba buses stop outside a stone mosque surrounded by food stalls. From the mosque there is a path to the top but it's a strenuous multi-hour climb. Instead you can drive to the ridge-top car park (around AZN20 return by taxi),

AZERBAIJAN BAKU TO QUBA

SHAHDAG NATIONAL PARK

Covering more than 1.3 million sq km, the vast **Shahdag National Park** (www.eco.gov.az/en/shahdag) encompasses many of the nation's most spectacular peaks and high-mountain trails. Behind Laza and Xınalıq a roadless crag-framed valley sweeps around to provide access to the base camps for some splendid 4000m-plus Caucasian peaks ripe for relatively nontechnical climbs. Best known are glacier crowned Şahdağ (4243m, three days), tough scree-plagued Bazarduzu Dağ (4466m, four days) and impressively pyramidal Tufandağ (4100m, three days). However, there are two huge bureaucratic 'buts'. Firstly the national park entrance ticket must be prepurchased (online), but standard tickets only apply to certain southern and western areas of the park. The bits you're most likely to want to see require a special high mountains ticket AND a special 'border zone' pass from the military authorities. And such passes have for years been essentially unavailable and soldiers might aggressively stop anyone walking unsanctioned even 100m into national park territory. So few have visited Azerbaijan's top outdoor highlights for years. However, as of 2015–16, things appear to have relaxed just an iota for those prepared to send off documents around three weeks in advance and to employ an officially sanctioned guide such as Mevlud Azizov (p234). Alternatively ask **Shahdag Mountain Tours** (☑ 077-2773205; mountaintours@shahdag.az; local/foreigner per day AN138/147) about its (pricey) mountaineering packages: they're brand new and evolving but still require serious advance planning. For alternative 'free' treks, explore the villages outside the park and perhaps make the multi-day crossing from Qarxun to Lahic via Babadağ.

Northern & Northwestern Azerbaijan

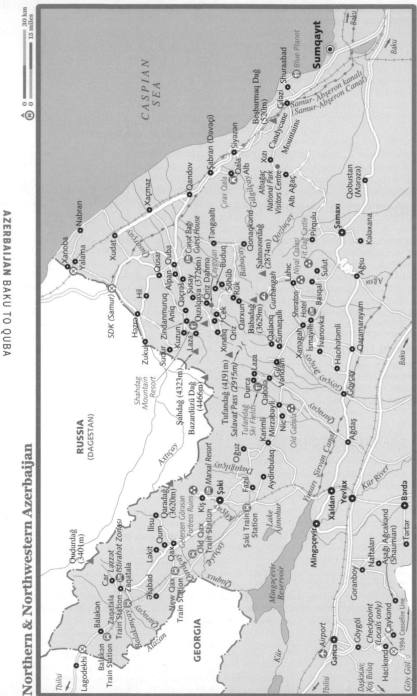

30 km
15 miles

CASPIAN SEA

Baku
Sumqayıt
Blue Planet
Şuraabad
Giləzi
Candycane
Beşbarmaq Dağ (520m)
Samur-Abşeron kanalı (Samur-Abşeron Canal)
Siyəzən
Altıağac National Park
Gilgilçay Altı
Altı Ağaç
Xızı
Qobustan (Maraza)
Mountains
Qala
Dəvəçi (Dəvəçi)
Çıraq Qala
Qandov
Şamaxı
Qozluçay
Piriqulu
Fit Dağ Castle
Nival Qalası
Qonaqkənd
Kalaxana
Sahnəzərdağ (2874m)
Lahıc
Altıağac
Visitors Centre
Qaçmaz
Nabran
Xudat
Xanoba
Yalama
Qusar
Cənət Bağı Guest House
Quba
Tənqəaltı
Çaygörən
Qıriz Dəhnə
Buduq
Sulut
Başqal
Ağsu
Ağsu
Şərcə
Dıvıççay
Susay
Qaçrəş
Alpan
Söhüb
Rük
Babaçay
Gurbangah
Hıl
Hazra
Zuxul
Sudur
Zindanmuruq
Anıq
Kuzun
Qızılqaya (3726m)
Qriz
Çek
Xınalıq
Qarxun
Qalacıq
Babadağ (3629m)
Xanagah
Sumaqallı
İsmayıllı
Sheraton Hotel
İvanovka
Hacıhatamlı
Qaramaryam
SDK (Samur)
RUSSIA (DAGESTAN)
Şahdağ Mountain Resort
Şahdağ (4323m)
Laza
Qriz
Laza
Tufandağ (4191m)
Salavat Pass (2915m)
Bazardüzü Dağ (4466m)
Durca
Güləf
Vəndam
Qəbələ
Axtıçay
Tufandağ Ski Fields
Mirzəbəylı
Nic
Old Gabala
Karimli
Aydınbulaq
Oğuz
Göyçay
Göyçay
Baku
Ağdaş
Dağlıqçay
Daşağılçay
Marxal Resort
Şəki
Kış
Fazıl
Fortress Ruins
Ağcaqşı
Qələrsən Görəsən
Fortress Ruins
Old Oax
Qax
Lakit
Oum
İlisu
Qaradağ (3620m)
Car
Lazzat
İstirahət Zonası
Zaqatala
Lake Ajnohur
Şəki Train Station
Kışçay
Mingəçevir Reservoir
Yuxarı Şirvan Canal
Xaldan
Yevlax
Kür River
Tərtər
Bərdə
Mingəçevir
Qudurdağ (3401m)
Balakan
Zaqatala Train Station
Əlabad
Balakən
Balkan Train Station
Lagodekhi
New Qax Train Station
Qanıx
Qanıx
Balakənçay
Alazan
Tbilisi
GEORGIA
Qanıx
Ağdam
Naftalan
Aşağı Ağcakənd (Shaumian)
Goranboy
Qaymaq
Caykand
Checkpoint (Locals only)
Göygöl
Xoş Bulaq
Daşkəsən
Ganca
Airport
Tbilisi
Hacıkənd
1994 Ceasefire Line
Göy Göl

which is around 6km up an unpaved track off the Siyəzən spur road.

Çirax Qala
CASTLE

One of rural Azerbaijan's best-preserved castle ruins, Çirax Qala's spindly, three-storey keep rises on a forested bluff, high above Qala Altı, a big, modern sulphur-water sanatorium complex. You see the silhouette while driving past on the Siyəzən–Şabran back road but access requires a muddy 4km offroad plus 15 minutes' walk.

Blue Planet
WINDSURFING

(☑ 050-2770730; kitesurfing.az; Shuraabad Beach; kiteboard set per hr/day AZN30/110, paddleboard AZN20/60; ☺ 9am-7pm May-Oct by appointment, restaurant 1.30-8pm Thu-Sun) Azerbaijan's brand-new kitesurfing centre offers a unique opportunity to go skimming across a Caspian lagoon with glorious sunsets, reliable wind yet relatively calm shallow water. Lessons available (from AZN180). Consider booking a few days ahead.

Along with its cafe-restaurant, the centre is set on an isolated headland beach, 16km off the main Baku–Quba Hwy via Shuraabad.

Quba

☑ 02333 / POP 24,000

Famous for apples and carpet-making, Quba is a town in three parts. Old Quba is a grid of low-rise streets raised above the deep-cut Qudiyalçay River. This had been the 18th-century capital of local potentate Fatali Khan, but later became a provincial backwater once the khanate had been absorbed into the Russian Empire (1806). North across the river is Qırmızı Qəsəbə, a unique Jewish settlement. And to the east, the new town stretches 3km to Flag Sq where a monumental trio of 21st-century public buldings boast proud stone facades and pediments. Quba is a popular getaway in itself but more particularly a gateway to Azerbaijan's most interesting and remote mountain villages.

◉ Sights & Activities

Quba's main attraction is just wandering the quiet leafy streets of the Old Town area centred on the Meydan.

Cümə Məscid
MOSQUE

This octagonal mosque is Quba's most distinctive historic building, painted a dull red and topped with a metallic dome forming a central point like a Prussian helmet.

Nizami Park
PARK

This little park has a more natural vibe than most of the over-manicured equivalents in other towns. Old chaps in flat caps sip tea and slap dominoes beneath shady chestnut and plane trees. There's an ornamental 'castle' tower, a museum, a metal spired *turbe* (tomb tower) and statues of poets repainted to look like bronze. Similarly gilded sportswomen give the stairway to the Qırmızı Qəsəbə pedestrian bridge an uplifting sense of Soviet optimism.

Hacı Cəfər Məscid
MOSQUE

(Ərdəbil küç 60) This colourfully painted brick mosque is the most eye-catching of several minor historic structures giving Ardəbil küç a modest appeal for casual strolling. You'll also find a few typical old-Quba houses with rounded door shields and overhanging upper windows.

Quba 1918 Genocide Memorial Complex
MEMORIAL

(Quba Soyqırımı Memorial Kompleksi; ☺ 9am-6pm Mon-Fri, 10am-5pm Sat & Sun) FREE Skulls and human bones protruding in awful profusion form a key part of this powerfully emotional if politically charged monument. The mass grave site was found in 2007 when digging to rebuild a stadium. Today there's also a startling pair of concrete spike-pyramids atop a subterranean museum commemorating the massacres of April to June 1918 in which 167 villages in the-then Quba district were ravaged by predominantly Armenian Bolshevik forces. Some 16,782 mostly unarmed civilians died – Azerbaijanis, Jews, Avars and Lezghins.

To find the site from Nizami Park, walk west past the decrepit Şahdağ Hotel and descend to the right after 15 minutes.

Qırmızı Qəsəbə
AREA

(Krasnaya Sloboda) Across the river from central Quba, Qırmızı Qəsəbə is a wealthy and much celebrated Jewish village with two active synagogues. Its comfortable existence is often cited as proof of Azerbaijan's history of religious tolerance, though to the casual observer the townscape's biggest difference from the rest of Quba is that of conspicuous wealth. From Nizami Park descend the long stairway adorned by statues of Greco-Soviet Adonis youths and across the pedestrianised bridge.

History Museum
MUSEUM

(Tarix-diyarşünaslıq Muzeyi; Nizami Park; admission AZN1; ☺ 10am-1pm & 2-6pm Tue-Sat) A facade

Quba

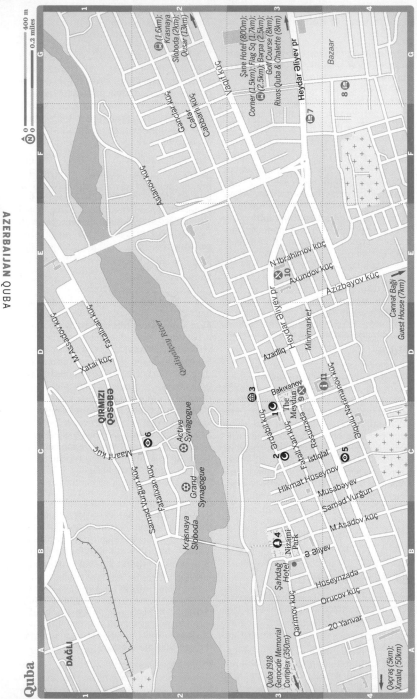

400 m
0.2 miles

N

DAĞLI

QIRMIZI
Qəsəbə

Krasnaya
Sloboda

Qaçraş (5km);
Xınalıq (50km)

Quba 1918
Genocide Memorial
Complex (350m)

Šahdağ
Hotel

Nizami
Park

Cənnət Bağı
Guest House (7km)

Bazaar

Heydər Əliyev pr

Şanе Hotel (800m);
Corner (1.5km); Flag Sq (1.7km);
(2.5km) Barpa (2.5km);
Golf Course (8km);
Rixos Quba & Chalette (8km)

(1.6km);
Krasnaya
Sloboda (2km);
Qusar (13km)

Qağıyçay River

Active
Synagogue

Grand
Synagogue

Minimarket

Azadlıq

Bakıxanov

The
Meydan

İstiqlal

Hikmat Hüseynov

Musabəyev

Samed Vurğun

M.Asadov küç

ə.Əliyev

Hüseynzadə

Orucov küç

20 Yanvar

Qarımov küç

Əhməd Rəsulzadə küç

Fatali Xan küç

Ərdəbil küç

Rəsulzadə

N.İbrahimov küç

Axundov küç

Əzizbəyov küç

Heydər Əliyev pr

Aşarıov küç

Məktəb küç

Samed Vurğun küç

Fatalıxan küç

Maarif küç

Xatai küç

M.Asadov küç

Fatalıxan küç

Genclar küç

Cəfər küç

Cabbarlı küç

Vaqif küç

Quba

like a stylised castle lures visitors to investigate this unusually professional new regional museum. Along with the typical displays of pots, swords and Bronze Age jewellery, there's a fine collection of classic local carpets and a refreshing emphasis on women's roles in local history. One guide speaks some English.

Qadim Quba   CARPET WORKSHOP
(☑02333-53270; Heydər Əliyev pr 132, ⊗8am-noon & 1-5pm Mon-Fri) Quba is famous for its handmade carpets and this workshop is one accessible place where visitors can see the process in action.

Azerbaijan National Golf Course   GOLF
(☑012-4042880; http://tnagolfclub.com; Amsar–Ispik Rd; 9/18 holes from AZN60/115, shoes/clubs/trolley/cart rental AZN10/40/20/50; ⊗9am-5pm Mon-Fri, 7am-dusk Sat & Sun) Azerbaijan's leading golf course is up to international PGA standards and open to nonmembers. Ask about off-peak day-play packages.

Bərpa   BOWLING
(☑050-3134530; www.lsh-resort.az; bowling lane per hr AZN30, paintball per shot 15q, karting per 5 laps AZN10; ⊗noon-midnight) Bored in the evening? Then hop in a taxi to Bərpa, a modern six-lane bowling centre with bar, billiards, paintball and a carting circuit.

It's all in a quiet, semi-rural spot amid orchards. Just beyond the Şane Hotel, turn south through a gateway then follow signs for 1.5km.

🛏 Sleeping

As well as the city options recommended, there are also hotels and many bungalow resorts along the road to Qəçrəş.

Oskar Hotel   GUESTHOUSE $
(☑070-8678022, 02333-51516; Heydar Əliyev pr 200; d/tr AZN30/45) Inexpensive but cheerier than the other bazaar guesthouses, Oskar is a collection of compact rooms with private bathroom above the entrance to a tree-shaded yard-cafe. You get hot showers and frilly curtains, but the partly tiled, plywood floors give a slightly jerry-built feel.

It's at the town end of the bazaar on the main street facing Bank Standard.

Xınalıq Hotel   GUESTHOUSE $
(☑050-3493463, 02333-54445; xinaliqotel@mail.ru; 22-ci Məhəllə 22; s/tw/tr AZN15/20/35, without bath dm/tr/q AZN5/15/20) This traders' guesthouse is basic and male-orientated, but the 19 well-maintained rooms cover a variety of qualities and styles – some even have private (squat) toilet and shower.

It's perched above the chaotic bazaar area: through the triple stone arch, 300m on your right.

Şane Hotel   HOTEL $$
(☑02333-56171; www.shane.az; Heydar Əliyev pr 227t; d AZN60-70; 🅿❄🛜; 🖵1) Quality pure-white sheets, chestnut stained-wood furniture and comfortable new beds at a decent price means it's easy to forgive the occasional elements of kitsch and the edge-of-town, main-road location. Little English is spoken, but the restaurant menu does make a valiant, sometimes comical, attempt to suggest otherwise.

★Rixos Quba   RESORT $$$
(☑sales office 012-4043434; http://quba.rixos.com; Amsar–Ispiq road; r from AZN160; 🅿❄🛜🏊) Preening above the Azerbaijan National Golf Course, this sumptuous 21st-century palace has all the five-star trappings yet midweek in the low season you can sometimes score a room for just AZN99.

It's 8km south of central Quba, with no nearby shops. During the low season the only eateries are the hotel's excellent but pricey restaurants (AZN35 dinner minimum). In summer there's a fast-food cafe in Planet Quba, the resort's funfair park (rides AZN1 to AZN5).

AZERBAIJAN QUBA

✗ Eating

Several cheap beer-and-tea places lie around the bazaar area, the Meydan and Nizami Park. Kebab barbecues dot the forest for several kilometres along the Qəçrəş road (towards Xınalıq). A local speciality sweet-snack is *bükmə*, like shredded wheat filled with syrupy nut fragments.

Mahir AZERBAIJANI, TURKISH $
(Heydar Əliyev pr 182; meals/kebab AZN3/1.50; ☺8am-10pm) Great-value canteen-style food along with *lahmacun* (when available) served in a bright, pleasant, if hardly world-beating, setting.

Ayləvi Kafé KEBAB $
(Meydan; kebab AZN1; ☺8am-11pm) If you want tea or a sit-down kebab, this new log cabin is a great central choice with summer seating facing the chestnut and willow trees of the Old Town's central square.

Chalette STEAK $$$
(☑012-4043434; Rixos Hotel; steak meals AZN35-45; ☺noon-11pm) If meat means more to you than money, try the 28-day chill-aged T-bone at this log-chalet-style steak house. It's surely the only non-ski restaurant in the Caucasus to be accessed by its own private cable car.

⬤ Drinking

Corner PUB
(Heydar Əliyev pr 30; ☺11am-last customer) 'Corner' is the nearest Quba comes to a real pub, with heavy wooden furniture and Belgian beers on tap (sometimes). There's a good range of meals and barman Coşgun speaks English. It's southeast of the town centre before Flag Sq, 700m beyond Hotel Şane on bus route 1.

ⓘ Information

Tourist Office (Quba Turizm İnformasiya Mərkəzi; ☑070-2383038, 02333-53618; http://gubatourism.az; Heydar Əliyev pr; ☺9am-1pm & 2-6pm Mon-Fri) The obliging tourist office is hidden in a drab lump of Soviet concrete that faces Meydan, the main Old Town square.

ⓘ Getting There & Away

Quba's cylindrical new bus station is on the Qusar-bound bypass, 800m north of Flag Sq. Destinations include the following:
Baku Buses (AZN4, three hours) depart at least hourly till 5.30pm.

Qusar (for Laza) Buses (50q, 25 minutes, three hourly till 6pm) plus shared taxis may collect passengers at the bazaar roundabout saving the hassle of going first to the bus station.
Xaçmaz Twice-hourly *marshrutky* (80q, 45 minutes).
Xınalıq (via Cek) Shared 4WDs (per person/car AZN10/40 westbound, 1¾ hours) depart from opposite Xınalıq Hotel if there's custom. That's most likely between 2pm and 4pm. If you're in a hurry, you might need to pay the whole vehicle (AZN40). Returning cars leave Xınalıq around 7am for as little as AZN3 per seat. Charming **Xeyraddin Gabbarov** (☑050-2259250; www.xinaliq.com) usually works in Quba but comes from Xınalıq, speaks fluent English and for a relatively modest fee can organise tailor-made visits.

ⓘ Getting Around

By day, bus 1 (20q) runs regularly from the bus station via Flag Sq, Heydar Əliyev pr, the bazaar and through the Old Town turning around just short of the main access lane to the Genocide Memorial. It returns along Əliqulu Nərimanov küç then continues the route again.

Around Quba

Amid sheepy Caucasian foothills and dramatic canyons lie Azerbaijan's grandest mountain panoramas and its most fascinating villages.

Quba to Xınalıq

The fabled ancient village of Xınalıq is an unforgettable rustic getaway but the beautiful route from Quba is an attraction in itself. The road starts out through woodlands past a string of barbecue cafes, then navigates several canyons before emerging above the treeline into an almost deserted upland valley. Traffic is very light, except perhaps on midsummer weekends, making the road's western section viable as a safe, easy hiking route.

Cavid Qara's Camping Azerbaijan (p218) offers regular weekend trips and tailor-made hikes in this region often including homestays in remote, little-visited villages like Qrız.

⊙ Sights & Activities

Çaygoşan PICNIC AREA
(Quba–Xınalıq Rd, Km 37-39) One of the most dramatic stretches of the Quba–Xınalıq road starts when it enters a deep, narrow

canyon at around Km 34.5. It emerges over 2km later at an uninhabited grassy picnic spot called Çaygoşan, where there are two seasonal tea places in an achingly beautiful valley. A small bridge across the river at Km 37 leads 4km up a very rocky track to the spooky village of Qriz.

Cek   VILLAGE
(Quba–Xınalıq Rd, Km 43) The minuscule village of Cek (pronounced 'Jek') is a handful of farmsteads around a rocky knob that protrudes from a sweep of grassy mountainside. There's no shop or accommodation infrastructure, but as a viewpoint or as a starting point for hikes, the wide open landscape here is hard to beat.

Xınalıq   VILLAGE
(Quba–Xınalıq Rd, Km 51-52) By some definitions Xınalıq (2335m) is Europe's highest village. Its upper half retains many ancient stone houses that form distinctively austere stepped terraces up a steep highland ridge. And the whole scene is often magically wrapped in spooky clouds that part sporadically to reveal 360-degree views of the surrounding Caucasus.

Apart from examining the one-room museum and gazing at the hypnotic views, the main attraction is meeting and staying with Xınalıq's hardy shepherd folk who have their own language (Ketsh) and still live much of their lives on horseback. Bring warm clothes – nights can be icy cold.

Ateşgah   HIKING
Ateşgah, a small ever-burning natural fire-vent high on a valley slope, should be a roughly five-hour return stroll from Xınalıq, but it's in the Shahdag National Park (p227) whose rules for now essentially prevent access (along with blocking the lovely Xınalıq–Laza trek).

Qalay Xudat   HIKING
(Quba–Xınalıq Rd, Km 48.5) For an appealing but easy, permit-free round-trip hike from Xınalıq follow the Quba road back 8km to Km 48.5, climb up the side lane to the attractive little village of Qalay Xudat, then follow the unpaved upper track back to Xınalıq high above the valley.

🛌 Sleeping

There's no hotel in Xınalıq but several families offer informal homestays for around AZN20 to AZN25 including breakfast, dinner and plenty of tea. None have signs,

WORTH A TRIP

XAÇMAZ

Most locals rush through Xaçmaz en route to the hopelessly over-estimated Nabran beaches but it's worth coming here to peruse the town's comical plethora of bizarre monuments – gigantic lanterns, a two-storey clothes peg, three biblical magi and kitschy ornamental spring-houses that light up in rainbow colours. A reduced scale Tower Bridge built in sandstone spans the main road junction. There are three good-value hotels within a short walk of Xaçmaz bus station. A Xaçmaz–Moscow train leaves Friday mornings at 6am (*platskart* AZN110).

indoor toilets or much spoken English. For accommodation with private bathroom there's a wide selection in the first 10km west of Quba but only a couple of options further on and none west of Km 34.

Hajibala's Homestay   HOMESTAY $
(☑ 02333-49051; www.cbtazerbaijan.com/xinaliq; Xınalıq; incl breakfast/half-board AZN20/25) The affable village historian speaks good Russian and has a comparatively comfortable Old Town house decorated with local historical curiosities. The guest bedroom has a novelty light that changes effect by remote control. You'd probably prefer an indoor toilet but don't dream, this is Xınalıq.

MəstDərgah   RESORT $$$
(☑ 077-732400; www.mestdergah.com; Quba–Xınalıq Rd, Km 32; d AZN150) At the roadside in the cliff-backed village of Qriz Dahna (not Qriz), this boutique cottage resort is by far the smartest and most comfortable accommodation option on the Quba–Xınalıq road.

Laza & Shahdag Ski-Area
📞 02338 / POP 150
A newly paved road speeds some 30km from Qusar (13km north of Quba) towards the looming peaks of the High Caucasus. The noble bulk of Şahdağ (4243m) is visible for miles ahead on a clear day, looking especially impressive when viewed from near the historic village of Əniğ. Around 10km later, just after Aladaş, is Azerbaijan's foremost ski resort with seasonal cable cars and ultra-luxurious hotels with gourmet restaurants. Some 5km further on a much

rougher road is contrastingly modest Laza, which has what is arguably Azerbaijan's most spectacular setting.

◉ Sights & Activities

Laza
VILLAGE

Encircled by soaring mountains with grass-clad slopes and ribbon waterfalls cascading over perilous cliff edges, Laza's setting is remarkably impressive. The tiny village is diffuse and its houses somewhat banal, but a rocky pinnacle beside the metal-roofed little mosque adds foreground for photos of the mind-blowing panorama.

Just beyond Laza, exploration is hindered by the strict visiting requirements of Shahdag National Park (p227).

Shahdag Mountain Resort
SKIING

(Şahdağ Turizm Kompleksi; www.shahdagmountain resort.com; Qusar–Laza road, Km39; ☺ ski lifts mid-Jun–Sep & Dec-Mar, weather dependent) Azerbaijan's top ski resort is a work in progress but it already proves a godsend for expats seeking winter sports opportunities. Four chairlifts and a gondola are currently operable and 160 snow-guns keep 17km of pistes in condition. The upper resort hotels have oodles of style.

As yet there's nothing much other than the hotels to vary your apres-ski experience. Kit rental is far cheaper from the ski base (boots, poles and skis AZN20) than from the big hotels. Note that only one hotel stays open year-round, and between seasons the lifts stop running.

🛏 Sleeping & Eating

Azizov Family
HOMESTAY, BUNGALOWS $

(☑ Khaled 051-4172600, Zahid 070-9213599; Laza; per person AZN12-18) Near the entrance to Laza there's a small shop. The houses facing and behind it are homestays owned by brothers Zahid and Khaled Azizov. Both also have self-contained bungalows at the other end of the village (AZN30 to AZN50) close to the waterfalls en route to Suvar. A third brother, experienced mountain guide Mevlud, works seasonally at the ski resort and speaks English.

Park Qusar
RESORT $$

(☑ 055-4243333; www.parkqusar.az; Qusar–Laza Rd, Km 30.2, Əniq; d/q from AZN80/150) Offering spectacular panoramic views of the whole Şahdağ Massif, this top-quality rural resort offers fully equipped pine bungalows, a

range of sports, and a restaurant that is remarkably well priced.

It's across the valley from Əniq village, 10km short of the Shahdag ski lifts, 1.4km off the Qusar–Laza road after Km 30. Taxis cost AZN12 from Qusar. Open year-round.

Shahdag Hotel & Spa
HOTEL $$$

(☑ 012-3101110, from local mobile 1110; s/d from AZN 79/195, low season AZN119/135; P ☎ 🛋) Şəbəkə (stained-glass) panels and lamps like upturned oriental parasols create a warm yet stylish ambience in the suave Shahdag Hotel. It's an upper-market resort with over 170 rooms, an Ovdan-branded spa and good-sized indoor pool. Most importantly it is the only hotel in the direct ski-area that stays open year-round.

ℹ Information

Mevlud Azizov (☑ whatsapp 070-9014048; misha_971@mail.ru) Mevlud, aka Misha, speaks some English and has years of experience as a mountain guide around Laza. For AZN45 per person plus guide fee he might be able to organise the permits for a Laza–Xinaliq trek if you can get him scanned copies of your passport etc around three weeks in advance.

ℹ Getting There & Away

Frequent buses from Baku and Quba (25 minutes) connect to the Lezgin town of Qusar. From there the ski resort is around 45 minutes' drive (share/private taxis AZN3/20). Buses leave Qusar at noon and 4.30pm to Aladaş (AZN1, 70 minutes) returning at 7.30am and 1.30pm. Get off at the roadside and continue 1.7km to the lower ski station, 3km to the upper resort/Shahdag Hotel, or 6km to Laza. There is no bus to Laza.

If hitching, start from the westernmost end of Qusar accessed by marshrutka route 1.

NORTHWESTERN AZERBAIJAN

If you're heading from Georgia to Baku, the fastest route is via Gəncə. But if you aren't in a terrible rush, it is far more pleasant to transit through northwestern Azerbaijan via Zaqatala and historic Şəki. The route traverses a spectrum of scenic and climatic zones from stark semi-deserts to views of mountain peaks poking above woodland foothills and fields where spring poppies add impressionistic splashes of colour.

Baku to İsmayıllı

Rolling semi-desert starts to become greener as you skirt Şamaxı, with a superbly rebuilt mosque but little else to show for centuries as northern Azerbaijan's leading cultural and trading capital. Beneath forested foothills, İsmayıllı has a leafy town centre and an almost comical plethora of recently built fortress-style walls, but for most travellers it's simply a transit point for reaching Lahıc on public transport.

Lahıc

☑ 02028 / POP 910

Lahıc is a pretty, highland village that's locally famous for its Persian-based dialect and traditional coppersmiths. It can feel just a little touristy at weekends when Bakuvians arrive to get photographed in vaguely preposterous sheepskin costumes. But stay a day or two and listen to the mellifluous mosques as mists swirl around the part-forested crags and you'll find it a delightful starting point for hiking and meeting locals who, more than in any other village in Azerbaijan, have a smattering of English.

◉ Sights

Hüseynov küç   STREET

Lahıc's main street is unevenly paved with smooth pale river-stones and lined with older houses built traditionally with interleaving stone and timber layers. Many have wooden box-balconies.

The village's once-famous workshops have mostly been superseded by little boutiques, but the smithy at Hüseynov küç 47 remains little changed and feels almost like a museum, hung with dusty old metalwork.

Lahıc History Museum   MUSEUM

(Nizami küç; donation expected; ⊙ 9am-2pm & 3-6pm Tue-Sat) This quaint little one-room collection of cultural artefacts is housed in a former mosque next door to the tourist office. Posted opening times are far from fixed.

School Museum   MUSEUM

(Hüseynov küç) During summer Lahıc's village school welcomes visitors to look around and has a tiny little 'museum room'.

Zərnava Bridge   LANDMARK

(Girdimançay Asma Körpü; Lahıc access Rd, Km 9) Tourist photos often feature the wobbly,

İVANOVKA

Although lacking any real 'sights', this unique hilltop village is culturally Russian-Molokan and is about the last place in the country to maintain its Soviet-style collective farm. It's famed for fresh produce, wine and honey. Best of all you can converse in fluent English when staying at **John & Tanya Howard's Guesthouse** (☑ John 050-2258861, Tanya 055-6791614; http://ivanovkaguesthouse.com; Sadovaya ul 86; s/d AZN15/30), a wonderfully homely Anglo-Azeri B&B where five guest rooms with private bathroom have super-comfy beds, framed-lace decor and a shared kitchen room across the garden. Full English/continental breakfast costs AZN10/5. İvanovka is around 15km south of İsmayıllı, around AZN10 by taxi.

vertigo-nightmare that is the suspension footbridge to Zərnava. That's at the roadside around 11km south of Lahıc. Elsewhere the road has other spectacular sections and some geological wizardry.

⚡ Activities

Hiking up the steep wooded hillsides you emerge on bare mountaintop sheep meadows (qaylağ) with views towards snow-topped Caucasus peaks that are majestic on clear days. For easy access you could walk (or possibly hitch) 4km up the zigzag Müdrü track from the conspicuous Girdmançay Bridge then walk along the upper ridge roads. There are rumours of a fire vent on a mountainside above Həftəsov village. Or with a horse and guide you could make a full-day excursion via the **Fit Dağ castle ruins** emerging at Sulut or Mucu, from where there's a driveable 4WD route back to the main İsmayıllı road via Basqal. The tourist office offers many more suggestions.

Niyal Qalası   HIKING

(Girdaman Qalası) This utterly ruined castle site is a barely recognisable heap of stones, but for a half-day hike (1½ hours up, less back) it is arguably more interesting than heading up the riverbed to a 4m waterfall. Both relatively easy-to-follow walks start up the Kişcay valley beside Cənnət Bağı Guest House. For Niyal, cross then climb and stay high.

Babadağ
HIKING

Babadağ is Azerbaijan's 'holy mountain', a 3629m bald peak with 360-degree views and a reputation for making climbers' wishes miraculously come true. While steep and tiring, the walk to the summit is entirely non-technical and in season (July and August) there's the added fascination of meeting an assortment of pilgrims as you hike. Out of season there's the danger of snow on top.

The starting point is Gurbangah, a seasonal camp that's two hours' very rough 4WD ride from Lahıc (per vehicle one-way AZN80 to AZN100, return AZN120 to AZN150, often impassable before June). From there most walkers start before dawn on a well-trodden trail taking around six hours up, four hours back. Around an hour before reaching the summit, a less-frequented alternative path leads northwards, descending in around seven hours to a basic camp called Amanevi. That's 11km up a rocky riverbed from Qarxun village, from where an early-morning shared 4WD runs to Quba via Rük, Söhüb and Təngəaltı.

🛌 Sleeping & Eating

Numerous families offer homestay rooms. Many now charge AZN20 to AZN30, cheaper places with only outdoor toilets cost less. Check whether showers cost extra.

Cənnət Baği Guest House
HOMESTAY, CAMPING $

(Garden of Paradise; ☑ 02028-77200, 070-2870140; mr.casarat@mail.ru; per person homestay/camping AZN15/5, cottages AZN40-60) This large, simple homestay is set in lovely landscaped orchards right at the entrance to the village. Four cottages with private bathroom are nearing completion. The attractive house has shared toilets and shower on the yard but its private *hamam* is a popular bonus (free for homestayers, extra for campers).

English-speaking Cəsarət İsmailov ('Jessy') is almost always in residence and can rustle up guides and horses at relatively short notice. Meals (extra cost) are available in the garden cafe.

Hidayat Haciyev's Homestay
HOMESTAY $

(☑ 050-6320732, 02028-77357; per person AZN10, breakfast/dinner AZN3/5) Ultra-simple with shared outdoor toilet but it's the cheapest homestay in town, owner Hidayat speaks some English and there's wi-fi. Ask at the small shop between Cənnət Baği and the main square.

Lahıc Riverside
HOTEL $

(☑ 050-6761444; Bridge Approach; d/tr without bathroom AZN20/30, beer/salad/kebab AZN1/1/4) With an attractive location facing the river near the Girdman Bridge, this bare-bones guesthouse has five acceptable rooms sharing indoor toilet and shower. The associated restaurant has garden dining booths and an upstairs view-section that's the nearest Lahıc comes to a pub.

★Rustam Rustamov's Guesthouse
HOMESTAY $$

(☑ 050-3658049; http://lahijguesthouse.com; Aracit; d AZN60-90; Ⓟ ⊜ ⓐ) With the comfort of a midrange hotel but the personal charm of a great homestay, this is far and away the most appealing choice in Lahıc with verandah seating, a pretty orchard garden, great private bar-lounge, and dining room lavished with local handicrafts and swords. Affable English-speaking host Rustam can help with hiking suggestions.

The best room has a big balcony with rocking chairs. Delicious dinners from locally sourced produce cost AZN15 to AZN22. To find Rustam's place go right down the main street to Aracit Sq then turn right.

Evim Otel
HOTEL $$

(☑ 02028-77111; www.evimotel.net; s/d/tr AZN50/70/70; ⊙mid-Mar–Oct; Ⓟⓐ) This well-signed 24-room hotel near the central bridge has pleasant, pine-floor rooms and semi style-conscious bathroom fittings, albeit some shower booths jam. Some rooms including all singles share bathroom and kitchenette between pairs – handy for families. The restaurant only works for groups or when nearly full.

Mikail Humbatov's Restaurant
RESTAURANT $

(Pavilyon; ☑ 050-3119475, 055-5322233; mikail_humbatov@mail.ru; kebab/buglama AZN5/5; ⊙9am-8pm Sun-Fri, 9am-midnight Sat; Ⓟ) Unsigned and invisible behind an unfinished five-storey hotel building, this inviting restaurant has tree-shaded garden seating with mountain views high across the river, while the main dining hall is festooned with carpets, animal hides and assorted bric-a-brac. Menu choice is limited unless you order ahead but it's open year-round. Four guest rooms share two minuscule bathrooms.

ℹ Information

Tourist Office (☑ 02028-77571, 050-6777517; lahij.tourizm@mail.ru; Nizami küç; ⊙10.30am-

2pm & 3-5pm or call) Dadaş Aliyev's helpful little office is beside the Lahıc History Museum: climb the stairway that starts beside Hüseynov küç 40. then turn right. It's a good first call if you're thinking of hiring guides or horses, and Dadaş can suggest around 40 homestays (including his own great-value place with wi-fi and indoor bathroom). English spoken.

ⓘ Getting There & Away

Lahıc is 20km off the main Baku–İsmayıllı road. Transport departures leave from the small square where Hüseynov küç narrows into a shop-lined cobbled lane.

Baku Some days a direct minibus leaves at 8am from the Lahıc bus stop (AZN7, four hours) but you'll need to contact the driver (Mehrab ☑ 050-3010484) to reserve/confirm. From Baku take an İsmayıllı minibus (AZN5, hourly till 5pm) then change. You could save distance but not necessarily comfort/time by getting off at the LukOil station at Km29 (11km before İsmayıllı) and flagging down passing vehicles up the 20km Lahıc lane. İsmayıllı–Baku minibuses start from İsmayıllı's inconvenient old bus station but pick up near the new stand where Baku shared taxis are also available.

İsmayıllı Minibuses to Lahıc (AZN1.50, 1½ hours) depart at 7am, 11am, 2pm and 4pm from a small new bus station on the Baku Hwy at the northeast edge of town (where the castle wall starts). They return from Lahıc at 8.30am, 11am, 1pm and 4pm (AZN1.50, 1½ hours). For photo stops consider paying a taxi one-way (around AZN15).

Şəki/Qəbələ A direct taxi to Şəki/Qəbələ costs from AZN50/30. Ask at your homestay. From İsmayıllı you could try flagging down Şəki/Oğuz/Qəbələ minibuses outside Könül Market at the Heydar Əliyev pr junction, 2km west of the new bus stand. However, these originate in Baku and often arrive already full. If seeking a shared car here, note that 55 number plates are from Şəki.

Qəbələ

☑ 02420 / POP 17,400

Azerbaijan's top provincial holiday centre, Qəbələ is a string of flashy new hotels and a burgeoning ski resort spread up into the foothills of some glorious forested mountains. Bakuvian families form the main clientele but a series of events and meetings also attract a wider audience.

◉ Sights & Activities

Durca   VILLAGE
(Duruja) Once a seasonal village only occupied by shepherd families during the midsummer grazing season, Durca has a few new holiday homes under construction, but the upper village remains essentially unspoilt with several older stone houses and plenty of walking opportunities in the valley behind.

There's an unpaved road but it's far more fun to get there by cable car. Get off at the end of the third ropeway leg and walk a couple of minutes.

Tufandağ Ropeway & Ski Fields   SKIING
(all-day pass AZN10; ◔ 9am-9pm May-Oct, 9am-6pm Nov-Apr) Whether for skiing, or just for memorable summer views of the Alpine scenery behind Qəbələ, jump aboard the Tufandağ network of four cable cars. If you're in a hurry just take the first, a white-knuckle vertigenous swoop up from behind the Qafqaz Riverside hotel to the Qəbələ Restaurant. Ski rental is available from the Qafqaz Tufandağ Hotel near Durca.

Qabaland   AMUSEMENT PARK
(www.gabaland.com; admission AZN3 plus per attraction AZN1-4; ◔ noon-midnight Jun-Aug, 9am-8pm Sep-Jan & Mar-May, weekends only Feb) It's not quite Disneyland, but Azerbaijan's first theme park is a godsend for local families and has something for all ages. All rides are paid through a precharged cash card.

It's 3km north of central Qəbələ, 300m east of the grand congress centre building.

★☆ Festivals & Events

Gabala International Music Festival   MUSIC
(www.gabalamusicfestival.com; ◔ Jul) Qəbələ's highbrow music festival is certainly not Glastonbury. Collared shirts trump tie-dyes here and the focus is on classical music. Concerts are mostly at the Qafqaz Resort Hotel around 2km towards Durca from the Qafqaz Riverside hotel and ropeway station.

🛏 Sleeping & Eating

Hotel Qəbələ   MOTEL $
(☑ 02420-52408; 28 May küç 31; s/d AZN30/50; ❄🖐) The town's central hotel is a clean, no-fuss budget option. Rear rooms face the mountains.

Qafqaz Karavansaray   HERITAGE HOTEL $$
(☑ 02420-54455; qafqazhotels.com; Elçin Kərimov küç; s/d from AZN80/90) The best value of Qəbələ's new slew of design hotels, the courtyard design is stylised to evoke a caravanserai while its rooms are more interested in neo art deco touches.

AZERBAIJAN Qəbələ

OLD GABALA

The town we now call Qəbələ was known as Kutkashen until the early 1990s when re-named in honour of an ancient city of Caucasian Albania. The site of that original **Old Gabala** was in fact some 20km further southwest. Mentioned in Pliny the Elder's *Natural History* (AD 77), Old Gabala was so comprehensively trashed by the 18th-century invader Nader Shah that even its location was entirely forgotten. Rediscovered in 1959, the large, peacefully rural **site** (admission AZN2; ⊙ 9am-1pm & 2-6pm) is mostly a raised grassy field, but there are a couple of interesting excavations plus the brick-and-stone stumps of two massive brick gate-towers at the southern end, around 10-minutes' walk from the en-trance. Tickets include access to a brand-new museum showing found artefacts.

The site is 4km off the Qəbələ–Şəki road, turning south at Mirzəbəyli. There's no public transport. Consider chartering a taxi between Qəbələ and Oğuz (around AZN20 with a side trip to Old Gabala) and perhaps also add another short diversion to see the Albanian churches in the ethnically Udi village of **Nic**.

Qafqaz Riverside RESORT $$$
(✆ 02420-54330; www.qafqazriversidehotel. com; s/d/ste Jun-Sep AZN90/120/140, Oct-May AZN75/100/120) Glitzy but tasteful with pale colour schemes, Qəbələ's luxurious seven-storey top dog stares up the valley to-wards a lovely mountain panorama. There are indoor and outdoor pools and the spa features a classic marble Turkish Bath.

It's 4km north of central Qəbələ, 6km from the bus station but ideally placed for accessing the steepest ski lift.

Qəbələ Xanlar AZERBAIJANI $$
(✆ 050-5877300; kebab AZN5-6, sac AZN25) Thatched dining platforms are set behind a series of amusing water-powered mobiles in one of Qəbələ's longest-running and best-respected rustic kebab restaurants. There's no menu.

If you don't want kebab, the main alterna-tive is a *sac* (chicken, veggies and potatoes on a sizzling hotplate), but be aware that it's a dish for at least three people costing AZN25.

Qəbələ Restaurant INTERNATIONAL $$
(Tufandağ Ropeway; mains AZN4-30, kebab AZN6-12, beer/espresso from AZN3/2; ⊙ 10am-8pm Jun-Sep, 10am-5.30pm Oct-May; 🛜) Stunning panoram-ic views from this mountain-top restaurant make it ideal for an early beer or daytime cof-fee. The decor is loungey with period-style ski posters, but like so many ski restaurants the world over, the food wins no prizes.

☆ Entertainment

Gabala FC FOOTBALL
(FK Qəbələ; www.gabalafc.az) Qəbələ's talented soccer team, Gabala FC, once managed by ex-Arsenal defender Tony Adams, qualified for the Europa League in 2015.

Their big new stadium should be complet-ed by the time you read this.

❶ Getting There & Away

The **bus station** (Avtovağzal; Qutqaşınlı pr) is 2km south of the town centre, beyond the splen-did 21st-century stone mosque. Pay 20q/AZN1 by *marshrutka*/taxi. Useful services:

Baku Buses (AZN6, five hours) around twice hourly from 7.20am to 6pm, fewer in after-noons. For İsmayıllı pay the full Baku fare or risk being refused a seat.

Gəncə Buses (AZN5) at 8.15am, 8.40am, 9.30am and 3pm.

Şəki (AZN2, two hours) via Oğuz at 9am, 11.10am and 3pm. Alternatively try to find a space on a Baku–Oğuz bus. Oğuz has two small, inexpensive hotels near its bus station and onward services to Şəki (AZN1, 40 minutes) running hourly 8am to 3pm plus 5pm. Beautiful scenery.

Şəki

✆ 02424 / POP 64,500

Snoozing amid green pillows of beautifully forested mountains, Şəki (Sheki) is Azerbai-jan's loveliest town, dappled with tiled-roof old houses and topped off with a glittering little khan's palace.

History

Historic Şəki was originally higher up the valley around the site now occupied by Kiş. That town was ruined by floods in 1716 but rebuilt by rebellious Khan Haci Çələbi, who set up a defiantly independent khanate there in the 1740s.

He built a second fortress at Nukha (today's Şəki). When the original Şəki was obliterated by a second, even more catastrophic flood in 1772, Nukha became the new royal capital.

After 1805, when the khanate was ceded to Russia, Nukha continued to flourish as a silk-weaving town and was a trading junction between caravan routes to Baku, Tbilisi and Derbent (Dagestan), with five working caravanserais at its peak. Nukha was renamed Şəki in the 1960s.

◉ Sights

◎ Within the Fortress Walls

The sturdy stone perimeter wall of Haci Çələbi's Nukha Fortress today encloses an 18th-century palace, tourist office, craft workshops and a decent cafe-restaurant, all set in patches of sheep-mown grass. There are also two largely forgetable museums (each AZN2), one in a circular former church that has a photogenic exterior.

★ Xan Sarayı   PALACE
(Fortress grounds; admission/guide AZN2/5; ◎ 10am-6pm) This ornate 1762 palace building features vivid murals and dazzling coloured light streaming through *şəbəkə* (stained-glass) windows making it Şəki's foremost 'sight' and one of the South Caucasus' most iconic buildings. It was originally the Şəki Khan's administrative building, just one of around 40 now-lost royal structures within the fortress compound.

It's set in a walled rose garden behind two huge plane trees planted in 1530. The facade combines silvered stalactite vaulting with strong geometric patterns in dark blue, turquoise and ochre.

The petite interior is only one-room deep, but lavished with intricate designs. Most are floral but in the central upper chamber you'll find heroic scenes of Haci Çələbi's 1743 battle with Persian emperor Nader Shah complete with requisite swords, guns and severed heads. No photos are allowed inside.

Şəbəkə Workshop   WORKSHOP
(Şəbəkə Şənət Evi; ☑ 050-6483015; Castle grounds; ◎ 9am-7pm Sun-Fri) **FREE** The *şəbəkə* stained-glass windows featured at Xan Sarayı are laboriously made by slotting together hundreds of hand-carved wooden pieces to create intricate wooden frames without metal fastenings. You can see them being made at this no-hassle family workshop (no English), where young apprentices are learning the trade. Opening times vary.

◎ Beyond the Fortress Walls

A canalised stream parallels MF Axundzadə pr from the fortress area to the new town's main square, passing two **19th-century mosques** and numerous halva shops en route. Away from this road, it's fun to delve into the maze of residential Old Town alleys full of typical tiled-roof homes.

Winter Palace   PALACE
(Şəkixanlarının Evi; Hikmət Ələkbərzadə küç, Otağ Eşiye; admission/photography AZN2/2; ◎ 9am-9pm) Be among the first foreigners to discover the Şəki Khans' recently restored yet little publicised 'other' palace. Like a slightly smaller Xan Sarayı, it has its own rose garden, and while five of the six rooms are essentially plain, the sixth has a stunning series of original 1765 murals depicting scenes from Nizami classics.

Unlike at the Xan Sarayı, photography inside is permitted. The English-speaking guide lives next door.

Karavansaray   CARAVANSERAI
(MF Axundzadə pr 185) Even if you don't stay here, do peep inside this historic caravanserai whose twin-level arcade of sturdy arches encloses a sizeable central courtyard. Stride through the imposing wooden gateway door and if questioned say you're heading for the restaurant in the garden behind.

Dili Qala   FORT
An intriguing landmark on the ridge above town, there's nothing historic about this curious castle-like folly, which was designed to be a hotel but so poorly constructed that it was never finished. Good for city views, though.

◎ Kiş

Kiş Albanian Church   CHURCH
(Kiş Alban Məbədi; adult/student AZN2/1, guide AZN5; ◎ 9am-dusk) The brilliantly renovated round-towered Albanian church in pretty Kiş village has been lovingly converted into a very well-presented trilingual museum. It's the best place anywhere to learn about mysterious Caucasian Albania, the Christian nation that once covered most of northern Azerbaijan. In fact, the church site goes back well beyond the Christian era, and glass-covered grave excavations allow visitors to peer down on the bones of possibly Bronze Age skeletons.

To find the church, take the first lane to the right after Kiş' main street becomes

AZERBAIJAN ŞƏKI

Şəki (Sheki)

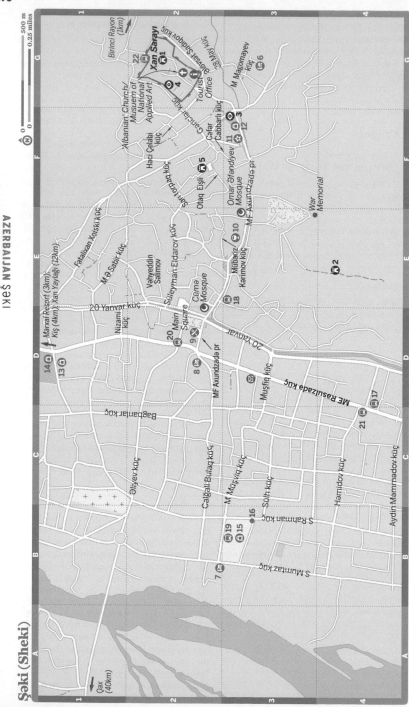

Şəki (Sheki)

cobbled. The church is well signed, 800m up a double-back loop.

🏃 Activities

Xan Yaylağı   WALKING

High above the city, a plateau of summer pastures known as Xan Yaylağı offers superb viewpoints over the valley and on towards high Caucasian peaks.

The easiest access is by a 12km switchback of forest track that zigzags up from Marxal Resort (off the Kiş road). However, at the time of research, access was usually blocked by the security guards of a major resort construction project that is redeveloping Marxal. An alternative path up starts from the terminus of *marshrutka* 17 in Şəki's Birinci Rayon district. Either route takes around

3½ hours one-way. Bears live in the forest so hiking alone isn't recommended.

🛏 Sleeping

There are several rural alternatives located around Kiş.

★ Karavansaray Hotel   INN $

(📞 055-7555570, 02424-44814; MF Axundzadə pr 185; s/d/tr/q AZN20/30/36/48, ste AZN50-80) Staying in this converted caravanserai is justification enough to visit Şəki. Rooms have arched brickwork ceilings and while they're certainly not luxurious, all have sitting areas and Western toilets in the humorously dated little bathrooms.

Booking ahead can be wise, especially if you want a single room, of which there are only two.

İlhamə Hüseynova   HOMESTAY $

(📞 02424-98833; ilhame633@mail.ru; homestay/guesthouse per person AZN10/15) Up in Kiş village, the English-speaking lady who manages the church site can also readily organise homestays and has built her own eight-room guesthouse just a few doors away. Rooms share modern bathrooms and a kitchen.

İlqar Ağayev   HOMESTAY $

(📞 055-6238295; www.cbtazerbaijan.com/sheki; M Magomayev 20; beds AZN16-20) Kindly, pious and proficient in English, İlqar can arrange beds in a selection of Şəki homes including his own family's place, with a great Old Town location. There's a hot shower and, unlike many traditional homestays, an indoor toilet. Ask about local hikes and horse riding.

Pensionat Sahil   MOTEL $

(📞 02424-45491; S Mumtaz küç; r AZN20-50; 🅿❄🛜) Aimed at market traders, Sahil has simple but perfectly survivable rooms with private if sometimes musty bathrooms. The cheapest rooms lack air-con

Access is through tall iron gates directly west of the bazaar. Enter from the back of the building via the good-value restaurant-garden, where Aysberq beer costs AZN1.

★ Şəki Saray Hotel   BOUTIQUE HOTEL $$

(📞 02424-48181; www.shekisaray.az; ME Rəsulzadə küç 187; s/d/tw/ste AZN80/90/100/250; ❄🛜) Local, oriental and modernist touches combine with original photography and spacious unfussy rooms to make this 21st-century hotel a splendid choice right in the centre of town. Staff speak English.

AZERBAIJAN ŞƏKI

WORTH A TRIP

FAZIL'S ANCIENT SECRETS

More than a dozen close-packed grave sites from the 2nd to 7th centuries BC have been excavated but left exactly as they were found with pots, talismans and the bones of sacrificed animals in situ, at **Fazıl Labarynth** (Fazıl Village; adult/ child AZN2/1; ⊙ by arrangement, typically evenings in summer). One can almost 'feel' the evolution of humanity in the space of 70m as you walk through the little brick-vaulted catacomb created for the site's protection.

This place has been a lifetime endeavour for two local archaeologists, who open the site by appointment, best arranged through the Şəki tourist office. They don't speak English but each burial site has a summary title in English. The rural site is 25km southeast of Şəki. Turn south off the Oğuz road turn towards Ibrahimkənd, then left in Fazıl at Km8.1 and go 200m east. Aşağı Kungut buses departing Şəki at 7am, 1pm and 5pm pass through Fazıl.

H.İ.İ. Hotel
BOUTIQUE MOTEL $$

(Servis Motel; ☑ 055-4679395; www.hotelservis. com; Oğuz Hwy; s/d AZN50/60) Rooms are smart, fully equipped and very spacious, and the views from north-facing windows encompass a sweep of Şəki's high mountain backdrop that is invisible from the town itself. But unless you're travelling by car, the location is simply too far from town to be convenient and the place can often feel eerily deserted.

✖ Eating

There are numerous very cheap, if forgettable, eateries around Təzə Bazaar. Şəki is famous for its confectionery. Shops along MF Axundzadə pr flog lurid *nöğul* (sugar-coated beans) and much more palatable *mindal* (nuts in a crisp caramel coating). But by far their best-known offering is *Şəki halvasi*, a misnomer for a kind of *paxlava* (baklava). *Piti* (two-part stew) is a popular main course here and Şəki also specialises in miniature vine-leaf dolma.

Çələbi Xan Restoran
AZERBAIJANI $$

(Main Sq; mains/kebabs from AZN4/3; ⊙ 9am-11pm; ▣) The restaurant's striking exterior combines classic *şəbəkə* with modern

smoked glass while the pine interior is as eccentric as a cuckoo clock. There's lots of tree-shaded outdoor seating and for just AZN2 you could fill up on bread and borscht. The *piti* (AZN4) is excellent but if you fancy the *aş* (a multiperson platter of fruity *plov*; AZN30), you'll need to preorder. There's a 15% service charge.

☕ Drinking

Buta Bar
LOUNGE

(Şəki Saray Hotel, ME Rəsulzadə küç 187; espresso AZN2; ⊙ 8am-midnight) Decked with Moroccan-style lamps, the inviting little Buta Bar brews Şəki's best coffee and is a rare place where unaccompanied women won't be ill-judged for ordering alcoholic beverages.

Ovuçlar Məkanı
AZERBAIJANI

(MF Axundzadə pr; beers from AZN1; ⊙ 9am-2am) If you're not put off by the animal trophies, this rustic-themed 'hunters' corner' makes a relatively comfortable place to sink beers after everywhere else has closed. It also has a pleasant garden area and serves local meals including kebabs (AZN2.90) and *qutab* (50q). Male dominated.

🛍 Shopping

Many tourist-friendly trinket-merchants occupy small shop-units tucked into the side of the Karavansaray.

Təzə Bazaar
MARKET

(▣ 5, 8, 11) Everything from pottery, metalwork and carpets to masses of fresh food. Saffron comes in a wide variety of qualities, the cheapest just AZN1 a cupful.

House of Craftsmen
SOUVENIRS

(Şəki Şənətkarlar Evi; Fortress Grounds; ⊙ 10am-dusk) Although the wide range of knick-knacks is mostly fairly corny tourist tat, this two-storey complex also includes genuine craft artists' workshops and is worth perusing en route to the tourist office, which is upstairs in the same historic building.

Halvaçi Yəhyə
FOOD

(MF Axundzadə pr 185/20; Şəki halva per box from AZN3; ⊙ 10am-11pm) Şəki is famed for its super-sweet, syrup-soaked halva, which is actually more like a form of *paxlava*. Yəhyə is our favourites of countless local brands.

Şəki İpek
SILK

(ME Rəsulzadə küç; ⊙ 9am-6pm; ▣ 2, 8) The showroom of Şəki's silk factory *(kombinat)* stocks high-quality carpets and some attractively simple silk scarves (from AZN20).

☆ Entertainment

Çingis Klubu   CINEMA

(MF Axundzadə pr 91; admission 40q; ⊙ shows 3pm & 5pm) Small gallery, one-room 'museum' and mini-cinema screening kids' movies at 3pm, adults' at 5pm.

ℹ Information

Several banks directly south of Şəki Saray Hotel have ATMs and currency exchange.

Tourist Office (☑ 02424-46095, 04427-71340; http://sheki.travel/en; 1st fl, Sənətkarlar Evi; ⊙ 9am-6pm daily Apr-Oct, 10am-5pm Mon-Fri only Nov-Mar) Well-organised, friendly tourist information office with English- and German-speaking staff.

ℹ Getting There & Away

BUS & TAXI

There's one well-organised **bus station** (☑ 02424-44617; ME Rəsulzadə küç). Useful services:

Baku Up to 25 services daily. Buses (AZN6.40, seven hours) drive via Xaldan and Kürdamir, most minibuses (AZN7) and all shared taxis (AZN15, six hours) go via İsmayıllı.

Balakən (AZN3, three hours, 10.10am and 2pm)

Gəncə (AZN4, 3½ hours, 8am, 9.10am, 11.50am and 1.30pm)

Qax (AZN1, one hour, seven daily)

Zaqatala (AZN2.50, 2½ hours, seven daily)

TRAIN

The Baku night train departs at 9.43pm from Şəki train station, 17km south of town. You can prebook tickets at the Aviakassa on the southeast corner of Təzə Bazaar. Bring a photocopy of your passport and apply at least by lunchtime, ideally much earlier. Pick up the physical ticket at the station at least one hour before departure.

Arriving by train at Şəki station, if you don't manage to find a shared taxi into town, you could walk 700m east to the AzPetrol roundabout then flag down any northbound bus (40q).

ℹ Getting Around

Marshrutky (20q) run till around 8pm, or 9pm in summer. *Marshrutka* 8 and 11 both connect Təzə Bazaar to the town centre, picking up at the Hәmidov küç/ME Rəsulzadə küç junction a half block north of the bus station. *Marshrutka* 11 continues to the Karavansaray and passes near the Xan Sarayı. Route 17 does the same but continues into Birinci Rayon. Route 8 goes on past the Silk Factory. Route 15 goes to Kiş.

Taxis charge AZN2 for rides within town, around AZN6 to the train station.

Qax & İlisu

☑ 02425 / POP 15,000

Qax (pronounced 'gakh') has a partly Georgian-speaking population and three historic churches, one containing a modest museum. From its gently quaint centre, the town straggles up through beautiful landscapes towards İlisu (15km north), somewhat over-grandly nicknamed Qax's 'mini-Switzerland'. The upper valley in-between has many rural restaurants and several hotels.

◉ Sights

İçəri Bazaar   AREA

Old Town Qax is centred on İçəri Bazaar, a streetscape where older houses have been given a faux-antique look on a lane guarded by castle-style gateways and warrior statues. The centrepiece is a small open-air theatre that's especially attractive on summer evenings when colonised by tea tables whose dim lights twinkle amid the trees.

A very short block north, tree-shaded İ Mustafaeyev küç leads west, hugging a canalised stream and overhung by the wooden box windows of a few traditional houses.

İlisu Village   VILLAGE

Two beautiful high-altitude valleys meet at charming little İlisu. Amazingly this diminutive village of photogenic old homes was once the capital of a short-lived 18th-century sultanate. Many houses retain box windows, arched doorways and red-tiled roofs, there's an antique mosque and several remnant fortifications. The square-plan, five-storey Summaqala Tower at the very southwestern end of the village commands a picture-perfect valley view towards distant snow-topped peaks.

At the northernmost end of Ilisu there are fine views from the Uludağ restaurant-resort. Turn right and hike 40 minutes uphill to find a locally famous waterfall (Şəlalə). Walking up the main valley towards Russia isn't allowed (closed border zone).

🛏 Sleeping & Eating

Hotel Qax   HOTEL $

(Mehmanxana; ☑ 02425-54868; Nərimanov küç 3; s AZN5-8, d AZN10-16, ste AZN20; 🛜) Friendly and good value, most rooms in the simple little Hotel Qax share clean if seatless communal toilets. Some suites have their own bathrooms. It's in central Qax just north of the Heydar Əliyev statue between İçəri Bazaar and the Kiş road. The cafe next door serves remarkably edible AZN3 meals.

İlisu Pansionat
COTTAGES $

(☑ 050-3285615; per person with/without 3 meals AZN30/15) Assuming you can get past the gruff gatekeeper, this is the best value of three bungalow resorts in a pretty meadow area around the 17th-century Ulu Bridge, 3km south of İlisu village.

Most of the sturdy cottages with private bathroom sleep four or six people but outside peak weekends individuals and couples get a whole unit at the same per-person rate. There's a small zipline, a climbing wall and the friendly family owners know hiking and mountaineering routes into the forest ridge behind. No English, though.

El Resort
HOTEL $$$

(www.elresort.az; Heydar Əliyev pr; d/tw AZN98/108; P ✳ 🛜 🏊) Formed wood and well-placed decorative stones give a faintly Japanese vibe to Qax's one big resort hotel that comes complete with indoor swimming pool, gym and conference centre.

It's 5km north of central Qax.

Səngər Qala Restaurant
AZERBAIJANI $$

(kebab/salads/beer from AZN4/2/2) Even if you don't eat here, it's worth a quick stop to photograph Səngər Qala Restaurant, which takes the form of a fantasy castle built within crenellated dark stone walls and full of quirky oddities.

It's 1km before Ilisu. Directly north are nearly a dozen smaller restaurants.

❶ Getting There & Around

The bus station is on the main street (Heydar Əliyev pr) at the far southwestern edge of town. Useful services:

Şəki (AZN1, one hour, seven daily)

Tbilisi (three buses daily) Book at least a few hours ahead.

Zaqatala (AZN1, 1¼ hours, seven daily direct) There are also three services that use a longer loop road (these are denoted 't.y.').

Sporadic *marshrutka* 1 drives from the bus station to the Flag Roundabout (1.5km), loops through the Old Town then continues north as far as El Resort.

For **İlisu**, *marshrutky* (40q, 20 minutes) depart the bus station at 7.20am, 9.30am, noon, 2pm

and 5pm, returning almost immediately. A Qax–İlisu taxi costs around AZN5.

Zaqatala & Car

☑ 02422 / POP 21,400

Azerbaijan's hazelnut capital sits at the confluence of two wide mountain rivers descending steeply from the Great Caucasus. The lower town (bazaar, bus station) is unremarkable but a useful place to stay and organise transport. The older town centre is 2km uphill. Climbing steeply into the wooded foothills behind is the pretty village of Car (pronounced 'jar').

◉ Sights

Old Town Square
GARDENS

(Old Town Sq) Zaqatala's Old Town is centred on a pretty garden-square, above which rise two 30m-tall *çinar* (plane) trees planted in the 1780s.

To the south, there are numerous old-style house facades on the upper reaches of Heydar Əliyev pr. Follow a path past the maudlin shell of a drum-towered Orthodox church to find the fortress entrance.

Car Village
VILLAGE

Car is a chocolate-box village half-hidden in blossoms and greenery. Picturesque houses are hidden behind mossy dry-stone walls in abundant orchards. Several rustic restaurants are tucked away in its woodland fringes.

Fortress
FORTRESS

(adult/student AZN2/1; ◷ 9am-1pm & 2-6pm Mon-Fri) Built between 1830 and 1860, Zaqatala's Russian fortress is a sprawling affair with sturdy grey stone walls. It originally guarded against attacks from the Dagestan-based guerrilla army of Shamil and later imprisoned sailors from the battleship *Potëmkin*, whose famous 1905 mutiny at Odessa foreshadowed the Russian revolution.

Arguably the walls look more appealing from the outside as within are several banal 20th-century buildings: until around 2005 the fortress was still in military use.

Historical Museum
MUSEUM

(30 Heydar Əliyev pr; admission AZN1; ◷ 9am-1pm & 2-6pm Mon-Fri) The small Historical Museum is worth a five-minute glimpse to peruse faded photos of the area's attraction amid old pots, jewellery, priceless books and local costumes. There's minimal English.

Zaqatala

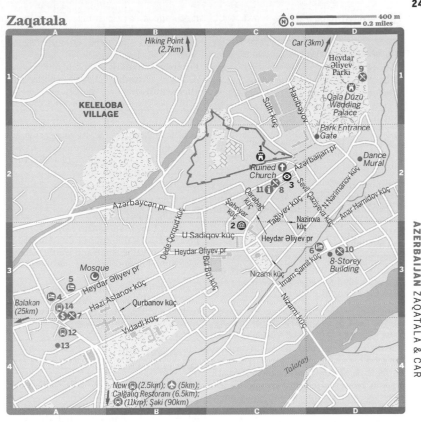

0 400 m
0 0.2 miles

Activities

Alpine Treks
HIKING

High Alpine pastures above the treeline offer some of the loveliest vistas in Azerbaijan. The only way up is on foot or by horse. The easiest access route follows the sheep up from the western side of Car on a fairly obvious trail following a sloping forest ridge.

The route is easily discernible from a Google Earth image. To get to the starting point, get off the Car *marshrutka* at Amin Market, cross the metal-plate bridge and walk 900m west turning left at each of the two main junctions. The sheep trail should be on your right before a small stream starts to cut away a valley beside you. If that sounds too tough, it's possible to engage a hiking guide through the tourist office (AZN50 per day). Or pay AZN100 for the popular two-day return trip to Xalaxı Göl mountain lake, sleeping overnight in one of the summer shepherd's hut-camps.

AZERBAIJAN ZAQATALA & CAR

🍽 Sleeping & Eating

🛏 Old Town Area

Turqut Motel   INN $
(☎02422-56229; Imam Şamil küç; d/ste AZN20/50, without bathroom d/tr AZN10/15) Recently redecorated rooms come with functioning bathrooms and toiletries, simpler ones share a seatless sit-down toilet. If reception is dormant, seek out a waiter in the fountain tea-garden behind. No English.

Meydan Kafesi   CAFE $
(Old Town Sq; mains from AZN3, coffee AZN1; ⊙11am-11pm) This cosy cafe doesn't have the advertised espresso but does an excellent Turkish coffee served with *lokum* (Turkish delight).

It's most popular on summer evenings once the blazing sun is off the outdoor terrace. Pizza and *khajapuri* (cheese pie) also available.

Qala Düzü   AZERBAIJANI, TEAHOUSE $
(Heydar Əliyev Park; qutab for 3 AZN1.50, kebab AZN4, beer AZN2; ⊙10am-midnight, summer only) The big main building is a wedding palace, but food, tea and a limited menu are available from the clifftop booth seats in the park outside. Some tables have views across the river valley and of the forested mountains beyond. No alcohol during Ramadan.

Qaqaş Restoran   AZERBAIJANI $
(☎050-6378192; Imam Şamil küç; mains AZN2-4, beer 80q; ⊙10am-11pm) Inexpensive yet original restaurant with a facade of bottle-ends, an interior of quirky timber rooms and a series of wooden perches behind as dining platforms. Cheap beer on draught.

🛏 Bus Station Area

Hotel Zaqatala   HOTEL $
(☎02422-55709; Heydar Əliyev pr 92; dm/tw/tr/ste AZN8/25/35/40; ❄🔊) Handy for the bus station, this sensibly pitched, no-nonsense budget hotel has good standards for the price and private bathroom even in the six-bed (men only) dorm, though you'll need your own toilet paper.

Choose even-numbered rooms to reduce road noise. Only the suites have air-con. A simple tea-honey-cheese breakfast is included.

Grata Hotel   HOTEL $$
(☎02422-53353; Grata-hotel@mail.ru; Heydar Əliyev pr 100; s/d/tr/ste AZN40/50/75/140; ❄🔊) The best choice in town with European-standard rooms featuring high ceilings, closeable shower booths and effective air-con.

Can Ailəvi Restoran   TURKISH $
(Türkeli Kafe; F Əmirov 6; mains AZN1.50-4, kebab AZN4-5; ⊙9am-11pm; ❄) It seems that the staff never stop polishing the glass-topped tables in this neat if generic place for Turkish pizza, kebabs or dolma.

🛏 Car (Jar)

Ləzzət Istirahət Zonası   GUESTHOUSE $
(☎070-2064663; s/d cottage AZN20/40) In a pretty woodland corner of Car, Ləzzət has several fair-value stone-and-wattle cottages with old-tiled roofs, polished wooden floors and functional bathrooms. The restaurant, a series of rustic dining pavilions including one in a tree house, serves Georgian, Azerbaijani and Dagestani. Many items require considerable preparation time.

🛏 Aşağı Tala

★**Calğalıq Restoranı**   AZERBAIJANI $$
(☎02422-67700; www.facebook.com/pages/ Calğalıq-Restoranı/240023086189092; mains AZN3-10, beer AZN2.50) The most characterful restaurant for miles around, Calğalıq is packed with more antique handicrafts than the average museum and the enchanted garden is all acroak with frogs. There are some Georgian options and very local seasonal specialities like *maxara* (*sac*-cooked savoury pancakes).

The location is utterly improbable: around 2.5km east of the flag roundabout/old bus station take the Aşağı Tala turn-off and drive 4km south.

ℹ Information

Several phone shops opposite the bus station sell SIM cards. Internet cafes are sprinkled along Heydar Əliyev pr.

Bank Respublika (F Əmirov 4; ⊙9am-5pm Mon-Fri) Has an ATM and changes US dollars at good rates. So-so rates for euros.

Tourist Office (Zaqatala Turizm və İnformasiya Mərkazi; ☎02422-54341; www.facebook.com/ Zagatala-Tourism-Information-Centre; Heydar Əliyev pr 2; ⊙9am-6pm) The friendly tourist office can organise trekking guides and help you find homestays/house rentals in Car. Tarlan speaks English.

ⓘ Getting There & Away

AIR

At the time of research the normally thrice-weekly Baku–Zaqatala flight was not operating.

BUS & SHARED TAXI

The following services depart from the **old bus station**.

Baku via İsmayıllı (per seat AZN20 to AZN25) Shared taxi.

Baku via Kürdamir (AZN8, eight to nine hours, 9.40am, 10am, 11am, noon, 3pm, 3.30pm, 4pm and 10pm)

Balakən (*marshrutka;* 60q, 35 minutes; shared taxi per seat/car AZN1/4) *Marshrutky* leave when fairly full till 5pm.

Other services leave from the **new bus station** (Yeni Avtovağzal) at the far eastern end of town, though before departure they may cruise back through town collecting passengers.

Gəncə (AZN4, 8.15am, 8.45am, 11am, 3pm and 4.30pm)

Qax (80q, 1¼ hours, 7.50am, 8.30am, 10.15am, 12.20pm, 2pm, 3.30pm and 5.05pm) Pay aboard. An 11am service goes via the long route.

Qəbələ (AZN4, 9.30am)

Şəki (AZN2, 2½ hours, 8am, 8.30am, 9.15am, 10.30am, noon, 1.15pm, 3pm and 5pm) Bypasses Qax.

Marshrutky to local villages start from various points between the bazaar and old bus station. These include three daily minibuses to Lahıc but that's NOT the Lahic near İsmayıllı that you probably wanted.

TRAIN

Trains to Baku (*platskart/kupe* AZN7/10, 11 hours) depart at 7.20pm from Zaqatala train station, 8km southeast of town. When arriving you might prefer to copy other passengers and get off at the Naib Bulaq (Zaqatala Yolu) halt, which has no ticket office or station building but is on the Baku road: Aliabad- and Mosul-bound minibuses pass by. Buy train tickets in advance from the **Dəmir Yol Kassa booth** (Dəmir Yol Kassa; Old bus station; ☉ 9am-2pm & 4-7.30pm) tucked almost invisibly into the rear courtyard of the old bus station.

ⓘ Getting Around

Marshrutky marked 'Qala Düzü' go from the bazaar to the old bus station roundabout then up to the Old Town area. Three or four times an hour (7am to 6.30pm) a minibus does the same route then continues to Car (30q). A new midsized bus links the two bus stations.

Balakən

☑ 02429 / POP 10,200

Balakən is the first town you'll reach on arrival from Georgia (via Lagodekhi). A large flagpole marks the central junction near the bazaar. Comfortable **Hotel Qubek** (☑ 050-4929272; www.qubekhotel.az; Səttar Gözəlov küç; s/d AZN50/60; ⓟ✷⊛🖥) is a short walk north of here beside a large park with its entertainingly pointless horizontal cable car. *Marshrutky* 1, 9 and 10 run west then south past the fine central mosque, or east 1.5km to the bus station, turning around 600m beyond at the AzPetrol filling-station-motel where there's an ATM.

ⓘ Getting There & Away

There's a night train to Baku but waiting for it in Zaqatala is more interesting.

Travel via taxi, minibus and *marshrutky* is available from Balakən:

Georgia Shared/private taxis to the border cost AZN1/5 from MMOil petrol station at the flagpole roundabout.

Şəki Minibus (AZN3, three hours) departs 8.30am from the bus station.

Zaqatala *Marshrutky* (60q, 40 minutes) leave once or twice hourly when nearly full from Culture Centre Park, 700m west of the flagpole roundabout. Last at 5.30pm.

CENTRAL AZERBAIJAN

Most travellers' memories of the main highway across Central Azerbaijan are likely to be of monotonous flat steppe. However, on very clear days, high distant mountains rise like ghostly apparitions on both north and south horizons. And roughly halfway between Baku and Tbilisi, Azerbaijan's historic second city, Gəncə, is putting considerable efforts into making itself more interesting for visitors.

Gəncə

☑ 022 / POP 328,400

Azerbaijan's second city has relatively little to show for millenia of history, unable to decide itself whether it's 2500 or 4000 years old. But 21st-century reinvention is starting to make the most of its surviving heritage, dust off its Soviet-era austerity and add some twinkles of new architectural daring.

Gəncə

Most proudly the town was home to Azerbaijan's national bard Nizami Gəncəvi (1141–1209). However, it was leveled by earthquakes, razed by the Mongols in 1231 and rebuilt by Shah Abbas in its present location after the city changed hands several times in the 17th-century Ottoman-Safavid wars. As capital of a later khanate, in 1804 Gəncə put up a suicidally brave stand to eventually victorious Russian forces, which renamed the city Elisavetpol and later Kirovabad. From a building that is now the city's agricultural institute, the Azerbaijan Democratic Republic first declared the nation's independence in 1918. Gəncə served for a few months as the capital of that short-lived republic until Baku was recaptured from the socialist revolutionaries.

⊙ Sights

The area around Heydar Əliyev Sq has a curious architectural mixture of Stalinist power, early-20th-century red brickwork and oddments of 21st-century pseudo-Classical revival. There's a small clutch of 17th-century structures too, but many of the city's more memorable sights are in the outskirts.

⊙ City Centre

City Hall ARCHITECTURE
(Heydar Əliyev Sq) Gəncə's central square is dominated by the arcade-fronted City Hall, a powerful example of Stalinist architecture that contrasts with the tree-shaded 17th-century mosque at the square's southern end.

Cümə Mosque MOSQUE
(Şah Abbas Məscidi) The early-17th-century Cümə Mosque features a disconnected double minaret and is credited to Persian Shah Abbas in whose reign it was built.

Cavadxan küç AREA
The city's most appealing street has been recently beautified with attractive sculptures and restored housefronts on a succession of brick buildings, which date mostly from around 1900.

Bottle House BUILDING
(Qəmbər Hüseynli küç) Worth a 20-second stop if you're passing, this residential home has been transformed into a quirky artwork using hundreds of beer, champagne and glass water bottles.

⊙ Outskirts

Heydar Əliyev Park PARK
(**P**; 🚃 11) In the unofficial 'Top Park' competition between Azerbaijani cities, Gəncə's vast new Heydar Əliyev Park wins hands down. Along with a fairground, modern art museum, culture centre and amphitheatre for occasional free concerts, there's what looks like a full-sized Arc de Triomphe.

It's at the western edge of town, accessible by bus 11.

İmamzadə ISLAMIC
(🚃 18) The İmamzadə, Azerbaijan's most impressive Islamic structure, is a masterpiece of brickwork and Central Asian–style blue majolica tiles nearing completion on the northern edge of Gəncə, replacing a far-more-modest 19th-century equivalent. Though evidence seems sketchy, the site is considered to be the grave of Maulana Ibrahim, son of the 5th Shiite Imam, Muhammad al-Baqir. Access is by hourly bus 18 from Gəncə train station (7km).

Gəncə Darvazası GATE
(Ganja Gates; M2 Hwy) This pair of gigantic brick gateways dates from 2014 but is designed to evoke the idea of ancient Gəncə's long-lost citadel portal from which the iron gates were plundered by an 1139 Georgian attack and removed to Gelati. The site is near the M2 Hwy bypass intersection several kilometres east of Gəncə via a long feeder avenue that also passes 2km of mock fortress walls and a space-ship-shaped mausoleum to the city's great 12th-century poet Nizami Ganjavi.

Göygöl VILLAGE
For a surreal slice of transplanted Teutonic history, take a 20-minute, 20q bus ride south of Gəncə to this agreeable small town founded as Helenendorf by German winemakers in the 1830s. Stalin bundled the Germans' descendants off to permanent exile in Kazakhstan during WWII. However, the tree-lined town centre has been extensively reworked with wooden house-frontages to rekindle the Germanic flavour. The old Lutheran Church houses a small museum.

South of Göygöl are numerous woodland restaurants, then after Hacıkənd the road emerges onto a ridge with magnificent views of the Lesser Caucasus range, crowned by the beaklike peak of Mt Kəpəz. Further still is the idyllic lake Göy Göl for which Göygöl is named. The lake had been out of bounds for two decades but reopened to visitors in late summer 2015. Entrance to the park area costs AZN2 per person, a taxi from Göygöl costs around AZN30 return. Continuing 7km further to see even lovelier and less-visited Maral Göl costs an additional AZN20 return because of the poor state of the track.

🛏 Sleeping

Ganja Homestay HOMESTAY $
(☑ 050-3210121; www.facebook.com/GanjaHome Stay/posts/338622466164506; Qacaq Nabi 23; tw AZN25; ❄ 🛜; 🚃 4) The very real family experience would be attraction enough. But the great bonus of this modest homestay is the thoughtful, ever-obliging host, Afgan Mehtikhanov, who speaks excellent English and, outside work hours, can help you get a really personal insight into this underestimated city.

The homestay is a short hop on bus 4 or *marshrutka* 25 from the central area.

Kəpəz Hotel HISTORIC HOTEL $
(☑ 022-2566013; Abbaszadə küç; s/d AZN20/35) The cheapest city-centre option, better rooms have water heaters and new toilets but the building is a monstrous Soviet-era hulk of decomposing concrete. Only the 4th floor functions and there's no lift. Try bargaining.

Cinema Boutique Hotel HOTEL $$
(☑ 022-2566999; Cavadxan küç 2; s/d from AZN50/70) Small, comfortable midrange option handily placed near the riverside at the top of Gəncə's most appealing commercial street.

★ Vego Hotel BOUTIQUE HOTEL $$$
(☑ 022-2640182; www.vegohotel.com; Cavadxan küç 38; s/d AZN97/108; ❄ @ 🛜) Gəncə's best central choice has the comfortable standards of a business hotel but adds plenty of quirky artistic touches. Best of all you get to use a large, genuine 17th-century *hamam* to which the hotel is connected by a mural-covered tunnel.

Şah Abbas Karvansarayı HERITAGE HOTEL $$$
(Şeyx Bahəddin küç 61) This hefty brick caravanserai has been under reconstruction since 2011 and is due to open as a heritage-style hotel. Eventually!

🍴 Eating

In summer, anyone with a vehicle should consider driving up towards Hacıkənd to dine at one of the woodland eateries along the way.

Kafe Mağara
AZERBAIJANI **$**

(Cavadxan küç; mains AZN1.5-3, salad AZN1, bread 50q; ⊙10am-11pm; ✳) This basement restaurant has displays of handicrafts, wagon-wheel lamps and partly stone-clad 'cave' walls, yet big portions of typical *yeməkxana* fare are very inexpensive and of reasonable quality.

Epikur Bağı
INTERNATIONAL **$$**

(☑022-2662070; www.facebook.com/epikurbagi; Heydar Əliyev pr 157; mains/sushi from AZN5/3; ⊙11am-11pm; ✳) Gəncə's widest selection of non-local cuisine served in a cutesy snow-queen palace setting. Enter from Şeyx Bahəddin küç.

❶ Information

There are several **moneychangers** (MUM, Heydar Əliyev pr) north of the Univermaq department store.

Internet Klub Ref (Cavadxan küç 22; per hr 40q; ⊙9am-11pm) Airy internet club with photocopy service.

❶ Getting There & Away

AIR
Globus Travel (☑022-2521121; www.safar.az; Cavadxan küç 41; ⊙9am-6pm) sells air tickets. Gəncə's airport is 8km northwest of the city centre, around AZN7 by taxi. Flights include the following:

Baku (AZN31, daily)

İstanbul (AZN190 to AZN450, daily) Flights with Turkish Airlines, some days via Naxçivan.

Moscow (AZN180, at least daily)

Mineralnye Vodi (Russia; AZN194, Sunday) Flights with Ural Airlines.

BUS
Buses to Baku and all destinations east use the new Yevlax Avtovağzal, accessible by bus 17 or 23 from central Gəncə. *Marshrutky* to Göygöl (20q, 25 minutes) leave frequently from Nərimanov küç just south of the Nizami küç junction.

Through buses to Krasny Most (Qırmızı Körpü, the Georgian border; three hours) pick up at Yeni Gəncə junction opposite Ramada Plaza hotel.

The Yeni Şəmkir Avtovağzal, 300m southwest of the Ramada Plaza by bus 4, handles *marshrutky* to Daşkəsən (80q, last 6.30pm), Şəmkir, Gadabey and Qazax (AZN2, last 7.30pm).

TRAIN
The train station is 4km north of the city centre by bus 1, 4 or 12. Sleepers run overnight to Baku (*kupe* AZN9 to AZN11, nine hours) at 10.20pm, 11pm and around 12.30am. The daytime 'express' (AZN6) departs at 3.50pm on alternate days arriving in Baku antisocially around midnight.

SOUTHERN AZERBAIJAN

Worth a look if you're heading to/from Iran, Southern Azerbaijan's coastal strip is the lush breadbasket of the country, where tea plantations line the roadsides and trees are heavy with citrus fruit. Inland, bucolic forested mountains offer tempting streamside getaways and there's hiking potential in the grassy uplands beyond. The area is home to the Talysh people, famed for their hospitality and for living to great ages.

Biləsuvar

Heading for Tabriz, Iran? From Biləsuvar bus stand, walk two blocks northwest to the junction of Axundov küç (just before the giant flagpole) to find AZN2 shared taxis to the border (*gömrük*), 18km west of Biləsuvar.

Lənkəran

☑02525 / POP 51,600

The southern region's biggest town, likeable Lənkəran (Lenkoran) is famous for flowers, tea and its trademark *ləvəngi* cuisine. The city is short on must-see attractions but exudes a laid-back charm, is full of relentlessly hospitable people and serves as a springboard for visiting the Talysh Mountains.

◉ Sights

★Bazaar
MARKET

(Mir Mustafaxan küç; ⊙6am-6pm) Lənkəran's sprawling bazaar is centred on an architecturally drab concrete hangar, but it's loaded with colourful produce and equally colourful local characters. Remarkably friendly.

Stalin's Prison
LANDMARK

(Dairəvi Qala; Fikrət Məmmədov küç; ⊙10am-1pm Mon-Fri) **FREE** This sturdy brick-barrel tower once imprisoned Joseph Stalin during his early revolutionary days, yet for now there's no attempt to commemorate the fact.

Instead the ground floor hosts a rather sparse gallery, the second is unused and the top floor is in urgent need of repairs after an unusual heavy snowfall in early 2015 damaged the old tile roofing.

Hazi Aslanov Statue
STATUE

(H Aslanov xiyabani) The figure standing proudly in front of the train station is local WWII hero Həzi Aslanov, whose plinth rises from a stylised concrete tank.

Southern Azerbaijan

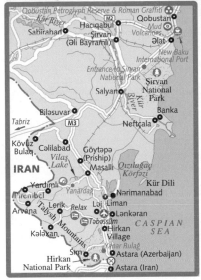

John Toshack, better known as a star of the 1970s Liverpool squad.

🛏 Sleeping & Eating

A southern speciality is *ləvəngi*, chicken or fish stuffed with nut paste, sold relatively cheaply from little stalls and house windows around the region. *Ləvəngi* makes a great picnic best savoured with hot bread (*isti çörək*) fresh-baked in the same *tandir* (hive-shaped clay stove).

★ Xan Lənkəran · HERITAGE HOTEL $$
(☑ 050-3905446, 02525-42580; xanlankaran@gmail.com; Ləvəngi bus station; s/d from AZN40/48; ❋🗟) Oh for more hotels like this. If you don't mind staying out by the bus station, this handicraft-filled complex combines an air of well-contrived antiquity with all modern conveniences, including Grohe bathroom fittings, fluffy dressing gowns and underfloor heating. There's a village-style dining room, a Tolkienesque garden and a reception desk fashioned from two vast tree trunks.

Some walls are made of traditional mud-wattle, and in sitting areas you can lounge like a khan on piles of carpets and *mutəkə* (elbow cushions). Shelves are hewn from logs and 'hung' from chains, lamps are designed like 19th-century lanterns and even the cleaners wear traditional village costumes. The restaurant offers excellent-value meals.

Hotel Səda · GUESTHOUSE $$
(☑ 050-6711141, 02525-51664; Nəsirli küç 7; s/d/tr/q AZN30/50/60/70; ❋) Despite the name, the Səda isn't so much a hotel as two collections of high-ceilinged if rather characterless rooms. The better, newer ones plus a communal kitchen are in the less obvious section, which is accessed via a side alley. There's no real reception.

AB Qala · HOTEL $$
(☑ 02525-50284; www.abqala.az; Mir Mustafaxan küç; s/d from AZN30/50; ❋) Entering the Qala there's a certain restrained elegance in the spacious lobby cafe, and at least some staff speak English. The rooms are acceptable but don't quite live up to the promise, some in the lower category feeling a tad dowdy.

The lift seems ever out of action.

Uzbek Kafesi · AZERBAIJANI $
(mains AZN3.50; ⊙9am-9pm) Inexpensive, hearty meals, notably *plov* with *ləvəngi* or *giymə* (vegetable dolma) are served at this unmarked but distinctive brick building

Lighthouse Tower · LANDMARK
Still functioning as a lighthouse despite being set well inland beyond the train station, this whitewashed structure is similarly shaped to Stalin's prison, formed of two concentric cylinders.

Fisherman's Beach · BEACH
Lənkəran's grey-sand beaches aren't a big attraction if you want to swim and many are dotted with debris, but the coastal area around 1km north of the train station is nonetheless a fascinating place to drink tea at one of many simple cafes while watching local fishermen cast their lines.

Heydar Əliyev Mərkəzi · CULTURAL CENTRE
(Dosa Park; ⊙10am-1pm & 2-6pm Mon-Sat) **FREE** Pop into this refreshingly air-conditioned centre to peruse the photographic exhibition on the life and times of the 'National Leader'. Or simply to cool down when the temperature and humidity make it less appealing to stroll between the fountains and shrubberies of Dosa Park, the city's social hub.

Xəzər Stadium · STADIUM
(www.lankaranfc.com) Just across the river from the town centre, the Xəzər Stadium is home to the local premier-league football team, which was managed during 2013 by

AZERBAIJAN LƏNKƏRAN

Lənkəran

Lənkəran

surrounded in summer by simple outside seating.

a'love
FAST FOOD **$**

(Qala xiyabani 17; pizza AZN3.40-9; ⊙8am-midnight) Bold yellows and oranges with alcoves of little camel figures make this place feel a little step above most fast-food options.

Gənclər Mərkəzi
ITALIAN **$$**

(Dosa Park; pizza AZN3-5.80, pasta AZN5.50, mains AZN5-12; ⊙8am-10.45pm; ✹🔊) A cinema, arcade games and three dining options are combined in this three-storey glass cylinder in Dosa Park. There's a summer terrace for

tea, a 'Chicken House' doing Western-style fast food, and the top-floor restaurant is upper market yet casual with an Italian menu, fresh-squeezed orange juice (AZN4) and real coffee if they can make the machine work.

ⓘ Information

Şəfaq Ekoturizm (☑ 055-7192068, 02525-50582, Tahmina 055-3926226; www.south tourism.az; Zərifə Əliyeva küç 120/10) This passionate, southern-specialist agency is essentially just two people – well-connected, ever-daring fixer Vamiq Babayev and English-speaking Tahmina Jafarova. As long as you give them a little notice they can organise almost anything you need for getting into the wilds of the fascinating Talysh mountains. Ask about village homestays.

Call to arrange a meeting as their office is virtually impossible to find unaided.

Tourist Office (Mir Mustafaxan küç; ⊙10am-5pm Mon-Fri) Friendly but almost useless.

❶ Getting There & Around

AIR

Lənkəran International Airport is just off the bypass on the Lerik road. The only regular flights are to Moscow (AZN150 to AZN180, thrice weekly).

BUS

Long-distance services start from **Ləvəngi bus station** (Lənkəran bypass), 3km northwest of the town centre. Buses to Baku (AZN5, five hours) run at least hourly until 5pm, and to Biləsuvar and/or Masallı (AZN3) twice hourly till 5pm. For Şəki, take the 8.30am Mingəçevir bus (AZN8) and change at Xaldan junction.

Most local services depart from around the bazaar. Take Ləj buses for the airport, Lıman buses for the Qafqaz Sahil Hotel and Fisherman's Beach, and Dairevi bus for Ləvəngi bus station (20q, last around 4pm). Marshrutky to Astara (AZN1) leave from Sabir küç, one block further north. For Lerik, shared taxis (per person/car AZN4/15) start from Dört Yol Lerik, the bypass junction near the airport. Getting there costs AZN2 by taxi from the back of the bazaar.

TRAIN

The sleeper train to Baku (*platskart/kupe* AZN5.50/7, 10 hours, departs 8.32pm) is far slower but more pleasant than the long bus ride through mostly dreary plains.

Talysh Mountains

The Talysh Mountains are not as high nor as spectacular as the Caucasus but their attractive mix of forest, canyon and sheep-mown uplands makes the area a delightful place to hike, as long as you don't stray too close to the sensitive Iranian border. The hub of this upland region is the overgrown village of Lerik. In summer Lerik is refreshingly cool but spring can be foggy and in winter it can get seriously cold, so bring appropriate clothing.

Lənkəran to Lerik

The Lənkəran–Lerik road leads some 50km up through extensive deciduous forests then continues into the bare, rolling Talysh Mountains. The first 22km has become a little degraded due to heavy truck traffic but beyond

OTHER TALYSH MOUNTAIN EXCURSIONS

There are several alternative routes into the Talysh Mountains. Relatively easy and satisfying is the Masallı–Yardımlı–Arvana road with hot springs after 13km, a little fire pool at Yanardağ (Km 15), a waterfall at Km 27 and a simple but great-value en-suite hotel in little Yardımlı. A new posibility opened up by roadbuilding in 2015 is the previously inaccessible village of Sım, with its own very impressive waterfall, small watermill and assorted mystery stones that reputedly date back to a period of cultural importance around the 7th century. Tourism there is as yet totally unknown but if you want help exploring this or other backwoods villages, it's worth dropping a line to the charming folks at Şəfəq Ekoturizm in Lənkəran.

Piran you're into idyllic greenery with a wide variety of rest areas which, for most Azerbaijani tourists, are the Lerik region's main attraction. They range from very basic dining areas to rustic getaways to full-blown family resorts, and while some can be used as the starting point for random strolls or longer hikes, most are seen as relaxation destinations in and of themselves. Addresses are kilomere-marker post readings from central Lənkəran. Once the Lənkəran bypass is finished (still a couple of years away at the time of research) the Lerik junction will be at Km 9.

🛏 Sleeping

Təbəssüm   CABINS $

(☑050-2263027; Lənkəran–Lerik Rd, Km 27; d/tr/q AZN30/40/60; ☎) Təbəssüm is a particularly appealing small-scale rural restaurant-resort that prides itself on not cutting any trees. Indeed some foliage grows right 'through' the kitchen buildings. Long footbridges link dining pavilions that nestle into the mossy rocks, overlooking a rear fork and minor waterfall. Pine-fragrant huts are good value with freshly ironed sheets for you to make your own bed. There's an en-suite toilet but no paper and the shower might never run hot. Wi-fi in the restaurant area.

Cənub Resort   RESORT $$

(☑050-4333636; www.cenub.com.az; Lənkəran–Lerik Rd, Km 36; d/q AZN80/100; ✳☎) Cənub's pine cottages are a definite knotch above most of the competiton – well built with ample natural light, indoor and terrace seating, and air-con. Larger units overlook the river. The characterful double-level wooden restaurant unusually has a menu in English and there's a bar shaped as a pirate ship. In summer, music can disturb the tranquility.

From October to May the resort is relatively calm and AZN20 cheaper.

Relax　　　　　　　　　　RESORT $$$
(☑ 050-2508464; www.relax.com.az; Lənkəran–Lerik Rd, Km 34; ✳ ☒) Relax provides the plush room standards and range of facilities that holidaying Bakuvian families seek. It might prove ideal if you're travelling with kids who want to splash in the vast waterpark while you go hiking in the forest. For some tastes the place is too big and brash for the rural surroundings, but most cottages are built with local materials and traditional tiled roofs.

Lerik

☑ 02527 / POP 6900

Often lost in the clouds, Lerik climbs a steep Talysh mountainside and makes a great starting point for regional hikes.

◉ Sights & Activities

Several bracing walks are possible by simply striding out of town in any direction. Simple maps of some well-tested options are available to guests at the Heydarov Homestay.

Viewpoints　　　　　　　　VIEWPOINT
There are numerous points from which to savour wide panoramas over highland fields and serrated crags. One relatively easy area to find such views can be found by climbing the long stairway behind the central Flag Sq onto the main suburban ridge. For still wider views hike/drive up to the TV tower across the valley.

Centenarians Museum　　　　　MUSEUM
(Uzunömürlülər Muzeyi; local/foreigner 40q/AZN1; ☺ 9am-1pm & 2-5pm Mon-Sat) This modest little museum celebrates the Talysh mountain people's statistically high proportion of centenarians. Most famous was Şirəli Müslümov (aka Shirali Muslimov), cited as the world's oldest man when he died in 1973, supposedly aged 168. The museum is hidden away on the short but circuitous route that leads from Flag Sq to the culture house.

Kəlvəz Road　　　　　　DRIVING, HIKING
If you're driving, don't miss the lovely country lane that leads on from Lerik as far as Kəlvəz near the Iranian border. You'll pass through a beautiful area of crags and gorge-viewpoints plus several flower-filled valley villages set between rolling high fields that are often sunny when Lerik hides in fog.

The road has only very recently been paved, so this is a new frontier for tourists, but hiking opportunities abound and miniresorts are already nearing completion at Kalaxan and Qosmalion.

🍴 Sleeping & Eating

Most visitors sleep at one of the resorts en route to Lerik, so options in town are very limited, but Lerik does have two backpacker fallbacks.

Gussein Baba's Cafe　　　　HOSTEL $
(Heydar Əliyev meydanı 4; dm AZN7, without indoor bathroom AZN5) Central but utterly unmarked, Gussein Baba's Cafe has acceptable if very basic rooms. The best two share an indoor squat toilet and shower but the four-bed small dorms require a short walk across the garden to an outdoor toilet hole. The place has been run since 1974 by ebullient, Russian-speaking Gussein, who's now in his seventies and thinking of selling up.

To find Gussein's place, take the short road opposite the central hospital that leads past the Royal Bank (ATM) and it's behind a wall where the road dead-ends at a car-repair workshop.

Heydarov Homestay　　　　HOMESTAY $
(http://cbtazerbaijan.com/portfolio/lerik; Nariman Narimanov 6; half/full board per person AZN12/15) Two large homely guest rooms share an indoor toilet that's accessed through the family kitchen. Father and son are *meyxana* performers and might show you DVDs of the art, but no English is spoken.

If walking from the city gate/share taxi stand, take the first alley on the right after the memorial garden and it's the first house on your right.

ℹ Getting There & Away

Between 6am and 9am numerous minibuses leave for Baku (AZN12) via Lənkəran, plus there's an old Ikarus bus (AZN8) at 9am from the *avtovağzal* (bus station), an area of teahouses at the valley bottom, around 800m steeply downhill from the bazaar.

NAXÇIVAN

Naxçivan (Nakhchivan) is a historic cradle of culture, once a trade crossroads but now a disconnected lozenge of Azerbaijani territory wedged uncomfortably between hostile Armenia and ambivalent Iran. Ancient monuments and oasis villages are dotted about a fascinating landscape of deserts and melon fields rimmed by craggy, barren mountains. The only direct transport from Baku is by air or on buses that transit Iran (creating a double visa problem for most foreigner visitors). However, there is a useful sliver of border with Turkey through which İstanbul–Naxçivan City buses pass several times daily. And for those with appropriate visas, crossing the pedestrian border to Iran at Culfa is relatively painless.

The main hub and almost all accommodation is in Naxçivan City, a surreally over-manicured town of neat streets, free museums and new administrative buildings. The city's one visibly ancient monument is the 26m-tall **Mömina Xatun** (⊙9am-1pm & 2-6pm Tue-Sun) FREE tomb tower dating from 1186. It's beautifully decorated with geometric patterns of blue tiles and stands in a garden fronting a heavily renovated 18th-century royal palace. Over-renovation of the 'ancient' citadel has been so complete that the site is essentially new. Just outside is the supposed Tomb of Noah, amusingly marked as being from the 7th-millenium BC but actually built in 2013, albeit on an earler site. Its reconstruction helps underline a local myth that the Biblical arc crashed through the cleft-top of Ilan Dağ, a very photogenic rocky pinnacle that dominates the landscape east of town.

Beyond Naxçivan City, highlights within the exclave include the pretty oasis town of **Ordubad**, the 14th-century tomb tower at **Qarabağlar** and the Soviet-era salt mine turned asthma spa hotel, **Duzdağ** (☑0436-5444901; www.duzdag.com; d AZN130, ste AZN250-350; ❋ 🛜 🖾).

Very few people speak much English and even Russian usage is limited, but reliable agency **Natig Travel** (☑050-5672506; www.natigtravel.com) can help and there's usually at least one English speaker employed at Naxçivan City's central **Hotel Tabriz** (Meh-manxanə Tabriz; ☑0136-447701; s/d/tr/ste AZN70/100/120/150).

Shared taxis to Lənkəran (per person/car AZN4/15) leave in the morning from the bus station, but after around 11am you might also find them leaving from the castle-styled city gate (*arka*) at the eastern edge of town .

Astara

☑02522 / POP 16,200

Wide beaches present Astara with a semblance of seaside resort potential but travellers mostly use the town as a transit point for Iran. The pedestrian **border crossing** (⊙9am-1pm & 2.30-6pm) is an intimidating, unmarked series of grey metal gratings, five minutes' walk along Azərbaycan küç from Astara's central square, where you'll find a 24-hour ATM and the semi-smart **Hotel Şindan** (☑02522-54177; Azərbaycan küç 11; d/ste AZN50/70; ❋🛜). Nearby **Hotel Xəzər** (☑050-7976373; Heydar Əliyev pr 69; d AZN15) is a simple, budget alternative with shared but clean squat toilet and shower.

Marshrutky to Lənkəran (AZN1, 50 minutes) depart regularly till 3pm from be-side Azərbaycan küç 36, two minutes' walk north of Hotel Şindan. Taxis cost AZN12. Ask them to stop en route at **Yanar Bulağ** (Burning Spring) where 'water burns' at a roadside standpipe 9km north. Bring your own matches.

A sleeper train departing Astara at 7.30pm (*platskart/kupe* AZN6/8) arrives in Baku 6.25am. However, Astara's station is inconveniently located so you might prefer to board in Lənkəran.

UNDERSTAND AZERBAIJAN

Azerbaijan Today

In June 2015 Baku hosted the first ever European Games, a kind of regional Olympics. To a remarkably short deadline the city created a whole raft of sparkling new stadia and set things going with a truly spectacular opening ceremony. The Games were probably envisaged as a kind of coming-out party to show the world how this once-obscure corner of the Caspian had dusted off its dowdy Soviet past and used a decade's oil bonanza to create a stylishly efficient vision of modernity. The performance was almost faultless and Azerbaijan's athletes managed an impressive second place overall. Anyone watching on TV would surely have been heartily impressed by the the backdrop of the capital's shimmering architecture. To Baku's chagrin, however, the world's media barely seemed to cover the event. Or worse, they decided to focus not on Azerbaijan's gigantic leaps forward in economic development, but on questions of press-gagging and corruption, a situation exacerbated by the arrest under spurious charges of several prominent civil-society champions in the run-up to the games.

Given Azerbaijan's membership (and recent chairmanship) of the Council of Europe, such heavy handedness seemed utterly self-defeating. But the regime appears to see even the most minor criticism of itself as an attack on the very survival of the state. The chaotic aftermaths of Arab Spring movements and the unrest in Ukraine have been seen from Baku as showing the dangers of so-called 'democracy promotion', and since 2014 many pro-Western NGOs along with the US Peace Corps have been effectively shut down. Baku would prefer that attention focussed on Azerbaijan's dramatically improved living standards, economic diversification and the virtual elimination of poverty over 10 years (at least statistically). And most of all, to the nation's apparent stability in the eye of a geopolitical storm, sandwiched between big powers (Russia and Iran) and still technically at war with a neighbour (Armenia) with some 16% of its territory under occupation.

Critics might venture that many of Azerbaijan's achievements are skin deep – facades – like the splendid stone frontages that now hide so many once-dreary Soviet-era buildings. Some decry a system of regional development controlled by clan-owned monopolies and many locals feel that education standards are sinking. Many older folk look back fondly to the 'fairer days' of the USSR when everyone had work and relatively equal incomes. Some younger people are turning towards relatively low-key religion as political expression becomes silenced. But others seem more genuinely supportive of the president, recognising the difficult balancing act for any leader, even one whose late father enjoys a full-scale personality cult.

History

Early History

From the 6th century BC (and indeed for much of its later history) proto-Azerbaijan was part of the Persian Empire, with Zoroastrianism developing as the predominant religion. Around the 4th century BC the ill-defined state of Arran, emerged also known as 'Caucasian Albania' (no link to the present-day Balkan republic). From about AD 325 these Albanians adopted Christianity, building many churches, the ruins of some of which still remain today. The history of the Caucasian Albanians is of great political importance to modern-day Azeris, largely for the disputed 'fact' that they weren't Armenian.

The Muslim Era

Islam became the major religion, starting with the Arabs' 7th-century advance into Albania. For later waves of Turkic herder-horsemen, proto-Azerbaijan's grassland plains presented ideal grazing lands. So it was here that the Caucasus' Turkic ethnicity became concentrated while original Caucasian Christians tended to retreat into the mountain foothills.

A classic cultural era bloomed in the 12th-century cities of (old) Qəbələ, Bərdə and Naxçivan. Şamaxı emerged as the capital of Şirvan and Gəncə's regional pre-eminence was symbolised by the classical 'national' poet Nizami Gəncəvi. However, from the 13th century these cities were pummelled into dust by the Mongols, Timur (Tamerlane) and assorted earthquakes.

After two centuries and an improving caravan trade, Şirvan had revived. Its rulers, the Shirvanshahs, scored an important home victory in a 1462 battle against Arbadil (southern Azerbaijan, now in Iran) only to lose in the 1501 rematch. Subsequently converted to Shia Islam, Şirvan bonded with (south) Azerbaijan under the originally Azeri Safavid shahs who came to rule the whole Persian Empire.

In the early 18th century, a collection of autonomous Muslim khanates emerged across Azerbaijan. However, to preserve their independence against a rebounding Persia, several khanates united and asked Russia for assistance. They got more than they bargained for. The Russian Empire swiftly annexed many northerly khanates. Persia's bungled attempts to grab them back ended with the further Russian annexation of the Şirvan, Karabakh, Naxçıvan, Talysh and Yerevan khanates, recognised under the humiliating treaties of Gulistan (1813) and Turkmenchay (1828).

The Russian Era

To consolidate their rule over their new conquests the Russians encouraged the immigration of Christians, particularly non-Orthodox religious sects from Russia, Germans from Würtemburg and Armenians from the Ottoman-Turkish Empire. This indirectly sowed the seeds of ethnic conflicts that broke out in 1905, 1918 and 1989.

In the 1870s, new uses for petroleum suddenly turned little Baku into a boom town. By 1905 it was supplying half the world's oil, creating immense wealth and a cultural renaissance, but also an underclass of workers suffering appalling conditions. Exploited by a young Stalin, their grievances ballooned into a decade of revolutionary chaos that resulted in several horrific interethnic clashes.

Independence & Soviet Conquest

Following the Russian revolution of 1917, and with WWI still undecided, Azerbaijan declared itself the Muslim world's first 'democracy'. Baku only became part of this formulation once its pro-Russian socialist revolutionary leaders were driven out, helped by an invading Turkish army. The Turks rapidly withdrew, leaving the Azerbaijan Democratic Republic (ADR; Azərbaycan Xaiq Cümhuriyyəti) independent. This forward-thinking secular entity, of which Azeris remain intensely proud, lasted barely two years as the Bolshevik Red Army invaded in 1920. The short-lived Transcaucasian Soviet Socialist Republic (SSR) was formed with Georgia and Armenia as a prelude to the USSR. Border changes diminished Azerbaijan's area in favour of Armenia, leaving Naxçıvan entirely cut off from the rest of the Azerbaijan SSR. The passionate insistence of Azer-baijan's 'father of communism', Nəriman Nərimanov, kept Nagorno-Karabakh within the nation, but for his pains Nərimanov was poisoned in 1925. His replacement, Mir Jafar Bağirov, oversaw Stalin's brutal purges in which more than 100,000 Azeris were shot or sent to concentration camps, never to return. Following the Khrushchev 'thaw' Bağirov was himself arrested and shot.

During WWII, one of Hitler's priorities was grabbing Baku's oil wealth for energy-poor Germany. Luckily for Baku, the German army became divided and bogged down trying to take Stalingrad on the way. Nonetheless, realisation of Baku's potential vulnerability later encouraged Soviet engineers to develop new oil fields in distant Siberia.

Perestroika (Soviet restructuring) in the late 1980s was also a time of increasing tension with Armenia. Tit-for-tat ethnic squabbles between Armenians and Azeris over the status of Nagorno-Karabakh bubbled over into virtual ethnic cleansing, as minorities in both republics fled escalating violence. On 20 January 1990, the Red Army made a crassly heavy-handed intervention in Baku, killing dozens of civilians and turning public opinion squarely against Russia. Azerbaijan declared its independence from the Soviet Union in 1991.

Independent Again

The Karabakh conflict reached its nadir with the massacre of over 600 Azeri civilians by Armenian forces at Xocalı (26 February 1992). Dithering post-independence president Ayaz Mütəllibov was thereupon ousted. His replacement, Əbülfəz Elçibəy, himself fled a year later in the face of an internal military rebellion. This was comeback time for Parliamentary Chairman Heydar Əliyev, an ex-USSR politburo member who had been Azerbaijan's Communist Party chairman in the 1970s. Əliyev stabilised the fractious country, kick-started international investment in the oil industry, and signed a ceasefire agreement with Armenia and Nagorno-Karabakh in May 1994. However, around 16% of Azerbaijan's territory remained (and remains) under Armenian occupation. For two decades the 'frozen conflict' has left around 800,000 Azeris displaced. Azerbaijan's 21st-century oil boom belatedly allowed funds for many rehousing projects, but has also led to a vast spurt of military spending sending a barely disguised message that the nation is one day

AZERBAIJAN HISTORY

intent on getting back at least part of the 'lost territories'.

Azerbaijan's new oil boom really got started in earnest when the US$4 billion Baku–Tbilisi–Ceyhan (BTC) pipeline began pumping Caspian oil to Turkey. The resultant building boom started in Baku, followed in Qəbələ and is now evident in regional centres nationwide. Heydar Əliyev is still unblinkingly referred to as Azerbaijan's 'National Leader', even though he died in 2003. His photos appear everywhere and each town has a cultural centre and park named in his honour. Meanwhile the dynasty continues under his son İlham.

Arts

Azerbaijan's cultural greats are revered across the country. Their busts adorn Baku's finest buildings, their names are commemorated as streets and their homes are often maintained as shrine-like 'house-museums' (ev-muzeyi), where fans can pay homage.

Cinema

Film-making in Azerbaijan dates back to footage of the Abşeron oil wells dated 1898. Ever since, Baku has offered a tailor-made set that has appealed to many directors. Its best-known Hollywood appearance was in *The World Is Not Enough*, with Pierce Brosnan as James Bond driving a BMW Z8 through the (now rehabilitated) old oil fields at Bayıl. In the 1968 Soviet cult classic *Brilliantovaya Ruka* (Diamond Arm), Baku's Old City formed the exotic backdrop to a De Funes–style comedy farce about an accidental gem smuggler. Baku also features heavily in Ayaz Salayev's *Yarasa* (The Bat), a contrastingly slow-moving art-house film that won the Grand Prix at the 1996 Angers Film Festival (France).

The **Azerbaijan Film Commission** (http://afc.az/eng/az_films/tarix.shtml) has an online history of the local movie industry.

Literature

Azerbaijan has a long and distinguished literary tradition. Best known is the Azeri 'Shakespeare', Nizami Gəncəvi (1141–1209), whose ubiquitous statues almost outnumber those of Heydar Əliyev. Nizami wrote in Persian rhyming couplets, but Mehmed bin Suleyman Füzuli (1495–1556) was the first to write extensively in Azeri-Turkish.

His sensitive rendition of Nizami's classic 'Leyli and Majnun' (a Sufi parable wrapped up as a tale of mad, all-engrossing love) influenced many later writers, including poet Khurshudbanu Natavan (1830–97), playwright Mirza Fatali Axundov (1812–78) and satirist Mirza Sabir (1862–1911), as well as inspiring Eric Clapton's hit song 'Layla'. Azerbaijan's 20th-century star writer was Səmət Vurğun, who remains especially popular in his native Qazax district. For recent fiction, a great read is Ella Leya's 2015 novel *The Orphan Sky* set in Soviet-era Baku.

Music

Azerbaijan's *muğam* music is recognised by Unesco as being one of the world's great forms of intangible cultural heritage. To some Western ears it sounds more like pained wailing than singing, but at its best it's intensely emotional, an almost primal release of the spirit. The greatest living *muğam* superstar is Alim Qazimov. Traditional music was also performed by *aşıgs* (wandering minstrels), some of whom would compete in contests similar to the bardic competitions of the Celtic world. A more upbeat, light-hearted latterday form known as *meyxana* has bantering lyrics and cantering synthesiser accompaniment.

In Baku, jazz grew popular in the 1950s and '60s and took an original local flavour under Vaqif Mustafazadeh (1940–79), who fused American jazz with traditional Azeri *muğam* improvisation. His multitalented daughter Aziza Mustafazadeh (b 1969) has further blended *muğam* jazz with classical music. Other contemporary jazz-*muğam* pianist sensations include Shahin Novrasli and Isfar Sarabski, both Montreux Jazz Festival champions.

Much of Azerbaijani pop is based firmly on the Turkish mould. There is also a minor rap, R&B and rock scene, and many up-and-coming DJs. Listen to a wide range of artists on www.rockzone.az

Painting & Sculpture

Azerbaijani art blossomed in the later Soviet era and today the works of neo-impressionist superstar Səttar Bəhlulzadə cost hundreds of thousands of dollars. Similarly admired, Tahir Salaxov's work ranges from thoughtful Soviet realism to densely coloured portraiture and semicubist landscapes. Much of the expressive pre-Independence public statuary has been removed of late in favour of fountains or replaced by images of Heydar Əliyev, but great works remain, notably by Omar Eldarov, whose swirlingly creative statue of Hüseyn Cavid dominates Baku's Landau Sq. In the 21st century there's been an explosion of interest in contemporary art as well as a rediscovery of modern painting genres, with Baku full of exciting galleries.

Food & Drink

Azeri cuisine lacks the garlic-walnut fascination of Georgian cookery but has great strengths in fruity sauces, wonderful fresh vegetables and mutton-based soups. Outside Baku, the main problem can be getting beyond restaurants' obsession with barbecued meat.

Note that in most rural restaurants, there will not be a menu. Almost all charge AZN4 to AZN5 for a kebab, but sizes and quality vary considerably – in many places you'll want two portions per person – and the quoted price won't include the bread, salad, cheese and other assorted plates that can very easily double or triple the cost.

Staples & Specialities

Baku restaurants offer a wide range of cuisines, but beyond the capital Azerbaijani and Turkish food is almost all you'll find. And in rural areas, the only dining options – commonly known as İstrahət Guşasi or Istrahət Mərkəzi – rarely serve anything other than flame-grilled kebabs.

Standard *tikə* kebabs consist of skewered meaty chunks, often including a cube of tail fat that locals consider a special delicacy. *Lülə* kebab is minced lamb with herbs and spices. Pricier kebab types include *leaber antreqot* (ribs) and *dana bastirma* (marinated beef strips). Barbecued vegetables are often available, too, though vegetarians might be alarmed to find lurking morsels of lamb fat inserted into barbecued aubergines to make them more succulent.

Whatever you order, don't be surprised if a series of fresh vegetables, fruits, salads, cheese and bread arrive. Each costs extra, so refuse anything you don't want to pay for.

In towns, for a cheap, unpretentious non-kebab meal look for a *yeməkxana*, which is likely to serve *qazan-yeməkləri* (plate foods) including various potato-and-mutton stews, such as *buğlama*,

bozbaş (with *kuftə* meatballs plus the odd cherry) and *piti* (with chickpeas, requiring mashing). But the classic non-kebab dish is dolma. A common dolma meal is a baked-vegetable trio (tomato, pepper and mini-aubergine) stuffed with a herb-infused mixture of rice and minced lamb. You can also find *kələm* (cabbage leaf) or *yarpaq* (vine-leaf) dolma with similar fillings. Şəki dolma means a pot full of mini vine-leaf dolma.

Fish such as *sudak* (pike-perch) or *farel* (trout) are sporadically available, tasting best when smeared with tangy sauces made from sour-plum *(alça)* or pomegranate juice *(narşərab)*.

Typical of southern Azerbaijan, deliciously fruity Talysh cuisine is best known for *ləvəngi* (chicken or fish stuffed with walnuts and herbs).

Çoban ('shepherd') salad comprising chopped tomato, cucumber, raw onion, dill and coriander leaves is served as a preamble to most meals.

Azerbaijani breakfast foods *(səhər yeməkləri)* are bread *(çörek)*, butter *(yağ)* and cheese *(pendir)*, maybe with some honey *(bal)* or sour cream *(xama)*, all washed down with plentiful sweet tea *(çay)*. Scrambled eggs *(qayğana)* or fried eggs *(qlazok)* might be available on request.

Quick Eats

Azerbaijan's foremost fast food is the döner kebab. Much as in Europe, a large cone of compounded meat *(ət;* essentially mutton), or perhaps chicken *(tovuq)*, is flamed on a rotating grill then sliced into small morsels that are served with mixed salad in *lavaş* (thin flour tortilla) or *çörək* (bread). Judge the quality by the queue of waiting diners.

EATING PRICE RANGES

The following price ranges refer to a typical main course with garnish.

$ less than AZN5

$$ AZN5–AZN10

$$$ more than AZN10

For Baku, the following price ranges are used:

$ less than AZN8

$$ AZN8–AZN20

$$$ more than AZN20

MENU DECODER

antreqot	lamb ribs
aş	fruity rice-pilaf meal generally served on huge multi-person platters; also known as *plov*
badımcan	aubergine
balıq	fish, sturgeon
borş	borscht, hearty cabbage-based soup
bozbaş	stew-soup usually featuring a meatball formed around a central plum
buğlama	mutton-and-potato stew slow-cooked to condense the flavour
çığırtma	soft omelette incorporating chicken, tomato and garlic (not a soup as in Georgia)
cız-bız	fried tripe and potato
çörek	bread
doğrama	a cold soup made with sour milk, potato, onion and cucumber
dolma	various mince-stuffed vegetables
dovğa	a hot, thick yoghurt-based soup
düşbərə	lightly minted broth containing tiny bean-sized ravioli and typically served with sour cream and garlic
düyü	rice
gurcu xinqal	Georgian spiced dumplings
kabablar	kebabs
kotlet	meat patties
kuftə	köfte
kükü	thick omelette cut into chunks
lahmacun	Turkish wafer-thin version of *pide* that you should fill with salad then squeeze on lemon juice
lavaş	very thin bread-sheets
ləvəngi	Talysh-style *toyuq* (chicken) or *baliq* (fish) stuffed with a paste of herbs and crushed walnuts
qızıl balıq	salmon
qovurma	mutton fried in butter with various fruits
qreçka	boiled buckwheat or a meal served with such buckwheat as the main filler
qutab	thin, pancake turnover filled with spinach (*göyərti*) or meat (*ətlə*)
pide	Turkish 'pizza' but without the cheese
piti	two-part soupy stew
püre	mashed potato
sac	sizzler hot-plate meal, usually served for multiple diners
sosiska	frankfurter-style sausage
tabaka	pricey, flattened whole chicken
xama	sour cream
xaş	heavily garlic-charged soup made from bits of sheep that Westerners prefer to avoid; wash down with a hair-of-the-dog vodka
xinqal	meaty chunks served with lasagne-like leaves of pasta
yağ	butter

Regaining popularity is the *qutab,* a very thin semicircular folded breadypancake lightly stuffed with either ground meat or sorrel-greens. *Peraşki* are greasy, Russian-style savoury doughnuts.

Drinks

The national drink is *çay* (tea), usually served in pear-shaped *armudi* glasses and sucked through a sugar lump for sweetness, or ac-

EATING PITI

So you've taken our suggestion and ordered *piti*. But all you can see in the conical earthenware *dobu* (pot) is a lump of lamb fat floating lugubriously in broth. Don't panic! Before eating anything, start by tearing up pieces of bread into a separate bowl. Sprinkle with *sumac* (the purple condiment you'll see on the table) and then pour the *piti* broth over the top. Eat the resultant soup as a first course. Then transfer the remaining *piti* solids to the dish and mush together using spoon and fork. Yes. Including that lump of fat. Without it the dish just won't taste right. Another sprinkling of sumac and your 'second course' is ready to eat. Delicious.

companied by jams and candies. Coffeeshops are a recent fad in Baku but in the provinces you'll rarely find espresso machines beyond top hotels.

Azerbaijan has long made decent *konjak* (brandy) but recently its wines (*şərab*) are steadily improving. Bottles of cheap, cheerful Ivanovka red (AZN3) are inoffensive, but for a good drop, reliable choices include the Savalan and Fireland brands. Be aware that many locals prefer their wine *şirin/kəmşirin* (very sweet/sweet). *Kəmturş/turş* (semi-dry/dry) options are generally closer to Western tastes.

Xırdalan lager is the best known of several unsophisticated beers (*piva*). Toasting with vodka (*arak*) remains an important social ritual between older men with significant social standing (and bellies) to maintain. However, it is less formalised than in Georgia and less compulsive than in Russia.

Drinking water (*su*) from the tap is fine in mountain villages, but not recommended in lowland towns. Bottled water is widely available: choose from sparkling (*qazli*) or still (*qazsiz*).

SURVIVAL GUIDE

ⓘ Directory A–Z

ACCOMMODATION

Camping
➡ In the mountains one can generally pitch a tent almost anywhere but do be sensitive about

damaging meadows – flower-filled grass is a crop.
➡ Beware of fierce dogs anywhere near sheep.

Homestays
➡ **AirBnB** (www.airbnb.com) has fairly limited penetration in Azerbaijan.
➡ **Couchsurfing** (www.couchsurfing.com) has far fewer active hosts since Peace Corps was shut down in the country.
➡ There are active homestay networks in Şəki.
➡ Many families in Lahıc, Laza and Xınalıq offer simple accommodation.
➡ Homestays in the south are being developed by Şəfəq Ekoturizm (Lənkəran).
➡ **CBT Azerbaijan** (www.cbtazerbaijan.com) was an early promoter of homestays but seems semi-dormant at present.

Hostels
➡ Don't exist in the European sense, though plans are afoot to start a new hostel association in coming years.
➡ The very few places that currently use the term hostel are either overstuffed rooms in private apartments or larger rooms in Baku hotels charging per bed.

Hotel (*mehmanxana* or *otel*)
➡ A hotel can mean anything from the (now-rare) unreconstructed Soviet-era dives, to Baku's five-star business hotels.
➡ There are a few glitzy rural getaways, notably at Qəbələ and Shahdag ski resort, plus a handful of jawdropping palaces run by the Rixos chain.
➡ Any room under AZN20 is likely to have shared-bathroom facilities, and such places can be hard to find.
➡ There's a growing supply of provincial accommodation in the AZN40 to AZN70 range, every AZN10 often connoting a marked improvement

ACCOMMODATION PRICE RANGES

The following price ranges are based on the cost of typical accommodation for two people, including taxes but without meals.

$ less than AZN40

$$ AZN40–AZN100

$$$ more than AZN100

For Baku, the following price ranges are used:

$ less than AZN70

$$ AZN70–AZN150

$$$ more than AZN150

in standards, though relatively few have much personality.

➡ A 'motel' or *'qonaq evi'* (guesthouse) is typically just another name for a lower midrange hotel.

Rural Rest Centres/Zones *(istrahət mərkəzi or istrahət zonası)*

➡ The most common form of rural accommodation, usually a set of cottages or cabins associated with a getaway restaurant.

➡ Cottages usually come with bathrooms but many can be a little ropey and prices generally work out somewhat higher than in hotels for an equivalent quality level. That's partly because most cottages could (and do) accommodate whole families.

➡ Such places typically favour peaceful woodland settings while paradoxically having a penchant for blaring music.

ACTIVITIES

Many rural hotels are well placed for exploring glorious scenery yet seem bemused by the idea that you'd want to do much more than eat, drink or soak in the spa between selfie opportunities.

Climbing & mountaineering The most appealing areas for mountaineers fall within the Shahdag National Park, which is currently awkward to access due to complex bureaucracy. For paperwork-free mountain hikes the best starting points are Zaqatala and Lahic.

Skiing Azerbaijan's two rapidly expanding ski resorts are at Şahdağ/Laza and Tufandağ/Qəbələ. Seasons are short and you'll find more visitors come to be photographed than to actually ski.

Spa cures Oil bathing in Naftalan, sulphurwater springs at Altı Ağaç and salt-mine accommodation at Duzdağ near Naxçivan City are major attractions for local, Russian and Central Asian tourists.

Swimming & watersports Pollution means that the Caspian isn't the most pristine sea for swimming, especially at Shikhov where the beach has a curious offshore backdrop of oil rigs. In summer, locals flock to the somewhat better beaches at Nabran and on the northern Abşeron Peninsula where jet skis can be rented. Kiteboarding is possible at Blue Planet on a pretty, lonely lagoon southeast of Şuraabad.

BUSINESS HOURS

The following are typical opening hours.

Bazaars Busiest 8am to 2pm

Offices 9am to 5pm Monday to Friday, but late starts, early closing and long lunch breaks are common

Restaurants 11am to 11pm, cafes 9am to 11am or later

Shops 10am to 7pm but often later, seven days a week

CUSTOMS REGULATIONS

Export restrictions include the following:

Artworks & artefacts Export can prove awkward, as you'll often need written permission from the Ministry of Culture.

Carpets Exporting new carpets bigger than 2 sq metres requires a certificate from the Baku Carpet Museum (AZN46/26 issued in one day/week). Baku carpet shops can usually organise this for you. Antique carpets may not be taken out of Azerbaijan at all.

Caviar Limit of 125g per person.

Importing vehicles is complex and expensive.

EMBASSIES & CONSULATES

Addresses of Azerbaijani embassies abroad are listed in the 'Diplomatic Service' section of http://mfa.gov.az

Most embassies and consulates are located in Baku, and include the following:

Chinese Embassy (Map p204; ☑ 012-4936129; http://az.chineseembassy.org; Xaqani küç 67, Baku) For years this Chinese embassy has only issued tourist visas for Azerbaijanis and official residents of Azerbaijan, though recently a few nonresident travellers have managed to get visas with a relevant invitation.

French Embassy (Map p204; ☑ 012-4908100; www.ambafrance-az.org; Rəsul Rza küç 7, Baku)

Georgian Embassy (Map p202; ☑ 012-4974560; www.azerbaijan.mfa.gov.ge; Yaşar Hüseynov küç 13-15, Baku) Most nationalities don't require a visa for Georgia.

German Embassy (Map p208; ☑ 012-4654100; www.baku.diplo.de; 10th fl, ISR Plaza, Baku)

Iranian Consulate (Map p202) The consulate in Baku (☑ 012-4341976; baku.mfa.ir/; Abbas Mirzə Şərifzadə 269, Baku; 🚌18, 77, 96, Ⓜ İnşaatçilar) where you go for visa applications is completely separate from the embassy. There is also a consulate in Naxçivan (Atatürk küç 13, Naxçivan; ⊙10.30am-noon Mon-Thu).

Kazakhstani Embassy (Map p202; ☑ 012-4656247; Ak Həsən Əliyev küç, 15-ci kecid 8-10, Baku; ⊙ 9.30-11.30am Tue-Fri)

Russian Embassy (Map p202; ☑ 012-4986016; Bakixanov küç 17, Baku)

Tajikistan Embassy (Map p202; ☑ 012-5021432; www.tajembaz.tj; Baglar küç, 2nd Lane, 20, Baku; ⊙ consular section 3-5pm Tue-Fri) Get off bus 3 or 5 where you see the sign to AEF Hotel and the embassy is around 200m east then southeast.

Turkmenistan Embassy (Map p202; Ak Həsən Əliyev küç 266, Baku; ⊙10am-noon Mon & Fri only; 🚌 61) Terrible queues, visas rarely issued.

UK Embassy (Map p204; ☑ 012-4377878; www.gov.uk/government/world/azerbaijan; Xaqani küç 45, Baku) Represents Commonwealth citizens.

US Embassy (Map p204; ☑ 012-4883300; http://azerbaijan.usembassy.gov; Azadlıq pr 111, Baku; ☐ 88)

Uzbekistan Embassy (Map p202; ☑ 012-4972549; Badamdar Şosesi, 9th Lane, 437, Baku; ☐ 3, 5) Visa applications take around a week. Get off bus 3 or 5 near the small Citimart store and walk 500m west along the residential lane one block further north. There's an alternative shorter lane access from opposite the Kempinski hotel.

MONEY

Azerbaijan's manat (AZN1) is denoted locally by a special 'M' that looks like a euro symbol rotated through 90 degrees. A manat is divided into 100 qəpiq (100q).

See p200 for exchange rates and costs. Note that just prior to printing this guide, the manat devalued against all currencies and the rate quoted reflects this. For up-to-date rates see www.xe.com.

PUBLIC HOLIDAYS

New Year's Day 1 January

Noruz Bayramı 20 to 24 March

Genocide Day 31 March (mourning day for those killed in Baku, 1918)

Victory Day 9 May

Republic Day 28 May (founding of first Azerbaijan Democratic Republic in 1918)

National Salvation Day 15 June (parliament asked Heydar Əliyev to lead the country in 1993)

Armed Forces Day 26 June (founding of Azerbaijan's army in 1918)

Ramazan Bayram Varies (the day after Ramazan)

Gurban Bayramı Varies (Festival of the Sacrifice)

National Independence Day 18 October (date of Azerbaijan's breakaway from the USSR)

Flag Day 9 November (celebrates the 2010 unfurling on what was then the world's tallest flagpole)

Constitution Day 12 November (framing of constitution in 1995)

National Revival Day 17 November (first anti-Soviet uprising in 1988)

Solidarity Day 31 December (breaking down of border fences between Azerbaijan and Iran in 1989)

TELEPHONE SERVICES

➡ Azerbaijan's country code is ☑ 994. Many landline city codes changed in 2014.

➡ Payphones are very rare.

➡ SIM cards typically cost from AZN5 for pay-as-you-go, with SMS messages costing 4q, calls per min 4q and data from AZN6 per GB. To buy one you'll need your passport.

The Azeri Alphabet

AZERI	ROMAN	PRONUNCIATION
A a	a	long, as in 'far'
B b	b	as in 'bit'
C c	c	as the 'j' in 'jazz'
Ç ç	ch	as in 'chase'
D d	d	as in 'duck'
E e	e	as in 'bet'
Ə ə	a	short, as in 'apple'
F f	f	as in 'far'
G g	g	like the 'gy' in 'Magyar'
Ğ ğ	gh	a soft growl from the back of throat (like French 'r')
H h	h	as in 'here'
X x	kh	as the 'ch' in Scottish 'loch'
I ı	ı	neutral vowel; as the 'a' in 'ago'
İ i	i	as in 'police'
J j	zh	as the 's' in 'leisure'
K k	k	as in 'kit'
Q q	q	hard 'g' as in 'get'
L l	l	as in 'let'
M m	m	as in 'met'
N n	n	as in 'net'
O o	o	short as in 'got'
Ö ö	er	as in 'her', with no 'r' sound
P p	p	as in 'pet'
R r	r	a rolled 'r'
S s	s	as in 'see'
Ş ş	sh	as in 'shore'
T t	t	as in 'toe'
U u	u	as in 'chute'
Ü ü	ew	as in 'pew'
V v	v	as in 'van'
Y y	y	as in 'yet'
Z z	z	as in 'zoo'

Words in Azeri are usually lightly stressed on the last syllable. Note that in many parts of the country, the hard **k** is pronounced more like a 'ch', so that Bakı sounds like 'ba-chuh' and Şəki becomes 'sha-chee'.

➡ Mobile phones not purchased in Azerbaijan can be used for up to 30 days but after that you'll need to register the phone's IMEI-code through www.imei.az (costs AZN5) or at a post office (costs AZN5.50). To find your phone's IMEI code tap *#06#.

TOURIST INFORMATION

Tourist information offices are a relative novelty. Most are friendly and generous with glossy pamphlets but few really understand the concept of individual travel. The best are in Lahıc and Şəki.

VISAS

Visas are required for most visitors and obtaining one can be a headache, except for Turks and

Israelis who can get a visa on arrival at Baku's Heydar Əliyev International Airport. Fees vary by nationality based on what your country charges an Azerbaijani applicant (free for Japanese, US$35 to US$60 for most EU nationals, US$118 for Brits, US$160 for US citizens). But on top of that, almost all visa applications require a Letter of Invitation (LOI) from an agency such as **Baku Travel Services** (www.azerbaijan24.com) or from a contact or business in Baku. Occasionally, however, certain consulates or embassies will grant visas without invitation – the best bet being in Georgia. Things change fast but currently Tbilisi accepts a Booking.com hotel reservation in lieu of an invitation while some travellers have received visas without any paperwork in Batumi.

Some consulates further demand that an LOI be approved by the Azerbaijani foreign ministry, adding considerably to the cost and annoyance of procuring one. If you want a multi-entry visa, such approval is always required. Certain consulates only accept applications from residents of that country (or delegated others).

The option of an e-visa also exists. This has the huge advantage of letting you apply for a visa without visiting an embassy, but it still often takes at least two weeks to come through and you will still need the help of a travel agency to whom a fee will be due. It's often cheaper to book a couple of nights' basic accommodation than to pay an agency for visa service only. Baku Palace Hostel (p213) offers an e-visa support for backpackers who book with them. Polish travellers report painless e-visa success in a week using www.aina.pl.

Be aware that the visa situation remains highly unpredictable and recent public pronouncements from the president suggest that easier visa rules are being considered to encourage more visitors. Your best bet for up-to-date information is often through lonelyplanet.com/thorntree or http://caravanistan.com/visa/azerbaijan/. The latter has a well-collated collection of traveller reports reflecting the viability of various consulates.

Note: if you have an Iranian visa, it is usually possible to get a five-day single/10-day double transit visa for Azerbaijan in Tbilisi for $20/40 regardless of nationality.

Registration

If you plan to stay more than 10 days, police registration *(müveqqəti qeydiyat)* is a legal requirement. This will be done for you at most hotels but you may need to insist. Otherwise you can register in a regional Migration Office or online. For the latter you'll need to download, print and fill out the form from website www.migration.gov.az > Useful References > Required

Documents – choosing the bottom option. Scan the signed form along with copies of your passport, visa and entry stamp plus the front and back of your host's ID card. Email all of this to the given address. Staying in a hotel for at least a night might prove easier! Not registering carries a penalty of AZN300 to AZN400 charged as you exit the country.

One original registration currently suffices for a whole stay.

Visas for Onward Travel

Rules change frequently so the following information is a transitory snapshot. Visa fees are often paid into a local bank. You then need to return with the pay-in slip, so don't apply late in the day.

Iran Always hit-and-miss but easier lately for many Westerners who can get visas on arrival at six airports. That is not (yet?) true for UK, US and Canadian citizens who need to book a tour and can't travel unaccompanied. Land entry requires a visa in advance. Applying in Baku you must apply at a separate consulate that's miles from the embassy. You'll usually do better applying in your country of residence, if necessary with an invitation organised through a reputable agency such as www.persianvoyages.com.

Kazakhstan Many nationals are now exempt from visas for 15-day Kazakh tourist visits. If your nationality requires a visa or you want a longer stay, a one-month tourist visa is relatively painless (no LOI) and takes a couple of days. Pay the fee into an IBA bank branch, eg at the nearby Hyatt complex.

Tajikistan Forty-five day tourist visas painlessly processed in four days. You keep the passport.

Turkey Most Westerners now require e-visas, which are issued almost instantly online for US$20.40.

Turkmenistan Applying in Baku is a nightmare. Transit visas are typically not issued. Even when you have all necessary paperwork for a full tourist visa, the embassy's very limited opening times means a scrum to get in and many travellers have been flatly refused. However, with a prebooked tour through a reputable Turkmen tour agency you can get visa pre-approval LOI (allow two weeks) and collect the tourist visa on arrival in Turkmenbashi once you get off the ferry and are met by the agent. At least for now you can board the Caspian Ferry in Baku without a Turkmen visa as long as you have such a LOI.

Uzbekistan Friendly and helpful if a little hard to find. LOI requirement depends on nationality. Allow one week, but graciously you don't have to leave your passport while you're waiting.

Nagorno-Karabakh

📞 374 / POP 146,500

Best Historic Sites

➡ Tigranakert (p272)

➡ Dadivank Monastery (p272)

➡ Shushi (p270)

➡ Gandzasar Monastery (p272)

Best Places to Stay

➡ Vallex Garden Hotel (p268)

➡ Park Hotel Artsakh (p268)

➡ Saro's B&B (p271)

➡ Karina Guesthouse (p268)

Why Go?

Nagorno-Karabakh is the fourth piece of the South Caucasus jigsaw, a geopolitical product of the Soviet Union and a self-declared republic recognised by no one. The subject of a brutal war between 1990 and 1994, this small region is Armenian culture on land claimed by Azerbaijan. Its name sums up its myriad cultural influences: *nagorno* means mountainous in Russian, *kara* means black in Turkish and *bakh* means garden in Persian. To further confuse matters, Karabakhtis call their land Artsakh.

While there exist many questions about Nagorno-Karabakh and its political status, the beauty and cultural richness of its remote mountain landscape are undeniable. The Karabakh War left deep psychological scars on the people but the Karabakhtis are moving on, rebuilding their land stone by stone. Travel here is still an adventure, but rapidly improving infrastructure means better hotels, restaurants and hiking trails, while Karabakhti hospitality makes the challenges a joy, even in difficult times.

When to Go

➡ Summer and early autumn (June to September) are the best times for hiking.

➡ An excellent time to visit is the 9 May Victory Day, which also marks the Day of Liberation in Shushi.

➡ Spring (March to mid-May) is often wet and foggy.

Nagorno-Karabakh Highlights

❶ Visiting **Gandzasar Monastery** (p272), the most important building in Karabakh with its rich friezes and magnificent detail.

❷ Wandering around the lovely hilltop town of **Shushi** (p270), Karabakh's cultural capital.

❸ Winding your way through Karabakh's rugged landscape to reach little-visited **Dadivank Monastery** (p272), an overgrown masterpiece on the edge of Kelbajar.

❹ Hiking the excellent **Janapar Trail** (p272), a well-marked 190km-long walking trail that takes you past many of Karabakh's most important sights.

❺ Exploring the ancient remains of **Tigranakert** (p272), one of the four cities built by Tigran the Great and home to an excellent museum.

FAST FACTS

Currency
Dram (AMD)

Language
Armenian

Visas
All foreigners need to buy a visa (AMD3000) on arrival at the Ministry of Foreign Affairs in Stepanakert.

Resources
➡ **Nagorno-Karabakh Republic Ministry of Foreign Affairs** (www.nkr.am)
➡ **Office of the NKR, Washington DC** (www.nkrusa.org)

Daily Costs
➡ **Homestay room** AMD10,000
➡ **Midrange hotel** AMD25,000
➡ **Two-course evening meal** AMD6000
➡ **Tour guide service per day** AMD15,000
➡ **Beer at a bar** AMD500

Stepanakert

☑ 0479 / POP 55,000

Stepanakert, Karabakh's rather inadvertant capital, is a bustling and prosperous place spread out along a steep hillside over the distant Karkar River. Despite a recent construction boom, there's still plenty of the town's Soviet heritage visible, as well as many rambling, typically Caucasian family homes. Little different in many ways from a typical medium-sized Armenian town, its unusual position as the capital of a breakaway republic means that it's an interesting place to explore, and with more infrastructure than anywhere else in the region, it makes a good base for trips to the rest of Karabakh.

☉ Sights

Museum of Fallen Soldiers   MUSEUM
(☑ 5 07 38; btwn N Stepanyan & Vazgen Sargsyan Poghots; ☉ 9am-6pm Mon-Sat) FREE This extremely disturbing and sad museum honours those who died in battle during the 1990–94 war with Azerbaijan. The walls are lined with thousands of photographs of soldiers killed in action and there are displays of weaponry and other artefacts from the brutal conflict. The sheer scale of the deaths is chilling, as is sadly the commentary you'll hear from any guide who takes you around. Inevitably this is not a place for objectivity, but rather indignation.

The entrance to the museum is tricky to find; go into the courtyard behind the white building that stands on Vazgen Sarksyan Poghots. There is no sign, but locals all know where it is.

Artsakh State Museum   MUSEUM
(☑ 4 36 69; 4 David Sasuntsi Poghots; ☉ 9am-5pm Mon-Fri, until 4pm Sat) FREE This rather dry museum nevertheless contains many interesting local artifacts, most of which can be better understood by taking a free English-language tour. Downstairs there's lots of taxidermy, archeological finds and ethnographic displays, while upstairs is devoted entirely to Karabakh's 20th-century turmoil, from the arrival of communism to the fight for independence.

Papik Tatik   MONUMENT
On the outskirts of town on the main road towards the north of the region is the primitivist statue of a bearded elder and a woman with a veil. It is named 'We are our mountains', their stony gaze embodying the indomitable local spirit.

☞ Tours

Dima Ekorov   HIKING
(☑ 091 14 15 48; mazzoniguide@gmail.com) Dima is an English-speaking walking guide who, though based in Kelbajar, can meet groups or individuals in Stepanakert. He has pioneered his own network of walking trails and is very knowledgeable about the region.

✹ Festivals

Karabakh's national holiday is celebrated on 9 May. The day commemorates the liberation of Shushi and the foundation of Karabakh's army. Concerts, military parades, fireworks and related ceremonies are held in Stepanakert and Shushi.

🛏 Sleeping

The homestay business is not well developed in Stepanakert; try contacting the English-speaking travel agent Susanna Petrosyan (p270), who has contacts in the city and can help find a host family for AMD10,000 per person including breakfast. Susanna also plans to open her own homestay in the city in 2016.

Stepanakert

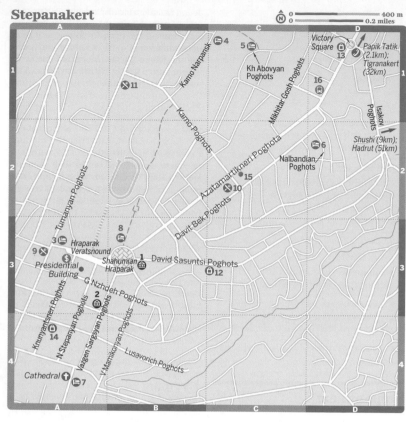

★ **Karina Guesthouse** GUESTHOUSE $
(☑097 33 52 88, 097 26 16 16; carinerooms7@
gmail.com; 27 Nalbandian Poghots; r per person incl
breakfast AMD10,000; @ 🛜) This unsigned but
thoroughly charming guesthouse just off the
city's main drag has three guestrooms and
a self-contained apartment inside a family
house. The rooms are clean and comfortable, and overlook a rose garden. Enter
through the gate and walk around to the
back of the building. Karina provides free
coffee and biscuits all day.

Ella & Hamlet Guesthouse GUESTHOUSE $
(☑4 77 38, 5 21 55; 10 Kamo Narpansk; r per person AMD5000) The cheapest place in town,
this spotless guesthouse is the closest Stepanakert gets to having a hostel. It has five basic but spacious rooms that share a bathroom
in a huge villa, as well as its own communal
kitchen. Ella, who speaks no English, is nevertheless a kind and conscientious host.

★ **Vallex Garden Hotel** HOTEL $$
(☑7 33 97; www.vallexgarden.com; 35 Nelson Stepa-
nyan; r/ste from AMD30,000/80,000; ℗ ❄ 🛜 ☋)
The best hotel in town, the Vallex Garden
is housed in a building that mashes up the
White House with the taste of an Armenian
millionaire. Inside it's a sleekly run affair,
however, with professional English-speaking
staff, spacious and seriously comfortable
rooms, and a basement gym and full swim-
ming pool, both of which are free for guests.

★ **Park Hotel Artsakh** HOTEL $$
(☑7 19 71; www.parkhotelartsakh.com; 10
Vazgen Sargsyan Poghots; s/d incl breakfast
AMD24,000/36,000; ❄ 🛜) This boutique hotel in the building of a former hospital has
been tastefully redeveloped in the classic
Karabakhti style. The distinctive stone and
wood facade lends a traditional atmosphere
but facilities inside are thoroughly modern,
though they include ethnic touches and big

Stepanakert

balconies. There's a traditional Armenian restaurant in the basement.

Armenia Hotel
HOTEL $$

(📞5 09 10; www.armeniahotel.am; Hraparak Veratsnound; s/d/ste AMD29,000/34,000/50,000; ✳🛜) Once the plushest hotel in town, the Armenia now has some competition, but its location on the main square, along with its fitness centre, sauna and cable TV access, make it a comfortable and convenient option. The on-site restaurant is also recommended.

Hotel Heghnar
HOTEL $$

(📞097 26 66 66, 4 86 77; www.heghnarhotel. com; 39-41 Kh Abovyan Poghots; s/d/deluxe incl breakfast AMD18,000/24,000/40,000; ✳🛜) This clean and functional place doesn't have the best location, but its rooms all have balconies with green valley views and are quite cosy and comfortable. Extras include flatscreen TVs and fridges. In summer breakfast is served outside in the garden.

✕ Eating

Stepanakert has a motley selection of eating options, and sadly nothing outstanding. Self-caterers and hikers can head for the bazaar or the best supermarket in town,

Luch (Azadamartikneri Poghota; ⏱8am-midnight). Locals tend not to eat very often in restaurants, preferring to visit a *pavilyon,* a combination of a private home and a restaurant where guests are served meals in self-contained booths within the house. The best of these are in Shushi.

★Ureni
ARMENIAN $

(📞4 45 44; Tumanyan Poghots; mains AMD1000-3000; ⏱noon-midnight; 🛜) This is the best option in Stepanakert, with friendly staff and a charming garden setting. The menu encompasses Karabakhti dishes such as *tanov apur* (a soup made from yoghurt and sour cream), as well as more general Caucasian standards including large sharing plates of grilled meats (AMD6000 to AMD7000).

Tashir Pizza
PIZZA $

(20 Azatamartikneri Poghota; pizza AMD300-800; ⏱10am-11pm; 🛜) Cheap, central and with a photographic English menu, Tashir is ideal for travellers hungering for a change from *shashlyk.* With a choice between thin and thick crusts, as well as pasta and salads to choose from, even the screaming children can't ruin this perennially popular place.

Florence Garden
ARMENIAN $

(57 Tumanyan Poghots; mains AMD2000-4000; ⏱9am-midnight; 🛜) A sprawling recent addition to the local eating scene, the Florence Garden is rather misleadingly named as it mainly offers Karabakhti specialities rather than anything Italian. While it's easily the city's smartest restaurant and the food is generally very good, its lack of an English menu and painfully disinterested staff can make dining here quite a challenge.

🛍 Shopping

Bazaar
MARKET

(David Sasuntsi Poghots; ⏱8am-6pm) This bustling market is a great place to wander about and soak up some local colour, as well as to buy local honey, cheese, fruit and vegetables. Two local specialities worth trying here include *jengyalov hats* (a dough pancake filled with greens and herbs) and *trteruk* (a sweet bread).

Nereni Arts & Crafts
CRAFTS

(📞0471-4 87 11; 10 Lusavorich Poghots; ⏱10am-7pm) Run by a diaspora Iranian and his Australian wife, this shop carries a range of unique handicrafts created by local jewellers and artisans.

KARABAKH STATUS QUO

According to nearly all international protocols, the territory of Nagorno-Karabakh is still legally part of Azerbaijan. It is not officially recognised as a sovereign state and we do not regard it as such. It is an independent state only according to the Nagorno-Karabakh Declaration of Independence and can only be visited from Armenia, which controls the territory. Note that in addition to Nagorno-Karabakh, there are other areas controlled by Armenia such as Kelbajar and Agdam that are historically not a part of Karabakh but were taken by Armenian forces during the war and remain a de facto part of Nagorno-Karabakh today. Visiting Nagorno-Karabakh will disbar you from entry to Azerbaijan, so if you plan to visit both, go to Azerbaijan first, or simply ask for the Karabakh visa not to be placed in your passport, which is totally possible and will not cause offense.

ⓘ Information

Karabakh Telecom (www.karabakhtelecom.com/en/; 15 Admiral Isakov Poghots) This central office sells SIM cards that can be used in unlocked phones.

Ministry of Foreign Affairs (☑ 95 07 68, 94 14 18; www.nkr.am/en/; 28 Azatamartikneri Poghota; ☺ 9am-1pm & 2-6pm Mon-Fri, noon-4pm Sat) This is where all visitors must go upon arrival to obtain visas.

Susanna Petrosyan (☑ 097 24 66 73, 097 23 78 73; susanna.petrosyan80@gmail.com) English- and French-speaking Susanna has pioneered tourism in Karabakh and can arrange homestays (including in rural villages), guided tours, transfers, hiking and almost anything else if you give her some notice. She knows everyone in the country and can give excellent advice about how best to approach a trip here.

ⓘ Getting There & Away

Buses and *marshrutky* (public minivan transport) depart from the **bus station** (☑ 4 06 61; Azatamartikneri Poghota) near Victory Sq. Marshrutky to Yerevan leave when full from 7am until 11am (AMD4500, seven to eight hours). These all pass through Goris (AMD1500, two hours). Chartering a taxi to Goris/Yerevan costs AMD15,000/40,000, or a seat in a shared taxi AMD4000/10,000.

Marshrutky to Shushi depart once or twice hourly between 7am and 7pm (AMD200, 30 minutes). Two buses a day run to Gandzasar (AMD600, one hour) at 9am and 4pm. Nine buses a day go to Martakert between 8.30am and 5pm (AMD800, 1½ hours). Buses to Martuni (AMD800, one hour) leave at 8.30am, 1pm, 1.30pm and 3pm. Buses to Karmir Shuka (AMD500, 50 minutes) depart at 9am, 9.30am, 2pm and 3pm.

The airport in Stepanakert, closed during the war, has been rebuilt but lies unused, as Karabakh's airspace remains contested.

ⓘ Getting Around

There are plenty of *marshrutky* (per ride AMD50) that ply the main boulevards of Stepanakert. Nos 10, 13, 14 and 17 shuttle up and down Azatamartikneri Poghota.

Shushi

☑ 0477 / POP 3500

Shushi (Şuşa to Azeris) stands on a plateau 9km from Stepanakert, with high walls and views over a wide swath of central Karabakh. The city was once a centre of Armenian and Azeri art and culture, and during the 19th century it was one of the largest towns in the South Caucasus with a multicultural population and a reputation for tolerance and peaceful coexistence. The city suffered badly during the war and much of its population left, but recovery has been under way for some time now. There are some excellent B&Bs in town, so if you want to experience village life in Karabakh consider spending a couple of nights up here, as it makes a good base for exploring the rest of the region.

◉ Sights

Shushi Fortress FORTRESS
FREE Shushi's fortress was built in 1750 by Panah Khan. During the Karabakh War the Azeri army fired Grad missiles from here down onto Stepanakert and its surrounding villages. It was conquered by a stunning night assault up the cliffs on 8 to 9 May 1992, a crucial turning point in the conflict. Today you can wander along the fortress walls.

Shushi History Museum MUSEUM
(☺ 9am-5pm Mon-Sat) **FREE** Housed in an impressive old stone mansion, Shushi's Museum holds an excellent collection of local artefacts. English-language descriptions of the exhibits help to make sense of it all,

but to get a better understanding talk with curator Saro Saryan, who will show you around the museum for free and who also runs a popular local B&B. In the same complex there's also a small Museum of Geology.

Ghazanchetsots Cathedral   CHURCH
The restored Ghazanchetsots Cathedral is an impressive white structure originally built in 1868. It was closed by the Soviets in 1920 and used as a storage depot, and was where Azeri forces stored their Grad missiles during the war. It was reconsecrated in 1998. Ask if you can go down to the crypt to hear the unusual echo in the middle of the room.

Carpet Museum   MUSEUM
(⊙10am-6pm Mon-Sat) FREE This new museum on the main road between the upper and lower town houses a wonderful collection of local carpets from the 17th to 20th centuries. Upstairs there's an art gallery.

Jerderduz   VIEWPOINT
This area of grazing land on the outskirts of Shushi overlooks the beautiful Hunot Gorge. Take a walk out here for some stunning views.

🛌 Sleeping & Eating

There aren't many restaurants in Shushi, but there are several *pavilyon,* private houses where meals are served up to visitors in much the same way as a restaurant. Ask at your hotel if you'd like to organise a meal.

★ Saro's B&B   GUESTHOUSE $
(☑097 23 17 64; saro.saryan@gmail.ru; Melik Pashayan 19; r per person incl breakfast AMD10,000; 🛜) English-speaking owner Saro Saryan is an enthusiastic host and knows much about Shushi's history. His tranquil home has several large rooms and a garden full of mulberry trees. It's in the lower part of Shushi near the hospital, but Saro can usually be found at his office in the Shushi History Museum.

Staying here is a great opportunity to experience traditional village life in Karabakh.

Hovik Gasparyan B&B   GUESTHOUSE $
(☑097 29 07 24, 097 26 17 36; mariamartur8@mail.ru; r per person incl breakfast AMD10,000; 🛜) This large family house has four multibed guestrooms. No English is spoken, but the welcome is warm and you'll get a good feel for life in a typical Karabakhti homestead. The head of the family, Hovik, is a well-known local painter and his works adorn the walls.

Avan Shushi Plaza Hotel   HOTEL $
(☑3 15 99; www.avanshushiplaza.com; 29 Ghazanchetsots Pohoda; s/d incl breakfast AMD10,000/20,000; ❄🛜) Right in the middle of town, the rooms at this high-rise place may feel a little worn, but they're still a great deal. There are sweeping views from the top floor, though it's sadly underused and was filled just with a ping pong table and an exercise bike on our last visit.

Shushi Grand Hotel   HOTEL $$
(☑73 33 37; www.shushigrandhotel.com; 2b Aram Manukyan Poghots; s/d incl breakfast AMD22,000/27,000; 🛜) Shushi's best hotel has spacious and comfortable (if not particularly characterful) rooms, all with balconies in a modern and clean environment. The Lebanese restaurant here is good, and breakfast on the terrace is an enjoyable experience.

❶ Getting There & Away

Buses between Shushi's main square and the bus station in Stepanakert, 9km downhill, leave every 30 minutes or so during the day (AMD200). By taxi the trip costs about AMD2000.

Southern Karabakh

Southern Karabakh was spared the intense fighting that afflicted the rest of the region during the Karabakh War, and so it's generally a well-preserved area, with little sign of war damage.

◉ Sights

Amaras Monastery   MONASTERY
Founded by St Gregory the Illuminator and completed by his grandson, Bishop Grigoris, the Amaras Monastery dates from the 5th century. It's a hugely important place for Armenian culture, as at the same time the creator of the Armenian alphabet Mesrop Mashtots founded a school to spread the written form of the language here. The current structure is a modest church surrounded by monastic cells, and the complex is enclosed by impressive walls you can wander around.

Azokh Cave   CAVE
The extraordinary Azokh cave, not far from the village of Azokh, is 14km south of Karmir Shuka (also known as Krasny Bazar). About 200m before the village, look for the trail to the right that leads uphill to the cave. The cave has six bat-filled chambers connected by tunnels. Remains of ancient

NAGORNO-KARABAKH SOUTHERN KARABAKH

humans have been found here, as well as tools and pottery shards. The cave entry is large and stunning, but you'll need a strong torch to view the inner chambers.

Plane Tree   PICNIC AREA
Just before the village of Karmir Shuka (also known as Krasny Bazar) if you're coming from Stepanakert, follow the signs uphill to the home of a 2000-year-old *platan* (plane) tree so large you could hold a party inside its core. Locals love to come here for picnics, in the shade of the trees and amid the chorus of the cicadas.

Northeast Karabakh

Northeastern Karabakh saw the worst fighting during the war and remains only partially open, as the front lines are here with towns such as Agdam still out of bounds to locals and visitors alike. Keep to the main roads and do not approach the front line.

◎ Sights

Tigranakert   RUIN
(admission AMD250; ⊙8am-6pm Tue-Sun) Tigranakert is one of the four cities founded by Tigran the Great, but the only one known to historians today. It was founded in the 1st century BC, and vanished from history in the 14th. Archaeologists are uncovering the remains of a 5th-century church and a 1st-century fortress wall, while inside the reconstructed fortress building an **Archaeological Museum** (☑097 20 86 78; ⊙10am-6pm Tue-Sun) FREE details the existence of Tigran's great kingdom, with pottery shards, jewellery and bronze tools on display.

Vankasar Church   CHURCH
This attractive 7th-century church is perched on a hillside high above Tigranakert and affords wonderful views of the otherworldly landscape in the area. It's a good one-hour hike to get up here from Tigranakert, or can be easily reached by car.

Mayraberd Fortress   FORTRESS
Just outside the town of Askeran, 14km north of Stepanakert, is the impressive ruin of Mayraberd Fortress. Built by Panah Khan in the 18th century, it once stretched 1.5km across the valley and still boasts huge medieval walls and towers.

Northwest Karabakh

Northwestern Karabakh is an area of rich cultural heritage for Karabakhtis, and includes two of the region's most important historical sites, the monasteries of Gandzasar and Dadivank.

◎ Sights

★**Gandzasar Monastery**   MONASTERY
Probably the most important structure in Karabakh, the Gandzasar Monastery signifies the millennia-old Armenian presence in Karabakh to locals. Dating from the 5th century, the monastery is centred on the church of Surp Hovhannes Mkrtich (St John the Baptist), which has exceptional carved friezes around its central drum. There are well-preserved inscriptions and *khachkars* (carved stone crosses) in the church's antechamber, which is filled with the floor-slab tombs of former bishops and nobles of the region.

★**Dadivank Monastery**   MONASTERY
This overgrown masterpiece has a bell tower, fine *khachkars* and monastic cells around the main 13th-century Surp Dadi church. Watch out for holes into underground cisterns and chambers as you walk

---

THE JANAPAR TRAIL

Dedicated hikers may want to consider crossing Karabakh on foot, taking advantage of a traditional walking path that stretches from Hadrut in the south to Kelbajar region in the north. The 190km-long Janapar Trail is marked with blue signs that depict a yellow footprint, and takes walkers through startling landscapes including waterfalls, gorges, mountain villages, ancient bridges, rivers and mountains. Starting from Hadrut, the trail connects the Azokh cave, the giant plane tree in Skhtorashen, Shushi, Stepanakert, Gandzasar and Dadivank. If you have Kelbajar listed on your travel permit, you can follow the trail to the hot springs at Zuar and finally Nor Manashid. The entire route takes 14 days, and there is no need for a tent as there are places to stay in every village and town along the way – just ask around for the local homestay. See www.janapar.org for more details.

around. The princes of Upper Khachen are buried under the floor of the main church's *gavit,* the distinctive Armenian entrance to the church that also functions as a mausoleum. The monastery has the most extraordinary position, and is quite a challenge to reach, but well worth the effort.

Vank VILLAGE

Vank is unlike any other village in Karabakh – if not the world – thanks to the patronage of native son Levon Hairapetian. The Moscow-based lumber baron has funded the large-scale redevelopment of the town, including a school, hospital and two super-kitsch hotels. The **Eclectic Hotel** (☑ 097 33 00 99; www.gandzasartour.com; s/d AMD25,000/30,000) resembles the Titanic, while the **Seastone Hotel** (www.gandzasar tour.com, s/d AMD12,000/20,000, ❄) has a giant roaring lion's head built into the rock next to it. The entire village is beyond bizarre, but it's definitely a worthwhile detour.

Nikol Duman Memorial Museum MUSEUM (☑ 0479-4 47 58; ⊗ 10am-6pm) The wonderfully named village of Ghshlagh houses this unique museum, which honours the life of the leader of the Dashnaks, a late-19th-century left-wing Armenian nationalist movement. The home, once occupied by Duman himself, is fully restored to its 19th-century condition.

Kelbajar

This wild, mountainous region between Armenia and northern Karabakh is ringed by 3000m peaks, with rivers cutting through high gorges and a scattering of villages that have been resettled by Armenians. Most of the population before the war were Muslim Kurdish farmers and herders, and as this is occupied Azerbaijan (and was never a part of Nagorno-Karabakh) its inclusion in the region is an anomaly due to where the ceasefire line fell.

The main artery through here is a rough road (currently being upgraded) that leads across the Sodk Pass, the second and far less used border crossing into Armenia proper. This is a superb drive, and well recommended as a way of returning to Armenia without retracing your route through Goris. There's little in terms of sights to see, and no major towns, but the scenery is the best in the region by a long way.

UNDERSTAND NAGORNO-KARABAKH

Nagorno-Karabakh Today

Together the Karabakhti diaspora abroad and Armenia proper provide the vast majority of investment in Karabakh. The local economy is otherwise lacklustre and most people outside the few urban centres are farmers. While outside investment has brought new life to Karabakh, especially in Stepanakert, the region still faces high levels of unemployment and poverty. The government believes increasing the population will stimulate development and pays large cash handouts to newlyweds and newborns.

The conflict with Azerbaijan remains static, though there are still regular exchanges of fire across the ceasefire line. Nagorno-Karabakh's biggest single problem is the lack of recognition as an independent state even by its sponsor Armenia.

History

In this region, names and history are as contested as the land itself. Azeris claim 'Qarabaq' as their cultural heartland, and point to the role of Şuşa (Shushi) in the growth of their literature and language. In Azeri accounts, the Christian inhabitants of Karabakh are descendants of the Christian nation of Albania (unrelated to the present-day state of Albania). Caucasian Albania lost independence after the Arab invasion in the 7th century, and most Albanians converted to Islam, while the remnants of the Albanian Church were usurped by the Armenian Church. Certainly the locals say they're culturally as Armenian as anyone, with 4000 churches, monasteries and forts on their hills to attest to this.

During the Middle Ages the region was under the control of Persia, with local rule in the hands of five Armenian princes known as Meliks. The Karabakh Khanate, with Panahabad (Shushi) as its capital, passed into Russian hands in 1805. During the 19th century many native Muslims left for Iran while Armenians from Iran emigrated to Karabakh.

Stalin, always keen on divide and rule policies, separated Karabakh from Armenia in the 1920s and made it an autonomous re-

ACCOMMODATION PRICE RANGES

The following price ranges are based on double rooms with private bathroom, in high season:

$ less than AMD25,000

$$ AMD25,000–70,000

$$$ more than AMD70,000

gion within Azerbaijan. The natural growth of the Azeri population outpaced growth of the Armenian one and Azeri settlers were moved to Armenian villages. By the 1980s the territory's population was down to about 75% Armenian.

Demands to join Armenia Soviet Socialist Republic (SSR) grew in 1987–88, until the local assembly voted for independence from Azerbaijan SSR in December 1989, and hostilities commenced. From 1989 to 1994 the area was racked by war, which, in its first stage, pitted the Karabakhtis against overwhelming Azeri and Soviet forces. Grad antitank missiles fell on Stepanakert from Shushi until 1993, while bands of local men, organised into *fedayeen* (irregular soldier) units, scavenged for weapons and ranged them against the Soviet army. After the fall of the USSR, the war escalated into a heavily armed clash between Armenian troops and *fedayeen* commandos on one side and the Azeri army assisted by Turkish officers on the other. A ceasefire was declared in May 1994 and the line of control has remained unchanged since then. The war cost around 30,000 lives. It also resulted in a mass emigration of Azeris: figures for those who fled Nagorno-Karabakh and surrounding war-affected areas of Azerbaijan range between 500,000 and 750,000, in addition to 150,000 other Azeri refugees from Armenia.

International negotiations have repeatedly failed but there are plenty of options on the table. The hope is that at some point an internationally recognised referendum can be held, but this would only be considered legitimate after the return of Azeri refugees who fled the region during the war. Armenia wants the referendum to be held as soon as possible, while Azerbaijan prefers a timetable of 15 to 20 years.

Bako Sahakyan, Nagorno-Karabakh's president since 2007, was re-elected in 2012 with a large majority. Running on a pro-independence platform, he remains popular even though his lofty title belies the fact that all political decisions are essentially handed down from Yerevan.

SURVIVAL GUIDE

❶ Directory A–Z

DANGERS & ANNOYANCES

Unless the stalemate between Armenia and Azerbaijan suddenly changes, foreign travellers should have almost no safety worries. That said, the conflict is ongoing and does have the potential to flare up at any time, so it is a good idea to keep an eye on local news before and during your visit. Unexploded ordnance (UXO) does occasionally injure people and livestock and it is unwise to venture into open pastureland anywhere near the front line. Warning signs are prominently displayed in areas close to the main roads. Regarding personal safety, crimes against visitors are almost unheard of. Do be aware that due to its unrecognised status, there is no diplomatic representation in Karabakh; you will need to return to Armenia to seek consular services.

VISAS

All foreigners need to buy a visa on arrival at the Ministry of Foreign Affairs (p270) in Stepanakert. This can be done the following day if you arrive late, or even after the weekend if you arrive after Friday afternoon. You simply need to fill out a single-page form that includes the towns you're heading to in Karabakh. No passport photo is required and a 21-day visa is issued on the spot for AMD3000. Multiple-entry visas valid for up to 90 days are also available. The entire process is quick and easy, and English is spoken.

Note that you will not be permitted to enter Azerbaijan if you have a Karabakh visa in your passport, so if you plan to visit Azerbaijan, request that the visa be left outside the passport: this is quite normal.

While no checks on your papers are likely to be made while travelling in Nagorno-Karabakh, the visa will be checked on departure at one of the two exit checkpoints to Armenia, so it's essential to have your paperwork in order.

EATING PRICE RANGES

The following price ranges are based on the price of one main dish and a drink.

$ less than AMD3000

$$ AMD3000–5000

$$$ more than AMD5000

Understand Georgia, Armenia & Azerbaijan

Georgia, Armenia & Azerbaijan Today

The three South Caucasus nations have travelled radically different roads since they became nations during the disintegration of the Soviet Union. The new era of tension between Vladimir Putin's Russia and the West now presents each of them with a different balancing act to perform, falling as they do within the territories of the old tsarist and Soviet empires, which Russia considers its rightful 'sphere of influence'.

Best on Film

The Colour of Pomegranates (1969) Sergei Paradjanov's dreamlike classic about troubadour Sayat Nova.

Tangerines (2013) Zaza Urushadze's Oscar-nominated film set in the Abkhazian war.

Repentance (1984) Ground-breaking Soviet-era film about a dictatorial politician (director Tengiz Abuladze).

Ali and Nino (2016) Movie version of Kurban Said's wonderful novel (director Asif Kapadia).

Best in Print

Ali and Nino (Kurban Said; 1937) Magical cross-cultural love story set in early-20th-century Azerbaijan

Bread and Ashes (Tony Anderson; 2003) Adventures and laughs walking the Caucasus.

The Crossing Place (Philip Marsden; 1993) Journeys among the Armenians, in Armenia and elsewhere.

Georgia: In the Mountains of Poetry (Peter Nasmyth; 1998) Exploring Georgia's landscapes and literature.

Journey to Karabakh (Aka Morchiladze; 1992) Two young Georgians suddenly find themselves in midst of the Karabakh War.

Entwined with Russia

The South Caucasus economies are still deeply entwined with Russia as a trade partner and as a source of remittances from migrant workers – which in Armenia's case amount to 20% of its entire GDP. Disappointing economic growth since 2013 has been made worse by Russia's own problems from the oil price slump and Western sanctions following its Ukraine interventions.

Armenia

Serzh Sargsyan of the Republican Party was reelected president in 2013, in an election boycotted by several opposition groups citing expectation of electoral fraud. Anger about economic stagnation and corruption erupted in the huge 'Electric Yerevan' street protests in summer 2015 over a planned electricity price hike.

A big part of Armenia's problem is that its borders with Turkey and Azerbaijan are closed because of the dispute over Nagorno-Karabakh, leaving Armenia economically isolated and dependent on aid and investment from Russia. Russia is also Armenia's military protector, with a large base at Gyumri. Under Russian pressure, in 2013 Armenia decided against signing an EU association agreement and instead joined the Russian-dominated Eurasian Economic Union.

Georgia

The Georgian Dream coalition launched by billionaire Bidzina Ivanishvili softened the fiercely pro-Western, anti-Russian stance of Mikheil Saakashvili (Georgia's president from 2004 to 2013), but maintained a westward course. In 2014 it signed an association agreement and free trade deal with the EU. It seemed little coincidence that Russia subsequently signed new alliances with the breakaway Georgian regions of Abkhazia and South Ossetia, tying them ever closer to it, including in matters of defence.

Georgians liked Georgian Dream's reforms of the previously Draconian justice system, but became disenchanted with its perceived lack of action on the economy. At least the transfer of power from Saakashvili and his United National Movement to Georgian Dream had been peaceful and electoral, and a similar success for democracy was anticipated for the parliamentary election of 2016.

Azerbaijan

Azerbaijan has continued to enjoy the fruits of its oil boom, with a dramatic rise in living standards and new buildings and infrastructure transforming the face of Baku and regional centres. There are serious worries, however, that the oil price slump of 2014–15 could turn things sour. Though the government of İlham Əliyev is continually criticised internationally and by some at home over allegations of corruption, rigged elections and the muzzling of criticism, it also has its admirers who appreciate the wealth and stability it has brought.

Azerbaijan has looked to the West as an investor and customer for its energy resources, but increasingly resents Western criticism and feels the USA and EU have not given it sufficient credit for channelling Caspian oil and gas to the West. Seen from Azerbaijan, the West is to blame for destabilising Ukraine and thus the whole Russian 'sphere of influence' in the name of democracy. The regime now sees the West as a threat to its own stability, hence the crackdowns on media and civil society groups in the run-up to the 2015 European Games in Baku.

Society & Religion

At grass-roots level, society at large in all three countries remains very traditional despite outward appearances of Western dress, bars, nightclubs, and the ability to have a great time at social gatherings with music, food, wine and vodka. The traditional family and traditional gender roles reign.

Conservative morality is bolstered by religion, especially in Georgia and Armenia where the Georgian Orthodox and Armenian Apostolic churches are the most powerful social forces. More than 40% of Georgians and over 30% of Armenians attend church at least monthly. Islam in Azerbaijan is relatively low-key: few women cover their hair and fewer than one in five Azerbaijanis attend religious services monthly.

The age-old town/country gap has not gone away. While the big cities experience building booms and life in their cafes and shops is bright, modern and dandy, out in the sticks things can still be much tougher. Codes of behaviour are more traditional too: take what might seem the minor matter of wearing shorts – in Yerevan, perfectly acceptable on both women and men, but in the Armenian countryside a no-no; in Baku now fashionable on men in informal situations, but in some other parts of Azerbaijan, positively offensive!

POPULATION: **17 MILLION**

AREA: **181,000 SQ KM**

GDP PER HEAD:
(AZERBAIJAN)
US$7884 (2014)

(ARMENIA & GEORGIA):
US$3640–3670 (2014)

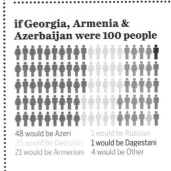

if Georgia, Armenia & Azerbaijan were 100 people

48 would be Azeri
25 would be Georgian
21 would be Armenian
1 would be Russian
1 would be Dagestani
4 would be Other

belief systems
(% of population)

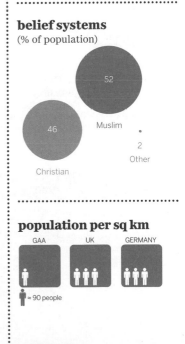

52 Muslim

46 Christian

2 Other

population per sq km

GAA   UK   GERMANY

≈ 90 people

History

This mountainous isthmus between the Black and Caspian Seas stands at the frontiers of Europe and Asia and of Islam and Christendom, an eternal crossroads of cultures and empires with one of the most complicated, and fascinating, stories in the world. Today's three South Caucasus nations are just the latest of scores of republics, kingdoms, principalities, emirates, khanates and satrapies that have blossomed and wilted here down the centuries, as Romans, Persians, Byzantines, Arabs, Ottomans, Russians and others used the local peoples as pawns in their grand imperial games.

Early Empires

Some aver that South Caucasus history began at the unspecified time when Noah's Ark grounded on Mt Ararat (in modern-day Turkey, just west of the Armenian border). What is known is that the 1.8-million-year-old early human remains found a few years ago at Dmanisi, 80km southwest of Tbilisi, are the oldest discovered outside Africa. It may also well be that the world's first wine was made in the region: archaeologists have found evidence of wine-making in Georgia 8000 years ago.

Greeks, Persians and Romans brought the classical pagan faiths and philosophies to the South Caucasus in the 1000 years before Christianity took hold, helping to create rich local cultures. The Greeks established colonies in Colchis (western Georgia) perhaps as early as the 8th century BC. The Armenians trace their origins back to the Urartu kingdom of about 1000 to 600 BC centred on Lake Van in eastern Turkey. They were incorporated successively into the Persian Achaemenian Empire, the Greek Macedonian Empire and the Middle Eastern Seleucid Empire. After the Romans defeated the Seleucids, Tigranes the Great (r 95–55 BC) built an Armenian empire stretching from the Caspian Sea to the Mediterranean. But Rome moved into Armenia and Georgia after Tigranes unwisely allied against it with Mithridates of Pontus (in northern Turkey). Armenia ended up as a buffer between the Romans and the Persians, who fought long wars for control of the region.

Top History Reads

The Caucasus (Thomas de Waal)

The Ghost of Freedom (Charles King)

Black Dog of Fate (Peter Balakian)

The Oil and the Glory (Steve LeVine)

TIMELINE

1st Century BC	AD 301	642–661
Tigranes the Great builds an Armenian empire stretching from the southwest corner of the Caspian Sea to the eastern shores of the Mediterranean, with its capital at Tigranakert.	Armenia becomes the first state officially to embrace Christianity, after King Trdat III's conversion. The eastern Georgian kingdom of Kartli (Iveria) follows suit in 327.	Muslim Arabs take over the South Caucasus, reaching Azerbaijan in 642, setting up an emirate in Tbilisi in 654 and gaining control of Armenia in 661.

NATION CREATION

Modern Armenia is just a small eastern part of historic Armenia, much of which lay in what are now eastern Turkey and northwest Iran. Back in the 1st century BC ancient Armenia held sway from the shores of the Caspian Sea to those of the Mediterranean, but for many later centuries there was no Armenian state at all. The predecessor of the modern republic was born in 1918.

Georgia did not come together as a single entity with approximately its current extents until several small principalities were united in the 11th century. It disintegrated by the 15th century, and was only reunified (under Russian rule) in the 19th century

What is now Azerbaijan was for centuries part of a jigsaw of small khanates on the northern fringe of the Persian empire. The first unified, independent Azerbaijan, or indeed any sense of an Azerbaijani nationality, did not emerge until the 20th century.

First Christian Kingdoms

Christian apostles were already visiting the South Caucasus in the decades after the death of Jesus. In 301 Armenia's King Trdat III was converted to Christianity and Armenia became the first nation officially to embrace the religion. The eastern Georgian kingdom of Kartli (or Iveria), and the state of Albania in what's now Azerbaijan (no relation to Balkan Albania), followed suit within the next 30 years or so.

As the Christian Byzantine Empire expanded eastward from Constantinople, western Armenia and western Georgia fell under its sway, while their eastern areas came under Persian control.

Islam & Asian Conquerors

Arabs, carrying Islam beyond the Arabian Peninsula after the death of the Prophet Mohammed in 632, took over the South Caucasus by 661. In the 9th century the Arabs recognised a local prince of the Bagratid family, Ashot I, as king of Armenia. By the 11th century, another Bagratid branch controlled most of Georgia.

Nomadic Turkic herders arriving from Central Asia from about the 9th century were probably the ancestors of modern Azerbaijanis. Another group of Turks from Central Asia, the Seljuks, brought death, plunder and destruction to the Caucasus region in the 11th and 12th centuries, but Georgian king Davit Aghmashenebeli (David the Builder, 1089–1125) managed to drive the Seljuks out of Georgia, initiating its medieval golden age. David's great-granddaughter Queen Tamar (1184–1213) controlled territory from western Azerbaijan to eastern Turkey, including many Armenian-populated regions.

A Hero of Our Time (1840), Mikhail Lermontov's masterpiece about a bored, cynical Russian officer in the Caucasus, was the first – and shortest – Great Russian Novel. An entirely different fictional experience, *The Girl King* (2011) is Meg Clothier's hard-to-put-down imagining of the great medieval Georgian Queen Tamar's life.

11th–13th centuries	13th & 14th centuries	16th century	1783
Georgia enjoys a golden age under rulers including Davit Aghmashenebeli (David the Builder, 1089–1125) and Tamar (1184–1213).	The South Caucasus is devastated by the Mongol invasion in the 1230s, the Black Death (1340s) and the ruthless Central Asian conqueror Timur (Tamerlane) in the late 14th century.	The Constantinople-based Ottoman Turks take over nearly all of Armenia; the Azeri/Persian Safavids take control of Azerbaijan and the khanate of Yerevan; Georgia is divided between the Ottomans and Safavids.	The Treaty of Georgievsk sees east Georgian King Erekle II accept Russian control in exchange for protection from Muslim foes. Russia goes on to take over the whole South Caucasus in the 19th century.

The whole region was floored by the next great wave from the east, the Mongols, who invaded in the 1230s. They were followed in the late 14th century by another ruthless Asian conqueror, Timur (Tamerlane). Şirvan, a Muslim khanate in modern Azerbaijan, managed to retain some autonomy, and by the 15th century Baku was a prospering trade-route centre. In 1501 Şirvan was conquered by fellow Azeris from what's now northern Iran, who converted it from Sunni to Shia Islam.

The next pair to compete for the South Caucasus were the Azeri Safavid dynasty from Persia and the Ottoman Turks, who had taken Constantinople and swept away the Byzantine Empire in 1453. In 1514–16 the Ottomans took over nearly all of Armenia, and kept most of it for nearly 400 years. After the Safavid collapse in 1722, a new Persian conqueror, Nader Shah, installed Bagratid princes in eastern Georgia, and autonomous Muslim khanates emerged in Azerbaijan.

Russia Arrives...& Stays

Peter the Great began the great Russian push into the Caucasus region in the 1720s. Russia took over the whole of South Caucasus in the 19th century, wresting the Yerevan khanate and those comprising modern Azerbaijan (including Karabakh and Naxçivan) from Persian claims, annexing the Georgian princedoms one by one, and taking the Batumi area (southwest Georgia) as well as Kars and Ardahan (northeast Turkey) from the Turks in the 1870s.

A good half of historic Armenia and perhaps 2.5 million Armenians remained in the Ottoman Empire after the Russo-Turkish War in the 1870s. Unrest among them led to massacres of Armenians in the 1890s, and in 1915 the Young Turk government in Istanbul ordered the dispossession and deportation of virtually all Armenians within the Ottoman Empire. Deportation meant walking into the Syrian deserts. In all, 1.5 million are thought to have been killed or to have died in the desert.

Following the Russian Revolution, the South Caucasus declared itself an independent federation in 1918, but national and religious differences saw it split quickly into three separate nations: Georgia, Armenia and Azerbaijan. The Turkish army pushed into the region before the Red Army came south to claim it in 1920–21. Georgia, Armenia and Azerbaijan were thrown together in the Transcaucasian Soviet Federated Socialist Republic, one of the founding republics of the Soviet Union in 1922. This in turn was split into separate Georgian, Armenian and Azerbaijani Soviet Republics in 1936.

The later Soviet period, after Stalin's death in 1953, was relatively calm, despite worsening corruption. But the wider Soviet economy stagnated, and Mikhail Gorbachev's efforts to deal with this through *glasnost* (open-

1915	1918–21	1930s	1989–94
The Young Turk government in Istanbul orders the dispossession and deportation of the Ottoman Empire's Armenian population. About 1.5 million Armenians are killed or die in the Syrian desert by 1922.	Following the Russian Revolution, Georgia, Armenia and Azerbaijan exist briefly as independent nations, before being taken by the Red Army and incorporated into the new USSR in 1922.	Antinationalist repression, led by Georgian Bolsheviks Stalin, Beria and Ordzhonikidze, and the Great Terror see hundreds of thousands of people from the region executed or imprisoned.	Fighting over Azerbaijan's Armenian-majority region kills 30,000 and displaces hundreds of thousands. Karabakh becomes de facto independent of Azerbaijan; Armenia occupies surrounding areas of Azerbaijan.

ness) and *perestroika* (restructuring) unlocked nationalist tensions that would tear both the Caucasus region and the whole Soviet Union apart.

Independence

In 1988 Azerbaijan's Armenian-majority region of Nagorno-Karabakh declared its wish for unification with Armenia. Armenians were massacred in the Azerbaijan town of Sumqayıt, violence spiralled in both republics, and Azeris in Armenia and Armenians in Azerbaijan started to flee. By 1990 Armenian and Azerbaijani militias were battling each other in and around Nagorno-Karabakh.

In Georgia, the national independence movement became an unstoppable force after 19 hunger strikers died as Soviet troops broke up a protest in Tbilisi in 1989. Georgia, Armenia and Azerbaijan all declared independence in 1991, and the Soviet Union formally split into 15 different nations in December that year.

Strife in the South Caucasus only got worse. In Karabakh, several years of vicious fighting ended with a 1994 ceasefire and a victory for the Armenian and Karabakhti forces over the Azeri army. Nagorno-Karabakh has been de facto independent ever since. In Georgia the first post-independence president, Zviad Gamsakhurdia, was driven out in a civil war, and bloody interethnic fighting left the Georgian regions of South Ossetia and Abkhazia effectively independent by 1993. These wars cost around 40,000 lives and displaced about a million people.

Into the 21st Century

All the region's economies nosedived in the 1990s, but took an upturn in the 2000s. In Georgia, President Eduard Shevardnadze, formerly Gorbachev's Soviet foreign minister, managed to stabilise the political situation but did not quell crime or corruption. He was booted out in the peaceful Rose Revolution of 2003 led by the modernising, pro-Western Mikheil Saakashvili. The new broom effectively eradicated crime and corruption, liberalised the economy and attracted a good deal of foreign investment which helped to modernise Georgia's infrastructure. But Saakashvili's attempt in 2008 to regain control of Russian-backed South Ossetia by military force ended disastrously in a brief, humiliating Russian invasion of Georgia. Following this 'Five Days War', Russia went on to tighten its grip over South Ossetia and Georgia's other breakaway region, Abkhazia. Saakashvili's star waned further as his style of government became increasingly autocratic and intolerant of opposition, with Georgians especially angered by the Draconian justice system where acquittals were virtually nonexistent. The Saakashvili era came to an end when the rival Georgian Dream

HISTORY INDEPENDENCE

Post-Soviet Wars & Politics

Black Garden: Armenia and Azerbaijan through Peace and War (Thomas de Waal)

Azerbaijan Diary (Thomas Goltz)

Georgia Diary (Thomas Goltz)

The Guns of August 2008 (Svante E Cornell and S Frederick Starr)

1991	1991–93	1990s	2003
Georgia, Armenia and Azerbaijan all declare independence from the USSR, which formally dissolves itself in December. The region is already wracked by interethnic unrest.	Interethnic conflict in Georgia's South Ossetia (1991–92) and Abkhazia (1992–93) leaves both regions de facto independent. Abkhazia ethnically cleanses its ethnic-Georgian population (about 230,000 people).	Economic collapse throughout the region due to internal wars, refugee problems, corruption, infrastructure collapse and the end of Soviet state support for industry and agriculture.	İlham Əliyev succeeds his father Heydar Əliyev as Azerbaijan's president, inheriting an economic boom based on the country's large reserves of oil and natural gas.

A TANGLED WEB

Just how interwoven are the stories of the South Caucasus' different peoples is well illustrated by the life of the famed 18th-century poet and Armenian cultural hero Sayat Nova. Though Armenian, Sayat Nova was part of the court of the Georgian king Erekle II in Tbilisi. Exiled for his forbidden love of the king's daughter, Sayat Nova lived as a wandering troubadour and as a monk in Armenian monasteries. He wrote more than 200 songs, some of them still sung today, in Armenian, Georgian, Persian and, most of all, in Azeri, which was spoken by Armenia's large Muslim population of the day and was also a *lingua franca* for much of the South Caucasus. Sayat Nova died helping defend Tbilisi from the Persians in 1795 and his tomb stands outside the city's Armenian Cathedral of St George. His life is the subject of one of the great Soviet-era films, *The Colour of Pomegranates,* directed by another Tbilisi-born Armenian, Sergei Paradjanov.

coalition, led by billionaire Bidzina Ivanishvili, won the parliamentary and presidential elections of 2012 and 2013.

In Azerbaijan, ex-communist boss Heydar Əliyev had returned to power in 1993 and negotiated a highly lucrative deal with Western oil companies over Azerbaijan's Caspian Sea oil reserves. The oil deal brought on an economic boom, which his son İlham Əliyev presided over following a seamless transition of power on his father's death in 2003. Azerbaijan enjoyed a steady rise in living standards and massive investment in new infrastructure (of which Baku's startling new tower architecture is only the most eye-catching), but this came with a politically repressive regime that tolerated little opposition or dissent.

Armenia was left economically isolated by the Karabakh War, which closed its borders with both Azerbaijan and its ally Turkey. Relations with Turkey were also bedevilled by a long-standing dispute over whether the mass deaths of Armenians at Turkish hands in 1915–22 should be labelled genocide. In 2009 the two countries attempted to normalise relations, with their foreign ministers signing protocols to establish diplomatic ties and open their mutual border. But the deal was rejected by nationalists on both sides and has never been ratified by their parliaments. Armenia's democratic credentials remained wobbly with elections routinely criticised as unfair by opposition parties and/or international observers. Many Armenians chose emigration as the way out: the population fell below three million in 2011, down from 3.5 million in 1990.

OIL

At the peak of its first oil boom, in the early 20th century, Baku was supplying half the world's oil.

2003	2008	2012	2015
Georgia's peaceful Rose Revolution brings in a pro-Western, anti-Russian, modernising government led by Mikheil Saakashvili to replace the regime of former Soviet boss Eduard Shevardnadze.	Russia inflicts a humiliating defeat on Georgia in a brief war over South Ossetia, then recognises South Ossetian and Abkhazian independence and starts military build-ups in both territories.	Billionaire Bidzina Ivanishvili's Georgian Dream coalition defeats Mikheil Saakashvili's United National Movement in parliamentary elections, heralding the end of Georgia's Saakashvili era.	Baku stages the first-ever European Games, showing off the city's stylish new modern face to the world, but international media focus on issues of press-gagging and corruption in Azerbaijan.

People of Georgia, Armenia & Azerbaijan

The Caucasus region is home to so many peoples and languages that the Arabs called it the 'Mountain of Languages'. Kept alive by rugged terrain that divides every valley from its neighbours, over 40 mutually incomprehensible tongues are spoken between the Black and Caspian Seas. Each defines a people. The southern side of the Caucasus is home to at least 16 languages. Some number only a few thousand speakers, isolated in remote mountain valleys.

Strained Relations

The region's major peoples give their names to the region's three countries: the Georgians, Armenians and Azeris, who form more than 90% of the region's nearly 17 million people. Differentiated by religion, language, alphabets, geography and more, these three peoples have nevertheless lived interwoven existences for centuries, which makes it all the sadder that the region today is riven by intractable ethnic and territorial quarrels.

Until the 1990s, communities of (Muslim) Azeris and (Christian) Armenians had coexisted for centuries across much of what are now Armenia and Azerbaijan, under Persian, Turkish or Russian rulers. Before WWI Muslims outnumbered Armenians in what is now Armenia's capital, Yerevan – and Armenians outnumbered Georgians in the Georgian capital, Tbilisi.

Today Armenians and Azerbaijanis are deeply divided over the Karabakh issue; Armenians and Georgians harbour a strange mutual distrust; while Georgians and Azerbaijanis rub along OK, without having too much to do with each other. Only Georgia has sizeable communities of the other two main nationalities – around 250,000 each of Azeris and Armenians, chiefly close to the borders of Azerbaijan and Armenia respectively.

Origins

The Armenians are an ancient people who trace their origins back to the Urartu kingdom of about 1000 to 600 BC, centred on Lake Van in eastern Turkey. Historic Armenia was a much larger area than today's Armenia, encompassing sizeable expanses of what are now eastern Turkey and northwest Iran.

Georgians' origins are shrouded in the mists of distant antiquity, and they still identify strongly with their local regions (Samegrelo, Adjara, Svaneti, Kakheti and so on), but they are united by shared, or similar, languages, and a shared culture and history going back at least 1500 years.

Azeris are a Turkic people whose animal-herding ancestors probably arrived on the southwestern shores of the Caspian Sea from Central Asia from about the 9th century AD.

EMIGRANTS

After centuries of emigration, many more Armenians (possibly 10 million) live outside Armenia than in it. Diaspora Armenians include Cher, Andre Agassi, the members of System of a Down, Charles Aznavour, Garry Kasparov, William Saroyan, Herbert von Karajan, Kim Kardashian and US billionaire Kirk Kerkorian (a big benefactor of Armenia).

RELIGIOUS REVIVAL

For seven decades until 1991, the South Caucasus was part of an officially atheist state, the USSR. But underlying religious sentiments never died and were a major part of the national independence movements in the late Soviet years. Today Christianity in Georgia and Armenia, and Islam in Azerbaijan, are ubiquitous; very few people call themselves atheists, and religious authorities are now strong, socially conservative forces. Churches and mosques, many of them newly built or recently renovated, are busy with worshippers; monasteries and convents have been repopulated by monks and nuns. Old traditions of tying bits of cloth to wishing trees, visiting shrines and graves, and spending lavishly on funerals, remain common everywhere.

The Armenian Apostolic Church was the first legal Christian church in the world, dating back to AD 301. The Georgian Orthodox Church was the second, dating from the 320s. While the Georgian church is part of the Eastern Orthodox tradition, like the Greek and Russian Orthodox churches, the Armenian church belongs to the separate Oriental Orthodox branch of Christianity, along with the Coptic Egyptian and Ethiopian churches. The Armenians diverged from Eastern Orthodoxy back in AD 451, when they disagreed with the authorities in Constantinople over the nature of Jesus Christ: the Armenian church sees Christ's divine and human natures combined in one body (monophysite), while the Eastern Orthodox churches see each nature as separate.

Azerbaijan is the only Turkic country to follow Shia Islam, established there in the 16th century by the Safavid dynasty. Azerbaijan is religiously very tolerant, with little fundamentalism. Women are not obliged to cover their hair and few do. Restaurants stay open during the fasting month of Ramazan, though in more conservative towns a few stop serving alcohol.

Common Traditions

Despite ethnic differences, the way of life around the region has much in common. The three large capital cities, home to a quarter of the total population, are large, cosmopolitan places (above all, oil-boom Baku) with layers of 21st-century Western lifestyle over much older traditional ways filtered through seven decades of attempted Soviet regimentation.

With their pubs, clubs and contemporary fashions, city dwellers might appear to live like Londoners or Parisians, but deeply ingrained social traditions keep the paternalistic family, and extended-family loyalties, supreme. Even in Georgia, the most socially liberal of the three countries, women are generally considered to be failures, or weird, if they are not married by the age of 26, and the concept of unmarried couples living together is unheard of.

Most city dwellers still have roots in the countryside, where life remains slow-paced and very conservative. Family homesteads often house three or more generations. Wives are expected to have food ready whenever their husband appears, and in Azerbaijan women never even set foot in the teahouses that are the hub of male social life. Wedding and funeral customs, and rituals held 40 days after death, are similar throughout the region.

Equally strong are traditions of hospitality and toasting (wine and brandy are produced in all three countries). Throughout the region it is both a custom and a pleasure to welcome guests with food and drink. People everywhere enjoy meeting, helping and hosting foreigners: as a visitor you will see the locals' warmest side, which will undoubtedly provide some of the best memories of your trip.

In churches and mosques, covered shoulders are obligatory, as are long skirts for women and long trousers for men. Headscarves for women show respect and are often obligatory in mosques in Azerbaijan. The required items are often available to borrow if needed (except trousers – but men too can don a wraparound skirt in extremis).

Landscape

Longer and higher than the Alps, the main Caucasus range strides from the Black Sea to the Caspian in a spectacular sequence of snowcapped rocky peaks, high passes, mountain pastures, deep, green valleys and rushing rivers. Its beauty is perhaps the greatest of all the region's attractions – though there is plenty of dramatic scenery further south in the Lesser Caucasus too. Mostly verdant and lightly populated, and with about a quarter of their territory still classed as natural habitat, the South Caucasus countries are a landscape- and nature-lover's delight.

The Lie of the Land

Great Caucasus

The Great Caucasus divides Russia from Georgia and Azerbaijan. Some contend that it also separates Europe from Asia, although the nations on its south flank would dispute that. Several of its peaks reach above 5000m, and in all its 700km length, the Caucasus is crossed by only three motorable roads. Its rugged topography, with valleys connected only by high, often snowbound passes, has yielded fascinating ethnic diversity. Yet feet and hooves can travel where wheels cannot: mountain peoples on both flanks of the Caucasus share cultural traits, and historically have always had contact with each other.

The Plains

The Great Caucasus' fertile lower slopes give way to broad plains running west–east along central Georgia and Azerbaijan, and it's these lower areas (along with Armenia's valleys) that are home to most of the region's all-important agriculture. Most of central Azerbaijan is monotonous steppe, semidesert and salt marsh, though it's intensively irrigated for cultivating cotton and grain.

The Rioni River drains the western Georgian plains into the Black Sea. The Mtkvari flows eastward through Tbilisi and on into Azerbaijan where it becomes the Kür (Kura) and enters the Caspian Sea. The Araz (Araks, Axaxes) River forms the western and southern borders of Armenia and Azerbaijan along much of its course from eastern Turkey, before joining the Kür in Azerbaijan.

Lesser Caucasus

South of the plains rises the Lesser Caucasus, stretching from southwest Georgia across Armenia to Nagorno-Karabakh. Less lofty than the main Caucasus range, the Lesser Caucasus still packs in some spectacular mountain, gorge and forest scenery, and has plenty of peaks above 3000m. Western Armenia and the Azerbaijani enclave of Naxçivan sit on the edge of the Anatolian Plateau, with historic Armenia's highest peak, Mt Ararat (5165m), sometimes in view across the border in Turkey.

Beasts of the Hills & Forests

With habitats embracing deserts and glaciers, alpine and semitropical forests, steppe and wetlands, the South Caucasus is a biodiversity hotspot. Mountain areas are home to brown bears (under 3000 in the whole Caucasus region including Russia), wolves, lynx, deer, chamois and more. Many of the most exciting species are, sadly, endangered.

Deforestation had been going on for millennia – the stark plains around Georgia's Davit Gareja monastic complex were once covered in woodlands – but increased with the energy shortages of the 1990s. Fuel-wood collection, illegal logging and poaching are among the biggest threats to wildlife here.

To learn more about the Caucasus region's special species and ecological value, check http://caucasus-naturefund.org and www.cepf.net.

GETTING OUT INTO NATURE

Hiking & Horse Riding

For the most scenic hiking in the Great Caucasus, home in on Georgia's Svaneti, Tusheti, Khevsureti and Kazbegi areas, and the Quba and Zaqatala hinterlands in Azerbaijan. Georgia's Borjomi-Kharagauli National Park and Armenia's Mt Aragats and Dilijan, Ijevan and Tatev areas and Yeghegis Valley offer further excellent walking. Trail marking is most advanced in Borjomi-Kharagauli, Svaneti and Tusheti. Dedicated long-distance hikers might like to try Nagorno-Karabakh's 190km Janapar Trail. If you prefer to enjoy scenery from a saddle – or have a horse carry your gear while you walk – horses are available in the same Georgian areas, and places such as Lahıc (Azerbaijan), and Tsaghkadzor and the Yeghegis Valley (Armenia).

Climbing

Mt Kazbek (5047m) on the Georgia–Russia border is the most popular high summit for mountaineers – a serious challenge but technically uncomplicated, and easy to organise locally. Mt Chaukhi, east of Kazbegi, presents some great technical challenges. Twin-peaked Mt Ushba in Svaneti is the greatest and most perilous challenge of all.

Skiing

With the expected opening of the new Tetnuldi ski resort in Svaneti for 2016, skiers now have three good, up-to-date resorts to choose from in Georgia. Azerbaijan has glitzy new resorts at Qəbələ and Shahdag. Armenia has newish if modest facilities at Jermuk and older ones at Tsaghkadzor.

Other Activities

Rafting on Georgia's upper Mtkvari and the branches of the Aragvi River north of Tbilisi is an ever-more popular activity, best from late April to July on most rivers. And you can go paragliding in the Caucasus around Kazbegi, or near Tbilisi. With 380 known bird species, the region attracts bird-watchers too. Raptors including the majestic lammergeier (bearded vulture), with its 2.5m wingspan, love the craggy, mountainous zones, while the Black Sea and Caspian coastlines are key summer and autumn migration corridors.

A small number of Persian leopards survive in places like Azerbaijan's Zangezur and Hirkan National Parks and possibly Armenia's Khosrov State Reserve (the leopard's stronghold is Iran, where 500 to 800 remain). The two species of Caucasian *tur* (large mountain goats found in the Great Caucasus) are down to perhaps 4000 for the western species and 25,000 for the eastern one.

Until recently the elegant little goitered gazelle (also called the Persian gazelle or ceyran) had its last South Caucasus refuge in Azerbaijan's Şirvan National Park; however, groups have recently been reintroduced to southeast Georgia's Vashlovani Protected Areas and Azerbaijan's Ağgöl National Park.

Animal herders still move their flocks up and down between the lowlands and mountains seasonally, but Azeri herders can no longer take their livestock up to Nagorno-Karabakh in summer as a result of the Karabakh conflict.

Parks & Reserves

National parks, nature reserves and other protected areas cover about 8% of the total land area. The degree of genuine protection these are-as receive is steadily increasing. Georgia has the most visitor-friendly network, with good infrastructure (including helpful visitors centres) in places such as Borjomi-Kharagauli National Park and the Tusheti, Lagodekhi and Vashlovani Protected Areas. In Azerbaijan, some national park tickets must be prepurchased before arrival, which can frustrate visitors. In some higher Caucasus areas of the Shahdag National Park, complex bureaucratic rules mean that it takes at least a couple of weeks to gain the necessary permits for a visit, effectively shutting down Azerbaijan's most popular longer-distance hike (Laza–Xınalıq–Vandəm).

Architecture

The charm of the old and the shock of the new – South Caucasus builders have been putting a wow factor into their work since the 4th century AD. And they have a wonderful sense of landscape, creating structures that enhance the already-beautiful scenery they are part of. From the quaint, conical-towered, old churches perched on Georgian and Armenian hilltops to the dazzling 21st-century towers of Baku's bayfront, the region's architecture is a continuous visual feast.

Georgia & Armenia

Armenia and Georgia were the world's first two Christian kingdoms, and their unique churches and monasteries, often erected in the most beautiful locations, are a highlight of both countries. Until the last couple of centuries, most other buildings were constructed in perishable materials and so have not survived – the chief exceptions being defensive constructions such as the impressive forts at Amberd, Armenia, and Narikala, Georgia, and the picturesque towers that dot Georgia's high Caucasus valleys.

Early Christian Architecture

Georgian and Armenian church architecture developed out of common roots. The earliest churches here were basilicas, a rectangular edifice (often divided into three parallel naves) that was originally devised by the Romans for meeting or reception halls. Armenian and Georgian basilicas usually had vaulted stone roofs, and domes began to appear above these roofs as early as the 6th century.

Church designs soon began to transmute from the rectangular basilica to symmetrical constructions with a dome above the centre. Such churches could be square, or take the form of an equal-armed cross, or of a four-leafed clover (known as a quatrefoil or tetraconch). Tall, windowed drums supporting the domes let light into the church.

In some churches a quatrefoil inner space is enclosed within a rectangular or square exterior. Such are the very typical and architecturally influential Surp Hripsime church at Vagharshapat, Armenia, and Jvari Church at Mtskheta, Georgia, both completed in the early 7th century. Symmetrical design reached its ultimate form with Armenia's circular Zvartnots Cathedral (641–661), which was as high as it was wide (about 45m).

Almost all the key features of Armenian and Georgian church design were established before the Arab invasion of the 7th century and new churches even today still imitate these original forms.

Later Christian Architecture

Church building revived under the Bagratid dynasties of both Armenia and Georgia from the 9th century onwards. Quite a lot of this new work, especially the Armenian, took place in what's now Turkey – buildings like the Holy Cross Cathedral on Akhtamar Island in Lake Van (on the Hripsime model), and the cathedral of the ruined Armenian capital Ani.

In Georgia the old basilica form was developed into the elongated-cross church, with a drum and pointed dome rising above the

World Heritage Sites in Georgia & Armenia

Mtskheta (Georgia)

Bagrati Cathedral, Kutaisi, and Gelati Monastery (Georgia)

Ushguli (Georgia)

Geghard Monastery (Armenia)

Zvartnots Cathedral (Armenia)

Echmiadzin (Armenia)

Haghpat and Sanahin Monasteries (Armenia)

THE CUTTING EDGE

Over the past decade or so the skyline of oil-rich Baku has sprouted dozens of concrete, steel and glass towers, some of which are among the world's most stunning contemporary architecture. The three blue-glass Flame Towers (a hotel, offices and apartments) twist their way up to pointed tips 28 or more storeys high, while the Korean-designed Crescent Moon and Full Moon hotel buildings (still under construction) will plant a giant upside-down crescent moon and a giant sphere (dubbed the Death Star Hotel by *Star Wars* fans) at the two ends of the city's seafront, both 30-plus storeys high. More earthbound but perhaps even more wonderful is the vast Zaha Hadid–designed Heydar Əliyev Cultural Centre, which ripples sinuously over the contours of its site in a form vaguely reminiscent of a large conch shell. The 21st century is also giving Azerbaijan its most impressive Islamic structure – the İmamzadə complex, a masterpiece of brickwork and blue Central-Asian-style tiles at Gəncə, nearing completion at the time of writing.

Much of the architectural energy of post-Soviet Georgia and Armenia has gone into building new churches and restoring old ones. Tbilisi's Tsminda Sameba (2004) and Yerevan's Surp Grigor Lusavorich (2001) are their countries' biggest cathedrals. But Georgia's modernising Saakashvili government also added spectacular new secular architecture such as the sinuously elegant Peace Bridge in Tbilisi, the six-storey-high glass bubble that is the new Parliament building in Kutaisi, and the avant-garde Public Service Halls that have sprouted in a dozen towns around the country.

crossing. Such are the beautiful tall Alaverdi, Svetitskhoveli (Mtskheta) and Bagrati (Kutaisi) cathedrals. This was also the major era of monastery construction in Georgia and Armenia.

The Mongol and Timurid invasions brought another hiatus in Christian construction, but it revived again under Persian Safavid rule from the 16th century.

19th- & 20th-Century Architecture

The 19th and early 20th centuries brought international influences via Russia, with Georgia putting a quirky twist on styles such as neoclassicism and art nouveau. Yerevan was almost totally rebuilt in heavy Soviet style in the 20th century. Gyumri's old quarter, Kumayri, is the most complete 19th-century urban area in Armenia. Tbilisi's Open-Air Museum of Ethnography is the best place to get a feel for some of the region's traditional wooden domestic architecture.

World Heritage Sites in Azerbaijan

Baku's Walled City

Qobustan Petroglyph Reserve

Azerbaijan

Little early architecture survives in Azerbaijan because of earthquakes and invaders like the Mongols and Timur. The few churches remaining from the early Christian Albanian culture, in places like Nic, Oğuz and Kiş, bear a strong resemblance to Georgian and Armenian churches. Outstanding among Azerbaijan's medieval Muslim buildings are some tomb towers, notably the 26m-high Möminə Xatun in Naxçivan, with its turquoise glazing, and some of old Baku's stone buildings, especially the 12th-century Maiden's Tower and the 15th-century Palace of the Shirvanshahs.

The finer buildings from later centuries include Gəncə's twin-minareted Cümə Mosque, credited to Persia's Shah Abbas (17th century), and the beautiful Xan Sarayı (Khan's Palace) and Karavansaray in Şəki (18th century). Baku's first oil boom a century ago spawned numerous fine mansions in eclectic European styles. Many of these have recently been restored, while many newer buildings in the city have been adorned with similar mansard roofs and stonework facades, creating a Parisian effect that contrasts with the 'New Dubai' pizzazz of Baku's more cutting-edge constructions.

Survival Guide

Directory A–Z

Accommodation

Lodgings in the capital cities tend to be considerably more expensive than elsewhere. Outside the capitals, the range of accommodation is smaller, but value for money is generally much better.

Budget

In Georgia and Armenia there are plenty of inexpensive hostels, homestays, guesthouses and B&Bs (generally with shared bathrooms boasting hot showers), but in Azerbaijan hostel supply is minimal and homestays limited to a few destinations.

Camping There are very few commercial campgrounds and most of those have pretty basic facilities. There are few restrictions on wild camping, but be sensible and sensitive about where you camp – it's not always safe to camp just anywhere, so get good information on local conditions, and if you're near a village, ask if it's OK to camp there. Camping gas is available in Tbilisi but hard to find elsewhere.

Homestays, Guesthouses and B&Bs Home-cooked meals often available and the opportunity

to get a feel for local life. Don't always assume that English will be spoken. **Couchsurfing** (www. couchsurfing.com) and **AirBnB** (www.airbnb.com) have limited local homestay/room-rental opportunities in the region. Signs saying 'Kiraya Otaq' (Room for Rent) are increasingly common in country villages.

Hostels Generally provide dormitory beds or bunks, guest kitchens and hang-out areas. Better hostels frequently dispense useful local information and can be very good places to meet fellow travellers.

Motels Not necessarily just for drivers, many no-nonsense mini hotels offer double rooms with private bathroom for around US$40 or less.

Soviet-era and Trucker Hotels Some rock-bottom budget dives still offer beds from as little as US$5, typically near bus stations or in small unreconstructed Soviet-era places. Expect to share a squat toilet.

Midrange

There's a good selection of comfortable midrange hotels within all three countries, many of them on a refreshingly small scale,

with professional, amiable staff. They range from pine cottages in the woodlands of Azerbaijan to modern art nouveau mansions in Batumi, Georgia. Most offer comfortable rooms with private bathroom (air-conditioned where necessary), and usually a decent restaurant, and often a bar and a couple of leisure facilities.

Top End

Several international top-end chains have Caucasus properties, and in Azerbaijan and Georgia the glitzy Turkish chain Rixos is growing fast.

Children

Family is important in the Caucasus, and children are considered treasured gifts from God. Local people love meeting children and are very relaxed with them – it's perfectly normal for strangers to strike up a conversation over kids, and for the most part people will be extremely considerate towards travellers with children.

➡ Children are only likely to enjoy travel in the region if they enjoy the things most travellers do here, such as hiking, horse riding and visiting monuments.

➡ Journeys in sweltering, crowded minivans and buses can be trying, and delays and minor inconveniences can make life difficult travelling on a budget.

BOOK YOUR STAY ONLINE

For more accommodation reviews by Lonely Planet authors, check out http://lonelyplanet.com/hotels/. You'll find independent reviews, as well as recommendations on the best places to stay. Best of all, you can book online.

➡ Resort areas such as Batumi (Georgia) and Qəbələ (Azerbaijan) have some child-friendly attractions.

➡ Most Azerbaijani woodland retreats have toddler play areas.

➡ Disposable nappies are sold in the larger towns, but may be hard to come by elsewhere.

➡ Extra beds for children sharing a parents' room are often available at no, or low, cost.

Electricity

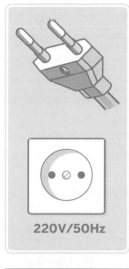

220V/50Hz

Embassies & Consulates

➡ If you are worried that your trip could take you to areas of potential danger, if might be reassuring to register with your home embassy, though the scope of embassies to help you out in an emergency is very limited. For some nationals registration is possible online, eg for US citizens through **STEP** (https://step.state.gov/step).

➡ In Nagorno-Karabakh, Abkhazia and South Ossetia, you're on your own: assistance from your embassy is not possible as these unrecognised if de facto independent territories are outside the control of their nominal national governments.

➡ Some countries may only have one embassy in the region, or none at all. Thus Australia, Canada, Ireland and South Africa hand consular responsibility for certain of the South Caucasus countries to their embassies in Moscow, Ankara, Sofia (Bulgaria).or Kiev (Ukraine).

Gay & Lesbian Travellers

Homosexual acts are legal in all three countries, but social acceptance or understanding is minimal and extremely few LGBT individuals openly display their orientation. Traditional and religious values and a patriarchal society make homosexuality pretty much taboo. There are small gay-rights movements in Georgia and Armenia, but no public gay scenes, and homophobia is still quite widespread. This is even the case in comparatively tolerant Georgia, where there have been anti-gay demonstrations. In general, however, LGBT travellers should encounter no problems if they are discreet. Two men or women sharing a bed is not automatically construed as having a sexual motive and indeed will often be considered far less scandalous than

Climate

Baku

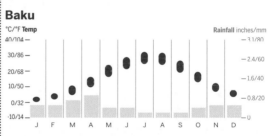

Tbilisi

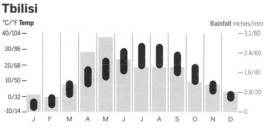

Yerevan

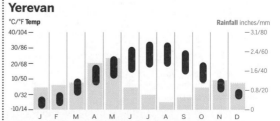

PRACTICALITIES

➡ **Weights & Measures** Georgia, Armenia and Azerbaijan use the metric system of measurements.

➡ **Discount Cards** An ISIC card is useful to prove student status and score discounts on entertainment and museums, plus some shops, restaurants and even certain places to stay. See www.isic.org.

➡ **Smoking** Smoking is near universal among local men, less common among women; only Georgia has a significant number of lodgings with nonsmoking rooms or eateries with nonsmoking areas.

an unmarried mixed couple doing the same.

Advocacy & Support Groups

Gay.az LGBT support website, mostly in Russian with forum in Azerbaijani.

Identoba (http://identoba. com) Georgian LGBT activist and civil-rights organisation.

Pink Armenia (www.pink armenia.org) Promoting LGTB acceptance and equality in Armenia.

We for Civil Equality (www. wfce.am) Armenian LGBT rights group.

Websites

Gay Batumi (http://gay batumi.wordpress.com) Practical information for Georgia, with an active message board.

Unzipped: Gay Armenia (www.gayarmenia.blogspot. com) Wide-ranging blog.

Insurance

It is important to be properly insured against theft, loss and medical problems. Health insurance should cover you for emergency air evacuations in addition to visits to private clinics in the capitals. These generally provide the best medical care, but can be expensive. Check that your policy covers any activities you plan, such as horse riding, climbing, skiing and even hiking. Keep the policy details to hand as many policies require you to inform the insurer promptly

for validation before incurring a major claimable expense like hospitalisation. Worldwide travel insurance is available at www.lonely planet.com/travel-insurance. You can buy, extend and claim online anytime – even if you're already on the road.

Internet Access

Many places to stay, at all price levels, have wi-fi and/or internet-connected computers for guests to use. These services are usually, though not always, free. Increasing numbers of cafes, restaurants and bars also offer free wi-fi. Almost all towns have internet cafes, rarely charging more than the equivalent of US$0.60 per hour. SIM cards with 3G and computer dongles are relatively inexpensive.

Legal Matters

You might be questioned by police or soldiers if you visit sensitive areas around military installations, border areas or ceasefire lines. In Azerbaijan sensitivity extends to some government buildings and economically strategic installations such as oilfields. Outsiders can be viewed with some suspicion in less-visited areas of Azerbaijan with minimal experience of tourism.

➡ Visiting Nagorno-Karabakh from Armenia is illegal under Azerbaijan law. Evidence that you have done so, such

as a Nagorno-Karabakh visa in your passport, will prevent you from entering Azerbaijan.

➡ Entering Abkhazia or South Ossetia from Russia is illegal under Georgian law, with a maximum penalty of five years' imprisonment. If you have entered Abkhazia from Russia, don't attempt to continue across Abkhazia's southern border into undisputed Georgia.

➡ It's sensible always to carry at least a photocopy of your passport and visa. Carry the real thing, too, if you are going anywhere where you might be questioned.

➡ There is a zero limit on blood alcohol for drivers in all three countries.

➡ Cannabis grows in the region and the seeds are sometimes used as a cooking ingredient, but consuming drugs in any other way carries the risk of long prison sentences.

Maps

Rapid road building means that virtually no map is fully accurate, though you might still find a regional map such as ITMB's *Caucasus Region* (1:650,000 scale) or Freytag & Berndt's *Caucasus* (1:1 million) useful for planning.

For your smart phone, Maps.me is a useful offline map app, while runners' apps like Endomondo can prove excellent for recording and mapping your hiking exploits.

Google Maps and regional sites like gomap.az are great for cities but near useless for rural hamlets.

Money

The easiest way to carry money is with a Visa or Mastercard debit/credit card for use in local ATMs. Those are plentiful in cities and can be found in almost every town. But check with your issuer as to overseas transaction charges. Other than in ATMs, credit card acceptance is relatively low compared to other parts of Europe: you can use them at better hotels, restaurants and some shops in the capitals, but less frequently elsewhere.

It's wise to have a stash of US dollars or euros as back-up in case of emergencies. Money-changing offices are common in towns and cities with generally excellent rates for US dollars and euros at zero commission. Rates for Russian roubles are bearable but changing other currencies can be more problematic outside the capitals. Where they are accepted at all, British pounds, Australian and Canadian dollars and Swiss francs will score far-poorer rate splits than US dollars, but not necessarily bad enough to warrant the comparatively huge costs you'd incur in converting those currencies to US dollars in your home country.

Before leaving any one of the Caucasian countries, it's usually wiser to change remaining local currency back into US dollars rather than trying to change large quantities of, say, Georgian Lari into Armenian dram or Azerbaijani manat into lari. Changing manat into dram or vice-versa isn't possible.

There are Western Union offices in many places in case you need to arrange a money transfer.

Travellers cheques are generally a real pain to change. Only a few banks in the three capitals will recognise them.

Photography

It's unwise to start pointing your camera anywhere near border areas that might be considered sensitive. This includes pretty much anywhere near a border, ceasefire line or military base. Azerbaijani police and security guards can get suspicious at anyone photographing government buildings or 'unflattering' or 'inappropriate' scenes (factories, transport infrastructure, metro stations etc). When photographing people, extend the usual courtesies – people (especially men) will often happily pose if you ask their permission to snap them, and it's a good way to break the ice. Be sensitive if photographing at religious sites.

Lonely Planet's *Travel Photography* is a comprehensive, jargon-free guide to getting the best shots of your travels.

Safe Travel

➡ These countries have generally very low crime rates.

➡ Take normal precautions – don't flash large amounts of cash, keep a close eye on your belongings in crowded places and transport, and don't walk alone along dark, empty streets.

➡ Any border area is sensitive, but be specially careful to avoid the Nagorno-Karabakh ceasefire line and Armenia–Azerbaijan border. The borders of Abkhazia and South Ossetia are also tense. Conflicts might flare up at any time in or around these areas. Keep an ear to the ground.

➡ Landmines and/or unexploded ordnance (UXO) still lie near sections of the Armenia–Azerbaijan border and the Nagorno-Karabakh ceasefire line. Away from the ceasefire line and any military exercises, Nagorno-Karabakh is generally no less safe than Armenia.

➡ Climbing and hiking in the mountains have their potential risks. Seek local advice and go with company or take a guide, especially if you're heading into isolated areas. Give sheepdogs a wide berth in the mountains: they are bred for fending off wolves!

Telephone Services

➡ All three countries use the GSM standard for mobile phones.

GOVERNMENT TRAVEL ADVICE

Government websites have information on potential danger areas and general safety tips. They sometimes err on the side of excessive caution:

➡ **Australia** (www.smartraveller.gov.au)

➡ **Canada** (www.voyage.gc.ca)

➡ **Germany** (www.auswaertiges-amt.de)

➡ **Japan** (www.mofa.go.jp)

➡ **Netherlands** (www.minbuza.nl)

➡ **New Zealand** (www.safetravel.govt.nz)

➡ **UK** (www.fco.gov.uk)

➡ **USA** (https://step.state.gov/step)

➡ If your mobile is unlocked for international use, it's often worth buying an inexpensive local SIM card even if you are only spending a few days in country.

Time

➡ All three countries are four hours ahead of Greenwich Mean Time (GMT +4), making them three hours ahead of most of Western Europe, four hours ahead of the UK and nine hours ahead of New York.

➡ Armenian and Azerbaijan change to Daylight Saving Time (GMT +5) from the last Sunday in March to the last Sunday in October.

➡ Georgia doesn't use Daylight Saving Time, putting it one hour behind Armenia and Azerbaijan in the main summer tourist season.

Toilets

➡ Public toilets are rare and may not have toilet paper, so it's a good idea to carry some.

➡ Except in top-end hotels, it's generally bad form to flush toilet paper into the toilet as drains block easily – use the small bin provided.

➡ Some basic homestays and guesthouses have squat toilets in an outhouse across the yard.

➡ Larger bus and train stations usually have toilets but they're often the squat variety and typically incur a small fee to the attendant.

Travellers with Disabilities

There are minimal facilities for travellers with disabilities. Cracked and potholed pavements make wheelchair use problematic, hotel lifts aren't usually planned for them and public transport certainly isn't. On the plus side, the cost of renting a car and driver-helper isn't extortionate. Some of the best local travel agencies will be able to discuss specific needs.

Travel for All (https://plus. google.com/communities/ 114049628154087345562; https://www.lonelyplanet. com/thorntree/forums/ travellers-with-disabilities) Lonely Planet's forum for travellers with disabilities.

Visas

Armenia Most European and CIS nationals (plus Argentines) can enter visa-free. Many other visitors can get a visa trouble-free at borders: 21 day (AMD3000) and 120 day (AMD15,000). Children under 18 years pay nothing. Some nationals, predominantly African, need invitations.

Azerbaijan Visas required. Procedures change frequently, and rules vary between different embassies, but don't assume things will be easy. Also note that fees vary vastly by nationality from free (Japanese) to US$160 (US Citizens). Most EU citizens pay US$35 to US$60, Brits pay US$118, or UK£100 plus processing in London.

Visas are available on arrival at Baku's Heydar Əliyev Airport but only for Turks (US$10), Israelis (US$40) and those with official ministerial approved invitations. Everyone else should obtain their visa well in advance. At present this seems easiest at the embassy in Tbilisi with average waits of just three days and no awkward paperwork, though at least one hotel booking might be demanded. Most other consulates require an invitation letter from an agency, contact or business in Azerbaijan. Some will not process tourist visas at all, telling applicants to get an **e-visa** (evisa.mfa.gov.az). Those are, on paper, cheap (US$20) but they're primarily designed for those on package tours with applications made through an approved travel agency. Some 50 agents could use this scheme but in reality only a handful are prepared to help those who don't want to book a full package, and you'll often find that there's an agency fee, that you still need to book every night of your stay (with confirmations) and that organising all this will take around three weeks.

As well as a visa, you must also register with the migration service after arriving at least once within the first 10 days of your stay. If you stay less than 10 days, the registration isn't necessary.

Georgia Many nationalities, listed on www.geoconsul.gov.ge need no visa for visits of up to a

---

RELIGIOUS FESTIVAL DATES

Some Christian and Muslim festivals have movable dates. The exact dates of Muslim festivals that are calculated by the Islamic lunar calendar must be pronounced locally by clerics, based on moon sightings. Dates given below are for the predicted dates.

YEAR	ARMENIAN EASTER SUNDAY	GEORGIAN EASTER SUNDAY	RAMAZAN	GURBAN BAYRAMI	AŞURA
2016	27 Mar	1 May	6 Jun–7 Jul	11 Sep	11 Oct
2017	16 Apr	16 Apr	27 May–26 Jun	1 Sep	1 Oct
2018	1 Apr	8 Apr	16 May–15 Jun	21 Aug	20 Sep
2019	21 Apr	28 Apr	6 May–5 Jun	11 Aug	10 Sep

year. Those who need visas can usually get them online through evisa.gov.ge (US$20.40, allow five days).

Nagorno-Karabakh You need a visa from the Ministry of Foreign Affairs in Stepanakert (obtainable on arrival there) or the Nagorno-Karabakh representative in Yerevan.

Important: you will not be permitted to enter Azerbaijan if you have a Karabakh visa in your passport, so if you plan to visit Azerbaijan after Nagorno-Karabakh request that the visa be left outside the passport.

Abkhazia Apply online for visa clearance then collect your visa from the Abkhazia Foreign Ministry in Sukhumi. Allow about a week's lead time.

Visas for Onward Travel

Central Asia The situation changes frequently. A fine up-to-date source for latest reports is www.caravanistan.com. Kazakhstan can be visited visa-free by many nationals, and for many others visas are available without any awkward paperwork in three to five working days at the Kazakhstan embassies in Tbilisi, Yerevan and Baku. The procedure can prove quicker if you have a Letter of Invitation (LOI). Baku is relatively good for Uzbekistan and Tajikistan visas, though some nationals will require an LOI for Uzbekistan. Getting Turkmen visas at the Baku embassy can prove a frustrating dead end even with visa support.

It's generally better to organise a Turkmen tourist visa on arrival through a reputable Turkmen tour agency.

Iran Untill recently obtaining a visa required a foreign ministry authorisation number obtainable through agencies such as **Persian Voyages** (www.persian voyages.com). Happily for many European nationals, Iranian visas recently became a whole lot easier and are even available on arrival at Tehran airport. Hopefully things should also improve for US and UK nationals once the nuclear talks conclude but for now those nationals are required to engage a tour guide for a visit. Start the process a few weeks in advance. You can nominate the embassy at which you will collect your visa: Tbilisi is a convenient collection point, Baku can be more difficult.

China For years Chinese visas were not issued except to residents in the relevant South Caucasus country but during summer 2015 some travellers did manage to get a tourist visa in Baku when armed with an invitation from a friend in China. Don't count on it!

Turkey Most nationals need to apply online at www.evisa.gov. tr/en for an e-visa. It's a painlessly simple procedure costing US$20 and requiring minimal documentation.

Women Travellers

➡ The capital cities are relatively liberated, but in

some provincial areas it's wise to dress modestly, keeping shoulders covered in public places. This is obligatory in mosques and churches, where you'll normally also need to don a headscarf.

➡ Other than in mosques, covering the hair is a woman's personal choice and an expression of piety (unlike in neighbouring Iran it is certainly not a legal requirement).

➡ Moderate drinking is generally fine in the capitals but women ordering alcohol or smoking publicly can raise eyebrows in conservative towns such as Zaqatala or Şəki.

➡ Sitting alone at male-dominated restaurants can be uncomfortable. In Azerbaijan a *çayxana* (teahouse) is usually an all male preserve and few local women dine in a typical *yeməkxana* (cheap local restaurant) either. But there are plenty of family restaurants and cafes, some offering private booths or rooms or discreet vine-covered pavilions.

➡ Some cheap lodgings aimed at truck drivers are uncomfortably male-dominated.

➡ In the Georgian mountain region of Tusheti, women are not permitted to approach the traditional animist shrines known as *khatebi*.

Transport

Travelling to and between the South Caucasus countries is complicated by the fact that both the Armenia–Turkey and Armenia–Azerbaijan borders are completely closed.

GETTING THERE & AWAY

Three major and several smaller international airports welcome those who fly into the region. Some flights can be booked online at www.lonelyplanet.com/bookings. Getting here is also possible by road from Iran, Russia and Turkey (but not Turkey–Armenia), by rail (Russia–Azerbaijan only) and by boat, albeit on somewhat irregular Black Sea services (Georgia–Ukraine/Bulgaria) or using often-frustrating Caspian cargo ferries (Azerbaijan–Turkmenistan/Kazakhstan).

Entering the Region

Arrival procedures at airports are generally straightforward and quick. Some land borders can take an hour or two to cross, especially if you're on a through bus and must wait for fellow passengers.

Air

Airports & Airlines

Flag carriers are **Azerbaijan Airlines** (www.azal.az) and **Georgian Airways** (www.georgian-airways.com). **Turkish Airlines** (www.turkishairlines.com) often proves good value and flies to five Caucasus airports (Baku, Batumi, Gəncə, Naxçivan and Tbilisi), with a vast array of connections via İstanbul.

Tbilisi International Airport (☑arrivals 2310341, departures 2310421; www.tbilisiairport.com) and **Heydar Iiyev International Airport** (www.airport.az; Bina; ☑H1, 116), Baku, are busy international airports.

Zvartnots Airport (☑49 30 00, flight information 187; www.zvartnots.aero), Yerevan, has more limited connections.

David the Builder Kutaisi International Airport (☑237 000; kutaisiairport.ge/) in Kutaisi, Georgia, has a growing network of flights by budget airlines to Eastern Europe and İstanbul.

Gəncə Airport is a useful alternative gateway to Azerbaijan via İstanbul on Turkish Airlines.

Tickets

Finding major carrier e-tickets to South Caucasus destinations is easy enough. But there are several ticketing alternatives that you might not have thought of.

CENTRAL ASIA

Watch for airport visa rules for transit flight on **Uzbekistan Airways** (www.uzairways.com) via Tashkent and **Air Astana** (www.airastana.com) two-stop flights via Kazakhstan. Alternative carriers include **SCAT** (www.scat.kz) and **AZAL** (www.azal.az) for Aktau, Kazakhstan, and AZAL for Bishkek, Kyrgyzstan. **Lufthansa** (www.lufthansa.com) makes the only cross-Caspian flight hop to Turkmenistan.

EUROPE

Unlike most major Western European carriers, if you want one-way connecting fares it is often worth looking at **Pegasus Airlines** (www.flypgs.com; via İstanbul), **Ukraine International** (www.flyuia.com; via Kiev) and **Air Baltic** (www.airbaltic.com; via Riga, Latvia).

Another option is **Wizz-Air** (wizzair.com), a budget airline that's due to restore its Budapest–Baku service and flies very cheaply into Kutaisi, Georgia, from several Eastern European cities. WizzAir connections further afield (eg Kutaisi–London Stansted) sometimes only work in one direction so pairing with another one-way flight to make an open jaw can be a clever way to score a bargain.

GULF COUNTRIES & EAST ASIA

Choices include **Qatar Airways** (www.qatarairways. com), **Etihad** (www.etihad. com), **China Southern** (www.flychinasouthern.com; via Urumqi), **FlyDubai** (www. flydubai.com) and **AirArabia** (www.airarabia.com). AZAL has a direct Baku–Beijing overnight flight.

IRAN

Iran Air (www.iranair.com) flies to/via Tehran from each capital. **Mahan Air** (www.maha.aero) and **Iran Aseman** (www.iaa.ir) both fly Yerevan–Tehran.

ISRAEL

Arkia (www.arkia.com) flies from Tel Aviv to Batumi, Tbilisi and Yerevan.

NORTH AMERICA

AZAL's Baku–New York service is the only direct transatlantic flight to the Caucasus. Various other airlines connect via European hubs.

RUSSIA

Numerous airlines operate: notably **Aeroflot** (www. aeroflot.com), **S7 Airlines** (www.s7.ru), **Transaero** (www. transaero.com), **Ural Airlines** (www.uralairlines.com) and **UTair** (www.utair.ru). Before booking a connecting flight via Russia double-check that

visa conditions allow you to transit between flights.

TURKEY

Links to Georgia and Azerbaijan are numerous, but Armenia–Turkey flights are limited to twice-weekly İstanbul–Yerevan services on **Atlasglobal** (www.atlasglb. com). These do not appear on the airline's website and tickets can only be purchased in Armenia or Turkey.

Land

Assuming you have the requisite visas, it is possible to enter the region by land from Iran, Russia or Turkey.

Iran

ARMENIA

➡ Tehran–Tabriz–Yerevan buses (US$60/25,000AMD, 24 hours) run daily using the Agarak border east of Jolfa. Ex-Yerevan departures are at noon from Kilikya bus station, but book tickets in advance through **Tatev Travel** (Map p134; ✆52 44 01; www.tatev.com; 19 Nalbandyan St; ◷9.30am-6pm Mon-Fri, 9.30am-3pm Sat).

AZERBAIJAN

➡ Tehran–Baku buses (about US$40, 19 hours) drive daily via the border at Astara. Several companies operate but it is often quicker, cheaper and more interesting to do this route in sections covering the

Baku–Lənkəran section by overnight train.

➡ Tabriz–Baku buses (12 hours) along with several daily 'domestic' Baku–Naxçivan services cross the border at Biləsuvar–Bileh Savar.

➡ Culfa–Jolfa (open 24 hours) is the relaxed, main Naxçivan–Iran road border. Pedestrians can walk across and onward transport is easy to organise on the Iran side. Train services are suspended.

Russia

AZERBAIJAN

➡ International buses on numerous routes cross at Samur-SDK, a busy 24-hour road border. However, all routes go through Dagestan, which has security issues. Trains are more comfortable and usually safer. If crossing the border in hops, the advantage of Samur-SDK is that some minibus services operate right from the border gate to Baku, but the border crossing can be painfully slow.

➡ Moscow–Baku trains travel weekly. Currently departures from Moscow's Kurskii station are 8.25pm on Saturdays (53 hours).

➡ Two more weekly trains enter Azerbaijan via Russia, originating in Kharkov, Ukraine. They depart from Kharov Yuzhni at 10.20pm Mondays and Thursdays (55 hours).

CLIMATE CHANGE & TRAVEL

Every form of transport that relies on carbon-based fuel generates CO_2, the main cause of human-induced climate change. Modern travel is dependent on aeroplanes, which might use less fuel per person than most cars but travel much greater distances. The altitude at which aircraft emit gases (including CO_2) and particles also contributes to their climate change impact. Many websites offer 'carbon calculators' that allow people to estimate the carbon emissions generated by their journey and, for those who wish to do so, to offset the impact of the greenhouse gases emitted with contributions to portfolios of climate-friendly initiatives throughout the world. Lonely Planet offsets the carbon footprint of all staff and author travel.

➜ Both trains travel via Makhachkala. You get stamped into Azerbaijan at Yalama around midnight, two nights after departure. Border guards can be very pedantic about changing their date stamps at the exact stroke of midnight. Even if you are stamped in at 11.59pm that single minute still counts as a day's stay so it's very wise to have your Azerbaijani visa set to start a day earlier than your planned arrival in Baku.

➜ Xanoba is a quiet, relatively easy road-crossing border point close to Yalama. Crossing is faster than at Samur-SDK but transport is limited to taxis.

➜ Zuxul border crossing is closed to non-locals.

GEORGIA

➜ International transport uses the Larsi (Verkhny Lars) vehicles-only crossing on the beautiful Georgian Military Hwy north of Kazbegi. Pedestrians cannot walk across but bicycles are allowed. A wide variety of Tbilisi–Russia buses depart from both Ortachala and Didube bus stations in Tbilisi. Prices from the latter can be considerably lower.

➜ Tbilisi–Vladikavkaz buses (four hours) travel twice daily from Ortachala bus station (around US$15), and from the Okriba section of Didube bus station (US$9), from where seven-seat minivans also depart (US$30, when full).

➜ Tbilisi–Moscow buses (about 32 hours) cost US$60 from Ortachala bus station, US$45 from Didube bus station.

GEORGIA & ABKHAZIA

➜ Beware. This route is feasible northbound if you have the visas, but don't try it southbound as entering Abkhazia from Russia is considered a crime in Georgia and you could be liable for a jail sentence on arrival.

➜ No Georgia–Abkhazia train service.

Turkey
AZERBAIJAN

➜ İstanbul–Trabzon–Baku buses (US$60 to US$70, 32 to 40 hours) operate at least daily through four companies including Metro and **LuxÌstanbul** (www.luksÌstanbul.com), departing from the Eminiyet Otogar off Küçük Langa Caddesi in the Aksaray area of İstanbul. Some drive via Ankara and are thus slower. All go via Georgia. When booking check if they go via Ankara, or if they transport cargo – both add delays.

➜ İstanbul–Iğdır–Naxçivan buses (US$35, 30 hours) operate several times daily through IğdırTurizm. Boarding in Iğdır, the short journey to Naxçivan (US$5) can take almost all day due to time-zone changes, border formalities and inter-bus station transfers. Buses use the Sədərək border post where pedestrians may not walk across no-man's land. Be aware that continuing from Naxçivan to Baku the only domestic route is by air.

GEORGIA

➜ International buses to/ from various Turkish cities use the 24-hour Sarp–Sarpi border, where passengers are usually required to get off the bus and carry their own bags through customs. İstanbul–Batumi–Tbilisi buses (US$40 to US$50, around 26 hours) run

---

BRINGING A VEHICLE TO THE SOUTH CAUCASUS

Drivers bringing vehicles into the region will need the vehicle's registration papers and liability insurance.

Crossing into Georgia or Armenia is relatively problem free. With some companies it is possible to rent a car in either Georgia or Armenia and drop it off in the other country.

Bringing a vehicle into Azerbaijan is more complex. Vehicles older than 2006 might be refused entry to Azerbaijan or be charged a hefty emissions tax. Any vehicle is liable to a massive cash deposit that is payable on arrival to ensure that you re-export it, the exact sum being dependent on the vehicle's value. However, you can avoid paying more than a US$20 transit fee by driving through the country within 72 hours (or in some cases 30 days); the exact time given seems to vary somewhat randomly so do ask for longer. If you have only 72 hours and are planning to transport your vehicle on the notoriously unpredictable Caspian Ferry, you should take the vehicle to the **Customs Compound** (Map p202; ☑055-5551757; 57-ci Priçal, off Nobel pr; 🚌2, 46, 95, 175), 8km east of the city centre at 'Elli-Yeddiji Pirchal' in Əhrnədli. If you get there after your deposit-free period has expired, you'll need to pay a AZN21 fine at **Customs HQ** (Bakı Baş gömrük idarəsi; Map p204; ☑012-4402501; http://customs. gov.az; Mixail Kaveroçkin 30a; 🚌83) near the US embassy. Drivers overlooking such payments have been refused boarding to the ferry and lost their tickets.

at least five times daily year-round via Trabzon. Trabzon–Batumi buses and minibuses (US$9) run almost round the clock but some eastbound 'Batumi' services actually terminate at the border, leaving passengers a local bus hop or US$10 taxi ride into town. Crossing this border in hops using local transport is usually painless via Hopa.

➡ Ardahan–Akhaltsikhe buses run once daily leaving Ardahan at 1pm eastbound. They cross the Vale–Posof border (open 10am to 11pm, Georgia Time), 18km from Akhaltsikhe. Walking across that border is allowed but it's a lonely spot, there's minimal waiting transport and westbound, even if you are the first to cross, you'll usually miss the last official *domuş* (public minibus) from Posof to Ardahan or beyond.

➡ İstanbul–Kars–Tbilisi trains are due to start operation by 2017, crossing at the remote new Kartsakhi–Çıldır border post,which should also allow road transport once open.

Sea

Georgia

Black Sea services connect Batumi to Bulgaria, Ukraine and Russia. Schedules, routes and fares fluctuate and the information on companies' websites can be inaccurate: contact them directly for latest details.

VARNA (BULGARIA) & ILYICHEVSK (UKRAINE)

UkrFerry (www.ukrferry.com) and **NaviBulgar** (www.navbul. com) both operate several monthly ferries between Batumi and Ilyichevsk, Ukraine, and/or Varna, Bulgaria. Varna–Batumi takes 2½ days direct, via Ilyichevsk 4½ days. Batumi–Ilyichevsk direct (50 hours) costs US$300/222 for a car/motorbike plus US$115 to US$140 per person in a two-

berth cabin including three meals daily.

BURGAS (BULGARIA)

PBM (www.pbm.bg) runs a weekly Burgas–Batumi ferry (2¼ days) that returns in 4¼ days via Novorossiysk, Russia, where you can't currently disembark. The fare in either direction for a car/motorbike plus driver is €250/100 (with a cabin berth and three meals daily). Extra passengers or pedestrians cost €100/150 in four-/two-bed cabins

SOCHI (RUSSIA)

Hydrofoils (passenger-only) leave Batumi for Sochi on Thursday mornings (US$100, five hours), returning Fridays. A second weekly service may operate midsummer.

Azerbaijan

Cross-Caspian Sea ships are rail-cargo vessels for which passengers and private vehicles are a minor afterthought. So don't expect a comfortable ferry. Strict timetables don't exist: they leave when they have enough freight.

Ticket price theoretically includes a sleeping berth and basic meals, though latecomers might have to sleep in public areas on some ships. Bicycles are accepted for the standard passenger fare, motorbikes cost double, cars are charged per metre's length (ie US$500 to US$800 per standard vehicle). The ticket purchasing process can be a surreal palaver. Start by calling the ticket office daily till your name is put on the departure list, then pay when and where you are directed. Go through the main shipping company, **Caspian Ferry** (Map p204; ☑Vika 055-2665354; www. acsc.az; ☺call ahead; 🚌30, 46, 49), rather than using a travel agency – few know the system well and you'll probably add both cost and frustration.

There are two routes:

TURKMENBASHI (TURKMENISTAN)

➡ Ships should leave from Baku roughly every two days (vehicles per metre length/ passenger US$80/90).

AKTAU (KAZAKHSTAN)

➡ Departures are from the new port at Ələt, 75km south of Baku (passenger/ vehicles per metre length US$110/100). These might leave every couple of days, but then maybe not again for a week.

➡ Sometimes the lack of an available dock at the destination can result in hours (or days) of delays, so while Baku–Turkmenbashi could be as fast as 12 hours, either route might easily take 30 to 50 hours. Consider taking extra food and water in case delays mean that the ship supplies run out. Some travellers report spurious requests for boarding and disembarkation 'ramp' fees but these are unofficial and widely ignored.

GETTING AROUND

Air

Interregional Tbilisi has air connections with Baku on AZAL and Qatar Airways, and with Yerevan by Georgian Airways (thrice weekly).

Georgia Georgian Airways flies Tbilisi–Batumi five times weekly (35 minutes, 150 GEL/US$68) and Kutaisi–Tbilisi very late on Thursday nights (30 minutes, 100 GEL/US$44). Tbilisi–Mestia flights run some years.

Azerbaijan AZAL flies Baku–Naxçivan ($65/AZN70, several daily), Baku–Gəncə (AZN31 to AZN35, daily) and Gəncə–Naxçivan (thrice weekly). Flights are more sporadic between Baku and Lənkəran, Qəbələ and Zaqatala.

Border Crossings

Following are the main border crossings within the region and the transport options for crossing them. Visa requirements vary for crossing these borders (see p294); ensure you have the latest information.

Georgia–Azerbaijan

Remember that most visitors require visas for Azerbaijan.

Tbilisi–Baku Trains (*platskart/kupe* US$20/30, 14 to 15 hours) run overnight daily using the Böyük Kəsik border crossing. Foreigners can only cross there on the train and NOT on foot/by taxi, though locals often do. It's marginally cheaper to take bus/*marshrutka*/taxi combinations from Tbilisi to either Balakən (via Postbina) or Qazax (via Krasny Most) and take domestic overnighters from those cities to Baku.

Matsimi–Postbina The quieter border between Lagodekhi and Balakən. Coming this way is scenic and relaxed, and leads through Kakheti, which is an attraction in itself. Baku–Lagodekhi and Qax–Tbilisi buses come this way. Shared taxi hops are inexpensive and straightforward. There's a Balakən–Baku overnight train.

Krasny Most (Tsiteli Khidi, Qırmızı Körpü, Red Bridge) The big road border on the main Baku–Tbilisi Hwy. Baku–Tbilisi–Turkey buses come this way. *Marshrutky* (minibuses) from Qazax and buses from Baku go right to the border on the Azerbaijan side. Shared taxis on the Georgian side shuttle to Tbilisi train-station concourse.

Georgia–Armenia

Yerevan–Tbilisi Trains (*kupe* around US$30, 11 hours) run overnight on alternate days in low season but daily from mid-June to mid-September when service is extended to Batumi. They cross the border at Sadakhlo–Bagratashen, which is also the main road border south of Tbilisi. Trains stop for just one minute at Alaverdi. Shared

taxis Yerevan–Tbilisi (8000AMD, six hours) are much more comfortable than *marshrutky* (6500AMD). Marneuli–Sadakhlo *marshrutky* go right to the border post on the Georgian side. Tbilisi–Alaverdi taxis cost AMD15,000.

Zhdanovi–Bavra Road border between Ninotsminda and Gyumri. One daily Gyumri–Akhaltsikhe *marshrutka* runs this way.

Guguti–Gogovan A potholed road border crossing near Tashir southwest of Marneuli, currently being redeveloped.

Armenia–Azerbaijan

All Armenia–Azerbaijan borders are closed and heavily militarised, the fallout of the unresolved Karabakh conflict. There are no Armenia–Azerbaijan flights either. So if visiting both Armenia and Azerbaijan on one trip you'll have to transit via Georgia or Iran. Should you plan to visit the unrecognised entity of Nagorno-Karabakh the only starting point is Armenia, and once you have been you will be persona non grata in undisputed Azerbaijan, which considers such visits illegal entry to its territory, so you'd best go to Azerbaijan first!

You could request that the Nagorno-Karabakh visa be put on a separate piece of paper, but if the truth emerges, you'll be barred from Azerbaijan and there's a chance that you could be prosecuted if you do get in.

Abkhazia–Georgia

Enguri River checkpoint Heading into Abkhazia from Zugdidi is allowed for foreigners with pre-approved clearance from Sukhumi. But don't enter undisputed Georgia from Abkhazia if you arrived from Russia. That's illegal under Georgian law, with a maximum penalty of five years' jail.

South Ossetia–Georgia

South Ossetia's creeping border with undisputed Georgia is closed to foreigners.

Bus & Minibus

Almost every town and village has some sort of bus or (more commonly) minibus service, the latter being known widely as a *marshrutka* (plural *marshrutky*). Services can run hourly between larger towns but rural villages often have just one single minibus that leaves for the regional centre in the morning then returns from the bazaar after lunch.

Cross-border bus/minibus routes include Tbilisi–Vanadzor–Yerevan, Tbilisi–Gəncə–Baku and Akhaltsikhe–Gyumri–Yerevan.

Domestic fares average around US$1.50 per hour of travel. Standards can vary considerably. Vehicles can get loaded up with freight (sacks of potatoes, crates of drinks) as well as people. It's rarely necessary (and often not possible) to book ahead except for a few international services. *Marshrutky* usually have a destination sign inside the windscreen but it will use the local alphabet. To hail one out on the road, stick out your arm and wave. If you want to get off, say 'stop' in the local language, ie *kangnek* in Armenia, *sakhla* in Azerbaijan or *gaacheret* in Georgia.

Car & Taxi

Driving in the capital cities can be very tough due to convoluted one-way systems, rush-hour traffic jams and uncertain parking conditions. Elsewhere parking is usually uncomplicated and traffic light, though it can prove challenging to adapt to sometimes-anarchic local driving styles. Roundabout priority is typically reversed from European norms (give way to oncoming vehicles), signs are often poor and sections with preposterously slow speed limits might be watched by hawkish police cameras. Fines now generally come with a receipt and may have to be paid into a bank.

The capital cities have branches of major international car-rental companies as well as (usually cheaper) local outfits. Hiring a local driver for intercity trips or excursions is worth considering especially if you locate someone who makes the proposed route regularly as a shared taxi (ie he won't need you to pay for his return drive). You can often find such drivers around bus and train stations, though in some cities shared taxis have their own recognised waiting points. Hostels can also find you a driver at prices that can prove favourable to finding a taxi on the street (around US$0.30 per kilometre).

Remote roads call for a 4WD. Car-rental agents usually want at least US$80 a day for such vehicles, but you'll often do better finding a local driver with an old Niva or UAZ 4WD at the starting village of any off-road adventure; you'll generally need the rudiments of the local language (or Russian) to organise things. You can drive yourself in mountain areas; it's safest to travel in a convoy of at least two vehicles with winches and tow cables for mud patches. Mountain roads are often very poorly surfaced and sometimes blocked or washed away by landslides or flash floods.

➡ Driving is on the right-hand side of the road.

➡ The legal maximum blood-alcohol level for driving in all three countries is zero.

➡ It is usually acceptable to drive using a driving licence from most Western counties but it is wise to get an International Driving Permit before departure to carry in addition, especially if your license does not have a photo.

➡ Filling stations are fairly common along main roads, but if you are going into remote areas fill up beforehand.

Hitching

In rural areas with poor public transport, local people sometimes flag down passing vehicles. If you do the same, it's customary to offer a little money (the equivalent of the bus or marshrutka fare). Hitching along main roads between cities is less common, though not impossible. Locals may pick you up because they're interested to talk with you.

Hitching is never perfectly safe anywhere and refusing rides from drunk drivers is crucial. Travellers who decide to hitch should understand that they are taking a small but potentially serious risk. People who do choose to hitch will be safer if they travel in pairs and let someone know where they are planning to go.

Local Transport

All three capitals have cheap, easy-to-use metro systems. Other urban transport comprises a mixture of *marshrutky* and buses. *Marshrutky* will stop to pick up or drop off passengers anywhere along their routes, but they can get very crowded.

Route boards are often in local script. Taxis are plentiful. Most in Yerevan and some in Baku are metered. For others, agree on the fare before you get in. A ride of 3km or so normally costs around US$2 in Tbilisi or Yerevan, US$3.50 in Baku if metered, much more unmetered.

Train

Trains are slower and much less frequent than road transport. But they're cheap, and overnight services have comfortable sleeper berths included in the price.

Sleeper classes:

1st class (*luks* or in Russian spainy vagon; SV) Upholstered berths, two people per compartment; only available on a few trains.

2nd class (*kupe*) – four to a compartment, harder berths with fold-down upper bunks. Good value, rarely over US$10 for a domestic overnight journey.

3rd class (*platskart*; reserved) – open bunk accommodation without closable compartment door. Two of the six bunks are placed lengthways in the corridor and aren't ideal for a good night's sleep.

Once a night train is underway and bedtime approaches, an attendant will dole out sheets for you to make up your own bed. Each carriage has an attendant who, in better trains, will fire up a samovar for boiling water with which to make tea or instant noodles. But bring your own food as there is usually no restaurant carriage.

You need your passport both for buying tickets and for boarding trains whether domestic or international but not for suburban/local day trains, commonly known as an *elektrichka*.

Health

Prevention is the key to staying healthy while travelling. A little planning before departure will save trouble later: visit a doctor in good time to discuss vaccinations and prepare any medications that you need to take with you; carry spare contact lenses or glasses.

The South Caucasus is generally a pretty healthy region, but as you would anywhere, minimise the risk of problems by avoiding dodgy food and water, and taking precautions against insect and animal bites.

BEFORE YOU GO

Insurance

EU citizens are entitled to free public medical and some dental care in Georgia, Armenia and Azerbaijan under reciprocal arrangements. However, standards of public health care in the region are very patchy and if you want to use far better but expensive Western-standard clinics in the major cities, good insurance coverage is essential.

Ideally get a policy that will make payments directly to providers, rather than reimburse you later.

Recommended Vaccinations

You should be up-to-date with the vaccinations that you would normally have back home, such as diphtheria, tetanus, measles, mumps, rubella, polio and typhoid. Further vaccines may be advisable for children or the elderly.

Hepatitis A Classed as an intermediate risk in the region: vaccination may be recommended for those who are staying for long periods, particularly in areas with poor sanitation.

Hepatitis B Has high endemicity: vaccination may be recommended for some groups, including people who are likely to have unprotected sex.

Tuberculosis (TB) Vaccination is a good idea for young people who plan to work in high-risk areas such as refugee settlements.

Rabies Exists in all three countries. Consider vaccination if you plan a lot of activities that might bring you into contact with domestic or wild animals, such as cycling, hiking or camping, especially in remote areas where post-bite vaccine may not be available within 24 hours.

Websites

There is a wealth of travel-health advice online. The following include country-specific information:

wwwnc.cdc.gov/travel The US Centers for Disease Control and Prevention.

www.nathnac.org The UK's National Travel Health Network and Centre.

IN GEORGIA, ARMENIA & AZERBAIJAN

Availability & Cost of Health Care

The capital cities have some expensive, Western-standard clinics. Public medical care is available in all towns, though clinics and hospitals may be ill supplied, and nursing care limited (families and friends are often expected to provide this). In Georgia some formerly public hospitals have been privatized and will charge fully for treatment, although the cost is still modest by Western standards.

In past years it was typically the custom to give cash tips to nurses or doctors for hospital treatment. This is no longer common and in places where it does still happen, foreigners would usually be forgiven for not knowing about it. If you want to give a cash tip for special attention, do it discreetly by putting money in an envelope, with a card saying something like 'for coffee and cakes in the office'.

Traveller's Diarrhoea

In general the South Caucasus countries are healthy places and stomach upsets are not noticeably more common than in other parts of Europe. If you do develop diarrhoea, however, be sure to drink plenty of fluids, preferably in the form of an oral rehydration solution such as Gastrolyte. If diarrhoea is bloody, persists for more than 72 hours or is accompanied by fever, shaking, chills or severe abdominal pain, seek medical attention.

Environmental Hazards
Altitude Sickness

Altitude sickness may develop in anyone who ascends quickly to altitudes above 2500m. It is common at 3500m and likely with rapid ascent to 5000m. The risk increases with faster ascents, higher altitudes and greater exertion. Symptoms may include headaches, nausea, vomiting, dizziness,

fatigue, insomnia, undue breathlessness or loss of appetite.

Severe cases may involve fluid in the lungs (the most common cause of death from altitude sickness), or swelling of the brain. Anyone showing signs of altitude sickness should not ascend any higher until symptoms have cleared. If symptoms get worse, descend immediately.

Acclimatisation and slow ascent are essential to reduce the risk of altitude sickness: fit, fast climbers are often the most at risk – less dynamic hikers being more likely to pace themselves on steep ascents. Drink at least 4L of water a day to avoid dehydration: a practical way to monitor hydration is to check that urine is clear and plentiful. Avoid tobacco and alcohol. Some climbers credit mint, ginger and garlic as being helpful, though that is largely apocryphal. Diamox (acetazolamide) reduces the headache pain caused by altitude sickness and helps the body acclimatise to the lack of oxygen. It is normally only available on prescription and it is not usually recommended for preventative use.

Hypothermia

Hypothermia occurs when the body loses heat faster

than it can produce it. Even on a hot day in the mountains the weather can change rapidly, so carry waterproof garments, warm layers and a hat, and inform others of your route. Hypothermia starts with shivering, loss of judgement and clumsiness. Unless rewarming occurs, the sufferer deteriorates into apathy, confusion and coma. Prevent further heat loss by seeking shelter, warm dry clothing, hot sweet drinks and shared bodily warmth.

Insect Bites & Stings
Mosquitoes are found in most parts of the Caucasus. Malaria is present, though uncommon, from May or June to October in southeast Georgia, the rural lowlands of southern Azerbaijan and some parts of Armenia. Bring a good insect repellent that can be applied to exposed skin and clothing. Repellents containing DEET are generally effective and last longer than plant-extract oils, but wash hands carefully after use as DEET can perish rubber and damage certain plastics, including many types of sunglasses.

Travelling with Children

➡ Make sure children are up-to-date with routine vaccinations, and discuss possible travel vaccines well before departure as some are not suitable for children.

➡ Be extra wary of contaminated food and water. If your child has vomiting or diarrhoea, lost fluid and salts must be replaced.

➡ Children should be encouraged to avoid and mistrust unfamiliar dogs or other mammals because of the potential risk of rabies and other diseases. Shepherd dogs are not pets and can be extremely fierce.

TAP WATER
Tap water is generally safe to drink in most of the region, though in Baku and the lowland areas of Azerbaijan, you're better off with bottled purified water, which is easily available. If you aren't sure of your tap water's quality, boil tap water for 10 minutes, use water purification tablets, or use a filter. The South Caucasus is also home to some regionally famous mineral waters of which Georgia's sparkling Borjomi is best known. Keep your empty bottles to refill at springs, which you'll often find beside country roads in upland areas. Most are safe and indeed positively healthy, but check with locals, especially if a spring seems little used, as there can always be a slight risk of contamination.

Languages

This chapter offers basic vocabulary to help you get around the south Caucasus. If you read our coloured pronunciation guides as if they were English, you'll be understood.

RUSSIAN

Russian is widely spoken in all three countries, and few people will ever object to being spoken to in it. If you speak passable Russian, you'll be able to get by. Note that kh is pronounced as in the Scottish *loch*, zh as the 's' in 'pleasure', r is rolled in Russian and the apostrophe (') indicates a slight y sound. The stressed syllables are shown in italics.

Basics

Hello.	Здравствуйте.	*zdrast*·vuyt·ye
Goodbye.	До свидания.	da svee·*dan*·ya
Excuse me./	Извините,	eez·vee·*neet*·ye
Sorry.	пожалуйста.	pa·*zhal*·sta
Please.	Пожалуйста.	pa·*zhal*·sta
Thank you.	Спасибо	spa·*see*·ba
Yes./No.	Да./Нет.	da/nyet

What's your name?
Как вас зовут?   kak vaz za·*vut*

My name is ...
Меня зовут ...   meen·ya za·*vut* ...

Do you speak English?
Вы говорите   vi ga·va·*reet*·ye
по-английски?   pa·an·*glee*·skee

I don't understand.
Я не понимаю.   ya pye pa·nee·*ma*·yu

Accommodation

campsite	кемпинг	*kyem*·peeng
guesthouse	пансионат	pan·see·a·*nat*
hotel	гостиница	ga·*stee*·neet·sa
youth hostel	общежитие	ap·shee·*zhi*·tee·ye

Do you have   У вас есть ...?   u vas yest' ...
a ... room?

single	одноместный номер	ad·nam·*yes*·ni *no*·meer
double	номер с двуспальней кроватью	*no*·meer z dvu·*spaln*·yey kra·*vat*·yu
How much is it ...?	Сколько стоит за ...?	*skol*'·ka *sto*·eet za ...
for two people	двоих	dva·*eekh*
per night	ночь	noch'

Eating & Drinking

What would you recommend?
Что вы   shto vi
рекомендуете?   ree·ka·meen·*du*·eet·ye

Do you have vegetarian food?
У вас есть овощные   u vas yest' a·vashch·*ni*·ye
блюда?   *blyu*·da

I'll have ...
..., пожалуйста.   ... pa·*zhal*·sta

Cheers!
Пей до дна!   pyey da dna

I'd like the ..., please.	Я бы хотел/ хотела ... (m/f)	ya bi khat·*yel*/ khat·ye·la ...
bill	счёт	shot
menu	меню	meen·*yu*
(bottle of) beer	(бутылка) пива	(bu·*til*·ka) *pee*·va
(cup of) coffee/tea	(чашка) кофе/чаю	(*chash*·ka) kof·ye/cha·yu
water	вода	va·*da*
(glass of) wine	(рюмка) вина	(*ryum*·ka) vee·*na*

Numbers – Russian

1	один	a·*deen*
2	два	dva
3	три	tree
4	четыре	chee·*ti*·ree
5	пять	pyat'
6	шесть	shest'
7	семь	syem'
8	восемь	*vo*·seem'
9	девять	*dye*·veet'
10	десять	*dye*·seet'

Emergencies

Help!	Помогите!	pa·ma·*gee*·tye
Go away!	Идите отсюда!	ee·*deet*·ye at·*syu*·da
Call ...!	Вызовите ...!	*vi*·za·veet·ye ...
a doctor	врача	vra·*cha*
the police	милицию	mee·*leet*·si·yu

I'm lost.
Я потерялся/ потерялась. (m/f) — ya pa·teer·*yal*·sa/ pa·teer·*ya*·las'

I'm ill.
Я болею. — ya bal·ye·yu

Where are the toilets?
Где здесь туалет? — gdye zdyes' tu·a·*lyet*

Shopping & Services

I'd like ...
Я бы хотел/ хотела ... (m/f) — ya bi khat·*yel*/ khat·ye·la ...

How much is it?
Сколько стоит? — *skol*'·ka *sto*·eet

That's too expensive.
Это очень дорого. — e·ta o·cheen' *do*·ra·ga

bank	банк	bank
market	рынок	*ri*·nak
post office	почта	*poch*·ta
tourist office	туристическое бюро	tu·rees·*tee*·chee·ska·ye byu·ro

Transport & Directions

Where's the ...?
Где (здесь) ...? — gdye (zdyes') ...

What's the address?
Какой адрес? — ka·*koy* a·drees

Can you show me (on the map)?
Покажите мне, пожалуйста (на карте). — pa·ka·*zhi*·tye mnye pa·*zhal*·sta (na *kart*·ye)

One ... ticket, please. Билет ... — beel·yet ...

one-way	в один конец	v a·*deen* kan·*yets*
return	в оба конца	v o·ba kant·*sa*

boat	параход	pa·ra·*khot*
bus	автобус	af·*to*·bus
plane	самолёт	sa·mal·*yot*
train	поезд	*po*·yeest

ARMENIAN

Armenian is an Indo-European language, with its own script and heavy influences from Persian evident in its vocabulary. It has also borrowed many words and phrases from Russian, Turkish, French and Hindi. The standard eastern Armenian is based on the variety spoken in Ashtarak, close to Yerevan. People from Lori *marz* have a slower, more musical accent, while speakers from Gegharkunik and Karabakh have a strong accent that can be difficult for outsiders to understand, and vocabulary that is sometimes unique to one valley.

Below we've provided pronunciation guides (in blue) rather than the Armenian script. Note that zh is pronounced as the 's' in 'measure', kh as the 'ch' in the Scottish *loch*, dz as the 'ds' in 'adds', gh is a throaty sound and r is rolled. See p194 for the alphabet.

Basics

Hello.	barev dzez **(pol)** barev **(inf)**
Goodbye.	tsetesutyun **(pol)** hajogh **(inf)**
Yes.	ayo/ha **(pol/inf)**
No.	voch/che **(po/inf)**
Please.	khuntrem
Thank you.	shnorhakalutyun
No problem.	problem cheeka
How are you?	vonts ek/es? **(pol/inf)**
I'm fine, thank you.	lav em shnorhakalutyun
And you?	eesk' duk?
What's your name?	anunut eench eh?
My name is ...	anuns ... e
Do you speak English?	khosum es angleren?
I don't understand.	chem haskanum

LANGUAGES AZERI

Accommodation

Do you have a room?	unek senyak?
guesthouse	panseeonat
hotel	hyuranots

Emergencies

Where is the toilet?	vortegh e zugarane?
I'm sick.	heevand em
doctor	bjheeshk
hospital	heevandanots
police	vosteegan

Shopping & Services

How much?	eench arjhey?
bank	bank
chemist/pharmacy	deghatun/apteka
currency exchange	dramee bokhanagum
expensive	tang
market	shuka
open	bats
post office	post
shop	khanut
telephone	herakhos

Time & Dates

When?	yerp?
yesterday	yerek
today	aysor
tomorrow	vaghe

| Monday | yerkushaptee |
| Tuesday | yerekshaptee |

Numbers – Armenian	
1	mek
2	yerku
3	yerek
4	chors
5	heeng
6	vets
7	yot
8	ut
9	eenuh
10	tas

Wednesday	chorekshaptee
Thursday	heengshaptee
Friday	urpat
Saturday	shapat
Sunday	keerakee

Transport & Directions

When does ... leave?	yerp jampa gelle ...?
When does ... arrive?	yerp gee hasne ...?
Stop!	kangnek!
airport	otanavakayan
bus	avtobus
bus station/stop	avtokayan/gankar
car	mekena
minibus	marshrutny/marshrutka
petrol	petrol/benzeen
plane	eenknateer/otanov
taxi	taksee
ticket	doms

Where?	ur/vortegh?
here	aystaeegh
left	dzakh
right	ach

AZERI

Azeri is a member of the Turkic language family, and shares its grammar and much of its vocabulary with Turkish. Originally written in a modified Arabic script, and during the Soviet rule in Russian Cyrillic script, it's now written in a modern Azeri Latin alphabet (used below; see p263 for more on the alphabet).

Note that r is rolled, ğ is pronounced at the back of the throat, g as the 'gy' in 'Magyar', ç as the 'ch' in 'chase', c as the 'j' in 'jazz', x as the 'ch' in the Scottish loch, j as the 's' in 'pleasure', g as the 'g' in 'get', ş as the 'sh' in 'shore', ı as the 'a' in 'ago', ə as in 'apple' (short), ö as the 'e' in 'her', and ü as the 'ew' in 'pew'. In many parts of the country, the hard 'k' is pronounced more like a 'ch'. Words are lightly stressed on the last syllable.

Basics

Hello.	*Salam.*
Goodbye.	*Sağ olun/ol.* (pol/inf)
How are you?	*Necəsiniz?* (pol)
	Necəsən? (inf)
Yes.	*Bəli./Hə.* (pol/inf)

No.	Xeyr./Yox.
Please.	Lutfən.
Thank you.	Təşəkkür edirəm.
You're welcome.	Buyurun.
Excuse me./Sorry.	Bağışlayın.
Do you speak English?	Siz ingiliscə danışırsınız?
I don't understand.	Mən anlamıram.
Cheers!	Deyilən sağlığa!

Accommodation

hotel	mehmanxana
room	otaq
toilet	tualet

Emergencies

ambulance	tacili yardım maşını
doctor	hakim
hospital	xastaxana

Shopping & Services

How much?	Nə qədər?
bank	bank
chemist/pharmacy	aptek
currency exchange	valyuta dayışma
expensive	baha
market	bazar
open	açıq
post office	poçt
shop	dukan/mağaza
telephone	telefon

Time & Dates

When?	Nə vaxt?
yesterday	dünən
today	bu gün
tomorrow	sabah

Monday	Bazar ertəsi
Tuesday	Çərşənbə axşamı
Wednesday	Çərşənbə
Thursday	Cümə axşamı
Friday	Cümə
Saturday	Şənbə
Sunday	Bazar

Numbers – Azeri

1	bir
2	iki
3	üç
4	dörd
5	beş
6	altı
7	yeddi
8	səkkiz
9	doqquz
10	on

Transport & Directions

When does ... leave?	... nə zaman gedir?
When does ... arrive?	... nə zaman gəlir?
Stop!	Saxla!
airport	hava limanı
bus	avtobus
bus station	avtovağzal
bus stop	avtobus dayanacağı
car	maşın
ferry	bərə
minibus	mikroavtobus
petrol	benzin
plane	təyyarə
port	liman
taxi	taksi
ticket	bilet
train	qatar
train station	damir yolu stansiyası
Where?	Hara?/Harada? (for verbs/nouns)
avenue	prospekt
lane/alley	xiyaban
square	meydan
street	küçə

GEORGIAN

Georgian belongs to the Kartvelian language family, which is related to the Caucasian languages. It is an ancient language with its own cursive script. See p125 for the alphabet.

Below we've provided pronunciation guides (in blue) rather than the Georgian script. Note that q is pronounced as the 'k' in 'king' but far back in the throat, kh as the 'ch' in the Scottish *loch*, zh as the 's' in 'pleasure', dz as the 'ds' in 'beds', gh is a throaty sound (like an incipient gargle) and r is rolled. Light word stress usually falls on the first syllable.

Basics

Hello.	gamarjobat
Goodbye.	nakhvamdis
Yes.	diakh/ho (pol/inf)
No.	ara
Please.	tu sheidzleba
Thank you.	madlobt
How are you?	rogora khart?
Excuse me.	ukatsrovad
Sorry.	bodishi
It doesn't matter.	ara ushavs
Do you speak English?	inglisuri itsit?
I don't understand.	ar mesmis
Cheers!	gaumarjos!

Accommodation

hotel	sastumro
room	otakhi
toilet	tualeti

Emergencies

doctor	ekimi
hospital	saavadmqopo
police	politsia/militsia

Shopping & Services

How much?	ramdeni?
bank	banki
chemist/pharmacy	aptiaqi
expensive	dzviri

Numbers – Georgian

1	erti
2	ori
3	sami
4	otkhi
5	khuti
6	ekvsi
7	shvidi
8	rva
9	tskhra
10	ati

market	bazari/bazroba
open	ghiaa
post office	posta
shop	maghazia
telephone	teleponi

Time & Dates

When?	rodis?
yesterday	gushin
today	dghes
tomorrow	khval
Sunday	kvira
Monday	orshabati
Tuesday	samshabati
Wednesday	otkhshabati
Thursday	khutshabati
Friday	paraskevi
Saturday	shabati

Transport & Directions

When does it leave?	rodis midis/gadis?
When does it arrive?	rodis modis/chamodis?
Stop here!	gaacheret!
airport	aeroporti
boat	gemi
bus	avtobusi/troleibusi
bus station	avtosadguri
bus stop	gachereba
car	mankana
minibus	marshrutka
petrol	benzini
plane	tvitmprinavi
port	porti
taxi	taksi
ticket	bileti
train	matarebeli
train station	(rkinigzis) sadguri
Where?	sad?
avenue	gamziri
road/way	gza
square	moedani

GLOSSARY

You may encounter some of the following words during your time in Georgia (Geo), Armenia (Arm) and Azerbaijan (Az). Some Russian (Rus) and Turkish (Tur) words, including the ones below, have been widely adopted in the Caucasus.

abour (Arm) – soup

ajika (Geo) – chilli paste

alaverdi (Geo) – person appointed by the toast-master at a *supra* to elaborate on the toast

Amenaprkich (Arm) – All Saviours

aptek/apteka/aptiaqi (Az/Rus & Arm/Geo) – pharmacy

Arakelots (Arm) – the Apostles

ARF (Arm) – Armenian Revolutionary Federation; the Dashnaks

aşig (ashug) (Az) – itinerant musician

astodan (Az) – ossuary

Astvatsatsin (Arm) – Holy Mother of God

aviakassa (Rus) – shop or window selling air tickets

avtokayan (Arm) – bus station

avtosadguri (Geo) – bus station

avtovağzal (Az) – bus station

baklava – honeyed nut pastry

baliq (Az) – fish, usually sturgeon, often grilled

basturma (Arm) – cured beef in ground red pepper

berd (Arm) – fortress

bulvar (Az) – boulevard

caravanserai – historic travellers inn, usually based around a courtyard

Catholicos – patriarch of the Armenian or Georgian churches

çay (Az) – tea

çayxana (Az) – teahouse

chacha (Geo) – powerful grappalike liquor

chakapuli (Geo) – lamb and plums in herb sauce

churchkhela (Geo) – string of nuts coated in a sort of caramel made from grape juice and flour

chvishdari (Geo) – Svanetian dish of cheese cooked inside maize bread

CIS – Commonwealth of Independent States; the loose political and economic alliance of the former republics of the USSR (except Georgia and the Baltic states)

çörək (Az) – bread

dacha (Rus) – country holiday cottage or bungalow

darbazi (Geo) – traditional home design with the roof tapering up to a central hole

doğrama (Az) – cold soup made with sour milk, potato, onion and cucumber

dolma (Arm, Az) – vine leaves with a rice filling

domık (Rus) – hut or modest bungalow accommodation

dram – Armenian unit of currency

duduk (Arm) – traditional reed instrument; also *tutak* (Az)

dzor (Arm) – gorge

elektrichka (Rus) – local train service linking a city and its suburbs or nearby towns, or groups of adjacent towns

eristavi (Geo) – duke

gavit (Arm) – entrance hall of a church

ghomi (Geo) – maize porridge

glasnost (Rus) – openness

halva (Az) – various sweet pastries, often containing nuts

hraparak (Arm) – square

IDP – internally displaced person

Intourist (Rus) – Soviet-era government tourist organisation

ishkhan (Arm) – trout from Lake Sevan

istirahət zonası (Az) – rural bungalow resort

jvari (Geo) – religious cross; spiritual site in mountain regions

kamança (Az) – stringed musical instrument

kartuli – Georgian language

Kartvelebi – Georgian people

kassa (Rus) – cash desk or ticket booth

katoghike (Arm) – cathedral

khachapuri (Geo) – savoury bread or pastry, usually with a cheese filling

khachkar (Arm) – medieval carved headstone

khamaju (Arm) – meat pie

khash/khashi (Arm/Geo) – garlic and tripe soup; also *xaş* (Az)

khashlama (Arm) – lamb or beef stew with potato

khati/khatebi (Geo) – animist shrine in Tusheti, Georgia

khevi (Geo) – gorge

khidi (Geo) – bridge

khinkali (Geo) – spicy meat, potato or mushroom dumpling

khoravats (Arm) – barbecued food

kişi (Az) – men (hence 'K' marks men's toilets)

köfte/kyufta/küftə (Tur/Arm/Az) – minced beef meatballs with onion and spices

körpü (Az) – bridge

koshki/koshkebi (Geo) – defensive tower in Georgian mountain regions

kubdari (Geo) – spicy Svanetian meat pie

küçəsi (Az) – street

kupe/kupeyny (Rus) – 2nd-class compartment accommodation on trains

kvas (Rus) – beverage made from fermented rye bread

lahmacun/lahmajoon (Tur/ Arm) – small lamb and herb pizzas

lari – Georgian unit of currency

lavash/lavaş (Arm/Az) – thin bread

ləvəngi (Az) – casserole of chicken stuffed with walnuts and herbs

lich (Arm) – lake

lobio/lobiya/lobya (Geo/ Rus/Az) – beans, often with herbs and spices

luks (Rus) – deluxe; used to refer to hotel suites and 1st-class accommodation on trains

manat – Azerbaijani unit of currency

marani (Geo) – wine cellar

marshrutka/marshrutky (Rus) – public minivan transport

marz (Arm) – province, region

matagh (Arm) – animal sacrifice

matenadaran (Arm) – library

matsoni (Geo) – yoghurt drink

mayrughi (Arm) – highway

mehmanxana (Az) – hotel

merikipe (Geo) – man who pours wine at a *supra*

meydan (Az) – square

mədrəsə (Az) – Islamic school

moedani (Geo) – square

most (Rus) – bridge

mtsvadi (Geo) – shish kebab, shashlyk

muğam (Az) – traditional musical style

mushuri (Geo) – working songs

muzhskoy (Rus) – men's toilet

nagorny (Rus) – mountainous

nard, nardi (Az/Arm) – backgammonlike board game

obshchy (Rus) – general-seating class (unreserved) on trains

oghee (Arm) – fruit vodkas; sometimes called *vatsun* or *aragh*

OSCE – Organisation for Security and Co-operation in Europe

OVIR (Rus) – Visa and Registration Department

paneer (Arm) – cheese

paxlava (Az) – honeyed nut pastry

pendir (Az) – cheese

perestroika (Rus) – restructuring

pir (Az) – shrine or holy place

piti (Az) – soupy meat stew with chickpeas and saffron

pivo (Rus) – beer

pkhali/mkhali (Geo) – beetroot, spinach or aubergine paste with crushed walnuts, garlic and herbs

platskart/platskartny (Rus) – open-bunk accommodation on trains

plov – rice dish

poghota (Arm) – avenue

poghots (Arm) – street

prospekti (Az) – avenue

qadım (Az) – woman (hence 'Q' marks womens toilets)

qala, qalasi (Az) – castle or fortress

qəpiq – Azerbaijani unit of currency (100 qəpiq equals one manat)

qucha (Geo) – street

qutab (Az) – stuffed pancake

rabiz (Rus) – Armenian workers' culture, party music

rtveli (Geo) – grape harvest

sagalobeli (Geo) – church songs

sagmiro (Geo) – epic songs

sakhachapure (Geo) – café serving *khachapuri*

sakhinkle (Geo) – café serving *khinkali*

saxlama kamera (Az) – left-luggage room(s)

satrap – Persian provincial governor

satrpialo (Geo) – love songs

satsivi (Geo) – cold turkey or chicken in walnut sauce

şəbəkə (Az) – intricately carved, wood-framed, stained-glass windows

shashlyk – shish kebab

Shirvan – old Azerbaijani unit of currency, equal to two manat

shkmeruli (Geo) – chicken in garlic sauce

shuka (Arm) – market

soorch (Arm) – coffee

spalny vagon/SV (Rus) – two-berth sleeping compartment in train

suchush (Arm) – plum and walnut sweet

sulguni (Geo) – smoked cheese from Samegrelo

supra (Geo) – dinner party; literally means 'tablecloth'

supruli (Geo) – songs for the table

surp (Arm) – holy, saint

tabouleh (Arm) – diced green salad with semolina

tamada (Geo) – toastmaster at a *supra*

tan (Arm) – yoghurt

tetri – Georgian unit of currency (100 tetri equals one lari)

tikə kabab (Az) – shish kebab; commonly called *shashlyk*

tqemali (Geo) – wild plum, wild plum sauce

tonir (Arm) – traditional bread oven

tsikhe (Geo) – fortified place

tufa – volcanic stone famous to Armenia

tur – large, endangered Caucasian ibex

tutak (Az) – traditional reed instrument; also *duduk* (Arm)

vank (Arm) – monastery

virap (Arm) – well

vishap (Arm) – carved dragon stone

xaş (Az) – garlic and tripe soup; also *khash/khashi* (Arm/Geo)

xəzri (Az) – gale-force wind in Baku

yeməkxana (Az) – food house, cheap eatery

zhensky (Rus) – womens toilets

Behind the Scenes

SEND US YOUR FEEDBACK

We love to hear from travellers – your comments keep us on our toes and help make our books better. Our well-travelled team reads every word on what you loved or loathed about this book. Although we cannot reply individually to postal submissions, we always guarantee that your feedback goes straight to the appropriate authors, in time for the next edition. Each person who sends us information is thanked in the next edition – the most useful submissions are rewarded with a selection of digital PDF chapters.

Visit **lonelyplanet.com/contact** to submit your updates and suggestions or to ask for help. Our award-winning website also features inspirational travel stories, news and discussions.

Note: We may edit, reproduce and incorporate your comments in Lonely Planet products such as guidebooks, websites and digital products, so let us know if you don't want your comments reproduced or your name acknowledged. For a copy of our privacy policy visit lonelyplanet.com/privacy.

OUR READERS

Many thanks to the travellers who used the last edition and wrote to us with helpful hints, useful advice and interesting anecdotes:

A Alan Graham, Aliyev Kanan, Amy Singer, Antal Szabolcs, Astrid van Wintershoven **B** Barney Smith, Bernd Zimmermann, Birgit Karle, Brigitte Schumann **C** Claas Morlang **D** Daniel Scovenna, David Devine **E** Edo Berger & Nina Willemse, Edward Eve, Elisabetta Bonino **F** Florian Timmermann, Francesco Cisternino **J** Jacqueline Appleby, Janet Croft, Jillana Krause, Jiri Preclik **K** Katie Crysdale, Kato Hansen, Kent Kuran **L** Lidwien Verweij **M** Matthew Ruszala, Michael Garrood, Michele Beraldo **N** Nancy Metashvili, Nickos Yoldassis **P** Peter Francev **S** Sain Alizada, Seda Melkumyan, Svetlana Kasaeva **T** Thomas Mayer, Thomas Sarosy, Tom Wyss **W** Wieland Ulrichs **X** Xavier Alcober **Y** Yuri Victorovich **Z** Zuzana Orsagova

WRITER THANKS

Alex Jones

Çox Sağol to Kate Hunt, Ian Peart and family, Cavid Qara, Afgan Mehdikhanov, Rustam Rustamov, Mevlud, Zahid and Khaled Azizov, Francesco Ricapito, Sabina Qazimova, Vamiq Babayev, Tahmina Jafarova, Ilqar Ağayev, Nick Thomson, Shayl Majithia, Chris Jackson, Shani and Dave Bakstrom, Anna and Ollof, Andreas, Artur, Stephen and so many others. At Lonely Planet many thanks to a fine team including Kristin Odijk, Helen Elfer, Valentina Kremenchutskaya and stalwart fellow writers John, Virginia and Tom.

Tom Masters

Thanks to Susanna Petrosyan for her invaluable help before, during and after my trip. Thanks also to Saro Sarosyan, Virginia Maxwell and Helen Elfer for their advice and assistance.

Virginia Maxwell

Greatest thanks go to my travelling companions, Peter and Max Handsaker, my destination editor, Helen Elfer, and my co-authors John Noble, Alex Jones and Tom Masters. Thanks also to Arpine Yesayan, Lusine Melqonyan, Artush Davtyan and Armine Kalashyan.

John Noble

Thanks to so many in Georgia but especially, Dustin Gilbreath, Hans Gutbrod, William Dunbar, Giorgi Gardava, Geostat (National Statistics Office of Georgia), Gulnasi Miqeladze and Nazim and Sofia Ghoghoberidze, Giorgi Giorgadze, Ira Hartmann, Tiniko Ididze, Regina Jegorova-Askerova, Dodo Kevlishvili,

Darejan Khetaguri and Vakho, Robert Kodric, Dmitry Lemeshev, Cally and Rohan Lienert, David Luashvili, all the Rukhadzes, Roza Shukvani and Vitia Chartolani, Saša and Simona, Irakli Paniashvili and Giorgi Demetrashvili, and not least my super-talented, always-helpful co-authors Alex, Virginia and Tom.

ACKNOWLEDGMENTS

Climate map data adapted from Peel MC, Finlayson BL & McMahon TA (2007) 'Updated World Map of the Köppen-Geiger Climate Classification', Hydrology and Earth System Sciences, 11, 1633–44.

Cover photograph: Mt Ushba in the Svaneti region, Georgia. Yevgen Timashov / Alamy ©

THIS BOOK

This 5th edition of Lonely Planet's *Georgia, Armenia and Azerbaijan* was researched and written by Alex Jones, Tom Masters, Virginia Maxwell and John Noble, with William Dunbar a contributing writer. The previous two editions were written by Michael Kohn, John Noble and Danielle Systermans.

Destination Editor Helen Elfer
Product Editors Elizabeth Jones, Amanda Williamson
Coordinating Editor Kristin Odijk
Senior Cartographer Valentina Kremenchutskaya
Book Designer Mazzy Prinsep
Assisting Editor Bruce Evans

Cover Researcher Naomi Parker
Thanks to Gemma Graham, James Hardy, Victoria Harrison, Andi Jones, Kate Mathews, Catherine Naghten, Karyn Noble, Kirsten Rawlings, Angela Tinson, Laura Wellicome, Tony Wheeler

Index

Map Legend

Sights
- Beach
- Bird Sanctuary
- Buddhist
- Castle/Palace
- Christian
- Confucian
- Hindu
- Islamic
- Jain
- Jewish
- Monument
- Museum/Gallery/Historic Building
- Ruin
- Shinto
- Sikh
- Taoist
- Winery/Vineyard
- Zoo/Wildlife Sanctuary
- Other Sight

Activities, Courses & Tours
- Bodysurfing
- Diving
- Canoeing/Kayaking
- Course/Tour
- Sento Hot Baths/Onsen
- Skiing
- Snorkelling
- Surfing
- Swimming/Pool
- Walking
- Windsurfing
- Other Activity

Sleeping
- Sleeping
- Camping

Eating
- Eating

Drinking & Nightlife
- Drinking & Nightlife
- Cafe

Entertainment
- Entertainment

Shopping
- Shopping

Information
- Bank
- Embassy/Consulate
- Hospital/Medical
- Internet
- Police
- Post Office
- Telephone
- Toilet
- Tourist Information
- Other Information

Geographic
- Beach
- Gate
- Hut/Shelter
- Lighthouse
- Lookout
- Mountain/Volcano
- Oasis
- Park
- Pass
- Picnic Area
- Waterfall

Population
- Capital (National)
- Capital (State/Province)
- City/Large Town
- Town/Village

Transport
- Airport
- Border crossing
- Bus
- Cable car/Funicular
- Cycling
- Ferry
- Metro station
- Monorail
- Parking
- Petrol station
- Subway station
- Taxi
- Train station/Railway
- Tram
- Underground station
- Other Transport

Note: Not all symbols displayed above appear on the maps in this book

Routes
- Tollway
- Freeway
- Primary
- Secondary
- Tertiary
- Lane
- Unsealed road
- Road under construction
- Plaza/Mall
- Steps
- Tunnel
- Pedestrian overpass
- Walking Tour
- Walking Tour detour
- Path/Walking Trail

Boundaries
- International
- State/Province
- Disputed
- Regional/Suburb
- Marine Park
- Cliff
- Wall

Hydrography
- River, Creek
- Intermittent River
- Canal
- Water
- Dry/Salt/Intermittent Lake
- Reef

Areas
- Airport/Runway
- Beach/Desert
- Cemetery (Christian)
- Cemetery (Other)
- Glacier
- Mudflat
- Park/Forest
- Sight (Building)
- Sportsground
- Swamp/Mangrove

OUR STORY

A beat-up old car, a few dollars in the pocket and a sense of adventure. In 1972 that's all Tony and Maureen Wheeler needed for the trip of a lifetime – across Europe and Asia overland to Australia. It took several months, and at the end – broke but inspired – they sat at their kitchen table writing and stapling together their first travel guide, *Across Asia on the Cheap*. Within a week they'd sold 1500 copies. Lonely Planet was born.

Today, Lonely Planet has offices in Franklin, London, Melbourne, Oakland, Beijing and Delhi, with more than 600 staff and writers. We share Tony's belief that 'a great guidebook should do three things: inform, educate and amuse'.

OUR WRITERS

3 1969 02410 8465

Alex Jones

Azerbaijan The Azerbaijan chapter was written by an experienced Lonely Planet writer who has been visiting Azerbaijan and Georgia for two decades. He has chosen to use a pseudonym due to political and cultural sensitivities in the region. Alex also wrote the Plan Your Trip and Survival Guide sections.

Tom Masters

Nagorno-Karabakh Tom studied Russian at the University of London and first visited the Caucasus in 1999 on an extended escape from a provincial university study course in the Arctic. He's been back many times since then, in his work for the BBC World Service's Caucasus & Central Asian Service and as author of the Georgia and Azerbaijan chapters for a previous edition of this book. For this edition, he returned to Nagorno-Karabakh to find the region safe and thriving. You can find more of his work at www.tommasters.net.

Virginia Maxwell

Armenia Although based in Australia, Virginia spends much of her year travelling in the Middle East and Mediterranean Europe. The author of Lonely Planet's *İstanbul* and *Pocket İstanbul* guidebooks, she also co-authors the *Turkey* and *Iran* guidebooks, so knows this part of the world very well. This is the first time she has updated Armenia but she hopes it won't be the last.

John Noble

Georgia John, from the UK, first came to Georgia in 1990 when he was writing Lonely Planet's first (and last) guide to the USSR. Arriving in Georgia at Kazbegi was like a breath of fresh after Soviet regimentation and he has loved Georgians' sense of independence, hospitality, beautiful landscapes and architecture, food and of course wine ever since. This is the third time he has covered the country for this book. John also wrote the Understand section.

Read more about John at:
http://auth.lonelyplanet.com/profiles/ewoodrover

Contributing Author

William Dunbar William is a freelance journalist who has worked in Georgia since 2006. When not travelling the country covering political unrest or obscure mountain tribes, he likes to unwind in the less salubrious Tbilisi nightspots and then complain about the service. William contributed to our Tbilisi's drinking, nightlife and entertainment coverage.

Published by Lonely Planet Publications Pty Ltd
ABN 36 005 607 983
5th edition – May 2016
ISBN 978 1 74220 758 2
© Lonely Planet 2016   Photographs © as indicated 2016
10 9 8 7 6 5 4 3 2 1
Printed in China